A Dictionary of
POLLUTION

A Dictionary of POLLUTION

J.L. SHARMA M.Sc., Ph.D.
Department of Chemistry
K.M. College, University of Delhi, India.

P.L. BULDINI C. Chem., M.R.S.C.
Sezione di Chimica
C.N.R.-LAMEL, Bologna, Italy

CBS

CBS PUBLISHERS & DISTRIBUTORS (P) LTD.
11, DARYAGANJ, NEW DELHI - 110002 (INDIA)

ISBN 81-239-0348-0

First Edition : 1994
Reprint : 2001

Published by :
Satish Kumar Jain for CBS Publishers and Distributors,
4596/1-A, 11 Darya Ganj, New Delhi - 110 002 (India)

Printed at :
Asia Printograph,
Shahdara, Delhi - 110 032

Preface

Man has changed the atmosphere, rivers, lakes, oceans, and the local distribution of rocks and soil. Many living forms are destroyed because they cannot adapt quickly enough to new conditions. Changes in the environment are particularly important because of their effect on living beings. Saving the environment does not mean that man must give up the modern technology. But man must learn to live within nature's cycles. Governments are beginning to take measures to clean air and water, and to save many species that might become extinct in time to come; and changes are being made in the use of the earth in an attempt to preserve the natural environment.

This Dictionary addresses the problems of change and deterioration in the earth's environment due to human activities that threaten the planet's future. It has been compiled to provide information on regulations, standards, and relevant information of the hazardous chemicals, and brings together various diverse sources in one systematized alphabetical compilation. There are many terms in this dictionary which do not have obvious pollution connotations. They appear here because they represent concepts or terms essential to understanding all the aspects of pollution. Every aspect of its conception and layout has been planned to help the user to find the scientific information he needs with minimum difficulty. Most of the terms come from a wide range of disciplines- particularry chemistry, biology, ecology, meteorology, toxicology, and numerous branches of engineering and technology, that are concerned with the functioning of nature: living organisms and their ecological relationships, processes and cycles in atmosphere, hydrosphere, and lithosphere; hazards resulting from pollution, including the description of noxious substances working all the time on ourselves and our environment; and the disposal or recycling of the waste products. Restraint must prevail, particularly in a dictionary such as this of modest proportions; the terms included have been selected in a somewhat pragmatic manner, partly on the basis of those most frequently encountered by the authors within the context of general awareness of the environment.

J.L. SHARMA
P.L.BULDINI

Acknowledgments

Prof. G. Furlan
Head, ICTP-TRIL Programme
International Centre for Theoretical Physics
Trieste, Italy

Dr. (Mrs) Donatella Ferri
Water Analyst
Presidio Multizonale Prevenzione
Bologna, Italy

Miss Anna Mevoli
C.N.R.S.M., S.C.p.A.
Brindisi, Italy

Dr. Praveen Saxena
Senior Scientific Officer
Ministry of Non-Conventional Energy
Government of India, India

Dr. Rakesh Parashar
Department of Chemistry
Kirorimal College
University of Delhi, Delhi

Dr. Pramod K. Singh
Department of Chemistry
Kirorimal College
University of Delhi, Delhi.

Dr. J.N. Srivastava
Department of Chemistry
Kirorimal College
University of Delhi, Delhi

Dr. Nitin Kohli
Department of Chemistry
Kirorimal College
University of Delhi, Delhi

Mr. Saeed Raees
Ana-Gen Technologies, Inc.
Saratoga, USA

Ms. Susan Strong
Marketing Manager
Dionex Corporation, srl
Sunnyvale, USA

Dr. Silvano Cavalli
Dionex Corporation, srl
Milan, italy

Dr. V.K. Saxena
Department of Chemistry
University of Lucknow
Lucknow, India

Prof. Ishwar Singh
Department of Chemistry
M. Dayanand University
Rohatak, India

Prof. P.C. Mathur
Dean, Interdisciplinary Applied Sciences
University of Delhi, Delhi

Dr. J.P. Jain
Shyam Lal College
University of Delhi, Delhi

Dr. S. Ghosh
Department of Chemistry
Kirorimal College
University of Delhi, Delhi

Prof. R.P. Singh (Retired)
Department of Chemistry
University of Delhi, Delhi

A

a. A prefix meaning not or without; such as in acyclic, anaerobic, atactic and asymmetric.
AB. *See ABO* blood group system.
abatement. The process of minimizing pollution through reuse or the process of waste treatment.
abiogenesis. The development of living from non-living matter, as in the origin of life.
abiotic. A term referring to the absence of living organisms.
abiotic environment. All physical and non-living chemical factors such as soil, atmosphere, and water, which influence the living organisms.
ablation. 1.The process of absorbing and dissipating heat by a material at temperatures as high as 3000 K. The epoxy or phenolic resins reinforced with glass or graphite fibres are used to coat the surfaces of space capsules to protect them from the excessive heat due to atmospheric friction. The ablative coating effects cooling of the surface by convection and formation of gaseous decomposition products which prevent the heat from penetrating the interior, but are very harmful from pollution point of view. 2. Removal of molten surface layers of meteorites and tektites by direct vapourization during the passage through the atmosphere. 3. The removal of tissue or a part of the body by surgery.
ABO **blood group system.** One of the human blood group systems. It is the most important in blood transfusion serology because natural antibodies against *ABO* blood group antigens occur in serum. Humans belong to one of four groups: *A, B, AB* and *O*; the red cells of each group carry respectively the *A* antigen, the *B* antigen, both *A* and *B* antigens, or neither antigen. The antibodies in serum are specific for those *ABO* antigens not present on the red cells of the bearer, *e.g.*, persons of group *A* have serum antibodies to *B* antigen.
above-ground tank. Device that is situated in such a way that the entire surface area of the tank is completely above the plane of the adnacent surrounding surface and the entire surface area of the tank (including the tank bottom) is able to be visually in spected.
abrasion. The removal of surface material from any solid through the frictional act of another solid, liquid, or a gas or combination thereof; or by chemical degradation. Also, The wearing away or rounding of surface by friction or rubbing as from action of glaciers, wind, and waterborne sand on rock

fragments and minerals. It is most effective when the impact of particles on bedrock is vigorous, and the particles themselves are coarse, hard, and angular; and there is no vegetation to protect the rocks and soil, especially in deserts. It is effective along the coastline too, where it wears away the cliffs as well as the shore.

absolute stability. A meteorological term referring to the condition of the atmosphere in which the environmental lapse rate is less than the saturated adiabatic lapse rate. If air pockets are forced to rise, they will loose heat adiabatically at a rate such that they will be cooler than the surrounding air. Thus if upward movement is terminated, the air pocket will again sink to lower levels. The absence of such forced ascent there will be no upward movement of the air pockets in the first instance, since they would immediately become cooler and heavier than the surrounding air.

absolute temperature. Temperature that is measured as a function of energy possessed by matter. Absolute temperatures are expressed either in Kelvin or in degrees Rankine; corresponding respectively to the Centigrade and Fahrenheit scales. Degree Kelvin is obtained by adding 273 to the Centigrade temperature. Degrees Rankine are obtained by subtracting 460 from the Fahrenheit temperature. Also known as thermodynamic temperature.

absorbed dose. D. The amount of energy imparted to matter by ionizing particles per unit mass of irradiated material at place of interest. In SI system it is expressed in Grays.

absorbers. Pollution control devices that transfer soluble gases to be removed from a polluted gas stream, to a liquid. *See also* absorption.

absorbing boom. As applied to containment and collection of a major oil spill, this type of boom employing the absorbing materials, not only checks the spread of oil, but aids in its removal.

absorption. 1. Penetration of substance (absorbate) into body of another (absorbent). 2. Reduction in the flux of electromagnetic radiation on passage through matter. The radiation absorptive capacity of matter is utilized in analytical chemistry in various types of absorption spectroscopy. 3. The ability of some elements to pick up or capture thermal neutrons produced in nuclear reactors as a result of fission. 4. In immunology the term refers to the use of reagents to remove antigens or antibodies from a mixture. It is used to remove unwanted possibly cross-reacting antibodies from an antiserum absorption elution test to make it more specific; accomplished by adding antigen and then removing the antigen-antibody complex formed.

absorption bands. Dark bands or lines present in spectrum as a result of absorption by some intervening medium. Atoms absorb only a single wavelength, producing lines, such as the sodium D-line.

absorption spectrum. The spectrum arising as a result of the propagation of electromagnetic radiation through absorbing medium. When the light from a high temperature source producing a continuous emission spectrum is passed through a medium through a spectroscope, the spectrum reveals dark regions where absorption has taken place (continuous, line, and band types). In general, medium absorbs those wavelengths which it would omit if its temperature is raised high enough. Solids and liquids show broad continuous absorption spectra, while gases give more discontinuous types.

absorption tube. A tube filled with a absorbent (generally finely divided solid or paste); used to absorb gases and vapours.

ABS resin. Any of a group of tough and rigid thermoplastics made by blending acrylonitrile styrene copolymer with a butadiene-acrylonitrile rubber or by interpolymerizing polybutadiene with acrylonitrile and styrene. Varying the composition of the polymer by changing the ratios of the three monomers and the use of other comonomers and additives, results in ABS resins with a wide range of properties. These resins find numerous applications in making automobile body parts and fittings, luggage, packaging, refrigerator door liners, building panels, boats, radiator grills, and components used in making pollution control devices.

abstraction. A term used in water pollution, referring to the process by which a stream, by the lateral extension of its valley, takes over the catchments of neighbouring streams, thus leading to an overall reduction in number of streams. It usually occurs at the upper end of a drainage line.

abundance. 1. The relative amount (% by weight) of a substance in the earth's crust, including the hydrosphere and atmosphere. The abundance of some of the elements in the earth's crust is:

Abundance	*% by weight*
Oxygen	49.2
Silicon	25.7
Aluminium	7.5
Iron	4.7
Sodium	0.6
Calcium	3.4
Potassium	2.4
Magnesium	1.9
Hydrogen	0.9
Titanium	0.6
Chlorine	0.2
All others	0.9

It may be noted that on universal scale, most abundant element is hydrogen. 2. Content of particular isotope in given sample of the natural element, expressed as percentage, *e.g.*, 99.76% of oxygen-16 in natural oxygen. Also known as abundance ratio.

abyssal. Pertaining to the zones of greatest depth at which water has more or less uniform temperature, also pertaining to the organisms of that environment.

accelerated stabilization. In composting, this desired condition may be achieved by more frequent turning of the windrows, or by raising the temperature as the material is undergoing commination and fermentation before being set out in windrows. In sludge treatment, accelerated stabilization is achieved by use of the activated sludge treatment, by raising the temperature of the sludge itself, etc.

accelofilter. One of the high-rate biofilter employed for the treatment of sewage. It consists of a primary clarifier, trickling filter with four arms, and a secondary

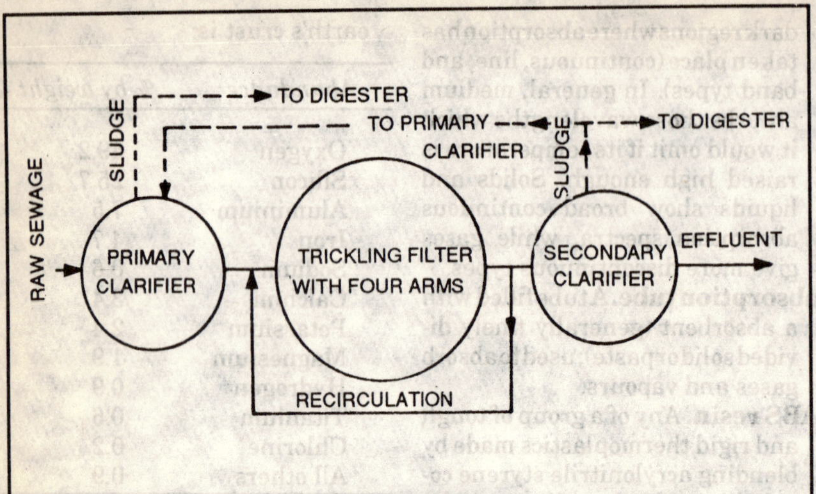

ACCELOFILTER

clarifier.

acclimated microorganisms. Bacteria, fungi and other microscopic organisms that can adjust themselves to changes in the environment, such as temperature, oxygen levels and pollution levels.

acenaphthene. A tricyclic compound obtained from coal tar; used in the manufacture of dyes, insecticides, pesticides, and plastics. It has been classified as pollutant and has been included in the list of potential occupational carcinogens. The available data for acenaphthene indicate that it is toxic to freshwater aquatic life at concentration as low as 1700 μg/L and would occur at even lower concentrations among the species that are more sensitive than those tested. It has also been found that toxicity to certain varieties of algae occurs at concentration as low as 520 μg/L.

acetaldehyde. A colourless, highly flammable, toxic liquid with a pungent smell; used in the manufacture of a large number of compounds, plastics, resins, and synthetic rubber. It has been assessed as a hazardous air pollutant. Its main hazard to the health is the irritant effect of the vapours on eyes and respiratory tract. The ingestion of acetaldehyde may cause nausea, vomiting, diarrhoea, narcosis, respiratory failure, fatty degeneration of the kidney, liver and heart tissue. Exposure to acetaldehyde should be controlled so that employees are not exposed at a concentration greater than 1000 part per million parts of air (ppm) by volume (about 180 mg/m^3) determined as time-weighted average concentration (TWA) concentration for up to a 10-hour workday in a 40-hour workweek over a working lifetime.

acetylene. A colourless, unsaturated, highly flammable, aliphatic hydrocarbon, existing as gas at room temperature; obtained by cracking petroleum hydrocarbons, or natural gas by partial oxidation, or by the action of water on calcium carbide. It is used in the manufacture of vinyl chloride, vinylidene chloride, vinyl acetate, acrylonitrile, acetaldehyde, acrylates, trichloroethylene, 1,4-butanediol, and carbon black. It is also used for cutting, welding, brazing, and localized hardening of glass and metals. The gas or vapours, when present in high concentrations in air, and act primarily as simple asphyxiant without other significant physiologic effects; but heavy concentrations have anaesthetic properties and may render a person unconscious. If the gas is impure, the symptoms of phosphine or hydrogen sulphide poisoning may also be present. The occupational exposure to acetylene is defined as exposure to airborne acetylene at concentrations greater than the environmental limit. If exposure to other chemicals also occurs, as would be the case with various commercial grades of acetylene, provisions of any applicable standard for these chemicals should also be followed. The occupational exposure to airborne acetylene should be controlled so that no employee is exposed to acetylene at a concentration greater than 2500 ppm (2662 mg/m^3 of air). The standard is designed to protect the health and provide safety of employees for up to 10-hour workshift, 40-hour workweek, over a working lifetime. Also known as ethane; ethane; and narcylene.

acid. 1. Any of the various compounds of hydrogen in which some or all of the hydrogen atoms may be replaced by an atom or atoms of a metal, and which is capable of forming hydrogen ions when dissolved in water. Acids may be classified as organic if they contain the -COOH, carboxyl group(s), as in acetic acid CH_3COOH; benzoic acid, C_6H_5COOH; and oxalic acid COOH.COOH. The aromatic organic acids are further classified as *ortho, meta,* or *para,* according to the location of the carboxyl group, -COOH, in relation to another subsistent in a cyclic compound 2. According to Bronsted and Lowry, an acid is a proton donor, and a base is a proton acceptor. An acid always becomes a base after proton transfer. This base is called conjugate base of the acid. By the same logic, when a base accepts a proton in a proton transfer reaction, it becomes an acid. This acid is the conjugate acid of the base. Because new acids and bases are created, the proton transfer reaction can reverse itself in order to continue proton transfer, although it may go largely to completion in one direction or the other. Since Lewis acids seek substances having electron pairs to which they can become bound, Lewis acids are said to be electrophilic (electron loving) in character and an acid displacement reaction is said to be electrophilic displacement. Of the various pollutants present in the atmosphere, ammonia is classified as basic, while hydrogen sulphide, carbon dioxide, nitrogen dioxide, and sulphur dioxide, are classified as acidic.

The wastes of some industries containing both organic and inorganic acids discharged commonly to rivers. Explosive factories, DDT factories, battery industries etc. contain acids, which when discharged in the body of water cause acidic pollution. This pollution causes corrosion of metal, concrete structures and harm to the aquatic life. The self-purification of streams due to natural process is reduced by the pollution of acids. Due to industrial pollutants there is usually a change in *p*H of water. Natural waters very in *p*H from 4.0 to about 9.5. Carbonic acid, formed by the reaction of carbon dioxide and water in the atmosphere, is picked upin the normal precipitation process, so that, rainwater is typically at about a *p*H of 5.6. Howevers, acid mine seepage, and particularly, acid rain, have a major effect on the *p*H of many lakes and streams. Acid rain, for example, can have a *p*H as low as 3.9.

acid clay. A variety of clay that gives off hydrogen ions when dissolved or suspended in water; it is used in the treatment of alkaline water and effluents.

acid deposition. *See* acid rain.

acid dew point. The temperature at which the condensation of water vapours along with small amount of sulphur trioxide and other acidic gases, arising from chimney gases takes place. It has been noticed that in such cases, the condensation takes place at a slightly higher temperature than the normal dew point temperature of water. Since the acid will cause corrosion of chimney and heat-recovery appliances, the chimney gases may be cooled only to a limited extent and the heat which may be recovered is reduced.

acidic gases. The gases such as sulphur dioxide, SO_2; sulphur trioxide, SO_3; hydrogen sulphide, H_2S; carbon dioxide, CO_2; which, when combine with or dissolve in, moisture, generally form corrosive acids.

acidimetry. The determination of the concentration of acid solutions or of the quantity of acid in a sample or of mixture. This is usually done by titration with a solution of base of known strength (standard solution) and an indicator is used to establish the end point.

acidity. 1. The amount of acid present, expressed for a solution either as the molecular concentration of acid, in terms of normality, molarity, etc., or the ionic concentration in terms of *p*H. The acidity of a base is the number of monobasic acid molecules which one molecule of the base can neutralize. 2. Characteristic feature of electrolyte solutions in which concentration of so called hydronium ions H_3O^+, is greater than that of hydroxyl ions, OH^-.

acid mine drainage. Drainage produced when water, passing through surface or underground mines, interacts with pyrites, an impurity in coal, to form sulphuric acid via bacterial action. This acidic water drains in to local streams and may adversly affect the aquatic ecosystem.

acid mine waste. One of the principal pollutants arising from mining operations. Water becomes acidic when it comes in contact with mine wastes containing sulphur containing ore.

acid pickles. The spent liquor from chemical processes that are used in industry to clean metal surfaces or to do bright dips is called and acid pickle. In some industries the wastewater contains various chemical compounds and acids form differing processes. Collectively this industrial wastewater is called acid pickles. The water form thee processes also includes the rinse water used o wash the metal items as a finishing tough to the pickling process.

acid rain. Rainfall occurring when atmospheric water vapour combines with oxides of sulphur and nitrogen. In relatively unpolluted atmosphere, acidity of rainwater is mainly due to dissolved carbon dioxide. The *p*H of rainwater in equilibrium with carbon dioxide is in the range of 5.6-5.7. The acid rain may cause:

(a) the direct leaching of potassium, calcium and magnesium from the leaves of trees;

(b) plant roots to become unhealthy and unable to extract nutrients from the soil. This appears to be due to the increased acidity mobilizing aluminium in the soil. The high levels of aluminium are responsable for killing the plant rootlets. In times of high rainfall, large amounts of aluminum (and other metals) can be flushed from the soil into water course where aquatic animals can be killed from metal poisoning and suffocation.

The origin of the acid rain is attributed primarily to the presence of sulphates, sulphites, and nitrates in the atmosphere. The pollutants result from the burning of fossil fuels, especially in thermal power stations, but they can also be caused by factories and car exhausts. Once they are in the atmosphere, pollutants can be washed down to earth by rainfall in the form of sulphuric and nitric acids. The oxides and other species of nitrogen and sulphur can be incorporated in to liquid water droplets in several different ways. They may be soluble enough to dissolve in water, may attach through diffusional processes, may be incorporated through impaction and collision; and acid aerosol species may act as nuclei for water droplet formation. The most important reactions for SO_2 and NO_x, are:

$$SO_2 + H_2O \rightleftharpoons SO_2.H_2O$$

$$SO_2.H_2O \rightleftharpoons H^+ + HSO_3^-$$

$$HSO_3^- \rightleftharpoons H^+ + SO_3^{2-}$$

$$O_2 + 2HSO_3^- \rightleftharpoons 2H^+ + 2SO_4^{2-}$$

$$H_2O_2 + HSO_3^- \rightleftharpoons H^+ + SO_4^{2-} + H_2O$$

$$O_3 + HSO_3^- \rightleftharpoons H^+ + SO_4^{2-} + O_2$$

$$\cdot NO_2 + O_3 \rightleftharpoons O_2 + \cdot NO_3$$

$$\cdot NO_3 + \cdot NO_2 + Z^* \rightleftharpoons N_2O_5 + Z^*$$

[Z* is a catalyst]

$$N_2O_5 + H_2O \rightleftharpoons 2H^+ + 2NO_3^-$$

$$2\cdot NO_2 + H_2O \rightleftharpoons 2H^+ + NO_3^- + \cdot NO_2$$

The catalysts as well as the *p*H play a very vital role for the above mentioned reactions. It has been revealed that if the *p*H of the medium is in the range of 5, then the presence of ozone, Fe^{3+}, and Mn^{2+}, and many other ions can significantly increase the conversion rates. At a *p*H of 4.5, however, the contribution by the trace metal ions add only about 1% per hour. Another chemical species that can enhance the conversion rates of SO_2 to SO_4^{2-} independently of acid levels in the rainwater is hydrogen peroxide. It dominates the aqueous chemistry process, and may cause conversion rates to reach 100%.h^{-1}, depending up on the cloud type, altitude, and other meteorological conditions, until the H_2O_2 is exhausted. Then O_3 becomes the dominant catalyst. In areas where neither H_2O_2 nor O_3 exist in significant amounts, NO_{3-} formation can control the production of sulphuric acid. H_2O_2 is not important in the NO_{3-} formation. The acids formed in the rainwater are although dilute, but they are powerful enough to poison lakes and rivers, leach soil, rocks, and pipes, damage crops, kill trees and speed up the erosion of buildings. Most industrial countries now have strict regulations to control the amount of pollution which is sent into the atmosphere. Also known as acid deposition.

acid slag. The furnace slag which contains more silica and silicates than lime and magnesia.

acid sludge. The residue left after the petroleum oil has been treated with sulphuric acid, for removing various impurities.

acid soot. Particulates of carbon that have absorbed acid in vapour form, such as hydrochloric acid as a by-products of incineration. Also, large soot particles that contain sulphurous or sulphuric acids formed in a furnace where sulphur in the fuel burns to form its oxides. If the soot particles gather on portions of the incinerate fuel, or on other metal surfaces, they can cause corrosion. The potential hazard can be reduced by using fuels of relatively sulphur content, operating plant with a minimum of excess air in order to reduce the formation of sulphur trioxide; elimination of air in-leakage to flues; the raising of back end temperatures; the use of additives; the insulation of chimneys and duct work; by the combination of such measures.

acid value. 1. The number of milligrams of potassium hydroxide required to neutralize the free acids present in one gram of oil, fat, or wax. The determination is made by titrating the sample in hot 95% ethyl alcohol using phenolphthalein as indicator. It is therefore, a measure of the degree of hydrolysis of the fat. Also known as acid number. 2. The acidity of a solution expressed in terms of normality.

acid wash. A solution of phosphoric acid applied to steel parts that neutralizes and removes the alkaline solutions used for grease removal after machining; it also forms a metallic phosphate coating that accepts paint and, of itself, provides a high degree of protection against corrosion.

acid water pollution. Acidic industrial wastewaters arise form manufacture of chemicals, insecticides, batteries, textiles, beer, mining, and pickling operations. Acid waters have a *p*H lower than 7·0.

acoustic dissipative element. Component of acoustic circuits associated with loss of energy. Operates by impeding the flow of gas through fine cloth, slits or porous material.

acoustic emissions. The Internal sounds generated by a structural material when placed under stress. Acoustic emissions are a kind of forewarning of structural failure, hence the equipments designed to detect them is an important mean for preventing hazardous materials spills caused by ruptured tanks or pipelines.

acoutic feedback. Feedback in which the feedback path is from a loudspeaker to a microphone in an electroacoustic amplifying system, either by direct air path or via room reflections or reverberations. The feedback will be maximum and positive for those frequencies for which the correspoinding standing sound wave in the room has antinodes at the microphone and speaker positions and for which the total loop gain of the system and feedback path has a maximum real part. Apart from oscillations that may be set up, acoustic feedback may give rise to udesirable echoes of impulsive sounds. Positive acoustic feedback is undesirable if it givesrisetoringingorhowling,but it is deliberately used in certain concerthallsto extendthe low-frequency reverberation times.

acoustic filter. System which transmits acoustic waves only over certain desired bands offrequencies while highly attenuating neighbouring frequency bands which are not required.

acoustic labyrinth. Loudspeaker enclosure designed to present an acoustic resistance to the rear of a loudspeaker diaphragm in such as way as to absorb all the sound radiated form this side. This may be achieved by a series of lined sound-absorbing partitions which produce a long convoluted path for sounds form the rear of the loudspeaker.

acoustic perfume. Unobtrusive broad-band noise generated in reading-rooms, libraries, etc. for the purpose of masking othrwise distracting noises such as pages being trurned or chairs being moved.

acoustic shielding. Means of protecting a location from sound, usually involving enclosure.

acoustic tile. Rigid prefabricated unit, consisting of or containing sound-absorbing material available in range of compositions, and surface characteristics with corresponding differences in acoustical properties. Tiles and panels are differentiated only on the basis of unit size, panels being the larger.

acoustic trauma. Noise-induced hearinglossresultingfromasingle briefexposure toanintensesound, as from gunfire or an explosion. Distinguishedform noise-induced hearing loss of gradual onset in workers exposed to steady noise in their occupations.

acoustical comfort. Situation of a hearer where his reception of sound is subjectively satisfying; in particular, the absence of unwanted sound. In 1951 an acoustial comfort index gives 100 as ideal conditions of acoustical comfort, 0 as bearable conditions and -100 as intolerable ones.

acoustic vault. Concave ceiling of an auditorium giving (usually undersired) concentration of sound over parts of the ausience area.

acquired immunity. The immunity that develops as a result of exposure to a new environment, foreign substance, or organism.

acquired immunodeficiency syndrome (AIDS). Severe immunodeficiency appearing in adults, and characterized by repeated bizarre and severe infections and an otherwise rare skin tumor, Kaposi's sarcoma. Common in homosexuals and heroin addicts. Patients appear to have a deficiency of helper *T* lymphocytes. Probably caused by *T* cell leukemia virus (HTLV-3).

acquired tolerance. Immunological tolerance induced by injecting very small or very large doses of antigen, and persisting only so long as that antigen remains in the body; in contrast to immunological tolerance arising naturally. *See also* adoptive tolerance.

acridine. A tricyclic compound containing nitrogen; it is used in the manufacture of many dyes, especially acriflavine and proflavine; recognized to have carcinogenic or cocarcinogenic potential.

acrolein. A colourless aliphatic, compound containing -CHO group; used as an intermediate in the manufacture of synthetic glycerol, polyurethane, and polyester resins. The available data for acrolein indicate that acute and chronic toxicity to fresh water aquatic life occurs at concentrations as low as 68 and 21 µg/L, respectively. For the protection of human health from the toxic effects of this compound, if ingested through water and contaminated aquatic organisms, the ambient water criterion has been determined to be 320 µg/L. For the protection of human health from toxic properties of acrolein ingested through contaminated aquatic organisms alone, the ambient water criterion has been determined to be 780 µg/L. It has been enlisted as a hazardous air pollutant.

acrylamide. An organic compound containing -$CONH_2$ group, used in synthesis of dyes, paper and textile sizes, soil conditioning, and sewage and waste treatment. It is quite irritant to skin and mucous membranes. The workplace concentration of acrylamide should be properly controlled so that no employee is exposed at a concentration greater than 0.3 mg/m^3 of air determined as TWA concentration for up to 10-hour workshift, 40-hour workweek.

acrylonitrile. A compound used in the manufacture of a large number of polymers and other products. It is highly flammable, and toxic by inhalation as well as skin absorption. It has been classified as potential occupational carcinogen. It is important that no employee should be exposed to an airborne concentration of acrylonitrile in excess of 2 ppm (in air) as an 8-hour time-weighted average (TWA); and 10 ppm as averaged over any 15-minute period during the workday. The available data for acrylonitrile indicate that acute toxicity to fresh water aquatic life occurs at concentrations as low as 7550 µg/L.

actinic rays. The radiations effective in producing chemical changes and biological reaction. This term is usually applied to the violet and ultraviolet portion of the electromagnetic spectrum which consists of radiations relatively effective in causing these changes, as contrasted with radiation in the long wavelength region of the electromagnetic spectrum.

action level. The level at which provisions of the proposed Occupational Safety and Health Act of 1970 (OSHA) of U.S. standards must be initiated, such as periodic measurements of employee exposure, training of employees, and medical surveillance (if appropriate for the particular substance).

activated adsorption. The phenomenon of chemisorption characterized by fairly high energy of activation.

activated alumina. A highly porous and granular form of aluminium oxide having preferential adsorptive potential capacity for moisture from gases, vapours, and some liquids. It is employed as catalyst and as drying agent in various pollution control processes.

activated carbon. A highly porous form of carbon obtained by destructive distillation of carbon-rich materials in the absence of air, to eliminate the volatile portions, followed by high-temperature treatment of the carbon with steam or carbon dioxide. The product ob-

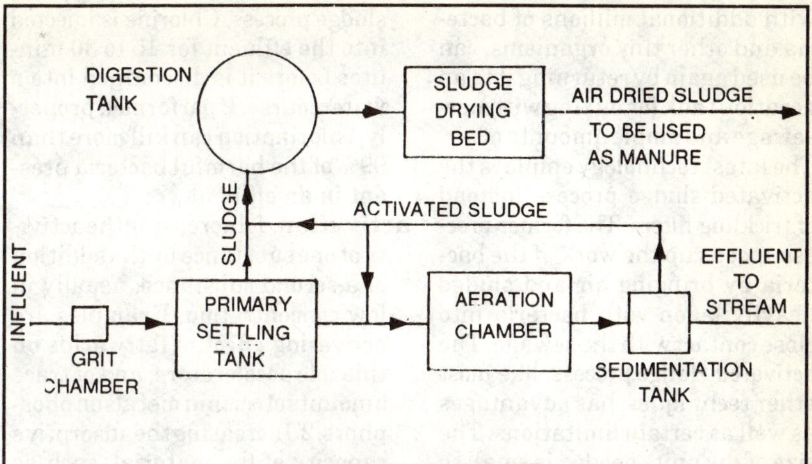

ACTIVATED SLUDGE PLANT

tained may have an internal surface area ranging from 420 to almost 1500 m^2/g. This enables it to strongly absorb molecules of gases and vapours or colloidally suspended particles from liquids. Activated carbon is used to reclaim solvents from the vapour phase, and to decolourize liquids. It is an important material used in the absorption processes that removes odours and toxic substances form industrial stack gases. It is also widely used in sewage sludge treatment. Also known as activated charcoal.

activated charcoal. *See* activated carbon.

activated clay. Clay whose absorbent character or bleaching action has been enhanced by acid treatment. Bentonite clay is most frequently treated in this way, which is used in sludge treatment.

activated complex. Unstable configuration of reactant atoms corresponds to maximum of potential energy in reaction path. Such chemical species are frequently encountered in the photochemical reactions taking place in the atmosphere. Also known as transition state; transition complex; critical complex.

activated sludge. A biologically active sediment resulting from the repeated exposure of organic waste materials to atmospheric oxygen, permitting the growth of aerobic bacteria and other unicellular organisms that feed upon and destroy the pollutants in the waste. *See also* activated-sludge process.

activated-sludge process. A process for the treatment of waste waters, in which the sewage from the settling tank during primary treatment is pumped to an aeration tank where it is mixed with air and sludge loaded with bacteria and allowed to remain for several hours. During this time, the bacteria break down the organic matter. From the aeration tank the sewage, known as mixed liquor, flows to another sedimentation tank to remove the solids. Chlorination of the effluent completes the basic secondary treatment. The sludge, now activated with additional millions of bacteria and other tiny organisms, can be used again by returning it to an aeration tank for mixing with new sewage and ample amounts of air. The latest technology employs the activated-sludge process instead of trickling filters. The former process speeds up the work of the bacteria by bringing air and sludge heavily laden with bacteria into close contact with the sewage. The activated-sludge process, like most other techniques, has advantages as well as certain limitations. The size of the units needed is small so that it requires comparatively less land space. Also, the process is free from insects and odours. But it is more expensive to operate than the trickling filter, and it sometimes loses its effectiveness when certain noncombatible substances are present in industrial wastes.

An adequate supply of oxygen is essentially needed for the activated-sludge process to be effective. Air is mixed with sewage and biologically active sludge in the aeration tanks by three different methods. The first, mechanical aeration, is accomplished by drawing the sewage from the bottom of the tank and spraying it over the surface, thus causing the sewage to absorb large amounts of oxygen from the atmosphere. In the second method, a large amount of air under pressure is pumped into the sewage and forced out through openings in the pipe. The third method is a combination of mechanical aeration and the forced-air method.

The final phase of the secondary treatment consists of the addition of chlorine to effluent coming from the trickling filter or the activated-sludge process. Chlorine is injected into the effluent for 15 to 30 minutes before it is discharged into a watercourse. If performed properly, chlorination can kill more than 99% of the harmful bacteria present in an effluent.

activation. 1. Increasing the activity of one substance by the addition of a second substance, usually in low concentration. Examples are activating effect of fatty acids on thiazole accelerators, and of trace amounts of certain metals on phosphors. 2. Increasing the adsorptive capacity of the material, such as charcoal or alumina by exposing it in a finely divided state to steam or carbon dioxide at high temperature; this treatment creates a high degree of porosity and thus increases the interior surface area. 3. Supplying of air and oxygen continuously to sewage sludge to promote growth of aerobic bacteria which digest (decompose) organic waste material.

activator. 1. Any substance which renders a material or a system active; commonly a catalyst. For example, certain metal ions act as activator during the formation of aerosols and photochemical smog. A special use of this term occurs in the flotation process, where an activator assists the action of the collector. 2. A substance which increases the effectiveness of rubber vulcanization accelerator, *e.g.*, zinc oxide, zinc laurate, litharge. 3. A substance which is required in trace quantities to impart luminescence to certain crystals. Silver and copper are used as activators for zinc sulphide and cadmium sulphide pigments.

active immunity. The protection

due to development of an immune response in an individual following stimulation with antigen, *e.g.*, in a vaccine or during infection.

active immunization. Stimulation of an individual's immune responses in order to confer protection against disease. It is effected by exposure to protective antigens either during the course of infection (which may be subclinical) or by vaccination. The protection effected usually takes a week or more to develop, but is then long lasting.

active life of a facility. The period from the initial receipt of hazardous waste at the facility until the Regional Administrator receives certification of final closure.

active portion. That portion of a facility where treatment, storage, or disposal operations are being or have been conducted and that is not a closed portion.

acute. A term used in the pollution studies to refer a sudden onset, lasting for a short time. It is used to define either the exposure or the response to an exposure.

acute lymphoblastic leukemia. Leukemia in which the predominant cell-type is lymphoblast-like, and usually lacking *T* or *B* lymphocyte markers. Possibly a neoplasm of committed stem cells. In a minority of cases, the cells are identifiable as immature *B* or *T* lymphocytes.

adaptation. The emergence of structural and external morphological and physiological properties in the living organism or group of organisms which, under given environmental conditions, increase in vitality and fertility; it results in better development, more vigorous or more rapid growth, a longer life-span and better exploitation of matter and energy resources.

adaptive value. The degree of adaptability of an organism or a group of organisms to an environment, in relation to that of other organisms or populations.

additives. A nonspecific term referring to any substance added to a food, a petroleum product, or a rubber and/or plastic mixture, to impart a particular purpose or property. In most cases the proportion necessary to accomplish the desired results is 1% or less. Food additives usually include antioxidants, leveaning agents, emulsifiers, flavours, and colorants. While headlines are being made by the danger to human and other animal life form tailpipe pollution, the list of additives to gasoline, oil and other fuels involved in internal combustion during motor vehicle operations grows and grows. Some of the frequently used additives include:

(a) antiknock compounds;

(b) high-speed and low-speed additives;

(a) scavengers used to remove sludge form valves and spark plugs;

(c) modifier that alter chemical character of deposits in cylinders;

(d) deactivators capable of destroying metals such as copper;

(e) anti-rust agents in gasoline that inhibit corrosion in gas tanks, fuel lines and the engine itself;

(f) anti-icing agents to keep fuel lines free of winter ice;

(g) detergents to inhibit in carburetors; and

(h) lubricants loaded with chemicals to minimize valve and piston-ring sticking more difficult for the engine to burn gasoline efficiently.

Most additives undergo chemical change during engine operation and are swept out as pollutants through the exhaust. Indeed some secondary products formed from additives are more dangerous than exhaust from gasoline free of additives.

additive toxicity. The toxicity of a mixture of chemicals which is approximately equivalent to that expected from a simple summation of known toxicities of the individual chemicals present in the mixture.

adhesion. In general, a condition in which two discrete entities or particles remain in close contact, or the force as a result of which such a condition is maintained. Specifically, the term adhesion is often used in chemistry to denote the attraction between the unlike particles, as distinguished from cohesion, which is the internal force of attraction, molecular or otherwise within a single substance or phase.

adsorbate. A substance which is absorbed at the surface of a stationary phase in the process of adsorption. Also known as adsorptive. In some cases term adsorbate refers a substance which has already been adsorbed, whereas term adsorptive is restricted to substance (present in gaseous or liquid bulk phases) which can be adsorbed under given conditions.

adsorbent. Crystalline amorphous or liquid substance or gel with greatly increased outer or inner surface area at which adsorption takes place.

adsorbent installations. Pollution control devices that cleanse dirty gas by causing pollutants to cling to an adsorbent. In one of the applications of continuous adsorption, a rotating fixed-bed adsorbent installation is employed. In large applications, fluidized bed adsorbent installations in a series might be employed.

adsorption. The attachment of the molecules of a gas or liquid to the surface of another substance (usually a solid); these molecules form a closely adherent film or layer held in place by electrostatic forces that are considerably weaker than chemical bonds. This process is widely used for extracting a pollutant by causing it to be attached to an adsorbent cleaner. In industry this physical-chemical method of collecting vapours containing recoverable solvents is initiated by use of any of the following:

(a) activated carbon,
(b) alumina (Al_2O_3),
(c) molecular sieves,
(d) silica gels (bentonite), and
(e) ion exchange resins.

advanced incineration concepts. Among the latest innovations put forth by manufacturers all over the world, three distinct types are:

(a) slugging incinerators,
(b) Fluidized-bed incinerators,
(c) pyrolysis.

advection. In the parlance of air pollution control and meteorology, advection is referred to horizontal convection.

aeration. The capturing of air and the forcing of it into water is called aeration. One use of aeration occurs when air is artificially introduced into sewage wastewater or effluent in order to create aerobic conditions and faster biological and chemical purification. Aeration is also used to purify water after filtration in a water supply system. It can be accomplished in two ways:

(a) the air can be bubbled into or

through the effluent; or

(b) the effluent undergoing aeration can be sprayed into the air and caught in a pool.

Stream and bubbling brooks undergo natural aeration as they bubble along on their merry route to river or sea.

aerator. A mechanical device used to inject air into effluent in order to facilitate aerobic action. In operation an aerator subject the greatest possible amount of water to be treated to the oxygen in the air in continuous fashion.

aeroacoustics. The study of the noise generated by jet engines and rocket tubes during fuel combustion in flight; investigations of aircraft noise in general including the noise sources, the external and internal sound fields (particularly form aircraft treavelling at supersonic speed), and thir effect on the enviromnent.

aeroallergen. Pollen or organic dust which cause hay fever and other allergic condition.

aerobacter aerogens. Non-faecal coli, usually originating in soil and decaying vegetable matter, without creating any offensive odour.

aerobic. Organisms requiring the presence of air or oxygen to live, grow, and reproduce; the term is applied to micro-organisms of various types, especially those used in activated sludge process for industrial and municipal waste treatment. Aerobic condition is good for the flowing rivers, the rate of cleansing depending on the concentration of the dissolved oxygen available. Its opposite term, anaerobic, refers to an organism that can live without air or oxygen, or to a digestion process from which air is excluded. *See also* activated sludge.

aerobic-anaerobic interface. The meeting point of bacterial action involving both anaerobic and aerobic micro-organisms on a body of sewage sludge, processed solid waste undergoing composting, or both is called the aerobic anaerobic interface. It is at this point that the material undergoing decomposition has been stabilized.

aerobic waste treatment. The process of treating the effluent from industrial processes by oxidation.

aerodynamic roughness. A term referring to the roughness of a surface over which a fluid flows, such that the boundary layer becomes turbulent at lower flow speeds than would be the case with a similar surface; with a blunt object turbulent flow leads to a decrease in total drag with a stream lined object viscous drag constitutes the total drag, which therefore remains at a lower level if the boundary layer is maintained in the laminar state.

aerodynamic sound. Term used to indicate sound fields which are products of airflows; sound fields which do not emanate from vibrating solids but from the movement through the air of some solid body *e.g.* a propeller, or fluid *e.g.* a jet stream.

aerofilter. A modified form of high-rate trickling filter; used for sewage treatment.

aerogel. A colloidal solution of a gaseous phase in a solid phase, obtained usually by replacement of the liquid in the dispersed phase by air or gas.

aerology. The study of the free atmosphere *i.e.*, that portion of the atmosphere above the friction layer, in which the air motion is affected

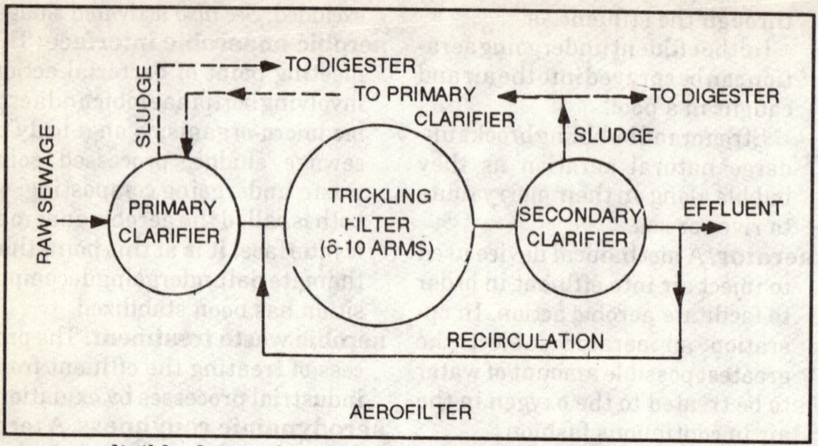

to a negligible degree by surface friction.

aerometric waste treatment. A method employed in treating effluent from industrial processes; this method subjects the waste water to aeration, and the water is partly purified by oxidation.

aerosols. Liquid particles with or without particulates, that are larger than molecules, but small enough to remain suspended and dispersed in a gas for a period of time. It can be regarded as a gas containing particles with a very low settling velocity. Thus, atmosphere can be regarded as an aerosol since it always has some particulate matter of small size, for example, in a smoke-filled room there may be as much as 1,000,000 to 10,000,000 particles per cm^3. Combustion products from cars, industry and heating represent by far the biggest source of air pollution caused by man's activities. Of the substances released into the atmosphere in this way, over 100 have been identified as contaminants. The proportion of organic compounds is much higher, which includes aromatic (unsaturated as well as annular) hydrocarbons, phenols, acids, bases, and many other compounds. Due to photochemical and other reactions, between contaminants upon their arrival in the earth's atmosphere, new compounds can also be formed. Among the atmospheric pollutants, substances in suspension consisting of solid and/or liquid particles are known as aerosols. These emanate either form condensation processes, by which molecular, masses combine to form bigger particles (*e.g.,* cloud formation from liquid particles), or form dispersion processes, by which coarse, material is split into finer particles (*e.g.,* flue dust form coal dust combustion). An essential feature of aerosols is the size of their particles. Coarse dust and soot, flue dust and the like, whose particles are over 10 μm in size, settle very quickly from the atmosphere under the force of gravity. Finer particles, on the other hand, with a diameter of less than 5 μm, remain suspended in the atmosphere. In this case the force of gravity is outweighed by the Brownian molecular movement in the atmosphere. For particles so small, the force of gravity is over ruled by Brownian movement, or the random motion of particles caused by their collision with molecules in the surrounding air. The velocity of aerosol particles due to Brownian movement is greater than their rate of vertical descent. Consequently, aerosols can be distributed by air currants almost like gases. Owing to their low concentrations, natural particles such as fog (1-40 μm), bacteria (1-15 μm), plant spores (10-30 μm), and pollen (20-60 μm) do not usually cause atmospheric pollution; and from a medical point of view, furthermore, they are generally harmless (except for possible allergic reactions). Particles released by artificial processes, such as cement (10-150 μm), flue dust (3-80 μm), quartz and asbestos (0.5-10 μm), oil smoke (0.03-1 μm), tobacco smoke (0.01-0.15 μm) and radioactive aerosols (0.1-20 μm), can give rise to serious atmospheric pollution depending up-on their concentration. On an extended area, aerosols can display considerable surface powers. This enables them to accumulate gas molecules, which facilitates chemical reactions of aerosols with the surrounding gases. Many substances which in the compact state combine very slowly with oxygen, react immediately when they enter the atmosphere as fine powder. Finally, the effects of energy radiation from the sun can be severely modified by solid or liquid particles dispersed in the air. Such particles absorb the radiation and pass on rapidly to surrounding gas molecules, which for their part can be fully previous to radiant energy, so that without the aerosols no heating would occur. Owing to their effect as condensation nuclei, on which water vapour can be deposited, they also affect the formation of mist or fog. Aerosols can be a particularly dangerous form for pollutants to take because they can be breathed into the lungs, where they can both damage sensitive lung tissue and be absorbed directly into the blood stream without the protection afforded by the digestive system.

after burner. A combustion chamber in which any smoke, carbon monoxide or other organic substances in the exhaust gases from furnaces or certain types of engine can be completely burned. The chamber normally contains oil or gas-fired burners to maintain the necessary high temperature, and the oxygen content of the gases is adjusted by admitting air as required. After-burners are also used to burn malodorous organic substances in gases arising from various processes. If the gases entering the after-burner are sufficiently hot, the use of a catalyst sometimes enables complete combustion to be achieved at a lower than normal temperature enables complete combustion to be achieved at a lower than normal temperature, and the provision of fuel to the after-burner may be necessary only when starting-up or at low through-put. Catalytic after-burners are widely used industry and have received a great deal of attention as a means of purifying motor vehicle exhaust gases.

agglomeration. The combination or aggregation of small particles in a liquid into clusters of approximately spherical shape. The agglomerates have varying degrees of voids, loosely bound, and have foamlike structures. They are formed by mechanical means in chamber spray driers, tubes, or fluidized beds, usually in the presence of moisture.

agitation. The act of bringing about intimate mixing and uniform dispersion of the components of a solid or liquid mixture. This is usually performed by stirring, grinding, kneading, shaking, or plowing with the help of mechanical

aggregation. A general term describing the combination or coalescence of particles dispersed in a suspension into clusters or clots, which either precipitate or are removed by filtration. Various types of aggregation includes agglutination, coagulation, flocculation, and agglomeration. It finds numerous applications in the treatment of industrial affluents and liquid wastes.

aggressions. Diffusible substances produced by pathogenic bacteria; though not necessarily toxic themselves, interfere with normal defence mechanisms and enhance the ability of organism to establish itself in the host's tissues.

agricultural pollution. The liquid and the solid wastes from all types of farming, including truck farming, dairy farming etc. Complicating agricultural pollutants include pesticides applied to both ground and crops. Special types of farming such as duck farming and poultry farming, and cattle feed lot operations create special pollution problems because of concentration wastes form the animals. Finally carcasses of dead animals and detritus from grain stalks dried leaves all form part of the soil enrichment and pollution. The surface water and the ground water included in farmland and rangeland are also endangered by erosion and the dust raised during ploughing, fertilization, rainwater runoff and snow melt.

agricultural wastes. Solid and liquid wastes arising from animals harvesting of crops, pesticides, erosion sediment, logging debris, dried stalks of harvested grain, etc.

air. The mixture of gases that envelops the earth's crust. Its composition varies with the altitude and the locality from which the sample is collected. The composition of dry air at sea level is:

Substance	*% by volume*
Nitrogen	78.0
Oxygen	20.95
Argon	0.93
Carbon dioxide	0.033
Neon	0.0018
Helium	0.0005
Methane	0.0002
Krypton	0.0001
Nitrous oxide	0.000,05
Hydrogen	0.000,05
Xenon	0.000,008
Ozone	0.000,001

There is no term such as pure air because air is a changing mixture of gases and solids. If there is a certain arbitrary minimum of solids present in the air sample, it may be classified as clean air. Air without any solid particulates is nicknamed as 'pure air'. When loaded with pollutants air may be classified as satisfactory, hazardous, unhealthy, dangerous, etc, according to the whim of the air pollution control authorities in the affected area. Air that is outdoors is called ambient air. Outdoor air that is still is often mistakenly called stagnant air. Air that is partly opaque due to suspended soils and oxidants is called either smog, smuts or smaze. Fresh air and stale air are descriptions that went out with the running boards and luggage racks on antique autos. *See also* atmosphere.

air basin. A geographic area in which owing to meteorological factors and topographic features, the air is more of less homogeneous and across whose boundaries pollutant transport is minimal. the concept is little used because of the difficulty at the present stage of development of meteorology and diffusion theory in defining such areas.

airchange rate. The actual or anticipated rate at which the volume of air within a built space is replaced, either by means of mechanical air-handling plant or by natural infiltration. The control of airchange rate is a significant factor in the pollution conscious design of buildings.

air classification. The separation of solid particles according to weight/size, by suspension in and settling from an air stream of appropriate velocity, as in air-floated clays and other particulates.

air curtain. One of the methods for mechanical containment of oil spills/dust particles. In this method, a pipe containing many holes is placed above (for dust containment), or below (for oil spill containment) the surface and air is vigorously pumped into the pipe. The exiting air (or air bubbles) retards the rapidly spreading of dust (or oil).

air-ground interface. The boundary where the lower atmosphere comes in contact with the topography of the earth; and where there is an exchange of certain physical and chemical factors, along with exchanges of light and energy This interface is of immense importance to life processes.

air pollutant incineration. A process for the incineration of contaminated gases and emissions, which cannot be cleaned from emissions by normal processes such as absorption and adsorption. It involves the disposal of pollutants such as aerosols, hydrocarbons, oxides of sulphur, ammonia, *etc.*, in a flame afterburner using a fuel. Combustion occurs in the afterburner between oxygen and the contaminated gases. The modification of this process involves the use of direct-flame incineration in the presence of a suitable catalyst. In this process the waste stream of gases is passed through a catalytic bed, where it causes the cleansing to occur at much lower temperature. This method finds application in oil refining, chemical and plastic industries, and pollution control.

air pollutants. In general, liquids, solids, or gases that are not normal constituent of the air, that in certain concentrations may be hazardous to animal and plant life, including human beings. These include oxides of carbon and sulphur, inorganic and organic acids, halogenated hydrocarbons, inorganic particulate trace elements and their compounds, insecticides, bacteria, viruses, dust and more much more.

air pollution. Introduction into the atmosphere of substances that are not normally present therein and that have a harmful effect on man, animals, or plant life. Among all the effects of pollution, the one of most immediate interest and concern is the impact on human health. Each day an adult inhales a volume of air normally in the range 10 to 15 m^3. While the lungs provide a very effective means of absorbing oxygen in to the blood stream, they provide similar facilities for many other gaseous impurities in air. Also, any small solid particles in the atmosphere can be drawn in to the lungs with each breath and a proportion may be deposited on the lung surface. Occupational diseases such as silicosis, which can arise among workers subjected to high levels of dust, have been recognized for many years. Estimates of global problems created by anthropogenic pollutants are often based on incomplete data and computer models. However, there is a growing concensus in the scientific community that such problems as acid rain, the greenhouse effect, and stratospheric ozone depletion are serious, and that governmental and economic actions are required to limit their impacts. Air quality problems in some developing countries, such as India, Mexico, Brazil, and China,are now reaching levels which can have severe adverse impacts on their populations and their environment. It is only throuh international acceptance and understanding of global air pollution problems, and international willingness to act, that the problems can be minimized.

air pollution control. Methods of controlling emissions loaded with solid, liquid and/or gaseous pollutants introduced into the atmosphere by both industrial and governmental polluters involve mechanical collection absorption, adsorption, air pollutant incineration and catalytic combustion. At the same time, the emission of contaminants to the atomosphere should be reduced by making proper changes or modifications in raw materials operation, and system control at the industries. The emission of pollutants may be due to presence of non-essential ingradients is the raw material, which act as the main source of pollutants. For reducing the air-pollutions from emission we usually follow the important illustrations are as under:

(a) Unleaded petrol should be used to reduce load concentration in ambient air due to vehicles.

(b) The vehicles should be driven on electricity, hydrogen, or methane as a source of energy to eliminate the concentration of various pollutants such as carbon monoxide and oxides of nitrogen.

(c) Bauxite flux should be used in place of fluorine containing flurospar.

(d) To reduce the emission of NO_2 two stage combustion should be adopted.

For eradication of Man-made hazards the sense of social and hygenic conciousness at national and international level are needed for preventing air pollution by anti-exhaust, locomotives in the stations yards, thermal power stations, etc., and training of the drivers by the the Transport Department and the establishment of suitable laboratories in co-operation with the industrialists and philanthropists.

air pollution control goals. Air quality control efforts are made to fulfill the following criteria:

(a) reduce concentrations of generation of sulphur and carbon oxides;

(b) reduce the volume of particulates emitted to the atmosphere;

(c) lessen concentration at heavy source points; and

(d) monitor and control the natural air resource for better cleaner air.

To some extent this can be achieved by equipping existing and future incinerators with adequate electrostatic precipitators, in order to effectively scrub flue gases, toxic oxides and particulates. Further suggestion in this regard is to convert all transportation modes to vehicles powered by hydrogen, methane, propane, butane, electricity, or anything else that will end diesel or combustion engine emission.

air pollution emissions inventory. An information collection and processing system containing data on emissions of, and sources of, air pollution from both man-made and natural causes.

air pollution episode. The occurrence of exceptionally high concentration levels of air pollution during a period of the order of a few days.

air pollution index. An arbitrary function of the concentration of one more pollutants that is taken as a measure of the severity of pollution. For example, the following index has been used in the USA: 10 times the sulphur dioxide concentration plus the carbon monoxide concentration (both in ppm by volume) plus twice the coefficient of haze. It was considered to be a cause for alarm when the value of this index deviates from its average of about 12 to 50 or more. Several such indices are used, but none has more than local use, nor has any been found fully satisfactory.

air purification. The process of the removal of the substances from air, that are not the normal constituents. Air purification and the recovery of valuable raw materials, especially from fine powder, is often possible only by means of an electrostatic precipitator. The construction, size and performance of such a dust extractor depend got a large extent, on the working conditions existing; and they will also be geared to the volume of gas, in particular to its temperature, condensation point, and dust content and to the physical and chemical properties of the dust and the supporting gas. Electrostatic precipitators are available for the separation of dust particles in whatever quantity and of whatever size. They are used in almost all dust-producing plants in industrial sectors such as mining, the chemical industry, blast furnaces, foundries, power stations and garbage disposal. According to the method of dust extraction (scaling or rinsing), a distinction is made between dry and wet electric precipitators, though their construction and method of operation do not differ greatly from one another. The general installation of dust extractors in industry has made a considerable contribution to the improvement of the emissions situation. It may be assumed, therefore, that despite increasing industrialization, the emission of dust would decline considerably if all old plant installations were equipped with dust extractors.

air quality. Since presence of pollutants in most urban areas is an accepted way of life for normal day-today air resource status, air quality involves the degree of concentration of undesirable pollutants such as oxides of sulphur and carbon, and hydrocarbons. Conditions affecting air quality involve weather, topography of the affected area meteorology of the region activity of both motorists and industrial processors, and the volume and type of emissions from governmental polluters.

air quality assessment. A general term for the collection, handling, evaluation, analysis and presentation of data necessary to understand the air pollution problem of a certain area/region, and its causes. Such data normally refer to geography, topography, land use, sources and emissions, ambient air quality, meteorology, climatology, atmospheric chemistry etc.

air quality class. The rating system established to determine allowable levels of air pollution in various regions. The air quality classification system divides the country into airsheds and categorizes each airshed into one of the three classes:

Class I: No deterioration allowed; it includes national parks and wilderness areas, and other pristine or reasonably pristine regions.

Class II: Some deterioration allowed; and it varies from region to region. In such cases the allowable ambient levels of pollutants are set by the state, as long as they do not exceed the national standards.

Class III: Deterioration allowed up to national standards; these are primarily industrial regions and large municipalities where ambient quality standards are largely ignored as long as pollutants do not reach unhealthful levels as defined by the Environmental Protection Agency (EPA).

air quality criteria. Air quality standards set down by the federal government involving precise amounts of pollutants and maximum exposure times permissible for good health. the criteria are usually expressed in parts per million related to a set number of hours.

air quality management strategy. The air quality management strategy, sometimes referred to as the air resource management strategy, involves designating the level of pollution deemed acceptable in terms of a set of ambient air-quality standards and then controlling pollutant emissions.

air quality simulation model. Any of the various models, usually in the form of a set of mathematical equations, which relates the air quality in an area to emissions. Many models are in practice for the routine application in environmental impact studies and form the basis of regulatory air-quality modelling. Some of the frequently used models are: BLP, CRSTER, CDM, HIWAY, ISCST, ISCLT, LONGZ, MESOPUFF, MPTDS, MPTER, PAL, PALDS, PTPLU, RAM, ROADCHEM, and ROADWAY.

air quality standard. In contrast to air quality criteria based on possible effect on a receptor air quality standards are designed to set levels for the air resource itself. Thus an air quality standard simply the prescribed level of a pollutant that cannot be exceeded in a specific area during a set period of time. This standard is set for oxides of sulphur and carbon for hydrocarbons and for most other solid, and gaseous pollutants possibly present in the atmosphere.

air shed. The envelope of air encompassing a specific region. The pollutants in one part of an airshed are swiftly transferred to other parts of the same airshed but not to the neighboring airsheds.

aldrin. The assigned common name for an insecticidal product containing 95% or more of the compound 1,2,3,4,10,10-hexachloro-1,4,4a,5, 8,8a-hexahydro-1,4,5,8-endoexodimethanonaphthalene. It is highly toxic by ingestion and inhalation, and has been enlisted as a potential occupational carcinogen. Occupational exposure to airborne aldrin should be controlled so that no employee is exposed to aldrin at a concentration greater than 0.25 mg/m^3 of air. For freshwater aquatic life concentration of aldrin should exceed 3.0 µg/L at any time, while for saltwater aquatic life it should not exceed 1.3 µg/L.

In all species examined (mouse, rat, rabbit, rhesus monkey, chimpanzee) 1,2-hydroxydieldrin and 4,5-aldrin-*trans*-dihydrodiol were the major metabolites. Regarding the ratios of these two metabolites, the rats and primates seemed to metabolize dieldrin mainly by direct oxidation resulting in 12-hydroxydieldrin, whereas in mice and rabbits the main metabolic process seemed to be the opening of the epoxide ring to the diol. This metabolic pathway, together with a high rate of metabolism compared with other animal species examined may result in relatively high concentrations of 4,5-aldrin-trans-dihydrodiol in the mouse liver. In humans, neither unchanged dieldrin nor the urinary metabolites found in rats were identified in workers occupationally exposed to dieldrin or in monkeys fed the insecticide. Dieldrin is a powerful inducers of microsomal enzymes. Mice react rather anomalously and, therefore may not be an appropriate model for humans. The results of prolonged enzyme injection are proliferation of the endoplasmic reticulum in the cells and hypertrophy and hyperplasia of the liver. No measurable microsomal enzyme induction occurs in man after long exposure to approximately 0.01 mg/kg of body weight per day. The calculated half-life of dieldrin in workers who were removed from exposure was seven months. The mean dieldrin concentration in blood during the last half-year of exposure was 0.1 mg/L, which corresponded to an average daily oral intake of about 0.17 mg/kg of body weight.

For the maximum protection of human health from the potential carcinogenic effects due to exposure of aldrin through ingestion of contaminated aquatic organisms and water, the ambient water concentration should be zero based on the nonthreshold assumption for aldrin. However, zero level may not be attainable at present time. Therefore, the levels that may result in incremental increase of cancer risk over lifetime are estimated at 10^{-5}, 10^{-6}, and 10^{-7}. The corresponding criteria are 0.74 ng/L, 0.074 ng/L, and 0.0074 ng/L respectively. If the above estimates are made for the consumption of aquatic organisms only (excluding consumption of water), the levels are redefined as 0.79 ng/L, 0.079 ng/L, and 0.0079 ng/L respectively.

alfisol. An order of soils with grey to brown surface horizons, a medium-to-high base supply, and horizons of clay accumulation.

algae. A large and diverse group of chlorophyll containing photosynthetic organisms. The majority of the approximately 25,000 known species of algae are one-celled organisms, although multicellular forms exist. The algae are not now regarded as a taxonomic group, although they are sometimes grouped with other simple organisms in the kingdom *Protista*. Usually, however, the component groups are recognized as taxonomic divisions. The separation in these divisions is based primarily on the composition of the cell wall, the nature of the stored food reserves, and other photosynthetic pigments present. Algae are found in almost every habitat. In the oceans, vast numbers of minute species float suspended in the upper levels of the water while the shores are covered with many and varied forms. In freshwaters, they are equally abundant, but due to their smaller size are seldom so conspicuous as the marine forms. They are found on the surface of the ground, on the bark of trees, on rocks, and even underground to a depth of several metres. In fact, wherever they find support and can obtain the necessary materials for growth, there algae may be found.

algaecides. Chemicals that destroy algae. These chemicals generally contain copper, aluminum and other metallic elements, which in combination cause reactions lethal to algal life. They are used to destroy an algal bloom and to reverse eutrophication in stagnant lakes and ponds.

algal bloom. Algal bloom on the surface of lagoons, ponds, lakes, and even rivers, is primarily caused by proliferation of living algae aided by phosphate enrichment. This enrichment comes from increasing amounts of phosphate in the water, an increase due to sewage and phosphorous based detergents. Nitrate enrichment can also cause algal bloom. The primary sources of such enrichment are farm fertilizers. Water temperature and the presence of sunlight can both affect the speed of algal growth. This explains why most problems with nuisance algae take place in shallow water during warm weather. The source of this nutrient may be either natural or artificial. The excess nutrients feed a cycle of rapid growth, reproduction, and death for the algae. The dead algae fall to the bottom in enough quantity that they have been likened to an underwater storm. Their decay uses up dissolved oxygen and releases toxins, making it difficult for other forms of aquatic life to survive. Under natural eutrophic conditions, there are often two blooms per year; the first as temperature rises in the early summer, and the second in the fall as the nutrients taken up by the first bloom are rereleased into water through decay and build back to more than limiting levels.

alkali. 1. Carbonate of sodium or potassium, or any bitter-tasting salt, occurring at near the surface in arid and semi-arid regions. 2. A strong base (hydroxide): *e.g.*, NaOH or KOH. 3. Minerals rich in sodium or potassium; *e.g.*, alkali feldspar. The alkaline wastes from the industries, when discharged in the body of water cause alkalies pollution. Alkalis cause demage to rivers and streams by altering the *p*H values of the water resulting in a breakage in the natural buffer system. This pollution also has the same effect as of acids, destroying bacterial and other micro-organisms. It is important to mention here that every alkali produces asphyxiation by the coagulation of gill secretion of fish. *See also* alkalinity; alkali water pollution.

alkalinity. In pollution control and water treatment, a term used to refer the acid neutralizing capacity of a substance. It is the sum of all the titrable bases. The measured values may vary significantly with the end point *p*H used. Alkalinity is significant in many uses and treatments of natural waters. Because the alkalinity of many surface waters is primarily a function of carbonate, bicarbonate, and hydroxide content, it is taken as indication of the concentration of these constituents. The measured values also may include contributions from borates, phosphates, silicates or other bases if these are present. Alkalinity in excess of alkaline earth metal concentrations is significant in determining the suitability of the water for irrigation. Alkalinity measurements are used in the interpretation and control of water and waste water treatment processes. The anaerobic digesters have supernatant alkalinities in the range of 2,000 to 4,000 mg calcium carbonate ($CaCO_3$)/L. *See also* alkalinity; alkali water pollution.

alkali water pollution. Caustic conditions in industrial wastewaters arise form the effluent from laundries and preparation of cotton and wool for the textile industry. This raises the *p*H of the waste water to higher than 7, making it alkaline. Alkalinity in waste water is due to the presence of bicarbonates, carbonates and hydroxides of metal such as calcium, magnesium, potassium, and sodium. In addition, salts of weak acids and ammonia present in waste waters also contribute to the total alkalinity. It is measured by titrating the sample with a standard acid such as 0.01M sulphuric or hydrochloric acid. Determination of alkalinity is of importance in water softening, chemical treatment of waste waters corrosion control, and in removal of ammonia by air stripping.

alkalized alumina process. A process developed in U.S. for the removal of sulphur from flue gases. In this process, the dust free flue gas is fed to a reactor wherein the absorbent, a porous form of sodium aluminate ($Na_2O.Al_2O_3$), adsorbs sulphur dioxide at about 600K.

alkane. One of the group of hydrocarbons of the paraffin series having the general formula C_nH_{2n+2}, *e.g.*, methane, ethane, propane, butane, *etc.*, and are mainly used as fuel. For alkanes, action level is defined as an airborne time-weighted average (TWA) concentration of 200 mg/m^3 of air of the alkanes for up to a 10-hour work-shift, in a 40-hour workweek. Occupational exposure to alkanes is defined as exposure above the action level. Occupational exposure to C_5-

C_8 alkanes should be controlled so that no employee is exposed to concentrations greater than 350 mg/m^3 as a TWA concentration; which is equivalent to about 120 ppm of *n*-pentane, 100 ppm of *n*-hexane, 85 ppm of *n*-heptane, and 75 ppm of *n*-octane. If a person is exposed to a mixture of C_5-C_8 alkanes, total alkane exposure should not be greater than 350 mg/m^3. In addition, no employee should be exposed to individual C_5-C_8 alkanes or mixtures of these alkanes at ceiling concentrations greater than 1800 mg/m^3, as determined over a sampling time of 15 minutes. The standard is designed to protect the health and provide safety of workers for up to a 10-hour workshift in a 40-hour workweek over a working lifetime.

alkylating agents. Chemicals such as mustards, diethyl sulphate, β-propiolactone, ethylmethane sulphonate, etc., belong to the class of mutagens. The mode of action of all these agents appears to be similar. Under physiologic conditions of temperature and *p*H, they can react with nitrogen atoms of the bases, causing their alkylation. It has been found that under suitable conditions, essentially the only base affected is guanine and the alkyl group is attached only to N-7 of this base. Such a reaction produces a positive charge on this nitrogen atom and attaches a bulky group to the base; both changes create serious disturbances and cannot be accepted in the mechanism of replication of DNA.

allergen. Any substance that induces the formation of an antibody in the bloodstream of a susceptible individual; the allergen and antibody combine to form a histamine-like substance, which in turn weakens the blood vessels sufficiently to release fluids. Protein-containing substances are the most common allergens (wool, hair, pollen, *etc.*), but allergic reactions may be experienced by a few individuals from exposure to almost any substance.

alpha factor. For an aerator in an activated sludge plant, the rate of oxygen transfer in clean water divided by the rate of transfer in mixed liquor.

alum. One of a group of minerals existing as double salt of general formula $(M(III))_2(SO_4)_3.(X(I))_2SO_4.24H_2O$ in which *M* may be aluminium, iron, or chromium and *X* may be either sodium, potassium, lithium, rubidium, ammonium, thallium or silver. Alums crystallize as octahedrals or as cubes. Ordinary alum has the formula: $Al_2(SO_4)_3.K_2SO_4.24H_2O$, and is frequently used for the purification of potable water.

aluminium adjuvants. The compounds of aluminium, such as aluminium hydroxide gel. aluminium phosphate, aluminium sulphate and alums like ammonium alum $(NH_4)_2SO_4.Al_2(SO_4)_3.24H_2O$ and potash alum, that strongly adsorb protein antigens from solution to form a precipitate. When injected into an animal these precipitates form deposit from which the antigens is slowly released. *See also* adjuvants, depot forming adjuvants, alum granuloma and adsorption.

aluminium air pollution. After being mined, bauxite is calcined at high temperature. Polluting effluent from this process contains valuable alumina which is removed by a collector. Thereafter, the alumina is converted into aluminium by electrolysis. The effluent is either scrubbed or sent up a high chimney.

ambient air. A professional designation of the air outdoors. More specifically it is the air subjected to meteorological and climatic changes including changes in the weather. It is the kind of air that gets polluted through combustion caused by automobiles, trucks power plants inculcators. Ambient air fills the portion of the atmosphere most important to daily deep breathing exercised the troposphere. in brief the ambient air from ground level to about 15 km in altitude is of abiding concern to pollution control people.

ambient air quality criteria. Quantitative relationship between a pollutant's dose, concentration, deposition rate or any other air quality-related factors, and the related direct and/or indirect effects on receptors, *e.g.*, humans, animals, plants, or materials. Air quality criteria serve as the scientific basis for formulating ambient air quality standards or objectives.

ambient noise. Unlike air noise surrounding human beings falls into only one category ambient noise. And this is the background noise in any environment, indoors or outdoors.

amenity. Anything that contributes to comfort, convenience, or pleasantness of life. In the air pollution literature, the expression loss of amenity: is taken to mean an adverse effect on such factors (*e.g.*, the presence of dirt or unpleasant odours, or the diminution of sunshine). Air pollution that cause loss of amenity is not necessarily sufficient to be injurious to health or to have serious economic effects.

ammonia. A colourless gas with a highly irritant odour; it is used in enormous quantities for soil fertilizers in the form of its sulphate and nitrate; as a refrigerant; in the preparation of a large number of chemicals and pharmaceuticals. It poses great hazard in accidental exposure to sudden high concentrations as a result of valve failure of the storage tanks, leakage etc. Ammonia can also be a component of industrial wastewater from gas, coke, and a number of chemical manufacturing industries. Most of its production has been attributed to the NH_3 release from animal urine. It is a known product of the deamination of proteins and in the oceans there are bacteria capable of producing NH_3 from nitrates. In its way it is the 'de-acid' agent of the atmosphere as it combines in the gaseous phase with sulphuric acid and sulphur dioxide and neutralize their acidity. It also tends to catalyze the oxidation of SO_2 in water droplets. One way or the other it tends to form the ubiquitous ammonium sulphate particles that are major components of almost every aerosol; also it is a good fertilizer. About 0.3% of ammonia is man made, being manufactured by Haber process from N_2 and H_2; it is even injected directly in to the soil as fertilizer. In the atmosphere, NH_3 is quickly removed by clouds, rain or acidic gases, and so is highly variable. In the lower levels of the atmosphere it has a residence time of few hours though in a clear, dry environment it may remain for weeks. Inhalation of ammonia vapours in high concentrations may cause chemical burns of the upper respiratory tract, showing symptoms such as severe burning pain in the throat, difficulty in breathing, and cough with copious watery sputum. The simple contact with ammonia vapours may result in burning pain in the affected areas with redness and swelling of eyes and mucous membranes and, to a lesser extent, the skin. Occupational exposure to ammonia should be controlled so that no employees are exposed to ammonia at a concentration greater than a ceiling concentration of 50 ppm, as determined by a 5-minute sampling period. The standard is designed to protect the health and provide safety of workers for up to a 8-hour workshift, 40-hour workweek over a working lifetime.

ammonifiers. Bacteria that liberate ammonia from organic matter in either sewage of solid waste deposits. Since ammonia is created by the activities of these bacteria they are called ammonifiers.

amphoteric. Capable of acting either as an acid or as a base, *i.e.*, as a proton donor or acceptor, according to the nature of the environment. Thus, aluminium hydroxide dissolves in acids to form salts of aluminium, and it also dissolves in strong bases to form aluminates.

anabatic wind. An up-slope wind caused by lower air density along the slope than at some distance, horizontally, from it. The wind is associated with strong surface heating of the slope.

anaerobe. A microorganism that can thrive and survive in an oxygen-free atmosphere.

anaerobic-aerobic system. A scientific description of any system that utilizes both anaerobic bacterial action and aerobic bacterial action to covert solid wastes or sludge or a combination of both into relatively inert or stabilized material.

anaerobic contact process. In manner not too dissimilar from the anaerobic treatment of sewer sludge, industrial wastes are stratified and subjected to breakdown by anaerobic bacteria. The effluent is drawn off, and the remaining solids are recirculated into the incoming liquids wastes in order to continue and accelerate the process.

anaerobic filter. A vertical filter bed filled with stone ballasts, gravel, coke, and plastics; suitable for treatment of wastewaters at high loading rates and with a satisfactory treatment efficiency.

anaerobic sediment. Sediment that occurs in basins where the limited circulation of water results in the absence or near absence of oxygen at the sediment surface.

ancilliary equipment. Any device, including, but not limited to, such device as piping, fittings, flanges, valves, and pumps, that is used to distribute, or control the flow of hazardous waste from its point of generation to a storage or treatment tank, between hazardous waste storage and treatment tanks to a point of disposal on-site, or to a point of shipment for disposal off-site.

anhydride. A compound formed by removing two atoms of hydrogen and one atom of oxygen from another compound (*i.e.*, water molecule) *e.g.*, sulphur trioxide (SO_3) is the anhydride of sulphuric acid (H_2SO_4), and carbon dioxide (CO_2)

is the anhydride of carbonic acid. In organic chemistry, phthalic anhydride $C_6H_4(CO)_2O$, is formed from phthalic acid. $C_6H_4(COOH)_2$ by the elimination of one water molecule on heating.

anhydrous. A term literally meaning without water, it is used to describe a substance in which no water is present in the form of a hydrate or water of crystallization. Anhydrous is not synonymous with anhydride and should not be confused with it.

animal black. Finely divided carbon made by calcination of animal bones or ivory; used in making pigments; decolourizers, and purifying agents. Its varieties include bone black and ivory black.

animal charcoal. Charcoal obtained by destructive distillation of animal matter at high temperatures; it is mainly used to absorb organic colouring matter.

anionic detergents. Detergents that contain as soluble groups, sodium sulphates and sulfonates. they also have additives including phosphates, surfactants, enzymes, etc. These are the household detergents most widely used for clothes-washing.

annual layer. Any sedimentary or precipitated layer of material of variable composition and thickness, presumed to have been deposited during the course of one year. Annual layers are most frequently utilized in the study of varved deposits laid down in glacially fed lakes.

anode. The positive electrode in an electrolytic cell to which negatively charged ion, molecules, or colloidal particles migrate under the influence of an electric current. In a primary cell (battery) the anode is negative terminal. In electrochemical corrosion, the material corroded, attacked, or dissolved is generally the anode in the galvanic circuit.

anode mud. An insoluble substance or mixture of substances that collects at the bottom of anode in an electrolytic refining or plating process. Also known as anode slime.

anode slime. *See* anode mud.

anodic reaction. The reaction in the mechanism of electrochemical corrosion in which the metal forming the anode dissolves in the electrolyte in the form of positively charged ions. Such reactions are responsible for the rusting of iron.

anoxia. A condition indicating a deficiency in the amount of oxygen reaching human tissue. It may be caused by too much smoking.

anthropogenic hydrocarbons. The hydrocarbons (other than methane) in the atmosphere that affect the life on the earth. These are generally released from motor vehicles, solvent evaporations, intentional bush-fires or stubble-burning. From these hydrocarbons a multitude of secondary products are created in smog conditions. These include formaldehyde and other doubly bonded organic compounds that are highly reactive. It has been realized that the interaction of anthropogenic hyrocarbons with the atmosphere is not confined to a local or regional scale.

anti-antibody. Antibody especially rheumatoid factor which is able to combine specifically with an immunogolbulin molecule that is bound to an antigen, but not with free immunoglobulin. It probably represents antibody against hidden determinants on the antibody molecule revealed by alterations in molecular shape that occur during the combination of immunoglobulin with antigen.

antibody. Protein with the molecular properties of an immunoglobulin and capable of specific combination with antigen carries antigen binding sites that link non-covalently with the corresponding antigenic determinant. Antibodies are produced in the body by the cells of the lymphoid cell series, especially plasma cells, in response to stimulation by antigen.

anticaking agent. An additive used primarily in certain finely divided food products that tend to be hygroscopic, to prevent agglomeration and thus maintain a free-flowing condition. Starch, calcium metasilicate and magnesium carbonate, are used for this purpose in table salt, flours, sugar, coffee and similar food products.

anticatalyst. A substance that slows down the action of a catalyst; for example, lead inhibits the catalytic action of platinum.

antichlor. A term used chiefly in the textile and paper industries to refer to any substance that will neutralize chlorine-containing bleaching agents (such as sodium hypochlorite) in order to improve the colour of the products and to remove the undesirable odour and irritating effects of residual chlorine. The compounds most widely used for this purpose are sodium thiosulphate and sodium bisulphite.

anticoagulant. Any substance possessing the ability to extend the normal clotting time of blood. Many anticoagulants are polysaccharides or complex carbohydrate polymers, an example is heparin, one of the most widely used types, which inhibits or prevents formation of thrombin from its precursor prothrombin.

anticyclone. An area of high pressure in subsiding, causing dry weather. The winds are normally light and the weather is settled. The major high pressure regions are found in the horse latitudes, about 20° to 30° north and south of the equator.

antidote. A substance given to counteract the effect produced by the ingestion of a poisonous or toxic chemical.

antiknocking agent. A substance commonly added to the fuel of an internal combustion engine to prevent premature excessively rapid and irregular combustion of the fuel-air mixture. The knocking properties of various fuels vary widely with their chemical structures and are expressed by their octane rating.

antimony. A metallic element placed in Group VA of the periodic table. The major source of antimony is stibnite ore (Sb_2S_3). Its chief uses are as an additive to harden lead and in metal bearings; it also has some application as a solder and in type metal. The highly purified metal has semiconducting properties, and finds numerous applications in the production of electronic materials. Antimony forms many compounds which are quite toxic, as are fumes of the metal itself; the toxicity depends largely upon the chemical state of the metal or compound. It is less toxic than, though possessing similar toxic properties to arsenic. It is capable of entering the body through the skin, by inhalation, or accidently by ingestion. Industrial poisoning is rare and occurs mainly in mining and refining the ore, and in typesetting in the printing industry. Its acute poisoning may result in vomiting and diarrhoea; weakness and collapse; and irregularities of heart-beat. Inhalation of antimony dust over the years may lead to pneumoconiosis, irritation of the skin, ulcer formation, and sometimes carcinoma of the lung, liver damage with jaundice, and irritation of the mucous membrane of the nose and throat.

Occupational exposure to antimony is defined as exposure to antimony at a concentration greater than one-half the recommended environmental limit. If exposure to other chemicals occurs (*e.g.*, from contamination of antimony with arsenic or free silica), provisions for any applicable standards for other chemicals should also be followed. Exposure to antimony should be controlled so that no employees are exposed to antimony at a concentration greater than 0.5 mg/m^3 of air determined as a time-weighted average (TWA) concentration limit for up to a 10-hour workshift in a 40-hour workweek. The available data for antimony indicate that acute and chronic toxicity to freshwater aquatic life occur at concentrations as low as 9000 and 1600 μg/L, respectively. For the protection of human health from the toxic effects of antimony ingested through water and contaminated aquatic organisms, the ambient water criterion to be 146 μmg/L; while for the protection of human health from the toxic properties of antimony ingested through contaminated aquatic organisms alone, the ambient water criterion has been determined to be 45,000 μg/L.

antioxidant. Generally, an organic compound which has the power to greatly reduce the normal tendency of oxygen to combine chemically with hydrocarbons in petroleum products, animal fats, vegetable oils, rubber, and similar substances, with consequent degrading effects on the material. The protective effect is considered to be due to free radical mechanisms and is obtained with extremely low percentages.

antiozonant. An inhibitor effective in preventing ozonation by atmospheric oxygen.

anti-pollution device. The device which could possibly be applied to other types to of pollution control devices, it is generally confined to such items as catalytic mufflers and other devices designed to reduce emissions of pollution of pollutants from internal combustion engines.

antiscorch. A substance used to retard the catalytic activity of rubber accelerators during processing.

Appiko movement. A non-violent action to save the destruction of natural forests launched by especially youths of Balegadde village under the leadership of famous environmentalist Sunderlal Bahuguna in 1983. The Appiko movement has three main objectives, "Ulisu" (to conserve); "belesa" (to grow), and "balasu" (rational use). It began when a groups of youth in balegadde village, worte to forest officials to stop clearing the natural forests, and protested against moves to establish teak plantations. No forest official could take action but ignored the appeal. At last, villagers of Balegadde launch Appiko movement by taking an oath to protect the trees from destruction. It was in September 1983 when the axe-men came for cutting to the kalase forest, the villagers embraced the trees, thus the "Appiko movement" was lunched, and this movement was joined by people in many forest areas of the western Ghats of India.

Appiko movement is really the movement of social, cultural, and educational awakening of the people to act effectively to conserve over precious forests. The message of this movement to the mass was conveyed by performing various activities such as padayatras, Yakshagana (a form of folk dance), slide shows and street plays. In Dakshina Kannada, the authorities of the Subramanya temple restored the Appiko movement for saving the evergreen forests.

application. The EPA standard national forms for applying for a permit, including any additions, revisions or modifications to the forms; or forms approved by EPA for use in approved states, including any approved modifications or revisions.

application factor. A unitless chemical-specific measure calculated as the threshold chronically toxic concentration of a chemical divided by its acutely toxic concentration; *i.e.*, the ratio between that concentration of a substance that produces a particular chronic response in an organ and that which causes death in 50% of the population with in a given period of time. The application factor is used to determine the maximum rate concentration of substance for organisms under consideration. In practice, the AF is calculated by dividing the limits (NOEC and LOEC) of the MATC by the time independent or incipient LC_{50}, or if that value is not available by the 96-h LC_{50} (or 48-h LC_{50} for daphnids) from a flow-through acute toxicity test.

aquiclude. A porous formation that absorbs water slowly but will not transmit it fast enough to furnish an appreciable supply for a well or spring.

aquifer. A geological term for a body of rock that contains water and releases it in significant quantities for use. The rock contains water-filled pore spaces that are sufficiently connected to allow the water to flow through the rock matrix to wells and springs.

aquitard. A geological term for a confining bed that retards but does not completely stop the flow of water to or from an adjacent aquifer. Although it does not readily release water to wells or springs, it may function as a storage chamber for groundwater.

aramid. Generic name for a distinctive class of highly aromatic polyamide fibres characterized by their flame-retardant properties.

arctic smoke. The name given to steaming fog, produced when very cold air passes over warm water, off the coast of Norway, and on rivers warmed by power stations on cold mornings.

arene. Class name for unsaturated cyclic (aromatic) compounds, of which benzene is typical; several rings may be present, either chemically bonded, as in diphenyl, or fused, as in anthracene. A large number of such compounds have been detected in the emissions from the automobiles and industries; and many of them have been classified as potential health hazards.

aridity. A geological term denoting dryness because of lack of rainfall. An arid area receives less than 250 mm of rainfall per annum, and only specialized drought resistant plants can survive. Such areas are prone to higher levels of pollution.

arsenic. An element placed in group VA of the periodic table. Arsenic occurs naturally in all environmental media and is usually present in the form of compounds with sulphur and with many metals (copper, cobalt, lead, zinc, etc.). The average concentration in the earth's crust is about 2 mg/kg. Although arsenic exists in various valency states and in both organic and inorganic forms, the levels of environmental arsenic are normally reported in terms of total arsenic. In some localized geographic areas, commercial use and production of arsenic compounds have resulted in significant elevation in the amounts of environmental arsenic above natural background levels.

Many arsenic compounds are water-soluble and, thus, contamination of water can occur. The chemical form of arsenic in water has not been identified; a few species of organic arsenic have been found in water. Geothermal discharges have been found to contain significant quantities of arsenic. In spite of its ubiquitousness in nature, most of the arsenic found in water derives from industrial discharges; the highest concentrations other than those occurring naturally in spring-waters are usually in areas of high industrial activity. A large number of water supplies contain very low levels of arsenic, *i.e.*, well below 10 μg/L. In special situations, gross contamination of well supplies has occurred and several thousand micrograms of arsenic per litre of water, have resulted.

Arsenic is present in most foodstuffs at concentrations generally below 1 mg/kg of dry weight. Marine fish can contain higher levels than this, and shellfish may contain levels well over 50 mg/kg; the arsenic in seafood is mainly in an organic form. The average dietary sources of arsenic seem to give rise to an intake of about 30 μg/kg of body weight per day. Some what higher estimates have been quoted for certain countries.

The air in non-urban and non-industrial areas contains very low levels of arsenic, *i.e.*, generally less than 0.01 μg/m^3. In urban areas and particularly industrial towns, levels of arsenic have exceeded 1 μg/m^3. A typical airborne exposure might be about 0.2 μg/m^3 of air, mainly as inorganic arsenic.

Industrial exposure to the fumes containing arsenic compounds does arise, especially in smelting operations; the levels of arsenic exceeding 1 μg/m^3 of air have been recorded. Levels of arsenic as high as 380 mg/kg have been reported in soil near smelters. Certain pharmaceutical products contain arsenic and, for some individuals, the exposure to arsenic *via* these sources can be high. For the general population, the contribution from such routes of exposure to arsenic is negligible in comparison with those from food, water, and air.

Based simply on intake of total arsenic, the contribution from the normally low levels in water in relation to general overall exposure is relatively small; however, at an arsenic level of 0.05 mg/L in drinking-water, this may equal or even exceed the total dietary intake in a nonoccupationally exposed individual. It is not possible to make estimates of the amounts of arsenic taken up by the body *via* various routes because the sufficient information about the particular forms of arsenic in food and water is notavailable.

Arsenic and some of its compounds, especially its oxide, are general protoplasmic poison. Most of the cases of acute poisoning result from accidental or suicidal drinking of solutions of arsenic compounds, which may cause nausea, vomiting, diarrhoea, and abdominal pain; pain in the chest, cough, shortness of breath; collapse with weak pulse and cold sweats; and sometimes coma or death. Chronic poisoning arises from inhalation of the fumes or dust containing solid arsenic compounds. This can result in burning pain and tenderness of limbs with difficulty in walking; damage to liver and jaundice; and inflammation and ulceration of skin, particularly in exposed or moist areas. Cases of conjunctivitis, laryngitis, and perforation of the nasal septum have also been reported due to its chronic poisoning.

It has been found that the chemical form of arsenic affects its absorption. Elemental arsenic is very poorly absorbed. Some trivalent and pentavalent inorganic arsenic compounds are readily absorbed; organic arsenic, too, is generally well absorbed. Following exposure to arsenic, it enters the blood and subsequently it is found mainly in the liver, muscles, kidneys, spleen, and skin; smaller quantities are also found in the brain, heart, uterus, thyroid, and pancreas, as well as in the hair and nails. Arsenic is transferred across the placenta. The biological half-life of arsenic appears to be between about ten hours and a few days. Human subjects are able to transform inorganic arsenic into monomethyl and dimethyl compounds; the overall mechanism of biotransformation is very little understood, however, the excretion of arsenic compounds is mainly *via* urine. Trivalent arsenic may inhibit the activity of many enzymes by reacting with sulfydryl groups; the reactions involving such groups are considered to be responsible for the toxic action of arsenic compounds.

Exposure to arsenic is defined as exposure at or above 0.002 mg arsenic/m^3. Arsenic and its gaseous compounds should be controlled to the same concentration as other forms of inorganic arsenic. Exposure to arsenic should be controlled so that no person is exposed to arsenic at a concentration greater than 10 $\mu g/m^3$ of air determined as a time-weighted average (TWA) concentration limit for up to a 10-hour workshift in a 40-hour work-week. Inorganic arsenic should be controlled so that no employees are exposed to arsenic at a concentration in excess of 0.002 mg/m^3, as determined by a 15 minute sampling period. The standard is designed to protect the health and provide safety of employees for a 40-hour workweek over a working lifetime. Compliance with all sections of the standard will prevent noncarcinogenic adverse effects of exposure to inorganic arsenic in the workplace air and by skin exposure.

For freshwater aquatic life the concentration of total recoverable trivalent inorganic arsenic should not exceed 440 μg/L at any time. Short-term effects on embryos and larvae of aquatic vertebrate species have been shown to occur at concentration as low as 40 μg/L. The available data for the total recoverable trivalent inorganic arsenic indicate that acute toxicity to saltwater aquatic life occurs at concentrations as low as 508 μg/L and would occur at even low concentrations among the species that are more sensitive than those tested. For the maximum protection of human health from the potential carcinogenic effects due to exposure of arsenic through ingestion of contaminated aquatic organisms and water, the ambient water concentration should be zero based on the nonthreshold assumption for arsenic. However, zero level may not be attainable at present time. Therefore, levels that may result in incremental increase of cancer risk over lifetime are estimated at 10^{-5}, 10^{-6}, and 10^{-7}. The corresponding criteria are 2.2 ng/L, 0.22 ng/L, and 0.022 ng/L respectively.

artificial radioactivity. Radioactivity induced in stable elements by bombardment with alpha particles, protons, deutrons, neutrons, gamma rays, etc. Thus aluminium on alpha ray bombardment emits a neutron, forming radiophosphorus of mass 30.

$${}_{13}Al^{27} + {}_{2}He^{4} = {}_{15}P^{30} + {}_{0}n^{1}$$

There are also radio-elements which decay by emission of alpha particles, by capturing one of their own *K*-electrons, etc.

aryl. A univalent group derived from aromatic hydrocarbons and having a ring structure of benzene, naphthalene, etc. Some of the examples are phenyl (C_6H_5–) and naphthyl ($C_{10}H_7$–). Such groups are often represented in general formulas by the letter R. Compounds made up of both aryl and alkyl groups are sometimes called aralkyl (a shortened form of arylalkyl), depending on where the available bond is located.

arylide. A compound formed from a metal and an aryl radical, *e.g.*, PbR_4, where R is an aryl radical.

asbestos. Any one of a group of fibrous amphibole minerals (amosite, crocidolite (blue asbestos), tremolite, anthophyllite, and actinolite) or the fibrous serpentine mineral chrysotile. Chysotile is a member of the serpentine group; the others belong to the amphibole group. These various forms of asbestos are composed of 40-60% silica, as well as oxide of iron, magnesium, and other metals. It has widespread commercial uses because of its resistance to heat, chemical inertness, and high electrical resistance. Its fibres may be spun and woven into fireproof cloth for use in protective clothing curtains, brake linings, etc., or moulded into blocks. Although not as highly publicized as poisonous hydrocarbons emanating from internal combustion engines, asbestos pollution is mounting considerably.

Available studies provide conclusive evidence that exposure to asbestos fibres causes cancer and asbestosis in humans. It has been found that the disease associated with asbestos are all caused by inhalation of dust over a long period of up to 20 years or even more. Pneumoconiosis and lung cancer usually occur in people who at some period of their working life have been associated with the manufacture or processing of asbestos material. Mesothelioma of either pleura or peritoneum on the other hand does occur in workers whose connection with asbestos is extremely tenuous though the connection does exist.

Asbestos is introduced into natural waters by the dissolution of asbestos-containing minerals and ores and from industrial effluents. There is some indication that atmospheric pollution may also contribute to asbestos content of natural water. Sedimentation, resuspension, migration, and chemical reactions affect the movement, abundance, and fate of asbestos fibres in water. The length of time from introduction of asbestos fibres into water until their disappearance is unknown.

It has been realized that the use of asbestos-cement (which contains about 170 g of asbestos per kg-80% chrysotile and 20% crocidolite) for pipes in water-distribution systems could contribute significantly to the asbestos content of drinking-water. It is commonly found in domestic water supplies. Typical background levels in rivers and lakes are considered to be about 1 million fibres per litre, although reported values range from less than 1 million to 10 million fibres per litre. Levels vary considerably, depending upon proximity to industrial sources. Generally, ordinary sand filtration removes about 90% of the individual asbestos fibres from water supplies. The most effective method for its removal involves chemical coagulation with iron salts and polyelectrolytes followed by filtration.

The extent of asbestos contamination of solid food stuffs has not been fully researched, owing to the lack of a practical, reliable analytical method. Foods that contain soil particles, dust, or dirt almost certainly contain asbestos fibres. Foodstuffs can also derive asbestos from water or impure talc used in their preparation (talc may be used as a dusting powder in chewing gum, on coated rice, and as an antisticking agent for moulded foods). Asbestos may also be introduced into foods from impure mineral silicates, such as talc, soapstone, or pyropohyllite, which are used as carriers for spray pesticides. Asbestos fibres make excellent filter materials, and at one time asbestos was widely used in the food industry for clarification of beverages and other liquids. In some cases, the use of asbestos filters has been found to increase the concentration of asbestos in the finished product.

Evaluation of all available human data provides no evidence for a threshold or for a safe level of asbestos exposure. Under such conditions, the standard should be set at the lowest level detectable by available analytical techniques. The level defined on the basis of phase contrast microscopy is 100,000 fibres 5 μm in length/m^3, on 8-hour TWA basis with peak concentrations not exceeding 500,000 fibres 5 μm in length/m^3 based on 15 minute sample period. The recommended standard of 100,000 fibres 5 μm in length/m^3 is intended to:

(a) protect against the noncarcinogenic effects of asbestos;

(b) materially reduce the risk of asbestos-induced cancer (only a total ban can assure protection against carcinogenic effects of asbestos); and

(c) be measured by techniques that are valid, reproducible, and readily available to the industry and official agencies.

For the maximum protection of human health from the potential carcinogenic effects due to exposure of asbestos through ingestion of contaminated aquatic organisms and water, the ambient water concentration should be zero on the nonthreshold assumption for asbestos. However, zero level may not be attainable at present time. Therefore, the levels that may result in incremental increase of cancer risk over lifetime are estimated at 10^{-5}, 10^{-6}, and 10^{-7}. The corresponding criteria are 300,000 fibres/L, 30,000 fibre/L, and 3000 fibres L respectively. No saltwater and fresh water organisms have been tested with any asbestiform mineral and thus no information is available about acute or chronic toxicity.

ash. The inert residue from a fire or burning fuel. It consists mainly of alumina and silica. The average ash residue for coal is about 15%. Fuel oil combustion also creates ash that can cause wear on delicate oil burner parts, such as the nozzle. Ash from the flue of an incinerator is called fly ash. When the ash is extracted from stove, furnace, or incinerator it is called ashes.

ash rock. The material of arenaceous texture produced by volcanic explosions.

asphalt. A sticky black substance derived from petroleum through the evaporation of some of the lighter hydrocarbons, and partial oxidation of the remainder. It is used in building, paving, and caulking. Because it is a residue, *i.e.*, everything that can volatilize or leach from it has already done so, it does not represent much of a threat as a pollutant. *See also* asphalt fumes.

asphalt fumes. The cloud of small particles created by condensation from the gaseous state after volatilization of asphalt. It is considered to be potential occupational carcinogen.

The occupational exposure to asphalt fumes is defined as the exposure in the workplace at a concentration of one-half or more of the recommended occupational limit. If exposure to other chemicals also occurs, as is the case when asphalt is mixed with a solvent, emulsified, or used concurrently with other chemicals such as tar or pitch, provisions of any applicable standard for the other chemicals should also be followed. Occupational exposure to asphalt fumes should be controlled in such a manner so that no person is exposed to asphalt fumes at a concentration greater than 5 mg/m^3 of air during any 15 minute period. The standard has been designed to protect the health and safety of workers for up to a 10-hour workshift, 40-hour workweek over a working lifetime.

asthenosphere. The layer or shell of the earth directly below the lithosphere. Its upper boundary begins about 100 km below the surface and extends to a depth of about 300 km. The upper limit is marked by an abrupt decrease in the velocity of seismic waves as they enter this region.

asthma. A form of allergic reaction in which the bronchial tissues in the lungs become inflamed, swelling up and secreting mucus and thus constricting or blocking the bronchial passages. The causative allergen may be present in the bloodstream, either from being ingested or from being absorbed through the skin. Smoking as well as air pollution can increase susceptibility to asthma-causing allergens.

atmolysis. The separation of a mixture of gases by means of their relative diffusibility through a porous portion, as burned clay. The rates of diffusion are inversely proportional to the square roots of the densities of the gases. Hydrogen, thus, is the most diffusible gas.

atmosphere. 1. The gaseous envelope surrounding the earth (or other heavenly body). The composition of the earth's atmosphere varies very slightly in different localities and according to altitude. For volume composition of dry air sea-level, *see* air.

The atmosphere is separated by gravity, centrifugal force, and the influence of the sun into a number of concentric layers, or spheres. These spheres may be defined with respect to each other in a number of different ways, one of which is based on temperature gradient. According to which, in the lowest level of atmosphere, the troposphere, temperature decreases gradually with altitude. Approximately 10 km above the surface, the tropopause, the temperature curve suddenly levels off and, a few kilometres later, begins rising. This sphere of rising temperature gradient is called stratosphere. At about 45 km appears a second break in the curve, the stratopause, above which temperature begins falling once more through the mesosphere. Finally at mesopause, 80 km up, a third and final change in the direction occurs, and the gradient begins rising again through the thermosphere, which extend outward to the limit of the atmosphere, an ill-defined zone of escaping gases that may lie as high as 4,000 km above the surface. Because the thermosphere is layered by molecular size, with nitrogen on the bottom, followed by the layers of oxygen, helium, and hydrogen, it is sometimes called heterosphere. In this case, the troposphere, stratosphere, and mesosphere, are usually grouped together as the homosphere. Another commonly recognized layer in the atmosphere is the chemosphere, a zone from 20 to 150 km up where chemical reactions commonly take place. It includes both the ozone layer and the ionosphere, a zone of ionized gases that occupies roughly the lower 300 km of the atmosphere.

2. A unit of pressure. The pressure that will support a column of mercury 760 mm high (29.92 inches) at zero sea-level and latitude 45°.

1 normal atmosphere is equal to 101325 newtons per square metre.

Atmospheric pressure fluctuates about this value from day to day.

atmospheric chemistry. The branch of meteorology concerned with the chemical composition of the atmosphere, and with the chemical and photochemical processes that occur in the atmosphere. Of particular importance to air pollution control are reactions by which pollutant (*e.g.*, photochemical smog) are formed and those by which they are changed into inoffensive materials.

atmospheric corrosion. The gradual destruction or alteration of a metal or an alloy by contact with substances present in the atmosphere, such as oxygen, carbon dioxide, moisture, and compounds of nitrogen, chlorine, and sulphur.

atmospheric dust. Dust entrained in the atmosphere scatters, sunlight, reflects it back into space, and causes cooling. Currently there is no systematic watch of this type of dust, but the continued pollution of the atmosphere through an increase in atmospheric dust burden might affect long term heat balance between the temperature to the earth's surface and the temperature of the earths surface and the temperature of the air surrounding it. Some scientists believe future concentrations of atmospheric dust will so lower the air temperature that the ice age will return.

atmospheric gases. Gases that are commercially derived through an air separation process. For purposes of this subchapter, atmospheric gases means argon krypton, neon, nitrogen, oxygen, and zenon.

atomspheric noise. Noise resulting from interference with radio transmissions by natural electrical disturbances. The magnitude and nature of the noise varies with such factors as the time of year and day, sunspot activity, etc.

atmospheric stability. In meteorology and air pollution control, the resistance of an air mass to vertical mixing, that is, the degree to which the air mass either damps out vertical currents or encourages them to form. The atmospheric stability depends upon the relationship of the lapse rate to the adiabatic rate.

atomic cloud. The cloud of hot gases, smoke, dust, and other matter that is carried after explosion of a nuclear weapon in the air or near the earth's surface; generally it has a mushroom shape.

atomic fallout. The radioactive dust that enters the atmosphere after atomic bomb tests or detonations is called atomic fallout, or just plain fallout. Obviously, intelligent onlookers are increasingly concerned not only with increasing amounts of fallout introduced into the atmosphere, but also with the fact that this fallout lasts and lasts accumulating ominously with the passage of the time. it certainly would seem sensible to end testing above and underground and once and for all get rid of the atomic bomb and the hydrogen bomb forever.

atomic wastes. Radioactive material discharged as waste after use but because the radioactivity persists for long times, these wastes are health hazards. The isotope cemeteries and abandoned salt mines are used for this purpose.

ATP (adenosine triphosphate). A compound that contains adenine, ribose, and three phosphate groups and occurs in cells. The chemical bonds of the phosphate groups store energy needed by the cell, for muscle contraction; this energy is released when ATP is split into ADP or AMP. ATP is formed from ADP or AMP using energy produced by the breakdown of carbohydrates or other food substances.

attenuation. The reduction of a radiation quantity upon passage of radiation through matter resulting from all types of interaction with that matter. Attenuation usually does not include geometric attenuation. Attenuation of solar radiation is the loss of energy suffered by a beam of radiant energy which traverses the earth's atmosphere. Losses are caused by scattering by air molecules, by selective absorption by certain, and by scattering ay aerosols.

attrition. In air pollution parlance, attrition is considered the wearing away of a substance or the grinding down of a substance by friction. Thus dust caught up by the wind is atmospheric attrition from the soil while asbestos in the air from the application of so many brakes on parkways is another form of attrition.

autocatalysis. A condition obtained when one of the products of a reaction, or one of the factors, acts as a catalyst and accelerates or retards the velocity of the reaction, *e.g.*, in the hydrolysis of esters the acid products formed exert an influence to increase the velocity of the hydrolysis. Autocatalysis may be positive or negative according as the result of the catalytic action is acceleration or retardation.

auto pollution. Emissions from moving and idling car, asbestos worn from brakes linings and spread into the air every time a car squeals to a stop, are major parts of auto pollution problem. Flying hubcaps, lost mufflers, and tailpipes and the wreaked autos are also parts of the increasingly large auto pollution problem. Emissions, however, are the major concern of the environmentalists. The hydrocarbons, oxides of carbon, nitrogen, and sulphur are the toxic pollutants burdening thickly populated urban areas. The metals such as lead, cadmium, nickel, and other additives used in the automobile manufacture/functioning can create other substances that cause undesirable effect on the human health.

autoxidation. An oxidation reaction that takes place spontaneously in a substance exposed to air or oxygen at temperatures below and around 400K. It is activated by a free radical chain mechanism (autocatalysis) and is characteristic of many hydrocarbons; thus it is applied to a number of industrial operations in the chemical industry, such as the production of acetone and phenol from cumene.

auxiliary. A term used almost exclusively in chemical industry to include a large number of functional materials which have no chemical relationship; among these are fats and oils used to lubricate fibres, natural and synthetic surface-active agents, film-forming materials (starches, gums, etc.) for coating and sizing, delustering agents, and water-proofing materials. Dyestuffs are not usually regarded as auxiliaries as their function is essential. These substances are one of the major sources of water pollution.

available fresh water. The surface source of fresh water available to any community. According to water quality this resource may be safe to use for drinking, cooking, washing, swimming, recreation or transportation. The planners are always concerned with the available fresh water before they plan to bring thousands of persons into any specific locality. The total available fresh water supply on earth is only 0.325% of the entire earth's water supply, and the great lakes contain 25% of the available fresh water found in lakes.

azeotrope. A term used to denote a mixture of two components in such proportions as to result in either the lowest or the highest constant boiling point attainable with any mixture of the same components. Thus, a blend of ethyl alcohol (b.p. 351.6K) and water (b.p 373K) when mixed in the mole fraction of 89.4% alcohol and 10.6% water, has the lowest boiling point, 351.3K of any possible mixture of these substances.

azine. A heterocyclic compound of six atoms in the ring one or more of which is nitrogen and a ring structure resembling benzene. Thus pyridine, C_6H_5N, is an azine. Many compounds of this class have been classified as carcinogenic.

azinphos-methyl. A non-systemic broad-spectrum insecticide and acaracide of relatively long persistence, with contact and stomach action. It forms white crystals, almost insoluble in water but soluble in most organic solvents. It is unstable at temperatures above 200°C and is rapidly hydrolyzed by cold alkali and acid. The acute oral LD_{50} for rats is 16.4 mg/kg. It has been found to be effective against Lepidoptera, mites, aphids, whiteflies, leafhoppers, sacles, psyllids, sawflies, thrips, grasshoppers, fly larvae, and some beetles. It is suspected of possessing carcinogenic activity, hence the exposure to workers by all routes should be carefully controlled. Also known as Gusathion.

azobenzene. The compound having boiling point 293°C, is a crystalline solid which has proved useful in the past for the control of mites in greenhouses. In acts as a vapour formed by heating the pure crystals by means of steam pipes, hot plates or lamps; it is also evolved by igniting a powder in a pressure fumigator. Many glasshouse plants and blooms are tolerant, but there has been some discoloration of red flowers. Flowers of the African violet (Saintpaulia) are reported to be susceptible to damage.

B

Bacharach smoke scale. A scale of ten shades from white to black, used for the assessment of smoke concentrations in flue gases; a smoke stain is obtained by drawing a sample of flue gases through a filter paper in a prescribed manner, the resultant stain being compared with the scale.

background. 1. Ionizing radiations coming from sources other than the radiation to be detected or measured, *e.g.*, from naturally occurring radioactive nuclides, cosmic radiation or radioactivity contamination in laboratory. 2. Absorption due to all components except for the one to be determined. 3. Counting rate recorded by a counter in absence of a radioactivity sample.

background pollution. The pollution that would exist at a given point if it were unaffected by pollution arising from a specified source. Thus, with respect to a given factory, the background pollution in a nearby town is the observed pollution less that part to it arising from the factory. The term is also applied to pollution as observed in the interiors of the country, unaffected by any nearby sources.

background station. A site for the observation of air pollution that is not affected by local sources of pollution. It may be in the interior of the country or at depth in the sea.

bacteria. A diverse group of ubiquitous micro-organisms all of which consist of only a single cell that lacks a distinct nuclear membrane and has a cell wall of a unique composition. A bacterial cell may be spherical, rodlike, spiral, comma -shaped, cordscrew-shaped, or filamentous, resembling a fungal cell. The majority of bacteria range in size from 0.5 to 5 pm. Many are motile, bearing flagella, possess an outer slimy capsule, and produce resistant spores. As well as being extremely simple, these organisms are extremely old; microfossils of them have been found in sedimentary rocks laid down more than 3.2 billion years ago. Their DNA is identical to the basic structure of our own, and is almost certain that we share a common remote ancestor. In general bacteria reproduce only asexually, by simple division of the cells, but a few undergo a form of sexual reproduction. They are widespread in all parts of the environment and are necessary for the operation of nearly all ecosystems. Many act as decomposers, breaking down the bodies of dead animals and plants, and re-releasing their component minerals for use by other organisms. Bacteria are resident in the digestive tracts of most animals, including humans, where they aid in the digestion of food. They live in nodules on the roots of some plants, especially the legumes, assisting them in the take up of nitrogen from the air and the soil. Some are able to decompose environmentally dangerous compounds such as petrochemicals. A few bacteria obtain their food by means of photosynthesis, some are saprophytes, and others are parasites, causing disease in man, animals, plants, and other microorganisms. It has been estimated that the weight of all living bacteria, taken together, equals or exceeds the weight of all other organisms on the earth.

bacteriological quality of drinking water. The most common and widespread danger associated with drinking-water is contamination, either directly or indirectly by sewage by other wastes , or by human or animal excrement. If such contamination is recent and if among the contributors there are carriers of communicable enteric diseases, some of the living causal agents may be present. The drinking of contaminated water or using it in the preparation of certain foods may result in further infection. *See also* waterborne bacterial pathogens; coliform organisms; faecal coliform organisms; sulphite-reducing clostridia; pseudomonas aeruginosa; colony counts; nuisance organisms; disinfectant residuals, and disinfection efficiency.

baffle. A refractory structure whose function is to change the direction of flow of air, fuel, or the products of combustion.

bag filter. A device for removing particulate matter from the waste gases of industrial processes. The filter medium is generally a woven or felted fabric usually in the form of a tube, whose upper end is closed, while the lower end is connected to a gas inlet which also serves as a hooper to catch the dust which is shaken down from the bags the by mechanical or air-reversal methods.

baghouse. A device used in air pollution control terminology for removing particulates from stack emissions by filtering them through a filter bag. The device is similar to a domestic vacuum cleaner, but very large in size, and is one of the most effective means of air pollution control.

Bahco centrifugal dust classifier. An apparatus for dividing the samples of dust into size fractions by means of centrifugal force acting against an inward air current. By using different inward air velocities with constant centrifugal force, the sample can be divided into a number of size grades.

ballast gas. An inert gas introduced into a mixture of combustible gases to adjust the specific gravity, in order to avoid the incomplete combustion and thereby increasing the fuel efficiency.

balloons, zero weight. Special hydrogen-filled balloons, adjusted to zero weight, used in air pollution research into the rise of chimney plumes under varying meteorological conditions. The balloons are introduced into a chimney and carried aloft into the general atmosphere by the chimney gases, their trajectory tending to follow the path of the chimney plume. A specially mounted range finder can be used to plot the distance and the height of each balloon from time to time.

bar. A unit of pressure in centimetre-gram-second (CGS) system;

$= 10^5$ pascals

$= 10^6$ dynes/ cm^2

$= 10^5$ newtons/ m^2.

barbiturate. Any of a group of drugs, derived from barbituric acid, that depress activity of the central nervous system. Most barbiturates, including amobarbital and pentobarbital, are taken as sleeping pills. Very slow-acting barbiturates (such as phenobarbital) are used as sedatives and to control epilepsy; those with a rapid and short-lived effect (such as thiopental) are injected as anesthetics. Because they produce tolerance and psychological and physical dependence, have serious toxic side effects, and can be fatal following large overdosage, barbiturates have been largely replaced in clinical use by safer drugs. The use of barbiturates with alcohol should be avoided since these drugs reinforce each other, producing serious effects.

barium. A heavy, alkaline-earth metal placed in group IIA of the periodic table. Barium is present in the earth's crust in a concentration of 0.5 g/kg. Traces of barium are present in most soils. Barium compounds are used in oil drilling, production of paints, the processing of diesel fuels, the manufacture of paper, rubber, linoleum and similar products, the manufacture of ceramic glazes and enamels, and in medical diagnostics.

Most waters contain some barium, but the concentration is generally well below 0.1 mg/L, although some underground sources may contain levels as high as 10 mg/L in geothermal brines. The source is normally natural mineral matter; although barium sulphate, the predominant form, is only slightly soluble in water in the presence of certain common anions the solubility of barium can be markedly enhanced. The chemical form of barium in tap-water is not definitely known.

Barium is present in traces in many foodstuffs, Brazil nuts are an especially rich source and contain up to several thousand mg/g. There is relatively little published information on dietary intake, but some values ranging between less than 0.1 to nearly 2 mg/day have been published. As the levels of barium in drinking-water are unlikely to exceed 0.05 mg/L, the intake in relation to normal total intake is unlikely to be more than about 15%. However, where the barium levels in water are high, *i.e.*, over 1 mg/L, more than three-quarters of the total barium intake could result from drinking-water. The uptake of barium is difficult to quantify accurately. Barium in food is poorly absorbed, but since a high proportion could be absorbed if ingested as a soluble salt in water, then the contribution made by drinking-water to the absorption of the element could be especially large.

There is no evidence that barium is essential for human nutrition. Insoluble forms of barium, such as barium sulphate (used medicinally), are very poorly absorbed, and have a very low toxicity. Soluble barium salts are readily and rapidly absorbed in this form, 50% or more of ingested barium is absorbed. Only a small fraction of barium in normal foodstuffs appears to be absorbed. Most absorbed barium is present in bone, but it has also been detected in a number of other tissues, such as kidney, liver, and heart. The metabolic pathways for barium are similar to those for calcium. Excretion of barium occurs more readily than with calcium; about a quarter of any ingested barium is excreted within 24 hours.

Animal experiments using drinking water suggest that 5 mg of barium per litre, as barium acetate, would cause no toxic effects even after prolonged exposure. In rats, a total dose of 250 mg of barium over period of 4-13 weeks also caused no adverse effects.

Barium is acutely toxic when soluble salts are ingested in excess; if taken as the chloride, the fatal dose of barium for an adult is about 550-600 mg. In high doses, it induces a strong prolonged stimulant action on all muscles, including those of the heart and gastrointestinal tract. The acute toxic dose has been found by one research group to be 200-500 mg. In another study, 125 mg as a single dose has been suggested to be the threshold for acute toxic effects. In certain industries, it is claimed that a benign form of pneumoconiosis is associated with the inhalation of dusts containing barium. Exposure to barium compounds should be controlled so that no employees are exposed to soluble barium compounds at a concentration greater than 0.5 mg/m^3 of air, determined as a time-weighted average (TWA) concentration limit for up to a 8-hour workshift in a 40-hour workweek.

bar screen. A screen made of closely

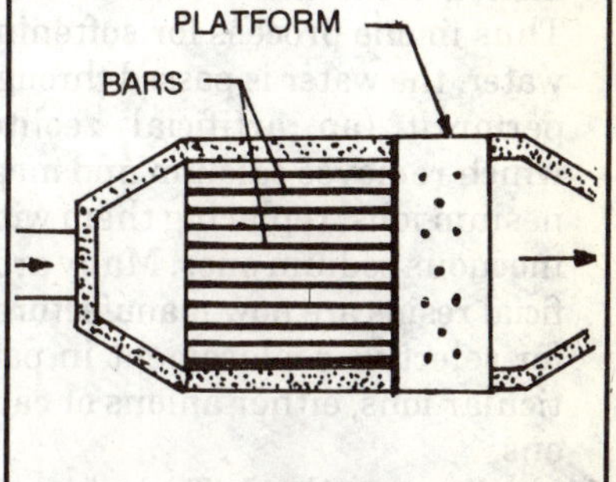

BAR SCREEN

spaced bars used in sewage pumping stations to arrest floating matter and solid particles. Also known as bar rack.

base. A substance that:

(i) liberates hydroxyl ions when dissolved in water;

(ii) that liberates negative ions of various kinds in any solvent;

(iii) that receives a hydrogen ion (proton) from a strong acid to form a weaker acid;

(iv) that gives up two electrons to an acid, forming a covalent bond with the acid (Lewis base); Lewis bases are considered hard if they have high electronegativity and are difficult to oxidize and soft if they have low electronegativity and are easily oxidized. These properties relate to the presence or absence of vacant orbitals. Bases react with acids to form salts and water; when the proper proportions are used, neutralization occurs. All bases in water give solutions having a pH of more than 7.0.

base exchange. This process occurring place when a solution is passed through a medium and the latter removes certain cations from the solution, replacing them with different, but equivalent, ions furnished from the medium itself. Thus in one process for softening water, the water is passed through permutit (an artificial zeolite) which removes calcium and magnesium ions, replacing them with inocuous sodium ones. Many artificial resins are now manufactured for selective replacement in particular ions, either anions or cations.

base line method. Technique in quantitative spectrophotometric analysis. In order to set up reference point for absorption evaluation of the determined component and to eliminate base influence, supplementary line is drawn on absorption curve.

base load. A steady demand equal to a high percentage of the insta lled capacity of a plant.

base metals. 1. In contradistinction to the noble metals, metals that corrode, tarnish, or oxidize on exposure to air, moisture, or heat. 2. The principal metal of an alloy.

Battersea process. A method of removing sulphur dioxide from stack gases, first used at Battersea power station, London. The gas is washed with water containing a little lime under such conditions that the resulting solution of calcium sulphate is not saturated and can be discharged into the river from which the water for washing is taken. The efficiency of the removal of sulphur dioxide is of the order of 90-95%. The process has several drawbacks:

(i) the plume is cooled and the residual sulphur dioxide and moisture fall readily on to the surrounding district;

(ii) the sulphur is not recovered in the form of useful compounds;

(iii) huge quantities of water are required which leads to water pollution; and

(iv) it accelerates the corrosion problems.

Becquerel rays. Radiations emitted by radioactive substances; later renamed as alpha, beta and gamma rays. These rays have harmful effects on living beings, and their presence in the environment is considered as serious pollution.

beneficial use. The use of environment or any element or segment of the environment which is conducive to public benefit, welfare, safety or health, and that requires protection from the effects of waste discharges, emissions, deposits, and despoliation. The beneficial uses include:

(i) potable water supply for drinking, domestic and municipal use;

(ii) agricultural and industrial water supply;

(iii) habitats for the support and propagation of fish and other aquatic life;

(iv) recreational activities such as bathing, boating, and fishing;

(v) navigation; and

(vi) wildlife habitats.

benthic obliteration. Destruction of bottom-dwelling plants and animal life in a specific section of a sea, bay or estuary. Dreading also is a sure method of destroying bottom life.

benzene. A colourless, mildly odiferous, highly flammable aromatic compound; it is very slightly miscible with water (about one part per 1500), and is an excellent solvent for a large number of organic compounds including oils, fats, resins, etc.

It is highly volatile with explosive vapours; and is moderately toxic, both in vapour and liquid forms, whether ingested, inhaled, or absorbed through the skin, and has recently been demonstrated to be carcinogen. Acute poisoning due benzene may result in narcosis, producing unconsciousness, convulsions, and paralysis leading to coma and death. Chronic poisoning due to benzene affects on the blood and blood forming organs and ultimately lead to haemorrhages. Exposure to benzene should be controlled in such a manner so that no human is exposed to benzene vapours at a concentration greater than 30 mg/m^3 of air (10 ppm), determined as a time-weighted average (TWA) concentration limit for up to a 8-hour workshift in a 40-hour workweek; and no employee should be exposed to an airborne concentration in excess of 15 mg/m^3, as averaged over 15 minute period, as the ceiling limit.

The available data for benzene indicate that acute toxicity to freshwater aquatic life occur at concentrations as low as 5300 μg/L; and toxicity to saltwater aquatic life occurs at concentrations as low as 5100 μg/L. For the maximum protection of human health from the potential carcinogenic effects due to exposure of benzene through ingestion of contaminated aquatic-organisms and water, the ambient water concentration should be zero on the nonthreshold assumption for benzene. However, zero level may not be attainable at present time. Therefore, the levels that may result in incremental increase of cancer risk over lifetime are estimated at 10^{-5}, 10^{-6}, and 10^{-7}. The corresponding criteria are 6.6 μg/L, 0.66 mg/L, and 0.066 mg/L respectively. If the estimates are made for the consumption of aquatic organisms only (excluding consumption of water), the levels are redefined as 400 mg/L, 40.0 mg/L, and 4.0 mg/L respectively.

benzidine. An organic compound used in organic synthesis, manufacture of dyes, and as stiffening agent in rubber industry. It has been classified as a potential occupational carcinogen, and no exposure by any route- respiratory, skin, or oral, is permitted. The available data for benzidine indicate that acute toxicity to freshwater aquatic life occur at concentrations as low as 2500 μg/L, and would occur at even lower concentrations among the species that are more sensitive than those tested. For the maximum protection of human health from the potential carcinogenic effects due to exposure of bezidine through ingestion of contaminated aquatic organisms and water, the ambient water concentration should be zero on the nonthreshold assumption for benzidine. However, zero level may not be attainable at present time. Therefore, the levels that may result in incremental increase of cancer risk over lifetime are estimated at 10^{-5}, 10^{-6}, and 10^{-7}. The corresponding criteria are 1.2 ng/L, 0.12 ng/L, and 0.012 ng/L respectively. If the above estimates are made for the consumption of aquatic organisms only (excluding consumption of water), the levels are redefined as 5.3 ng/L, 0.53 ng/L, and 0.053 ng/L respectively.

benzopyrene. A hydrocarbon present in coal and cigarette smoke; considered to be carcinogenic for humans.

benzoyl peroxide. A white, crystalline, hazardous solid, having active oxygen; employed as bleaching agent for flour, fats, oils, and waxes; and as polymerization catalyst. Occupational exposure to benzoyl peroxide is defined as any work involving handling, storage, use, or manufacture of benzoyl peroxide at a concentration above the action level. Exposure to benzoyl peroxide should be controlled so that no employees are exposed to benzoyl peroxide at a concentration greater than 5.0 mg/m^3 of air, determined as a time-weighted average (TWA) concentration limit for up to a 10-hour workshift in a 40-hour workweek, over a working lifetime.

beryllium. Beryllium is found as part of feldspar mineral structures and may exit as the mineral beryl in small localized deposits. The amounts mined have been very small. It is an excellent neutron reflector (better than graphite for slow neutrons), and it is a good source of neutrons, especially when mixed with radium. Hot pressed blocks of beryllium are used for aerospace instruments and inertial guidance equipment, as well as in nuclear reactors. In metallurgical applications, it is used as an alloying agent (with copper) in the manufacture as well as of springs and diaphragms.

The metal and its compounds are quite toxic, especially in the form of powder, dust or fume. The primary source of beryllium in the environment is the burning of fossil fuels, although contamination is normally slight. Because of its light weight and high tensile strength, the metal is valuable as a constituent of special alloys for applications such as space vehicles, X-ray windows, and certain electrical components. Industrial processes in which exposure to beryllium can occur include the mining and extraction of beryllium, aerospace equipment, alloy machining, electroplating, and atomic energy industries. Exposure to beryllium in industries is via inhalation and skin contact. Without ventilation, concentrations of beryllium in air as high as 23 mg/m^3 have been reported.

Dermal absorption of beryllium is negligible, since beryllium becomes bound to certain epidermal constituents, but there have been reports of beryllium dermatitis and granulomatous ulcerations of the skin at sites where insoluble beryllium compounds were embedded; conjunctivitis has also been described. Compounds of beryllium are not readily absorbed when ingested, since they tend to form insoluble compounds at physiological *p*H levels. Less than 1% of ingested beryllium is absorbed. Inhaled soluble compounds of beryllium are absorbed from the lungs into the blood and are transported mainly as orthophosphate colloids, being ultimately deposited in the bone as insoluble hydroxide. Insoluble beryllium compounds tend to remain in the lungs indefinitely after inhalation. Absorbed beryllium is either excreted in the urine or deposited in the kidneys or bone. Excretion of beryllium is fairly rapid.

The inhalation of beryllium has been demonstrated to be harmful to human beings. Acute respiratory exposure can result in severe health effects, including rhinitis, pharyngitis, pneumonitis, and pulmonary oedema. Beryllium is very poorly absorbed from the gastrointestinal tract, and its toxicity via this route of entry is low. Inhalation, intratrachel installation, and intravenous injection have been shown to induce tumors in experimental animals. Although firm evidence of human cancer induction by exposure to beryllium is lacking, the evidence is suggestive. Some studies of tumour induction in experimental animals as a result of ingestion of beryllium compounds at levels up to 500 mg/kg of diet have been inconclusive.

Exposure to beryllium should be controlled so that no employee is exposed to total airborne beryllium as particulate at a concentration greater than 2.0 μg/m^3 of air, determined as a time-weighted average (TWA) concentration limit for up to a 8-hour workshift in a 40-hour workweek, and no peak concentration of beryllium to which workers are exposed should exceed 25 μ/m^3 as determined by a minimum sampling time of 30 minutes.

The available data for beryllium indicate that acute and chronic toxicity to freshwater aquatic life occur at concentrations as low as 103 and 5.3 μg/L, respectively; and would occur at even lower concentrations among the species that are more sensitive than those tested. For the maximum protection of human health from the potential carcinogenic effects due to exposure of beryllium through ingestion of contaminated aquatic organisms and water, the ambient water concentration should be zero on the non-threshold assumption for beryllium. However, zero level may not be attainable at present time. Therefore, the levels that may result in incremental increase of cancer risk over lifetime are estimated at 10^{-5}, 10^{-6}, and 10^{-7}. The corresponding criteria are 37.0 ng/L, 3.7 ng/L, and 0.37 ng/L respectively. If the above estimates are made for the consumption of aquatic organisms only (excluding consumption of water), the levels are redefined as 641 ng/L, 64.1 ng/L, and 6.41 ng/L respectively.

best available retrofit technology. In air pollution control, the best control technology that can be added onto a currently polluting source at reasonable cost.

best available technology. In water pollution control, the best means currently available for reducing or eliminating the discharge of pollutants into the natural waters from the industrial point sources.

best practicable technology. In water pollution control, the best technology currently available on a practical basis for controlling point source pollution from industrial sources. Publicly owned treatment works are required to meet a modification of these standards that calls for the best technology practically available over the life of the project rather than currently.

bilge water. Water trapped within the hull of a ship. It must be pumped out frequently to keep the ship from foundering. However, since it is usually polluted by oil, fuel, human wastes, and the dregs of whatever cargo the ship may have been carrying, pumping should not be done directly into the harbor or the open ocean but should be processed through a waste treatment facility, either on board the ship or as a part of the harbor complex.

bio-. A prefix indicating life or the presence and activity of living organisms, as in biomass, biodegradable, bioluminescence, etc. It is also appears in words in other sciences as well as in literature (biology, biography).

bioassay approach. The analytical method used to determine the measure of biomass in a certain water environment. The biologists take a sample of water filter it through fibres, and inoculate the filtered water with a culture to test algae. Subsequently the inoculated sample is incubated for about ten days. The amount of growth during that period is a measure of the biomass in the test region from which the sample were taken.

bio-bubble. The ecosphere is often referred to as a bio-bubble in which all living orders are particles held together bt non-living forces.

biochemical oxygen demand (BOD). The amount, in milligrams per liter, of dissolved oxygen required by aerobic bacteria to decompose organic matter in water solution. BOD is not a pollutant, but is a measure of the effect of certain types of pollutants on the receiving waters. Generally, a high BOD in body of water or a waste stream means that high levels of nutrients are present, along with a high number of microorganisms feeding the nutrients. These are the conditions associated with eutrophication. BOD is thus an indicator of degraded conditions in a body of water, but it cannot tell us specifically what may be causing the degradation. The BOD is determined by adding oxygen-saturated water to sample of the contaminated water and then measuring the dissolved oxygen in the mixture at once and again after several days. The BOD value is thus an index of the contamination of the water. It is an important consideration in sewage treatment, in which proper aeration of the organic material is essential. Also known as biological oxygen demand. *See also* chemical oxygen demand.

biochemorphology. The science dealing with the chemical structure of foods and drugs and their reactions and living organisms.

biocide. General name for any substance that kills or inhibits growth of microorganisms, such as bacteria, molds, slimes, fungi, etc. Any chemical that is toxic to any living thing is technically a biocide, however the term is generally reserved for chemicals that kill a large number of different species. *See also* disinfectant; fungicide.

biocolloid. A general term including all biochemically active aggregates in the colloidal size range, such as protein macromolecules, nucleic acid complexes, and various coenzymes, bacteria, and viruses.

bioconversion. The conversion of the energy stored in plant materials such as trees, crops, algae, and water plants, to produce ethanol, methanol, methane, or other useful products. Agricultural wastes, urban wastes, sewage, and animal excreta can also be converted into liquid and gaseous fuels, such as methane and hydrogen. Also known as biological conversion.

biodegradability. The susceptibility of an organic material to decomposition as a result of attack by micro-organism. The term is applied especially to detergents and insecticides, which vary widely in this respect.

bioenergetics. The study of transfers between plants and animals, between plants and plants, and between animals and animals. This is an important aspect of environmental investigations. Naturally much of bioenergetics is calculated with computers instead of measuring with measuring instruments. These calculations are based on unbiased, intelligently prepared parameters.

bioengineering cycles. The circulation of nutrients from the environment to living organism and back. In this regard there are three main cycles:

1. The carbon cycle
2. The nitrogen cycle, and
3. The phosphorus cycle

Unlike business cycles, these kinds of cycles are regularly occurring and are continuous.

biofiltration plant. A sewage treatment plant in which BOD is removed to a great extent by passing the settled sewage through a bed of stone blocks, brick bets, ballasts, etc. The plant may be single-stage or two-stage; and the plant layout may be designed in series, series-parallel, or parallel.

biogas. The gas produced by the microbial decomposition of organic matter in the absence of oxygen. It consists of a gaseous mixture of methane and carbon dioxide in approximate volumetric ratio of 2:1. In this state, it has a calorific value of about 20-25 MJ/m^3, which

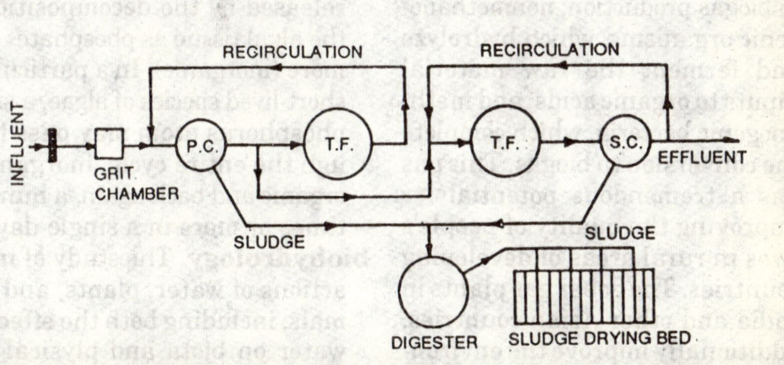

BIOFILTRATION PLANT

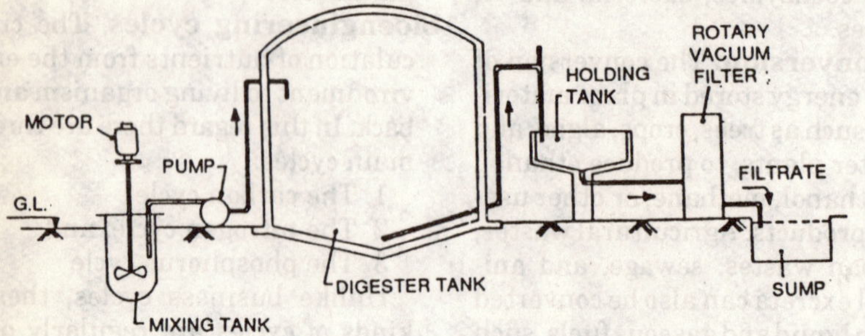

BIOGAS PLANT

can be further upgraded by reducing the amount of carbon dioxide. It is a renewable source of energy and has been used on a small scale to drive motor engines and as a substitute for firewood in different parts of India. Sewage and human/animal manure are the most common organic wastes used for the production of biogas, though waterweeds, algae, and agricultural residues have also been employed for this purpose. Two major classes of bacteria are involved in biogas production; nonmethanogenic organisms, which hydrolyze and ferment the raw material inputs to organic acids, and methanogenic bacteria, which complete the conversion to biogas. This gas has a tremendous potential for improving the quality of people's lives in rural areas of developing countries. The gobar gas plants in India and other Asian countries, additionally improve the environment by lessening the need for firewood energy, which in turn reduces the possibility of deforestation and soil erosion.

biogeochemical cycle. The path taken by a chemical element as it passes from inorganic matter to organic matter and back again. Phosphorus, for example, may exist in water in the form of dissolved phosphates(inorganic); the phosphates may be used as a food by algae, which break them down and use the phosphorus to build DNA and other complex living molecules(organic); and when the algae die, the phosphorus may be released by the decomposition of the algal tissue as phosphates once more (inorganic). In a particularly short-lived species of algae, a single phosphorus atom may pass through the entire cycle, inorganic to organic and back again, a hundred times or more in a single day.

biohydrology. The study of interactions of water, plants, and animals, including both the effects of water on biota and plysical and chemical changes in water or its environment caused by biota.

biological accumulation. Accumulation of elements and compounds in living organisms; it is a specific characteristic of certain species or it can be determined by the geochemical environment. Biological accumulation is a frequent phenomenon in alga and aquatic weed species in waters. These are capable of accumulating certain elements by a factor of 10^4 or 10^5. Some of the known harmful accumulates are DDT, aldrin, dieldrin, cadmium, lead and mercury.

biological assay. *See* bioassay.

biological balance. In every living community there are balances between the animals and plants, between the plants and plants, and between the animals and the animals, including humans. Any balance of any of the aforementioned types is considered a biological balance, because it involves life. For other types of balance necessary to support life on earth as we know it.

biological clock. The mysterious attribute that causes white collar workers to get up each morning five minutes before the alarm goes off. In some species the biological clock tells them when to work, when to eat and when to sleep. thus some creatures are nocturnal and diurnal. Ecologists are concerned that continued pollution will stop these clocks.

biological conversion. *See* bioconversion.

biological degradation. The biochemical process of the breakdown of complex, large organic molecules into small, simple molecules. In other words, this is the process of decay or decomposition of organic matter accomplished by bacteria or by secretions and chemicals involving these bacteria, fungi and other microorganisms. Any organic matter that can be broken down by bacteria is called biodegradable matter because it undergoes biodegradation, an abbreviated description of biological degradation.

biological effects of radiation. Effects that have been studied for many victims, survivors of the atomic bomb explosion at Hiroshima and Nagasaki, patients undergoing radiotherapy, persons exposed to radiation in their work, and in animal experiments. These biological effects can be broadly classified as somatic, occurring with in the exposed individual, and genetic, affecting the descendants of the exposed individual. An acute exposure of the whole body to a radiation dose of hundreds of rads produces almost immediate effects, known as acute radiation syndrome. These usually include nausea, vomiting, loss of hair, severe blood changes with haemorrhage and increased susceptibility to infection. Genetic effects of the ionizing radiation arise from the mutations induced in the DNA of germ cells. These changes to the genetic material are usually considered to be detrimental and will be transmitted to any offspring, in whom their effects may range in severity from inconspicuous to lethal and may not be revealed for many generations.

biological oxidation. Oxidation of chemical compounds caused by enzymes, which act as electron or hydrogen atom carriers.

biological oxygen demand. *See* biochemical oxygen demand.

biological shield. Layer of material of suitable absorption characteristics and thickness, placed between source of ionizing radiation and operator, securing attenuation of radiation to admissible level.

biological treatment process. Means of treatment in which bacterial biochemical action is intensified to stabilize, oxidize and nitrify the unstable organic matter present. Trickling filters, contact stabilization and lagoons are examples that have been used for treatment of combined sewer overflows.

biologic artifact. An organic compound whose chemical structure demonstrates its derivation from living matter.

biomass. The total organic matter contained by plants and/or animals, and other living beings, usually expressed in terms of ovendry weight per unit area. In other words, it is the weight of all producers, consumers, and reducers that exist in an ecosystem at a particular time. Biomass of living and dead material may be calculated separately, depending on kind of data needed. Weights given for biomass may be measurements of fresh (live) or wet materials or of dry materials. For plants, dry weight is generally preferred because the amount of water that plants contain, varies with the change in season. The weights are usually obtained for specific areas of land or for volumes of water. Yields, such as tons of hay per hectare, etc., is another way for expressing biomass. To calculate the biomass in a forest, all of the roots, stems, and leaves would have to be collected over a specified area, dried and then weighed. To obtain an energy equivalent for biomass, the samples of plants and/or animal material are dried, weighed and burned in a bomb calorimeter, and the results expressed as kilojoules per unit of dry weight.

biomaterial. Any of the various materials, used either within the body or as a prosthetic device in contact with external tissue under the supervision of a surgeon of dentist. Such materials must meet standards of tissue compatibility, resistance to degradation, toxicity, and functional dependability.

biome. A large naturally occurring assemblage of animal and plant species that are of the same general type, being adopted to the particular conditions in which they occur; for example, the deep forests and woodlands with their vast herds of browing and grazing animals and associated predators, constitute a biome.

biometeorology. A combination of various desciplines of science that examines and investigates physical and chemical factors in the atmosphere as they are related to life. It involves the studies related to pollutants and infectious agents, and the interaction of pollutants and weather factors. Specializations of this discipline include: bioclimatology, physiological ecology, environmental science, aerobiology, micrometeorology, aeronomy, synoptic meteorology, and climatology.

biomonitoring. The use of living things to detect changes in the environment. Coal miners, for example once carried canaries into the mines with them; the birds are extremely sensitive to carbon monoxide poisoning, and their behaviour enabled the miners to detect the presence of this deadly gas at the levels far below those which would be dangerous to human health.

biophile. 1. Said of those elements that are concentrated in and by living plants and animals. 2. Also said of those elements that are the most typical in organisms and organic material.

biophotolysis. The biological splitting of water molecules into hydrogen and oxygen in the presence of sunlight. The experimental processes have been accomplished by living organisms such as blue-green alga *Anabaena cylindrica* under conditions of nitrogen deficiency; in the absence of molecular nitrogen the enzyme nitrogenase liberates hydrogen from water instead of beginning the usual reactions of photosynthesis. Hydrogen is also evolved by adding extracted hydrogenase enzyme to isolated plant chloroplasts as well as to photosynthetic artificial membranes. The latter are more stable than the living systems and generate a potential difference through the initial transference of electrons, thereby developing an electric current.

bioprecipitation process. A process for the treatment of raw sewage, in which te waste liquid is pretreated in a counter current oxygenation unit and is passed upward through a sludge blanket.

biosorption process. A sewage treatment process in which sewage is pretreated with activated sludge in a mixing chamber for 30 minutes during which biosorption takes place. This is followed by the aeration of the sewage in an aeration tank for about 2-3 hours.

biosphere. All living organisms of the earth and its atmosphere. 2. All the area occupied or favourable occupation by living organisms. It includes parts of the lithosphere, hydrosphere and atmos-

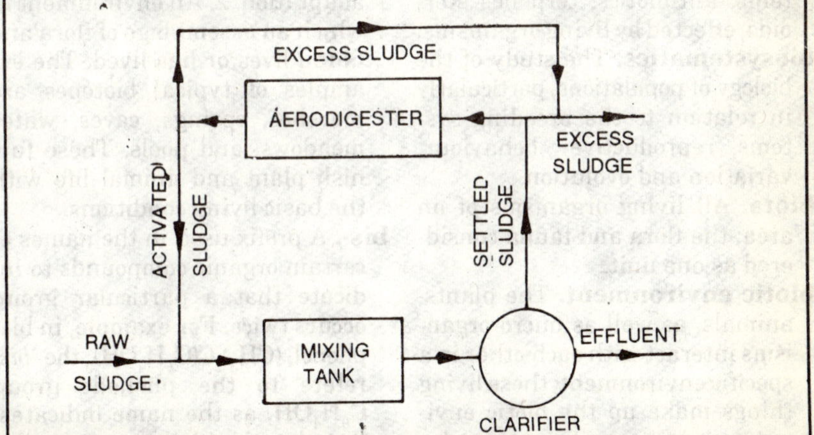

BIOSORPTION PROCESS

phere. It extends about 10 m down into the soil, about 100 m into the sea or freshwater, and into the atmosphere about 300 m above land or water surfaces. The majority of living organisms arbiocycles. These are:

(a) marine;

(b) freshwater; and

(c) terrestrial.

Since most birds get their food from land or sea, they are arbitrarily made a part of the terrestrial biocycle portion of the biosphere. The biosphere has also been sectioned into two larger portions or ecological pie called the hydrosphere and the pedosphere. The hydrosphere contains swimming creatures and the pedosphere contains walking creatures-including humans who are accelerating their deaths by not walking. Putting all the pieces of this complicated cake together we find biosphere synonymous with environment.

biosynthesis. Synthesis of organic compounds, *e.g.*, alkaloids, proteins, antibiotics, terpenes steroids, effected by living organisms.

biosystematics. The study of the biology of populations, particularly in relation to the breeding systems, reproductive behaviour, variation and evolution.

biota. All living organisms of an area; the flora and fauna considered as one unit.

biotic environment. The plants, animals, as well as micro-organisms interact with each other in a specific environment; these living things make up the biotic environment in a specific area under study. They in turn are inextricably interrelated with the abiotic environment, consisting of physical and chemical and inorganic ingredients in the total environment. Interactions within the biotic environment consist of birth, death, density, distribution, *etc.* Pollution is a man-made factor that impairs or degrades this relationship.

biotic potential. The ability of a populations to grow, or put another way, the growth potential of a living species or community. How much pollution saps or accelerates the biotic potential of differing species of plant and animals life has never quite been determined, but there is little doubt that pollution can affect the biotic potential of any species if the amount of pollutants and the length of time of exposure are great enough.

biotic province. A geographic area that supports one or more ecologic associations which are distinct from those of adjacent provinces.

biotope. 1. An area characterized by uniform ecology and organic adaptation. 2. An environment in which an assemblage of flora and fauna lives or has lived. The examples of typical biotopes are marshes, springs, caves, water meadows, and pools. These furnish plant and animal life with the basic living conditions.

bis-. A prefix used in the names of certain organic compounds to indicate that a particular group occurs twice. For example, in bisphenol, $(CH_3)_2C(C_6H_4OH)_2$ the '*bis*' refers to the phenolic group C_6H_4OH, as the name indicates, though two methyl groups are also present.

black acids. Sulphonates in the

sludge formed during treatment of petroleum products with sulphuric acid; soluble in water but insoluble in naphtha, benzene, and carbon tetrachloride.

black ash. A carbon product made by furnace heating of black liquor from paper making processes.

black center burning. The condition in a fuel bed in which an area or areas of unignited coke appear at the surface. It may result in under-feed stoking if the air rate is too high. It may also result due to the formation of coke trees from strongly coking coals. Black center burning is accompanied by smoke emissions.

blackdamp. The poisonous gas containing carbon dioxide, carbon monoxide, or other suffocating material, sometimes found in pockets in underground workings.

black smoke. Smoke produced when particulates of carbon are derived from the cracking of hydrocarbon gases, following sudden cooling. Smoke is a visible evidence of incomplete combustion. Ships, factories, mills, and other necessities like power plants use bituminous coal as fuel. The resulting emissions are mostly black; and thus, black smoke is a symbol of a coal fire, a wood fire, or any other fire resulting from fossil fuel. The blackness in black smoke is caused by carbon particulates and char.

black smoker. A vent on the deep-sea floor that releases a large, rapidly moving plume of extremely hot mineral laden water. Upon contact with the cold water of the ocean, the vent water cools rapidly, releasing its minerals in the form of fine particulates, which turn the plume black. Some of the metallic minerals are deposited around the vent mouth, building a chimney and others are dissolved in water. It is believed that the black smokers, by circulating ocean water through the earth's crust, are responsible for much of the sea's mineral content.

black water. The component of the household sewage that carries urine, fecal matter, or other biologically active substances. More specifically, black water is the effluent from toilets and from garbage disposals.

blank. Test carried out under specified conditions with all reagents with exception of determined substance to account for content of this substance in reagents used. Also known as blank test; blank determination.

blast furnace gas. Waste combustible gases generated in a blast furnace when iron ore is being reduced with coke, to metallic form. The gas contains high proportions of nitrogen and carbon monoxide, and smaller amounts of carbon dioxide and hydrogen. Excess carbon monoxide in the gases of the furnace are usually flared, which creates excessive particulates because it has to take place inside the furnace.

bleaching. The process of decolourizing impurities occurring in numerous materials, including textiles, paper pulp, vegetable and mineral oils, as well as such earth products as barytes and clays in order to achieve whiteness. Bleaching usually involves a chemical reaction such as oxidation or reduction. Some of the commonly used bleaching agents are sodium/

calcium hypochlorite, hydrogen peroxide, organic peroxides, sodium perborate, and sodium bromide. These substances and their reaction products, when discharged as waste, account for the water pollution.

bleaching assistant. A material added to textile bleach baths to cause better penetration by bleach; includes pine oils, borax, and sulphonated oils.

bleaching clay. Absorbed clay contacted with petroleum, vegetable, and other oils to obtain decolourized products.

blow-down. The release of water from the lowest part of the boiler to free it from sludge and reduce the dissolved solid content of the water. The amount of blow-down required per day depends upon the maximum total dissolved solids which can be tolerated without risk of priming.

BLP. Buoyant line and point-source description model. A Gaussian plume-dispersion model designed to handle the unique modelling problems associated with aluminium reduction plants, and other industrial sources where plume rise and downwash effects from stationary line sources are important.

blue tide. An overgrowth of certain blue-green algae that secrete toxins harmful to cattle. The toxins kill cattle that drink water covered with such algae, but probably do not harm man because he'd either have to be blind or dying of thirst to touch the scummy stuff.

BOD. *See* biochemical oxygen demand.

bog. A rich, organic deposit formed when a lake or pond underwent intense europhcation. As living organisms, botanical matter, plants and algae thrived and died, their remains settled to the bottom to form a slimy sediment where the organic matter underwent decomposition anaerobically. As the lake or pond aged, the slimy matter grew in size and eventually the water covering it either evaporated of seeped away. this lift, exposed to the sun the slimy sapropel. As the sun baked the sapropel it become converted into a solid mass rich in hydrocarbons.

bog lake. A lake undergoing severe eutrophication, already rimmed with areas called bogs. Eventually when the water covering the centre of this lake disappears entire lake will become a bog. Nutrients from man-made pollutants such as phosphate and nitrate, hasten this process.

bog soil. An intrazonal, hydromorphic group of soils having a mucky or peaty surface horizon and an underlying peat horizon. These soils developed in swamps or marshes in humid or subhumid climates. Bog soils are now classified as histosols.

boiler. An enclosed device using controlled flame combustion and having the following characteristics:

(a) The unit must have physical provisions for recovering and exporting thermal energy in the form of steam, heated fluids, or heated gases.

(b) The unit's combustion chamber and primary energy-recovery section must be of integral design. To be of integral design, the combustion chamber and the primary energy-recovery section (such as waterwalls and superheaters) must be physically formed into one manufactured or assembled unit. The following units are not precluded from being boilers solely because they are not of integral design: process heaters (units that transfer energy directly to a process stream) and fluidized bed combustion units.

(c) While in operation, the unit must maintain a thermal energy recovery efficiency of at least 60%, calculated in terms of the recovered energy compared with the thermal value of the fuel.

(d) The unit must export and utilize at least 75% of the recovered energy, calculated on an annual basis. In this calculation, no credit shall be given for recovered heat used internally in the same unit. (Examples of internal use are the preheating of fuel or combustion air, and the driving of induced or forced draft fans or feedwater pumps).

boiler scale. An extremely hard incrustation of calcium and/or magnesium compounds formed on the inner surfaces of boilers and hot-water lines after so-called hard water has been in contact with them for a long period of time.

bone seeker. Any element that tends to concentrate in the bones and teeth of animals and man. Most important are calcium, an essential component of bony structure, and fluoride, which in very low concentration (1 ppm) can inhibit tooth decay. Strontium also belongs to this class; the radioactive isotope strontium-90 is extremely dangerous, as it replaces calcium and cause radiation damage in blood-and marrow-forming structure.

bottle. A container having a neck of relatively smaller cross section than the body and an opening capable of holding a closure for retention of the contents.

bottled gas. Butane, propane, or butane-propane mixtures liquified and bottled under pressure for use as domestic cooking fuel.

Bowen ratio. In climatology, the ratio of the sensible heat to the latent heat in the earth's atmosphere. This ratio varies from place to place and time to time. It is lowest where evaporation is actively tying up heat inputs as latent heat. Where the ratio is low, temperature change is slow and the range between the low and high temperature is quite narrow. Where the ratio is high (as in deserts), temperature change is fast and the low and high temperatures tend to be extreme.

brackish water. Water containing from 1000 to 3000 mg/L salinity. It results from inter-mixing of ocean water and riverine mixing at the liquid-liquid interface, where ocean tides bring the salt water to the river mouth and where the river current brings the fresh water to the edge of the ocean; brackish water may be successfully desalinated by such methods.

break-bulk. Packages of hazardous materials that are handled individually, palletized, or unitized for purposes of transportation, as opposed to bulk and containerized freight.

breathing. The movement of oil and other volatile substances or, air in and out of the relief valves or vent lines of storage tanks due to alternate heating and cooling of the contents.

broad-spectrum pesticide. A pesticide such as DDT, which kills a wide variety of living organisms. The 'shotgun approach' that the broad-spectrum pesticides represent is now discredited as a pest-management tool due to the indiscriminate killing of non-target species (including bees, ladybugs, and other beneficial insects) following their use.

bromine. A highly reactive element, placed in group VIIA of the periodic table; exists as a liquid at room temperature, though it is highly volatile; it does not occur naturally in elemental form but always in combined state. It is obtained commercially from brines, and was the first element to be recovered from sea water. The vapour is over five times as dense as air. Its major industrial use has been in making antiknock gasoline (as ethylene bromide), where it acts to keep cylinders free from lead oxide deposits; this use is excepted to decline in the future. Bromine is also important in organic synthesis, as a laboratory reagent. It is toxic by inhalation and strongly irritant to eyes and skin, and therefore should be handled with proper protective measures. The acute poisoning due to bromine results in irritation and watering of eyes; choking and coughing; deep and severe skin burns. Chronic poisoning due to bromine results in skin rashes. Exposure to bromine should be controlled so that no employees are exposed to bromine vapours at a concentration greater than 0.7 mg/m^3 of air, determined as a time-weighted average (TWA) concentration limit for up to a 8-hour workshift in a 40-hour workweek.

bromochloromethane. A colourless liquid mainly used as a fire extinguishing fluid, as a solvent, and as a refrigerant. It has anaesthetic properties especially if used in confined spaces. The acute poisoning can lead to unconsciousness which may ultimately lead to death unless the affected worker is removed to fresh air at earliest. Exposure to bromochloromethane should be controlled so that no employees are exposed to bromochloromethane at a concentration greater than 1050 mg/m^3 of air (200 ppm), determined as a time-weighted average (TWA) concentration limit for up to a 10-hour workshift.

bronchitis. Inflammation of the mucous membrane of the bronchial tubes existing in either an acute or chronic form. Epidimiological studies have indicated that there is a correlation high concentration of air pollution and morbidity and mortality among chronic bronchitis, although the ultimate progress of the disease is sensitive, particularly in winter, to many stimuli, of which air pollution is but one. Despite the complexity of the problem, the medical research has concluded that cigarette smoking and air pollution are two important factors in the causation of this disease.

Brownian motion. The discontinuous movement-of colloidal particles in a gaseous or liquid suspension, giving the appearance in a micro scope of a 'dance' or zig-zag effect. It was later shown that the motion is caused by the impact of the molecules of the suspending medium, and it thus provides visible evidence of molecular kinetics.

bubble. In air pollution regulation, the treatment of an entire industrial plant or complex of plants as a single point source for regulatory purposes, as if all of its separate stacks, vents, and other sources of pollutants were enclosed in a giant plastic bubble with only one opening from which all emissions emerged. The concept of bubble is to allow all plant managers to meet overall emission standards with a choice of alternate strategies that may include decreasing emissions more from some stacks than from others, rather than forcing them to meet specific emission goals on each stack. This permits those processes from which emissions are technologically and/ or economically easier to control to be reduced below the overall standard, offsetting the application of more costly and difficult controls on other processes, which are then allowed to relax to levels greater than the imposed standards.

buffer. An acid-base balancing or control reaction by which the *p*H of a solution is protected from in small quantity change when acids or bases are added to it. The protection is afforded by the presence in the solution of a weak acid and related salt (for example, acetic acid and sodium acetate), which maintain the equilibrium by means of ion transfer and neutralization. The same effect can be obtained by use of a blend of two acid salts; phosphates, carbonates, and ammonium salts are common buffering agents.

bulk packaging. A packaging, other than a vessel or a barge, including a transport vehicle or freight container, in which hazardous materials are loaded with no intermediate form of containment and that which has:

(a) an internal volume grater than 450 litres (118.9 gallons) as a receptacle for a liquid;

(b) a capacity greater than 400 kgs (881.8 pounds) as a receptacle for a soild; or

(c) a water capacity greater than 1,000 pounds (453.6 kgs) as a receptacle for a gas.

Bunsen coefficient. The volume of gas under standard conditions of temperature and pressure (S.T.P.) which is absorbed by a unit volume of gas solution. Also known as absorption coefficient.

buoyancy. The upward force that acts on a body that is totally immersed in a fluid. It is equal to the weight to the fluid displaced by the body, so if the density of the immersed body is less than that of the fluid, there will be a net upward force on the body. As the density of a gas decreases with temperature, the upward force on a parcel of warm air will be greater than its weight and it will rise. This will continue until the parcel of air cools to the temperature of its surroundings. The behaviour of a plume of hot gas issuing from a chimney provides an example.

burn. To oxidize so rapidly that the products of the oxidation are rendered incandescent.

burnable poison. A means of controlling the radioactivity of certain types of nuclear reactor. In pressurized water reactors, a very dilute solution of boric acid, is employed to capture neutrons and control excess reactivity in a newly fuelled reactor.

burn-up. In radiochemistry, destruction or transformation of specified nuclei as a result of neutron capture reaction. In reactor technique, degree of consumption of initial load of reactor fuel as a result of reactor operation.

***n*-butyl acetate.** A colourless, flammable liquid with fruity odour; it is slightly soluble in water but readily soluble in ether, hydrocarbons and ethyl alcohol. It is used as a solvent in nitrocellulose lacquers, leather dressings, perfumes, and a solvent for natural gums and synthetic resins. It is moderately toxic and skin irritant. Exposure to *n*-butyl acetate should be controlled so that no worker is exposed to this compound at a concentration greater than 710 mg/m^3 of air (150 ppm), determined as a time-weighted average (TWA) concentration limit, and 950 mg/m^3 as the short-term exposure limit. The guidelines have been recommended for up to a 10-hour workshift in a 40-hour workweek, over a working lifetime.

***sec*-butyl acetate.** A colourless, and flammable liquid; readily soluble in ether and hydrocarbons, and is used as a solvent in nitrocellulose lacquers, thinners, nail enamels and leather finishes It is moderately toxic and skin irritant. Exposure to *sec*-butyl acetate should be controlled in such a manner so that no worker is exposed to this compound at a concentration greater than 950 mg/m^3 of air (200ppm), determined as a time-weighted average (TWA) concentration limit, and 1190 mg/m^3 as the short-term exposure limit. The guidelines have been recommended for up to a 10-hour workshift in a 40-hour workweek, over a working lifetime.

***tert*-butyl acetate.** A colourless, and flammable liquid; it is readily soluble in ether and hydrocarbons, and is used as a solvent as as gasoline additive It is moderately toxic and skin irritant. Exposure to *tert*-butyl acetate should be controlled in such a manner so that no worker is exposed to this compound at a concentration greater than 950 mg/m^3 of air (200 ppm), determined as a time-weighted average (TWA) concentration limit, and 1190 mg/m^3 as the short-term exposure limit. The guidelines have been recommended for up to a 10-hour workshift in a 40-hour workweek, over a working lifetime.

***n*-butyl acrylate.** A colourless, flammable liquid; used as in the manufacture of adhesives, binders, emulsifiers, and paints. It is moderately toxic and skin irritant. Exposure to *n*-butyl acrylate should be controlled in such a manner so that no worker is exposed to this compound at a concentration greater than 55 mg/m^3 of air (10 ppm), determined as a time-weighted average (TWA) concentration limit.

***n*-butyl alcohol.** A colourless, flammable liquid with vinous odour; it is soluble in water and is miscibile with ether, hydrocarbons and ethyl alcohol. It is used as a solvent in nitrocellulose lacquers, perfumes, and in the preparation of plasticizers and detergent formulations. It is toxic on prolonged inhalation and irritant to eyes. It has been enlisted as hazardous by Environment Protection Agency (EPA). Exposure to *n*-butyl alcohol should be controlled so that no worker is exposed to this compound at a concentration greater than 150 mg/m^3 of air (50 ppm), determined as a time-weighted average (TWA) concentration limit, The guidelines have been recommended for up to a 10-hour workshift in a 40-hour workweek, over a working lifetime.

butyl rubber. A synthetic rubber that is a copolymer of iso-butylene and isoprene. Owing to its low permeability to gases, butyl rubber is used in the manufacture of tyre inner tubes. The industry manufacturing butyl rubber causes a lot of air pollution.

byerit. Bituminous coal that does not crack in fire and melts and enlarges upon heating.

by-product. A secondary product of a reaction or of manufacture obtained in addition to the primary product. Byproducts are not due to malfunctioning of the reaction vessels or processes, but arise from the nature of the operations themselves, as for example, smoke from the burning of wood to obtain heat in a stove or heat from the burning of wood to obtain smoke in a smokehouse. The byproducts of coal gas manufacture include ammonia, coke, and coal-tar. If they are thrown away, byproducts are also called waste products. An efficient process, however, minimizes the production of byproducts or produces byproducts that are useful in other contexts, and check pollution.

byssinosis. Disease of workers in vegetable fibre industry, *e.g.*, cotton, flax, jute, hemp. Presents with chest tightness after a period of absence from work.

bystander phenomena. The non-specific effects (including lysis) of an immune response on tissues which are not themselves specific targets of that response, but which are susceptible to the action of non-specific factor released during the response.

C

caballing. The mixture of two water masses to produce a blend that sinks because it is denser than either of the parent components. The phenomenon occurs when two water masses have same density but different salinities and temperatures.

cabot control. An effective method of adding a wick to the surface of an oil spill and then setting the spill afire, so that combustion of the oil will clean the sea.

cadmium. A silvery white metal, placed in group IIB of the periodic table. It occurs in various minerals in association with zinc. It is used in industry for galvanic plating to protect iron and steel from corrosion, for low-melting-point alloys, and to moderate the chain reaction in nuclear power stations. Cadmium sulphur (yellow) and cadmium selenide (deep red) are basic substances for dyes, which are used in ceramic glazing, porcelain dying and plastics. In the agricultural field, cadmium occurs in artificial phosphate fertilizers and in certain plant protection agents. Like lead and mercury, cadmium is a toxic heavy metal. Whereas the toxic effects of lead and mercury have been known for a long time, the dangerous nature of cadmium has only recently been recognized. The hazard arises when cadmium coated metal is heated, soldered, welded, or burnt and the fumes are given off. Acute poisoning due to inhalation of fumes may result in tightness of chest, dry and uncontrollable cough, headache and shivering, and in some cases even death. Chronic poisoning due to cadmium may cause shortness of breath, impaired sense of smell, loss of weight, and golden-yellow staining of teeth.

The solubility of cadmium in water is influenced by the nature of the source of the cadmium and the acidity of the water. Surface-waters that contain more than a few micrograms of cadmium per litre have probably been contaminated by discharges of industrial wastes or by leaching from areas of landfill, or from soils to which sewage sludge has been added. Unpolluted waters generally contain less than 1 mg/L.

The levels of cadmium in public water supplies are normally very low, since generally only tiny amounts exits in raw water and even where levels are somewhat elevated, many conventional water-treatment processes will remove much of the cadmium.

Higher levels of cadmium in tap-water are associated with plated plumbing fittings, silver-base solders, and galvanized iron piping materials.

Drinking-water normally contains very; low concentrations of cadmium of the order of 1 μg/L or less; occasionally, levels up to 5 μg/L have been reported and on rare occasions levels up to 10 μg/L have been detected. In some areas, well-water may contain elevated concentrations of cadmium. It is probable that the levels of cadmium could be higher in areas supplied with soft water of low *p*H, since this would tend to be more corrosive to any plumbing systems containing cadmium. The level of cadmium in a sample of water is likely to be a function of how long the water has been in contact with the plumbing, and as a consequence there is likely to be a variation in concentration when water is drawn at different times of day from the same tap. It would be difficult to define the average exposure unless a large number of samples were collected.

Estimated daily exposure to cadmium via water, based on a water consumption of 2 litres per day, ranges from substantially less than 1 μg to over 10 μg per day. Such estimates are, of course, based on the presumption that all the cadmium from the water is ingested; it is likely, however, that in the preparation of certain beverages, *e.g.*, tea, not all the cadmium will be consumed since some could become attached to the surface of the utensils, etc.

Most foodstuffs, contain traces of cadmium; crops grown in polluted soil (from industrial contamination and from use of sewage sludge as fertilizer) or irrigated with polluted water may contain increased concentrations, as may meat from animals grazing on contaminated pastures. The kidneys and livers of animals concentrate cadmium, and people who eat these food items will tend to ingest more cadmium than those who do not. Shellfish also tend to accumulate the metal. Cadmium is present in tobacco, one cigarette normally containing 1-2 μg. Because cadmium is volatile at elevated temperatures, some of the metal will be inhaled during smoking. Estimates have been made of the contribution made by various types of tobacco in different countries. Typically, 2-4 μg of cadmium per 20 cigarettes is inhaled; probably 50% will be deposited in the lungs.

Cadmium is fairly readily absorbed through ingestion or through the lungs. Alimentary absorption is affected by a number of factors, such as age, calcium, iron, zinc, and protein deficiency, and the chemical form of the cadmium ingested. As with lead, the state of the stomach is likely to influence the amount absorbed, with a fasting stomach probably providing the maximum uptake in contrast with a full stomach. In human subjects given labelled cadmium, between 4.7% and 7% (mean 6%) of orally administered cadmium was absorbed. Dietary factors, such as iron, calcium, and protein deficiency, may increase the gastrointestinal absorption rate. In iron-deficient women, up to 20% of ingested cadmium was found to be absorbed. Pulmonary absorption is dependent on the size and solubility of the particles containing cadmium and will be affected, too, by the depth and rate of breathing. Approximately 50% of 0.1 mg particles will be retained by the lung in contrast to 20% for particles as large as 2 mg. From information on the particle size distribution of cadmium in the general air and for tobacco smoke, it has been estimated that typically 25% and 50% of the particles will be retained, respectively

Absorbed cadmium when enters the blood, become concentrated in certain parts of the human body. Both the liver and the kidneys act as stores of cadmium (about 50% of any accumulated cadmium is found in these organs). The cadmium is to a large extent bound to a protein of low relative molecular mass, known as metallothioneine this metal-binding proteins believed to be involved in cadmium transport and absorption. Cadmium has a long biological half-time in the body (13-38 years) and accumulates with age. It has been found that, because the placenta acts as a fairly efficient barrier to cadmium, the newborn are virtually free of cadmium (approximately 1 μg only in contrast to non- occupationally exposed people of age 50 who may have 10-50 mg stored in their bodies. Grossly exposed industrial workers have been discovered to have levels of over 1000 mg. Blood levels are usually below 20 μg/L for non-smoking members of the general population. Cadmium in blood reflects recent exposure rather than body burden. Excretion of cadmium is usually rather slow, mainly via the urine. On a group basis, urinary cadmium is generally regarded as a good indication of the body burden. Cadmium interacts with other metals, especially zinc, and may influence the relative distribution of zinc in the body.

Acute effects have been seen where food has been contaminated by cadmium from plated vessels; severe gastrointestinal upsets have been reported. The acute oral lethal dose of cadmium for man has not been established, but it is estimated to be several hundred milligrams. Health effects have been demonstrated in industrial workers heavily exposed to cadmium oxide fumes and dust Bronchitis, emphysemas, anaemia, and renal stones have been reported. The renal cortex is generally accepted with proteinuria, glucosuria, and aminoaciduria. Where the exposure has been high, as was the case in Japan in the outbreak of Itai-Itai disease (a bone disease), irreversible renal injury occurred in those most severely exposed, especially in elderly women. There have been no reported effects from the low levels of cadmium that can be found in drinking-water, although contaminated beverages made from dispensers containing cadmium-plated fittings have caused acute effects in children.

Occupational exposure to cadmium is defined as any work involving handling, storage, use of cadmium at a concentration above the action level. Exposure to cadmium should be controlled so that no employee is exposed to cadmium at a concentration greater than 40 μg/m³ of air, determined as a time-weighted average (TWA) concentration limit for up to a 10-hour workshift in a 40-hour workweek, over a working lifetime. The ambient water quality criterion for cadmium is recommended to be identical to the drinking water standard which is 10 μg/L.

Caisson disease. A disease occurring when a person remains under high atmospheric pressure for a prolonged period, usually a matter of hours and is suddenly exposed to a lower pressure. This is generally experienced by deep sea divers and workers in compressed air compartments of tunnels and caissons. It is due to formation of nitrogen bubbles in the body as nitrogen comes rapidly out of solution. When blood passes through the lung capillaries, it picks up nitrogen along with oxygen from the alveoli (minute air sacs). The amount of nitrogen picked up depends on the pressure of the air or atmosphere. As pressure increases, so does the amount of nitrogen picked up by the blood (along with nitrogen, oxygen is also picked up but this presents no problem, as the extra oxygen diffuses rapidly and metabolizes into the system). The additional nitrogen in the blood is carried to the body tissues and gradually saturates them under continued high atmospheric pressure. If the atmospheric pressure is suddenly dropped, the nitrogen (unlike oxygen) forms bubbles, which can block blood vessels and can do other damage by their pressure. In Caisson's disease, These bubbles affect portions of the central nervous system. especially the parts of the spinal cord. The usual first symptom of this disease is pain in legs and sometimes the arms. The other symptoms are dizziness, disturbances of vision, paralysis, a rash, a choking sensation in the chest, headaches, and inability to speak and coma. These symptoms may appear in the victim within a few minutes or until as many as six hours have passed. Usually they appear within an hour.

calcination. Heating an inorganic material such as limestone, gypsum, magnesium carbonate, or a metallic ore to a temperature below its melting point but high enough to effect evolution of carbon dioxide, and removal of bound water and of other impurities by oxidation, reduction, etc. Calcination also induces phase changes in some metal ores and in glass. In metallurgy it is called roasting when oxidation is involved and while smelting a reduction reaction occurs. Calcination of ores adds to the carbon mono/dioxide level of the atmosphere.

calcium cycle. The circulation of calcium atoms brought about mainly by living things. Calcium is taken up from the soil by the trees and other plants and deposited in roots, trunks, stems, and leaves. Rain may leach some of the calcium from the leaves and return it to the soil. Creatures such as insects, rabbits, and oyster herbivores, obtain their share of calcium from the plants and leaves, birds acquire it by eating the insects. When animals and insects die, and the leaves and branches fall and decay, the calcium is returned to the soil. Some calcium may be lost from the ecosystem by leaching and surface runoff and carried to the bodies of water. It is recycled through phytoplankton, zooplankton, fish and lake and ocean water.

cancer. A malignant tumor with the production of epithelial cells. A pathological disorder caused by an anarchical (complete disorder) proliferation of certain cells and characterized by the filtration of abnormal cells into all parts of the organism (metastasis). It can be in all living beings including plants (the brown gall of the oak) as well as in animals and man. Moreover, it can be in all kinds of living tissues even nerve tissues. The real causes of cancer are still unknown. Several theories have been put forward, but these may all be summed up under two main categories: According to the first, cancer is a form of infectious disease in which the infectious agent a virus-invades the organism and causes a cell disturbance that results in a disordered multiplication of cells. According to the other theory, there is a genetic predisposition to cancer which, under the influence of a chemical agent (tar) or physical agent (ultra-violet or X-rays), or by a hormonal disorder, is transformed into the true cancer.

The experimental study of cancer on animals has resulted in great progress in our knowledge of how the disease appears and the way in which cancers are transmitted from one organism to another. Cell and tissue cultures of cancers have also led to an appreciable amount of knowledge about physiological modifications (*p*H, metabolism etc.), which occur within the cancer cell. According to the most recent researches, the virus theory appears to be in the lead. It has been possible to obtain a certain condition of immunity against cancer and this also has lent support to this theory. But the possibility of genetic modifications (mutations) cannot be entirely excluded.

Anti-cancer treatment is usually of three kinds: surgical, radiotherapy and chemical. Surgery and radiotherapy are used in localized cancerous tumors. Chemotherapeutic treatment is used particularly for generalized cancers of leukemia (blood cancer- a great increase in the number of leucocytes in the blood). It is based on the use of antimetabolites which blocks the metabolism of cancerous cells or of substances that prevent these cells from dividing.

Types of cancer: There are two general types or classes of cancer. One, *carcinoma,* which develops from epithelial tissue which lines the inner passages of the body or composes the outer covering *i.e.*, skin. The other type is *sarcoma,* which develops in connective tissue. There are also many variations of these two types usually named for the specific tissue involved, such as, *adenocarcinoma,* (epithelium or glands); *lymphosarcoma* (cancer of the lymphatic glands and vessels); *myeloma* (cancer of the bone marrow and *rhabdomyosarcoma* (cancer of the voluntary muscle tissue). There are certain conditions which one can take as cancer's warning signals:

(a) change in bowel or bladder habits;
(b) a sore that does not heal;
(c) unusual bleeding or discharge;
(d) thickening or lump in breast or elsewhere;
(e) indigestion or difficulty in swallowing;
(f) obvious change in wart or mole; and
(g) nagging cough or hoarseness.

Inspite of all the complications and varieties involved, there are certain scientifically based actions which the average person can take to help prevent cancer.

canceroid. Like cancer; growth of tissues with characteristics of cancer, but which are not necessarily malignant are termed canceroid. For example, an abnormal proliferation of cells resulting in a tumor which is not a cancer is canceroid.

canning industries waste treatment. The objectionable matter in the wastes from canning industries comprises decomposing organic solids in suspension. The wastes contain suspended, colloidal, and dissolved organic solids from 50 to 3000 ppm which have BOD varying from 3000 to 4000 ppm.. The treatment processes may include screening, chemical sedimentation, lagooning, broad irrigation, soil absorption, biological filtration, incineration, animal feeding of solid wastes, dumping into to waste treatment about 300 ppm may be followed by 800 ppm of ferrous sulphate, as a result of which BOD is reduced by 35-80% Liquid sulphuric acid is added to neutralize the alkalinity of the molasses. The BOD of distillary wastes, brewery wastes and antibiotic wastes are 15000-25000, 500-1200 and 10,000 ppm repectively. These wastes can be treated by settling, lime flocaulation centrifugation, broad irrigation, evaporation, activated sludge process with high aeration and trickling filters etc.

capacity. When the capability of any pollution control service has been established in connection with control of a specific pollutant or pollutants, the capacity of the device involves the volume by weight or size the device can handle during a set period of time, thus if the capability of a certain incinerator is reduce solid wastes and its is designed to handle a capacity of 500 tons a day, a community requiring processing of 1,000 tons a day would need at least three incinerators with a 500-tons capacity.

carbofuran. A broad-spectrum systemic insecticide, acaricide and nematicide, used against both foliage feeding insects and mites and soil pests. In plants its half-life is less than five days; in soil the half-life is 30-60 days. It is a white, odourless, crystalline solid, fairly soluble in water and acetone; non-inflammable, but unstable in alkaline media. The acute oral LD_{50} for rats is 8-14 mg/kg. Effective against various sap-feeding insects and mites, especially leafhoppers on rice, root-eating caterpillars and beetle larvae on cereals. Also known as Furadant.

carbonate balance. A state of water, at which it will neither dissolve nor deposit calcium carbonate. It is the most desirable condition of water from the view point of its corrosiveness or the possibility of clogging pipes. This can be determined by laboratory tests.

carbonate cycle. The biogeochemical carbonate pathways involving the conversion of carbonates to carbon dioxide and bicarbonates, and the metabolism and regeneration of it in biological systems.

carbonation. 1. In beet sugar refining, the process of precipitating, with a stream of carbon dioxide, the lime which has been added to the juice to neutralize the free acids and precipitate the albuminoids. 2. The reduction of carbon containing compounds to elemental carbon. 3. Saturation with carbon dioxide. 4. The introduction of a carboxyl group (COOH) into an organic carboxylic acid) by the action of carbon dioxide on certain organic compounds, especially alkylmagnesium halides.

carbon black. The material consisting of more than 85% carbon in the form of near-spherical colloidal particles and coalesced particle aggregates of colloidal size obtained by the partial combustion or thermal decomposition of hydrocarbons. If carbon contains polycyclic aromatic hydrocarbons (*i.e.*, if it contains cyclohexane-extractable substances at a concentration greater than 0.1%), occupational exposure to carbon black is defined as any work involving any contact, airborne, or otherwise, with this substance. If the amount of cyclohexane-extractable substances present in carbon black is equal to or less than 0.1%, occupational exposure to carbon black is defined as any work involving exposure to carbon black at a concentration greater than half the recommended environmental limit of 3.5 mg/m^3. Some aromatic hydrocarbons such as pyrene, 1,2-benzpyrene, and 3,4-benzopyrene, are formed during carbon black manufacture and their adsorption on the carbon black could pose a risk of cancer after exposure to the carbon black. Occupational exposure to carbon black should be controlled so that no employees are exposed to carbon black at a concentration greater than 3.5 mg/m^3 of air, or to polycyclic aromatic hydrocarbons at a concentration greater than 0.1 mg, measured as cyclohexane extractable fraction, per cubic metre of air, determined as a time-weighted average (TWA) concentration limit for up to a 10-hour workshift in a 40-hour workweek.

carbon cycle. This term refers to two quite different phenomena; one occurring in the sun and other stars, while the other in the earth's biosphere.

1. As to the first, carbon acts as a catalyst of the thermonuclear reactions responsible for the sun's energy, namely, the formation of helium from four hydrogen nuclei (protons). The carbon is not transformed in the process. *See also* carbon-nitrogen cycle.

2. The second meaning involves the complex reactions involving photosynthesis, in which carbon is absorbed from the air by plants as carbon dioxide, then moves through photochemical reactions catalyzed by chlorophyll, and finally through decay or combustion sequences wherein it reappears as carbon dioxide; microbial decomposition processes, and respiratory chain of animal organisms. A large part of the carbon

assimilated by the plants serves to maintain their life functions and is immediately emitted again. The remainder is incorporated as a structural or reserve substance in the plant cells. By day, the assimilation rate of plants is higher than the transpiration rate, so that an increase in amount of organic matter is achieved. At night, photosynthesis stops, and by their transpiration the plants lose biomass, *i.e.*, they draw on reserve substances. Animal organisms which do not have the capacity to assimilate carbon, also contribute by their respiration too the return of carbon to the atmosphere

carbon dioxide. A colourless, odourless, non-toxic, asphyxiant gas present in the atmosphere. In one form or the other CO_2 is represented in the atmosphere and lithosphere. In primitive times it is thought that the atmosphere itself was primarily CO_2. Since those early times most of the CO_2 has been trapped in the lithosphere as carbonates. The approximate present distribution of carbon is:

1 part in the atmosphere as CO_2, 30,000 parts in the lithosphere as carbonate, 10,000 parts in the lithosphere as reduced carbon (coal), 60 parts in the hydrosphere as ions in the deep sea, 1.2 parts in surface waters, 0.5 parts as land plants, and 1.7 parts as humus.

The carbon dioxide levels in the atmosphere are increasing at a rate greater than 1 ppm per year. The present levels are about 350 ppm. Since CO_2 and other greenhouse gases such as CH_4, H_2O absorb infra-red radiation, increases in its concentrations may cause a general warming of the earth. The net effect may be an increase of 0.5 °C in mean temperature of the earth by the year 2000. However, though the CO_2 levels are increasing, the mean temperature actually fell between 1940 and 1970. This may be an effect of blanketing due to aerosols or, has been suggested, increased absorption of the IR radiation by the oceans, higher water vapour in the atmosphere with increased deposition of snow on the poles and, thence, cooling due to the increased polar reflectivity. Some scientists are of a view that man's activities are generating increasing amount of carbon dioxide that may be effecting changes in the global weather patterns. If man continues to increase the atmospheric content of carbon dioxide by, for example, burning fossil fuels, the earth's surface temperature will rise sufficiently, some others feel that other components of air pollution, such as particular (atomic) matter, have a cooling effect on earth temperature as they absorb and scatter the sun's radiation. In this way there is little effect of carbon dioxide on pollution of the atmosphere. At a rough estimate, the annual formation of carbon dioxide by the photosynthesis of land plants amounts to about 13.22×10^{19} kg. The carbon dioxide taken up by the water plants should be well in excess of that for land plants. Under favorable conditions the annual absorption of carbon dioxide by the sea algae is estimated to be 0.36 kg per square metre of the sea's surface.

Data over the last 20,000 years,

mainly from the ice shells of Greenland and the Antarcitic, have given a picture of the changing carbon dioxide concentraion. Chemical analysis of the air, contained in ice bubbles of different ages shows that around 20,000 years ago, during the last glaciation when the avarage global surface temperature was 4.5°C cooler the now, carbon dioxide concentration was as low as 200 ppm. From that value, it reached 280 ppm, some 10,000 years back; from the glacial 200 ppm to the stable 280 ppm it took around 5,000 years. This level continued upto about 200 years back when the Industrial Revolution began. Since then the carbon dioxide concentration has been increasing at a very rapid rate and has now reached at a level of 353 ppm. Thus the single most important gaseous. constituent reponsible for global warming is now on the path of runaway increase.

The acute poisoning due to carbon dioxide results in respiratory distress, loss of consciousness followed by death, and burns of the skin, if exposed to solid carbon dioxide. Occupational exposure to carbon dioxide is defined as exposure to a concentration greater than the time-weighted average (TWA) environmental limit. Overexposure to carbon dioxide is defined as any exposure at a concentration sufficient to produce signs of respiratory difficulty or central nervous system effects. Employee exposure to carbon dioxide should be controlled so that no employee is exposed to carbon dioxide at a concentration greater than 10,000 ppm parts of air by volume (1%) determined as a time-weighted average (TWA) concentration limit, with a ceiling concentration of 30,000 ppm parts of air (3%) by volume, as determined by a sampling period not exceeding 10 minutes.

carbon disulphide. A colourless, hazardous liquid with a characteristic odour. It ignites readily and has a very low flash point. It is used as a solvent, in the manufacture of man-made fibres, and optical glass and oil industries. Carbon disulphide is one of the oldest soil fumigants. It is only marginally good as a nematicide, but has been outstanding in the practical control of *A. mellea* in the root rot of date palms. The main interest in this chemical arises from its effective but indirect control of *A. mellea* in orchards and citrus grove soils. Here, its use not only appears to weaken the pathogenic *Armillaria*, but also to stimulate the powerful fungal antagonist, *T. viride*. The latter is so enhanced in its development in treated soil that it completely destroys the pathogen. Judged on the basis of lethal dosages, CS_2 ranks rather low among the insect fumigants because relatively large dosages by weight are required. Carbon disulphide is toxic to man. Because it is used in certain manufacturing processes, it is an important industrial poison. High concentrations of the vapour produce a narcotic effect and if exposure is continued unconsciousness and death may ensue from paralysis of the respiratory centre. Repeated exposure to low concentrations for periods of a few weeks or longer may result in a variety of nervous manifestations which may make correct diagnosis difficult. Persons exposed to low concentrations may lose their ability to detect the odour of the chemical and thus may continue to work in a toxic atmosphere without being aware of it. Absorption of high concentrations may take place through the skin as well as by inhalation. Prolonged contact of the skin with high concentrations of vapour or with the liquid may result in severe burns, blistering or neuritis.

Carbon disulphide produces a profound narcotic effect and leads to damage to nervous system including mental disturbance. In addition, it affects the kidneys and blood vessels. Acute poisoning due to carbon disulphide leads to reddening of face, stupor and restlessness, unconsciousness, and paralysis of respiration; while chronic poisoning is characterized by insomnia, and bad dreams, loss of apatite and indigestion, pallor and fatigue, headache, depression or excitability. The occupational exposure to carbon disulphide should be controlled in such a manner so that no employee is exposed to carbon disulphide at a concentration greater than 3.0 mg/m^3 of air, determined as a time-weighted average (TWA) concentration limit for up to a 10-hour workshift in a 40-hour workweek, or to more than 30 mg/m^3 of air as a ceiling concentration for any 15 minute period. The standard is designed to protect the health and provide safety of employees for up to a 10-hour workshift, 40-hour workweek over a working lifetime.

carbon monoxide. A colourless, odourless, inflammable, toxic gas, present in large quantities in the waste from burned gases, especially in exhaust fumes from motor vehicles. This is the one pollutant which is mostly produced by mankind, who generates about 70% of the total. Carbon monoxide is produced when the fuel to oxygen ratio is too high or the temperature of combustion is too low. Motor vehicles are normally operated at a slight excess of petrol, which gives maximum power and performance, and produces high carbon monoxide levels.

The toxic effect of carbon monoxide arises from the fact it combines with the red blood cell pigment hemoglobin and so impedes the combination that normally occurs in the lungs of oxygen with hemoglobin. It thus arrests the transport of oxygen through the blood and leads to symptoms similar to those that occur in suffocation. Carbon monoxide has a 200 to 300 times greater affinity with hemoglobin than oxygen. A measure of the degree of acute carbon monoxide poisoning can be established from the proportion of hemoglobin in the blood that has reacted with carbon monoxide molecules (carboxyhemoglobin). With as little as 2% carboxyhemoglobin (corresponding to 10 ppm of carbon of carbon monoxide in the air inhaled), sensitive tests have disclosed the first effects on the central nervous system in the form of impairment of time judgment. At 30% carboxy hemoglobin (corresponding to 20 ppm of carbon monoxide in the air inhaled), disturbances are observed in light sensitivity and clarity of vision. At 4.5%

to 5% carboxhemoglobin (corresponding to 30 ppm to carbon monoxide in the air inhaled) impairment of vision and psychomotor disturbances can be established. These effects of low carbon monoxide concentrations have been recognized only recently. Earlier it was assumed that at between 10% to 20% carboxyhemoglobin level no distinguishable symptoms of poisoning would occur. Only at 30% carboxyhemoglobin does the individual affected himself perceive the damage occurring in the form of headaches. Carboxyhemoglobin concentrations of 45% to 50% normally result in collapse and loss of consciousness, and higher saturations result rapidly in death. From the results of more recent investigations, it is concluded that lower carbon monoxide concentrations produce chronic toxic effects. Carbon monoxide exerts a special influence on the performance of vehicle drivers. An investigation revealed that drivers involved in road accidents showed particularly high carboxyhemoglobin levels. With an increase of about 10% in the catboxyhemoglobin level, drivers of vehicles on the motorway at night were found to react more slowly to stoplights and changes in speed limits. In order not to exceed the probably quite harmless carboxyhemoglobin value of 2%, carbon monoxide concentrations in big cities should not rise above 9 to 10 ppm. In some big cities, however, hourly values of 30 and even as high as 50 ppm are recorded at present, and peak values of 100 to 300 ppm are by no means rare.

The occupational exposure to carbon monoxide should be controlled in such a manner so that no person is exposed to carbon monoxide at a concentration greater than 35 ppm, determined as a time-weighted average (TWA) concentration limit for up to a 8-hour exposure, or to more than 200 ppm, as a ceilıng concentration for any 15 minute period. Because of the well-defined relationship between smoking and the concomitant exposure to carbon monoxide in inhaled smoke, the recommended standard may not provide the same degree of protection to those workers who smoke, as it will to nonsomkers. Similarly, under conditions of reduced ambient oxygen concentration, such as would be encountered by the workers at high altitudes, the permissible exposure limit should be lowered to compensate for loss in the oxygen-carrying capacity of the blood. The recommended standard is designed to protect the health and safety of workers for up to a 8-hour workshift, 40-hour workweek over a working lifetime.

carbon tetrachloride (CT). A colourless, heavy, nonflammable liquid with a characteristic odour. It is used as a solvent for fats, oils and grease; paint remover, fumigant and dry-cleaning agent; and in fire extinguishers. Carbon tetrachloride may be used as a fumigant but on account of its low toxicity to insects high dosages or greatly prolonged exposure periods are needed. It has however, been used for grain fumigation. It is a narcotic causing drowsiness and unconsciousness, and is a potent kidney and liver poison. When used as fire extinguisher, it is converted into phosgene. In case of acute poisoning due to carbon tetrachloride, the outcome may be rapidly fatal, or death may be delayed from a few hours to several days.

Carbon tetrachloride is readily absorbed through the lungs and more slowly but still completely absorbed through the gastrointestinal tract. It can also enter the body by penetration through the skin. The rate and amount of absorption is enhanced by the simultaneous ingestion of fat and alcohol. In an investigation of the absorption of carbon tetrachloride from the gastrointestinal tract of dogs, Robbins found that considerable quantities were absorbed from the small itestine, less from the colon, and tittle from the stomach.

When carbon tetrachloride is administered to mammals, it is metabolized to a small extent, but the majority is excreted through the lungs. The metabolites include chloroform, hexachloroethane and carbon dioxide. Research has revealed that these metabolites play an important role in the overall toxicity of carbon tetrachloride.

The occupational exposure to carbon tetrachloride should be controlled in such a manner so that no employee is exposed to carbon tetrachloride at a concentration greater than 12.6 mg/m^3 of breathing zone air, determined as a time-weighted average (TWA) concentration limit for up to a 10-hour workshift in a 40-hour workweek, over a working lifetime. The available data for carbon tetrachloride indicate that acute toxicity to freshwater aquatic life occur at concentrations as low as 35,200 μg/L, and would occur at even lower concentrations among the species that are more sensitive than those tested. For the maximum protection of human health from the potential carcinogenic effects due to exposure of carbon tetrachloride through ingestion of contaminated aquatic organisms and water, the ambient water concentration should be zero on the non-threshold assumption for carbon tetrachloride. However, zero level may not be attainable at present time. Therefore, the levels that may result in incremental increase of cancer risk over lifetime are estimated at 10^{-5}, 10^{-6}, and 10^{-7}. The corresponding criteria are 4.0 μg/L, 0.4 μg/L, and 0.04 μg/L respectively. If thc above estimates are made for the consumption of aquatic organisms only (excluding consumption of water), the levels are redefined as 69.4 μg/L, 6.94 μg/L, and 0.694 μg/L respectively.

Carbophenothion. A non-systemic acaricide and insecticide, with a long residual action. It is phytotixic at high concentrations to some plants. 50% degradation in soil occurs in 100 days or longer, depending upon the soil type. It is a pale amber liquid; insoluble in water, but miscible with most organic solvents. It is relatively stable to hydrolysis, and is oxidized on the leaf surface to the phosphorothiolate; compatible with most pesticides, and is non-corrosive to mild steel. The acute oral LD_{50} for male rats is 32.2 mg/kg. It is used mainly on deciduous fruit, in cobination with petroleum oil, as a dormant spary for the control of overwintering mites, aphids and scale insects; on citrus as an acaricide. Also known as Trithion; Garrathion.

carboxyhaemoglobin. The compound of carbon monoxide and haemoglobin formed when carbon monoxide is present in the blood. The carbon monoxide displaces the oxygen and checks the respiratory function of the red blood corpuscles

carcinoembryonic antigen. An antigen normally found only in fetal gut; present in serum of patients with carcinoma (especially of colon and lung) but also in smokers and in subjects with inflammatory bowel disease; therefore of limited diagnostic value.

carcinogen. Any physical or chemical agent that may lead to the development of a cancer; although definite cause or causes of cancer are not known, yet certain agents in our environment or certain habits have been shown to cause cancer. Carcinogenic materials can be either chemical, viral, physical and hormonal.

There are more than one thousand chemicals which have been shown to produce various kinds of cancer in animals after application to the skin, injection into body organs, or oral feeding. These chemicals include compounds of chromium, lead, mercury, cadmium, selenium, antimony, arsenic, iron dextran, various insecticides and pesticides, such as D.D.T., industrial solvents such as benzene, mustard gas (a nerve gas) and several plastics. The chemical carcinogens which effect man most are the hydrocarbons inhaled with cigarette smoke. This produces bronchogenic carcinoma (lung cancer). The chemicals such as β-naphthylamine used in aniline dye industry is known to cause bladder cancer in man.

It has been studied that viral agents can induce cancer in experimental animals, but there is no positive proof to say that the viruses cause cancers in man. There are four large groups of viruses which are known to be carcinogenic in animals, which are: *papovirus, adenovirus, poxvirus, and myxovirus.*

The physical agents which can cause cancer include ionizing radiations produced by X-ray and atomic energy. Exposure to sunlight and other sources of ultraviolet (UV) light may also induce the formation of certain skin cancers. Some researchers have proved that the hormones act directly on the cells and produce malignant tumors particularly estrogens.

carcinogenesis. The totality of factors and elements that determine the origin and development of cancerous tumors.

cargo tank. Any tank permanently attached to or forming a part of any motor vehicle or any bulk liquid or compressed gas packaging not permanently attached to any motor vehicle that by reason of its size, construction, or attachment to a motor vehicle is loaded or unloaded without being removed from the motor vehicle. Any packaging fabricated under specifications for cylinders is not a cargo tank.

catalyst. Element or compound that changes rate of chemical reaction but remains unchanged in chemical composition after reaction. The catalysts most used in industrial processing are inorganic substances, chiefly metals or metallic oxides, usually in the form of powders or porous masses. They function by either physical or chemical adsorption. To be effective, catalysts must be in a finely divided state to furnish maximum surface area for adsorption as the reacting substances pass over or through them. Catalysis is conventionally divided into three categories; homogeneous, heterogeneous, and enzymatic.

catalyst poison. In heterogeneous catalysis, substance adsorbed at surface of catalyst, blocking access of substrates and therefore diminishing, or even destroying activity of catalyst. Also known as catalytic poison.

catalyst promoter. In heterogeneous catalysis, a substance which is not a catalyst or possesses weak catalytic properties, but which when mixed with a catalyst causes growth of its catalytic activity (sometimes also its selectivity of persistence).

catalyst stripping. Introduction of steam to remove hydrocarbons retained on the catalyst; the steam is introduced where the spent catalyst leaves the reactor.

catalytic mufflers. Air pollution control devices inserted along the exhaust lines or internal combustion engine vehicles. Three major pollutants are supposed to be controlled by these mufflers: carbon monoxide, hydrocarbons and oxides of nitrogen. Various metals such as chromium, nickel, vanadium, etc., are used as catalysts to aid in braking down the pollutants by causing them to diffuse onto the pores of the catalysts but lead salts in the exhaust fumes cause deactivation or the catalytic material by filling up the pore spaces between fragments of the catalyst that would normally trap pollutants.

catastrophe. A sudden and violent disturbance of nature ascribed to unusual or super natural agents, and affecting both physical conditions and inhabitants of the earth.

catenate. A term used in chemistry to indicate the tendency or ability of an element to unite with itself to form chains; carbon is notable in this regard. Several other elements, such as sulphur, phosphorus and silicon, exhibit this property to a limited extent.

cation. An ion, having one or more unit of positive charges, which migrates to the cathode when an electric current is passed through their solution. *See* also anion.

cation exchanger. Ion exchanger containing cations that can be exchanged for other cations present in solution. These are employed for the removal of cationic impurities from polluted water.

cationic detergent. A member of a group of detergents that have molecules containing a quaternary ammonium salt cation with a group of 12 to 14 carbon atoms attached to the nitrogen atom in the cation.

caustic. A term meaning 'corrosive' and is applied to the water-soluble hydroxides of the light metals to distinguish them from their carbonates. It is also used in medicine to designate substances that destroy body tissues; thus lunar caustic is silver nitrate.

CDM model. The climatological dispersion model that determines the long-term (seasonal or annual)

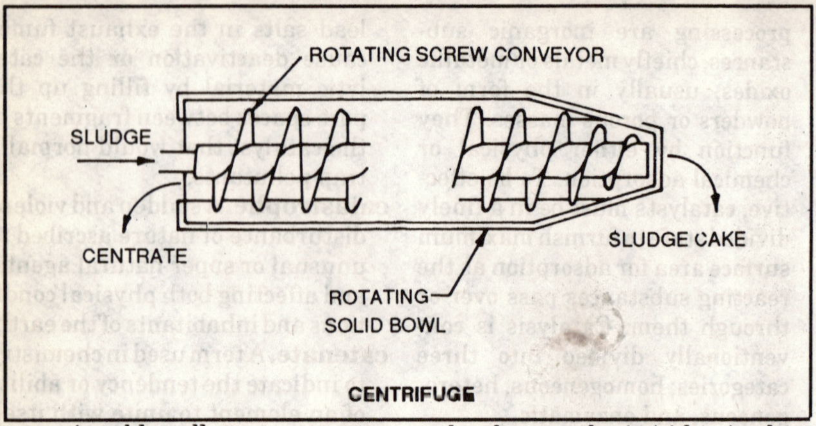

quasi-stable pollutant concentrations at any ground level receptor using average emissions rates from point and area sources and a joint distribution of wind direction, wind speed, and stability for the same period.

ceiling. The concentration that should not be exceeded even instantaneously. For some substances, for example irritant gases, only one category, the threshold level value-ceiling (TLV), may be relevant. For other substances, either two or three categories may be relevant, depending upon their physiologic action. It is important to observe that if any one of these three TLVs is exceeded, a potential hazard from that substance is presumed to exist. It is opined that limits based on physical irritation should be considered no less binding than those based on physical impairment. There is increasing evidence that physical irritation may initiate, promote, or accelerate, physical impairment through interaction with other chemical or biologic agents.

cellular respiration. A complex biochemical process which breaks down the carbohydrates produced by photosynthesis (either in plants themselves or in the animals that eat them). Cellular respiration is a slow oxidation process and the chemical energy thus liberated is used by the plants or animals for their living functions. The end products of cellular respiration are carbon dioxide and water which are returned to the atmosphere, completing the carbon dioxide cycle.

centrifuge. In sewage treatment, a power driven device used for dewatering sewage sludge, for thickening slurries, and for separating liquids of different densities.

centrifuged sludge. An advanced concept used in the thickening and dewatering of sewage sludges or industrial waste sludge. The solids are separated by centrifugal force from the liquids and the effluent is carried off for further treatment. The solids of course my then be disposed of by combustion or other treatment.

chain reaction. 1. chemical reaction in which many molecules undergo chemical reaction after one molecule becomes activated. It is initiated by a free atom, ion, or radical of transitory existence as a result of rupture of a chemical bond. Under certain conditions these set up a limited sequence of reactions ending in the formation of a stable compound. 2. A nuclear reaction in which each of the two or three neutrons released by the fission of one atomic nucleus splits another atomic nucleus, thus creating a continuous and self-sustaining energy release.

charcoal. A highly porous form of carbon obtained from wood by destructive distillation or from animal bones by calcination; it is also called char. It is used to remove odors and other impurities from gases by adsorption as a component of low, explosives, and for recovery of solvents from their vapours. Its efficiency can be increased by steam activation.

cheep. Sound similar to that of a chirp or peep; a shrill, short, feeble notes as uttered by a young bird.

chelate. Any of the various organic coordination (complex) compounds in which the metal ion is bound to atoms of nonmetals, *e.g.*, nitrogen, carbon, or oxygen, to form a heterocyclic ring having coordinate covalent bonds, Chelate formation is successfully applied in water softening and treatment of effluents from the heavy industries.

chemical burns. Burns produced by contact with chemicals. Strong acids and alkalies are most often responsible for chemical burns. Some chemicals that produce burns are ammonia, sulphuric acid, hydrochloric acid, phenol, sodium hydroxide and potassium hydroxide. These chemicals are widely in use in industry and in home. Whenever, a chemical burn may occur, the skin must be rinsed at once with large amounts of running water.

chemical coagulation. The agglomeration of molecules either suspended in a liquid or in colloidal suspension, produced by bunching the material to be removed in clumps or clusters which either float on the surface of the liquid. Chemical coagulation is generally more expensive than physical separation.

chemical conversion. The term for the chemical change from reactants to products of a chemical industrial process. The term is being used to an increasing extent for the entire chemical process industries in place of unit processes, since it is a more exact definition of industrial chemical reaction. The important chemical conversions are: alkylation, amination, ammonolysis, aromatization, calcination, combustion, condensation, dehydration, esterification (sulphation), fermentation, halogenation, hydroformylation, hydrogenation, hydrogenolysis, hydrolysis, hydration, ion exchange, isomerization, neutralization, nitration, oxidation, polymerization, pyrolysis, cracking, reduction, sulphation, and sulphonation.

All these terms refer to the classes of chemical changes, each embracing many individual reactions or chemical conversions into which chemical industrial processes can be divided.

chemical industry pollution. Most of the chemical reaction do not always go to completion, thus in addition to the desired product, by-product are also formed when the effluents of the chemical industry enter the atmosphere or discharged into the drainage system. The spectrum of products manufactured by the chemical industry is extraordinarily wide-ranging; inorganic substances such as sulphuric, nitric, hydrochloric, hydrofluoric and phosphoric acid and their salts; organic compounds such as hydrocarbons, fertilizers, plant protection and pest destruction agents, plastics, man-made fibres, paints and lacquers, pharmaceutical products, adhesives, detergents, cosmetic products, polishing powders, and leather and textile accessories. The principal emission given off by the chemical industry are gases and vapours of organic chemical compounds such as hydrocarbons and their halogen derivatives, aldehydes, ketones, carboxylic acids, and nitrogen and sulphur compounds (amines, mercaptans, disulphides); gases and vapours of inorganic chemical compounds such as hydrogen sulphide, hydrochloric acid, fluorine compounds, sulphur dioxide, and hydrogen phosphides; and finally toxic powders such as fluorides and carbides, and powders from iron alloys, arsenic and asbestos. Extensive control is necessary, partly because the human sense of smell is very sensitive to substances emitted by chemical industries (such as hydrogen sulphide and mercaptans), even when they are highly rarefied. Thiophenol, for instance, is still perceptible to the human sense of smell in concentrations as low as 10 parts per billion. Owing to the large number of noxious chemical substances in existence and the rapid changes that occur in chemical production, the over all technical development of specific filter appliances to meet all requirement is very hard to achieve.

chemical mutagens. Sources of mutations, other than radiation, which may give rise to mutations resulting in an increase in the incidence of congenital defects in future generations. Mankind is exposed to thousands of chemical mutagens whose mutagenic potential is unknown.

chemical oxygen demand (COD). A parameter of water quality which measures the amount of oxygen in parts per million required to oxidize organic and oxidizable inorganic compound in the water sample.

chemical treatment. Treatment of gases and emissions of a toxic odorous or corrosive nature may be accomplished by chemical solvents, emulsifiers and even by incineration. Treatment of undesirable solids by chemical means when they are present in water includes coagulation, precipitation, neutralization, etc.

chemical warfare. The use in war of toxic gases, incendiary mixtures and other chemicals for defensive or offensive purposes. There are many types of chemical agents used to make gases, smokes and incendiaries. They are choking gases, such as chlorine, phosgene and diphosgene. They are lung irritants and effect the respiratory system. They cause inflammation of bronchi, trachea and lungs. The effects on the body lasts from several minutes to three hours and the gas remains effective in the air for less them ten minutes. There are blister gases, such as mustard gas. They cause the skin to blister. They are also known as vasicants. These gases cause injury to any part of the body that comes in contact with the liquid or vapour. Inflammation, burns and tissue damage follow external or internal contact with no immediate pain or effect on the body. The sneeze gases or irritant smokes are also frequently used in warefares, which cause sneezing, respiratory pains and mental depression when inhaled.

The blood gases or systemic poisons are also employed in the chemical warfare; these include chemical agents which act on the heart or nerve reflexes or interfere with the absorption and taking in of oxygen. The carbon monoxide, hydrocyanic acid and cyanogen chloride are not used for war purposes because the chemical agents are too light to remain in the air long enough to be effective.

chemisorption. A phenomenon related to adsorption in which atoms or molecules of reacting substances are held to the surface atoms of a catalyst by electrostatic forces having about the same strength as chemical bonds. Chemisorption is an essential feature of catalytic reactions and accounts for large measure of the specialized activity of catalysts.

chemosmosis. The phenomenon of chemical action taking place through an intervening membrane.

chemosynthesis. The synthesis of organic compounds from carbon dioxide by micro-organisms using energy derived from chemical reactions.

chemotaxis. Sensing of and movement toward (or away from) a specific chemical agents by cells.

Chicago aerator. A device frequently combined with final clarifier which is beneath a splash plate. The aerator has an impeller at the upper end which discharges mixed liquor to a vaned splash plate. This facilitates further agitaion of the sludge.

chink. Short, sharp, ringing sound as made by coins or glasses gently

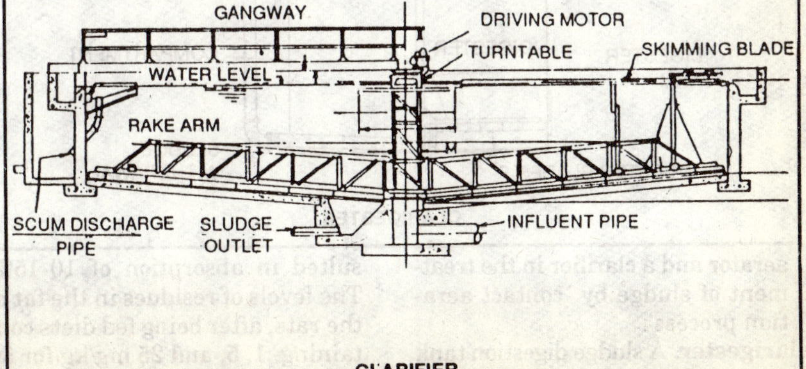

CLARIFIER

striking against each other.

chip. Abbreviation for *C*hemical *H*azard *I*nformation *P*rofile; documents prepared by the Environmental Protection Agency (EPA) on the hazards of specific chemicals.

chirp. Short, sharp note characteristic of the sound made by small birds and insects such as crickets.

clarifier. A circular tank with a hopper bottom for sludge accumulation. The clarification takes place through sedimentation of the suspended solids in the effluent. *See* diagram on last page.

clarifilter. A proprietary device combining features of a contacr aerator and a clarifier in the treatment of sludge by `contact aeration process'.

clarigester. A sludge digestion tank equipped with a clarifier mechanism. It consists of a two-storeyed tank in which the upper part is the clarifier, while the digester mechanism is in the lower chamber. The side depth of the clarigester is about 6 metres. It has been devised to make the processes of digestion and clarification economical.

chlordane. A polychlorinated hydrocarbon mainly used as insecticide; it has been included in the list of potential occupational carcinogens. A single oral dose of chlordane administered to rats resulted in approximately 6% absorption. Small daily doses resulted in absorption of 10-15%. The levels of residues in the fat of the rats, after being fed diets containing, 1, 5, and 25 mg/kg for 56 days, were approximately three

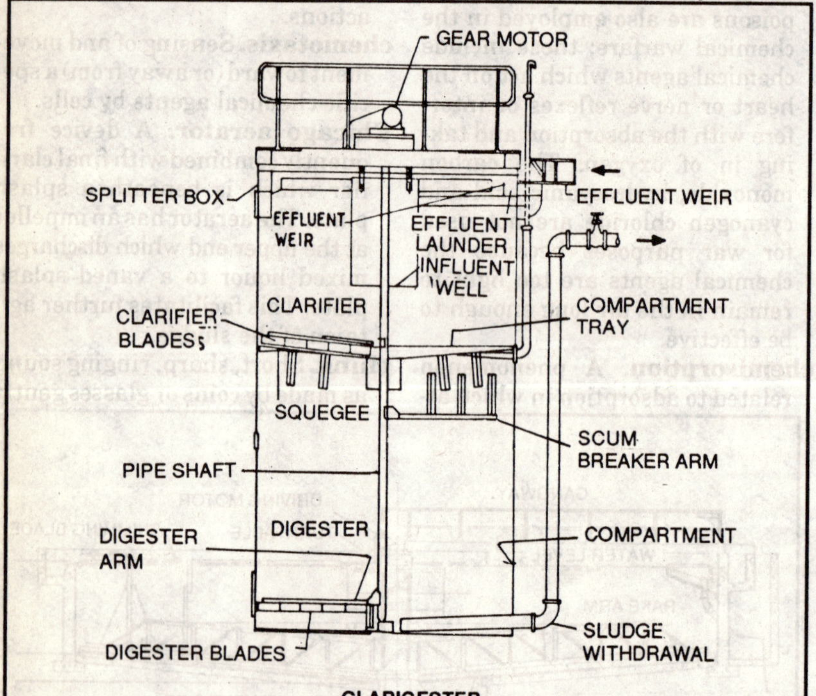

CLARIGESTER

times the concentration in the diet. Concentration in the liver, kidney, brain, and muscle were 12, 10, 4 and 2%, respectively, of the concentration in the feed. Once the chlordane was removed from the diet, all the residues declined steadily for 4 weeks, by which time the concentrations were reduced by about 60%. During the following 4 weeks, the residues declined only slightly.

For chlordane the criterion to protect freshwater and saltwater aquatic life are 0.0043 μg/L and 0.0040 μg/L respectively. For maximum protection of human health from the potential carcinogenic effects due to exposure of chlordane through ingestion of contaminated aquatic organisms and water, the ambient water concentration should be zero on the nonthreshold assumption for chlordane. However, zero level may not be attainable. Therefore, the levels that may result in incremental increase of cancer risk over lifetime are estimated at 10^{-5}, 10^{-6}, and 10^{-7}. The corresponding criteria are 4.6 ng/L, 0.46 ng/L, and 0.046 ng/L respectively. If the above estimates are made for the consumption of aquatic organisms only (excluding consumption of water), the levels have been redefined as 4.8 ng/L, 0.48 ng/L, and 0.048 ng/L respectively.

chloridization. Treatment of mineral ores with hydrochloric acid or chlorine to form the chloride of the main metal present in the ore.

chlorinated dioxins. A group of toxic chemicals formed in minute quantities in normal combustion processes, and during the manufacture of pesticides and herbicides.

chlorinated hydrocarbons. Any of a large number of organic compounds of varying structure, in which one or more hydrogen atoms are replaced by chlorine atoms. A feature common to almost all these compounds is that they are insoluble in water, but they dissolve readily in fats, oils and organic solvents.

Generally they are quite effective insecticides against insects with biting mouthpart than the sap-suckers. Because of their persistence they get taken up in food chains very easily and accumulate in the body fat of the vertebrate predators at the apex of the food chains. Under normal conditions this build-up in the body fat may not affect the animal but in times of starvation when body fat reserves are being utilized the amount of pesticide released into the blood may be critical or even fatal. Most countries in Europe and North America are in the process of restricting the use of chlorinated hydrocarbons where suitable alternatives are available, because of the long-term contamination dangers to the environment. It can also be observed that in most of these countries the major pests have already become or are now becoming resistant to the organochlorine compounds, and so their period of utility is ending. In some cases though suitable alternatives are not readily forthcoming.

The organochlorine compounds may be subdivided into several groups-the three most commonly used groups are represented by DDT, BHC, and aldrin (cyclodienes). Despite the structural differences between the subgroups they do possess several characteristics in common-they are chemically stable, have a low solubility in water, moderate solubility in organic solvents and lipids, and a low vapour pressure. The properties of stability and solubility make most of the group very persistent, and they also produce similar physiological responses in the insects.

The solubility of DDT in lipids enables the poison to penetrate the insect integument quite readily (as opposed to slow penetration through animal skin). This difference in penetrative ability would account for its selective toxicity to insects. Cuticle thickness does not seem to greatly influence the susceptibility of insects to DDT, although it may penetrate more readily through the flexible intersegmental membranes. Dissolution in the epicuticular wax is apparently the essential prerequisite to toxic action. Penetration rate of the poison increases with temperature, often nearly doubling for a 20°C rise in temperature.

Chlorinated hydrocarbons are also used as pesticides, solvents (*e.g.*, chloroform, ethylene tetrachloride), and polymers (*e.g.*, polyvinyl chloride). Chlorinated hydrocarbons, in particular pesticides (including DDT, dichlorodiphenyltrichloroethane) and PCBs, represent a serious threat to the environment. The available data indicate that the toxicity increases with the increasing chlorination. When DDT and other chlorinated hydrocarbons enter into the diet of man, which is the viable link in various food chains, they tend to concentrate, because of their fat-like character, mainly in the nerve tissues (including the brain), the liver, the gonads and the cardiac muscular system. A considerable concentration of such compounds has been found to occur in mother's milk.

chlorine. A highly reactive element, placed in group VIIA of the periodic table. It is a strong electron acceptor and thus is powerful oxidizing agent. It is estimated that 0.045% of the earth's crust is chlorine. Chlorine is unusually capable of forming ionic bonds and free radicals. It is used for bleaching paper and man-made fibres; and as disinfectant for water supplies, swimming pools, etc. It is toxic when inhaled as a gas and is a strong skin irritant in liquid form. Acute poisoning due to chlorine causes severe coughing, difficulty in breathing, burning sensation to the nose, throat, and eyes, and skin irritation. Occupational exposure to chlorine should be controlled so that no employee is exposed to chlorine at a concentration greater than 0.5 mg/m^3 of air, for any 15 minute sampling period. The recommended standard is designed to protect the health and safety of workers for up to a 10-hour workshift, 40-hour workweek over a working lifetime.

chlorine demand. The amount of chlorine by any given volume of sewage or polluted water to kill all pathogenic bacteria therein.

chlorine dioxide. A highly reactive, hazardous compound of chlorine; used for bleaching and as disinfectant. Occupational exposure to chlorine dioxide is defined as exposure to airborne concentration of this compound at or above one-half of the recommended workplace environmental limit. Occupational exposure to chlorine dioxide should be controlled so that no employee is exposed to chlorine dioxide at a concentration greater than 0.3 mg/m^3 of air (0.1 ppm), for any 15 minute sampling period. The recommended standard is designed to protect the health and safety of workers for up to a 10-hour workshift, 40-hour workweek over a working lifetime.

chlorine trifluoride. A highly reactive, hazardous and corrosive gas, used for cutting oil-well tubes, reprocessing reactor fuels and as oxidizing agent in propellants. Occupational exposure to chlorine trifluoride is defined as exposure to airborne concentration of this compound at or above one-half of recommended workplace environmental limit. Occupational exposure to chlorine trifluoride should be controlled so that the employees are not exposed to vapours of chlorine trifluoride at a concentration greater than 0.4 mg/m^3 of air (0.1 ppm), for any 10 minute sampling period.

chloroalkyl ethers. A large number of compounds with similar chemical behaviour, many of them have been enlisted as potential occupational carcinogens. Available data for chloroalkyl ethers indicate that acute toxicity to freshwater aquatic life occur at concentrations as low as 238,000 μg/L, respectively; and would occur at even lower concentrations among the species that are more sensitive than those tested. No definite results are available concerning the chronic toxicity of chloroalkyl ethers to sensitive freshwater aquatic life. For the maximum protection of human health from the potential carcinogenic effects due to exposure of chloroalkyl ethers through ingestion of contaminated aquatic organisms and water, the ambient water concentration should be zero on the nonthreshold assumption for chloroalkyl ethers. However, zero level may not be attainable at present time. The levels that may result in incremental increase of cancer risk over lifetime have been estimated at 10^{-5}, 10^{-6}, and 10^{-7}. The corresponding criteria are 0.038 ng/L, 0.0038 ng/L, and 0.00038 ng/L respectively. If the above estimates are made for the consumption of aquatic organisms only (excluding consumption of water), the levels are redefined as 18.4 ng/L, 1.84 ng/L, and 0.184 ng/L respectively.

For the protection of human health from the toxic effects of *bis*(2-chloroisopropyl) either ingested through water and contaminated aquatic organisms, the ambient water criterion has been set to be 34.7 μg/L; while for the protection of human health from the toxic properties of *bis*(2-chloroisopropyl) either ingested through contaminated aquatic organisms alone, the ambient water criterion has been determined to be 4.36 mg/L.

Chlorobenzilate. A non-systemic acaricide with very little insecticidal action, particularly effective against phytophagous mites. Some phytotoxicity has been notes on pear, plum, and some apple varieties. The technical products is a brown liquid, insoluble in water, but soluble in most organic solvents including petroleum oils. It is hydrolyzed by alkali and strong acids. The acute oral LD_{50} for rats is from 700 to 3100 mg/kg. It is effective only against phytophagous mites, but can kill all active and inactive stages, including eggs. It is suspected of possessing carcinogenic activity, hence the exposure to workers by all routes should be carefully controlled. Also known as Akar; Folbex.

chloroform. A colourless, volatile, hazardous liquid with characteristic odour and sweet taste; used as a solvent, fumigant, and analytical reagent. It is suspected of possessing carcinogenic activity, hence the exposure to workers by all routes should be carefully controlled. Occupational exposure to chloroform is defined as any work involving handling, storage, use, or manufacture of chloroform at a concentration above the action level. Occupational exposure to chloroform should be controlled so that no employee is exposed to chloroform at a concentration greater than 9.78 mg/m^3 (2 ppm) of breathing zone air in a 45-litre air sample taken over a period not exceeding 1 hour. The recommended standard is designed to protect the health and provide safety to workers for up to a 10-hour workshift, 40-hour workweek over a working lifetime.

The available data for chloroform indicate that the acute toxicity to freshwater aquatic life occurs at concentrations as low as 29,900 µg/L, and would occur at even lower concentrations among the species that are more sensitive than those tested. 27-day LD_{50} values indicate that chronic toxicity occurs at concentrations as low as 1240 µg/L. For the maximum protection of human health from the potential carcinogenic effects due to exposure of chloroform through ingestion of contaminated aquatic organisms and water, the ambient water concentration should be zero on the nonthreshold assumption for chloroform. However, zero level may not be attainable at present time. Therefore, levels that may result in incremental increase of cancer risk over lifetime are estimated at 10^{-5}, 10^{-6}, and 10^{-7}. The corresponding criteria are 1.9 µg/L, 0.19 µg/L, and 0.019 µg/L respectively. If the above estimates are made for the consumption of aquatic organisms only (excluding consumption of water), levels are redefined as 157 µg/L, 15.7 µg/L, and 1.57 µg/L respectively.

chloropicrin. A powerful tear gas; of the fumigants commonly used today it is one of the most toxic to insects. It is sometimes added in small proportions to other fumigants, *e.g.*, hydrocyanic acid and methyl bromide, to serve as a warning agent. Although the tear gas effect of chloropicrin is helpful in preventing persons from staying in dangerous concentrations during the fumigation process, it is also a handicap because fumigated commodities are unpleasant to handle for some time after fumigation. Even small amounts diffusing from the treated material may be extremely irritating. If it were not for this disadvantage, chloropicrin would be useful for commodity treatments because it penetrates effectively into many materials. Chloropicrin is also toxic to nematodes and certain fungi, and it has found wide application as a soil fumigant. Chloropicrin is corrosive to metals and care should be taken to protect metal surfaces and equipment during treatment. In man, a concentration of about 2.4 g/m^3 can cause death from acute pulmonary oedema in one minute. A concentration as low as 1 ppm of chloropicrin in air produces an intense smarting pain in the eyes, and the immediate reaction of any person is to leave the vicinity in haste. If exposure is continued, it may cause serious lung injury.

Chloropicrin is extremely phytotoxic and plants exposed to its vapours are often completely destroyed. Even added in small amounts to other fumigants for warning purposes, it is likely to be toxic. For instance, methyl bromide containing small amounts of chloropicrin should not be used to fumigate plants fruit or vegetables. Hence, when used for soil fumigation it kills weed seeds and any living plant material present.

choking. The interruption of breathing by pressure or by an obstruction. The blocking usually occurs in the larynx, or voice box, which opens into the throat. The cause of choking may be illness, injury, a foreign body, or breathing in polluted atmosphere.

chromatography. An analytical technique that make use of different rates of migration of components in a mixture in which one phase is immobile layer of developed surface and the other is a mobile stream of gas or liquid flowing through it. In general, chromatography involves passing a gaseous or liquid mixture called the mobile phase, through a column of porous material sometimes coated with a nonvolatile liquid, called the stationary phase. The components of the mixture are adsorbed selectively and pass through the porous material at different rates, emerging as distinct separation zones at the bottom of the column. A carrier gas or liquid is necessary to provide movement of the material through the adsorbent. When the components have been thus separated, the identity of each can be determined by an appropriate analytical method. The best-known types of chromatography are gas, liquid, paper, ion-exchange, and thin layer, the name depending on the characteristic aspect of the method.

chromium. A grayish-white, hard and brittle metal, though many of its compounds display various colours. It is obtained by reduction of chromite ore. The metal itself is not toxic except in the form of fume, but some of its compounds are irritant and damaging to the skin, especially those involving hexavalent chromium. Its major uses are as an alloying agent in stainless steel and other alloys and for electroplated coatings on exposed metal parts. It can also be plated on plastics. Current research show that the noncarcinogenic compounds of chromium(VI) are chromates and dichromates of lithium, sodium, potassium, rubidium, and ammonium, while most of the other compounds of chromium(VI) have been found to possess carcinogenic activity.

Chromium in its naturally occurring state is in a highly insoluble form; however, weathering, oxidation and bacterial action can convert it into a slightly more soluble form. Most of the more soluble forms in soil, especially any chromium (VI), are mainly the result of contamination by industrial emissions. Some contamination arises from the use of sewage sludge added to land. Contamination of air, water, and food has occurred as a result of man's use of chromium; traces of some natural chromium are present in food. Trivalent and chromium (VI) occur in biological media, but only the trivalent form is stable, since chromium (VI) is reduced by a variety of organic species.

Occupational exposure to carcinogenic chromium(VI) is defined as exposure to airborne concentration of carcinogenic chromium(VI) at or above one-half of the recommended workplace environmental limit; while occupational exposure to noncarcinogenic chromium(VI) is defined as exposure to airborne concentration of noncarcinogenic chromium(VI) at or above one-half of the recommended workplace environmental limit. The occupational exposure to noncarcinogenic chromium(VI) should be controlled so that no employee is exposed to noncarcinogenic chromium(VI) at a concentration greater than 25 $\mu g/m^3$ of air, determined as a time-weighted average (TWA) concentration limit for up to a 10-hour workday in a 40-hour workweek, over a working lifetime. For total recoverable chromium(VI), the criterion to protect freshwater aquatic life as 0.29 μg/L as a 24-hour average and the concentration should not exceed 21 μg/L at any time.

Because of the low solubility of chromium generally, the levels found in water are usually low (9.7 μg/L), however, there are examples of contamination of water, in some cases serious in which effluents containing chromium compounds have been discharged to rivers; the chromium may be in the trivalent or hexavalent form, either as a soluble salt or as insoluble particles and often as a chemical complex. The valency of the chemical form in natural waters is influenced by the acidity of the water. Trivalent chromium is converted to the insoluble hydroxide at neutral *p*H. Total chromium levels in raw water are usually 10 μg/L or less; rarely do levels exceed 25 μg/L except in highly contaminated situations. There is a tendency for the naturally occurring higher levels of chromium to be associated with waters of the greatest hardness.

Drinking-water normally contains very low concentrations of chromium (*i.e.*, 5 μg/L or less). It would be very rare to find chromium levels as high as 20 μg/L in tap-water. The level in tap-water may be a function of the period the water has been standing in contact with any plumbing fittings and as a consequence there could be variations in chromium levels when water is drawn at different times of the day at the same tap.

Based on a water consumption of 2 litres per day, it can be estimated that the daily exposure to chromium in water might vary from substantially less than 10 µg to perhaps 40 µg per day on rare occasions. Since apparently trivalent chromium rarely occurs in drinking-water that is chlorinated, it is assumed that most waterborne chromium is in the hexavalent form.

Foodstuffs vary considerably in their chromium content, which ranges from 20 to 590 µg/kg. Because varying and conflicting figures have been quoted, it is not possible to make proper comparison between different foodstuffs. Some seafoods appear to contain higher levels of about 0.02-0.21 mg/kg. Wines contain chromium concentrations up to 60 µg/L. The chromium in foodstuffs is in both the trivalent and the hexavalent form. Some contamination of food could result during its preparation where plated or stainless steel utensils are used.

Most of the chromium in the air is found in the form of fine particles, of which perhaps one half of those inhaled could become deposited in the respiratory tract. Based on a daily inspired volume of 22.8 m^3 and 50% alveolar retention, the daily quantity deposited in the lungs has been estimated to be about 0.2 µg.

Chromium is absorbed through both the gastrointestinal and respiratory tracts. The amount absorbed differs in each system and depends on the form of chromium. Trivalent chromium is an essential form of the element for human beings.

Discrepancies in values reported for chromium absorption from the digestive tract appear in the literature; exact values are not known. Trivalent chromium is poorly absorbed. From 0.1% to 1.2% of trivalent chromium salts are absorbed, whereas 25% of glucose tolerance factor (GTF), a chromium complex necessary for normal glucose tolerance, is absorbed. Natural chromium complexes in the diet seem to be more available for absorption than simple salts. It appears that at least 10% of the chromium in food is absorbed. Tissue chromium levels in rats exposed for one year to chromium (VI) in drinking-water at a level of 25 mg/L were approximately 9 times higher than the levels in tissues of rats similarly exposed to trivalent chromium. Hence it is assumed that the absorption rate for waterborne chromium (VI) is at least 9 times that for trivalent chromium, *i.e.*, approximately 10% and elevated waterborne chromium is usually hexavalent. No quantitative information was found concerning the rates of absorption through the respiratory tract. Respiratory absorption would be expected to be dependent on particle size and solubility. A reasonable estimate for the absorption of inhaled chromium is 50% of that inhaled.

Chromium is distributed in human tissues in variable, low concentrations. Chromium levels in tissues other than the lungs decline with age. The largest stores of chromium in man are in skin, muscle, and fat; tissue levels are a function of sex, age, and geographical location. A homeostatic mechanism, involving hepatic or intestinal transport mechanisms, prevents accumulation of excess trivalent chromium. Chromium is excreted slowly, mainly in the urine but also in the faeces. Chromium appears to be necessary for glucose and lipid metabolism and for utilization of amino acids in several systems. It also appears to be important in the prevention of mild diabetes and atherosclerosis in humans. The harmful effects of waterborne chromium in man are associated with chromium (VI); trivalent chromium, which is regarded as a form of chromium essential to man, is considered practically non-toxic and no local or systemic effects appear to have been reported. People living in areas of the world where atherosclerosis is mild or virtually absent tend to have higher chromium levels in tissues than people from areas where the disease is endemic.

Chromium (VI) at 10 mg/kg of body weight will result in liver necrosis, nephritis, and death in man; lower doses will cause irritation of the gastrointestinal mucosa.

Toxic effects have been observed in rats and rabbits when drinking water contained more than 5 mg of chromium (VI) per litre, although in other studies up to 25 mg/L produced no ill effects. A study of the effects of chromium (VI) and cholesterol on the development of atherosclerosis in rabbits appears consistent with the hypothesis that chromium inhibits the development of experimentally induced atherosclerosis. Serum cholesterol levels, too, are higher in rats fed diets low in available chromium.

Chromium (VI) in high doses has been implicated as the cause of digestive tract cancers in man, and there is firm evidence that there is an increased risk of lung cancer for workers who are exposed to high levels of chromium. Prostate cancer has been reported in workers in many chromium-using industries (chromium plating); however, the risk of cancers at sites other than the lung cannot be assessed on the basis of the current data. Exposure to a mixture of chromium compounds of different solubilities carries the greatest risk for human beings.

The available data for chromium(VI) indicate that chronic toxicity to freshwater aquatic life occur at concentrations as low as 44 μg/L, and would occur at even lower concentrations among the species that are more sensitive than those tested. For the protection of human health from the toxic effects of chromium(III) ingested through water and contaminated aquatic organisms, the ambient water criterion to be 170 mg/L; while for the protection of human health from the toxic properties of chromium(III) ingested through contaminated aquatic organisms alone, the ambient water criterion has been determined to be 3433 mg/L. The ambient water quality criterion for the total chromium(VI) is recommended to be identical to the existing drinking water standard, *i.e.*, 50 μg/L.

chromosome. One of the deeply staining bodies, the number of which is constant for the cells of the species, into which the chromatin resolves itself during cell division (karyokinesis and meiosis). The nucleus of a cell is made up primarily of chromosomes, which direct the activities of the cell, maintain protein production and control the reproduction of the cell and thus the whole organism. Chromosomes can only be seen when the cell is under division. Each plant and animal has an exclusive, individual set of chromosomes. This means that two distinct species can never together produce off spring.

Man has 46 chromosomes, arranged in twenty three pairs. Each chromosome looks quite different under the microscope. The chromosomes together contain all the information which makes man what he is. The information of heredity is written in the chemical DNA in genes in the chromosomes. At the moment of fertilization, in species that reproduce sexually, the two chromosomes of the same pair couple except for one pair, the sex chromosomes or heterochromosomes, which are different from one another and are responsible for the determination of sex. These heterochromosomes are usually called *X* and *Y*. In man and mammals, fish, amphibians and numerous groups of invertebrates, the female sex carries a pair of *X* chromosomes, and the male one *X* and one *Y*. In birds and reptiles, it is the other way round. Each chromosome replicates itself by autoduplication and then, in a daughter cell, each chromosome carries the hereditary character of the species. Anomalies of division of chromosomes, arrest duplication, translocation, fragmentation etc. and are the causes of chromosomic diseases, such as Mongolism in man. Recent research has demonstrated that chromosomes can be damaged by a number of chemical, physical and radiation factors. Such damage to chromosomes can in turn result in damage to offspring.

chronic toxicity tests. Chronic toxicity tests are conducted to determine if prolonged (*i.e.,* chronic) exposure (usually weeks, months or year) to a chemical (at sublethal concentrations) would have significant adverse effects on organisms. Chronic exposures involve entire reproductive cycle of organisms. In this long-terms toxicity (contrary to short-term toxicity involving acute exposure), studies are also performed due to subchronic exposures (intermediate between acute and also performed due to subchronic exposures (intermediate between acute and chronic exposures, generally of one to several months duration) involving less than a complete life cycle stages (sensitive early stages of life cycle) of organisms. Chronic toxicity threshold concentrations for a number of selected species of ecosystem, receiving the toxic chemical, is tested.

Three categories of tests are commonly used to predict the chronic and subchronic effects of toxic chemicals on organisms:

(i) life cycle toxicity tests,

(ii) sensitive early life stages tests, and

(iii) functional tests.

clarification. The removal of settleable and floating solid matter from the sewage.

clay. Sedimentary rock; an argillaceous rock composed of fine-grained clastic sediments; consists of minute, flaky crystals of minerals produced by chemical weathering of crystalline rocks. Its cohesive and plastic properties are derived from thin films of water enveloping flaky particles. When heated and water is driven off, it becomes hard and stone-like. It has adsorption and ion-exchange properties and comprises clay minerals, with varying amounts of quartz, feldspars, other silicates, carbonates and ferruginous or organic matter; used for the removal of oxygen, nitrogen and sulphur compounds from certain oils following refining.

clean water act. The act enforced in U.S. where Environmental Protection Agency (EPA) is required to periodically review and publish criteria for water quality accurately reflecting the latest scientific knowledge:

(i) on the kind and extent of all identifiable effects on health and welfare including, but not limited to plankton, fish, shellfish, wildlife, plant life, shorelines, beaches, esthetics, and recreation which may be expected from the pollutants in any body of water, including ground water;

(ii) on the concentration and dispersal of pollutants, or their byproducts, through biological, physical, and chemical processes; and

(iii) on the effects of pollutants on biological community diversity, productivity, and stability, including information on the factors affecting rates of eutrophication and rates of organic and inorganic sedimentation for varying types of receiving waters.

Section 304(a)(1) criteria contain two essential types of information:

(i) discussion of available data on the effects of pollutants on public health and welfare, aquatic life, and recreation, and

(ii) quantitative concentrations or qualitative assessments of the pollutants in water which will generally ensure water quality adequate to support a specified water use.

Under section 304(a)(1), these criteria are based solely on data and scientific judgments on the relationship between pollutant concentrations and environmental and human health effects. The criteria values do not reflect considerations of economic or technological feasibility, and no regulatory impact. Rather these criteria present scientific data and guidance on the environmental effect of pollutants which can be useful in the derivation of regulatory requirements based on considerations of water quality impacts. Under Clean Water Act, these regulatory requirements may include the promulgation of water quality-based effluent limitations under section 302, water quality standards under section 303, or toxic pollutant effluent standards under section 307. States are encouraged to begin to modify or if necessary, develop new programs necessary to support the implementation of regulatory controls for toxic pollutants. In partial fulfillment of this requirement, EPA (with guidance from a nationwide committee of experts) identified a list of 129 compounds and elements from the 65 pollutant categories. The list of elements and compounds (the priority pollutant list) includes substances with known toxic effects on human and aquatic life and those known or suspected to be carcinogens, mutagens, or teratogens. The original list which has since been modified included 13 heavy metals, asbestos, cyanides, and 114 organic compounds. The organic compounds are further categorized into the following broad groups: volatile compounds (31), acidic compounds (11), basic/neutral compounds (46), pesticides (25), and dioxan (1). EPA has conducted an extensive screening and verification sampling programme to determine the types and levels of priority pollutants present in waste-waters from those industries which are known or suspected users or manufacturers of these pollutants.

climax stage. The final stage of ecological succession, and therefore an ecological community which continue to reproduce itself over time; or a stage in ecological succession during which an ecological community achieves the greatest biomass or diversity.

closed portion. That portion of a facility that an owner or operator has closed in accordance with the approved facility closure plan and all applicable closure requirements.

coal. A readily combustible, naturally occurring containing more than 50% by weight and more than 70% by volume of carbonaceous material including inherent moisture, formed from compaction and induration of variously altered plant remains similar to those in peat. Coal is noncrystalline, brittle, and dull to brilliant in lustre. With increasing compaction, the colour changes from light brown to black, and the specific gravity increases from 1.0 to 1.7. Coals are classified according to their constituent plant materials (type), ratio of fixed carbon content to volatile matter (rank), and amount of impurities present (grade). Coal occurs in rocks of the early Proterozoic, but did not become widespread until the development of woody land plants in the Devonian. Pre-Devonian coals are composed of algal remains. Sedimentary rocks of the Carboniferous-age hold the greatest abundance of coal-bearing rocks. Large deposits of lignite also occur in rocks of early Tertiary age. Coal beds are commonly found with shales and fine-grained sandstones. In spite of increasing production, coal has shown a steady decline in importance due to environmental reasons. For example, when it is burned, it creates much soot and smoke, disclouring nearby buildings and polluting the air. Smoke in the atmosphere creates smog, which a health hazard.

Coal Ming leaves inevitable scars on the landscape. Open-cast pits can be enormous and even costly reclamation measures cannot restore the land to its former condition. Underground mining causes subsidence of the surface and the waste materials removed in tunnelling to reach the coaql accumulate on the surface in unsightly tip-heaps. Vast areas of the land may be covered by spoil heaps near the coal mines, and may thus be lost to other more valuable agricultural or urban uses.

coal gas. A fuel made by the carbonization of a high-volatile bituminous coal. Approximate composition by volume: 50% hydrogen, 30% methane, 6 to 8% carbon monoxide, 2 to 4% olefins and 7 to 8% carbon dioxide, nitrogen, and oxygen.

coal gasification. The conversion of coal, char, or coke to a gaseous product by reaction with air, steam, carbon dioxide, or mixture of these.

coalification. Formation of coal from plant material by the processes of diagenesis and metamorphism. Also known as bituminization; carbonification; incarbonization; incoalation.

coal tar pitch volatiles. The fused polycyclic hydrocarbons which volatilize from the distillation residues of coal, petroleum (excluding asphalt), wood, and other similar organic matter. These compounds have been recognized to have carcinogenic or cocarcinogenic potential. The exposure to coal tar pitch volatiles should be controlled so that no employee is exposed to coal tar pitch volatiles at a concentration greater than 0.2 mg/m^3 of air, determined as a time-weighted average (TWA) concentration limit for up to a 8-hour workday in a 40-hour work-week, over a working lifetime.

coal tar products. From the environmental pollution study point of view, the term 'coal tar products' refers to coal tar and two of its fractionation products- creosote and coal tar pitch. Coal tar, coal tar pitch, and creosote derived from bituminous coal often contain identifiable components such as benzo(α)-pyrene, benzanthracene, chrysene, and phenanthrene, which by themselves are carcinogenic. Other substances from coal tar products such as anthracene, carbazole, fluorathene, and pyrene may also cause cancer, but the casual behaviour of these compounds has not been adequately documented. Occupational exposure to coal tar products is defined as any contact with coal tar, coal tar pitch, or creosote in the working environment. Occupational exposure to coal tar products should be controlled so that no employee is exposed to coal tar, coal tar pitch, creosote, or a mixture of these, at a concentration greater than 0.1 mg/m^3 in air as the cyclohexane-extractable fraction of the sample, determined as a time-weighted average (TWA) concentration limit for up to a 10-hour workday in a 40-hour workweek.

cohort. All the individuals in a population born during the same period. Thus all people born during the year 1993 represent the world human cohort for that year.

coke. The solid residue of the distillation of coal at high temperature (above 1075 K). Since the sulphur content of coke is about the same as that of the coal from which it was produced, its use in place of coal has little effect on sulphur dioxide pollution; compared with coal, however, it causes very little smoke pollution. Blast-furnace coke, coke specially prepared in coke ovens for use in blast furnaces; usually large coke of a narrow size range. This type of coke can be burned only in special stoves or furnaces in which the conditions necessary for combustion can be maintained. Low temperature coke, the solid residue or the low temperature distillation of coal (775 K to 1075 K). Such coke is sufficiently reactive to burn on fire.

coliform organisms in drinking water. Coliform organisms have long been recognized as a suitable microbial indicator of drinking-water quality, largely because these organisms are easy to detect and enumerate in water. They are characterized broadly by their ability to ferment lactose in culture at 308 K or 310 K, and include *E. coli, Citrobacter, Enterobacter* and *Klebsiella* species. Coliform bacteria should not be detectable in treated water supplies, and if found suggest inadequate treatment or post-treatment contamination. In this sense, the coliform test is used as an indicator of treatment efficiency. Although coliform organisms may not be directly related to the presence of varuses in drinking-water, the use of the coliform test is still essential for monitoring the microbial quality of public water supplies. The cysts of some parasites are known to be more resistant than coliform organisms to disinfection. The absence of coliform organisms in surface water that has only ben disinfected will not necessarily indicate freedom from the cysts of *Giardia, amoebae* and other parasites. Furthermore coliform bacteria are derived not only from the faeces of warm-blooded animals but also from vegetation and soil. Under certain conditions coliform organisms may also persist on nutrients derived from non-metallic construction materials. For these reasons the presence of small numbers of coliform organisms (1-10 organisms per 100 ml), particularly in untreated groundwater, may be of limited sanitary significance provided faecal coliform organisms are absent.

collection efficiency. The ratio of the quantity of a substance retained by a device to that passed through it. In any air pollution control equipment, if M_1 is the mass of incoming dust M_c the mass of collected dust and M_o the mass of outgoing dust, then collection efficiency is:

$$M_c/M_1 = M_1\text{-}M_o/M_1 = 1\text{-}M_o/M_1$$

colony counts. A bacteriological term used to assess the general bacterial content of water. This term does not refer to the total number of micro-organisms present in water, but simply those that are able to form visible colonies in nutrient media under specified culture conditions. Colony counts are of little value in detecting the presence of faecal pollution and should not be considered essential for assessing the safety of potable water supplies, although a sudden increase in the colony count from a groundwater source may be an early sign of pollution of the aquifer. They are useful in assessing the efficiency of water-treatment processes, specifically coagulation, filtration, and disinfection, the objective being to maintain as low a density as possible in the treated water. They may also be used to assess the cleanliness and integrity of the distribution system and the suitability of water for use in the manufacture of food and drink where, to minimize the risk of spoilage, numbers should be low. The main value of colony counts lies in the comparison of results obtained from regular samples from the same supply so that any significant change from the normal range in a particular location can be detected.

colour of drinking water. Colour in drinking-water may arise due to the presence of coloured organic substances, usually humics; metals such as iron and manganese; or highly coloured industrial wastes, of which pulp and paper and textile wastes are the most common. The primary importance of colour in drinking-water is aesthetic but the sensory effects may be regarded as a health effect. Experience has shown that consumers whose drinking-water contains aesthetically displeasing levels of colour may seek alternative, possibly unsafe, sources. Most people can detect levels of colour above 15 TCU (True Colour Units) in a glass of water. The removal of excess colour, prior to chlorination, will reduce the production of trihalomethanes. Taste due to chlorinated organics is also mitigated. Limiting the colour in potable water also limits the concentration of undesirable substances that are complexed with or adsorbed on to human material.

The guideline value recom mended for colour in drinking-water is less than 15 TCU. The appearance of colour in drinking-water is caused by the absorption of certain wavelengths of normal white light, by the presence of cloured substances, and by light scattering caused by suspended matter is defined as apparent colour; true colour is measured on water samples from which particulate matter has been removed by centrifugation or filtration, colour then being due to human substances in true solution. In general, the true colour of a given water sample is substantially less than its apparent colour. Complaints of coloured water generally approach in number those collectively concerned with taste and odour. Colour in natural waters is due mainly to organic matter, primarily humus substances, originating from the decay and aqueous extraction of vegetation into surface-water. Iron and manganese may often be present in groundwater as well as in some surface-waters and impart a colour. Another important source of iron in drinking-water is dissolution of iron pipes conveying the water. Iron and manganese can give rise to red and black water respectively. Copper solubilized from copper pipes may give rise to blue-green discoloration of sanitary ware in addition to a faint blue colour to the water in extreme cases. Highly coloured wastewaters, in particular wastes from the pulp, paper and textile industries, any create cloured water problems.

The colour problem of microbiological origin is the production of red water, a phenomenon caused by the oxidation of iron(II) to iron(III), as a result of which, iron precipitates from solution as the hydroxide and imparts a characteristic reddish colour to water. In severe cases, distribution lines have been blocked by the action of these iron bacteria. Similarly, a black discoloration may be imparted to drinking-water by the action of bacteria capable of oxidizing dissolved manganese to its insoluble oxides. This colour problem occurs more frequently in groundwater than in surface-water supplies.

combined pollutant. When tailpipe pollutants ascend into the atmosphere they throw hydrocarbons, oxides of sulphur, nitrogen, and carbon, etc., into the ambient air; under certain climatic conditions, photochemical processes combine some of these pollutants into a more dangerous form than they each were before. This form, called an oxidant is symbolic of synergy, which is also a combined pollutant, or a secondary pollutant, because it is formed from a combination of primary air pollutants.

combined sewer. A single conduit or pipe intended for the removal of sludge, sewage and storm water, as distinct from a separate system in which the storm and rain-water is removed through a separate conduit.

commercial waste stream. An ever-growing torrent of solid wastes that encompasses all packing and packing material used in commercial operations and all solid wastes generated in shipping and handling of merchandise.

comminutor. A stationary, semicircular screen grid with a rotating circular cutting disc, placed in a channel or in a wet wall of a sewage pumping station. The larger solids intercepted by the grid are cut on the rotating part and pass through the drum slots.

competence. The ability of a stream/fluid current to carry detritus, as determined by particle size rather than amount. The diameter of the largest particle transported is known as the competence value.

competition. When different individuals, populations, or species compete for the same resource(s), and the presence of one has a detrimental effect on the other.

competitive exclusion principle. The idea that two populations of different species with exactly same requirements cannot persist indefinitely in the same habitat, that is, one will always win out and the other will go extinct. Which one wins depends on the exact environmental conditions.

composting. A biological process in which the organic material in

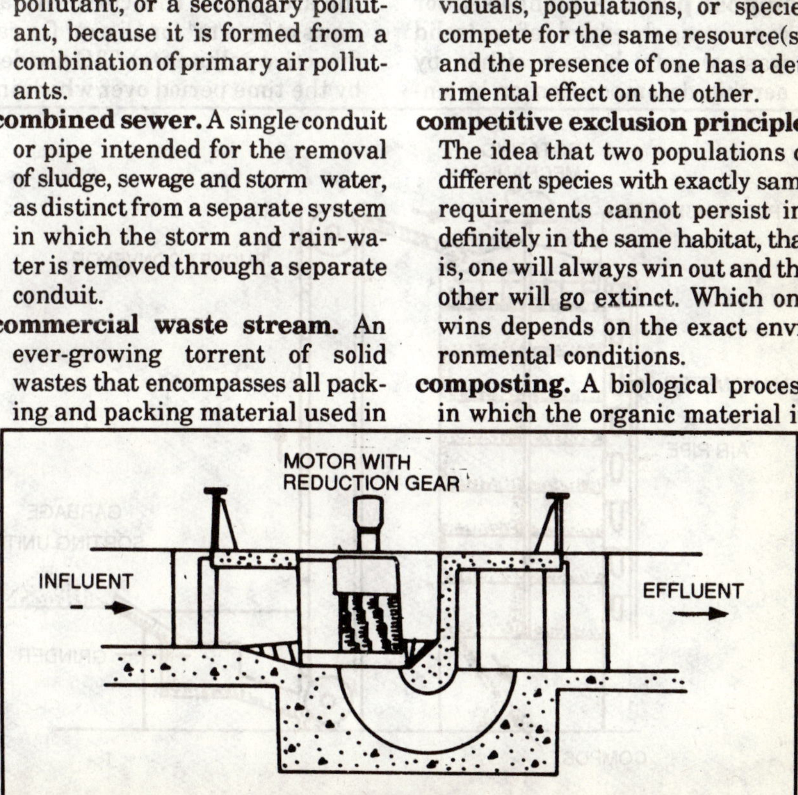

COMMINUTOR

refuse is converted to a usable stable material by the action of micro-organisms present in the refuse. After a period that may range up to five days, the refuse is fed through pulverizers and screened. The reject material is normally carted away to tips while the finest material is windrowed for several months, the windrows being turned periodically. Some plants pulverize the refuse initially and then windrow the screened material. It is quite common to add sewage sludge to the in the plant to serve as an additive to the compost and, of course, to dispose off the sludge.

compost plant. A plant used for converting shredded refuge (solid wastes) into humus either by aerobic decomposition or by anaerobic fermentation. The sectional view of a composting plant is shown in the given diagram.

compost stack. Round or square based stacks, more or less haycock-shaped or dome-shaped, of compostable materials.

compound air lift. A modified air-lift pump with two air-lift pipes used in places, where adequate depth of immersion is not available. The first pipe discharges water into the second pipe.

concentration, time integrated (TIC). The concentration at a point integrated with respect to time over a given period. If concentration is plotted against time, TIC is the area under this curve. It has units of $\mu g\ s/m^3$ (or $Ci\ s/m^3$ for radioactive pollutants). TIC divided by the time period over which in-

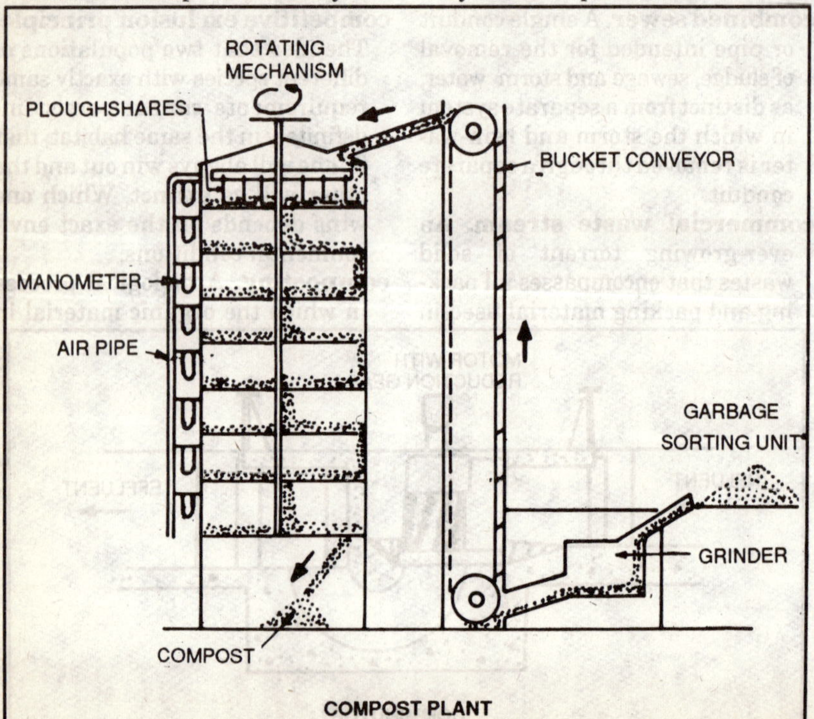

COMPOST PLANT

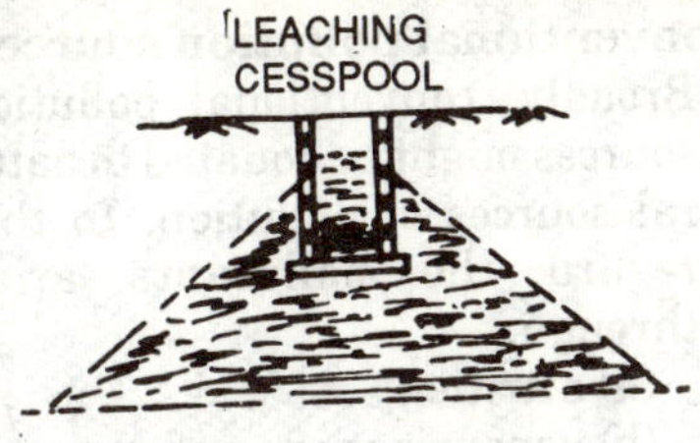

CONE OF CONTAMINATION

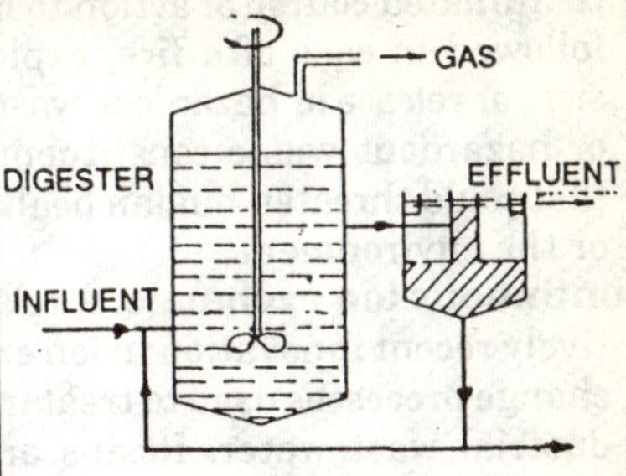

CONTACT PROCESS

tegration is done is therefore equal to average concentration over that period.

cone of contamination. The contamination of the subsoil in the form of a cone due to leaching of foul water from a cesspool.

confined aquifer. An aquifer bounded above and below by impermeable beds or by beds of distinctly lower permeability than that of the aquifer itself; an aquifer containing confined groundwater.

connote water. Water that is no longer in circulation or in contact with the existing water cycle; generally saline water trapped during the deposition of sediments.

conservation. The rational use of the environment to improve the quality of living for the mankind. It implies:

1. The use of some areas and resources for production to satisfy the requirements of humanity for goods and services.

2. The preservation or enhancement of other areas and resources for the contribution these can make to the scientific, educational, aesthetic, or recreational requirements of mankind.

consumer commodity. A material that is packaged and distributed in a form intended or suitable for sale through retail sales agencies or instrumentalities for consumption by individuals for purposes of personal care.

contact process. A sludge treatment process comprising a well-mixed digestion unit and a sludge settler. The wash out of the active anaerobic bacterial mass from the reactor is controlled by a sludge separation and recycle system.

container. Any portable device in which a material is stored, transported, treated, disposed of, or otherwise handled.

container ship. A cargo vessel designed and constructed to transport, within specifically designed cells, portable tanks and freight containers that are lifted on and off with their contents intact.

continental deposit. Sedimentary material deposited on land or in bodies of water not directly connected with the ocean, as distinguished from a marine deposit. The term thus includes lacustrine, glacial, fluvial, or eolian deposits originating in a non-marine environment.

contingency. A document setting out an organized, planned, and coordinated course of action to be followed in case of a fire, explosion, or release or hazardous waste or hazardous waste constituents that could threaten human health or the environment.

continuous ion exchange. A relatively recent innovation in ion exchange processes used to treat industrial wastewater. Resins are packed into what is called an exchange column, with the bottom of the column exposing the resins to the polluted liquid so that when the resin at the interface is spent is removed, regenerated and shifted to the top of the exchange column. In this manner the operation can be continuous and economical.

convection. The process of heat transfer through the movement of air masses. In meteorology, the term describes the vertical movements of the air within the atmosphere, arising from the different temperatures at different levels and in particular the high temperatures at ground level, due to the heating of the air in contact with the warm surface. Convection is associated with atmospheric instability, which causes the rising and cooling of the air pockets, condensation and cloud formation, convectional rainfall, and thunderstorms.

conventional lagoon. A lagoon in which the aerobic layer is locked on the surface, while the major portion of the sewage in the lagoon is subjected to anaerobic bacterial action. This type of lagoon is the least productive of sludges and in practice the most malodorous, since among other gases emitted to the atmosphere the major odour source is hydrogen sulphide.

conventional pollution sources. Broadly, conventional pollution sources might be equated to natural sources of pollution. In this regard the pollutants arise through:

(a) attrition;

(b) vapourization; and

(c) combustion.

A forest fire, for example, creates conventional pollutants such as particulates, gaseous oxides in smoke, and ashes, other processes also occur during the fire. For example, vapourization can cause liquids in the forest to change in to gases and the ashes creates grift that wears, causing attrition.

convectional rainfall. Rainfall caused by convectional currents. When the dew point is reached the water vapour condenses to form the cloud. If the convection current is strong, a very high cloud may form, with large quantities of water and dust particles, and produce heavy rain showers. In tropical areas, most of the rainfall is convectional; but in temperate latitudes convectional rainfall occurs only occasionally.

cooling pond. A large tank of water in which irradiated fuel elements from a nuclear reactor are stored to allow the short-lived fission products to decay. Also an artificial lake used for the natural cooling of the condenser-cooling water serving a conventional power station.

cooling tower. A device for conventional cooling of water by evaporation in the ambient air. A tower requires a flow of air and this may be induced by natural or mechanical means. The use of large cooling towers at power stations to dissipate recovered waste heat eliminates the problem of thermal pollution in masses of water, however, the make-up water for a cooling system is taken from river or stream, thus eliminating its subsequent use down-river. After being used several times for cooling purposes, it is finally dissipated in to the atmosphere as steam.

copper. A metal placed in group IB of the periodic table. Copper and its compounds are ubiquitous in the environment and are thus frequently found in surface-water. The nature of the copper in water depends on the *p*H and carbonate concentration in the water and the other anions in solution.

Water treatment processes usually result in the removal of trace metal from water but the copper concentration in drinking-water at the consumer's tap can be higher than in either the source water or the treated water entering the supply. Various chemical and physical characteristics of the distributed water influence the leaching of copper from the distribution system and household plumbing. Water stored in copper vessels tends to maintain the bacterial quality without deterioration. Copper in solution imparts a colour and an undesirable taste to drinking-water.

The copper content of soils depends on such factors as geographical location, proximity to industry, and use of fertilizers. Copper concentrations in inorganic-based fertilizers were found to range from 0.01 to 0.05 mg/g. The amount of copper present in food will vary with the copper content of the soil from which it derives. Foods such as vegetables, flour, and dairy and meat products normally have a copper content lees than 0.01 mg/g. Copper levels in drinking-water vary normally from 0.01 to 0.5 mg/L.

Copper is an essential element in human metabolism, having roles in erythrocyte formation, release of tissue iron and the development of bone, the central nervous system, and connective tissue. Copper is usually combined with proteins: haemocuprein in the erythrocytes and ceruloplasmin in the blood plasma contain copper as an integral part of their structure; metallothionein is a copper storage protein. A number of copper-containing enzymes have been isolated, notably cytochrome oxidase, ascorbic acid oxidase, and uridase.

As copper is widely distributed in foods, it is unlikely that human beings with the exception, perhaps, of infants on an exclusive milk diet, ever develop a dietary deficiency of copper. It is a beneficial adjunct to iron therapy in the treatment of nutritional anaemia in infants. in animals, however, a wide variety of clinical disorders have been associated with copper deficiency.

In take of excessively large doses by man leads to severe mucosal irritation and corrosion, widespread capollary damage, hepatic and renal damages, and central nervous system irritation followed by depression. Severe gastrointestinal irritation and possible necrotic changes in the liver and kidneys could occur. However, copper poisoning is rare in man and higher mammals owing to the powerful emetic action of copper. Application of copper salts to the skin is corrosive and may lead to papulovesicular eczema. Local action on the eye produces serious inflammation. Copper in water has an unpleasant, although taste is detectable in distilled water at 2.6 mg/L of copper ions.

The presence of copper in the water supply, although not constituting a hazard to health, may interfere with the intended domestic uses of water.

Copper in public water supplies enhances corrosion of aluminium and zinc utensils and fittings. Staining of laundry and plumbing fixtures occurs when copper concentrations in water exceed 1.0 mg/L and this value is recommended as a guideline value.

cotton dust. Dust generated into the atmosphere as a result of the processing of cotton fibres combined with any naturally occurring materials such as stems, leaves, bracts, and inorganic matter which may have accumulated on cotton fibres during the growing and harvesting period. Any dust generated from processing of cotton through the weaving of fabric in textile mills and dust generated in other operations or manufacturing process using new or waste cotton, or cotton fibre byproducts from textile mills, is regarded as cotton dust.

As per OSHA standards, it should be noted that exposure to cotton dust in cotton yarn manufacturing is controlled so that no employee is exposed to airborne concentration of lint free respirable cotton dust greater than 200 μg/L of air, determined as a time-weighted average (TWA) concentration limit for up to a 8-hour workday, measured by a vertical elutriator or a method of equivalent accuracy and precision. It should also be assured that no employee who is exposed to cotton dust in the textile processes (such as slashing and weaving) is exposed to airborne concentration of lint free respirable cotton dust greater than 750 μg/m³ of air, determined as a time-weighted average (TWA) concentration limit for up to a 8-hour workday, measured by a vertical elutriator or a method of equivalent accuracy and precision. It should be further assured that no employee who is exposed to cotton dust in yarn manufacturing, slashing and weaving) is exposed to airborne concentration of lint free respirable cotton dust greater than 500μg/m³ of air, determined as a time-weighted average (TWA) concentration limit for up to a 8-hour workday, measured by a vertical elutriator or a method of equivalent accuracy and precision.

creosote. *See* coal tar products.

crop damage due to pollution. Among the destructive agents that cause damage to plants, and so to agriculture and forestry in general, include sulphur dioxide and fluorides and fluorinated hydrocarbons. The substance that has been most thoroughly investigated so far is sulphur dioxide. This gas, which is released mainly by combustion processes, penetrates into the pores in the leaves of plants, combines there with water to form sulphurous acids, and so results in local poisoning. Individual kinds of plant react very differently to a particular maximum concentration of sulphur dioxide, which leads in all cases to the death of the plant cells. This probably depends in the first place on the different speeds at which the sulphur dioxide is absorbed by the leaves. Plants with sappy leaves and high physiological activity, such as corn, alfalfa, sulphur dioxide is transmitted more rapidly and its poisonous effects develop faster as a result. Plants with pithy leaves or needles, on the other hand, are more or less resistant. Even for these plants considerable damage has been reported. At many places, coniferous trees have been killed by the effects of sulphur dioxide. Plant growths that can keep their pores closed longer, such as corn and oak trees, are less sensitive to sulphur dioxide. In lower concentrations, sulphur dioxide will affect photosynthesis and respiration of plants. At higher concentrations the plant cells die off. The rate of photosynthesis can also be affected when sulphur dioxide concentrations that would cases, however, after a temporary drop in assimilation performance the plants are able to recover. The visible signs, if damage by sulphur dioxide are different for different plants. One-seed-leaf plants display something between a slight specking on the tips of the leaves and a complete bleaching of the leaves. In the case of two-seed-leaf plants, well-defined speckles appear, which can be red, brown or yellowish.

CRS model. Algorithm estimates ground-level concentrations resulting from up to nineteen collocated elevated stack emissions for an entire year and prints out the highest and second-highest 1-hour, 2-hour, and 24-hour concentrations as well as the mean concentrations at a set of 180 receptors. The algorithm is based on a modified form of steady-state Gaussian plume equation which uses empirical dispersion coefficients and includes adjustments for plume rise and limited mixing. Pollutant concentrations for each averaging time are computed for discrete, non-overlapping time periods (no running averages are computed) using measured hourly values of wind speed and direction, and estimated hourly values of atmospheric stability and mixing height.

cumulus cloud. A large and usually isolated cloud with considerable vertical extent. It has a dome-shaped upper surface, and nearly horizontal base, with many individual protuberances. Such clouds result from convection currents and develop under conditions of limited atmospheric instability.

cyanides. The salts of hydrocyanic acid (HCN), which are virulent poisons. Cyanides are used in many industrial processes, *e.g.*, in the production of acrylonitrile, adiponitile, and methylmethacrylate. Cyanides are also used for extracting gold and silver, in the production of steel, for electroplating, and for the preparation of some intermediates in chemical synthesis. In some of these processes, contamination of the air and water can arise.

Hydrocyanic acid dissociates to

give the cyanide ion in water; its dissociation is pH dependent, with the ionic from predominating above pH 8.2. Conversion of cyanide to the much less toxic cyanate will occur at pH levels of 8.5 and above. In general, the levels in raw water appear to be low (*i.e.*, less than 0.1 mg/L) except in the case of serious contamination, mainly by industrial discharges to river or other sources. Metal-treating industries, coke and gas manufacture, and a variety of chemical producers can be major sources of cyanide contamination of water. Chlorination of potable water to a free chlorine residual under neutral or alkaline conditions will reduce the concentration of cyanide in the finished water to very low levels. Chlorination of water (at pH 8.5) converts cyanides to innocuous cyanates, which can ultimately be decomposed to carbon dioxide and nitrogen gas.

Some foodstuffs (such as almonds) contain traces of cyanides; cyanides is also found in fish living in contaminated waters. Cyanides are decomposed on heating and, thus cooked foods will tend to contain lower levels. Typical daily intakes of cyanide from food do not appear to be properly known; in general, dietary intake is regarded to be low. The acceptable daily intake of cyanide residues via ingestion of fumigated foods has been set at 0.05 mg/kg of body weight.

The discharge of cyanides in effluents from various industrial sources (especially electroplating industry) is highly objectionable due to:

(a) the toxic effects which they have on aquatic life, and on bacteria in sewage works;

(b) their ability to absorb dissolved oxygen; and

(c) the formation of extremely poisonous hydrogen cyanide gas which can endanger the life of persons working in sewers.

The cyanide ion is readily absorbed in animal species, and its highly poisonous effects are induced rapidly. Cyanide blocks the oxidative processes in the cells of the carotid and aortic bodies, allowing anaerobic products, *e.g.*, lactic acid, to accumulate in them, thus stimulating respiration. This reaction is due to the combination of cyanide with the catalytic iron group of cytochrome oxidase, preventing the donation of electrons to molecular oxygen. The absorption of oxygen by the cells is inhibited, *i.e.*, cellular oxidation cannot proceed, and the main supply of energy to the cells ceases. Without oxidation of glucose, neurones convert glucose to lactic acid at a greatly increased rate. In animals the increase in the lactic acid content of the brain, even with small doses of cyanide, may cause coma and convulsions with irreversible cerebral damage, although the rest of the body is unharmed. Low exposures to cyanide are not fatal to human beings who have an efficient detoxification system where by the cyanide is converted to the thiocyanate ion, which is non-toxic at low levels.

A single dose of 50-60 mg for a human being is usually fatal. Exposures of 2.9-4.7 mg of cyanide per day are regarded as non-injurious to humans, owing to highly efficient detoxification system in the human body in which cyanide ion is converted to the relatively non-toxic thiocyanate ion through the rhodanase and thiosulphate enzyme system.

The action level for hydrogen cyanide or a cyanide salt is defined as one-half the corresponding recommended ceiling environmental limit. Occupational exposure to cyanide compounds is defined as exposure to airborne concentrations greater than the corresponding action levels. The exposure to hydrogen cyanide should be controlled so that no employee is exposed to concentrations greater than 5.0 mg/m^3 of air expressed as cyanide (4.7 ppm), determined as a ceiling concentration based on 10 minute sampling period. For free cyanide (sum of cyanide present as HCN and CN^-) the criterion to protect freshwater aquatic life is 3.5 μg/L as a 24-hour average and the concentration should not exceed 52 μg/L at any time. The available data for free cyanide (sum of cyanide present as HCN and CN^-) indicate that acute toxicity to freshwater aquatic life occur at concentrations as low as 30 μg/L; and would occur at even lower concentrations among the species that are more sensitive than those tested. If the acute-chronic ratio for saltwater organisms is assumed to be similar to that for freshwater organisms, chronic toxicity would occur at concentrations as low as 2.0 μg/L, and would occur at even lower concentrations among the species that are more sensitive than those tested. The ambient water quality criterion for cyanide is recommended to be identical to the existing drinking water standard which is 200 μg/L.

cyanophyceae. Blue-green algae, unicellular autotrophic organisms, reproducing by cell division, that form cell families or colonies; widely distributed all over the world. Several species of blue-green algae are toxic. They occur and thrive equally well on moist soil, cliff or bare rock faces, on the bark of trees, and on the surface of water. Several species (*Anabaena, Anabaenopsis, Microcystis,* etc.) cause the algal blooms of eutrophic waters. They are biological indicators of water pollution.

cyanosis. Blue discoloration of the skin due to lack of oxygen supply. It indicates that the protein hemoglobin of the blood is not carrying its normal quantity of oxygen. When the oxygen concentration in haemoglobin is within normal limits, the blood appears red, but when it is low, the hemoglobin turns purple. Nearly every major heart or pulmonary disease can result in cyanosis. It may occur in pneumonia, asthma, lung collapse, poisoning, congenital heart defects, bronchitis, tuberculosis, suffocation, and tetany. Cyanosis depends on a number of factors such as, the extent of the oxygen deficiency, the rate of blood circulation, the colour of the skin to begin with, and the thickness of the skin.

cycle of erosion. A concept in which the various stages in the erosion of a region are regarded as parts of a cyclic process. Ideally the cycle begins with uplift of a land surface followed by initiation and development of relief, and finally degeneration of relief and ultimate plantation. Further uplifts cause the cycles to recommence. It is very likely that complete plantation is never achieved, uplift occurring at almost any stage in the cycle. In certain circumstances traces of an earlier cycle may be preserved even after several later cycles of erosion have operated.

cycle of sedimentation. 1. An ordered repeated sequence of associated processes and conditions recorded in a sedimentary deposit. 2. The deposition of sediments in a basin between onset of any two successive marine transgressions.

cyclone. 1. A device for removing particulate matter from the waste gases of industrial processes. A simple cyclone consists of a cylindrical upper section and a conical bottom section. The dust-laden gases enter the cylindrical section tangentially. Centrifugal action throws the grit and the dust particles to the outer walls; these particles fall by gravity to the dust outlet at the bottom. The relatively clean gases leave through a centrally situated tube within the upper section. With a suitable pressure drop, separation of particles of about 40 µm can be achieved. 2. An area of low pressure, with a more or less circular pattern of isobars. The term is sometimes applied to mid-latitude frontal depression but is now increasingly restricted to tropical depressions of hurricane type. Cyclones depend for their development on an initial supply of heat and moisture and are sustained for the further release of the latent heat through massive condensation. When the storm moves over a cooler surface, it quickly decays. Cyclones generally move along westward tracks, either to the north or south of the equator, but then curve northwards along the eastern margins of continents to become components of the westerly wind-systems of the mid-latitudes.

cylinder. A pressure vessel designed for pressures higher than 40 psi and having a circular cross section. It does not include a portable tank, multiunit tank, car tank, cargo tank, or tank car.

D

damper. A device used to regulate the rate of flow of combustion gases through the flues of a fuel-burning appliance.

dark smoke. Commonly defined as smoke appearing to be as dark as, or darker than shade-2 on the Ringelmann chart.

d-block elements. The block of elements in the periodic table co consisting of scandium, yttrium, and lanthanum together with the three periods of transition elements: titanium to zinc, zirconium to cadmium, and hafnium to mercury. All these elements have two outer s-electrons and *d*-electrons in their penultimate shell, *i.e.,* an outer electronic configuration of the type $(n\text{-}1)\,d^x ns^2$, where x is 1 to 10. Though some of these elements are essentially required in small quantities for the growth of plants and animals, but their presence in air and water, in large quantities, is of serious concern as they exert ill effects on flora as well as fauna on the earth, and are therefore regarded as pollutants.

DDT and metabolites. [1,1,1-trichloro-2,2-di-4(chlorophenyl) ethane]. A chlorinated hydrocarbon used to destroy insects, mainly mosquitoes. It is a strong pesticide. The very characteristic that gained DDT its widespread use is now leading to its disuse. DDT is absorbed via both inhalation and ingestion. Absorption of small doses is virtually complete and is facilitated by the presence of fat in food. DDT is poorly absorbed through the skin. Levels of storage in adipose tissue increase rapidly at first and then more gradually until a steady state is reached. In man, the time necessary to reach storage equilibrium is at least one year. There is a gradual reduction in the amount of DDT stored in the tissue if exposure to the compound of discontinued. Like most species, man converts some DDT to DDE. A small amount of TDE (DDD), an intermediate in the formation of main excretory product 2,2-bis (4-chlorophenyl) acetic acid (DDA), may also be found in tissues.

Concentrations of total DDT in the blood of the general population of different countries lie within the range 0.01-0.07 mg/L. In the blood and other tissues of the fetus or newborn infants. DDT concentrations are lower than in the corresponding tissues of the mother. Levels of DDT in human milk have usually been reported to be in the range 0.01-0.10 mg/L, with the concentration of DDT plus its metabolites, especially DDE, being about twice as high. By accumulating in fatty tissues of animals.

DDT and its derivatives (DDD, DDE) enter into food chain and thus also into the human organism. Animal studies indicate that the concentration in serum most accurately reflects the concentration in the brain, the critical tissue. Its application has been prohibited in many developed as well as developing countries.

The available data for DDE indicate that acute toxicity to freshwater aquatic life occur at concentrations as low as 1050 μg/L, and would occur at even lower concentrations among the species that are more sensitive than those tested. No data is available about the chronic toxicity of DDE to sensitive freshwater aquatic life. For DDT and its metabolites the criterion to protect saltwater aquatic life is 0.001 μg/L as a 24-hour average and the concentration should not exceed 0.13 μg/L at any time. The available data for DDE indicate that acute toxicity to saltwater aquatic life occur at concentrations as low as 14 μg/L, and would occur at even lower concentrations among the species that are more sensitive than those tested. For the protection of human health from the potential carcinogenic effects of DDT through ingestion of contaminated water and contaminated aquatic organisms, the ambient water criterion to be zero on the nonthreshold assumption for DDT. However, zero level may not be attainable at present time. Therefore, the levels that may result in incremental increase of cancer risk over lifetime are estimated at 10^{-5}, 10^{-6}, and 10^{-7}. The corresponding criteria are 0.24 ng/L, 0.024 ng/L, and 0.0024 ng/L respectively. If the above estimates are made for the consumption of aquatic organisms only (excluding consumption of water), the levels are redefined as 0.24 ng/L, 0.024 ng/L, and 0.0024 ng/L respectively.

deactivation of catalyst. Loss of ability to catalyze by catalyst; it may so happen because of ageing, sintering, or poisoning.

deactivator. A substance used to modify selectively the action of an activator, reducing its effect upon an undesired substance.

deadspace. The part of the respiratory system constituted by the larynx, the trachea, the bronchi and the bronchioles in which the volume of air that penetrates the lungs on each inspiration is not entirely used for respiration. In every 500 ml that constitute the used air, 150 to 170 ml remain in the dead space. In the calculation of the coefficient of ventilation, this figure must be subtracted from that of the circulating air.

deaerator. A setup for removing the dissolved gases, particularly oxygen, from feed water supplied to the boilers and chemical reactors.

deafness caused by noise. Impairment of hearing caused by noise reflects metabolic exhaustion of the hearing cells in the inner ear accompanied by degenerative changes. Metabolic exhaustion under the effects of noise occurs when the oxygen requirements of the hearing sense cells exceed the amount of oxygen supplied from the bloodstream. During the hearing process, sound waves are carried via the eardrum and the ossicle apparatus to the inner ear fluid. In the inner ear fluid is a membrane composed of many hearing sense cells which absorb the oscillation of the inner ear fluid and pass them on for transmission to the brain. In this way the hearing sense cells receive the mechanical energy of the sound and their task is to convert the mechanical energy into nerve impulses.

deagglomeration. A scientific term for the size-reduction process in which loosely adhered clumps (agglomerates) of powders or crystals are broken apart without further disintegration of the powder or crystal particles themselves.

decalescence. Absorption of heat, usually by an alloy, without rise in temperature, due to an allotropic transformation.

decantation. Pouring, or siphoning, off the clear supernatant liquid after a substance held in suspension has settled to the bottom of the containing vessel.

decarbonization. Removal of carbon from any system which contains it. The substitution of oxygen for carbon dioxide in the blood in the lungs is termed decarbonization, as is also the burning out of a portion of the carbon in cast iron to make steel.

decarboxylation. The removal of carboxyl groups from the molecule of a compound by loss of carbon dioxide. The term is also applied to the loss of carbon dioxide from proteins or amino-acids by the bacterial action. The carboxylic acids having α–carbonyl group, or α–double bond often suffer loss of carbon dioxide on heating.

decay. 1. In atmospheric chemistry, the disappearance of a pollutant as a result of absorption or chemical reaction at the earth's sulphur, to removal by rain, or to transformation into some other substance. 2. The process of spontaneous transformation of one radioactive nuclide into a daughter nuclide, which may be radioactive or may not, with the emission of one or more particles or photons. The decay of N_0. nuclides to give N nuc' des after time t is given by:

$$N = N_0 \exp(-Y)$$

where, Y is the decay constant or the disintegration constant. The reciprocal of the decay constant is the mean life. The time required for half the original nuclides to decay (*i.e.*, $N = 1/2N_0$) is called the half-life of the nuclide. The same terms are applied to elementary particles that spontaneously transform into other particles.

decibel. dB. The unit of loudness or measure of physical pressure exerted by sound waves at a given point. It is a logarithmic ratio, defined as

$$dB = 10 \log(I/I_o)$$

where, I is the sound pressure of the source being measured, and I_o is the sound pressure of a sound at the threshold of hearing. Since the human ear is itself logarithmic in character, the average person can make out the difference in loudness between two sounds one decibel apart, even though the actual differences in sound pressures are much greater at the upper end of the scale than at the lower end. Nearly all audible sounds lie between 0 and about 140 dB; 0 dB is the threshold of hearing, while sounds above 140 dB are uncommon and unhearable. An increase of 10 dB that the noise perceived by a listener has doubled in loudness. The examples of typical decibel levels are:

rustle of leaves	10 dB
quiet library	30 dB
whisper	35 dB
normal conversation	60 dB
busy office	65 dB
moderate traffic	70 dB
alarm clock ringing	80 dB
very noisy factory	90 dB

The decibel measurement is widely used throughout the world for determining the approximate human reaction to noise, and is the basis of legislation to control noise in many countries.

decomposer. An organism that obtains energy from the chemical breakdown of dead organisms, or animal or plant wastes. Organisms such as bacteria and fungi, participate in the decomposition of organic matter. Many decomposers (*e.g.*, nitrifying bacteria) are specialized to break down the organic materials that are difficult for the other organisms to digest. Decomposers perform a vital role in the ecosystem by returning the constituents of organic matter to the environment in inorganic form so that they can again be assimilated by plants.

decomposition. The biodegradation of organic compounds such as proteins and lipids, into stable organic matter of smaller molecules and (finally) into organic compounds by the action of microorganisms. The final products are generally, carbon dioxide, ammonia, and water. Decomposition takes place under either aerobic or anaerobic conditions and plays vital role in the biogeochemical cycle and in the self-purification of waters. In connection with organic matter deposited either on land or in water, decomposition is the opposite of photosynthesis. During photosynthesis, carbon dioxide and water are used by plants, and oxygen is liberated to the atmosphere. In decomposition for example, the carbohydrates in the organic matter are oxidized with the aid of bacteria so that water and carbon dioxide are released, while the bacteria use up the oxygen. The more organic material is in the water, for example, the greater is the demand by the bacteria for oxygen.

decongestants. Any agent or drug which removes the blockade of nasal and bronchial passages. The most popular decongestant drug is epinephrine.

decontamination. In general, the removal of chemical, biological, or radiological contamination, from an area or a material; specifically this term refers to treatment of clothing, equipment, buildings, and the like to remove radioactive substances to which they have been exposed.

decontamination factor. Ratio of amount of radioactive impurities present in substance before purification to that present after purification.

decrepitation. A crackling noise produced when certain crystals are heated, caused by changes in structure resulting generally from loss of water of crystallization.

deduster. A term sometimes applied to the fine sieve or elutriator for removing fine dust from powders. *See also* dust separator.

defecation. A term used to refer of the process of clarification or removal of impurities from sugarcane or beet juice by heating in the presence of lime to precipitate undesirable substance. The resulting mother liquor is then drained off and concentrated by evaporation and boiling. *See also* clarification.

defervescence. The act of cessation or discontinuance of boiling or of effervescence.

deflagration. A chemical reaction accompanied by evolution of heat, flame, sparks, or sputtering of burning particles; usually containing potassium or sodium nitrate (black powder) or nitrocellulose (smokeless powder). It is induced by heat, friction, or impact. Deflagration occurs at the particle surfaces of materials classified as low explosives, in which the combustion products flow away from the unreacted material.

deflation. The removal of tiny particles of dust or sand by wind; a common process occurring in deserts.

deflocculation. The reverse process of flocculation, or the process of preventing flocculation, *i.e.*, the process of breaking up dispersing agglomerates to form a stable compound.

defoliation. A disgusting aspect of modern warfare used as a weapon in anti-guerrilla warfare, but the ecological harm it does by destroying chlorophyll-bearing leaves is irrevocable. The practice should be banned in all the countries along with biological warfare, chemical warfare, and bombardment. But defoliation often occurs unintentionally by action of industrial or governmental polluters. Cases of radioactivity leaks indicate that trees in the vicinity of atomic plants and laboratories have been defoliated and died. In less serious ecological incidents, leaves of sycamores in the cities and the suburbs curl up and down and drop off far earlier than they are supposed to because of local air pollutants.

degasification. Removal of gas, as applied particularly to the removal of the last traces of gas from wires used in vacuum tubes, from metals to be plated, and from substances to be used in other specialized applications.

degradation. The breakdown of complex chemical structures to simpler compounds by the influence of bacteria, usually accelerated by oxygen and sunlight.

degraded environment. Whenever any environment is saddled with undue amounts of any pollutants, making it either ugly or unsuitable to support human and animal life, it is degraded. Actually many environments that are perfectly fine, but only temporarily littered or invaded by undue amounts of pollution, are often mistakenly classified as degraded. Since most environments contain many species of life, healthy environment are considered complex. Degraded environments are exceedingly simple, containing few if any living species.

degraded water. Water that is polluted to such an extent that it is not suitable for its primary propose. This is quite understandable because in the case of fresh water, for example, the best grade is drinking water. When a certain coliform count is exceeded the water is degraded to wash water.

If still further degradation of the quality continues, the water may be unsafe to use for drinking, washing or swimming, but safe for boating, and so on down the grades.

degree-day, heating. A form of degree-day used as an indication of fuel consumption. One heating degree-day is counted for each degree that the daily mean temperature is lower than a base temperature. The total number of degree-days for the heating season are the algebraic sum of the degree-days for the different days of the season.

degree of polymerization. A number indicating the extent to which the molecules of a monomer have combined to form a polymer; it is determined by calculating the number of such molecules present in an average molecule of polymer in a sample.

dehydration. 1. Removal of 95% or more of the water from a food product by intensive over drying, spraying, or other means, for the purpose of saving space, weight, and transportation cost. 2. Elimination of water molecule from the molecule of a chemical compound.

dehydrocyclization. Elimination of hydrogen molecule from hydrocarbon molecule (open chain, aromatic or hydroaromatic) with formation of compounds containing one or more cyclic structures in molecule.

dehydrogenation. A chemical reaction, normally requiring a catalyst, in which hydrogen atoms are removed from a saturated compound (an alcohol, paraffin, or alicyclic compound) to unsaturated aldehydes, olefins, or aromatic compounds.

deletion mutation. Mutation resulting from deletion of one or more nucleotides from a gene.

deliquescence. The literal meaning of this term (from the Latin) is becoming liquid. Substances are said to be deliquescent if they absorb enough water from the air to dissolve themselves, and hence become liquid. Many substances are hygroscopic, but only a smaller number, such as caustic soda, calcium chloride, and magnesium nitrate, etc., are deliquescent.

Demephion. A systemic insecticide and acaricide effective against sap-feeding insects, and non-phytotoxic to most crops. It is straw-coloured liquid (a mixture of two isomers), miscible with most aromatic solvents, chlorobenzene and ketones; immiscible with most aliphatic solvents. It is generally non-corrosive and compatible with most, expect strongly alkaline, pesticides. The acute oral LD_{50} for rats is about 0.015 ml/kg; the acute dermal LD_{50} is about 0.06 ml/kg. It is mainly used against aphids-on all crops.

Demeton-S-methyl. A systemic and contact insecticide and acaricide, metabolized in the plant to the sulphoxide and sulphone; rapid in action; moderate persistence. It is a clourless oil, only slightly soluble in water, soluble in most organic compounds. It is hydrolyzed by alkali. The acute oral LD_{50} for rats is 65 mg/kg of the technical material, 40 mg/kg of the pure. It is quite effective against most sap-sucking pests (aphids, leafhoppers, etc.), sawflies and red spider mites.

Demotion. A systemic insecticide

and acaricide with some fumigant action, effective especially against sap-sucking insects and mites. No marked phytotoxicity has been recorded. The technical product is a light yellow oil, hydrolyzed by strong alkali but is compatible with most non-alkaline pesticides. It is almost insoluble in water but is soluble in most organic solvents. The acute oral LD_{50} for male rats is 30 mg/kg. This formulation is very effective against sap-sucking insects and mites.

demulsification. The international destruction of the undesirable emulsions such as that occur in petroleum extraction, where subterranean pressure has created a highly stable emulsion of saline water in the petroleum.

denaturation. A reordering of the molecular structure of some proteins (globulins) induced by a number of environmental factors, such as heating to just below the boiling point, change of *p*H, or exposure to various detergents. These factors cause rupture of the hydrogen bonds in the molecule, but not of the stronger peptide bonds. As a result the structure of the protein becomes somewhat more random, and its enzymatic activity is greatly reduced.

denitrification. 1. Any process for removing or altering the nitro group in an organic compound. The nitro group may be altered by reduction, being converted into the amino group and then the compound by diazotizing the reduction product and boiling with water or alcohol. 2. Bacterial decomposition of nitrates with production of gaseous nitrogen. The bacteria which effect the change are termed as denitrifiers. Also known as denitration. 3. In waste-water treatment, the removal of ammonia from waste-water through the use of denitrifying bacteria similar to those found in the soil. Bacteriological denitrification is a two stage process. Nitrogen fixing bacteria (nitrifiers) are first employed to change the ammonia to nitrates. The nitrates are then stripped of their nitrogen by denitrifying bacteria (denitrifiers). Nitrogen is released into the air. Denitrifying tanks are similar to anaerobic digesters, but the sludge is stirred less aggressively and the cover does not need to be airtight.

densification. The reduction, in bulk, of solids wastes. It can be accomplished by baling incineration, and compaction.

denudation. The end result of processes such as weathering and erosion which cause a lowering of the land surface.

deodorant. Substances capable of removing the objectionable odour. Deodorants used for the human body mask or diminish odours and inhibit bacterial growth. Their ingredients generally include perfume to mask odour and antibacterial agents to inhibit bacterial growth. One of the commonly used antibacterial ingredients is hexachlorophene. Others are zinc phenosulphonate and methylbenzethonium chloride.

deoxygenation. Removal of oxygen from a substance, such as blood or polluted water.

deoxyribonucleic acid. DNA. The most essential part of the nucleus of the cell. This substance is the primary determinant of hereditary traits passed on from generation to generation through the genes and chromosomes in a nucleic acid. The molecules are self-replicating, *i.e.*, they are able to manufacture exact copies of themselves, a characteristic that is driving force behind all multicellular organic growth and reproduction. The protection of DNA is of supreme importance for the preservation and orderly development of life, and those environmental factors that attack it are among the most dangerous of all pollutants.

dephlegmation. A process for increasing the efficiency of fractional distillation by forcing the vapours from the still to bubble through shallow, layers of condensate in a column or dephlegmator, whereby the amount of low-boiling component in the vapour is increased and a substantial portion of the higher-boiling components is retained in the condensate.

depletion. The act of seriously diminishing or exhausting a quantity of something, *e.g.*, natural resources.

designated facility. A hazardous waste treatment, storage, or disposal facility that has been designated on the manifest by the generator.

depleted materials. The material in which the amount of one or more isotopes of a constituent has been reduced by an isotope separation process or by a nuclear reaction.

deposition. The laying down of material which has been removed by denudation. Most of the material will be sediment and therefore, a possible source of sedimentary rocks when consolidated. After denudation has taken place, the material is transported, sometimes over considerable distances, before being deposited.

depressant. A chemical used to reduce the concentration of undesired substances in the air-solution interface; and consequently, to reduce the amount of these undesired substances appearing in the product.

depth dose. Dose of ionizing radiation at defined depth (mostly at 0.1 metre); usually depth dose is defined relatively to surface dose as percentage.

desalination. The process of removal of salt from sea water for irrigation of the land, or to provide drinking water. The methods employed include evaporation, often under reduced pressure (flash evaporation); freezing (pure ice forms from freezing brine); reverse osmosis; electrodialysis; and ion exchange.

desensitization. A therapeutic technique which aims at causing the disappearance of hypersensitivity reactions in certain individuals. Desensitization may be total or specific.

desiccants. 1. Chemicals that kill leaves of plants, the leaves may either drop off, or remain attached. These are used on many seed crops to hasten harvest; the leaves are cleaned from seed in harvesting. Such chemical have also been used during wars to destroy vegetation. 2. Substance used to withdraw moisture from other materials. *See also* desiccation.

desiccation. Removal of water vapour from a material by a hygroscopic substance, such as anhydrous calcium chloride, phosphorus pentaoxide, or silica gel, placed in an air-tight container with the material to be dried (often under vacuum). The term is conventionally restricted to laboratory control or chemical reagents, test samples, and the like and is not used for large scale drying or dehydrating operation.

desorption. The reverse of absorption or adsorption, as in the release of one substance which has been taken into another by a physical process, or the release of a substance which has been held in concentrated form upon a surface.

destructive metabolism. The retrograde chemical changes in the tissues of the body. The totality of reactions of cell respiration resulting in the transformation of living matter and cell reserves into waste matter with a low level of energy. Catabolic reactions lead to the liberation of energy. The final products of such reactions are carbon dioxide and oxygen.

desulphurization of fuel gases. The process of removal of sulphur from fuel gases; several methods are available for desulphurization of fuel gas; these include dry method, alkalized alumina process, and manganese dioxide process etc.

desulphurization of fuel oils. Method for the removal of sulphur with hydrogen over a catalyst at temperatures of 575-775 K and pressure of 10^6-10^8 Pa. Hydrogen reacts with organic sulphur compounds to form hydrogen sulphide.

detergents. Any substance used to enhance the cleansing action. These are surface-active compounds, either natural or synthetic. Oil soluble detergents are used in gasoline and lubricating oils to hold particulate impurities in suspension. Among the water soluble detergents, alcohols and common soaps are effective. Still more sc are the synthetic types (syndets) such as sulphonated dodecylbenzene and similar alkylates. The linear alkyl sulphonates (LAS) are more biodegradable than are the branched-chain type; they are made from petrochemicals by various cracking and polymerization techniques. Detergent action is promoted by phosphatic compounds called builders. These pollutants are generally regarded as enemies of clean water; are still highly popular in homes and industries alike. Basically, detergents lower the surface tension of wash water, make the water more wettable, emulsify oils and greases break up colloids cause flotation and create lather or foam. At the same time they utterly destroy useful bacteria and organisms. Moreover, detergents containing phosphate, can contribute to accelerated algal growth and other forms of enrichment of receiving waters. Three general types of detergents in use today are;

(a) anionic detergents,
(b) cationic detergents, and
(c) nonionic detergents.

detonation wave. The specific value for the rate at which an explosive combustion spreads throughout a body of gas when it is once started at any point. It is much faster than the velocity of sound in the same gas.

detoxification. The removal of poisons from the body, either by the body itself or by medical treatment. One form of detoxification takes place when the kidney cleanses the blood of waste products. When an individual sustains an infection due to bacteria or viruses, toxic or poisonous substances develop and are similarly removed. Another form of detoxification is used when a person is accidentally poisoned and is given an antidote. The liver is the most important detoxification organ. It converts harmful substances to less harmful ones, or to products which can be more readily excreted either in the bile or by the kidneys.

dew. Moisture condensed from the air and deposited on grass and other plants, especially during the night. Dew is formed in calm and settled condition generally associated with anticyclonic weather. During the night, the temperature falls and the air is unable to hold as much water vapour; some condensed on to plants as dew, and some may form mist or fog. The cooling which causes dew is the result of radiation during the night. The air cools from the ground upwards, and if dewpoint is reached condensation will occur. It is most frequent after sunny days, especially in winter in southeast Asia. *See also* dew point.

dewatered sludge. Sewage sludge with about three-fourths of the water-content removed. In Europe, it is widely used to blend processed solid wastes in composing; activated sludge is more difficult to dewater than digested sludge.

dew point. T_d. The temperature at which dew first appears on a solids surface whose temperature is steadily reduced below that of surrounding moist air. The dew points, or thermodynamic dew-point temperature, is technically defined as the temperature of moist air at pressure p and with mixing ratio r at which moist air, saturated with respect of water at the given pressure, has a saturation mixing ratio r_w equal to the given mixing ratio.

***di-*.** A prefix meaning 'two'; in the names of compound, it indicates the presence of two atoms of the same element (sulphur dioxide, SO_2). It also appears in more general terms such as dipole (two electric poles), diolefin (two double bonds), dimmer (two molecules united), and diatomic (two atoms); the last of these has no connection with diatom or diatomaceous earth, which are named from a biological genus. *See also dia-; bi-.*

***dia-*.** A prefix having several meanings: 1. passing through, as in dialysis, diaphragm, diametre; 2. opposite to, an in diamagnetic; 3. complete or throughout, as in diagnosis. It is not a prefix in the word diamond.

dialysis. The separation of a colloid from ions and molecules in solution by means of a parchment membrane. Ions and molecules pass through the membrane but the colloid is retained. If the mixture is placed in a parchment bag, and water is constantly flown round the bag, eventually a complete washing of the colloid will be effected.

diathermal wall. *See* diathermic partition.

diathermic partition. Partition which allows energy transfer in the form of heat but does not allow for mass or energy transfer in the form of work. Also known as diathermal wall; thermally conducting wall.

diatom. Unicellular algae having cell walls impregnated with silica that persists as a skeleton after death; forms a large proportion of plankton in both seawater and freshwater.

Diazinon. A non-systemic insecticide with some acaricidal action, used mainly against flies, both in agriculture and veterinary practice. At higher dosages it may be phytotoxic. It is a clourless oil insoluble in water, but is miscible with ethanol, acetone, xylene, and is soluble in petroleum oils. It decomposes above 393 K and is susceptible to oxidation; stable in alkaline media but is slowly hydrolyzed by water and dilute acids. It is compatible with most pesticides but should not be compounded with copper fungicides.

The acute oral LD_{50} for male rats is 108 mg/kg. This formulation is especially effective against flies and their larvae (*e.g.,* Anthomyiidae on vegetables and carrot fly), also used against mites, thrips, springtails, glasshouse pests, and some bugs (aphids, capsids, etc.).

dibasic. 1. A term used to describe an acid either inorganic or organic, whose molecule contains two hydrogen atoms that can be replaced by basic elements to form salts; *e.g.*, sulphuric acid (H_2SO_4) and oxalic acid (HOOCCOOH). Dibasic inorganic acids liberate two hydrogen ions when dissolved in water. 2. An inorganic compound whose molecule contains two atom of a basic univalent element, for example, dibasic sodium phosphate (Na_2HPO_4).

dibromochloropropane (DBCP). A chemical regarded as a potential cancer hazard. Occupational exposure to dibromochloropropane should be controlled so that no employee is exposed to dibromo chloropropane at a concentration greater than 1 ppb, determined as a time-weighted average (TWA) concentration limit for up to a 8-hour workshift in a 40-hour workweek. Occupational exposure to dibromochloropropane is defined as any work involving handling, storage, use, or manufacture of dibromochloropropane. The possible effects on the health of humans chronically exposed to dibromochloropropane may include sterility, diminished renal function, and degeneration and cirrhosis of liver.

dichlorobenzenes. The three isomers *ortho, meta-,* and *para-*, find their applications as insecticide, fumigant, moth repellant, degreaser for hides and wool, and intermediates in the production of a large number of dyes and pharmaceuticals. The available data for dichlorobenzenes indicate that acute and chronic toxicity to freshwater aquatic life occur at concentrations as low as 1120 and 763 μg/L, respectively; and would occur at even lower concentrations among the species that are more sensitive than those tested. For the protection of human health from the toxic effects of dichlorobenzenes ingested through water and contaminated aquatic organisms, the ambient water criterion to be 400 μg/L.

3,3'-dichlorobenzidine. A cancer-suspect agent, used as intermediate for dyes and pigments. For the maximum protection of human health from the potential carcinogenic effects due to exposure of this potential health hazard chemical through ingestion of contaminated aquatic organisms and water, the ambient water concentration should be zero on the non-threshold assumption for dichlorobenzidine. However, zero level may not be attainable at present time. Therefore, the levels that may result in incremental increase of cancer risk over lifetime are estimated at 10^{-5}, 10^{-6}, and 10^{-7}. The corresponding criteria are 0.103 μg/L, 0.0103 μg/L, and 0.00103 μg/L respectively. If the above estimates are made for the consumption of aquatic organisms only (excluding consumption of water), the levels are redefined as 0.204 μg/L, 0.0204 μg/L, and 0.00204 μg/L respectively.

Dichlorvos (DDVP). The commercial name of dimethyl 2,2-dichlorovinyl phosphate. It has high boiling point and low vapor pressure. For certain usages it is discharged as a true gas to control insects in the open spaces of structures. It is also used as a contact insecticide. On account of its low vapour pressure dichlorvos is unable to penetrate into materials. Therefore it is of no value as a commodity fumigant. When used as a fumigant this compound is effective at very low concentrations against houseflies, mosquitoes and mushroom flies. At higher concentrations it is effective against cockroaches and a wide range of stored product insects. It has been used against moths and the cigarette beetle in tobacco ware-houses. An important characteristic of dichlorvos is that it hydrolyzes slowly in the presence of water, and this process is accelerated in the presence of alkali and reduced in the presence of an acid. An end product of hydrolysis may be dichloroacetic acid. As a result of this, formulations and spaces treated with the insecticide may exhibit a vinegarish odour if hydrolysis has occurred.

The toxicological evaluation of dichilorvos is that 10 ppm in the diet, equivalent to 0.5 mg/kg of body weight per day, is the level that will cause no toxicological effect; estimated acceptable daily intake for man is 0 to 0.004 mg/kg of body weight. According to the threshold limit set by American Conference of Government Industrial Hygienists, the maximum permissible concentration of daily exposure to humans has been recommended to be 1 μg/L. This compund is easily absorbed through the skin and if only small amounts of formulations containing this insecticide are spilled on the clothes or body, these may produce very serious results requiring medical treatment.

Dicofol. A non-systemic acaricide, with little insecticidal activity, recommended for the control of mites on a wide range of crops. Although residues in soil decrease rapidly, traces may remain for a year or more. The pure compound is a white solid, practically insoluble in water, but soluble in most aliphatic and aromatic solvents. It is hydrolyzed by alkali, but is compatible with all but highly alkaline pesticides. Wettable powder formulations are sensitive to solvents and surfactants, which may affect acaricidal activity as well as phytotoxicity of the product.

The acute oral LD_{50} for male rats has been found to be 809±33 mg/kg. It has been found to be effective only against Acarina; kills eggs and all active stages of the mites. Also known as Kelthane.

dieldrin. A white, crystalline, chlorinated hydrocarbon; considered to be a potential occupational carcinogen; mainly used as insecticide. It has a high contact and stomach toxicity for most insects. Skin contact, inhalation, and food contamination with dieldrin should be completely avoided. For dieldrin, the criterion to protect aquatic life is 0.0019 μg/L, as a 24-hour average and the concentration should not exceed 0.71 μg/L at any time. For the maximum protection of human health from the potential carcinogenic effects due to exposure of dieldrin through ingestion of contaminated aquatic organisms and water, the ambient water concentration should be zero on the nonthreshold assumption for dieldrin. However, zero level may not be attainable at present time. Therefore, the levels that may result in incremental increase of cancer risk over lifetime are estimated at 10^{-5}, 10^{-6}, and 10^{-7}. The corresponding criteria are 0.71 ng/L, 0.071 ng/L, and 0.0071 ng/L respectively. If the above estimates are made for the consumption of aquatic organisms only (excluding consumption of water), the levels are redefined as 0.76 ng/L, 0.076 ng/L, and 0.0076 ng/L respectively.

dienes. Alkenes that contain two carbon-carbon double bonds. Dines are divided into three classes according to the arrangement of the double bonds. Double bonds that alternates with single bonds are conjugated. Double bonds that are separated by more than one single bonds are isolated. Double bonds that share a carbon are cumulated, and the compounds are called allenes. For example,

$CH_2{=}CH{-}CH{=}CH_2$
1,3-butadiene (conjugated diene)

$CH_2{=}CH{-}CH_2{-}CH{=}CH_2$
1,4-pentadiene (isolated diene)

$CH_2{-}CH{=}C{=}CH_2$
1,2-butadiene (cumulated diene)

The chemical properties of a diene depend upon the arrangement of its double bonds.

diesel engine pollution. The pollution caused during combustion by a diesel engine, as it generates highly toxic products such as nickel carbonyl and oxides of nitrogen. Also under certain operating conditions nitrogen oxide emissions may be higher in diesel engines than they are to be found in internal combustion engines. Diesel exhaust also contains 3,4-benzopyrene, a suspected contributor to lung cancer.

differential weathering. Weathering that occurs at varying rates because of the intrinsic differences in rock composition and resistance, or differences in the intensity and degree of erosion. It helps to develop and modify many upstanding forms such as columns, pillars and rock pedestals.

diffused aeration. Aeration of water or sewage by passing compressed air through porous plates or pipes in such a manner so that the air bubbles coming out from

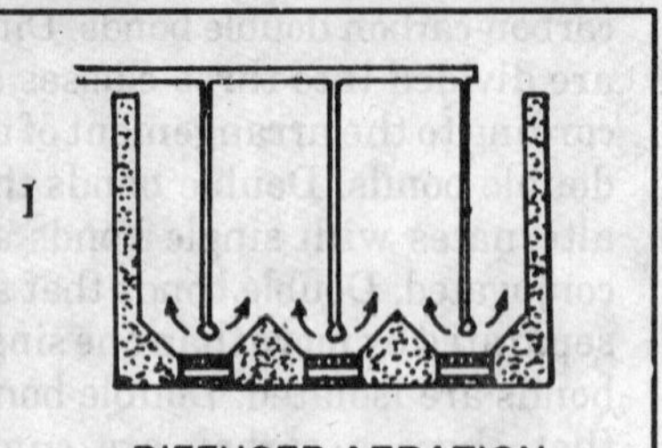

DIFFUSED AERATION

the pores aerate the liquid.

diffuse emission. Pollution entering the atmosphere from a large-sized area; the opposite of concentrated emission from a point source.

diffusion. The mutual permeation of two or more substances due to the kinetic activity of their molecules so that a uniform mixture of solution results. Gases of different densities will mix uniformly counter to gravity. For gases, the rate of diffusion is inversely proportional to the square roots of their densities. Two metals in close contact also show a slight tendency to diffuse. Diffusion also takes place when a barrier or film of a microporous solid (metal or cellulose) is placed between two gases or between two liquid solutions of different concentrations; in the latter case, the rate depends on the relative strength of the concentrations.

digested sludge. The sludge obtained form septic tanks, inmhoff tanks and sludge digestion tank. The volatile matter content of a well-digested sludges is 30 to 45%. It is dark brown in colour, homogeneous in texture having a tarry odour when wet. Its drainability is high and the solid particles separate easily.

digestion. The conversion of organic matter into simpler chemical compounds through the action of enzymes produced by living systems. When applied to sludge, digestion occurs in the primary treatment when the raw sludge is deposited in settling tanks. If the sludge remains in an imhoff tank,

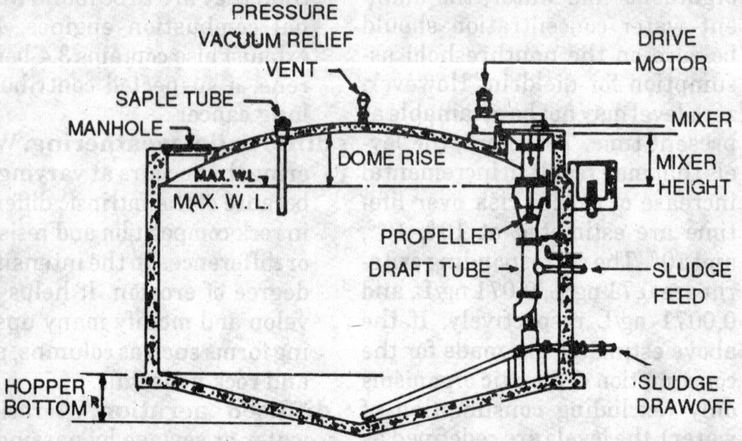

DIGESTION CHAMBER

it is subjected to anaerobic digestion. If it is subjected to an activated sludge process, it is aerobically digested. The primary difference is that in the anaerobic digestion the breakdown of the organic matter within the sludge does not result in the formation of cellular matter. In the activated sludge process the sludge is converted into cellular matter which causes problems in dewatering or concentrating the sludge.

dilatancy. The property of certain colloidal solutions of becoming solid, or setting under pressure. Dilatancy is one of the gel-sol transformations known under the general term of thixotropy.

dilatation. The increase in volume per unit volume of any continuous substance, caused by deformation.

dilution. The process wherein the concentration of solute decreases; it may occur as result of the increase in amount of the solvent. Due to the fact that nature has provided air and water with physical and chemical means of self-cleansing, it traditionally has been the concept to mix small volumes of sewage with large volumes of water to allow natural purification, or it has been the hopes of engineers that a high chimney will effectively disperse toxic emissions through dilution in the air. If the chimney is high enough, they reason, the air will whisk away the pollutants and the ground level will remain clean.

Dimefox. A systemic insecticide and acaricide of very high toxicity, used mainly for soil treatment against aphids and red spider mites; non-phytotoxic at insecticidal concentrations. It is a colourless liquid, miscible with water and most organic solvents. It is resistant to hydrolysis by alkali but is hydrolyzed by acids. It is compatible with other pesticides, but the technical product slowly attacks metals. The acute oral LD_{50} for rats is 1-2 mg/kg; the acute dermal LD_{50} for rats is 5 mg/kg; the hazards of vapour toxicity are high.

Dimethoate. A systemic and contact insecticide and acaricide, used mainly against fruit flies and aphids. The pure compound is a white soild, only slightly soluble in water, soluble in most organic solvents except saturated hydrocarbons such as hexane. It is stable in aqueous solution and to sunlight, but is readily hydrolyzed by aqueous alkali. It is incompatible with alkaline pesticides. The acute oral LD_{50} for rats is 250-65 mg/kg. It has been found to be effective against aphids, psyllids, some flies, sawflies, Woolly Aphid and red spider mites; and is mainly used against fruit olive fly and cherry fly, and aphids.

dimethyl sulphate. A reagent frequently used for the methylation of various organic compounds. Occupational exposure to dimethyl sulphate should be controlled so that no employee is exposed to dimethyl sulphate at a concentration greater than 0.5 mg/m^3 of air, determined as a time-weighted average (TWA) concentration limit for up to a 8-hour worksheet in a 40-hour workweek. It is suspected to have carcinogenic potential for humans. Worker exposure by all routes should be carefully controlled to the levels consistent with animal and human experience data.

1, 4-dioxane. A clourless, flammable liquid, used as solvent for cellulosics and wide range of organic products; paint and varnish removers; dispersing agent in textile industry, and fumigant. Because of the carcinogenic action of dioxane and its ability to penetrate the skin, occupational exposure to dioxane is defined as any work in workplaces where dioxane is handled, manufactured, or otherwise used, except where it is present as an unintentional contaminant in other chemical substances in quantities less than 1% by weight. Occupational exposure to dioxane should be controlled so that the workers are not exposed at airborne concentrations greater than 1 ppm, based on 30 minute sampling period. The recommended standard is designed to protect the health and provide safety to the workers for up to a 10-hour worksheet, 40-hour workweek over a working lifetime.

dioxin. The term dioxin is a generalization of a family of chlorinated organic compounds, some of which have been found to be extremely hazardous to life in minute quantities. A total of 75 dioxins are theoretically possible, depending upon the number and position of the attached chlorine atoms. No dioxin is completely safe. The symptoms of exposure are similar to those of the closely related polychlorinated biphenyls (PCBs) and dibenzofurans. They can cause chloracne, nerve and liver damage, weakness and pain in the hands and feet, fetal abnormalities, and miscarriages. The chemicals are strongly lipophilic and build up rapidly in the food chain. Trace amounts of dioxins have been found as contaminants in incinerator smoke, automotive exhaust, cigar and cigarette smoke, and indeed virtually anywhere where combustion of aromatic hydrocarbons has taken place.

1,2-diphenylhydrazine. A chemical classified as one of the potential occupational carcinogens. The available data for 1,2-diphenylhydrazine indicate that acute toxicity to freshwater aquatic life occur at concentrations as low as 270 μg/L, and would occur at even lower concentrations among the species that are more sensitive than those tested. No saltwater organisms have been tested with 1,2-diphenylhydrazine and therefore no data is available concerning acute and chronic toxicity. For the maximum protection of human health from the potential carcinogenic effects due to exposure of 1,2-diphenylhydrazine through ingestion of contaminated aquatic organisms and water, the ambient water concentration should be zero on the nonthreshold assumption for 1,2-diphenylhydrazine. However, zero level may not be attainable at present time. Therefore, the levels that may result in incremental increase of cancer risk over lifetime are estimated at 10^{-5}, 10^{-6}, and 10^{-7}. The corresponding criteria are 422 ng/L, 42.2 ng/L, and 4.22 ng/L respectively. If the above estimates are made for the consumption of aquatic organisms only (excluding consumption of water), the levels are redefined as 5.6 μg/L, 0.56 μ/L, and 0.056 μg/Lrespectively.

diphtheria. A contagious disease

caused by the Klebs-Loffler bacillus *Corynebacterium diphtheriae*. It is characterized by the production of false fibrinous membrane in the mucosa of the pharynx and the larynx, with general poisoning (paralysis, nephritis and cardiovascular disturbances) caused by toxins secreted by the bacillus. The bacteria generally gain entrance to the body through the mouth, trachea (windpipe), and lungs. During the early stages in diphtheria a mild sore throat is the only complaint. Fever and fatigue follow soon as the bacteria multiply and invade the throat and upper trachea. At this stage a characteristic gray-coloured membrane begins to develop and grows rapidly around the tonsil area and into the throat. This is called the pseudomembrane. Around this is a zone of redness (erythema) and swelling (edema). This goes on increasing and ultimately invades the larynx (voice box) and trachea so extensively that the complete air-passage is blocked and the patient suffocates.

The diphtheria organism also produces a chemical substance, called exotoxin, which is highly toxic. When the exotoxin comes in contact with the heart muscle (myocardium), an inflammatory reaction starts. This inflammation of the heart is called myocarditis. Myocarditis causes a rapid but weak pulse and with the continuance of this condition the heart beats irregularly and there is congestive heart failure. The exotoxins produced by these bacteria can also damage various nerves. The nerves become inflamed, producing the condition called neuritis. The cranial nerves (head and neck) are the first to be affected, causing speech difficulties, abnormalities in swallowing, and visual problems. The neuritis may advance to the rib cage and extremities.

Dipterex. A contact and stomach insecticide with penetrant action, recommended for use against flies, some bugs, some beetles, lepidopterous larvae, and ectoparasites of domestic animals. Its activity is attributed to its metabolic conversion to dichlorvos. Moderate persistence. It is a white crystalline powder, quite soluble n water, insoluble in petroleum oils, poorly soluble in carbon tetrachloride and identhyl ether; soluble in benzene, ethanol, and most chlorinated hydrocarbons. It is stable at room temperature but is decomposed by water at higher temperatures (and acid media) to form dichlorvos. The acute oral LD_{50} for male rats is 630 mg/kg. Effective against most lepidopterous larvae, flies and fly maggots, some Homoptera, many Heteroptera, some beetles. Used for household and veterinary pests, under different trade names. Also known as Trichlorphon.

discoloration. Pollutants in air or water often cause change in colour. This does not necessarily mean that the resource is unsafe to use for the purpose required. Iron for example can make a lake seem brown. That doesn't mean the lake isn't safe for swimming, Discoloration, however, is a form of aesthetic pollution. When a freshly-painted white home suddenly erupts with yellow spots the discoloration generally comes from hydrogen sulphide pollution.

disease causing agents. Water and air are potential carriers of pathogenic micro-organisms. These pathogens are carried into the water bodies by sewage and waters from farms and various industries, specially tanning and meat packaging industries. Water may also contain some animal parasites including the round worms, are the pork tape worms.

disinfectant. An agent that destroys germs is termed as disinfectant, and which inhibit their growth are termed as antiseptics. In other words, those compounds which kill bacteria (bactericidal) are disinfectants, while those which prevent their production (bacteriostatic) are called antiseptics.

disinfectant residuals. In addition to disinfection efficiency, another important consideration is the ability of pathogens to remain as residual disinfectants during the storage and distribution of potable water. Except for ozone, all of the other practicable disinfectants (chlorine, chlorine dioxide, and chloramines) can provide a persistent residual for continued microbial control once the finished water enters the distribution network. However, chloramines are such mild biocides that any decisions as to their use should be evaluated carefully with sufficient bacteriological data collected throughout the distribution system to demonstrate effectiveness in controlling microbial regrowth and providing protection against a moderate degree (1% sewage) of contamination from cross connections.

disinfection efficiency. A term used in the water pollution, referring to the comparative efficiency of disinfectants, and may be expressed in terms of either the relative rates of disinfection produced by the same concentration of disinfecting agent. However, because of the different nature of the microorganisms and the difficulty of standardizing test conditions, such as *p*H, temperature, and the chemical characteristics of the water, only generalized statements can be made about the comparative efficiencies of different disinfectants. Within these limitations, disinfecting agents may be grouped according to their efficiency. Thus, the use of chlorine, chlorine dioxide, or ozone is preferable, although for chlorine the *p*H should be less than 8.0 Because chloramines are only slowly biocidal, their use as primary disinfecting agents for water-treatment purposes is not recommended, although they may be used for the maintenance of residuals in distribution systems where the contact time is longer. Similarly, in decreasing order, the relative resistance of different types of microorganisms and their probable survival may be listed as follows: protozoans, cysts, enteroviruses, enterobacteria. Although there are distinct differences in the time required to inactivate enteroviruses as compared with enterobacteria, the minimum conditions of disinfectant-residual and contact-time required to ensure a microbiologically safe water supply can be achieved readily. It is, therefore, recommended that water from potentially polluted sources should always be disinfected. This would ensure inactivation of certain organisms, including some viruses, which may be relatively more resistant than faecal indicator bacteria.

dispersants. Chemical agents used to break up concentrations of organic material, for example, when oil slicks cover a water resource, one of the methods of dispersing the slick is to employ dispersants. These are classified as anionic, cationic, and non-ionic. Non-ionic dispersants are best suited for salt water applications.

dispersed medium. The medium in which a colloid is suspended, in a manner analogous to that of the solvent in a true solution. Also known as dispersive or dispersion medium; continuous phase.

dispersed phase. The distributed phase in a colloidal system, *i.e.*, the phase which is composed of the distributed particles.

dispersion. 1. A system comprised of two phases, one of which is in the form of finely divided particles, often in the colloidal size range, distributed throughout a bulk substance; the particles are usually called the internal or disperse phase and the medium in which they are distributed, the external or continuous phase. Dispersions of solids in liquids are called suspensions. If the solid or liquid particles are larger than colloidal. They will eventually agglomerate, coalesce, and settle out by gravity. 2. In optics, dispersion refers to the retardation of a light ray as it passes through or into a transparent medium; a change of direction is usually involved. The extent of the phenomenon depends on the frequency of the radiation and the refractive index of the medium.

disposal. The treatment of sewage and processing of solid wastes. Collecting and transporting these pollutants is called handling.

disposal by burning. The disposal of refuge from industries and residental area by heating. The refuge is loaded in the furnace by a mechanical charger on to a grating, where it is burned in to sterile slag. The noncombustible substances are left as slag. To recover the cost of this operation, the heat generated by combustion of the refuge, can be utilized to produce steam for the generation of electricity. In this manner, the volume of the refuge to be dumped is much reduced, and the energy contained in the refuge can be exploited in the interest of the community.

disposal facility. A facility or part of a facility at which hazardous waste is internationally placed in or on any land or water and at which waste will remain after closure.

dissipation. The interaction between matter and energy incident on it, such that the portion of energy used up in the interaction is no longer available for conversion into useful work.

dissociation. A specific kind of decomposition occurring (*a*) when a molecule of a diatomic gas (Cl_2) is separated by heat into its constituent atoms, and (*b*) when an inorganic compound in aqueous solution separates into charged particles (ions), *e.g.*, hydrochloric acid in water dissociates to form positively charged hydrogen ions (H^+) and negatively charged chloride ions (Cl^-) (electrolytic dissociation). In sense dissociation is synonymous with ionization.

dissolved oxygen. The amount of oxygen available for biochemical activity within a given volume of water; expressed as mg/L, g/m^3, or ppm. The saturation point depends on the temperature, barometric pressure, and the chemical characteristics of water. The amount of dissolved oxygen in water is of vital importance to living organisms. Under normal conditions, water is saturated when it contains about 10 ppm oxygen at 0°C. In still water, oxygen entering at the surface can only pass into a region of lower concentration by diffusion; under those circumstances, diffusion is a very slow process. The rate which oxygen diffuses into a body of water diminishes with increasing depth. In running water, however, turbulence will distribute the oxygen much more rapidly; the rate of dissolution in a swift flowing stream may be two hundred times as great as that in nearly stagnant water.

dissolved phosphate level. The amount of soluble phosphate in wastewaters or any waterbody; usually expressed as mg/L. Although municipal wastes may be subjected to primary or secondary treatment to degrade organic suspended solids the effluent will contain substantial amounts of phosphorus in the form of dissolved phosphates. This is a nutrient for plant and causes accelerated eutrophication. To lower the dissolved phosphate level in the wastewater, many processes, including chemical precipitation, are available.

dissolved solids. In pollution control, minerals and other materials that are carried in dissolved state in a body of water, as opposed to those that are carried in suspension, and those that are bounced along the bottom in a moving watercourse. These are classified as volatile fractions that evaporate when the sample is heated at 875 K for 30 minutes, and as fixed fraction that remain behind when the volatiles have been driven off.

Disulfoton. A systemic insecticide and acaricide used mainly as a seed dressing or granules to protect seedlings from insect attack. It is metabolized in the plant to the sulphoxide and sulphone. It is clourless oil with a characteristic odour only slightly soluble in water, but readily soluble in most organic solvents. It is relatively stable to hydrolysis at pH below 8.0. The acute oral LD_{50} for male rats is 12.5 mg/kg. It has been found to be effective against aphids on vegetables and fruit, and carrot fly. leafhoppers on rice, vegetables, cotton, some flies, some leafminers, and some beetles.

dizziness. The state in which objects seem to be whirling around, having a feeling of being faint, unsteady or lightheaded. Dizziness can be a normal physical reaction. Other terms almost similar to dizziness are giddiness and vertigo. Doctors call dizziness vertigo, when there is sensation of spinning, turning, or falling in space, or of standing still while the objects around are moving. Vertigo, on the other hand, is a severe disturbance, usually accompanied by nausea and vomiting. It almost always originates in the vestibular labyrinth-the center for the sense of balance in the inner ear, in the auditory (hearing) nerve, or in the vestibular nuclei or nerve terminals, on the brain stem or their connections. The disorders that cause vertigo often cause hearing loss and tinnitus, that is, ringing in the ears at the same time. Because there are nerve connections between the eye and the inner ear. Vertigo is also often accompanied by nystagmus, (an abnormal movement of the eyes). Sight plays an important part in the body's sense of balance, and its loss or impairment is often part of the problem in a condition called multisensory dizziness. This disturbance usually occurs in persons who are elderly or diabetic. Dizziness can also be a problem for people who hyperventilate, that is, breathe more than they used to. The result is a drop in the carbon dioxide in the blood, which causes constriction of the blood vessels in the brain, causing dizziness.

DNA. *See* deoxyribonucleic acid.

DNOC. It is a non-systemic stomach poison and contact insecticide; ovicidal to the eggs of certain insects. It is strongly phytotoxic and its use as an insecticide is limited to dormant sprays or on waste ground, *e.g.,* against locusts. It is also used (not usually on oil) as a contact herbicide for the control of broad-leaved weeds in cereals, and in the formulation for the pre-harvest desiccation of potatoes and leguminous seed crops. It forms yellowish, odourless crystals, only sparingly soluble in water, but soluble in most organic solvents and in acetic acid. The alkali salts are water soluble It is explosive, and is usually moistened with up to 10% water to reduce the hazard, though it is corrosive to mild steel in the presence of water. Effective against overwintering stages of aphids, capsids, psyllids, scale insects, red spider mites, and various lepidoptera on top, bush and cane fruit. Products containing DDT also control various weevils and tortrix moths in their overwintering stages; also used as a herbicide.

DO. An acronym for the dissolve oxygen content in a sample of water undergoing analysis. More formally it is called the DOL, or dissolved oxygen level, and this is a measure of the amount of oxygen found available for biochemical activity in aprescribed volume of water. Obviously, it the reverse of BOD, biochemical oxygen demand. Thus if the DO decline the BOD rises and *vica-versa*.

doldrums. The equatorial belt of low winds or clams, lying between the trade-wind belts occurring between 5° and 30° north and south of the equator. The doldrums constitute a zone of constantly high temperatures, high humidity and generally low pressure. However, there are no steep pressure gradients, and it is estimated that calm conditions exist for approximately one-third of the year.

domestic incinerators. The category that includes the wire baskets used to burn dying or dead plants leaves etc. auto.

domestic sewage. The sewage containing natural human waste, laundry water, and the discharge from regular household activities.

The great outcry against phosphate stems from the increasing use of detergent or without enzymes, that accelerate the eutrophication of lakes, rivers and estuaries and may be hazardous to marine and riverine live.

dose. 1. Industrially, the term is often used in reference to the percentage of an active ingredient added to a mixture as, for example, the accelerator dosage in rubber mixture. 2. In radiation therapy it refers to the amount of radiation of any type administered to a patient; the so-called permissible dosage of *X*-radiation is 0.3 roentgen a week. 3. In medicine, it refers to the amount of any medicine prescribed by a physician.

down-draught. A region of severe turbulence formed on the leeward side when the wind flows around and over a building. The region of down-draught begins at the top of the windward face of the building, and rises to almost two times the height of the building, and stretches to about six times the height of the building downwind. Chimney emissions discharged into down-draught zone will be brought rapidly to the ground. Thus, the chimneys should discharge their gases high enough for them to escape the influence of down-draught.

down-wash. The drawing down of chimney gases into a system of vortices or eddies which form in the lee of a chimney when wind is blowing. Down-wash affects the visual appearance of the plume and causes blackening of the stack. In extreme circumstances, it may also assist in bringing the flue gases prematurely to the ground level. To overcome the risk of frequent down-wash, it is necessary to discharge the gases from the mouth of the chimney at a sufficiently high velocity.

draft tube aerator. An aerator using a draft tube, which generally requires maintenance of a constant level of mixed liquor in the aeration tank. The draft is downward in the tube and air pipes aspirate air into the liquor. Agitation at the surface also aids aeration.

drainage. The natural path runoff, from rain and snow melt, covers on its way to surface receiving waters. It is also the subsurface pattern by which surface waters from all sources aid in replenishing the aquifers.

drainage density. A term describing the relative spacing of a stream network; it is expressed as the ratio of the total length of all streams within a drainage basin to the area of the basin. Thus it is a measure of the dissection or, of the topographic texture of the area. It depends on the climate geology and physical characteristics of the basin.

drainage patterns. A particular arrangement or configuration that is collectively formed by the individual stream courses in an area. These patterns reflect the influence of factors such as initial slopes inequalities in rock hardness and structural controls, and the geological and geomorphic history of the drainage basin.

dredge spoils. Solid material, such as sand, silt, clay, rock, or other material deposited from industrial and municipal discharges, that is removed from the bottom of water bodies to improve discharge rate of the effluents as well as navigation.

driftwood. A rare combination of both natural and man-made pollutant. Basically it signifies any significantly-sized pieces of wood floating on the surface of a body of water used for boating. Driftwood as an increasingly larger annual pollutant is a boon to propeller shops and a bane to boatman.

dross. Oxidized metallic residues, or other metallic waste-products, such as the scummaterial which forms on the surface of molten metals during refining or casting.

dry deposition. In pollution control terminology, the deposit of airborne pollutants directly onto the land or water surface, as opposed to toxic precipitation, in which the pollutants are washed from the air by raindrops. Dry deposition is not always 'dry', *i.e.*, the pollutants may be liquids as well as solids, or gases, the important distinction being that they are not carried down the rain. The process accounts for a significant proportion of organic pollutants reaching the large water bodies such as lakes, each year.

dry gas. A gas that does not contain fractions which may easily condense under normal atmospheric condition, for example, natural gas with methane and ethane.

dry ice. Solid carbon dioxide having temperature of 194 K; used to refrigerate foodstuffs in transit, for carbonation of liquids and for cold traps in laboratories. It sublimes from solid state to gaseous state with liquefying.

dry limestone process. An economic method of handling the air pollution problem posed by oxides of sulphur. The limestone is exposed to pollutants in the furnace and to stack gases and combines with the oxides to form calcium sulphite, which oxidizes to calcium sulphate. The mixture of sulphate, ash and limestone in the residue may be used for cinder blocks while the cleaned gas goes up the stack.

drying. 1. Evaporative loss of water or other solvent from a substance, usually a solid, with the aid of heat. Removal of water by a mechanical device such as a screen or filter is called dewatering or drying. 2. Polymerization of a vegetable oil or high polymer base in paints and varnishes, resulting in the formation of a protective film; it is catalyzed by oxygen and is quite distinct from evaporative drying, which occurs simultaneousl in paints.

drying agents. Substances used to absorb moisture, especially in a desiccator and in towers through which moist gases are passed. The principal laboratory drying agents are sulphuric acid, fused calcium chloride, solid sodium hydroxide, calcium oxide, and phosphorus pentaoxide.

duff. The partially decayed or reduced organic matter that make up the upper surface of the soil beneath trees, especially conifers.

dust. Industrial or natural particulates 76 microns or less in size are caught in a catch all called dust. Any dust smaller than 5 microns can pass through the nostril and lodge in the alveoli of the lungs. Dust larger than 5 microns becomes an observable nuisance and while not hazardous to human health causes economic loss. Dust is generated by combustion processes (in power stations, by motor vehicles and in homes), and in various forms of industrial undertakings (cement work, for example). From a medical point of view, dust can be classified of under two heads: coarse dust and fine dust. In recent times, the emission of coarse dust has been cut down considerably by the installation of dust filters in new industrial plants, which can have an efficiency, rating as high as 99% (electric dust filters). In the steel producing industry, for example, dust ejection has been reduced in the past ten years or so about one quarter. But this reduction relates primarily to coarse dust. In a medical context, coarse dust is less dangerous than the dust particles are so large that they cannot penetrate the lung vesicles (aeveoli). The real medical problem stems from fine dust (particles measuring 5-10 μ, which is only partially arrested by the filter mechanism in the human respiratory system. It gets the lung vesicles and can lodge there for some time. A complicating factor is that fine dust from coal tar distillates, often contains poisons, such as 3,4-benzopyrene which causes cancer, and heavy metal oxides, such as vanadium compounds, which act as catalyzers. These toxic substances can then develop their effects in the sensitive lung vesicles directly. By the catalytic effects of various metallic oxides, moreover, gaseous sulphur dioxide can be converted into the even more dangerous sulphur trioxide, which for its parting conjunction with the moisture present in the lung vasicles, forms sulphuric acid. According to the industrial process by which the fine dust is formed, the following poisons have been identified in it so far: arsenic, beryllium, cadmium, lead, selenium, thallium, uranium, and asbestos. Particular mention may also be made of fine dust composed of lead particles from automobile exhaust fumes and of fine dust emitted by refineries.

dust bowl. An area which has been changed from a grassy landscape into near desert. If grassland is ploughed and the land left, bare wind can blow away the topsoil and rain will also wash away soil and possibly form gullies. This eroded landscape is bare and useless for farming. It is also possible to expose the soil by overgrazing; if there are so many animals that they remove all the vegetation, wind and rain will erode the soil.

dust burden. The weight of dust suspended in a unit of medium, *e.g.*, flue gas. It is usually expressed in mg/m^3, at normal pressure and temperature.

dustfall. A measure of the settleable particulates in either air or chimney emissions it is usually measured by instruments as simple as an open bottle supported on a stand, or as complicated as an electronic analyzer hooked to a computer. The open bottle, or dust gage is only reflective of the amount of settleable particulates that are observable.

dust separator. An apparatus for separating solid particles from a gas stream in which they are suspended. Dust separators are widely used to remove dust and grit form stack gases and other industrial gases. They are of many different types, which may be broadly classified on the basis of whether they use or do not use a liquid to remove particles. Dust separators of the former type are known as washers. The cyclone, in gas cleaning is a dust separator of droplet separator using essentially the centrifugal force derived from the motion of the gas. A dust separator consisting of several cyclones in parallel is known as multicyclone. In the inertial separator particles are removed by a combination of inertial and centrifugal forces resulting from sudden change in direction of flow of the gas, together with impact on of the particles on a target. In the electrostatic precipitator the gas is passed between sets of electrodes across which a very high constant potential is maintained. The dust particles become charged and adhere lightly to one set of electrodes they are removed by sharp tapping, causing them to fall into containers. Although expensive to install, electrostatic precipitators are relatively cheap to operate and are one of the most efficient mend of removing fine dust from gases although strict maintenance is necessary to ensure unimpaired efficiency. They are widely used in power stations burring pulverized fuel cement works, steel works, etc. In the bubble washer dust separator, the gas is bubbled through the liquid; in a spray washer it is passed through a chamber in which a spray of the liquid removes the dust. In the venturi scrubber, the gas is drawn at high velocity through a conical restriction at the throat of which water is injected at the rate of about 1 m^3 of gas. The water is broken down into very fine droplets and the dust particles are thoroughly wetted; dust and water particles and subsequently removed in acycline. Such equipment will remove about 99% of particles smaller than 0.5 mm in diametre.

dystectic mixture. A mixture of two or more substances in such proportions as to yield the maximum melting point, so that upon altering the proportions the melting point is lowered.

dystrophic lake. A lake in which nutrient matter and oxygen are sparse. It is rich in humic matter, which consists mainly of undecomposed plant fragments. Dystrophic conditions are often associated with acidic peat bogs.

E

ear pollution. A kind of noise pollution in the matter of aesthetics. Noise pollution of course, covers every thing; but the ear pollution, like its parallel term eye pollution, involves ugly sounds instead of ugly sights. From this point of view, soft music or classical music, even jazz, are sensibly excluded.

earthquake. A sudden motion or trembling in the earth caused by the abrupt release of slowly accumulated strain. Earthquakes and volcanoes are manifestations of motion of crustal plates. Shallow earthquakes occur where plates are colliding or separating, and deeper earthquakes occur where the lithosphere plunges into the mantle (subduction zone). Many shallow earthquakes are caused by movement of one crustal block with respect to an adjacent block along a fault plane.

earth science. The science that deals with the study of the earth or any part thereof; includes geology, geography, geophysics and geochemistry (in their widest senses), geodetics, climatology and meteorology, oceanography, and the astronomical aspects of the earth-moon system.

earthwatch programme. A programme of global environmental assessment to assess trends in air, water, land, and human health; a part of action plan adopted by the United Nations Conference on the human environment in 1972. The programme includes a scheme for the establishment of ten baseline stations remote from all sources of pollution in order to monitor long-term global trends in atmospheric constituents and properties which may cause changes in meteorological properties, including climatic changes.

ECDIN. *E*nvironmental *C*hemical *D*ata *I*nformation *N*etwork. A data bank working within the framework of a programme elaborated by the EEC. It records physical, chemical, and technical properties of industrial and commercial products. The availability of such data can help to reduce the environmental impact of accidental release of toxic substances.

eco-city. A hypothetical term referring to a city that would be no-waste city. In other words the city would convert its garbage, its solid waste, its gaseous and liquid pollutants into harmless and useful substances, using the solid wastes as soil conditioners, the waste liquids and liquors from sewage for drinking and other beneficial purposes, the particulates as activated carbon which be continually used for pollutant removal.

ecocline. A genetic gradient of adaptability to an environmental gradient; formed by the merger of ecotypes.

ecological association. A complex of communities that develops in accord with variations in physiography, soil, and successional history within the major subdivision of a biotic realm.

ecological catastrophe. The extinction of one or more species of animal or plant life. This differs from ecological disaster in that in a catastrophe, once a species has been obliterated from the earth, it cannot be recreated, but in a disaster the species may recover and resume abundance either in the disaster area at a later stage or in another area of the environment.

ecological disturbance. The traditional controls by the factors such as predatorprey relationship, in all the communities. Man's disturbance of this relationship can in a way be considered as a form of pollution, because it can cause ecological catastrophes.

ecological efficiency. The concept involving a study of the energy required by a living organism to produce protoplasm. To determine this, several parameters, such as absorption ratio, assimilation ratio, growth ratio, and increase ratio, have to be calculated. Pollution or the changes caused by the pollution in the environment, can affect the ecological efficiency of living organisms and vegetation, to the detriment of all life on earth.

ecological factors. Collective name for inanimate (abiotic: climatic, edaphic, hydrographic, physiographic) and animate (biotic: plant and animal kingdom, and man) environmental factors determining the processes of living organisms and their distribution.

ecological murder. Death of the living plants and animals, caused by the polluters and pollutants.

ecological niche. The environment in which an organism lives to which it is better suited than any other organism, and which suits it better than any other environment. It is defined by the types of food it consumes, its predators, temperature tolerances, etc. Two species cannot coexist stably if they occupy identical niches.

ecological pyramid. A pyramid-shaped diagram showing the quantitative relationship between the number of organisms, energy and biomass of an ecosystem. The ecological law involved in such a pyramid is that the higher one goes the lower are the number of individuals in the population, and the larger their specimen size, *i.e.*, the numbers are highest for the lowest trophic levels (plants), and low for the highest trophic level (carnivores).

ecological succession. A gradual process incurred by the change in number of individuals of each species of a community and by the establishment of new species populations that may gradually replace the original inhabitants. The introduction of pollution can hasten the onset of ecological recession, which is the reverse of ecological succession in that during recession the complex community begins to loose its diversity of species and becomes simple again.

ecology. The study of interactions of organisms with one another and with their environment. As a science, it seeks to discover how an organism affects and is affected by its environment and to define how these interactions determine the kinds and number of organisms found in a particular place and at a particular time. Autecology is concerned with single organisms or species, and synecology with communities of species, although these artificial demarcations are no longer accepted by all the ecologists. Human ecology is the study of structure and development of human communities and societies in terms of the processes by which human populations adapt to their environments; as a subject it represents an application of the perspectives of the biological sciences to the investigation of topics included in the social sciences.

economic toxicology. The scientific study concerned with harmful or undesirable effects of drugs or combinations that are intentionally administered to biological systems to achieve a specific effect. This also refers to the risks involved using food additives including substances used in food processing such as preservatives, binding agents, colorants, flavorants etc. These chemicals are required for transport of foodstuffs over long distance and for storage for long periods.

economizer. A heat exchanger linked to a steam boiler in which the heat from the flue gases is transferred to the entering feedwater. The heat loss is thus reduced and the thermal efficiency of the boiler plant is increased. Also the gases issuing out of the exhaust are cooled and a number of pollutants are condensed and thus check the air pollution.

ecosphere. The bio-bubble that contains life on the earth, in the ocean, rivers and lakes, and in the air. It therefore consists of lithosphere, hydrosphere, biosphere, atmosphere, and all the living occupants therein.

ecosystem. A biological community and the physical environment associated with it. Living organisms are classified as biotic and inorganic substances that aid life are called abiotic. The organisms of a community, together with the atmosphere, soil, or water, form a functioning system. Matter and energy are taken up by the producer organisms from the physical surroundings, and passed from organism to organism through the food chain. Each ecosystem has an input of gases and mineral nutrients from the atmosphere, from the weathering of rocks and from other ecosystems, and input of energy as either light or organic matter or both. Also each ecosystem has an output of gases, and energy to the atmosphere, and often an output of nutrients and organic matters to the other ecosystems as well.

ecotope. Ecological interpretation of biotope, a type of landscape with ecologically homogeneous areas.

ecotype. Stabilized forms of one and the same species having adapted themselves to different environmental conditions. Systematically, they are equivalent to the category (taxon) of subspecies.

ectosymbiosis. A situation in which an oranism has a mutually beneficial relationship with a host organism while remaining physically separated from the host.

ectosymbiotic commensals. The insects that feed on feathers, sloughed-off flakes of skin, or waxy epidermal exudates; for example, fleas and house flies.

ectothermic. Capable of maintaining body temperature by gaining heat outside itself.

edaphic factors. Physical, chemical, and biological characteristics of a soil, which determine the distribution and metabolism of plants.

edaphon. Collective name for the bacteria, fungi, and lower animals living in the soil. They play a vital role in biological decomposition.

eddy. An element of fluid, within a turbulent mass of fluid, which has a certain identity and life history of its own. Atmospheric eddies may range from about 10 mm to several hundred kilometres in size. The dilution (by diffusion) of a plume of gas from a stack is controlled by small eddies; large scale eddies, such as those associated with cyclones and anticylones, play a role in the long-range transport of pollutants.

eddy diffusion. The process by which gases, including smoke, diffuse into atmosphere; molecular diffusion is extremely slow by comparison and may be ignored.

Edeleanu process. In petroleum industry, a finishing process based on solvent extraction using sulphur dioxide as a solvent. This process removes undesirable aromatics and other polar compounds, gum and coloured constituents, and has been widely used for the manufacture of kerosine. The process yields an unpleasant waste acid sludge, which can be further decomposed in a special kiln where sulphur dioxide is converted into sulphuric acid.

effective height of emission. The height above the ground level at which a plume of waste gases is estimated to become horizontal. It is usually higher than the height of the chimney due to upward momentum and buoyancy of gases.

effective temperature. 1. A meteorological term for the temperature at which motionless, saturated air would create the same sensation off comfort in a sedentary worker wearing ordinary indoor clothing as that created by actual conditions of temperature, humidity, and the air movement. 2. The surface temperature of a black body that has the same size as a star and radiates the same amount of energy per unit area.

effervescence. The formation of gas bubbles in a liquid as a result of chemical reaction. It occurs during fermentation, during the action of acids upon carbonates, etc. Boiling is not regarded as effervescence, nor is the frothing produced in such actions as that of concentrated sulphuric acid upon sugar.

efflorescence. The process in which a crystalline hydrate loses water, forming a powdery deposit. It depends on the partial pressure of water vapour in the air. When it is less than the dissociation pressure of the hydrated compound the latter gives up all or part of its water of crystallization and becomes powdery.

effluent. Any liquid, slurry, or gas emerging from a pipe or similar outlet. It is usually used in connection with waste disposal of chemical of manufacturing plants, such as stack gases and residual liquid or semi-liquid mixtures discharged into rivers or lagoons.

effluent charge. A fixed fee levied by a regulating body against a polluter for each unit of waste discharged into public waters. The fee may be uniform for all waste producers in that area, or may be selective according to the composition of individual wastes or the absorption capacity of the local environment. The fee may be charged continuously at all times or it may be levied only when the conditions deteriorate below a specified level.

effluent stream. A stream whose channel lies below the water table and into which water flows from the zone of saturation.

efflux velocity. The linear velocity with which gas leaves a stack, which is equal to the volume of gas issuing from the stack mouth per second divided by the cross-sectional area of the mouth. If the efflux velocity is low, downwash is liable to occur. If several furnaces are connected to a single stack the efflux velocity is often undesirably low when some of the furnaces are not in operation, and it is an advantage to provide furnace with a separate flue extending to the top of the stack, inside the outer casing.

effusion. The passage of gases through small apertures under pressure. The relative rates of effusion of different gases under the same conditions are inversely proportional to the square roots of their densities.

Egnell's law. A law stating that the velocity of nearly straight winds in the upper troposphere increases with height at approximately the same rate that the air density decreases in any one fixed place above this level.

Ehlers-Danols syndrome. A group of hereditary abnormalties linked to deficiencies in the production of collagen and caused by both autosomal and sex-linked genes, characterized by joint hypermotility, tissue fragility, and abnormally stretchable skin due to the lack of sufficient or healthy collagen.

Ekatin. A systemic insecticide and acaricide suitable for control of sucking insects and mites in orchards, vineyards, hop gardens and on beet. At 0.02% concentration systemic effects persist for 2 to 3 weeks. It is a colourless oil, fairly soluble in water slightly soluble in light petroleum oils but soluble in most other organic solvents.

The acute oral LD_{50} for rats is 120-30 mg/kg. It is mainly used for aphid control (and also mites) on fruit, potatoes, beet, cereals, and vegetables. Also known as Thiometon.

Ekman layer. The transition boundary between the free atmosphere and the surface boundary layer in which the shearing stress is constant.

electrical storm. 1. A popular name for a thunderstorm. 2. An infrequent disturbance of the electric field in the lower atmosphere caused by strong winds and blowing dust, but without thunderstorm activity.

electrodecantation. The modified electrodialysis in which concentration of dispersed phase occurs simultaneously with dialysis due to electrophoresis and gravitational sedimentation; clear solution lying above concentrated dispersed phase is removed by decantation.

electron probe microanalysis. A method of analyzing a very small quantity of a substance by directing a finely focused electron beam on to it so than an *X*-ray emission is produced characteristic of the elements present in the simple. The diameter of the beam is usually about 1 μm and quantities as small as 10^{-14}g can be detected by this method. The method may be used for quantitative determination of for elements whose atomic numbers exceed 11.

electrostatic precipitation. A widely used method of controlling the pollution of air or other gases. It is based on the principle that if a gas is passed between two electrodes, one of which is supplied with a very high negative voltage, and the other is earthed, the gas and any particles of dust in suspension become electrically charged; the dust attracted to the earthed electrodes, where it collects and is dislodged by the mechanical device. Such units installed at large new power stations are designed to operate at collecting efficiencies of 99.3%

elution. In general, a process for extracting a solid substance from a mixture of solids by means of a liquid; as in the recovery of a vitamin adsorbed on an adsorbent by means of a solution. Specifically, a process for the recovery of sucrose from molasses.

elutriation. A method of separating particles using the difference in apparent weight which may exist between the particles when they are suspended in a fluid. In practice, the particles are usually allowed to settle against to the bottom, while fine material remains suspended and is removed with the fluid.

eluviation. The downward movement of materials in suspension or solution that are being carried from *A*-horizon to *B*-horizon of a soil by descending soil water. The occurrence and the rate of eluviation is usually determined by the texture and structure of the soil and the climatic conditions under which the soil has formed.

emanating power. Ratio of magnitude of emission of radioactive emanation released by solid material to total emission produced in material in given time interval.

emanation method. Method used for studying structure and surface of solid materials, and changes occurring in the solids. It consists of the introduction into the materials studied of radionuclide (*e.g.*, Ra-226) which decays to give gaseous emanation, the rate of evolution of which is measured.

emanations. In general, a gaseous substance given off from radioactive material. Specifically, collective name for three radioactive gases (isotopes of the element radon) occurring in natural radioactive series.

emerged bog. A bog that grows above the water table by drawing water up through the vegetation.

emergency core cooling system. A system devised to protect a nuclear reactor against the consequences of loss of a coolant, with resultant over-heating; it is based on the principle of injecting of water into the reactor when failure occurs.

emissary sky. A sky of isolated or small, separated groups of cirrus clouds that indicates the approach of a cyclonic storm.

emission. The introduction of pollutants into the atmosphere; and concentration of trace elements and transformation products of emitted substances in the upper layers of the soil.

emission factor. The average amount of a pollutant emitted from each type of polluting source in relation to a specific amount of material processed or burned.

emission inventory. The compilation of data, either by measurement or (more usually) by estimation, from which a more or less detailed map of the distribution of emission over a given area may be constructed, showing the positions of the more important sources and the amounts they emit, and the areas in which smaller emitters are concentrated with the emission per unit area for each. Also called emission survey and source inventory.

emission source. Any factory or other plant, furnace, chemical process, etc., that discharges pollutants into the atmosphere. Point source is the name given to a plant whose total emission of a pollutant is sufficiently large to warrant separate consideration in an emission inventory, rather than inclusion with other, smaller, emission sources under average emission per unit area. An emission of the order of 100 tonnes per year or more may lead to a plant being considered as a point source.

emission standard. Legally binding maximum allowed emission for a certain type of process, plant of installation, *e.g.*, expressed in terms of concentrations or mass flow rates per pollutant; The standard can involve a mobile source such as an automobile, or a stationary source such as a power plant. Emission standards are usually set in relation to the desired environmental quality standard, as indicator of the maximum level of pollution which can be permitted without creating a hazard to human health or causing a decline in the visual quality of the environment.

emitter. In the context of air pollution control, an emitter is any air pollution source, mobile or stationary. But in popular usage the word is synonymous with industrial polluter.

emulsifying agent. A substance which aids the formation of an emulsion, or which extends the range of temperature, concentration, etc., over which the emulsion remains dispersed, and, in general, increases the stability of the emulsion.

emulsion. A permanent suspension or dispersion, usually of oil or fat particles in water; the reverse also may occur, in which water is dispersed in an oil or fat. These are often designated as o/w (oil in water) and w/o (water in-oil) emulsions, the latter occurring frequently in crude petroleum. The intimate and uniform mixture of naturally immiscible liquids is made possible by the action of an emulsifying agent, commonly fatty acids or long chain alcohols, at the oil-water interface.

emulsoid. Historical term used to

define lyophilic sol. A colloidal dispersion formed when a liquid phase is dispersed over a liquid medium.

endangered species. Any plant or animal species which can no longer be relied upon to reproduce itself in numbers which ensure its survival. A species may become endangered due to natural environmental change, or due to human activity. It has been realized that for every one species which become extinct, an average of 30 other species which were dependent on that species move into the endangered category.

endemic species. Any plant or animal species confined to, or exclusive to, an area. Remote oceanic islands or isolated mountain peaks often contain a large proportion of endemic species. The term has also been used for any pest or disease-producing species occurring continuously in a given area.

Endosulphan. A non-systemic contact and stomach insecticide and acaricide. The technical product is a brownish crystalline solid, practically insoluble in water, but moderately soluble in most organic solvents. It is a mixture of two isomers. It is stable to sunlight but subject to a slow hydrolysis to the alcohol and sulphur dioxide. It is compatible with non-alkaline pesticides. The acute oral LD_{50} for rats is 110 (55-220) mg/kg. It is quite effective against most crop mites, and certain Hemiptera (aphids, capsids) and beetles.

Endosulphan is highly toxic by ingestion, inhalation, and skin absorption, and has been classified as hazardous poison. For endosulphan, the criterion to protect freshwater aquatic life has been estimated to be 0.056 μg/L as a 24-hour average and the concentration should not exceed 0.22 μg/L; and the criterion to protect saltwater aquatic life is 0.0087 μg/L as a 24-hour average and the concentration should not exceed 0.034 μg/L. For the protection of human health from the toxic effects of endosulphan ingested through water and contaminated aquatic organisms, the ambient water criterion to be 74 μg/L; while for the protection of human health from the toxic properties of endosulphan ingested through contaminated aquatic organisms alone, the ambient water criterion has been determined to be 159 μg/L. Also known as Thiodan.

endrex. *See* endrin.

endrin. A very toxic, broad-spectrum, persistent insecticide and acaricide isomeric with dieldrin. It is non-systemic, and non-phytotoxic at insecticidal concentrations, but is suspected of damage to maize. It is a white crystalline solid practically insoluble in water, sparingly soluble in alcohols and petroleum oils, moderately soluble in benzene and acetone. The technical product is a light brown powder of not less than 85% purity. It is stable to alkali and acids but strong acids or heating above 200°C cause a rearrangement to a less insecticidal derivative. It is compatibles with other pesticides.

The acute oral LD_{50} for male rats is 17.5 mg/kg. It is quite effective against many insects and mites, and is used mainly on field crops.

For endrin, the criterion to protect freshwater aquatic life is

0.0023 μg/L as a 24-hour average and the concentration should not exceed 0.18μg/L; and the criterion to protect saltwater aquatic life is 0.0023 μg/L as a 24-hour average and the concentration should not exceed 0.037 μg/L. For the protection of human health from the toxic effects of endrin ingested through water and contaminated aquatic-organisms, the ambient water criterion to be 74 μg/L; while for the protection of human health from the toxic properties of endrin ingested through contaminated aquatic organisms alone, the ambient water criterion has been determined to be 159 μg/L. The ambient water quality criterion for endrin is recommended to be identical to the existing drinking water standard which is 1 μg/L. Also known as Endrex.

entrainment. The process of collecting and transporting of a substance by the flow of another fluid moving at a higher velocity. For example, when smoke moves up a chimney, it not only carries gases, vapours of water and other material in suspension, but also solids such as particles of char, soot, grit, etc. Many of these particles might remain at the bottom of the furnace, but they are captured and forced up the chimney by the velocity of the upward moving smoke.

environment. All the factors (living and nonliving) that actually affect an individual organism or population at any point in the life cycle. The term environment is also sometimes used to denote a certain set of circumstances surrounding a particular occurrence. The environment of an organism includes:

(i) the purely physical or abiotic milieu in which it exists, *e.g.*, geographic location, climatic conditions, and terrain; and

(ii) the organic or biotic milieu including nonliving organic matter and all other organisms, plants and animals in the region including the particular population to which the organism belongs.

The environment of human being includes the abiotic factors of land, water, atmosphere, climate, sound, odours, and taste; the biotic factors of animals, plants, bacteria, viruses, and the social factors of aesthetics. All energy supply and consumption affects the local environment to some extent. Of particular importance has been air and water pollution from various sources.

environmental archaeology. The study of the relationship of human activity to the environment and environmental change, as shown by the archaeological record.

environmental capacity. A term used in planning to indicate the capacity of an area to accommodate motor vehicles, whilest maintaining an acceptable level of pollution and standard of environment, *i.e.*, without ruining the general comfort, convenience and aesthetic quality of an area.

environmental chemicals. Chemicals in combination that are man-made, for alleged beneficial use in man's environment. Such chemicals may include pesticides, insecticides, cylamates, and monosodium glutamate.

environmental exploitation. Withdrawal of more natural resources from environment than are returned to it.

environmental forecasting. A forecasting programme capable of timely and effective warning of technologically induced perturbations of any given health-welfare parameter of the population.

environmental hazard. A natural occurrence which threatens, or actually causes serious damage and destruction to, human settlements, man-made structures such as historical monuments roads and dams, economic activities such as agriculture and mining. Among the most serious environmental hazards are river floods, earthquakes, tsunamis, volcanic eruptions, landslides, and glacial outbursts.

environmental impact assessment. A method of analysis which attempts to predict the likely repercussions of a proposed major development upon the social and physical environment of the surrounding area.

environmental impact statement. A written statement that assesses and explores possible impacts associated with a particular project which may affect the human environment. Each environmental impact statement must include:

(i) a detailed description of proposed action, including information and technical data adequate to permit a careful assessment of the environmental impact;

(ii) discussion of probable impact on the environment, including any impact on ecological system and any direct or indirect consequences that may result from the action;

(iii) the discussion of any adverse environmental effects that cannot be avoided;

(iv) an assessment of the cumulative, long-term effects of the proposed action, including its relationship to short-term use of the environmental versus the environment's long-term productivity.

environmental improvement. Any form of pollution abatement, such as sewage treatment, cleaning the river basins, addition of secondary and tertiary treatment plants to handle the sewage effluent and sludge.

environmental information system. The computerized collection, storage, and manipulation of environmental data. The data may include a large proportion of geographical information along with data specific to the description of plants, animals, and other habitats.

environmental insult. The careless and casual approach of the of human beings towards the environment, some of the examples of environmental insults are throwing of garbage at roadside, improper handling of domestic effluents, and dead animal lying at the roadside, covered with flies and bloated by the gas of putrescence. The environmental insults are not too serious if they occur in limited amounts intermittently, but they become problems when continually recurring.

environmental lapse-rate. The actual decrease of temperature with altitude in earth's atmosphere above a particular place at a specific time. The environmental lapse-rate has a mean value of 0.66°C/100 m. However, this is of little importance, since the actual lapse-rate (which is necessary for the calculation of atmospheric stability and instability) is highly variable. It changes with the passage of different air masses.

environmental pathology. The study of pathology resulting from abiotic environmental agents. social attitudes.

environmental perception. The manner in which an individual or a group of people regards its environment. Each person tends to regard his home environment as the norm and to see its resource possibilities in terms of his own cultural traditions.

environmental pollution. The disturbance of the natural environment resulting directly and indirectly from human activities often involving substances being in the wrong place, at the wrong time, in the wrong amounts, and in the wrong physical and chemical forms. In other words, environmental pollution is the unfavorable alteration of our surroundings, wholly or largely as a by-product of man's action, through direct or indirect changes in energy patterns, radiation levels, chemical and physical constitution, and abundance of organisms. The cause and source of pollution are many, ranging from atmospheric emissions associated with the burning of fossil fuels to the application of fertilizers and pesticides, from the discharge of domestic and industrial effluent into rivers and other water bodies to the generation of intolerable noise levels. The results of pollution are diverse, ranging from the creation of acid rain to the rising of sea-level, from the breaking or disruption of food chains to the hazarding of human health.

environmental protection. That part of resource management which is concerned with the discharge to the environment of chemical and biological waste materials, and of physical effects (*e.g.*, radioactivity and sound) with a aim of providing a defence against interference, damage, or destruction, in relation to those beneficial uses of natural resources valued by the community.

environmental quality. A catch-all covering pure air, clean water, fertile soil, beautiful architecture, soft music, no dangerous pesticides and radiation, no starvation, survival of present species of human, animal, and plant life. It is obvious that we cannot have such an ideal environment quality but the best way is to see to it that the environment meets certain criteria and standards of quality, with minimum degradation.

environmental resistance. 1. The factors within a particular environment that prevent an organism from achieving its full biological potential; for example, many species of trees being dwarfed by the cold weather on the tundra. 2. The restriction of population growth through the interaction of one or more environmental factors.

environmental tolerance. The tolerance of change of each natural resource in man's environment. When change is induced by various pollutants, the limit of environmental tolerance become strained and may be exceeded. For example, a stream consists of a physical and chemical self-cleansing setup. Excessive pollution can strain this setup to the point of irreversibility, and the stream can die.

environmental toxicology. The study concerned primarily with the harmful effects of chemicals that are encountered by man either directly or indirectly because they are in the atmosphere, hydrodphere, lithosphere or biosphere, or by contact during occupational or recreational activities or by ingestion as food additives or food residues. Environmental toxicology includes serval specialized areas such as pollutants having toxic effect on man, pollution disturbing the ecological balance of the bisophere *i.e.*, biodiversity, or pollution affecting the aesthetics of the environment.

environment protection act, 1986. The Act was promulgated to provide for the protection and improvement of environment and matters connected therewith. The Act consists of 26 Sections distributed among four chapters, and extends to the whole of India.

The Act provides general powers to the Central Government to take all necessary measures for the purpose of (a) protecting and improving the quality of the environment, and (b) preventing controlling and abating environmental pollution. Besides other powers, the Central Government shall have power for:

(i) planning and execution of a nation-wide programme for the prevention, control and abatement of environmental pollution;

(ii) laying down standards for the quality of environment in its various aspects;

(iii) laying down standards for emission or discharge or environmental pollutants from various sources whatsoever;

(iv) restriction of areas in which industry, operations or processes shall not be carried out or shall be carried out subject to certain safeguards;

(v) laying down procedures and safeguards for prevention of accidents which may cause environmental pollution;

(vi) laying down producers for handling of hazardous substances;

(vii) examination of such manufacturing processes, materials and substances as are likely to cause environmental pollution;

(viii) carrying out and sponsoring investigations and research relating to problems of environmental pollution;

(ix) collection and dissemination of information on environmental pollution; and

(x) preparation of manuals, codes or guides relating to the preventing, control and abatement of environment pollution.

EPA. Acronym for *E*nvironmental *P*rotection *A*gency, which formulates standards for the protection of the environment and also, inter alia, conducts research to study the adverse health effects of air and water pollution.

EPA hazardous waste number. The number assigned by Environmental Protection Agency (EPA) to each hazardous waste listed in Part 261, Subpart D, of 40 CFR and to each characteristic identified in Part 261, Subpart C, of 40 CFR.

EPA identification number. The number assigned by Environmental Protection Agency (EPA) to each generator; transporter; and treatment, storage, or disposal facility.

epicolous. Describing an organism that lives on the surface of another without any effect on the host.

epideictic display. A behaviour pattern in which the members of a group collectively show themselves to an outside, so as to display the size and territory of their group.

epidemiology. A branch of medical science concerned with the study of the environmental, personal, and other factors that determine the incidence of a disease. For example, epidemiological studies have revealed that the prevalence of bronchitis is closely associated with air pollution, and that mortality and morbidity varies very closely with changes in smoke and sulphur dioxide.

epilimnion. The upper layer of deep lakes, rich in oxygen and nutrients, in which the primary production of producers takes place.

epipelic. Of or relating to organisms that inhabit the surfaces of water or sediment, or where water and sediment meet.

episode. A term applied in the air pollution literature to a very restricted number of incidents when, under unusual circumstances (persistent temperature inversion and stagnant air over a city surrounded by hills, accidental escape of pollutants from industry, etc.) air pollution has risen to abnormally high levels and has remained at these levels for several days, producing marked increases in illness and death.

equatorial countercurrent. A current flowing eastward near the equator in all oceans, generally between the westward-flowing north and south equatorial currents.

equatorial current. Either of two currents, the north equatorial current, or the south equatorial currents.

equatorial dry zone. An arid region of the equatorial trough, such as the area just south of the equator in the central part of the equatorial Pacific.

equatorial easterlies. The very deep trade winds in the summer hemisphere that extend to at least 8-10 km in height.

equatorial trough. A zone of low pressure lying between the subtropical high-pressure belts of the northern and southern hemisphere.

equatorial westerlies. The westerly winds found in the equatorial trough, separated from the mid-latitude westerlies by a broad belt of easterly trade winds.

equilibrium. 1. A state of balance in terms of the molecular concentration of compounds undergoing a reversible reaction. The equilibrium constant, K, is the ratio of the molecular concentration of the reaction products to that of the starting materials. It is strongly affected by temperature, which increases the rate of the reaction. Equilibrium exists when the rates of the two reactions are equal at a given temperature. 2. Physical equilibrium is said to exist when, in a liquid partially filling a closed container, the number of molecules expelled from the surface by internal molecular impact is equal to the number of molecules attracted back into the liquid at the interface when the air-space has become saturated, that is, when it can retain no more molecules of vapour. Thus, there is a reversible physical reaction which reaches equilibrium condition between two molecular concentration (of the liquid and the vapour, though no chemical change occurs.

equinoxial storm. A violent storm of rain and wind that is associated with the time of the equinox.

equipotential surface. A surface along which the gravity is constant at all points and for which the gravity vector is normal to all points on the surface. The geoid is an equipotential surface.

equitability. A property of population distribution that refers to the numerical equality of various species populations in a community; maximum equitability is attained when all species maintain approximately equal populations.

Eradex. *See* Thioquinox.

etesian. Any of the prevailing northerly summer winds in the eastern Mediterranean, especially the Aegean Sea, that bring clear skies and dry as well as cool weather.

Ethion. A non-systemic insecticide and acaricide, used mainly in combination with petroleum oils on dormant fruit as an ovicide and scalecide. It is non-phytotoxic. It is a pale-coloured liquid very slightly soluble in most organic solvents including kerosene and petroleum oils. It is slowly oxidized in air and is subject to hydrolysis by both acids and alkalis. The actue oral LD_{50} for rats is 208 mg/kg (for the pure substance) and 96 mg/kg (technical grade). Effective against eggs and dormant stages of pests (scales, leafhoppers, red spider mites, Heteroptera) on fruit trees. Some use against anthomyiid fly maggots on cereals and vegetables (in the soil). It is suspected of possessing carcinogenic activity, hence the exposure to workers by all routes should be carefully controlled. Also known as Embathion, Nialate, Hylemox.

ethoate-methyl. A systemic insecticide and acaricide with contact action, that is particularly effective against fruit flies. The pure compound is a white crystalline soild, almost insoluble in water, but soluble n benzene, chloroform, acetone, ethanol. It is stable in aqueous solution but hydrolysed by alkali.

The acute LD_{50} for male rats is 340 mg/kg; non-irritant. It is quite effective especially against Olive Fly and fruit flies, and is recommended for control of aphids, and red spider mites on fruit, arable and vegetable crops. Also known as Fitios.

ethylbenzene. A highly flammable liquid, classified as a priority pollutant; used as intermediate in the manufacture of styrene and a number of other chemicals and dyes. The occupational exposure to ethylbenzene should be controlled in such a manner so that no employee is exposed to ethylbenzene vapours at a concentration greater than 435 mg/m^3 of air, determined as a time-weighted average (TWA) concentration limit for up to a 10-hour workshift in a 40-hour workweek. The available data for ethylbenzene indicate that acute toxicity to freshwater aquatic life occur at concentrations as low as 32,000 μg/L, and would occur at even lower concentrations among the species that are more sensitive than those tested. For the protection of human health from the toxic effects of ethylbenzene ingested through water and contaminated aquatic organisms, the ambient water criterion has been set to be 1.46 mg/L; while for the protection of human health from the toxic properties of ethylbenzene ingested through contaminated aquatic organisms alone, the ambient water criterion has been determined to be 3.28 mg/L.

ethylene chlorobromide. One of the promising fumigants against the oriental fruit fly, but it is not as toxic as the closely allied ethylene dibromide. It has a lower boiling point than ethylene dibromide. The effect of this fumigant on fruit and plant material is similar to that of ethylene dibromide. It has not come into general use, although it has been adequate in many fields of application for which ethylene dibromide is also suited.

ethylene dibromide (EDB). A chemical acknowledged as a mild fungicide, although its value in controlling certain fungus diseases or root-disease complexes is widely known. It has been observed that ethylene dibromide at high dosages inhibited species of phytophthora, but remained ineffective against *T. basicola* and *R. solani.* Other than the phytophtora species, fungitoxicity of EDB was also shown against *Ceratostomella fimbriata,* the sweet potato black-root fungus.

In field trials, good control of the cotton wilt pathogen, *F. oxysporum, F. vasinfectum* by ethylene dibromide, has been obtained with the field soil infested with *M. incognita*, too. Later, it was found that the effectiveness of ethylene dibromide against *F. oxysporum.* In these cases, the presence of *M. incognita* must be seen as the main cause of the disease and *F. oxysporum* as only a secondary cause. Therefore, the elimination of the nematodes can result in complete control of the disease complex caused by the nematode and the fungus. In another nematode-fungus interaction (*e.g.*, Pratylenchus penetrans, Verticillium sp.), the control of the nematode resulted in marked reduction in the appearance of the vascular disease. The effects of several fumigants in soil infested with a *Fusarium sp.* capable of causing damping-off of peas, have also been investigated. It was concluded from these studies (based on the percentage of emergence of peas in treated and nontreated soil) that chloropicrin was the most fungicidal of all fumigants tested. 1,2-Dicloropropene had some fungitoxicity, but at dosages above those required to be nematicidal, while ethylene dibromide had little or no fungitoxicity to the *Fusarium sp.* tested.

Although the root knot nematode has a predisposing effect on cotton to Fusarium wilt, there is little indication that these nematodes predispose cotton plants to Verticillium wilt. Ethylene dibromide was applied at the rate of 42.7 L/hactare one week before planting and at the planting time to a field on which root knot nematode *M. incognita var. acrita* had been a serious problem for two years. Although excellent control of the root-knot of nematode was obtained and growth was more rapid in fumigated plots, the average proportion of Verticillium wilt was not significantly reduced by any treatment. Therefore, it appears that effectiveness of ethylene dibromide depends on the mechanism of interaction between the nematode and the fungus.

Ethylene dibromide has been classified as a hazardous chemical found to have carcinogenic activity among the humans and animals. Occupational exposure to ethylene dibromide is defined as any work involving handling, storage, use, or manufacture of ethylene dibromide. The action level is defined as equal to one-half of the recommended workplace exposure concentration. Occupational exposure to ethylene dibromide should be controlled so that no employee is exposed to ethylene dibromide at a concentration greater than 1.0 mg/m^3 of air, determined as ceiling concentration for any 15 minute period. The recommended standard is designed to protect the health and provide safety to the workers for up to a 10-hour workshift, 40-hour workweek over a working lifetime. Also known as 1,2-dibromoethane; glycol dibromide.

ethylene dichloride (EDC). A flammable and hazardous chemical found to have carcinogenic activity among the humans and animals; used as general solvent, and as scavenger for lead in gasoline, varnish and paint remover, and degreaser.

Ethylene dichloride is not as toxic to insects as other commonly used fumigants but it is useful in the fumigation of grain and seeds. Because both the vapours and the liquid are flammable, ethylene dichloride is mixed with some non-flammable material usually carbon tetrachloride (carbon tetrachloride) in the proportion of 3 parts ethylene dichloride to 1 part carbon tetrachloride by volume. The mixture applied according to recommendations has no adverse effect on the germination of seeds or the milling qualities of grain. Care must be taken to avoid excessive exposure. Although some plants appear to be tolerant to ethylene dichloride, severe injury has been recorded with certain species. Some fruits are also tolerant. This fumigant, therefore, should not be used alone or in a mixture for fumigating nursery stock living plants or vegetables without careful preliminary experiments on the particular species or varieties concerned.

Ethylene dichloride has been used in emulsion with water against the peach tree borer when soil temperatures were too low for effective use of paradichlorobenzene. Some injury has been reported to peach trees. Because ethylene dichloride is soluble in fats and oils, it is not recommended for use on cereals or foods with a high oil content.

Ethylene dichloride has the property of causing injury to the human liver and kidney from either excessive single or repeated exposures. Acutely, it is somewhat more toxic than carbon tetrachloride and under these conditions is also a central nervous system depressant and lung irritant. Chronically it is safer than carbon tetrachloride.

Occupational exposure to ethylene dichloride is defined as any work involving handling, storage, use, or manufacture of ethylene dichloride. Occupational exposure to ethylene dichloride should be controlled in such a manner so that no employee is exposed to ethylene dichloride at a concentration greater than 4.0 mg/m^3 of air (1 ppm), as determined by a air sample collected at flow rate between 25 and 200 ml/minute. The recommended standard is designed to protect the health and provide safety to the workers for up to a 10-hour workshift, 40-hour workweek over a working lifetime.

ethylene oxide. An industrial substance; the principal use of ehthylene oxide has been for fumigation of bulk grain in recirculating systems and in the vacuum fumigation of packaged foods and tobacco. It has also proved to be effective both under vacuum and at atmospheric pressure for destroying several species of snails entering the United States in military cargoes from the Mediterranean area. In recent years, ethylene oxide has been used extensively for the cold sterilization of medical supplies and instruments and also for preventing spoilage in foodstuffs and spices.

Despite a general impression to the contrary, ethylene oxide must be regarded as poisonous to man by inhalation, although it is not as lethal in comparatively low concentrations as some other fumigants. The threshold limit of 50 ppm for continuous daily breathing is higher than that set for many fumigants. Headaches, vomiting, shortness of breath, diarrhoea and changes in the blood have been reported as resulting from excessive exposure. Skin injury may result from excessive freezing following spillage of the chemical. There have also been reports of skin allergies. Of the commonly used fumigants, ethylene oxide is about intermediate in toxicity to insects. Ethylene oxide reacts strongly with living plant material causing either death or extreme injury. It is not usually recommended for use on seeds nursery stock or any growing plants.

Ethylene oxide has been enlisted as a potential carcinogen for the humans, and has been assessed as a hazardous air pollutant. The occupational exposure to ethylene oxide is defined as any work involving handling, storage, use, or manufacture of ethylene oxide at a concentration above the action level. The exposure to ethylene oxide should be controlled so that no employee is exposed to ethylene oxide at a concentration greater than 20 mg/m^3 of air, determined as a time-weighted average (TWA) concentration limit for up to a 8-hour workshift in a 40-hour workweek, over a working lifetime.

eubacteria. The name given to those bacteria which have simple unbranched cells, rigid cell walls, and flagella for movement.

eugenics. The study of methods for improving the quality of human populations by the application of genetic principles. The positive eugenics would seek to do this by selective breeding programmes, while negative eugenics aims to eliminate harmful genes by councelling any prospective parents who are likely to be carriers.

euphotic zone. An ocean zone in which light penetration is sufficient for photosynthesis. The euphotic zone effectively filters out the red, orange, yellow and green wavelengths in approximately the top 100 metres leaving only the blue light which provides the colour of oceans and lakes. Plankton is confined to the euphotic zone. Net primary production (NPP) for this zone show great variation, ranging from a low of 125 g/m^2/year in algae beds and reefs. The extent of the open oceans (332 million km^2) means that despite a low NPP, their cumulative production levels of about 4150 million tonnes per year make them the greatest single source of protoplasm production on the planet.

EURATOM. The European Atomic Energy Community, internal organization which also deals with the question of environmental control arising from the use of nuclear energy. It lays down basic radiation standards for the protection of the health of both workers in the industry and of the general population.

eurybaric. Describing an organism that is able to tolerate a wide range of atmospheric or hydrostatic pressure in its environment.

eurybathic. Describing an organism that lives at the bottom of a body of water.

euryecious. Species of wide ecological amplitude. They can exist under varied ecological conditions and are capable of enduring greater changes in the environmental factors.

euryhaline. Describing an organism that is able to tolerate a wide range of saline levels in its environment.

euryhydric. Describing an organism that is able to tolerate a wide range of moisture or humidity in its environment.

eusaprobic. A concept for the qualitative assessment of water; water containing such an amount of pollutants that can be decomposed microbiologically.

eustatic. A term used for worldwide changes in sea level as distinct from local changes. The formation and subsequent decline of continental icesheets were the main cause of eustatic changes in sea level during the pleistocene epoch. However, for the last 20 million years plate tectonics and seafloor spreading are believed to have been important factors in sea level changes.

eusynanthropic. Describing an organism that lives or thrives in human habitats.

eutrophication. The process of aging of a body of water by the growth of vegetation, particularly algae; these plants flourish and then die, their decay using up the dissolved oxygen of water with serious impairment of water quality. In lakes, rivers, harbors, and estuaries, the accumulation of nutrients include carbon, oxygen, hydrogen, sulphur, nitrogen, potassium, magnesium, calcium, and phosphorus. Algal blooms, thriving on these nutrients may be blue-green, red or brown in colour. If present in small numbers, these plants are helpful, as they contribute to the oxygen balance in lakes and streams, and also serve as a food for the fish. Industrial and domestic activity may greatly accelerate an otherwise slow aging process by increasing the amount of nutrients entering the water.

eutrophic lake. A lake characterized by an abundance of dissolved plant nutrients and by a seasonal deficiency of oxygen in the bottom layers; its deposits usually have considerable amounts of rapidly decaying organic mud and its water is frequently shallow. It has been found that as the time passes oligotrophic lakes become shallower by two processes; by filling from the bottom up by the outlet stream bed cutting down, thus lowering the lake surface. Their sides may also be eroded away to some extent and thereby help to fill in the deeper parts of the basin. Exactly when a lake passes from the oligotrophic to the eutrophic stage, it is difficult to determine for there is great variation of physical and biological conditions in lakes. Criterion that has been used to designate eutrophic lakes is that they possess a hypolimnion smaller than the epilimnion. It is not always easy to use this criterion however, since thermoclines may not develop every summer, especially in shallow lakes. When a thermocline forms, the hypolimnion may be so small and organic materials so abundant that stagnation occurs in the hypolimniom.

Life is abundant in eutrophic lakes, and plankton populations become especially high in the spring and fall. In clear lake, a large standing crop of plankton occurs, despite high turbidity and a consequent shallow penetration of light sufficient for photosynthesis. In this lake the spring phytoplankton productivity is not as great as the autumnal. Lakes may vary with respect to the dominant phytoplankton species present. Among the zooplankton of eutrophic lakes, dominant types may include rotifer, cladocerans, copepods, and protozoa. Since zooplankton feed on phytoplankton, their populations may be determined by phytoplankton populations, but probably in a complex manner.

evapouration ponds. Shallow, artificial ponds into which sewage sludge is pumped, permitted to dry and either removed or buried by more sludge. Such ponds are very frequently used in connection with industrial waste water disposal.

evaporite. The deposits of physico-chemical origin mainly involving precipitation and crystallization from saturated solutions; forms lenticular masses (if of terrestrial origin) or well bedded occasionally, regularly interstratified, with fragmental or organic sediment (if laid down in lakes or the sea). It deposits mainly from evapouration processes from lakes seas or evapouration of ground water drawn up through soil by capillary action. Chemical deposition from springs leads to formation of calcareous sinter.

evergreen. A term used for a plant that bears leaves throughout the year, each leaf being shed independently of others after every two or three years. The leafs of evergreens are often reduced or adapted in some way to prevent excessive water loss.

evolution. The gradual process by which the present diversity of plant and animal life rose from the earliest and most primitive organisms, which is believed to have been continuing for the past 3,000 million years.

excess air. Air in excess of the amount required theoretically to burn completely a unit mass of a fuel. It is normally calculated and reported as a percentage of the theoretical air. In practice, most fuels require more than the theoretical air to prevent the production of smoke. The excess depends both on the nature of the fuel and the design of the combustion unit.

exhalation. The process by which radioactive vapour or gases escape from the surface of soil or loose rocks where they are formed by decay of radioactive substances.

exhaust gases. Gases produced as a result of the burning of petrol and diesel in internal combustion engines. Exhaust gases mainly contain carbon monoxide, unburnt hydrocarbons, oxides of nitrogen, sulphur and lead compounds, soot and water vapour. These are harmful to human beings, as well as to plants and animals. The vegetation along the motorways is found to accumulate significant amounts of lead. In many cities, a major part of air pollution is caused by the exhaust gases from the motor vehicles.

exhaust gas recirculation. Technique to improve the combustion of pollutants in internal combustion engines, or reducing pollutant emissions.

exhaust trail. A condensation trail that forms when water vapour from an aircraft exhaust mixes with and saturates the air in the aircraft's wake.

existing hazardous waste management facility. A facility has commenced construction if:

(a) The owner or operator has obtained the federal, state, and local approvals or permits necessary to begin physical construction; and either

(b) A continuous on-site, physical construction program has begun; or the owner or operator has entered into contractual obligations, which cannot be canceled or modified without substantial loss, for physical construction of the facility to be completed within a reasonable time.

existing portion. That land surface area of an existing waste management unit, on which wastes have been placed prior to the issuance of a permit.

existing tank system. A tank system or component which is used for the storage or treatment of hazardous waste and that is in operation. Installation will be considered to have commenced if the owner or operator has obtained all federal, state, and local approvals or permits necessary to begin physical construction of the site or installation of the tank system and if either

(a) a continuous on-site physical construction or installation program has begun; or

(b) the owner or operator has entered into contractual obligations, which cannot be canceled or modified without substantial loss, for physical construction of the site or installation of the tank system to be completed within a reasonable time.

exogenetic. The term used to describe processes or events which take place at or very near the surface of the earth, *e.g.*, weathering, erosion, etc.

exosphere. The outermost layer of the earth's atmosphere, in which the density is such that an air molecule moving directly outwards has a 50% chance of escaping rather than colliding with another molecule. The exosphere lies beyond the ionosphere and starts about 400 km above the earth's surface.

exotic species. Animals or plants that need protection from humans in order to exist. Man is now trying to make up for the extinction of some species by classifying dwindling species of animals, as endangered species. When endangered species are brought in a zoo, in the hopes of reproducing, they become exotic species.

explosive. An unstable chemical compound which decomposes more or less violently when shocked or ignited, particularly when confined. Low explosives, typified by black powder and smokeless powder, burn or deflagrate rapidly, with evolution of gases. High explosives detonate, with production of a rapidly travelling shock wave of destructive violence.

exponential growth. A form of population growth in which the rate of growth is related to the number of individuals present. Increase is slow when numbers are low but rises sharply as numbers increase.

extended aeration plant. The low-capacity sewage treatment plant, suitable for small colonies. The organic loading is kept low with long aeration time to avoid sludge handling problem. Oxidation ditch is an example of extended aeration plant.

extinction. 1. The eradication of all members of a specific group of animals or plants. If the group involved is merely a local population, the process is referred to as local extinction. It is a natural and common event in the long history of biological evolution. Of the estimated five hundred million species of organisms that are believed to have ever existed on earth since life began, perhaps five to ten million are currently active. This represents an extinction rate of 98 to 99%. Obviously, these numbers are estimates, but the fact remains that extinction

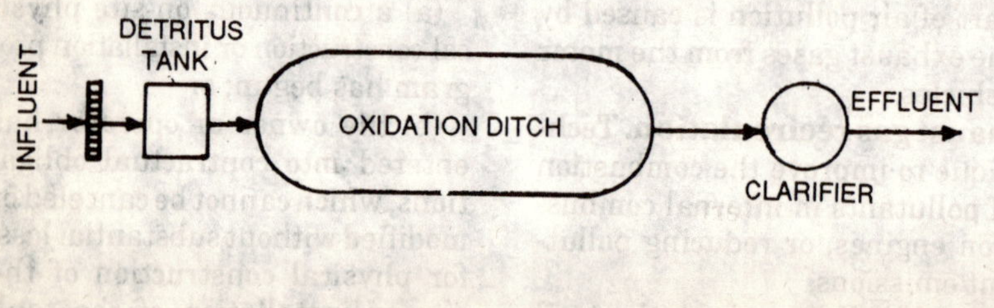

EXTENDED AERATION PLANT

has been the fate of most species of organisms. However, as some species were going extinct others were entering the biological arena for the first time. Studies of local extinctions suggest that certain kinds of species are more likely than others to become extinct. Species populations that already are low are prone to extinction because successful breeding is more difficult than in more numerous species populations. Many organisms at higher trophic levels such as carnivores, are usually low in numbers compared to their prey species and often have a lower reproductive rate than their prey. Thus, these species find responding to environmental change more difficult. Specialized organisms are also more likely to become extinct than are generalized ones. Since specialized organisms rely on a few key factors in the environment, anything that negatively affects these factors could result in their extinction. 2. A term that is by international agreement, reserved for application to certain quantities related to the diffusion. It should not be applied to the absorption of radiation.

extinct species. A species of animal or plant that has no living members. *See also* extinction.

extinguishing agent. In general, any compound used to put out fires. Water is, of course, the best-known fire extinguisher. It not only has a powerful cooling effect but also serves to keep oxygen away from the flame. Dry chemicals (such as a mixture of sodium chloride and sodium bicarbonate) are quite useful for extinguishing fires in metals and electrical equipment. Fires in hydrocarbon liquids are best controlled by use of chemical foam (carbon dioxide in water). The use of toxic halogenated hydrocarbons such as carbon tetrachloride and methyl bromide should be avoided. *See also* flame retardant.

extraction. 1. The separation method that makes use of differences in partition of various substances between two immiscible liquids. 2. In metallurgy, the term is applied to the mining of metals and separation of pure metals from their ores. Sometimes it is also called winning.

F

facility. All contiguous land, structures, other appurtenances, and improvements on the land used for treating, storing, or disposing of hazardous waste. A facility may consist of several treatment, storage, or disposal operational units (*e.g.,* one or more landfills, surface impoundments or combinations of them).

faculative lagoon. A lagoon used for the treatment of liquid organic wastes, in which aerobic action takes place in the upper layer, faculative in the middle layer, and anaerobic at the bottom of the lagoon.

faecal coliform organisms. Coliform organisms that are able to ferment lactose at about 313 K; frequently found in water, soil, and in contaminated foodstuffs; they comprise the genus Escherichia and to a lesser extent occasional strains of *Enterobacter, Citrobacter* and *Klebsiella.* Of these organisms, only *E. coli* is specifically of faecal origin being always present in the faeces of man, animals, and birds in large numbers and rarely found in water or soil that has not been subject to faecal pollution. Complete identification of *E. Coli* in terms of modern taxonomy would require an extensive series of tests, which would be impracticable for routine water examination. Therefore, detection and identification of these organisms as faecal organisms or presumptive *E. coli* is considered to provide sufficient information to assess the faecal nature of pollution. Regrowth of faecal coliform organisms in the distribution system is unlikely unless sufficient bacterial nutrients are present (biochemical oxygen demand BOD greater than 14.0 mg/L), water temperature is higher than 286 K, and there is no free chlorine residual.

faecal streptococci. The micro-organism frequently encountered in polluted waters. The occurrence of faecal streptococci in water generally indicates faecal pollution. This term refers to those streptococci normally present in the faeces of man and animals. It includes *S. faecalis, S. faecium. S. durans, S. bovis, and S. avium,* as well as strains with properties intermediate between them. These organisms rarely multiply in polluted water and they may be slightly more resistant to disinfection than coliform organisms. However, this indicator group has rarely been recommended for control of drinking-water quality because of their persistence in water with moderate salt concentration such as might occur with blended water supplies. Furthermore the widespread occurrence of *S. faecalis* var. liquefactions may detract from the significance of numbers of faecal streptococci less than 100 per 100 ml in drinking water, unless strain identification is part of the routine procedure. When used as a supplementary bacterial indicator, the ratio of faecal cloiform, organisms to faecal streptococci (greater than 3:1 for human wastes; and greater than 0.7:1 for other animal wastes) may be useful in locating the origin of faecal pollution in heavily contaminated sources of raw water, provided sufficient data are collected. In addition, these organisms can be used to assess the significance of doubtful results with the coliform test, particularly if coliform organisms are found in the absence of faecal coliform organisms. They can also be of much importance in checking water in the distribution system following repairs to mains.

fallout, radioactive. The descent to the earth's surface of the radioactive particles produced in a nuclear explosion; the radioactive particles themselves. It is often referred to simply as 'fallout', although this term is also applied to any solid particulate matter that settles out of the air on to the surface of the earth. This usage is sometimes broadened to include wash-out.

fanning plume. A smoke plume that occurs in stable air, when the gases quickly reach their highest level then travel horizontally, remaining visible for a long distance.

far infrared radiation. Electromagnetic radiation in the range of wavelength between 50 μm to about 800μm.

far ultraviolet. Electromagnetic radiation in the range of wavelength between 175 nm to about 300 nm.

fast breeder reactor. A type of fast nuclear reactor that used highly enriched fuel in the core, fertile material in the blanket, and a liquid metal coolant, having breeding ratio equal to one or more than one.

fast burst reactor. A nuclear reactor that produces microsecond pulses of fast neutrons which are used in biomedical research.

fast effect. Increase in neutrons due to fissions caused by fast neutrons in a thermal reactor.

fast neutrons. Neutrons moving with the speed at which they emerge from a ruptured nucleus and possess kinetic energies greater than 1 MeV as opposed to 'slow' or thermal neutrons whose speed has been reduced by impinging on a moderating substance such as graphite.

fast reactor. A nuclear reactor in which fission is produced by fast neutrons, with little or no mod erator to slow down the neutrons.

fatliquor. A mixture of meatsfoot oil and water, emulsified with a fatty acid or sulphonated oil. Fatliquors are used primarily in the leather industry to lubricate skins and hides, which tend to become hard and dry as a result of tanning; a major cause of water pollution, when discharged into rivers.

faucet. 1. A tap provided in ahousehold water filter or a water cooler. 2. The socket end of a pipe.

***f*-block elements.** The block of elements in the periodic table consisting of the lanthanide series (from cerium to lutetium) and the actinide series (from thorium to lawrencium). They are characterized by having two *s*-electrons in their outermost shell and *f*-electrons in their inner shell.

feces. The discharge of the bowels. Waste materials expelled from the bowels are called stereos or feces. They consists mostly of undigested cellulose (woody fibres from vegetable foods) and billions of useful bacteria that help to complete the digestive processes in the large intestine.

feeder. A channel for feeding water to a canal or a reservoir.

feeding main system. A system of water mains to feed the individual tanks at different levels from a water treatment plant.

feed-lot pollution. A kind of pollution resulting due to modern methods of raising beef on the hoof, that leads to the concentration of pollutants in small areas.

feed water. The water that is treated, pre-heated to boiling, and pumped for feeding a boiler.

Fenitrothion. A contact and stomach insecticide, particularly effective against rice stemborers, but a wide spectrum of activity, and a selective acaricide but of low ovicidal activity. It is a brownish-yellow liquid practically insoluble in water, but soluble in most organic solvents, and is hydrolysed by alkali of moderate persistence.

The acute oral LD_{50} for rats is 250-500 mg/kg. It is quite effective against lepidopterous larvae (rice stemborers especially), aphids, whitefiles, scales, mealybugs, capsids, psyllids, some fly larvae, some beetles, locusts, thrips, and sawflies. Also known as Accothion, Folithion, Sumithion.

Fenthion. A contact and stomach insecticide with a useful penetrant action, which, by virtue of low volatility and stability to hydrolysis, is of high persistence. It is a colourless liquid, practically insoluble in water, but readily soluble in most organic solvents. It is stable at temperatures up to 210°C and is resistant to light and to alkaline hydrolysis.

The acute oral LD_{50} for male rats is 215 mg/kg. It is of greater toxicity to dogs and birds, and is used for the control of weaver birds in Africa. It is effective against fruit flies, many caterpillars, leafhoppers and plant bugs, aphids, thrips, mites, sawfiles, some beetles; also weaver birds. Also known as Baytex; Lebaycid; Queleton.

ferment. A material which catalyzes certain organic reactions and which consists of an enzyme (a catalyst which is the product of a living organism or organisms, and which has an organic chemical composition) in association with other substances produced by the living organism, or with the organism or cell itself.

fermentation. An anaerobic, energy-yielding reaction brought about or catalyzed by enzymes or bacteria and involving the decomposition of carbohydrates (sugars and starches) to alcohol and carbon dioxide. The ethyl alcohol in spirituous liquors is derived in this way from cereals and fruits. The fundamental reaction is:

$$C_6H_{12}O_6 \rightarrow 2C_2H_5OH + 2CO_2$$

Yeast contains enzymes which activate this reaction, and the bacteria of some induce the fermentation responsible for growth of antibiotics. Bacterial action also accounts, for the souring of milk, spoilage of vegetables, and similar types of organic decomposition. Proteins can be obtained from petroleum by means of bacteria-induced fermentation. Several vitamins, including riboflavin and vitamin B_{12}, can be obtained as a result of fermentation.

fermentation, acetic. A fermentation reaction which produces acetic acid, commonly in the dilute form (vinegar) from alcohol-containing solutions or substances.

fermentation, alcoholic. A fermentation which produces ethyl alcohol, commonly by the action of a yeast, such as *Saccharomyces cerevisiae,* on a sugar, or a sugar-containing solution.

fermentation, amylolytic. In general, this term refers to the fermentation of starch; specifically, it refers to an incomplete fermentation of starch that does not yield simple sugars.

fermentation, butyric. A fermentation reaction which yields butyric acid.

ferricyanide process. A process for the removal of hydrogen sulphide from refinery emissions. The chimney gas is treated with a scrubber containing sodium ferricyanide, which reacts with hydrogen sulphide to form ferrocyanide, while hydrogen sulphide is oxidized to sulphur.

fertile material. Isotopes that can be transformed into fissile material by the absorption of neutrons, *e.g.*, thorium-232; uranium-238.

fertilizers. Materials which, when added to the soil, stimulate the growth of crops. Animal manures and vegetational wastes have been applied for thousands of years for this purpose. Natural organic fertilizers applied today include manure, compost and sawdust, while inorganic fertilizers include crushed limestone, gypsum, sulphur, and rock phosphate. In addition to this, vast amounts of manufactured chemical compounds of nitrogen, potassium, phosphorus, and sulphur are applied. Many of these manufactured fertilizers are quite soluble, and if not taken up by the plants are easily leached away; their movement out of the soil by run-off or by drainage may have a significant impact on water quality. Thus appreciable amounts of nitrates may be leached to water. Nitrate fertilizers may also pose a health hazard if excessive nitrates occur in food, particularly leafy vegetables, and in drinking water.

fibre glass. The name given to manufactured fibre in which the fibre-forming substance is glass; while glasses are a class of materials made from a mixture of silica and oxides of various metals and other elements, that solidify from the molten state without crystallization. A fibre is considered be a particle with the length-to-diameter ratio of 3 to 1 or greater. An action level is defined as half the recommended time-weighted average (TWA) environmental limit; while occupational exposure to airborne fibre glass is defined as exposure to airborne glass above the action level. Since the workers may be exposed to fibre glass by dermal or eye contact, occupational exposure includes contact with the skin or eyes to fibre glass where it is manufacture, used, handled, or stored. Occupational exposure to fibre glass should be controlled so that no employee is exposed to airborne concentration greater than 3 million fibres per cubic metre of air having a diameter equal to or less than 3.5 μm and a length equal to or greater than 10 μm, determined as a time-weighted average (TWA) concentration limit for up to a 10-hour workshift in a 40-hour workweek, over a working lifetime. The airborne concentration determined as total fibre glass should be limited to a time-weighted average (TWA) concentration of 5 mg/m^3 of air. The recommended standard is designed to protect the health and provide safety to the workers for up to a 10-hour workshift, 40-hour workweek over a working lifetime.

filter. In gas cleaning, an apparatus for separating solid or liquid particles from a gas stream in which they are suspended. This apparatus is generally formed of a porous or fibrous layer and/or of an assembly of porous and/or fibrous layers.

filter bag. An apparatus for removing dust from dust laden air, employing cylinders of closely woven material which permit passage of air but retain solid particles. The term 'breather bag' is deprecated. The bag may be up to 10 m in length and 1 m in diameter. An efficiency of 99-99.9% or better is quoted, depending on conditions. If a layer of chemically reactive dust is deposited on the fabric, gaseous pollutant in low concentration can be removed from stack gases (*e.g.*, fluorine compounds can be removed from the gases in the electrolytic production of aluminium). An installation containing many filter bags is known as a house.

filter bed. A bed comprising a filtering media of fine sand, coarse sand, pea-size gravel, medium-size gravel, and coarse gravel; used for filteraing water.

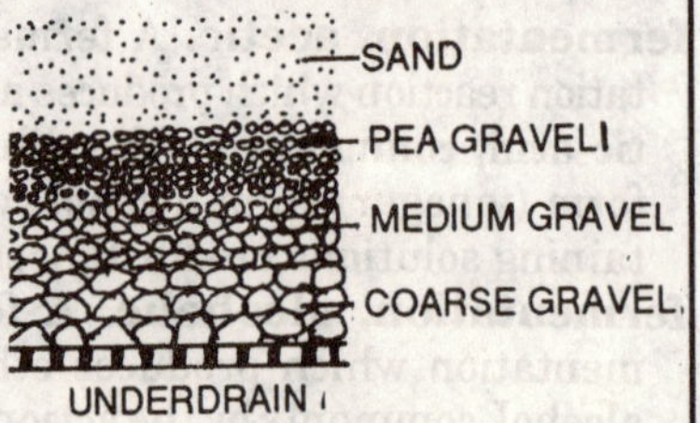

FILTER BED

filter blocks. Blocks of stone, concrete, or bricks, used in a trickling filter for the bio-filtration of sewage.

filter-feeding animals. Edible animals such as clams and oysters often act as pollutant amplifiers by filtering tainted water and concentrating the assimilated pollutants inside themselves. Since clams and oysters obtain their food by filtering the water in their immediate vicinity, the examination of such filter-feeding animals

FILTER UNDERDRAIN

is a method of determining whether or not the waters are fit for the humans to swim in.

filter underdrain. An under drainage system provided at the bottom of a filter bed to collect the filtered water.

filtrate. Solution separated from precipitate by filtration.

filtration. In general, an operation involving liquid-solid separation, used in chemistry and chemical engineering; it consists essentially of either gravity or forced flow of a liquid containing dispersed solid particles through a structure having a pore size small enough to retain the particulates. Filter paper, glass fibre mats, and similar materials are used for laboratory filtration.

final authorization. Approval by EPA of a state program that has met the requirements or section 3006(b) of RCRA and the applicable requirements.

final closure. The closure of all hazardous waste management units at the facility in accordance with all applicable closure requirements, so that hazardous waste management activities under parts 264 and 265 of 40 CFR are no longer conducted at the facility.

final cover. The layer of earth deposited over a completed sanitary landfill. The thickness of this cover varies from 0.5 to 1.0 metre.

fine chemical. A chemical produced in comparatively small quantities and in a relatively pure state. Pharmaceutical and biological products, perfumes, photographic chemicals, and reagent chemicals are examples of fine chemicals.

fineness. 1. The extent of subdivision of a substance. 2. The number of particles in a unit volume of a material. 3. The gold content of an alloy, expressed in parts per thousand.

fines. In the coal industry, coal having a maximum particle size usually less than 1.5 mm and rarely above 3 mm. In general, that fraction of a material that has been broken down into particles too small for a given use. If not properly contained, fines can cause much air pollution by dust.

fingerprint region. Spectral range in infrared from 650 to 1480 cm^{-1} with a number of bands characteristic for a molecule as a whole and non-characteristic for separate functional groups.

fining agent. A substance added to a liquid to clarify it. Examples are the addition of certain colloids or other materials to fermented beverages to remove suspended matter; and the use of certain oxides, such as arsenious oxide, in molten glass to aid in the removal of air bubbles.

finishing agent. A substance used to confer certain desired properties upon another substance, such as resistance to shrinking, oxidation, combustion, etc., and which is commonly applied or incorporated in the latter stages of the manufacturing process.

fire-damp. An explosive mixture of methane (CH_4) and air, formed in coal mines, due to decomposition of coal or other carbonaceous matter.

firing. The feeding of fuel into a furnace. It generally involves spreading of coal evenly over the entire fuel bed. Also known as stoking.

first flow. The condition, often

occurring in storm river discharges and combined river overflows, in which a disproportionately high pollution load in carried in the first-portion of the discharge overflow.

Fischer-Tropsch process. A process for the manufacture of liquid hydrocarbon fuels. It is basically a catalyzed reaction of carbon monoxide and hydrogen, yielding alphabetic hydrocarbons and oxygen- containing organic chemicals. The gaseous mixture of hydrogen and carbon monoxide can be obtained from petroleum or coal (water gas or synthesis gas). A number of metallic catalysts have been successfully used. Variations of this process are being applied to coal gasification.

fish mortality. The mass killing of fish, which indicates the rapid qualitative deterioration of waters. It can be caused by large amounts of poisonous substances getting into the water (such as ammonia, phenols, chlorine, detergents, cyanides, metal ions, greases, petrochemicals, etc.); chemicals leached out from agricultural lands and industrial wastes, and the thermal pollution of waters, that can result in reduction of dissolved oxygen.

fissile material. Material containing nuclides with nuclei undergoing fission with emission of neutrons in reaction with neutrons. Sometimes the term is restricted to isotopes that are capable of undergoing fission upon impact with a slow neutron (*e.g.*, U-233, U-235, Pu-239). Also known as fissionable material.

fission. A nuclear reaction brought about by direct impact of a neutron upon uranium-235 or upon the artificial element plutonium-239. This causes the nucleus to split or divide into two fragments (fission products); for example, U-235 yields radioactive isotopes of barium and krypton, the lost mass appears as energy. The process of fission is initiated by the bombardment with certain particles and radiations, especially neutrons of resonance energy, of certain fissionable atomic species, such as U-235, U-238, and Pu-239.

fission chain reaction. Chain of nuclear reactions; in neutron fission chain reaction, neutron hitting fissionable atom causes fission resulting in number of neutrons which in turn cause other fissions with emission of further neutrons; number of fission may diminish with time, remain constant or increase rapidly.

fission fragments. Nuclei formed in nuclear fission process with kinetic energy obtained during this process.

fission neutrons. Neutrons emitted in atomic nuclear fission reactions, immediately or with delay. Spectrum of fission neutrons is continuous with maximum at 1 MeV.

fission products. Fission fragments from atomic nucleus and products of their radioactive decay.

fission yield. Fraction of fissions leading to formation of product of specified mass number.

Fitios. *See* ethoate-methyl.

fixation. 1. In general, the act or process of making secure or permanent. Examples are found in microscopy, where the term is applied to the preparation of slides from specimens or sections cut from them; in photography, the term is applied to the removal from photographic film or other media, after exposure, of the unchanged light-sensitive substances, to prevent further change and hence marring the picture. 2. In immunology, the term fixation is applied to the method of preventing hemolysis by the complement; in perfume and flavour formulation, to the use of high boiling components to make the evaporation of the mixture uniform. 3. In chemistry, it refers to reactions and processes by which free nitrogen enters into chemical combination. *See also* nitrogen fixation.

flaky. In the description of particles, consisting of strata, laminae, or plate-like layers.

flame impingement. The impingement of a flame, or of a burning oil spray, against the wall of a combustion chamber. In addition to possible damage to the chamber, it may lead to the production of smoke by the immediate cooling of burning particles.

flame ionization analysis. A method of analysis based on the formation of ions when certain substances are introduced into a hydrogen-air flame. An electric field between the jet and a collector electrode accelerates the ions to the electrode. If the hydrogen, air, and sample flowwaters are maintained constant, the concentration of the substance undergoing analysis can be determined from measurement of the ion current. The technique, which was first developed as a gas chromatography detection system, is applicable to the determination of many organic air pollutants, particularly hydrocarbons.

flame retardant. A substance applied to, or incorporated in a combustible material to reduce or eliminate its tendency to ignite when exposed to a low-energy flame. Substances commonly employed for this purpose include compounds such as ammonium sulphamate, zinc borate, antimony oxychloride; alumina trihydrate, chlorinated organic compounds, certain organic phosphates and phosphonates.

flammability. A measure of the extent to which a material will support combustion. Any material which will catch fire instantly on exposure to spark or flame and which will burn rapidly and continuously, is termed as flammable material. Many solids which approach colloidal size in one or more dimensions are dangerous fire hazards, while others may take fire continuously at room temperature. Organic liquids having a flash point less than 300 K comprise a broad range of flammable materials. The U.S. National Fire Protection Association has assigned numbers to various flammable materials as follows:

4. Very flammable gases, very volatile flammable liquids, and materials that in the form of dusts or mists readily form explosive mixtures when dispersed in air. Shut off flow of gas or liquid and keep cooling water streams on exposed tanks or containers. Water spray is carefully used in the vicinity of dusts so as not to create dust clouds.

3. Liquids that can be ignited under almost all normal temperature conditions. Water may be ineffective on these liquids because of their low flash points. Solids that form coarser dusts, solids in shredded or in fibrous form that create flash fires, solids that burn rapidly, usually because they contain their own oxygen, and any material that ignites spontaneously at normal temperatures in air.

2. Liquids that must be moderately heated before ignition will occur and solids that readily give off flammable vapours. Water spray may be used to extinguish fire because the material can be cooled to below its flash point.

1. Material that must be preheated before ignition can occur. Water may cause frothing of liquids with this flammability rating number if it gets below the surface of the liquid and turns to steam. However, water spray gently applied to the surface will cause a frothing that will extinguish fire. Most combustible solids have a flammable rating of 1.

0. This rating is assigned to the materials that will not burn.

flare. The flame produced by the burning of surplus and residual gases at the top of a flame pipe at an oil refinery or other chemical factory. The gases cannot be released into the atmosphere owing to their unpleasant odour and to the explosion risk that would result. Flares can produce a great deal of smoke; this can be reduced by injecting steam or a water spray close to the point of ignition (this procedure, however, renders the flame noisy).

flash evaporation. Very rapid evaporation, especially as applied in industrial processes, in which liquids are heated under pressure is subsequently suddenly reduced causing the liquid, which is then superheated, to evaporate rapidly. Also known as flash drying.

floatation. A method of causing separation of undesirable substances from water or liquid wastes. The effluent is treated with chemicals causing the material desired to be collected to rise above the surface. Surface active agents and foaming agents are added in order to create a stable surface foam that will support the material rising to the top of the treatment tank; the loaded foam is then skimmed off.

floating boom. A device used in combatting oil spills to contain the size of the spill and prevent it from contaminating greater areas of the ocean surface. The floating boom is a mechanical barrier at the air-sea interface that extends sufficiently downward into water to prevent the oil from flowing under it, and projects high above the sea's surface to prevent the oil from slopping over the boom and into clean water. Thus a floating boom is like a floating fence, buoyed up by chambers, empty oil drums, etc., and dressed with a weighted skirt to keep it upright and functional as an effective barrier. The boom can be joined and premanufactured in sections.

floating suction pump. Spills of oil from containers and appliances in which it is stored or utilized are among the most serious forms of water pollution, as they spread very rapidly over wide stretches of water and seriously impair the exchange of gas and the other life functions of the biotop. For the most part, dispersal of the oil film is left to the self-purifying properties of the sea itself. The lighter constituents in the oil evaporate within one to two weeks. The less volatile components combine with the seawater to form a dark viscous slick, which after a few weeks either sinks to the seabed, drifts up onto beaches as lumps of tar, or collects in eddy currents. Chemical processes to get the oil to sink by the application of dispersion agents or emulsifiers encounter strong opposition. Their use is particularly questionable in shallow coastal waters, as they are capable of poisoning the creatures living on the seabed and in the water above it. The best solution seems to be to confine the oil spills to the sea's surface by appropriate means and there to destroy with a suction or pump them off. For dispersal of localized oil slicks of limited a suction appliance (floating suction pump) has been developed. It consists of a funnel- shaped pan, the outer rim of which is kept by means of floats a few mm below the surface of the sea. This outer rim is capped by a floating hollow rim. In the pan, the water is lowered by continuous supply of the water by means of a rotary pump. In this way the hollow rim is made to sink and the floating oil film runs into the. pan. When sufficient oil has collected, an oil pump sucks the oil away through suction funnels, the immersion level of which is controlled by another flow. If no more oil is present in the hollow, the oil pump switches off automatically. The water pump, on the other hand, runs continuously. Appliances of this type are built with performances of up to 40 cubic metres per hour. In addition to this system and similar substantially stationary systems which absorb oil from one spot, mobile oil collectors are being developed with performances of up to 60 cubic metres per hour.

flocculants. Chemical agents that cause clumping of undesirable solids in suspension and subsequent precipitation of these solids.

flocculation. A type of aggregation of finely divided solid particles dispersed in a liquid or semiliquid matrix; under certain conditions they tend to clump together to form small clusters or 'flocks' similar in appearance to tufts of fibre.

flock. A finely divided, low-gravity pulverized material made from vegetable fibres; it is flammable when suspended in air as a dust. Its uses are as a diluent in rubber, plastics and paint mixtures. Cotton linters can be considered as a type of flocculation. *See also* flocculation.

flow controller. An automatic device used to control the rate of filtration through a filter bed.

flow, laminar. Flow in which the air moves smoothly along streamlines which air arranged in parallel layers or sheets.

flue dust. Fine particles of alloys or metals emitted along with the gases of metallurgical furnaces.

flue gas. A catch-all term referring to the smoke emerging from incinerator flues to the stack, smoke coming out of the top of a chimney, or gases caused by incineration which are sent from the flue to a secondary combustion chamber, to be burned. Flue gas mainly consists of nitrogen, carbon dioxide, carbon monoxide, oxygen and oxides of nitrogen and sulphur; along with some moisture, and particulate matter.

fluidized bed. An apparatus in which finely divided solid, usually sand, is supported and rendered fluid-like (fluidized) by a column of rapidly moving gas, usually air, admitted from below. Conditions in a fluidized bed are such that fuel (*e.g.*, oil or coal) is rapidly distributed in it, without the need for special burner systems. If suitably crushed limestone or dolomite is also introduced, much of the sulphur in the fuel is fixed as sulphur and the emission of sulphur oxides in the stack gases is correspondingly reduced. The content of nitrogen oxides is also much lower than that of stack from ordinary furnaces, on account of the lower combustion temperature.

fluidized-bed combustion. A method of burning fuel in which the fuel is continually fed into a bed of reactive or inert material while a flow of air passes up through the bed, causing it to act like a turbulent fluid.

fluo- (or fluor- or fluoro-). A prefix indicating content of fluorine, as fluobenzene, fluorocholoroform. The prefix fluo- also indicates the presence of fluorescence.

fluoranthene. A tetracyclic hydrocarbon obtained from coal tar; classified as priority pollutant. The available data for fluoranthene indicate that acute toxicity to freshwater aquatic life occur at concentrations as low as 3980 μg/L, while acute and chronic toxicity to saltwater aquatic life occur at concentrations 40 and 16 μg/L respectively; and would occur at even lower concentrations among the species that are more sensitive than those tested. For the protection of human health from the toxic effects of fluoranthene ingested through water and contaminated aquatic organisms, the ambient water criterion to be 42 μg/L; while for the protection of human health from the toxic properties of fluoranthene ingested through contaminated aquatic organisms alone, the ambient water criterion has been determined to be 54 μg/L.

fluorescence. Type of the photoluminescence depending on emission of light during transition of atoms or molecules from electronically excited state to other energetically lower electronic state of like multiplicity.

fluoride. From pollution point of view, fluorides are defined as those compounds of fluorine that are inorganic solids at room temperature, having components that do not have exposure limits more restrictive than that proposed here for fluoride, and any gaseous fluorides that are emitted simultaneously with particulate fluorides as defined above. The addition of fluorides to drinking water to prevent dental caries (tooth decay) had been opposed by some doctors and toxicologists but now has been endorsed by all major U.S. and international health organizations. The application of fluorides in tooth pastes or for internal consumption hardens the enamel on teeth and so provides protection against destruction of the teeth by caries. Against the fluoridation of drinking water, various toxicological and legal arguments have been adduced. Fluoride at high concentration produces a corrosive effect on glass, steel and a number of other metals. Fluorides are now frequently added to certain pharmaceutical products, including toothpastes and vitamin supplements.

Traces of fluorides occur in many water sources of water and higher concentrations are often associated with underground sources. In areas that are rich in fluoride-containing minerals, *e.g.*, fluorapatite, well-waters may contain up to about 10 mg/L of fluoride or even more. The highest natural level reported is 2800 mg/L. Most waters contain below 1 mg/L of fluoride. Occasionally, fluorides may enter a river as a result of industrial discharges. The levels of fluoride in tap-water are very similar to those found in the source water, except where fluoridation of the supply is practised. In general, unfluoridated supplies contain less than 1 mg of fluoride per liter, but, depending on the type and situation of the source, may very occasionally contain up to 10 mg/L. In most parts of the world such sources have now been identified. Where fluoridation of water supplies is practised, fluoride concentration is normally within the range 0.6-1.7 mg/L, ambient air temperature usually being the deciding factor. With a consumption of 2 litres of water per day, between 1.2 and 3.4 mg of fluoride per day could thus be ingested from drinking-water in those areas where fluoridation is practised. Elsewhere, the daily exposure will range from a fraction of a milligram to perhaps 20 mg in very exceptional circumstances.

Fluorine-containing compounds are present in the air, mainly arising from industrial emissions. Concentrations in air will vary, depending on the type of industrial activity, but it has been estimated that the general exposure, equivalent to less th^n 1 μg/m^3 of air is insignificant in comparison with ingested fluorine.

Virtually all foodstuffs contain at least traces of the element. All vegetation contains some fluoride, which is absorbed from soil and water. Some foods may contain high levels, particularly fish, some vegetables, and tea. For example, the fluorine content of some fish can be as high as 100 mg/kg, and tea may contain more than twice that concentration, in contrast to most other foodstuffs, which rarely exceed 10 mg/kg. The use of fluoridated water in food processing plants can often double the level of fluoride in prepared foodstuffs.

Various consumable household products, such as toothpaste, tooth powders, mouth washes, chewing gum, vitamin supplements, and drugs, may contain added quantities of soluble fluoride, mainly in inorganic form. Such compounds are commonly added to dentifrices, typically at concentrations of about 1 g/kg. Studies have shown that significant quantities of fluoride can be absorbed by this route and a possible absorption of about 50 μg of fluoride per brushing has been demonstrated. The use of topical applications of fluoride solutions can contribute to an increased absorption. Mouth washes can provide as much as 2 mg of fluorides, including tablets containing sodium fluoride used as an anticarcinogenic agent. Regular use of such tablets can provide up to about 1 mg of fluoride per day.

Fluoride ingested with water is almost completely absorbed, while fluoride in the diet is not as fully absorbed as from water, but the absorption is still rather high, although in the case of certain foods (*e.g.*, fish and some meats) only about 25% of the fluorides may be absorbed.

Absorbed fluoride is distributed rapidly throughout the body. It is retained mainly in the skeleton and a small proportion is retained in the teeth. The amount of fluoride in bone increases up to the age of 55 years. At high doses fluoride can interfere with carbohydrate, lipid, protein, vitamin, enzyme, and mineral metabolism. Many of the symptoms of acute fluoride intoxication are the result of its binding effects with calcium. Fluoride is excreted primarily in the urine. The excretion is influenced by a number of factors, including the general health of the person and his previous history of fluoride exposure the rate of retention decrease with age, and most adults can be regarded for practical purposes as in balance. Under this steady state condition the fluoride present in the body is sequestered in calcified tissues; most of the remainder is present in plasma and thus available for excretion. Skeletal sequestration and renal excretion are the two major ways by which the body prevents the accumulation of toxic amount of the fluoride ion.

In high doses, fluoride is acutely toxic to man. Pathological changes include haemorrhagic gastroenteritis acute toxic nephritis and various degrees of injury to the liver and heart muscle. The acute lethal dose is about 5 g as sodium fluoride, *i.e.*, about 2 g of fluoride. In animals, a variety of serve symptoms have been observed as a result of environmental exposure to fluoride in highly contaminated areas. Chronic effects from high exposure in man are primarily related to mottling of teeth and fluorosis, in which bone structure is affected, sometimes to a very alarming degree, producing serious crippling. Chronic effects on kidneys have also been observed, generally in persons with renal disorders. Other less common problems, including effects on the thyroid, are known as a result of high exposure. Initial signs and symptoms of intoxication include vomiting, abdominal pain, nausea, diarrhoea, and even convulsions.

Epidemiological studies in areas where the concentration of fluoride in the water is naturally high have only rarely shown adverse effects which included mottling of teeth and skeletal fluorosis in areas of exceptionally high levels in water.

Occupational exposure to fluoride should be controlled so that no employee is exposed to fluoride at a concentration greater than 2.5 mg/m^3 of air, determined as a time-weighted average (TWA) concentration limit for up to a 10-hour workshift in a 40-hour workweek.

fluorine. At an estimated 0.065% of the earth's crust, fluorine is roughly as plentiful as carbon, nitrogen or chlorine, and much more plentiful than copper or lead, though much less abundant than aluminium or iron. Fluorine is the most reactive member of the halogen family. It is a strong oxidizing agent and therefore is a fire hazard in the presence of combustible materials. It has the highest bactericidal activity of all the halogens; and is classed as a bone-seeking element. A number of industrial processes are known to release fluorine-containing compounds into the air of the work place, and there are numerous documented examples of human exposure, in particular in aluminium smelters and glass manufacture. Such exposure to fluorine under these conditions (*i.e.,* concentrations of up to several milligrams per cubic metre of air) could provide the major contribution to the total exposure. However, with improvements in working conditions, this route of exposure becomes far less significant.

Occupational exposure to fluorine should be controlled so that no employee is exposed to fluorine at a concentration greater than 2.0 mg/m^3 of air, determined as a time-weighted average (TWA) concentration limit for up to a 10-hour workshift in a 40-hour work-week, over a working lifetime.

fluorocarbon. Any of the compounds of fluorine and carbon. Large numbers of such compounds are known; in many of their properties they resemble the hydrocarbons. The series C_nF_{2n+2} shows a sequence of increasing boiling points in successive members that is closely analogous to that of the paraffin hydrocarbons. The chemical inertness of the fluorocarbons makes them useful solvents, lubricants, and insulators.

fluorocarbon polymers. The polymers of substituted polyethylene monomers of the general formula $(XCX\text{-}XCF)_n$, where X = F, H, Cl, CF_3, or $CF_3\text{-}CF_2\text{-}CF_2\text{-}O$. Their decomposition products are defined as substances that are thermally generated from fluorocarbon polymers. In this case occupational exposure is defined as any exposure to fluorocarbons polymers that may involve the production of decomposition products. Due to lack of sufficient information regarding the impact of decomposition products of fluorocarbons on the human health, the employers as well as the employees should take all possible steps to keep occupational exposure to the decomposition products as low as possible.

flux. 1. In the metallurgical industries, a substance added to minerals or metals to promote fusion in a furnace; in brazing and soldering, a substance used to promote easy flow of solder and prevent oxide formation. 2. In physics, the rate at which particles, electricity, heat, fluid, etc., flow or are transferred, expressed in terms of quantity per unit area per unit time.

fly ash. The low density, finely divided, noncombustible particles in a flue gas. The combustible particles are called blackbirds because they are black, while fly ash is often grey.

fog. A suspension of very small water droplets in the air, generally reducing the horizontal visibility at the earth's surface. It is formed when the relative moisture content reaches 100%, that is, when the vapour pressure equals or exceeds saturation point. Advection fog is formed in the lower part of a moist air mass which moves over a colder surface. Evaporation fog is formed when saturation has caused a cold and stable air mass by rapid evaporation from an underling warm water surface. Sea fog is a form of advection fog which forms over the sea. Upslope fog is the fog formed on windward slopes of hills or mountains by forced ascent of air and associated adiabatic expansion and cooling. Frontal fog is caused along a front, in the formation of which there occurs mixing of the two air masses present. Ground fog is the name given to radiation fog of small vertical extent though often dense, through which the stars may often be seen by night and the sun by day. High inversion fog is caused by the extension downwards to the ground of a cloudy layer of stratus formed under an inversion. Mixing fog is formed when warm air is suspended above a layer of cold air close to the ground so that, owing to the interchange and turbulence of water vapour, the warm air can penetrate in to the cold air below it. As a result of the fall in temperature of the mixture caused by intermingling in relation to the saturated warm air, the saturated moisture pressure is reduced and the water vapour are condensed. Ice fog is the name given to a suspension of numerous minute ice crystals in air, reducing the visibility at the earth's surface. Mixing fog of thin and of short duration, is produced by the mixing of two moist but non-saturated air masses of different temperature. Radiation fog is caused by the radiational cooling of the earth's surface, and thus cooling of the surface air, to a degree sufficient to cause condensation of water vapour contained in the air.

Fonofos. An insecticide particularly suitable for the control of soil maggots and other soil insects. It has caused some damage to seeds when placed in their proximity. Persistence in soil is moderate, that is, of the order of eight weeks.

Fonofos is a pale yellow liquid; partically insoluble in water, but miscible with most organic solvents such as kerosene, xylene, etc. It is quite stable under normal conditions. Acute oral LD_{50} for male rats is 8-17 mg/kg. It is effective against most soil pests, such as root maggots, soil caterpillars, wireworms and other beetle larvae, crickets, symphylids.

food allergies. Many infants and adults have allergies to certain foods. These allergies (a hypersensitive state acquired through exposure to a particular allergen) may develop at any age. A person who is allergic to one food is often allergic to related foods. For example, peanuts belong to the pea family, and persons who cannot eat peanuts usually cannot eat beans and peas.

food poisoning. Illness caused as a result of intake of contaminated food. There are occasional outbreaks of food poisoning in which large groups of people have become violently sick after a picnic or public dinner. These outbreaks are usually due to contamination with *staphylococci* bacteria. The large outbreaks generally occur when nonacid foods like meats, potato salad and cream filled pastries are allowed to stand at room temperature for several hours before being consumed. The *staphylococci* multiply enormously, producing toxins (poisons) that cannot be destroyed by reheating. People with *staphylococci* food poisoning are miserably sick with cramps, diarrhea, and vomiting. This kind of illness can be most dangerous for young children and people in poor health. The other kind of food poisoning is botulism, which is due to a toxin produced by a bacterium called *Clostridium botulinum*. The outbreaks of botulism are generally due to improperly processed canned food. The third type of food poisoning can be due to *salmonella* infection. Many animals harbor various types of salmonellae, and outbreaks are usually traced to animal products. The organism is destroyed by cooking but not by freezing or drying. The symptoms of salmonella food poisoning are much like those of staphylococcus poisoning but are not due to a toxin but to intestinal infection. The shigella organisms are related to the salmonellae and have been found to be the cause of bacillary dysentery. Scientists have discovered that a bacterium called *Clostridium perfringens*, a normal inhabitant of the human intestine, can cause trouble if it gets into food. It can cause the very dangerous wound infection known as gas gangrene. Food can also be contaminated by the bacterium that causes strep throat-hemolytic streptococcus infection.

forensic toxicology. A subject closely related to clinical toxicology, and deals with the medical and legal aspects of the harmful effects of chemical on man, often in postmortem material, for instance, where there is a suspicion of murder attempted murder or suicide by poisoning.

formaldehyde. A colourless hazardous liquid with a pungent odour, found to possess carcinogenic activity in animals. Its vapours are irritant to eyes causing tear formation, and irritating to respiratory tract causing coughing and difficulty in breathing even in concentrations below the threshold limit value. Acute poisoning by the ingestion of formaldehyde causes intense upper abdominal pain, retching and vomiting, and unconsciousness; while the direct contact with the skin can cause eczema. The occupational exposure to formaldehyde is defined as exposure to formaldehyde in air at a concentration in excess of 0.6 mg/m^3, based on 30 minute sampling period. The occupational exposure to formaldehyde should be controlled in such a manner so that no employee is exposed to formaldehyde at a concentration greater than 1.2 mg/m^3 of air (1 ppm), for any 30 minute sampling period. This standard is designed to protect the health and provide safety to the workers for up to a 10-hour workshift, 40-hour workweek over a working lifetime.

Formothion. A contact and systemic insecticide and acaricide. In plants it is metabolized to dimethoate. In loamy soil the half-life is 14 days. It is a yellow viscous oil or crystalline mass, slightly soluble in water, miscible with alcohols, chloroform, ether, ketones, and benzene. It is stable in non-polar solvents, but is hydrolysed by alkali and incompatible with alkaline pesticides.

The acute oral LD_{50} for male rats is 375-535 mg/kg. It is effective against many sap-sucking insects and mites, especially aphids and red spider mites, and some fly larvae. Also known as Anthio.

formula weight. The sum of the atomic weights from the formula written for the molecule, although it may be known that the substance does not exist as separate molecules, *e.g.*, some proteins. For many substances it is molecular weight, but in the case of common salt, for example, 58.5 represents its formula weight rather than is molecular weights as any such crystal is a 'giant molecule' composed of a large number of sodium and chloride ions.

fouling. A form of marine pollution involving the attachment and growth of marine plants and organisms to hulls, pilling and other objects under water. Fouling is caused by barnacles, mussels, etc. Odour from a rendering plant can be considered a form of fouling in air. The difference is that the fouling of air is generally for a short period and atmospheric action normally cleans up the foul odour. But current flow or tidal action does very little to clean up the fouling of objects placed in a marine medium.

foundry pollution. Furnace effluent from the foundry where the alloys are manufactured or used at high temperature. The furnace effluent contains oxides of sulphur, carbon monoxide, waste gases, and entrained inorganic particulates. Because the fumes contain recoverable metals, the gases should be treated by scrubbing or in a bag house.

freeboard. The vertical distance between the top of a tank or surface impoundment dike and the surface of the waste contained therein.

free liquids. Liquids that readily separate from the solid portion of a waste under ambient temperature and pressure. (This is determined by the paint filter test).

free-living nitrogen fixers. Important component of the ecosystem, include certain bacteria (*nitrobacteraceae*), algae, and microorganisms.

free-living organisms in water. The free-living organisms generally considered significant in water supplies include plankton and macroinvertebrates. Plankton consists of macroscopic or small organisms that live primarily in suspension in the water column. Phytoplankton consists of the free-living bacteria, fungi, and algae. The algae are chlorophyll-bearing organisms, having different colours. They are autotrophic, unicellular or colonial, and motile or non-motile. The fungi and bacteria are largely heterotrophic. Zooplankton consists of free-living protozoa, rotifers, cladocera, copepods, worms and, in their early stages of development or during brief excursions, the larvae, of some aquatic insects and fish. The macroinvertebrates include the larger benthic animals, such as aquatic insect larvae, crustacea, and gastropods. Plankton organisms are important in water supplies because they interfere with water-treatment processes, produce substances toxic to humans, harbour human pathogens, and contribute organic matter, which may be converted to halogenated organic compounds during chlorination. The macro invertebrates may affect the efficiency of water distribution systems and the acceptance of water by consumers. The algae may present problems because of their occurrence in raw surface water, and uncovered storage reservoirs containing treated (finished) water. In addition to these, zooplankton may occur in open wells. The occurrence of macro-invertebrates related to water supply problems is limited to distribution systems. The abundance and species composition of algae in surface water supplies are governed by a combination of natural environmental conditions. Maximum algal counts in surface water range from only a few to many millions of organisms per ml. The algae in surface waters are most frequently dominated by the diatoms, followed by the coccoid green and blue-green algae. Winter populations are generally dominated by the pennate diatoms, whereas in summer, the centric diatoms, coccoid greens, and blue-green are most abundant. In late summer, or where temperatures remain above 298 K throughout the year, the blue-green algae often comprise the bulk of the algal biomass. A wide variety of free-living organisms has been found in water supply distribution systems, including fungi, algae, protozoa, rotifers, worms, water fleas, shrimps and other crustacea, spring-tails, midge larvae, mussels, and snails. Initial reports on these occurrences were based on investigations following complaints of the appearance of animals at consumers taps. More recently, systematic studies have revealed the presence of organisms in numerous networks even where there was no obvious reason to suspect their presence. There is mounting evidence that some toxic substances produced by some algae in water supplies may have a significant adverse effect on public health. Poisonous species occur in two major groups of algae; yellow-greens (*Xanthophyta*) and blue-greens (*Cyanophyta*). The toxic blue-green algae are the most important in fresh water supplies. Toxic substances released by algae may penetrate the treatment works. In laboratory experiments, aluminium coagulation, filtration, and chlorination were not effective in the removal of algal toxins. Even treatment by activated carbon in quantities similar to those used in water treatment was unsuccessful. The occurrence of public health problems related to algae is quite limited. Substances similar to the endotoxins of Gram-negative bacteria have been isolated from several blue-green algae. Algae and their extracellular products can represent a large part of the horny matter in surface water supplies and may be important sources of precursors in the formation of trihalomethanes during chlorination. The free-living animals that have been reported to occur in water supplies in temperate regions are not known to cause disease directly, but some have been shown to ingest and protect pathogenic organisms under laboratory conditions.

free radical. A molecular fragment or an ion that one of more unpaired electrons, rendering it highly reactive. Although free radicals are generally very short-lived in gaseous systems, their high reactivity enables them to take part in chemical reactions that would not otherwise occur. Thus, in the atmosphere, certain free radicals play a significant role in the production of aldehydes, ketones, acetylnitro peroxide and other constituents of photochemical smog.

French drain. A sloping trench back-filled with coarse stones, which drains away surface and surface water, usually with the help of a land drain.

fresh water zones. A portion of the world's aquatic environment, broadly divided into standing water and running water. Standing water generally includes bogs, lakes, ponds, swamps, while the running water includes rivers, springs, streams, and brooks.

front. The surface of separation of two air masses. The line of intersection of the surface of separation of two masses with another surface or with the ground. Cold front is any non-occluded front, the front separating two cold air masses which are brought into contact as the result of the process of occlusion. Warm front is referred to any non-occluded front which moves in such a way that warmer air replaces colder air.

frontal fog. The fog associated with the passage of the boundaies separating unlike air masses. Such boundaries are known as fronts. Frontal fog is formed chiefly through saturation of the cold surface layer of air by rainfall from the overrunning warm air aloft.

frother. Substances that make longer lasting air bubbles by reducing surface tension, *e.g.*, used in froth flotation process.

froth flotation. A method for separating different particles from a crushed ore. Its effectiveness depends on the fact that different particles have different 'wettabilities'. If a particle is easily wetted by a solution, it will sink; but if not it can be carried to the surface in a froth. The mixture used usually contains an oil, such as pine or eucalyptus, and the air is forced through the emulsion to create violent agitation and frothing. The mixture is made to flow through a series of cells and the oiled and unwetted particles are carried to the surface in the froth, continuously overflowing the rims of the cells. The method is particularly useful because, by altering the composition of the mixture, particles of different types can be removed in succession.

fuchsin-formaldehyde method. A method for the determination of sulphur dioxide. Air is passed through a solution of sodium hydroxide and glycerol; sulphur dioxide reacts to from sulphurous acid, which in turn reacts with a solution containing basic fuchsin, sulphuric acid, and formaldehyde to give a red or violet colouration, which is determined spectrophotometrically.

fuel. Any substance that evolves heat as a result of combustion can be used as a fuel. The most common materials used for heating and electric power production are the so-called fossil fuels (coal, petroleum and the gases or liquids derived from them). Economic feasibility is usually the critical factor in selection of a fuel for a given purpose. Quite distinct, from combustible fuels are the nuclear fuels whose energy is derived from controlled disintegration of atomic nuclei; they are used exclusively in electric power reactors.

fuel cell. An electric cell that converts the chemical energy of a fuel directly into electric energy in a continuous process. Such cell has total reaction consisting in oxidation of easily available fuels (*e.g.*, coal, hydrocarbons, water gas). An electrochemical reaction takes place at the electrodes and will continue as long as fuel is supplied. An electrolyte is necessary to act as a conducting medium. The electrodes are of generally porous carbon to permit diffusion of the gases, *e.g.*, hydrogen and oxygen, into the cell. The electrode reactions are comprised of the oxidation of hydrogen on the anode (the negative electrode) to hydrated protons with the release of electrons; and on the cathode the reaction of oxygen with protons to form water vapour with the consumption of electrons. Electrons flow from the anode through the external load to the cathode and the circuit is closed by ionic current transport through the electrolyte. In an acid cell, the current is carried by proton.

fuel, colloidal. Fuel oil containing pulverized coal.

fuel, fossil. A general term for any fuel (*e.g.*, coal and petroleum) formed from the remains of plants and animals. *See* coal.

fuel injection. The introduction under pressure of fuel into the combustion air (of an internal combustion engine). The system is now used in some spark-ignition gasoline engines, replacing the use of a carburetor; when properly adjusted it gives better control of the mixture and reduces emission of air pollutants.

fuel, petroleum. Any of a wide range of petroleum products used as liquid fuels for heating equipment or engine. They may be classified as distillate fuels and residual oils. The more important distllates include, in the order of increasing boiling range, gasoline, kerosine, and gas-oil (including some diesel fuels). Residual oil is the heavy oil that remains in a refinery still after removal of the different distillate. Diesel fuel is the name given to a group of products ranging from distillates (of low sulphur content) for high-speed engines to heavy residual blends (with a sulphur content of up to 4%) for large low-speed engines. Fuel oil is the heavy distillate, residue, or mixture of the two. It is used as fuel for the production of heat or power. Gas-oil is the name given to distillate (atmospheric or vacuum) hav-ing a viscosity and a distillation intermediate between those of kerosine and spindle oils. It is treated, if necessary for use as a fuel for the production of heat or power. The sulphur content of gas-oil is about 0.5-1%. A generic term for distillate fuel oils widely used for domestic heating, is heating oil.

fuel, pulverized. Finely ground coal, usually meeting specified particle size limits.

fuel, solid smokeless. A term commonly used in the United Kingdom for 'authorized fuel'. While such fuels produce much less smoke than bituminous coal, some of them are by no means smokeless.

fuel tank. A tank other than a cargo tank, used to transport flammable or combustible liquid, or compressed gas for the purpose of suppling fuel for propulsion of the transport vehicle to which it is attached or for the operation of other equipment on the transport vehicle.

Fulham-Simon-Carves process. A proposed process for removing sulphur dioxide from stack gases by scrubbing with solutions containing ammonia. The sulphur is recovered as ammonium sulphur, but with the decline in popularity of this substance as a fertilizer, the economic prospects of the process have also declined.

fuller's earth. A clay having a high adsorptive capacity. It is widely used as a bleaching agent, as a filter, and for removing grease from fabrics. It mainly contains montmorillonite with other hydrated aluminium silicates and accessory minerals such as quartz, mica and glauconite.

full life cycle tests. These are the typical chronic toxicity tests. These tests measure the effects of chronic exposure to a chemical on reproduction, growth, survival and other parameters over one or more generations of a population of test organisms. Groups of test organisms are exposed to a series of concentrations of test chemical. Chronic or full life cycle toxicity test is an important tool for understanding and evaluating the potential hazard of toxicants to organisms. A chronic toxicity test can indicate the concentrations of a chemical that will interfere with normal growth, development and attainment of reproductive potential of an organism.

fumes. Solid particles less than one micron in diameter, present in dirty gas stream, that are trapped in vapour in the gases as chemical reactions occur, form fumes. The term is used for the whole of the combustion gases and the particles entrained by them (smoke). By extension, also for the gases charged by particles resulting from a chemical process or a metallurgical operation; often used in the plural (fumes) for visible clouds of gases, vapours, or aerosols that usually have a choking or unpleasant smell.

fumigant. A pesticide or bactericide applied either indoors or in a closely restricted locality in the form of a vapour or gas. Common outdoor fumigants include *p*-dichlorobenzene, sulphur dioxide, and hydrogen cyanide. Phenol and naphthalene, as well as sulphur compounds are used for disinfection of sickrooms.

fumigation. In air pollution contexts, the appearance at ground level of pollutants that were previously (a) in a poorly dispersed smoke plume or (b) trapped in a temperature inversion (or between two inversion layers), as a result of turbulence (*e.g.*, turbulence arising from morning heating of the earth's surface by the sun).

functional tests. The tests performed for measuring chronic toxicity of chemicals through various physiological functions or functional responses of organisms. Functional responses includes, physiological and behavioural responses as affected due to exposure to sub-lethal concentrations of toxic chemicals. Among the types of functional responses that have been measured in different organisms exposed to toxicants are, changes in blood chemistry, histology, swimming performance, avoidance, respiration, enxyme activities, sensory perception, and disease resistance. Such tests have been used in studies on bioaccumulation and biotransformation processes also. Many of the functional responses are sensitive indicators of sublethal toxic effects. Some of the commonly used functional tests in toxicology are:

(a) behavioural responses;

(b) histo-patological examinations; and

(c) enzymatic activities.

fungal diseases. Disease caused in animals as a result of fungal invasion. Most fungi are harmless, but a few are pathogenic causing skin and systemic infections. Those which are pathogenic to the skin, hair and nails produce superficial fungal diseases. Those which invade the body produce deep fungal diseases. Commonest among the superficial fungal diseases is the ringworm or tinea; tinea of the body (*Tinea corporis*); tinea of the groin (*Tinea cruris*); infection of the feet (*Tinea pedis*); tinea of the nails (*onychonychosis*); tinea of hair and scalp (*Tinea capitis*). Among the deep fungal diseases the commonest are: coccidiomycosis (bones and skin); blastomycosis; *sporotrichosis* etc.

fungi. A group of simple plants lacking chlorophyll. Some authorities do not regard fungi as plants and include them with other organisms of uncertain affinities in the kingdom Protista. Fungi are classified in the taxonomic division Mycota or Fungi. They can either exist as single cells or make up a multicellular body called a *mycelium*, which consists of filaments known as hyphae. Most fungal cells walls composed chiefly of chitin. Fungi exist primarily in damp conditions on land and, because of the absence of chlorophyll, are either parasites or saprophytes on other organisms. The Mycota can be subdivided into four main classes, the Phycomycetes, Ascomycetes, Basidiomycetes, and Fungi Imperfecti. The principal criteria used in classification are the nature of the spores produced and the presence or absence of cross walls within the hyphae.

fungicide. Synthetic or biosynthetic compounds used to control fungal diseases. Fungicides used now-a-days include both inorganic and organic compounds. Older fungicidal agents for agricultural purposes included sulphur, lime, and their combinations; inorganic copper compounds such as Bordeaux mixture and copper oxychloride. Various metallic naphthenate have been used to impregnate tent fabrics and clothing.

fungistat. A substance that checks the growth of fungi.

fungitoxic. A substance that exerts a toxic effect upon fungi.

furan. Any of a large group of compounds containing furan ring, which consists of four carbon atoms and one oxygen atom bound together in a cyclic ring. The furans include a large number of compounds including some sugars, and many of these are beneficial. In popular sense, the term 'furan' has been referred to a relatively small subgroup of furans, the dibenzofurans. These compounds consists of a furan ring integrated into a pair of benzene rings, so that each benzene ring shares two carbon atoms with the furan ring. When chlorine atoms are attached to one or more outer carbon atoms of the benzene rings, the polychlorinated dibenzofurans (PCDF) are formed. Dibenzofurans are found as trace contaminants in most combustion products, including incinerator smoke, cigarette and cigar smoke, and automobile exhaust.

furfuryl alcohol. A colourless, mobile liquid becoming brown on exposure to air; may react vigorously with some mineral and organic acids; used in making wetting agents, corrosion resistant sealants and cements, and polymers. Occupational exposure to furfuryl alcohol is defined as exposure to airborne concentration of furfuryl alcohol at or above one-half of the recommended workplace environmental limit. Occupational exposure to furfuryl alcohol should be controlled so that no employee is exposed to furfuryl alcohol at a concentration greater than 200 mg/m^3 of air (50 ppm), determined as a time-weighted average (TWA) concentration limit for up to a 10-hour workshift in a 40-hour workweek, over a working lifetime. The recommended standard is designed to protect the health and provide safety to the workers for up to a 10-hour workshift, 40-hour workweek over a working lifetime. Also known as 2-furylmethanol, or 2-(hydroxymethyl) furan.

fyrite apparatus. A portable instrument for measuring the carbon dioxide content of flue gases. A known amount of the gas is introduced into the apparatus by means of a rubber bladder. When the instrument is turned upside down, the gas is bubbled through a solution of potassium hydroxide; a final reading is obtained in about one minute, within the limit of 0.5% error.

G

galactotoxin. A poisonous substance of ptomaine (a crystallizable, nitrogenous basic substance, produced by bacteria in dead animal or vegetable matter) generated in milk by the growth of microorganisms.

galvanic corrosion. Electrochemical corrosion associated with the current in a galvanic cell, caused by dissimilar metals an electrolyte because of potential difference of two metals.

galvanizing. Application of a protective layer of zinc on metal, chiefly steel, to prevent or inhibit corrosion. The length and extent of the protection are dependent upon the weight or thickness of the zinc coating. It is applied by (*a*) the hot-dipping process by passing the metal through molten zinc; or by (*b*) electrodeposition of zinc by a plating process, usually onto strip or wire.

Ganga action plan. The Central Ganga Authority was constituted in February 1985 to guide and oversee the implementation of a programme for restoring the quality of river Ganga. The Authority, under the Chairmanship of the Prime Minister reviews the overall progress of Ganga Action Plan at regular intervals and provides guidance. The Monitoring Committee and the Steering Committee of the Action Plan also review the progress from time to time. The three State Governments of U.P., Bihar and West Bengal are involved in the plan. The schemes are of six categories, *viz.*,

(a) interception and diversion,
(b) treatment of wastewater,
(c) low cost sanitation,
(d) river front development,
(e) electric crematorium, and
(f) other aspects.

Of these 50 schemes have already been completed.

gangue. A term used in extractive metallurgy to refer to the waste rocky or siliceous content of metal ores which is separated by floatation or elutriation. It is also a component of slag, which separates from the ore on smelting. Ore residues are sometimes called tailings; the latter term is also used in other industries for any residual processing waste.

Gardona. A selective insecticide used against lepidopterous and dipterous pests on the aerial parts of crops; very low mammalian toxicity; some translaminar action. It is a white crystalline solid, sparingly soluble in water, but soluble in chloroform (40% w/w), methyl chloride (40%); in xylene (15%) and acetone (20%). It is temperature stable, but slowly hydrolysed by water, particularly under alkaline conditions. The acute oral LD_{50} for rats is 4000-5000 g/kg. It is very effective against lepidopterous and dipterous pests of fruit, rice vegetables, cotton and maize. With certain exceptions it does not show high activity against Hempitera, and because of rapid breakdown is not effective in the soil and shows promise against pests of stored products. Also known as Tetrachlorvinophos.

gas carbon. A hard deposit consisting of fairly pure carbon, found on the walls of the retorts used for the destructive distillation of coal in the manufacture of coal gas. It is a good conductor of electricity, and it is used for making carbon electrodes. Also known as retort carbon.

gas chromatography. A very sensitive method of analysing the components of a complex mixture of volatile substances. The apparatus consist of a long narrow tube, packed with an inert support material of uniform particle size (*e.g.*, diatomaceous earth) that has been coated with a non-volatile liquid, called the stationary phase, the whole tube and its content being maintained in a thermostatically controlled oven. The sample to be analyzed is carried through the tube by a noble gas, carbon monoxide, or nitrogen, so that the passage through the tube of various components of the mixture is selectively interfered with the stationary phase, some components passing through the tube more rapidly than others. A detector measures the electrical or thermal conductivity, or some other characteristic property, of the gas leaving the column, differences being recorded on a strip chart, which indicates peaks corresponding to the various components. The instrument is calibrated by analysing samples of known compositions. Mixtures in small quantities can be separated into its constituents and thus detected without interference. This technique has been successfully applied for the detection of many pollutants present in the air.

gas, coal. A mixture of gases produced from bituminous coal by destructive distillation at high temperatures. The composition varies, the major constituents being hydrogen, methane, and carbon monoxide. It was formerly used for domestic and industrial heating and lighting but in many areas it has been replaced by natural gas.

gas, ideal. A hypothetical gas that obeys Boyle's law and Charle's law. In practice no gas is ideal, although a few (*e.g.*, helium and nitrogen) are very close to it a high temperature and low pressure. The gases in the atmosphere offer a reasonably close approximation to ideal behaviour if they are not saturated with water vapour.

gas, inert. A gas that does not react with materials with which it is in contact; nitrogen, for example, is widely used in the laboratory and in industry as an inert gas. For the inert gases, *see* noble gases.

gas, liquefied petroleum. A mixture of light hydrocarbons, gaseous under conditions of normal temperature and pressure and maintained in the liquid state by increase of pressure of lowering of temperature. The principal components are propane, propene, butanes, and butenes.

gas, natural. Gaseous hydrocarbons (mainly methane) from underground deposits, the production of which may be associated with that of crude petroleum.

gasohol. A fuel, chiefly for internal combustion engines, composed of a 9/1 ratio by volume of unleaded gasoline and water-free ethyl alcohol. Its octane number is essentially equivalent to that of gasoline.

gas oil. A liquid petroleum distillate with viscosity and boiling range between kerosine lubricating oil, usually includes diesel fuel, heating oils and light-fuel oils.

gasoline. A refined mixture of hydrocarbons having an octane number ranging from about 60 to 100 or more; highly flammable and hazardous; used primarily as a fuel for automobiles and airplanes. The mixture consists of more than 100 different hydrocarbons. Generally high octane gasoline is made by catalytic cracking, platinum being one of the most effective catalyst. Occupational exposure to gasoline is defined as any work involving handling, storage, use, or manufacture of gasoline at a concentration above the action level. Occupational exposure to gasoline should be controlled so that no employee is exposed to 300 ppm or more of gasoline vapours, determined as a time-weighted average (TWA) concentration limit for up to a 10-hour workshift in a 40-hour workweek, over a working lifetime. For the ways in which gasoline and the combustion of gasoline can contribute to air pollution, *see* carbon monoxide; nitrogen oxides; smog; and tetraethyllead.

gas, refinery. Gas produced in the refinery of crude petroleum and consisting mainly of hydrocarbons. It is used as a fuel in the refinery.

gas, reformed. A gas of low calorific value manufactured from one of high calorific value by thermal process.

gas, sewage. Gas produced during the treatment of sewage. It consists largely of methane and can be used as a fuel in the sewage disposal works.

gas, sour. Gas containing sulphur compounds (mainly hydrogen sulphide and mercaptans). The term is sometimes applied to natural gas that contains more than a specified amount of hydrogen sulphide. *See also* sweetening.

gas tar. Coal tar, the tarry matter produced in the distillation of bituminous coal, and obtained from coal gas by separation.

gastritis. Inflammation of the stomach; may be the result of eating irritating foods, drinking too much alcohol, infections with bacteria or viruses, allergies, or as a complication of other diseases. The general symptoms include anorexia (lack of desire for food), nausea, vomiting, diarrhea, cramps, and tenderness in the abdomen, hematemesis (spitting up of blood), fever chills, headache and muscular aching. Poisoning by contaminated foods or by chemicals can also be the cause of gastritis.

gas washbottle. An apparatus for passing a gas or mixture of gases through a liquid in order to remove an undesirable constituent. The gas may enter the liquid through a plain glass tube to from numerous tiny bubbles and so increase contact with the liquid (the same effect is also achieved by designs in which the gas is forced to follow a long spiral passage through the liquid). The device is frequently used in the chemical analysis of pollutants in air.

gas washing. A general term for gas cleaning or purifying processes that use a liquid as the collecting medium. If such processes are used to remove sulphur oxides from stack gases, the latter are cooled and on emission from the stack tend to descend rapidly to ground level, causing an unacceptable nuisance, no matter low satisfactory the efficiency of remove of sulphur oxides. *See also* Battersea process; Fulham-Simon-Carves process.

gel. A term used in colloid chemistry to denote a structure formed by substances of high molecular weight, in which the macromolecules consist of long chains or fibres. The substances which readily produce gels include certain proteins (collagen), and carbohydrates such as starches, complex sugars, and related compounds (pectin). They absorb many times their own weight of water, with consequent swelling and set to a viscous or semisolid jelly (gel) when cool.

gelation. Stiffening of colloidal system into uniform mass without separating dispersed phase and dispersion medium. Also known as gelling.

gel filtration. A chromatographic procedure for the separation of a mixture of molecules on the basis of size, through the capacity of porous polymers to exclude solutes above a certain size.

gene. The unit of inherital factors or characteristics. Genes ensure the transmission of specific character from one generation to another. The exact nature of genes is not yet fully known. The view currently held is that the genes, which are carriers of genetic information are made up of groups of four bases (thymine, cytosine, guanine and adenine). Each human being possesses an even number of chromosomes, which is characteristic of the species and fixed. In man the number is 46 (twenty three pairs). Each gene determines some particular characteristic by regulating the production of important proteins used by the cell. Paired genes, called alleles, regulate given characteristics of the body, such as eye colour or blood type. Sometimes one member (one allele) of a gene pair can over power the instructions of its partner. The powerful allele is said to be dominant while its partner is recessive. If the members of the gene pair are alike (both dominant or both recessive) the organism is said to be homozygous in respect to that gene. If one member of a gene pair is dominant and the other is recessive then the organism is heterozygous for that gene. The genetic make up of a given person is called his genotype. The physical appearance that result for the genotype is referred to as the phenotype. The characteristics of the organism are passed on to the offspring by the genes. In the gonad (the female ovary or the male testis), the production of egg or sperm is carried on, in a process called the meiosis. Chromosome pairs, containing these genes, are divided up so that the sperm or egg contains only half the number (haploid). Therefore, when sperm and egg unite during fertilization to form union cell, the original number (diploid) characteristic of the species is again present there. Sometimes mistakes occur during this process of meiosis and defective chromosomes or gametes (sperm or egg) result. In principle, a given gene is always found on the same chromosome in a given place (locus); the sequence of genes on a chromosome is thus invariable; but if a chromosome undergoes rearrangement (*e.g.*, translocation) this will lead to a modification of hereditary character *e.g.*, the appearance of chromosomal diseases, and in other cases, there is a sudden modification called a 'mutation' of a gene or a group of genes, either spontaneously or under the effect of a physical or chemical mutagenic agent.

generator. Any person, by site, whose act or process produces hazardous waste identified or listed in part 261 of EPA, or whose act first causes a hazardous waste to become subject to a regulation.

genetic conservation. The retention of plants and animals for the purpose of safeguarding their genetic information. In practice this can be done by establishing collections of plant and animal protoplasm, by conserving those geographical areas which show the greatest natural plant and animal diversity or by selective breeding in captivity.

genetic counsellor. The specially trained physicians usually pediatricians who possess knowledge about all kinds of congenital and hereditary defects. Some human diseases are the result of abnormal structure in a given gene. The genetic counsellor knows that these diseases may be transmitted to a certain percentage of the affected person's children. Among such disorders are diabetes insipidus, Huntington's chorea (chronic progressive involuntary muscular twitching), polycystic kidney disease, cystic fibrosis, muscular dystrophy, sickle cell anemia and albinism. The genetic counsellor can determine the probability that children with these diseases will be produced by affected parents. Other human disorders result from chromosome irregularities when cells contain the wrong number of chromosomes or when damaged chromosomes are passed on to the child.

genetic defects. The disorders in the body that result from abnormalities of the chromosomes. The process called meiosis which occurs in the human ovary and testes distributes one-half of the normal number of chromosomes to the egg or sperm. This assures that, after fertilization (joining of egg and sperm), the new embryo has the full complement of chromosomes. Normally the process of meiosis works well and the chromosomes are generally of proper structure and are of correct number (forty six). Sometimes, however, errors occur during meiosis and chromosomal abnormalities result. The identification of chromosomal abnormalities in a child involves the microscopic examination and photography of specially prepared human cells. There are twenty-two-pairs of chromosomes which determine body characteristics. These chromosomes are called autosomes. The remaining pair consists of sex chromosomes. Males have two different sex chromosomes, designated *XY*. Females have two *X* chromosomes and are designated *XX*. Abnormalities can occur in either the autosomes or the sex chromosomes.

Autosomal abnormalities. The twenty two pairs of autosomes are subject to various abnormalities of either number (more or less than twenty-two pairs) or structure. These variations cause deformity. Three major syndromes (disease entities) are associated with the incorporation of an extra autosome into the human organization. This type of arrangement, called trisomy. involves having three instead of two (a pair) given autosomes. Children with an extra number-21 chromosome (trisomy-21) have mongolism, also known as Down's syndrome. Trisomy-18 occurs once in every 6500 live births. These infants are usually females. They are mentally retarded, have low-set ears, a small jaw, and a deformed palate. The third syndrome involving an abnormal autosome number is trisomy-13, occurring once in every 4600 live births. The defects involve the face, palate, brain and frequently extra fingers.

Chromosome-structural abnormalities. Most of the abnormal structures seen in chromosomes are the result of so-called translocation (breakage and exchange of chromosome material during meiosis) or deletion of chromosomal material. Translocations involving chromosomes 15 or 21 can cause Down's syndrome. A deletion of part of one number 5 autosome brings about the *Cri du Chat* (cat cry) syndrome. These infants look like those of with Down's Syndrome but in addition have a poorly developed larynx (vocal cords). As a result, their cry sounds very similar to the plaintive mew of a kitten. Similarly severe malformations are associated with deletions involving chromosome 4 and 18.

Sex chromosome abnormalities. The major abnormalities in this category result from the usual *XX* (female) or *XY* (male) pattern.

(a) The sex chromosome pattern *XXY* - Klinefelter's Syndrome. These children are males, since they have one *Y* chromosome, but their testes fail to function normally. Most of them are infertile (no sperm production) and many are mentally retarded.

(b) The sex chromosome pattern *XYY*. They are all males. and there physical and sexual development is usually normal. Common characteristics include above average height, mental retardation, personality disorders, and often criminal behaviour.

(c) The sex chromosome pattern only one *X* chromosome *XO* pattern. They are females. This disorder is called Turner's Syndrome, or gonadal dysgenesis. The gonads (ovaries) are present only as small streaks of primitive tissue, causing definite infertility. Common features of Turner's Syndrome are infantile genitals, short stature, webbing (narrow and tapering) neck, and abnormalities of the heart and kidneys. Rarely, a female is born with three, four, or five X chromosomes; the child is always mentally retarded.

genetic information. Determination of hereditary character of the organism by the genes contained in the nucleus of the cell. It is very well established that the active element of the genes is deoxyribonucleic acid (DNA). The innumerable combinations of molecular arrangement of which preserve genetic information. This is transmitted by a mechanism that at the moment is still being sought to ribonucleic acid (RNA) which, in the cytoplasm of the cell, directly controls the synthesis of protein.

geobotanical prospecting. The visual study of plants and their distribution as indicators of soil composition and depth, bedrock lithology, the possibility of ore bodies, and groundwater conditions.

geostrophic wind. A theoretical wind which corresponds to equilibrium between the horizontal pressure force and the horizontal component of the deviating force due the earth's rotation; only these forces being supposed to act on the air. It blows parallel to straight isobars or contours.

germicide. A substance or chemical which kills disease germs and other microorganisms.

gnotobiotic. A scientific term used for germ-free conditions, especially those in which experimental animals are inoculated with known strains of microorganisms.

gradient wind. A theoretical wind which corresponds to equilibrium between the horizontal pressure force, the horizontal component of the deviating force due to the earth's rotation, and the centrifugal force due to air motion on a curved path; only these forces being supposed to act on the air. It blows parallel to curved isobars or contours.

graphite. An allotopic form of carbon, existing in finely divided form; found extensively throughout the world and contains many impurities such as quartz, feldspar, apatite, and iron sulphide. Hazards are associated with the mining and manufacture of graphite and its products rather than its industrial uses. Inhalation of graphite dust causes pneumoconiosis. Other dangers are associated with the minerals that are mined with graphite such as silica, and the chemicals used in the purification of graphite.

green belt. Any zone of countryside immediately surrounding a town, defined for the purpose of.restricting indiscriminate outward extension of the urban area. The original purpose of green belts, is to secure a permanent recreation area for people living in the polluted and unpleasant urban environment of the city, as well as controlling urban sprawl.

greenhouse effect. Warming of the lower layers of the atmosphere due to the fact that solar radiation of relatively short wavelength, penetrates the atmosphere without appreciable, and is, in large measure, absorbed only at the atmosphere to a much greater exent. The phenomenon is named by analogy with a greenhouse, whose glass is much more transparent to short-wave solar radiation than to the longer-wave radiation from the interior of the greenhouse. Fears have-been expressed that an increase in the concentration of carbon dioxide in the atmosphere could lead to an enhancement of the greenhouse effect with a consequent rise in temperature.

grit chamber. A detritus tank with a detention time of about one minute used in a sewage treatment plant for separation of sand, grits, pebbles, etc., from the sewage.

grit channel. A long narrow channel used in a sewage treatment plant for removal of grits, sand and other inert matters. The removal takes place by sedimentation of particles under the controlled velocity of flow of sewage in the channel.

gross weight. The weight of a packaging plus the weight of its contents.

ground level concentration. The concentration of a pollutant in air to which a human being is normally exposed, *i.e.,* between the ground and a height of some 2 m above it. It does not mean the concentration in a layer of air in direct contact with the ground is occurring. The upper limit of height is flexible if concentrations do not change very much with height from 2 m upwards. When the major source of pollution is a single stack or a small group of stacks the measured ground level concentration at any point will vary very rapidly with time on account of small but rapid changes in wind speed and direction, and 'ground level concentration' is meaningless without specification of the time over which the concentration is averaged.

growth retardation. Disturbances of growth, however, are more common in children whose growth was retarded within the uterus than in those whose birth weights fall within normal limits. Many other factors contribute to a child's slow rate of growth, of which, one is heredity. Others include diet, health, living condition, and family climate, and conditions leading to emotional disturbances-in fact, the entire environment of the child. It is well known that food affects health and growth. Children whose growth has been retarded by under nutrition also have a disturbed pattern of skeletal development. Not only are they thinner and shorter in stature than their well-nourished age mates but their bone growth is immature. Their lack of adequate caloric intake often incapacitates them physically and emotionally, leaving them indifferent, gloomy, apathetic and fatigued. Specific vitamin deficiency can also lead to a slowing of growth. Lack of a mother's love and her close presence also affect infant growth. The emotional and social tensions produced by maternal deprivation can retard the growth of young children, regardless of how well they

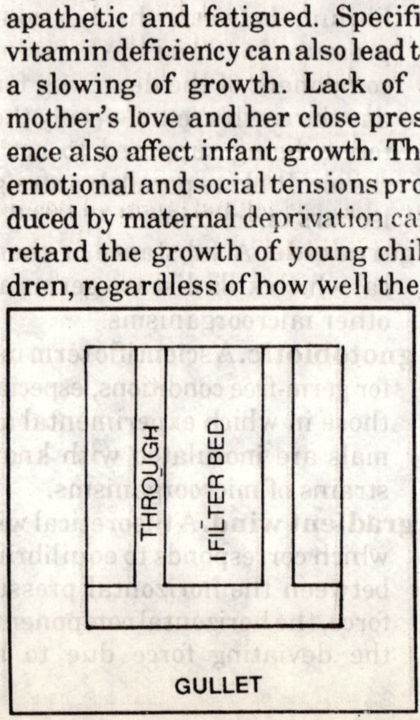

are fed. This type of growth failure due to neglect and rejection is found among children living in their own homes, and not solely among those in institutions.

gullet. 1. A narrow trench dug to the formation level in earth cutting to lay a track for movement of wagons carrying the spoil. 2. A channel in a rapid sand-filter for the entry of settled water and the exit of wash water.

gulley. A pit with grating on the roadside gutter for draining of the pipe from road surface. The pit is provided with a silt trap from which silt is removed periodically.

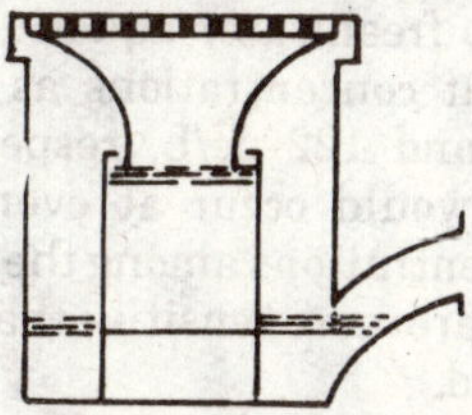

GULLEY

gulley sucker. A truck carrying large tank fitted with a vaccum pump and hose. The hose is introduced in the pit to suck the silt and slush mucks from it.

GULLEY TRAP

gulley trap. A trap with a seal of water provided in a gulley to prevent foul gases coming out of the drain. The silt deposited at the bottom is removed periodically.

gust. A transitory, positive or negative departure, lasting a relatively short time, of the wind speed (or of a component of the wind speed in a particular direction) from its mean value (or mean value of the component) over a specified interval of time.

gyro process. A petroleum-cracking process that operates on crude oil which is preheated and flashed. The reduced crude oil is introduced into the fractionator and the bottoms from the tower are sent to a viscosity-breaking coil.

H

haemagglutinin. A protein substance present in certain viruses, such as the influenza virus, which has the property of producing agglutination of red cells owing to its specific action on mucopolysaccharides of the membrane of those cells. The phenomenon of haemagglutination is one of the means most used to show that certain viruses are present, in particular those of influenza and mumps.

hafnium. One of the less abundant elements in the earth's crust. It is a lustrous, silvery-white, ductile corrosion-resistant metal. The chemistry of hafnium is almost identical with that of zirconium, which is a consequence of the lanthanide contraction. It is separated from zirconium by chlorination and solvent extraction, followed by reduction of hafnium chloride with magnesium (Kroll process). Several uses have been found for hafnium: (*i*) as a control material in water-cooled nuclear reactors; (*ii*) as a filament in gas filled incandescent light bulbs; (*iii*) as an alloying ingredient to add strength to tungsten and molybdenum filaments and electrodes used in high-pressure discharge (*iv*) as a cathode in X-ray tubes (*v*) as a getter material in vacuum tubes and system; (*vi*) as a minor alloying ingredient in nichrome heating elements where hafnium appears to significantly increase the lifespan of the elements; and (*vii*) usually with zirconium, as an ingredient of several alloys. The available data for hafnium indicate that acute and chronic toxicity to freshwater aquatic life occur at concentrations as low as 360 and 122 μg/L, respectively; and would occur at even lower concentrations among the species that are more sensitive than those tested.

hail. In meteorology, a form of precipitation consisting of almost round pallets of ice. Hail is formed in turbulent air masses containing strong updrafts within which temperatures range from above to below freezing.

half-life. 1. The time required for an unstable element or nuclide to lose one-half of its radioactive intensity in the form of alpha, beta, and gamma radiation. Half-lives of radionuclides range from micro-seconds to millions of years. *See also* decay; radiocarbon dating. 2. The time required for a reaction to be half-completed or for one-half of a reactant to be consumed.

half-thickness. The thickness of an absorbing medium necessary to reduce the intensity of the transmitted radiation to one-half its incident value. Also known as half-value layer.

half-value layer. *See* half-thickness.

halocarbons in atmosphere. Halocarbons play an important role in the photochemical process of the atmosphere, since they constitute the source of halogen radicals which catalytically destroy ozone. A variety of halocarbons is being released in to the atmosphere by both natural and anthropogenic processes. Since, natural sources are likely to remain essentially constant, it must be realized that the anthropogenic contribution and hence the atmospheric halogen content are increasing with time. Fully halogenated hydrocarbons such as trichlorofluoromethane, are almost inert in the troposphere. Consequently, they accumulate and gradually diffuse in to higher layers of the atmosphere, where they undergo photochemical reactions. Halogen atoms thereby released convert O_3 and O to molecular oxygen O_2 through catalytic reaction cycles. Partially halogenated hydrocarbons such as methyl chloride, CH_3Cl and methyl chloroform, CH_3CCl_3, are less stable. They react with hydroxyl radicals and are thus largely removed by tropospheric OH^- reactions. Only a fraction of the amounts emitted in to the troposphere reaches the stratosphere and can thereby augment the source of halogen atom catalysts. The same is true for halocarbons with double bonds such as tetrachloroethylene, $CCl_2{=}CCl_2$, and trichloroethylene, $CHCl{=}CCl_2$. The fully halogenated halocarbons contain about 3% of the organically bound chlorine present in the atmosphere.

halogen. The term whose literal meaning is saltmaker, refers to the five elements of Group VIIA of the Periodic Table. In the order of their activity these are fluorine, chlorine, bromine, iodine, and astatine; they are all electronegative and thus are strong oxidizing agents. They are classified as nonmetals.

halogenation. A chemical reaction or process which results in the formation of chemical bond between a halogen atom and another atom of some other element. Reactions resulting in the formation of halogen carbon bonds are especially important.

hallucinogen. The compounds acting on the central nervous system in such a way as to cause mental disturbance, imaginary experiences, coma, and even death. Many of these are narcotics and/or alkaloids; some of them are derived from plants and others are made synthetically. They differ in the degree of addiction and hallucinatory effect. Some of the common hallucinogens are hashish, marijuana, lysergic acid, amphetamine, and a number of morphine derivatives.

hard metal. A term referring to a mixture of tungsten carbide (WC), cobalt, and sometimes other metals and metal oxides and/or carbides. The tungsten carbide content of hard metal is generally 80% or more, and the cobalt content is generally less than 10%, but it may be as high as 25%. When the cobalt content exceeds 2%, its contribution to the potential health hazard is judged to exceed to that of tungsten carbide and all other components, and the recommended standard for such mixtures is based on the current U.S. federal standard for occupational exposure to cobalt, 0.1 mg/m^3. If nickel is used as a binder rather than cobalt and nickel content of the mixture exceeds 0.3%, then the recommended occupational exposure limit for nickel of 15 μg/m^3 is applied. The recommended limits for the airborne tungsten are different from 'insoluble tungsten', 'soluble tungsten', and 'cemented tungsten carbide' because of their differing potential biologic effects and inherent toxicities. These criteria and recommended standards should apply to places of employment involved in the manufacture, use, or handling of any of the defined materials. The action level is defined as one-half of the appropriate recommended time-weighted average (TWA) environmental limit. Occupational exposure to cemented tungsten carbide, cemented tungsten, or its compounds, is defined as exposure at a concentration greater than the appropriate action level, that is, except for the case of cemented tungsten carbide products in which nickel is the binder. It may be noted that occupational exposure to insoluble tungsten should be controlled so that the employees are not exposed to insoluble tungsten at a concentration greater than 5.0 mg, measured as tungsten, per cubic metre of air, determined as a TWA concentration for up to 10-hour workshift in a 40-hour workweek. Occupational exposure to soluble tungsten should be controlled so that employees are not exposed to soluble tungsten at a concentration greater than 1.0 mg, measured as tungsten, per cubic metre of air, determined as a TWA concentration for up to 10-hour workshift in a 40-hour workweek. Occupational exposure to dust of cemented tungsten carbide that contains more than 2% cobalt, should be controlled so that employees are not exposed to a concentration greater than 0.1 mg, measured as cobalt, per cubic metre of air, determined as a TWA concentration for up to 10-hour workshift in a 40-hour workweek. Occupational exposure to dust of cemented tungsten carbide that contains more than 0.3% nickel, should be controlled so that employees are not exposed to a concentration greater than 15.0 μg, measured as nickel, per cubic metre of air, determined as a TWA concentration for up to 10-hour workshift in a 40-hour workweek.

hardness. *See* hardwater.

hard radiation. Ionizing radiation of high energy and penetrating power.

hardwater. Water that does not form an immediate lather with soap, owing to the presence of calcium, magnesium, and iron compounds in dissolved form. The addition of soap produces an insoluble scum consisting of salts of these metals with the fatty acids of the soap, until no more is left in solution. Hardness is divided into two types:

(a) temporary hardness, due to hydrogen carbonates (bicarbonates) of the metals. These enter the water by the passage of the water, containing dissolved carbon dioxide, over solid carbonates (chalk or limestone deposits, etc.). Such hardness is removed by boiling, the soluble bicarbonate being decomposed into the insoluble carbonates, carbon dioxide and water.

(b) Permanent hardness, due to sulphates and carbonates of the metals. This is removed by the addition of washing soda, sodium carbonate, which precipitates the insoluble carbonates.

The principal natural sources of hardness in water are sedimentary rocks, seepage, and runoff from soils. Hard water normally originates in areas with thick topsoil and limestone formations. Groundwater is generally harder than surface-water. Groundwater rich in carbonic acid and dissolved oxygen usually possesses a high solubilizing potential towards soil or rocks that contain appreciable amount of the minerals calcite, gypsum, and dolomite, and consequently hardness levels up to several thousand milligrams per liter can result.

Although most calcium compounds are not easily soluble in pure water, the presence of carbon dioxide readily increases their solubility, and sources of water containing up to 100 mg of calcium per litre are fairly common sources containing over 200 mg of calcium per liter are rare. Many salts containing magnesium are easily soluble and water sources containing levels of magnesium at concentrations up to 10 mg/L are common. Water sources rarely contain more than 100 mg/L and calcium hardness usually predominates.

The buffering capacity of water normally described as alkalinity is closely associated with water hardness. Thus, such anions as hydroxide, bicarbonate, and carbonate have a significant influence and so to a lesser degree do phosphate and silicate molecular species of weak acids also contribute. Scaling of hot-water pipes, boilers, and other household appliances is due to hard water. In freshwater, the principal hardness causing ions are calcium and magnesium; the ions strontium, iron, barium, and manganese also contribute. Hardness is usually measured by the reaction of the polyvalent metallic ions present in a water sample with a chelating agent such as EDTA and is expressed as an equivalent concentration of calcium carbonate. Hardness may also be estimated by determination of the individual concentrations of the components of hardness their sum being expressed in terms of an equivalent quantity of calcium carbonate. The degree of hardness of drinking-water has been classified in terms of its equivalent $CaCO_3$ concentration as follows:

Soft	0-60 mg/L
Medium hard	60-120 mg/L
Hard	120-180 mg/L
Very hard	180 mg/L and above.

There is some suggestive evidence that drinking extremely hard water might lead to an increased incidence of urolithiasis. This has been suggested to account for urolithiasis in a small human population. Where the local tap-water contained 300-500 mg/L of calcium it has also been demonstrated in animals drinking extremely hard water (200-400 mg/L of calcium), when they had been subjected to a high ambient temperature of 303 K. The occurrence of drinking-water containing as much as 500 mg/L of calcium must, however, be very rare.

Alkalinity, an index of the buffering capacity of water, is closely linked to hardness. For the most part alkalinity is produced by anions or molecular species of weak acids mainly hydroxide bicarbonate, and carbonate; other species such as borates, phosphates, silicates and organic acids also contribute to a small degree of present. Whichever solute species contributes to the alkalinity of water, it is always expressed in terms of an equivalent quantity of calcium carbonate. When the alkalinity of a surface-water is due to the presence of carbonates and/or bicarbonates, the alkalinity value is usually close to the hardness value.

Soft water has a greater tendency to cause corrosion of pipes and consequently, certain heavy metals such as copper, zinc, lead, and cadmium may be present in the distributed drinking-water. The degree to which this corrosion and solubilization of metals occurs is also a function of *p*H alkalinity and dissolved oxygen concentration. In some communities, corrosion is so servere that special precautions must be adopted with the supply.

In areas with very hard water, household pipes can become choked with deposited scale hard water also deposits incrustations on kitchen utensils as well as increasing soap consumption. Hard water can thus be both a nuisance and an economic burden to the consumer. Public acceptance of water hardness varies among communities; it is often related to the hardness to which the consumer has over, the years, become accustomed, and in many communities a water hardness greater than 500 mg/L is tolerated. A hardness level of about 100 mg/L of $CaCO_3$ provides an acceptable balance between corrosion and the problems of incrustation, although, from aesthetic considerations, 500 mg/L is recommended as a guideline value.

There appears to be no firm evidence that water hardness causes ill effects in man. Conversely there have been a number of studies, where the results suggest that water hardness protects against disease. The hardness of water can be removed by passing the water through zeolites.

hazardous material. Any material which, if improperly handled, can be damaging to health and well-being of human being. These may be poisons or toxic agents, corrosive chemicals, flammable materials, explosives, and radioactive substances. The numbers allotted by U.S. National Fire Protection Agency, to various chemicals that are hazardous from health point of view, are as follows: A few whiffs of the gas or vapour could cause death; or the gas, vapour, or the liquid could be fatal on penetrating the fire fighter's normal full protective clothing which is designed for resistance to heat. For most of the chemicals having a health 4 rating, the normal full protective clothing available to the average fire department will not provide adequate protection against skin contact with these materials. Materials extremely hazardous to health, but areas may be entered with extreme care. Full protective clothing, including self-contained breathing apparatus, rubber gloves, boots, and bands around legs, arms and waist should be provided, and no skin surface should be exposed. Materials hazardous to health, but areas may be entered freely with self-contained breathing apparatus. Materials slightly hazardous to health, and it may be desirable to wear self-contained breathing apparatus. Materials which on exposure under fire conditions would offer no health hazard beyond that of ordinary combustible material.

hazardous waste. For the purposes of this chapter means any material that is subject to the Hazardous Waste Manifest Requirement of the U.S. Environmental Protection Agency.

hazardous waste constituent. A constituent that caused the Administrator to list the hazardous waste in Part 261, Subpart D, of 400 CFR or a constituent listed in table 1 of Part 261.24 of 40 CFR.

hazardous waste discharge. The accidental or intentional spilling, leaking, pumping, pouring, emitting, emptying, or dumping of hazardous waste into or on any land or water.

hazardous waste management unit. A contiguous area of land on or in which hazardous waste is placed, or the largest area in which there is significant likelihood of mixing hazardous waste constituents in the same area. Examples of hazardous waste management units include a surface impoundment, a waste pile, a land treatment area, a landfill cell, an incinerator, a tank and its associated piping and underlying containment system, and a container storage area. A container alone does not constitute a unit; the unit includes containers and the land or pad union which they are placed.

haze. A suspension in the atmosphere of extremely small, dry particles which are invisible to the naked eye but are numerous enough to give the sky an appearance of opalescence. Since the haze particles act as condensation nuclei, and the water vapour pressure over the droplets that may thus be formed is much lower (particularly if the haze particles are soluble) than that over larger droplets, it is difficult to draw a firm distinction between haze and mist.

haze, coefficient of (COH). A factor used for the assessment of the amount of smoke or other aerosol in air. It is 100 times the absorbance of the stain produced on white filter paper when air is passed through it(absorbance being determined from measurement of the light transmitted by the stain and by clean filter paper). A COH unit is the amount of particulate matter on the paper that gives an absorbance of 0.01; *i.e.*, if a given determination gives an absorbance of 0.01, the result is 1 COH unit. If the COH is multiplied by s/v, where s is the area of filter paper through which a volume v of air is passed, a value in terms of linear measure is obtained.

heat. Energy in the course of being transferred from one body or system to another as a result of a difference in temperature. Most cells cannot tolerate high temperatures. In case of dry bacterial cells, spores and dry plant seeds, temperatures upto 300-425K can be applied for a short time without killing all the cells; the survivors include a large proportion of mutants that are induced (not merely selected out) by heat. If DNA alone is heated under these conditions, an interesting injury can be detected in it, such as some of the purines become detached. Among cells surviving such treatment, an injury of this kind would be sufficient to produce loss of a proper base sequence in one or more sites of DNA molecule, and logically may be offered as an explanation of the observed loss of genetic information (mutation). Thus the first step of the mutational process is an injury which can occur without any replication of DNA. But this injury cannot be propagated as there is no known biochemical mechanism to utilize a sugar (or a sugar triphosphate) without its base as a building block for DNA synthesis. Thus during the replication DNA a second step must take place, *i.e.*, the translation of primary injury (loss of purines), nonacceptable in the mechanism of DNA replication, into a final acceptable one: replacement of missing purine by some normal base. Since the replicating strand of DNA has no information as to the missing base, perhaps the incorrect one (the wrong purine or even a pyrimidine) can sometimes be used for the synthesis of the new strand (replication); this represents an error in base sequence that is, by definition, a mutation. It has also been suggested that one of the effects of breaking hydrogen bonds by heat or other denaturing agents may be ionization of guanine in N-1 position, and such an ionization may cause guanine to pair with thymine instead of with cytosine, thus contributing to mutagenic effect of heat.

heating of rivers. Most power stations use river for cooling purposes. This in turn can give rise to far-reaching adverse ecological changes. The main problems are a reduction in the self-purification capacity of the river and the danger to river fauna caused by the heating of the river water, the extermination of water organisms in the condenser in the power station, and the climatic effect of heating of the waters. By the heating of river waters, the dissolving power for the oxygen that is vital to the needs of water organisms is lowered, and at the same time the metabolic processes of the water organisms are accelerated. A higher consumption of oxygen is thus accompanied by a reduction in the supply. This can result in the impairment of the self-purification capacity, in the disappearance of oxygen (with the consequent extinction of water organisms and the possible extermination of fish life) and, in extreme cases, in the complete disruption in bacteria. One result of this is that in addition to the physical reduction in the oxygen content of the water already caused by the rise in temperature, the remaining oxygen is consumed more quickly. The water acquires a musty smell and taste, which can seriously complicate the purification of drinking water from the river concerned. The bacterial cultures that develop can settle in quiet spots in the river, such as backwaters beside weirs, and putrefy there. As this problem was recognized fairly early on, and therefore in many countries, authorities have imposed limits on the extent to which river water might be heated. These limits have been set too high, however, as they only take account of the physical factors present in clean revers. The limits laid down stipulate that water temperatures may not be raised by more than 5°C so that the upper limit of 28°C is never exceeded. This threshold value takes no account of the fact that this range of temperature can give rise, in polluted river, to extensive disturbances in ecological processes to the point of complete disruption. A further problem consists in the sharp increase in temperature of the water drawn into the condenser at a power station, possibly to 40°C. This is precisely the optimum temperature for pathogenic such as typhus and enterococci (intestinal bacteria). In clean cold water, these disease germs do not multiply, but in polluted warm water well supplied with nutrients they do so freely. An increase in pathogenic bacteria is thus matched by the extermination of the creatures that prey on them. In a 1000-megawatt power station, about 40,000 litres of water per second are absorbed and heated, which seriously impairs the self-purification capacity of polluted rivers. Another problem arises from the influence on the climate of heating the river.

heat of combustion. The heat evolved when a definite quantity of a substance is completely oxidized (burnt); usually stated for a standard state at 298 K and one atmosphere pressure for reactants and products, in kilojoules per mole of the substance.

heavy metals. Metals having a specific gravity greater than four; *e.g.*, lead, mercury, cadmium, and bismuth. Sulphides of such metals are usually insoluble in water.

heavy water. A form of water also known as deuterium oxide (D_2O), in which the symbol D_2 stands for two atoms of heavy hydrogen (H_2), an isotope of hydrogen containing one proton and one neutron. The specific gravity of heavy water is 1.1 and its boiling point at normal atmospheric pressure is 374.4 K Its occurrence in ordinary water is in the ratio of approximately 1 to 6000 parts. It was used as moderator in early types of nuclear reactors.

hepatic water. A natural spring water that contains hydrogen sulphide or an alkali sulphide.

heptachlor. Heptachlor is readily metabolized by mammals to heptachlor epoxide. This metabolite is stored mainly in adipose tissue, but also in liver, kidney, and muscle. Both the rat and the dog rapidly metabolize ingested heptachlor to heptachlor epoxide and accumulate heptachlor epoxide primarily in adipose tissue. A positive relationship is found between the amount of heptachlor in the diet and the amount of heptachlor stored in the fatty tissue, female rats accumulating approximately six times as much heptachlor epoxide in their fat as males.

Although there is no direct evidence showing the conversion of heptachlor to its epoxide in humans, there is little doubt that the epoxide that has been found in human tissues is derived from heptachlor. Various levels of heptachlor epoxide have been found in the blood, fat, and milk of humans. Because of its high lipid content, milk is one of the major excretion routes for organohalogenated compounds, including heptachlor epoxide. An extensive survey carried out in the USA indicated that women who had lactated following several births had lower pesticide levels in milk than primiparae. Heptachlor epoxide, dieldrin, and oxychlordane were the most common pesticides found in human milk. Only 2% of human milk samples showed heptachlor residues the levels ranging from 15 to 2050 μg/L on a fat-adnusted basis, with a mean concentration of 91 μg/L. Of the high-residue group of women, 11% were either occupationally exposed or lived in households where a household member was occupationally exposed.

herbicide. Any chemical used to destroy or inhibit plant growth, especially of weeds or other undesirable vegetation. They may include weeds-killers, silvicides and defoliants.

herpesvirus. One of a group of complex DNA-containing viruses causing infections in man and most other vertebrates that tend to recur. The group includes *herpes simplex*, the agent of cold sores; *herpes varicella zoster*, the virus causing chickenpox and shingles; *Epstein-Barr* (EB) virus, thought to be the causal agent of glandular fever and also implicated in the cancer Burkitt's lymphoma; and the cytomegalovirus.

hetero-. A prefix having the meaning different or unlike, as in heterogeneous (different kinds) and heterocyclic (different atoms in the ring).

heterocyclic compound. An unsaturated cyclic compound containing one or more atoms other than carbon as part of the ring structure. The rings may be hexagonal or pentagonal, the latter appearing in the furan, purine, and pyrrole families of heterocyclics. Substances of cyclic structure, as acid anhydrides, lactides, lactams lactones, cyclic ethers, and cyclic derivatives of dicarboxylic acids which are formed by the elimination of water from alphabetic compounds, are not considered among the heterocyclic substances. Derivatives of pyridine, quinoline, thiophene, thiazole, pyrone, etc., which contain heterocyclic ring that persist in the compound through chemical reactions, are considered the true members of this class.

heterogeneous. Consisting of more than one phase. *See* equilibrium, reaction, catalysis.

heterogeneous catalysis. Catalysis in systems in which catalyst forms separate phase, most often solid.

heterogeneous equilibrium. The equilibrium between two or more phases, as between a solid and a gas, or a liquid and its saturated vapour. Such systems are usually studied at constant pressure, since at last one of the phases will be a solid or liquid. The imposed pressure may be that of an equilibrium gaseous phase, or it may be an externally controlled pressure. Other heterogeneous equilibria are solubility equilibria, reactions involving two immiscible phases, and reactions involving condensed and immiscible phases. Also known as polyphase equilibrium.

heterogeneous system. Thermodynamic system composed of finite (but greater than one) number of homogeneous phases. Also known as multiphase system.

heterolysis. *See* heterolytic dissociation.

heterolytic dissociation. Fission of covalent bond in molecule, resulting in formation of two ions bearing, different charges. Also known as heterolysis fission.

heterolytic fission. *See* heterolytic dissociation.

heteronuclear. A condition in which two (or more) substituents occur in different rings or nuclei of compounds which contain two or more rings, as, *e.g.*, 1, 8-dichloronaphthalene. When substituents are both located in the same ring condition is termed isonuclear.

heteropolar colloid. A colloidal system in which the dispersed particles are polar compounds.

hexachlorobenzene. A moderately toxic compound included in the list of potential occupational carcinogens; used as fungicide for seeds and as wood preservative. Studies have revealed that hexachlorobenzene administered orally to rats was absorbed slowly from the gut, mainly via the lymphatic system, and was stored extensively in the fat after 48 hours. The quantitative recovery of intraperitoneally and orally administered (^{14}C)-hexachlorobenzene in rats was dose-dependent, but more ^{14}C was recovered from the faeces than from the urine. The major urinary metabolites were pentachlorophenol, terta-chlorohydroquinone and pentachlorothiophenol. The other urinary metabolites that were detected were tetrachlorobenzene, pentachlorobenzene, 2, 4, 5- and 2, 4, 6-trichlorophenols, and 2, 3, 4, 6- and 2, 3, 5, 6- tetrachlorophenols; 2, 3, 4-trichlorophenol and other tetrachlorophenols were present in traces. These metabolites were excreted as conjugates or in free form in the urine. Unchanged hexachlorobenzene was found in the faeces and in fat. When (^{14}C)-hexachlorobenzene was given orally in a dosage of 110 μg/day tc Macaca mulatta monkeys for 11-15 minutes, 50% of the radioactivity found in the urine was in pentachlorophenol and 25% in pentachlorobenzene, the remainder being in unidentifield metabolites and unchanged hexachlorobenzene. In the faeces, 99% of the radioactivity was in unchanged HCB. During the last 10 days of the experiment, males excreted 7.2% of the administered dose in the urine and 52% in the faeces; females excreted 4.6% and 42.2% respectively.

hexachlorobutadiene. An industrial substance enlisted as potential occupational carcinogen; used as solvent for elastomers, heat-transfer liquid, and a wash liquid for removing C_4- and higher hydrocarbons. The available data for hexachlorobutadiene indicate that acute and chronic toxicity to freshwater aquatic life occur at concentrations as low as 90 and 9.3 μg/L, respectively; while the corresponding values for the saltwater aquatic life are 32 and 6.7 μg/L respectively; and would occur at even lower concentrations among the species that are more sensitive than those tested. For the maximum protection of human health from the potential carcinogenic effects due to exposure of hexachlorobutadiene through ingestion of contaminated aquatic organisms and water, the ambient water concentration should be zero on nonthreshold assumption for hexachlorobutadiene. However, zero level may not be attainable at present time. Therefore, the levels that may result in incremental increase of cancer risk over lifetime have been estimated at 10^{-5}, 10^{-6}, and 10^{-7}. The corresponding criteria have been assessed to be 4.47 ng/L, 0.45 ng/L, and 0.045 ng/L respectively. If the above estimates are made for the consumption of aquatic organisms only (excluding consumption of water), the levels are redefined as 500 μg/L, 50 μg/L, and 5.0 μg/L respectively.

hexachlorocyclohexane. A chlorinated hydrocarbon mainly used as a insecticide; included in the list of potential occupational carcinogens. It is highly toxic by ingestion, inhalation, and skin absorption, and has been classified as hazardous poison. For hexachlorocyclohexane, the criterion to protect freshwater aquatic life is 100 μg/L as a 24-hour average; and the criterion to protect saltwater aquatic life is 0.34 μg/L as a 24-hour average. For the protection of human health from the potential carcinogenic effects due to exposure of α–HCH, through ingestion of contaminated aquatic organisms and water, the ambient water concentration should be zero on the nonthreshold assumption for hexachlorocyclohexane and its isomers. However, zero level may not be attainable at present time. Therefore, the levels that may result in incremental increase of cancer risk over lifetime are estimated at 10^{-5}, 10^{-6}, and 10^{-7}. The corresponding criteria are 92 ng/L, 9.2 ng/L, and 0.92 ng/L respectively. If the above estimates are made for the consumption of aquatic organisms only (excluding consumption of water), the levels have been redefined as 310 ng/L, 31 ng/L, and 3.1 ng/L respectively.

For the protection of human health from the potential carcinogenic effects due to exposure of β-HCH, through ingestion of contaminated aquatic organisms and water, the ambient water concentration should be zero on the nonthreshold assumption for this chemical. However, zero level may not be attainable at present time. Therefore, the levels that may result in incremental increase of cancer risk over lifetime are estimated at 10^{-5}, 10^{-6}, and 10^{-7}. The corresponding criteria are 163 ng/L, 16.3 ng/L, and 1.63 ng/L respectively. If the above estimates are made for the consumption of aquatic organisms only (excluding consumption of water), the levels are redefined as 547 ng/L, 54.7 ng/L, and 5.47 ng/L respectively.

For the protection of human health from the potential carcinogenic effects due to exposure of tech-HCH, through ingestion of contaminated aquatic organisms and water, the ambient water concentration should be zero on the nonthreshold assumption for this chemical. However, zero level may not be attainable at present time. Therefore, the levels that may result in incremental increase of cancer risk over lifetime are estimated at 10^{-5}, 10^{-6}, and 10^{-7}. The corresponding criteria are 123 ng/L, 12.3 ng/L, and 1.23 ng/L respectively. If the above estimates are made for the consumption of aquatic organisms only (excluding consumption of water), the levels are redefined as 414 ng/L, 41.4 ng/L, and 4.14 ng/L respectively.

For the protection of human health from the potential carcinogenic effects due to exposure of γ-HCH (lindane), through ingestion of contaminated aquatic organisms and water, the ambient water concentration should be zero on the nonthreshold assumption for this chemical. However, zero level may not be attainable at present time. Therefore, the levels that may result in incremental increase of cancer risk over lifetime have been estimated at 10^{-5}, 10^{-6}, and 10^{-7}. The corresponding criteria are 186 ng/L, 18.6 ng/L, and 1.86 ng/L respectively. If the above estimates are made for the consumption of aquatic organisms only (excluding consumption of water), the levels have been redefined as 625 ng/L, 62.5 ng/L, and 6.25 ng/L respectively.

hexachlorocyclopentadiene. An industrial chemical which has been proposed to be a hazardous air pollutant; highly toxic by inhalation, ingestion, and skin contact; used as intermediate for dyes, resins, pesticides, fungicides, and pharmaceuticals. The available data for hexachlorocyclopentadiene indicate that acute and chronic toxicity to freshwater aquatic life occur at concentrations as low as 7.0 and 5.2 μg/L, respectively; while the corresponding values for the saltwater aquatic life are 7.0 and 4.5 μg/L respectively; and would occur at even lower concentrations among the species that are more sensitive than those tested.

high explosive. An explosive whose shattering power is due to detonation brought about by heat or mechanical shock. *See also* explosive.

high-pressure chemistry. Chemistry at very high pressures arbitrarily chosen to be above 10,000 bars, and mainly concerned with solid and liquid states. At 298 K, and 10 kilobars, nearly all ordinary gases are liquid or solid, and only a few liquids are not frozen; thus most high-pressure chemistry involves either high temperatures, at which chemical reactions can occur at appreciable rates, or studies of internal arrangements in solids. The traditional high-temperature chemistry deals with the chemical phenomena in the range of 500-3000 K, although exotic flames can produce temperature upto 25,000 K, electric arcs can be operated in constricted modes to produce temperatures upto 50,000 K, and nuclear processes begin to occur at temperatures in the millions of degrees range. Laser-excitation of selected energy states can produce species with effective temperature in the range of 10^8 K.

high rate digestion. The rapid digestion of sewage sludge, within a week or so, in a sludge digestor is accomplished by keeping the digestor contents thoroughly mixed with continuous addition of thickened seeded sludge and preventing stratification of sludge into scum, supernatant and sludge solids. Mixing is done by recirculation of sludge gas which facilitates substrate to come in contact with the methane formers and thus digestion proceeds rapidly.

Hill reaction. The oxygen evolution and photo-reduction of an artificial electron acceptor by a chloroplast preparation in the absence of carbon dioxide.

hindrance. Partial or complete blocking of a reaction resulting from the three-dimensional structure of a molecule, often referred to as steric hindrance.

histones. Basic proteins which occur in the nuclei of both plant and animal cells. They are less basic than the protamines, having isoelectric point at about *p*H 11. Some investigators restrict the term histone to only those basic proteins anatomically and chemically associated with DNA.

homo-. A prefix having the meaning of the ' same', as in the terms homogeneous, homologous, homopolymer, etc.

homoazeotrope. Homogeneous mixture of liquids, which distils without change of composition.

homocyclic. A ring or nucleus composed of atoms of the same element which is usually carbon.

homodesmic. Pertaining to a crystal, having atoms bonded in a single manner.

homogeneous catalysis. Catalysis in systems where catalyst and reactants constitute one phase.

homogeneous equilibrium. The equilibrium conditions in a system that constitutes a single phase, *i.e.,* reactions in solution or among gases the products of which remain in the same phase as the reactants.

homogeneous radiation. Radiation having an extremely narrow band of frequencies, or a beam of particles each having same energy.

homogeneous system. A thermodynamic system composed solely of one homogeneous phase.

homogenization. Reduction of the sizes of solid or semisolid particles in aqueous suspension to colloidal dimensions by mechanical action, the purpose being to stabilize the suspension so that the particles will neither rise to the surface nor precipitate.

homosphere. The part of the atmosphere in which the permanent constituents, that is, nitrogen, oxygen, and inert gases, are maintained in the same proportions by circulation. Up to a height of 80 km the mixing of the gases is perfect. In the homosphere three different regions exist, and the each region is separated by a boundary zone; these are:

(a) the lowest section, called the troposphere;

(b) a boundary zone, named the tropopause;

(c) a second region, called the stratosphere;

(d) a further boundary zone, the stratopause; and

(e) the third layer, called the mesosphere.

hormone. One of a number of complex organic substances which control or regulate various metabolic processes in plants and animals. In man they are formed in the so-called ductless glands (adrenal cortex, pituitary, pancreas, thyroid) and are secreted directly into the blood stream. Examples are adrenaline. ACTH, thyroxine, insulin, estrogen, and testosterone. They regulate such metabolic functions as blood-sugar level (insulin), reproductive functions (estrogen), metabolic rate (adrenaline), and other body processes.

horse latitudes. Either of two areas of high pressure found near 25° north and south of the equator. The air rises at or near the equator because of low pressure and then circles in the atmosphere, but much falls near the tropics of Cancer and Capricorn. The falling air gives rise to fairly permanent regions of high pressure, the horse latitudes. Both the trade winds, which blow from the horse latitudes towards the poles, are caused by the high pressure. It is suggested that the horse latitudes were so called because in the days of sailing vessels it was easy to become becalmed in these areas, in which case everything possible would be thrown overboard in order to lighten the vessel. Apparently it was not unknown for the horses to be discarded at this time.

Houdry process. A process for the catalytic cracking of the crude oil by the action of activated aluminium hydrosilicate. The charge is heated in a still to about 750 K, whence it passes to a vaporizer, from which the vapourized fraction's pass to catalyst chambers, after which they are fractionated. The process varies considerably with the nature of the oil changed and the products desired.

humectant. A hygroscopic liquid used to maintain constant moisture content in materials with which it is mixed or associated. Common types are glycerol, glycols, sorbitol, etc.

humidity of the air. The water vapour content of the air relative humidity of moist air with respect to water, at a given pressure p and temperature T, the percentage ratio of the mole fraction of the water vapour N_v to the vapour mole fraction N_{vw} which the air would have if it were saturated with respect to water at the same pressure p and temperature T. It is this relative humidity which is calculated, even at temperatures.

humus. The dark-coloured amorphous colloidal material that constitutes the organic component of soil. It is formed by the decomposition of plant and animal remains and excrement and has a complex and variable chemical composition. Being a colloid, it can hold water and therefore improves the water-retaining properties of soil; it also enhances soil fertility and workability. Acidic humus (mor) is found in regions of coniferous forest, where the decay is brought about mainly by fungi. Alkaline humus (mull) is typically found in grassland and deciduous forest; it supports an abundance of micro-organisms and small animals such as earthworms.

humus tank. The final settling or consolidation tank in a sewage treatment plant from which humus is obtained.

hydration. 1. A term referring to the combination of one or more molecules of water with a crystalline inorganic compound, usually a salt, without rupture of the H-OH bond. Such compounds are called hydrates, the structure being indicated by a centered dot. *e.g.*, $Na_2SO_4.10H_2O$. 2. The term hydration also refers to the strong affinity of water molecules for ions of dissolved substances, an interaction which is the fundamental cause of electrolytic dissociation. Ions and other charged particles thus acquire a tightly held film of water. Such particles are said to be solvated. This phenomenon may lead to hydrate formation, as defined in (1); it also exerts important effects in stabilization of colloidal solutions.

hydrazine. A colourless, fuming, hygroscopic liquid that is highly toxic by ingestion, inhalation, and skin absorption. It is strong irritant to eyes and skin; and poses severe explosion hazard when exposed to heat or oxidising materials. It finds numerous applications such as rocket propellant, and in the manufacture of drugs, as blowing agent, short-stopping agent, antioxidant, scavenger for gases, and as polymerization catalyst. It has been enlisted as one of the potential occupational carcinogen. The criteria and the recommended standard apply to the exposure of workers to hydrazine and its derivatives, such as methylhydrazine, 1, 1-dimethylhydrazine, 1, 2-dimethylhydrazine, and phenylhydrazine, and their salts. The occupational exposure to hydrazines is defined as any work involving handling, storage, use, or manufacture of hydrazines and their salts in such a manner that the vapours or aerosols may be released in workroom air or that the material may spill or splash onto the skin or into the eyes. Occupational exposure to hydrazines should be controlled so that no employee is exposed to hydrazines at a concentration greater than those shown below:

Hydrazine	0.04 mg/m^3
Methylhydrazine	0.08 mg/m^3
Phenylhydrazine	0.60 mg/m^3
1,1-dimethylhydrazine	0.15 mg/m^3.

These values are determined as ceiling concentrations in any 2-hour period. The recommended standard is designed to protect the health and provide safety to the workers for up to a 10-hour workshift, 40-hour workweek over a working lifetime.

hydrocarbon. Any compound composed of carbon and hydrogen. These are regarded as the parent substances in organic chemistry from which all other organic compounds may be considered derived. They are classed as saturated, unsaturated, alphabetic, aromatic, etc. Their chemical structure may be straight- or branched-chain, alicyclic.

hydrocolloid. A hydrophilic colloidal material used largely in food products as emulsifying, thickening and gelling agents. They readily absorb water, thus increasing viscosity and imparting smoothness and body texture to the product, even in concentrations of less than 1%.

hydrocooling. Removing heat from freshly harvested fruits and vegetables by immersion in ice water, then while still wet, subjected to vacuum. The evaporation of water chills the fruits and vegetables.

hydrocracking. Cracking of petroleum or its products in the presence of hydrogen and a suitable catalyst.

hydrocyanic acid (HCN). One of the oldest fumigants to be used extensively under modern conditions. Its use for treating trees under tents against scale insects. The use of HCN has been declining in recent years but it is still important in certain fields of application. Hydrocyanic acid is one of the most toxic of insect fumigants. The fact that it is very soluble in water has considerable bearing on its use in practice. Thus it cannot safely be used on moist materials such as fruit and vegetables because the solution of hydrocyanic acid in water is a dilute acid. Not only does this acid render these materials unpalatable and possibly hazardous for human consumption, but its action by causing burning wilting or discoloration may make them unmarketable. On the other hand, hydrocyanic acid has been widely used for fumigating dormant nursery stock that is sufficiently dry. It may be used for some living plants if they can be washed with water immediately after treatment to prevent burning by the acid.

Hydrocyanic acid may be employed for fumigating many dry foodstuffs, grains and seeds. Although it is strongly sorbed by many materials this action is usually completely reversible when they are dry, and, given time, all the fumigant vapours are desorbed. With many foodstuffs little, if any, chemical reaction occurs and there is no detectable permanent residue. Because of the high degree of sorption at atmospheric pressure, hydrocyanic acid does not penetrate well into some materials. It was largely because of this that vacuum fumigation was adopted. It is a powerful, quick-acting poison. In man and other warm-blooded animals it induces asphyxiation by inhibiting the respiratory enzymes, and renders tissues unable to absorb oxygen from the blood in the normal manner. The toxic action is reversible. In practice this means that a person who is completely unconscious from the effects of cyanide but whose heart is still beating may still recover if suitable antidotes and remedial measures are applied in time. Hydrocyanic acid may be absorbed in toxic amounts through the unbroken skin.

hydrodelkylation. A term used in petroleum technology to describe a method of removing alkyl groups from a hydrocarbon compound and replacing them with hydrogen. This is effected by treating the compound with hydrogen at high temperatures and pressures.

hydrodistillation. The removal of essential oils from plant components by using high temperature system.

hydrofining. A high-pressure catalytic process for the hydrogenation of low-grade petroleum fractions, to produce gasolines and lubricating oils that are exceptionally high in quality.

hydroforming. The operation of converting hydrocarbons of low octane number and other undesirable properties into a stable fuel of higher octane rating. During the process various reactions occur, including considerable cracking and aromatization.

hydrogasification. Production of gaseous of liquid fuels by direct addition of hydrogen to coal.

hydrogel. A colloidal gel in which water is the dispersion medium for example, coagulated silicic acid.

hydrogen. An element, by far the most abundant element in the universe. Hydrogen at standard conditions is a colourless, odourless, tasteless gas, suffocating, but not toxic. It is asphyxiant when present in high concentrations in air. Atomic hydrogen, made up of one proton and one electron, is represented by H; molecular hydrogen is a diatomic molecule represented by H_2; the isotope deuterium (one proton and one neutron in the nucleus) is represented by ^2H; or D; the isotope tritium (one proton and two neutrons in the nucleus) is represented by ^3H; or T. Normal hydrogen (protium) and deuterium are stable, whereas tritium is radioactive, with a half-life of 12.26 years. Hydrogen is the lightest of all elements and is extremely flammable over a concentration range of 4 to 75% by volume. As hydrogen is a major potential energy source, there is containing active research on its use as a fuel.

hydrogenation. The process of catalytic addition of hydrogen molecule(s) to organic compound containing multiple bond. Destructive hydrogenation, in which organic molecules split into smaller ones capable of reacting with hydrogen, occurs in catalytic hydrocracking of gasoline (hydrogenolysis). Reactions of hydrogen with inorganic materials are not considered as hydrogenation.

hydrogenation of coal. The manufacture of artificial mineral oil from coal by the action of hydrogen. This depends on causing the carbon in coal to combine with hydrogen to form hydrocarbons.

hydrogenation of oils. Artificial hardening of liquid animal and vegetable oils by the action of hydrogen. Liquid fats and oils contain a high percentage of liquid triolein, $C_{57}H_{104}O_6$, which may be converted into a solid tristearin, $C_{57}H_{110}O_6$, by the action of hydrogen in the presence of finely divided nickel as catalyst; the result being a hard fat of higher melting point.

hydrogen bomb. Explosion system based on synthesis reaction of light nuclei of deuterium and tritium, occurring at temperature of the order of 10^6 K.

hydrogen cyanide. *See* hydrocyanic acid.

hydrogen fluoride. A colourless, highly corrosive, fuming substance, highly soluble in water. It is highly toxic by ingestion, inhalation, and strong irritant to eyes, skin, and mucous membranes. It is used in steel industry, for cleaning glass, as a catalyst in the plating of steel, pickling of metals, in the electrolytic production of aluminium, and as on e of the ingredients in timber preservatives. Occupational exposure to hydrogen fluoride is defined as exposure to airborne concentration of hydrogen fluoride at or above one-half of the recommended time-weighted average environmental limit. Occupational exposure to hydrogen fluoride should be controlled so that no employee is exposed to hydrogen fluoride at a concentration greater than 2.5 mg of fluoride ion, determined as a time-weighted average (TWA) concentration limit for up to a 10-hour workshift in a 40-hour workweek, or to more than 5.0 mg/m^3 of air as a ceiling concentration for any 15 minute period. If both particulate and gaseous fluorides are present, the total fluoride exposure from all occupational sources should not exceed the recommended TWA concentration. The recommended standard is designed to protect the health and provide safety to the workers for up to a 10-hour workshift, 40-hour workweek over a working lifetime.

hydrogenolysis. Catalytic hydrogen reduction with partial destruction of substrate and formation of molecules of lower molecular weight (than original ones) or with ring opening. Also known as destructive hydrogenation.

hydrogen sulphide. A flammable, poisonous gas with a characteristic odour of rotten eggs. Hydrogen sulphide and sulphides of the alkali and alkaline earth metals are soluble in water. Soluble sulphide salts dissoçiate in water into sulphide ions, which react with the hydrogen ions to form hydrosulphide ion (HS^-) or hydrogen sulphide (H_2S). The relative concentrations of these species are usually function of the *p*H, hydrogen sulphide concentration increasing with decreasing *p*H. The sulphide ion is present in appreciable concentrations above *p*H 10. In well-aerated water, hydrogensulphide is oxidized to sulphate. Biological oxidation to elemental sulphur occurs and sulphides form an indispensable link in nature in the sulphur cycle.

Sulphide occurs naturally in mineral ores, oil, and coal deposits. Copper, lead, zinc, nickel, and other mined base metals may occur as simple or complex sulphides. Iron sulphides are often associated with these ores.

Sulphides are also present in industrial wastes from petroleum and petrochemical plants, chemical plants, gas works, papermills, heavy water plants, and tanneries. Sulphides are generated by suphate-reducing bacteria. The growth of suphate-reducing bacteria in distribution systems can be major cause of taste and odour problems in drinking-water.

Data on the sulphide content of foodstuffs are incomplete and thus the daily dietary intake of sulphides has not been estimated. Exposure may result from the consumption of beer and ale, seafoods, cooked meat, warm milk, and asparagus and other vegetables. In Europe, the maximum likely daily intake of dimethyl sulphide from artificially flavored sweets, soft drinks, creams and jellies was estimated to be 1.7 mg. The inhalation of 20 m^3 of air containing hydrogen sulphide in natural concentrations would result in a daily intake of 0.003-0.01 mg. The intake of the sulphide from drinking-water cannot be estimated owing to the absence of data on sulphide levels in drinking-water. The alkali sulphides are absorbed rapidly from the intestine. Hydrogen sulphide is transformed to alkali sulphide in the blood and tissues. Excretion of sulphide is via the kidneys and lungs, whereas metallic sulphides are excreted by the bowels. Sulphide may also be oxidized to sulpate and thiosulphate and excreted by the kidneys.

Hydrogen sulphide blocks the action of certain enzyme systems some of which are involved directly in celluar oxidative process. Such inhibitive effects have been reported for dehydrogenase (succinic) phosphatase (ATP ase) oxidase (dopa oxidase) carbonic anhydase, dipeptidase benzamidase and some iron-containing enzymes. Mechanism of enzyme inhibition is not completely understood, but is considered to be via the formation of metal sulphides which decrease the availability of cations to the enzymes.

Inhaled hydrogen sulphide gas causes death by paralyzing the respiratory centre; the threshold for acute inhalation poisoning is between 700 and 1000 mg/m^3 (length of exposure was not specified). Exposure levels of 1400-2100 mg/m^3 stimulate the nervous system and are fatal within 30 minutes; levels greater than 2800 mg/m^3 result in instantaneous death by means of nervous system paralysis. The progression of symptoms includes sudden fatigue, dizziness, intense anxiety, loss of olfactory function, collapse, respiratory arrest, and death. Olfactory paralysis prevents detection of hydrogen sulphide beyond concentrations of 225 mg/m^3. Hydrogen sulphide at levels of 0.12 mg/m^3 in air causes mental depression; levels of 1.5-43 mg/m^3 result in conjunctivitis and visual disorders. Levels of 70-700 mg/m^3 produce chronic intoxication resulting in psychic changes, dizziness, confused somnolence, tachycardia, coughing and vomiting.

Hydrogen sulphide in water has a disagreeable taste and odour and its presence is important cause of consumer complaints. The taste and odour thresholds for hydrogen sulphide in solution are estimated to be in the range 0.05-0.10 mg/L. For sulphides, the taste and odour threshold is about 0.2 mg/L. It is unlikely that a person would consume a harmful dose of sulfide because of the unpleasant taste and odour at concentrations much lower than the toxic levels; consequently, the guideline value has been chosen as not detectable by consumers. Exposure to hydrogen sulphide should be controlled so that no worker is exposed to hydrogen sulphide at a ceiling concentration greater than 15.0 mg of hydrogen sulphide per cubic metre of air, as determined for a sampling period of 10 minutes. Evacuation of working area is recommended if the concentration of hydrogen sulphide increases beyond 70.0 mg/m^3.

hydrolysis. The reactions of both organic and inorganic compounds wherein water affects a double decomposition with another compound, hydrogen going to one component, and hydroxyl to another.

hydrophilic. 1. A term with the literal meaning of 'water-loving'; this term refers to substances that tend to absorb and retain water; this results in swelling, often accompanied by formation of gels. Hydrophilic agents are widely used as stabilizers and thickeners in food products, pharmaceuticals, and coatings for textiles, paper, etc. The term should not be confused with hygroscopic. 2. The term is also applied to the surfaces of solids which are readily wetted by water or on which water is adsorbed easily. Thus, wetting is important, *e.g.*, in detergency and in the secondary recovery of oil which involves the displacement of oil from sand by water.

hydrophobic. A term referring to 'water-heating'; this term describes substances which repel water and thus are difficult to wet or emulsify. Most notable of these are fats, waxes, and oils, but this property is also found in many solids in finely divided form.

hydroquinone. A white, crystalline substance soluble in water; mainly used as photographic developer, dye intermediate, inhibitor, stabilizer in paints and varnishes and antioxidant for fats and oils. It is toxic by ingestion and inhalation. The occupational exposure to hydroquinone is defined as work in an area where it is stored, manufactured, used, or processed, except as a component of other materials at a concentration of 5% or less by weight. The use of hydroquinone should be controlled so that no worker is exposed at a concentration greater than 2.0 mg/m^3 (0.44 ppm) of air determined as 15-minute collection period. Other popular names of this compound are *p*-hydroquinone; and *p*-dihydroxybenzene.

hygi-aeration sewage treatement. A package treatment plant for sewage by employing extended activated sludge process.

hygroscopic. A term used to describe solid or liquid materials which pick up and retain water vapour from the air. Some solids having a high internal surface area are made especially for this purpose; by adsorbing vapour molecules they can maintain a small volume of air virtually free from moisture.

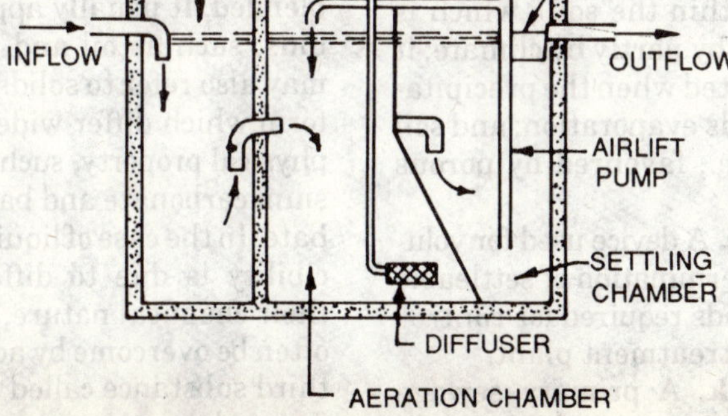

HYGI-AERATION SEWAGE TREATMENT PLANT

I

ignition. 1. The process of complete oxidation. 2. The initiation of such a process. 3. The process of heating a substance until it ceases to lose-weight, indicating that all thermal decomposition, including losses of moisture and volatile matter which may occur up to the temperature of heating, has been completed.

ignition point. Lowest temperature necessary to start combustion of substance in precisely defined and usually normalized conditions. It is also called ignition temperature.

ignition temperature. *See* ignition point.

illuviation. The deposition of colloids, soluble salts and small particles of minerals in an underlying layer of soil. It may be regarded as a kind of translocation (the movement of the solids and solutes within the soil), which is controlled by partly by climate; it is accelerated when the precipitation exceeds evaporation; and soil texture, *i.e.*, favoured by porous soil.

imhoff cone. A device used for volumetric determination of settleable sewage solids required for control of sewage treatment plant.

imhoff tank. A primary sewage treatment precess combining sedimentation with anaerobic sludge digestion in one tank; there is no mechanical equipment. The sewage flows through the upper or sedimentation chamber, the deposited sludge passing through slots into a digestion chamber below. The sludge removal is thus automatic; these tanks having certain advantages over separate sedimentation and sludge digestion tanks.

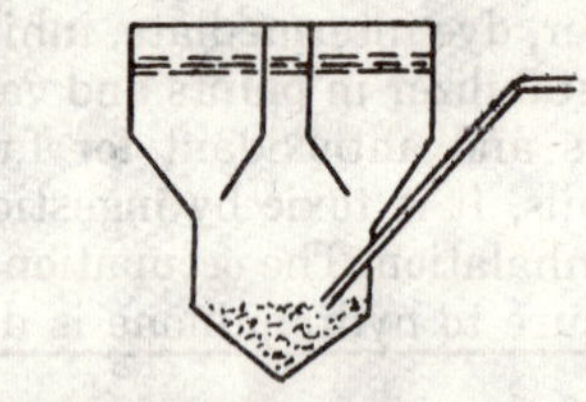

IMHOFF TANK

Imidan. *See* Phosmet.

immiscible. A term used to describe substances of the same phase that cannot be uniformly mixed or blended. It usually applies to liquids, such as oil and water, but may also refer to solids in powder form which differ widely in some physical property, such as magnesium carbonate and barium sulphate. In the case of liquids, immiscibility is due to differences in their chemical nature, which can often be overcome by addition of a third substance called an emulsifier or detergent.

immunity. The state of relative

insusceptibility of an animal to infection by disease-producing organisms or to the harmful effects of their poisons (toxins). Immunity depends on the presence in the blood of antibodies and white blood cells (lymphocytes), which produce an immune response. Inherited (natural) immunity is that with which an individual is born. Acquired immunity is of two types: active immunity, which arises when the body produces antibodies against an invading foreign substance (antigen), either through infection or immunization of serum taken from an individual already immune to a particular antigen. Active immunity tends to be long-lasting, while passive immunity is considered to be short-lived.

implosion. The sudden reduction of pressure by chemical or physical reaction which cause an inrushing of the surrounding medium.

impurity. An extremely low percentage of an extraneous substance either naturally present in a material or added to it accidentally or intentionally.

incineration. A method of treating refuse to reduce the volume and weight and to leave an innocuous residue. Early type of incineration plants were known as normally used continuous-feed plants. A modern incineration plant is usually constructed where landfill disposal sites are distant from the center of generation of refuse, making transfer and transportation of refuse a costly proposition. Incineration involves the burning of solid wastes at high temperatures, typical air pollutants from

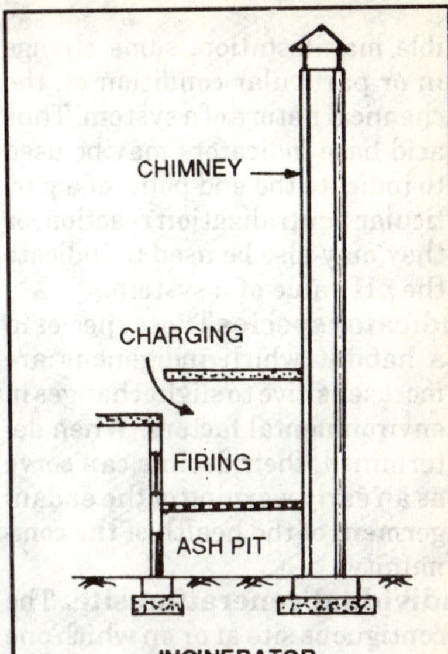

INCINERATOR

incineration are ash, oxides of sulphur and nitrogen, hydrogen chloride, and organic acids.

incipient lethal level. The level of a toxic substance beyond which 50% of a population of organisms cannot live for an indefinite period of time. Incipient lethal levels denote threshold concentrations.

incompatible waste. A hazardous waste that is unsuitable for:

(a) placement in a particular device or facility, because it may cause corrosion or decay of containment materials (*e.g.*, container inner liners or tank walls);

(b) commingling with another waste or material under uncontrolled conditions because the commingling might produce heat or pressure, fire or pressure, fire or explosion, violent reaction, toxic dusts, mists, fumes, or gases, or flammable fumes or gases.

indicator. A substance which shows by a colour change, or other visible manifestation, some change in or particular condition of, the chemical nature of a system. Thus acid-base indicators may be used to indicate the end point of a particular neutralization reaction, or they may also be used to indicate the *p*H value of a system.

indicator species Those species in a habitat which indigenous are most sensitive to slight changes in environmental factors. When determined, their decline can serve as an early warning of the endangerment of the health of the community.

individual generation site. The contiguous site at or on which one or more hazardous wastes are generated. An individual generation site, such as a large manufacturing plant, may have one or more sources of hazardous waste, but is considered a single or individual generation site if the site or property is contiguous.

induced reaction. A reaction that is accelerated when one or more, but not all, of its reactants enter into another reaction with one or more other substance. In system of coupled reactions, path of secondary reaction which depends on simultaneous run of primary, initiating reaction.

industrial effluent. The water- and air-borne wastes of industry. *See also* industrial waste.

industrial effluents standards. The rapid industrialization of India, make it necessary to introduce the minimum permisible limit of standard of industrial effluent, which can be allowed to discharge in the streams.

IS: 2490-1963 given the specifications of the industrial effluent allowed for discharge into the water courses. As per this standard, following are the standards of the 5 day BOD at 20°C of effluent to be discharged into inland surface water as 30 mg/L, in exceptional cases the BOD may be allowed upto 100 mg/L, but in exceptional case as far as possible, and practicable it should be free from colour and unpleasant odours. Its *p*H should be between 5.5 to 9.0. Oil grease, phenolic compounds, cyanides (as CN) and sulphides (as S) should not exceed 10.0,1.0 and 2.0 mg/L, respectively, total suspended solid should not exceed 100 mg/L, presence of arsenic, cadmium, barium, chromium, copper mercury, lead selenium, nickel, silver and zinc should not exceed 1.0 mg/L individually or collectively. Total residual chlorine and fluorides should not exceed 1.0 and 2 mg/L, respectively, and radioactive materials like and emitters should not exceed 10^{-9} and 10^{-8} respectively. The industrial effluent from food-processing industries, dairies, pharmaceutical industries, pulp and paper industries and if the industrial effluent is discharged into public sewers without proper treatment, it may create sewage treatment problems, deteriorates sewer and increase stream pollution. The toxic elements present in the effluent are undesirable for the biological activity in the treatment plant. Sulphates of effluent tend to form sulphuric acid which corrode the sewers.

According to IS:3306-1965, the tolerance limits for Industrial effluents discharged into public sewer are as follow :

(a) its pH value should be between 5.5 to 9.0,

(b) 5-day BOD at 20°C should not exceed 500 mg/L,

(c) lead, copper and zinc should not exceed 1.0, 3 and 15 mg/L respectively,

(d) effluent temperature should not exceed 318 K,

(e) quantity of suspened solids should not exceed 2% each,

(f) effluent containing solids, such as straw, plastic, wood, paint residue, gross solids from cannery wastes, cinder, ash, sand, tar, rag, hari, metal shavings, garbage, broken glass etc, should not be discharged into public sewers,

(g) phenolic compunds, sulphates and the total inorganic compounds (in dissolved form) discharged into public sewers, should not exceed 5,1000 and 1200 mg/L, repectively.

(h) suspended solids should not exceed 600 mg/L, while chloride and boron should not exceed 600 and 2 mg/L, respectively.

industrial furnace. Any of the following enclosed devices that are integral components of manufacturing processes and that use controlled flame devices to accomplish recovery of materials or energy:

(a) Cement kilns

(b) Lime kilns

(c) Aggregate kilns

(d) Phosphate kilns

(e) Coke ovens

(f) Blast furnaces

(g) Smelting, melting, and refining furnaces (including pyrometallurgical devices, such as cupolas, reverberator furnaces, sintering machines, roasters, and foundry furnaces)

(h) Titanium dioxide chloride process oxidation reactors.

(i) Methane reforming furnaces

(j) Pulping liquor recovery furnaces

(k) Combustion devices used in the recovery of sulphur values from spent sulfuric acid.

(l) Such other devices as the Administrator may, after notice and comment, add to this list on the basis of one more of the following factors:

(i) The design and use of the device primarily to accomplish recovery of material products.

(ii) The use of the device to burn or reduce raw materials to make a material product.

(iii) The use of the device to burn or reduce secondary materials as effective substitutes for raw materials, in processes using raw materials as principal feedstocks.

(iv) The use of the device to burn or reduce secondary materials as ingredients in an industrial process to make a material product.

(v) The use of the device in common industrial practice to produce a material product.

(vi) Other factors, as appropriate.

industrial waste. The materials (generally solid, occasionally liquid or gas) discarded from trading, commercial and industrial premises and requiring appropriate disposal. It can be divided roughly into five categories:

(a) general factory waste,

(b) relatively non-reactive wastes obtained during industrial operations,

(c) flammable process wastes,

(d) acid or caustic wastes, and

(e) indisputably toxic wastes.

industrial wastewater. Industries use huge quantities of the nation's waters and are the major factor in the continuing rise in water pollution. They utilize over 15 trillion gallons of water but, prior to discharge, treat less than 5 trillion gallons. In terms of a single pollution parameter, BOD the waste generated by industries is equivalent to that generated by a population of over 360 million people. Even more undesirable than the BOD loads of industrial effluents are the enormous quantities of mineral and chemical wastes from factories which steadily become more complex and varied. They include metals such as iron, chromium, nickel, and copper; salts such as compounds of sodium, calcium, and magnesium; acids such as sulfuric and hydrochloric; petroleum wastes and brines; phenols; cyanides; ammonia; toluene; blast furnace wastes; greases; many varieties of suspended and dissolved solids; and numerous other waste compounds. These wastes degrade the quality of receiving waters by imparting tastes, odors and colour; and through excess mineralization, salinity, hardness, and corrosion. Some are toxic to plant and animal life. The variety and complexity of inorganic and organic components contained in industrial effluents present a serious liquid waste-water treatment control problem in that the pollution and toxicity effects of these constituents are of greater significance than those found in domestic waste waters. The great variety of industrial pollutants argues against an attempt to classify them, but for the purpose of general discussion, at least five distinct categories of wastes from industrial sources have been recognized, which are as follows:

1. Oxygen-demanding materials wasted to water by industrial processes have been calculated to amount to 15 million tons of five-day chemical oxygen demand (BOD_5) per year having an aggregate discharged strength, after treatment, of 6.5 million tons of BOD_5 per year. The estimate, then places the oxygen demand of industrial wastes before treatment at 3.5 times that of sewered domestic wastes, and after-treatment strength at 5.5 times that of the after-treatment strength of domestic wastes.

2. Settleable and suspended solids wasted to water by industrial processes are calculated to amount to about 12 million tons per year before treatment, over 3.5 million tons after treatment, with the relationship between industrial and domestic wastes quite similar to that for BOD.

3. Many materials which impart acidity or alkalinity or which contain radioactivity are added to water in undeterminable amounts by manufacturing activities. Often these are directly toxic. Such materials cause a permanent changes in water quality that is not neutralization-the latter usually adding to the concentration of total dissolved solids-are the only remedies in such cases.

4. Heat in the amount of several million joules is currently discharged annually into water by industrial processes, most of it by the electricity generating indus-

try. Although some control is exercised through recycling procedures, particularly in arid areas, the major part of the industrial cooling water is discharged directly to streams. Waste heat is a pollutant in that it reduces the utility of water for additional cooling and may radically alter aquatic ecology. It also contributes to the polluting effect of water borne materials by accelerating chemical reaction rates and by reducing the solubility of gases-including oxygen.

5. Toxic compounds occur in water as a result of industrial processes, either through direct discharge by establishments producing such compounds(*e.g.*, factories engaged in the production of pesticides or pharmaceuticals), by the synergistic interaction of materials in water, or through the food chain. Again, no quantitative assessment is available, and for the second category of toxins, even determining probability of occurrence cannot be attempted.

inert. Having little or no chemical affinity or activity. The six elements comprising the noble-gas group of the Periodic Table are either wholly or relatively inert.

influent stream. A stream or reach of a stream that contributes water to the zone of saturation and develops bank storage; its channel lies above the water table.

infra red radiations. The emissions in the wavelength range 0.78 microns to about 300 microns; often produced as unwanted emissions during heating and rolling of metals and glass. Infrared radiations find applications in for applying controlled heat to industrial processes. Since these are associated with heat and may cause skin burns depending on intensity and duration of exposure. Over the years of exposure, they can cause cataract of the eye.

infra sound. Sound waves composed of mechanically induced pressure waves which are below the threshold of hearing in humans. The hazards due to infra sound waves include changes in the blood circulation, and in the tissues of fingers, hands, and arms in the operators who use various vibrating tools. In some cases it can lead to 'dead hand' or 'white fingers' when they are exposed to cold air or water as well.

inground tank. A device in which a portion of the tank wall is situated to any degree within the ground, thereby preventing visual inspection of that external surface area of the tank that is in the ground.

inhibitor. Any substance that retards or reduces the rate of a chemical reaction; the opposite of a catalyst. Antioxidants are well-known inhibitors of oxidation reactions in foods, rubber, and other organic materials.

injection well. A well into which fluids are injected.

initiator. A substance exhibiting unusual chemical activity, which enables it to set in motion, or induce, a chemical reaction such as polymerization, oxidation, or detonation. Well-known initiators are peroxides, which evolve oxygen, organic ions (carbanions and carbonium ions), and free radicals.

inner liner. A continuous layer of material placed inside a tank or container that protects the construction materials of the tank or container from the contained waste or reagents used to treat the waste.

in-place pollutant. A pollutant that has sunk to the bed of a body of water and has become incorporated in to the bottom sediments. Nearly any material heavier than water has the potential of becoming an in-place pollutant. Lighter materials may also become in-place pollutant if they have ability to sorb to particulates in the water, which then settle out, carrying the pollutants with them to the bottom. In these manners, bottom sediments in particular heavily used areas such as industrial harbors and shipping channels may actually come to contain more pollutants than sediments. In-place pollution adversely affect rooted aquatic vegetation and bottom dwelling invertebrates, easily entering the food chain through these creatures, where they become subject to biological magnification in fish, birds, and mammals, including humans. They also serve as reservoir from which pollutants may be resuspended in the water.

insecticide. A chemical compound that is lethally toxic to insects but not so much to human being or plants in small doses either by ingestion or by paralytic body contact; it is applied to vegetation, crops, and insect-breeding areas in dilute form in solid or liquid medium by spray. There are five major types; inorganic metallic compounds, for example, Bordeaux mixture (copper sulphate-lime); natural organic compounds, such as rotenone; chlorinated hydrocarbons, typified by DDT; organic phosphorus esters (parathion and its derivatives) methylcarbamates, such as carbaryl (1-naphthyl N-methylcarbamates). Of these the fourth is by far the most toxic to man. Insecticides are also classified according to the type of action on the human/animal body, such as: stomach poisons, systemic poisons, fumigants, repellents, attractants, insect growth regulators, *etc.* They may act in one or more than one way.

inspection chamber. A chamber with a manhole at the junction of small diameter sewers or at the point of change of direction of such sewers for having ready access for inspection and facilitating rodding operation for the removal of choking materials from the lines.

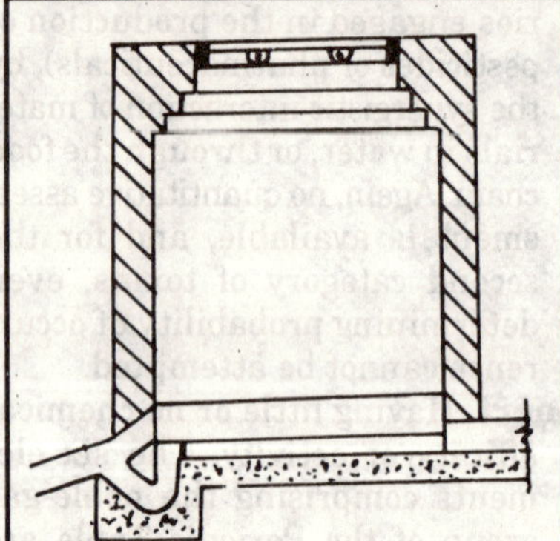

INSPECTION CHAMBER

installation inspector. A person who, by reason of knowledge of the physical sciences and the principles of engineering, acquired by a professional education and related practical experience, is qualified to supervise the installation of industrial plants and tanks.

intake well A well constructed on the river bed close to the bank of the river for drawing water from the river for the purpose of water

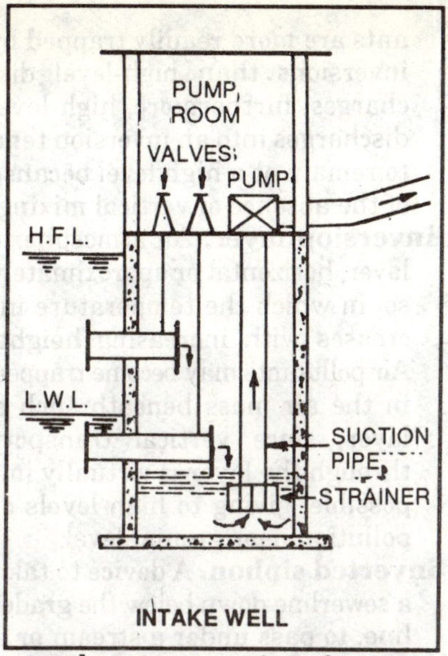

supply to a community, after treatment.

interceptor. A sewer that receives dry-weather flow from a number of transverse combined sewers and additional predetermined quantities of intercepted surface runoff and conveys such waters to a point for treatment.

intercept well. A well drilled into a contaminated aquifer in order to intercept the flow of contaminants and pump them out, thus protecting the downgrade portions of the aquifer. Intercept wells are generally drilled in groups, forming a curve line around the downgrade perimeter of the contaminant plume. They are commonly used to guard against seawater intrusion in coastal aquifers as well as to limit the pollution of the aquifers from the sewage of hazardous wastes.

interface. The area of contact or boundary layer between two forms of matter or two phases of a dispersion,

interfluve. The area of land between adjacent streams.

internal drainage. Surface drainage in which the water does not reach the ocean, such as drainage toward the central part of an interior or basin.

internal loading. In pollution control, the total amount of the pollutants entering a body of water by recycling from sediments in its bed. Internal loading tends to continue for some time after other pollution sources are controlled.

International convention for the prevention of pollution from ships. A convention held in London in 1973, at the end of the International Marine Pollution Conference, convened by the Intergovernmental Maritime consultative Organization (IMCO). The conference, the largest ever held on the subject, was attended by 500 representatives of the leading maritime nations.

The convention applied to any ship of any type whatsoever, including hydrofoil boats, air-cushion vehicles, submersibles, floating craft and fixed or floating platforms, operating in the marine environment. It covers all aspects of intentional and accidental pollution from ships by oil or noxious substances carried in bulk or in packages, sewage and garbage. But it does not deal with dumping which is covered by the Convention for the Prevention of Marine Pollution by Dumping from Ships and Aircraft, nor the release of harmful substances directly arising from the exploration, exploitation and associated offshore processing of sea-bed mineral resources.

International Referral System. A programme for the international exchange of information on environmental problems and solutions; part of the Action Plan adopted by the United Nations Conference on the Human Environment, 1972.

International shipment. The transportion of hazardous waste into or out of the jurisdiction of the United States.

inversion. A meteorological term for the phenomenon of temperature inversion in the atmosphere in which the temperature, instead of falling, increases with height above the ground. With the colder and heavier air below, there is no tendency to form upward currents and turbulence is suppressed. Inversions are often formed in the late afternoon when the radiation emitted from the ground exceeds that received from the sinking sun. Inversions are also caused by katabatic winds, *i.e.*, cold winds flowing down the hillside into a valley, and by anti-cyclones. In inversion layers, both vertical and horizontal diffusion is inhibited and pollutants become trapped, sometimes for long periods. Low-level discharges of various pollutants are more readily trapped by inversions than high-level discharges; furthermore, high-level discharges into an inversion tend to remain at a high level because of the absence of vertical mixing.

inversion layer. An atmospheric layer, horizontal or approximately so, in which the temperature increases with increasing height. Air pollutants may become trapped in the air mass beneath such a layer, since vertical transport through the layer is virtually impossible, giving to high levels of pollution near ground level.

inverted siphon. A device to take a sewerline down below the gradeline, to pass under a stream or a railway track and to raise it again to the regular gradeline beyond. The siphon should consist of two parallel pipes laid straight in grade and alignment and at either end, manhole should be palced. Self-cleansing velocity must always be maintained in the inverted siphon.

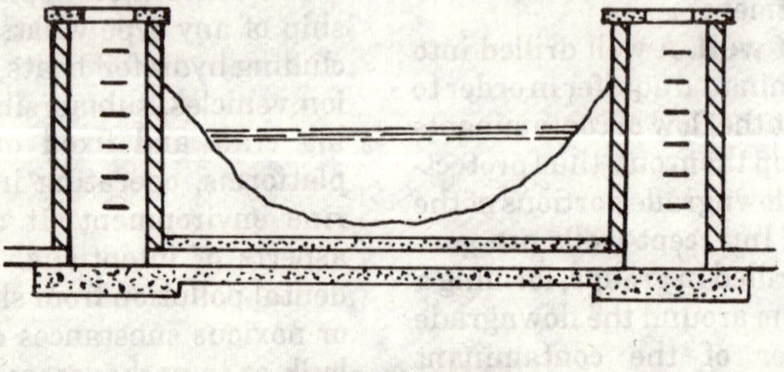

INVERTED SIPHON

iodine. One of the less active members of the halogen family of elements, and is classified as a nonmetal. In terms of abundance in the crust of the earth, the element ranks 53rd and is about as plentiful as tin, antimony, cesium, and barium. It is quite poisonous in the concentrated, state, and even the 3% solution used as an antiseptic is dangerously toxic if swallowed, though it can be applied topically without risk. It is extracted from Chilean nitrate, which contains about 0.2%, from natural brines and to a limited extent from seaweed. Acute poisoning due to iodine is intensely irritating to nose and throat causing coughing, soreness and tightness of chest. If swallowed, it usually induces violent vomiting. Iodine is not required by plants, but if iodine is present in the soil, it is taken up by most plants and moves on into the diets in certain forms that are effective in preventing goiter. Occupational exposure to iodine should be controlled so that no employee is exposed to iodine at a concentration greater than 1.0 mg/m^3 of air (0.1 ppm), determined as a time-weighted average (TWA) concentration limit.

ion. Atom or group of atoms with electrical charge equal to elementary charge or its multiple. The properties of ions are quite different from those of the neutral units from which they are derived, because of the presence of the electric charge.

ion exchange. In pollution control, the removal of dissolved pollutants by means of a chemical reaction which involves the exchange of ions of the same sign of electric charge between a solution and an inorganic or organic solid or liquid called an ion exchange. The ion exchanger is considered to be insoluble in the solution. The use of ion exchange processes has been found to be very effective for the removal of calcium, magnesium, iron and many other undesirable ions from polluted as well as hard water. It has also been employed for the removal of sulphur dioxide from stack gases.

ionic sieves. Ion exchangers (most often inorganic) of such pore dimensions which enable exchange of smaller ions while mechanically excluding larger ones; in case of big differences in counter ion dimension organic ion exchangers also can act as sieves.

ionosphere. The region of the earth's upper atmosphere in which free electrons arising from ionization occur, mainly as a result of ultraviolet radiation and *X*-ray from the sun. The ionosphere is useful in that it enables intercontinental radio transmission round the curved surface of the earth to be achieved, as a result of its property of reflecting electromagnetic waves of radio frequencies; but it is an obstacle to radio astronomy because it reflects a large proportion of the radiation that arrives from extra terrestrial sources.

iron. Iron is the fourth most abundant element by weight in the earth's crust; placed in group VIII of periodic table. In water it occurs mainly in the divalent and trivalent (ferrous and ferric) states. Both cast iron and steel pipes are employed for drinking-water distribution to the consumer. In the production of potable water, various salts of iron are used as coagulating agents.

Iron in surface-water is generally present in the ferric (Fe III) state. The concentration of iron in well aerated water is seldom high, but under reducing conditions which may exist in some groundwater, lakes or reservoirs and in the absence of sulfide and carbonate, high concentrations of soluble ferrous iron may be found. Concentrations of iron greater than 1 mg/L have been reported to occur in groundwater. The presence of iron in natural waters can be attributed to the dissolution of rocks and minerals, acid mine drainage, landfill leachates, sewage or iron-related industries.

Iron is an essential element in human nutrition. It is contained in a number of biologically significant proteins, for example, haemoglobin and cytochromes, and also in many oxidation-reduction enzymes. Estimates of the minimum daily requirement for iron vary from 7 to 14 mg, depending upon age and sex; pregnant women may require in excess of 15 mg per day. The average daily requirement is considered to be 10 mg.

Iron ingestion in large quantities result in a condition known as haemochromatosis (normal regulatory mechanisms do not operate effectively wherein tissue damage results from iron accumulation. This condition rarely develops from simple dietary overloading. However, the condition has resulted from prolonged consumption of acid foodstuffs cooked in iron kitchenware. Haemochromatosis has not been demonstrated in test animals receiving extremely high doses of iron. Small children have been poisoned following the ingestion of large quanties of iron tablets.

The presence of iron in drinking-water supplies is objectionable for a number of reasons unrelated to health. Under the *p*H conditions existing in drinking-water supplies, ferrous salts are unstable and precipitate as insoluble ferric hydroxide, which settles out as a rust coloured silt. Such water often tastes unpalatable and stains laundry and plumbing fixtures. The iron that settles out in the distribution system gradually reduces the flow of water. Iron also promotes the growth of iron bacteria. These micro-organisms derive their energy from the oxidation of ferrous iron to ferric iron, and in the process deposits a slimy coating on the piping.

The above problems usually arise especially in distribution systems when the iron concentration approaches 0.3 mg/L, and consequently whenever possible it would be prudent to maintain levels below this value.

iron bacteria. Any of several genera of bacteria that, through their metabolic processes, cause iron compounds to precipitate from seawater and become deposited in seafloor sediments. It is thought that this process is at least partially responsible for the concentration of iron into ore bodies suitable for mining in many parts of the world. Also known as iron-fixing bacteria.

irradiation. Exposure to rays, *e.g.*, *X*-rays and ultra-violet rays.

irreversible reaction. A chemical reaction that can proceed in only one direction, *i.e.,* to the right, giving a product (or products) that is/are more stable than the reactant(s) and that cannot revert to the original constituents.

ISCLT model. The industrial source complex long-term model is a steady-state Gaussian plume model which can be used to assess pollutant concentrations from a wide variety of sources associated with industrial source complex. This model can account for settling and dry deposition of particulates, the downwash, area, line and volume sources, plume rise as a function of downwind distance, separation of point sources, and limited terrain adjustment. ISCLT model has been designed to calculate the average seasonal and/or annual ground-level concentration or total deposition from multiple continuous point, volume and/or area sources. In this model provision is made for special discrete *x*, *y* receptor points that may correspond to sampler sites, points of maxima or special points of interest, and sources can be positioned anywhere relative to the grid system.

ISCST model. The industrial source complex short-term model is a steady-state Gaussian plume model which can be used to assess pollutant concentrations from a wide variety of sources associated with an industrial source complex. This model can account for settling and dry deposition of particulates, downwash area, line and volume sources, plume rise as a function of downwind distance, separation of point sources, and limited terrain adjustment.

isopropyl alcohol. A colourless liquid with pleasant odour; used in the manufacture of acetone and its derivatives, glycerol and isopropyl acetate, as solvent for essential oils and gums, deicing agent for liquid fuels and as denaturant. The reports suggest that it appears to have carcinogenic effect on humans during the course of its manufacture. The occupational exposure to isopropyl alcohol is defined as exposure to airborne concentration of isopropyl alcohol at or above one-half of the recommended workplace environmental limit. The occupational exposure to isopropyl alcohol should be controlled so that no employee is exposed to isopropyl alcohol or its vapours at a concentration greater than 984 mg/m^3 of air (400 ppm), determined as the time-weighted average (TWA) concentration limit for up to a 10-hour workshift in a 40-hour workweek, over a working lifetime.

isotope. Any of two or more forms of an element whose weights differ by one more mass units as a result of variation in the number of neutrons in the nuclei. Isotopes of an element have the same atomic number but different mass number *A*, *i.e.*, of the same number of protons but different number of neutrons.

itai-itai disease. The health problem caused as a result of chronic cadmium poisoning, first described in 1970 in Toyama, Japan, about 200 km northeast of Tokyo on the east coast of island Honshu. The city is located near a zinc smelter, and cadmium released by the smelter had poisoned the soil of the nearby rice paddies, thus raising the cadmium level in the rice consumed by the local residents. Symptoms of this disease include severe pains in bones and joints, softening of bones, kidney damage, and eventually death.

izal. An emulsion of tar oils, it is mainly used as a disinfectant and deodorant.

J

jar test. The test required to be carried out in a water treatment plant to determine the optimum dosage of coagulant for complete reaction in forming flocs with their settling characteristics depending up on the trubidity, *p*H and alkalinity of raw water.

jet fuel. Two types of petroleum fractions used as fuels for the gas turbines of jet aircraft. These are kerosine with a boiling range of 423-563 K and wide-cut gasoline with a boiling range 303-553 K. The former is considered as somewhat safer in use since it has a higher flash point and is less liable to be ignited accidentally if spillage takes place. It is thus preferred for civil aircraft. Since only 5% of crude petroleum is available as straight-run kerosine, military aircraft tend to be fuelled with wide-cut gasoline.

jet stream. A strong current of air blowing through the atmosphere at a high altitude. The main jet streams are in the middle and the sub-tropical latitudes. The temperate jet stream flows from west to east, though along a wave-like route, going north and south as it winds all round the world. It can blow at a speed of up to 350 km/h. Jet streams develop at or near the tropopause over very strong surface fronts, especially those connected with polar air masses.

Jetzer process. A process for composting and utilization of the refuge. It takes in to account the rapid increase in environmental pollution through the buildup of refuge in urban aggregates; and is commercially as well as ecologically viable. The compost formed after the household refuge is subjected to decomposition of easily reducible substances, is further subjected to Jetzer compost plate process, in which the fibre base is fed in to a horizontally rotating rotary drier, on one side of which hot air is injected at an input temperature of about 1050 K to heat up the damp fibrous material. The refuge is stirred thoroughly while exposed to the hot-air current for 2-7 minutes, the temperature of on leaving the drying drum falling to about 370-500 K. The high temperature and the steam together serve to kill protozoa, fungi, bacteria, and viruses completely. The complete elimination of water as a result of high temperatures and the decomposition in to individual fibre particles in constant movement result not only in coagulation of proteins but also in destruction of the cell wall or of the cytoplasmic membranes of the microorganisms. The resulting material is absolutely sterile, inert, stable fibre material. This is separated from air and steam in a cyclone and split up by sifting in to five fractions, each of which is submitted to special air separation. The materials are grouped in different sizes, and heavy items like ceramics, glass, and metals are segregated. The fibres are subsequently collected in intermediate bunkers. From the intermediate bunker, the fibres are mixed and metered, according to need and the desired plate quality, with wood chips and shavings. The fibres are treated with glue, combined in briquettes and finally compressed. The type of compression corresponds by and large to methods of plate pressing in general use. Finally, the plates are trimmed and polished. The fibre plates so produced are used primarily for building walls and as insulating material.

junction chamber. A manhole consisting of a masonry chamber constructed on sewer lines at junction points to have easy access for inspection and cleaning.

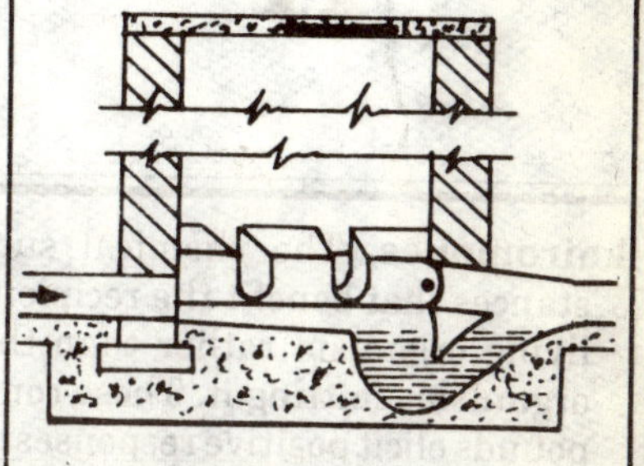

JUNCTION CHAMBER

juvenile water. Water formed from the chemical reactions within the earth, which has not yet existed as surface water or as atmosphere water vapour. The amount of juvenile water produced each year by the earth is not known, but it is thought to be extremely small.

K

kairomones. The chemical substances that benefit the recipient living organism rather than the organism emitting it. These compounds elicit positive responses of predators to their prey, herbivores to their food plants, and parasites to their hosts.

kaolin. A group of clay minerals with a two layer crystal structure in which each silicon oxygen sheet is alternately linked with one aluminium hydroxide sheet and having the approximate composition $Al_2Si_2O_5(OH)_4$. The kaolin minerals are generally derived from alteration of alkali feldspars and micas; classified as nuisance particulate. Occupational exposure to kaolin should be controlled in such a manner so that no employee is exposed to kaolin at a concentration greater than 10.0 mg/m^3 of the total dust, or 5.0 mg/m^3 of total respirable dust.

kaolinite. 1. $Al_2Si_2O_5(OH)_4$. A common clay mineral of the kaolin group. It is the characteristic mineral of most kaolins and is polymorphous with dickite and nacrite. Kaolinite is a high-alumina clay mineral that does not appreciably expand under varying water contact and does not exchange iron or magnesium. The mineral was formerly known as kaolin. 2. A name sometimes applied to the kaolin group of clay minerals and formerly applied to individual minerals of that group, *e.g.*, dickite and nacrite.

karyotype. The characteristics of the set of chromosomes (in respect of sizes, shapes and numbers) of a representative somatic cell of a given species or individual.

katabatic wind. A wind caused by cold air flowing downhill. When a sloping land surface cools by night-time radiation, the cold air in contact with the ground flows downhill and along valley bottoms; opposite of an anabatic wind.

katatectic layer. A layer of solution residue, usually composed of gypsum and/or anhydrite in salt-dome cap rock.

Kelvin. K. The SI unit of thermodynamic temperature defined as the fraction 1/273.16 of thermodynamic temperature of the triple point of water, *i.e.*, the triple point of water exists exactly at 273.16 Kelvins. The units of Kelvin and Celsius (centigrade) temperature interval are identical. A temperature expressed in degrees Celsius is equal to the temperature in Kelvins less 273.15°C. This is true both for thermodynamic temperatures as well as on the International Practical Temperature Scale. The name 'degree Kelvin' (symbol °K) was discontinued by the international agreement in 1967.

kepone. An insecticide which is toxic by ingestion and inhalation; classified as potential occupational carcinogen. Occupational exposure to kepone is defined as exposure to kepone at a concentration less than one-half the recommended environmental limit. Occupational exposure to kepone should be controlled so that no employee is exposed to kepone at a concentration greater than 1.0 μg/m^3 of air, determined as a time-weighted average (TWA) concentration limit for up to a 8-hour workshift. The recommended standard is designed to protect the health and provide safety to the workers for up to a 8-hour workshift, 40-hour workweek over a working lifetime.

kerma. Energy supplied to defined medium by gamma or neutron radiation as kinetic energy of secondary charged particles.

kerogen. The complex fossilized organic material which yields petroleum-type hydrocarbons on heating and distillation. It is also known as petroleum.

Kessener tank. A long tank used in Kessener process to agitate sewage, the flow being from end to end.

ketones. A class of reactive organic compounds whose formula is characterized by a carbonyl group to which two organic groups are attached: these groups may be either paraffinic (alkyl) or aromatic (aryl). The ketones are named in various ways:

(i) By combining the names of the radicals (alkyl or aryl) with ketone, as dimethyl ketone, ethyl methyl ketone, *etc.*

(ii) The Geneva names are formed by adding the suffix-*one* to the root of the parent hydrocarbon. Thus, acetone is propanone; ethyl methyl ketone is butanone. Ketones are used primarily as solvents, in lacquers, explosives, and textile processing. The recommended exposure limits for some of the ketones are shown below:

Acetone,	590 mg/m^3
Methyl ethyl ketone,	590 mg/m^3
Methyl *n*-propyl ketone,	530 mg/m^3
Methyl *n*-butyl ketone,	4 mg/m^3
Methyl *n*-amyl ketone,	465 mg/m^3
Methyl *iso*-butyl ketone,	200 mg/m^3
Methyl *iso*-amyl ketone,	230 mg/m^3.

kick. A surge or thrust against the normal fluid circulation in an oil well, as a result of a well pressure that exceeds the pressure exerted by the drilling mud arrival.

kiln. An oven, furnace, or any other similar device, for the heating certain materials or products. These days, car tunnel kiln is used for the firing of ceramic ware; it is heated by gas, oil or electricity; in contrast to the older intermittent type of kiln. It is smokeless and has made a great contribution to clean air. Claus kiln is another installation used in the last stage of the recovery of sulphur from petroleum and natural gas. Gas rich in hydrogen sulphide is produced in the earlier stages; part is burned to give sulfur- dioxide, which is mixed with the remainder over a catalyst to give elemental sulphur. In modern installations the process is conducted in two stages to increase the yield that must be disposed of. Hoffman kiln, is a commonly used brick-making kiln; it can give rise to intense pollution by smoke and by sulphur and fluorine compounds.

Kilval. A systemic insecticide and acaricide of high persistence of particular value against woodlly aphid. It is metabolized in the plant to the suiphoxide which has similar biological activity but grater persistence. It forms a colourless waxy solid, very soluble in water (4 g/ml) and most organic solvents, but almost insoluble in light petroleum and cyclohexane. It undergoes slight decomposition at room temperature. It is noncorrosive and compatible with most pesticides. The acute oral LD_{50} for male rats is about 100 mg/kg. The toxicity of the sulphoxide is reduced by about half. Kilval is especially effective against woolly aphid; used for control of sap-feeding insects and mites on fruit, rice, cotton, and many other crops. Also known as Vamidothion.

knick point. A point of sharp change of slope especially in the longitudinal profile of a stream or of its valley.

konimeter. An instrument used for the approximate determination of the amount of dust in suspension in the air. A form of the instrument is based on the fact that the intensity of the coloration produced in certain substances by the condensation of water vapour increases with the dust concentration in the air.

L

lacustrine. 1. Related to, inhabiting, or produced by lakes; *e.g.*, lacustrine environment. 2. A region populated by lakes is said to be lacustrine.

LAER. *See* lowest achievable emission rate.

lagoon. In pollution control, the term lagoon refers to an oxidation pond in which waste water is purified through sedimentation, and both aerobic and anaerobic biochemical action over a period of time. Lagoon treatment or 'ponding' involves storing liquid waste in natural or artificial lades, although this storage is provided in different circumstances to achieve different ends. The two main types of lagoon are:

(i) Stabilization lagoon. A lagoon in which crude sewage or industrial waste is treated. These are used in many countries where reasonably long periods of sunshine can be expected throughout the year. Careful maintenance is necessary otherwise this type of lagoon may become a nuisance as a source of odour and mosquito breeding. The technique gives a 60-80 per reduction in biochemical oxygen demand (BOD) and removes 75-85% of the solids. Improvement in performance may be achieved by installing surface aerators.

(ii) Maturation lagoon. A lagoon or pond for the tertiary treatment of sewage works effluent; a great improvement in the organic quality of an effluent is achieved. A fully oxygenated effluent is produced. The major disadvantage of this method of treatment is the large area occupied by the lagoons.

In geology, the term lagoon refers to: 1. A body of shallow water between a barrier island and the shore. 2. A body of water inside the coral reefs of an atoll. 3. A shallow pond or lake generally near but separated from or communicating with the open sea.

lagoon cycle. The sequence of events, and interval of time, involved in the filling of a lagoon with sediments followed by eventual erosion by wave action and refilling by deposition.

lake. 1. A term loosely applied to a sheet of water lying along a coast and connected with the sea. 2. Any inland body of standing water occupying a depression is the earth's surface, generally larger than a part and too deep to permit vegetation. The term includes an expanded part of a river, a reservoir behind a dam, or a lake basin intermittently or formerly covered by water. 3. An English term for a brook or small stream.

lake deposit. A sedimentary deposit laid down conformably on the floor of a lake, usually consisting of coarse material near the shore and sometimes passing rapidly into clay and limestone in deeper water.

Lamella separator. A recently developed device for sedimentation of suspended particles in water. The influent enters at the top of the clarification basin and is then directed to flow downward through a series of parallel plates. The sludge settle at the bottom of the basin, while the clarified water rises to the top of the basin by return tubes. The plates are inclined at 30° to 45° to the horizontal and are spaced at about 4 cm apart.

land breeze. The movement of air from land to sea. On clear nights the land cools faster than the water, cooling more quickly the lowest layers of air. The heavier land air spills seaward displacing the warmer sea air.

land-fill. The most common form of disposal of refuse; it appears that between 80-90% of the world's refuse will be disposed of by this method for several years to come. The type of sites being used for such disposal are:

(a) mineral excavations,
(b) low-lying land,
(c) valleys,
(d) areas involving the reclamation of land from water, and
(e) flat land to build up a feature.

Generally, in a sanitary landfill scheme, refuse is tipped in trenches or cells prepared to such a width that the daily input of refuse can be effectively covered, presenting a clean face each day. The refuse can be tipped either at the bottom of the face and dozed into the face, or tipped on top of the previous fill and dozed over the face. It is essential that the refuse be adequately covered and compacted to allow traffic over the fill. The land-fill method is also known as controlled tipping and sanitary land-fill; while the content of both expressions is identical, the former emphasizes the system by which the waste is deposited while the latter emphasizes the hygiene aspects.

landfill cell. A discrete volume of a hazardous waste landfill that uses a liner to provide isolation of wasters from adjacent cells or wastes. Examples of landfill cells are trenches and pits.

land treatment facility. A facility or part of a facility at which hazardous waste is applied onto or incorporated into the soil surface; such facilities are disposal facilities if the waste will remain after closure.

land use. The deployment of land for a variety of uses, such as agriculture. industry and commerce housing, and recreation. Land use planning has as its object the spatial coordination of such activities on a national, regional and local level. Through zoning, performance specifications, and building codes, governments cannot only specify the uses to which land can be put but also place restrictions on those uses. Controls can prevent the establishment of industries with a high air pollution potential in poorly ventilated basins and valleys; and the establishment of noisy or odorous processes near residential areas. The ways in which land is used can be ploted on maps. The present land utilization survey produces maps on a scale of 1:25,000. Land use maps can also be drawn for urban areas; they can reveal zones of industrial use, business use, expensive housing, etc., and on large-scale maps it is possible to show the use of each building.

Lannate. A new broad-spectrum, systemic and contact insecticide and acaricide. It is also effective as a nematicide. It is a white crystalline solid, slightly soluble in water, soluble in acetone, ethanol, methanol; the aqueous solution is non-corrosive. It is a non-skin irritant and is stable in solid form and aqueous solution under normal conditions, but decomposes in moist soil. The acute oral LD_{50} for male rats is 17 mg/kg. As a soil treatment it has given systemic control of certain insects and nemathodes. It is of promise as a foliar spray for many insects such as aphids, Colorado beetle, leaf-rollers and many other caterpillars, and red spider mites. Also known as Methomyl.

lapse rates. The rate of decrease of temperature with increasing height in the atmosphere. From the surface to a height of about 11 km, known as the troposphere, the lapse rate is, on average about 6° to 8°C per km. There are considerable departures from this average at all times and at all levels, and it is these departures which characterize the type of weather experienced. If the temperature shows to change with height the condition is described as isothermal. In the stratosphere, the layer of the atmosphere above the troposphere, the lapse rate is isothermal. If a parcel of air is displaced upwards without any heat being supplied or removed the air will expand and cool at a rate which is known as the *D*ry *A*diabatic *L*apse *R*ate (DALR), the value of which is 10°C per km. This is also known as a 'neutral gradient'. If a parcel of saturated air is similarly displaced, the cooling will be less than with dry air due to the latent heat made available from the condensation of moisture. The rate at which it cools, known as the *S*aturated *A*diabatic *L*apse *R*ate (SALR), is about 6°C per km. The saturated adiabatic lapse rate is not constant at all levels. An atmosphere in which the temperature decreases with height more quickly than the SALR is said to be unstable or superadiabatic. If the lapse rate is negative, *i.e.*, temperature increases with height, the atmosphere is said to be stable. Owing to the enthalpy of condensation, the value of the saturation adiabatic lapse rate is less than that of the dry adiabatic lapse rate. Sometimes the word 'stable' is attached to any atmosphere in which the lapse rate is less than the SALR. The actual lapse rate in the atmosphere is known as the *E*nvironment *L*apse *R*ate (ELR). Under average meteorological conditions, the actual temperature gradients lie between 0° and 12°C per km. Super-adiabatic lapse rate is defined as a temperature lapse rate of magnitude greater than the dry adiabatic lapse rate. This state of atmospheric instability is most likely of occur over a land surface strongly heated by the sun, and is usually very favorable to the dispersion of air pollutants. However, it causes looping of elevated plumes and can land to pollutants being brought down to ground level in high concentration for short periods.

LASERS. An abbreviation for *L*ight *A*mplification by *S*timulated *E*mission of *R*adiation. Lasers therefore, are amplifiers and particularly oscillators in the optical range. The difference in filament lamps or discharge lamps, which use spontaneous emission (in general, from thermal sources), is that the laser employs induced emission and nonthermal sources. The resulting radiation is monochromatic and has time and spatial coherence. As in high-frequency engineering, amplification requires an amplifying element and feedback; in the microwave and optical ranges, such elements are provided by invertible materials and optical cavities. Stimulated emission is basic to the operation of lasers (and also of masers, which is the acronym for microwave amplification by stimulation emission of radiation). When light passes through an optical material, it is exponentially attenuated or absorbed. This means that some of the quanta give up their energy to the atoms, which are excited; electrons are raised from the ground level to higher ones. The light leaving the material has an intensity lower than that on input. The stimulated atoms give up their energy spontaneously and in a statistically random fashion in the form of light or heat. The spontaneous emission (electron transition from a higher level to a lower one) is not dependent on an external radiation field. The light produced by a laser may be continuous or pulsed at intervals of sub-micro or sub-milliseconds. A laser beam is characterized by the following features: high collimation (resonator property), monochromaticity, partial and time coherence (induced emission), high power density at the focus of a lens, and high frequency (optical transition).

The main health hazard arising from the use of lasers is to the eye. The damage may be severe and permanent to both retina and the pupil. The lasers are also capable of damaging skin tissues. In addition, there is a danger of fire if the lasers are used in the presence of flammable materials. Apart from this, the more familiar hazards due to lasers are:

(a) high voltage electric current;
(b) low voltage electric current;
(c) static electricity on mirrors;
(d) flash tube brilliance;
(e) breakage of glassware;
(f) toxic and irrespirable gases:
(g) flash tube explosion;
(h) flash tube infra red and ultra violet radiation; and
(i) fusible materials in beam path.

latosol. A great group of zonal soils characterized by deep weathering and abundant hydrous-oxide material. They are developed under forested humid tropical conditions.

law of stream gradients. A general law expressing the inverse geometric relation between stream order and the mean stream gradient of a given order in a given drainage basin.

leachate. Any liquid. including any

suspended components in the liquid, that has percolated through or drained from hazardous waste.

leaching. The process by which material such as organic matter and mineral salts is washed out of a layer of soil or dumped material by percolating rain-water.

leaching field. A system of open pipes within covered trenches allowing the effluent from a septic tank to enter the surrounding soil.

leaching pit. A cesspool or a pit built underground with honeycombed walls so that the foul water in the pit drains out by leaching action and finds its way into the subsoil.

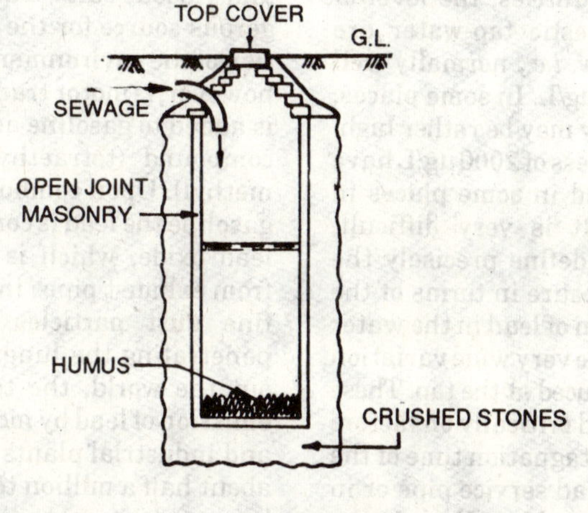

LEACHING PIT

lead. One of the heavy metals, placed in group IVA of periodic table. Lead is present in a wide variety of foodstuffs. The amounts vary depending on the type of food. For instance, canned foods tend to contain the highest levels if lead solders have been used in the manufacture of the can. Most of the fresh vegetables, cereals, and fruits contain small quantities of lead as a result of some limited absorption of the metal from the soil in which they are grown, and because of the deposition on surfaces from lead in the air. Lead is also present in milk and dairy products and in wine. Because of the large differences in individual diets, precise calculations of lead intake are not possible. Estimates of typical daily intakes range from less than 100 to over 500 µg of lead the worldwide average for adults is about 200 µg/day.

The natural lead content of lake and river water worldwide has been estimated to be 1-10 µg/L. Although higher values have been recorded where contamination has occurred, particularly from industrial sources, such situations are relatively rare, since there are a number o natural mechanisms that control the levels. The concentrations in finished water (*i.e.*, water after treatment) prior to its distribution are generally lower than in source waters since lead is partially removed by most conventional water-treatment processes. The levels in drinking-water, however, can be much higher owing to the use of lead service pipes running from the street to a dwelling, from lead plumbing, and/or lead-lined storage tanks. Particularly high lead levels can result when the water is aggressive, soft, or has a low *p*H. These conditions tend to produce the highest levels. Lead pipes have not been used extensively throughout the world, but in some towns and cities in certain countries lead is till being widely used. This occasionally results in undesirably high levels of lead in the tap-water.

In most countries, the level of lead in domestic tap-water are relatively low, *i.e.,* normally well below 10-20 μg/L. In some places, however, they may be rather high. Values in excess of 2000 μg/L have been recorded in some places in the world. It is very difficult, however, to define precisely the average exposure in terms of the concentration of lead in the water because of the very wide variation of levels produced at the tap. These levels depend critically on factors such as the stagnation time of the water in a lead service pipe or in household plumbing. Even in the same water supply area, there may be considerable home-to-home variations in the level of lead because of differences in the length of pipe, water-use patterns, and types of deposit that have built up.

An important consideration is the proportion of the lead in drinking-water that is actually absorbed when ingested. Although little is known about the absorption of fine particles of lead present in tap-water, some information exists on the intestinal uptake of lead from aqueous solutions containing dissolved lead. Generally a figure of about 10% is regarded as typical of the fraction absorbed for an adult, but this value depends on whether the water is consumed on a gastrointestinal tract, such as the presence of elements such as calcium, phosphorus, iron, copper, and zinc in the diet, and the age and physical state of the subject.

Lead dust is emitted by different industrial plants (through flues into the air) in the form of oxides and various salts. The most dangerous source for the contamination of the environment with lead, however, is motor transport. Lead is added to gasoline as an organic compound (tetraethyl or tetramethyl). Upon combustion of the gasoline the lead is converted into lead oxide, which is discharged from exhaust pipes in the form of fine dust particles capable of penetrating the lungs. Throughout the world, the total annual emission of lead by motor vehicles and industrial plants amounts to about half a million tons. Human beings, plants and animals absorb lead from the most diverse sources. From sewage water it gets into ground and river water; from waste gases it gets into the atmosphere, and from there into foodstuffs and beverages. By far the greatest volume is inhaled with the air we breathe, however. While some 5%-15% of the lead contained in the food we consume is absorbed by the intestines, the absorption by the lungs of lead from exhaust fumes in the air we inhale amount to almost 100%. The damage done by lead released into the atmosphere is extremely difficult to eliminate. Particularly worrying, therefore, is the long-term buildup of lead in the environment. The ground on both sides of busy streets and highways is seriously contaminated with lead to a distance of 0.5 to 1 km. The oceans of the world today have a lead content more than 50 times above the natural level.

Pulmonary absorption depends on the size of lead particles are deposited on the mucous lining of the respiratory tract, and are ultimately swallowed. Pulmonary retention is typically 40%. Absorbed lead enters the blood and is distributed to soft tissues and bone. After prolonged exposure an equilibrium is reached between the blood and soft tissues. In contrast, bone has the ability to accumulate lead with time. Postmortem studies indicate that the skeletal burden of lead increases with age; in fact, about 90% of the total body burden lies in the bone. The respective half-lives of lead in blood, soft tissues, and bone have been estimated to be 2-4 weeks,4 weeks and 27.5 years.

Lead passes through the placenta easily and fetal blood has almost the same lead concentration as maternal blood. Lead also passes the blood-brain barrier, although the brain does not accumulate lead. Relationships between lead intake and blood lead level have been extensively studied and reviewed. It appears that there is a curvilinear relationship between air lead and blood lead; as lead exposure increases the corresponding blood lead increments become smaller. The interrelationship between lead exposure from water and blood level is also curvilinear, and this has been demonstrated in human beings drinking household tap-water where lead was present in high concentrations, *i.e.,* exceeding 50 μg/L.

It should be stressed, however, that at the present time there is considerable uncertainty regarding the precise relationship between low-level exposure to lead and levels in the blood; consequently, great care need to be exercised when using data derived from such relationships.

Soluble lead salts, and insoluble lead compounds which can be rendered soluble by metabolic processes, are toxic. At the outset the symptoms of lead poisoning are: general upset, loss of appetite, loss of energy, etc. Later on, the persons affected lose weight and suffer from anemia. In woman the menstrual cycle is disturbed. Characteristic changes in the blood count set in; and the red blood cells appear granulated. In every case a blue line appears around the gums, and there is a slate-gray discoloration produced by a buildup of the metal in the oral cavity. The blue line, which is frequently the first specific sign of lead poisoning, may last a long time, well after the cause of the poisoning has been removed. At a later stage, more serious symptoms of lead poisoning, sometimes verging on the fatal, will manifest themselves in such forms as lead colic, feeble pulse and high blood pressure, cirrhosis of the kidney (nephritis), acute or nagging pains in the muscles, and finally bring fever (encphalopathy) accompanied by severe headaches, epileptic-type fits and psychosis. Also established are nervous ailments displaying symptoms of paralysis, arthritis, allergies and other skin reactions, anemia and various metabolic disorders. In cases of chronic lead poisoning severe damage can also be done to the chromosomes, which transmit hereditary factors.

Typical lead poisoning with clearly diagnosable symptoms mainly affects persons working in the lead industry, who in the course of their activity have absorbed large quantities of the heavy metal. Less prominent but probably more problematic is the gradual poisoning of the environment by smaller quantities of lead and the chronic lead poisoning of people, who from childhood onward, are exposed to higher accretions of lead throughout their lifetime. It must also be noted that the lead concentrations well below the levels that give rise to physical symptoms can still touch off marked behaviour disturbances. The occupational exposure to lead should be controlled in such a manner so that no employee is exposed to lead at a concentration greater than 50.0 μg/m³ of air, determined as a time-weighted average (TWA) concentration limit for up to a 8-hour workshift in a 40-hour workweek. The ambient water quality criterion for lead is recommended to be identical to the existing drinking water standard which is 50 μg/L. Analysis of the toxic effects data resulted in a calculated level that is protective to human health against the ingestion of contaminated water and contaminated aquatic organisms. The available data for lead indicate that acute and chronic toxicity to saltwater aquatic life occur at concentrations as low as 668 and 25 μg/L, respectively; and would occur at even lower concentrations among the species that are more sensitive than those tested. Exposure to inorganic lead is defined as exposure to compounds of lead such as its oxides, and salts (inorganic organic salts such as lead soaps but excluding lead arsenate). Occupational exposure to inorganic lead should be controlled so that no employee is exposed to lead at a concentration greater than 0.1 mg/m³ of air, determined as a time-weighted average (TWA) concentration limit for up to a 10-hour workshift in a 40-hour workweek. All workers subjected to exposure to inorganic lead should be offered biological monitoring at least every 6 months. If blood level of 0.06 mg Pb/100 g or greater is found, and confirmed by a second sample taken within 2 weeks, steps to reduce absorption of lead should be taken as soon as high levels are confirmed.

lead-uranium ratio. The ratio of lead-206 to uranium-238 and/or lead-207 to uranium-235, formed by the decay of radioactive uranium within a mineral. The ratios are frequently used as a part of the uranium-thorium lead age method of estimating the geologic age of a rock of mineral.

leaf area index (LAI). The ratio of the leaf surface area of a plant to 1 m² of the ground surface beneath it. For example, if the LAI is

3, the plants have developed a leaf surface three times larger than the soil surface beneath, that is, the leaf surface covers an area of 3 m^2. Ratios greater than 1:1 occur because plants can produce may layers of leaves, or grow in dense bunches. High LAI values are usually found in undisturbed plant communities while low LAI values are typical of agricultural crops and pioneer communities.

leak-detection system. A system that is capable of detecting the failure of either the primary or secondary containment structure or the presence of a release of hazardous waste or accumulated liquid in the secondary containment structure. Such a system must employ operational controls (*e.g.,* daily visual inspections for releases into the secondary containment system of above ground tanks) or consist of an interstitial monitoring device designed to detect continuously and automatically the failure of the primary or secondary containment structure or the presence of a release of hazardous waste into the secondary containment structure.

leaping weir. A device to divert the sanitary sewage of a combined sewer into a sanitary sewer during storm.

learning. A process by which an animal's response to a particular situation may be permanently altered, usually in a beneficial manner, as a result of its experience. Learning allows an animal to respond more flexibly to situations it encounters: learning abilities in different categories of learning have been proposed, but there is no general agreement on how many different processes are involved.

leukemia. A frequently fatal disease in which there is an uncontrolled over production of white blood cells.

levee. A raised bank formed by deposition, which allows the level of the river to rise above its flood plain.

licences. Means of controlling pollution in many developed countries, in which the waste discharges from large numbers of installations are controlled through the issue of licences, each licence containing a stringent set of conditions relating to the discharge in terms of volume, nature, and manner of release; licences may be waived or rescinded at any time.

LIDAR. A system, based on the same principle as radar, in which a light pulse produced by a laser is used to detect and measure the

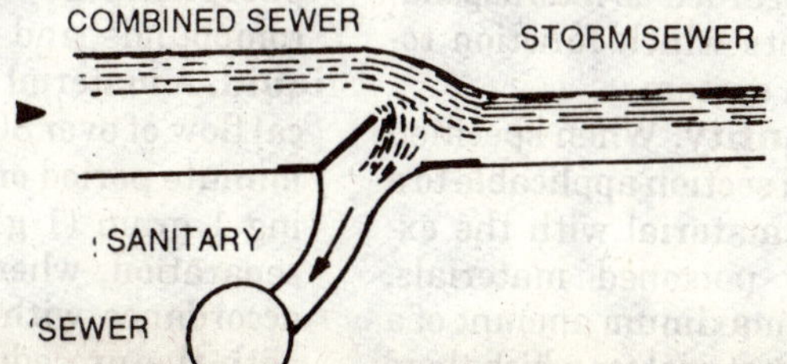

LEAPING WEIR

distance to an object. It is used in air pollution research to detect and track chimney plumes at considerable distances, long after they have become invisible to the naked eye. The term 'lidar' (*Li*ght *D*etection and *R*anging) has come to be applied to such optical radar. A lidar can readily detect the small particles which make up the aerosol content of the atmosphere and smoke plumes. Lidar equipment comprises:

(a) a laser transmitter which emits very brief, high intensity pulses of coherent light; and

(b) a receiver, which detects the energy at that wavelength backscattered from the atmospheric aerosol as a function of range. Lidar has been used for several different purposes in air pollution studies, but its most important application in this area is the measurement of the density of smoke plumes.

life system concept. The part of an ecosystem which determines the existence, abundance, and evolution of a particular population. A life system comprises a subject population and its effective environment; the latter includes all those biotic and abiotic and abiotic agencies influencing the population. Population and environment are regarded as interdependent elements which function together as a system.

limited quantity. When specified as such in a section applicable to a particular material with the exception of poisoned materials, means the maximum amount of a hazarodus material for which there is a specific labeling and packaging exception.

limiting factor. An ecological term referring to any environmental factor whose availability or presence serves as a limit to the growth of an organism, a community, or a population. In all these cases, growth is affected when the limits of the limiting factor are exceeded, even if all other factors contributing to growth are still underutilized. The common limiting factors for the growth of plants are light, temperature, rainfall, and nutrient availability.

limnology. The scientific study of the physical, chemical, and biological condition of lakes, ponds, and streams.

lindane. *See* hexachlorocyclohexane.

liner. A continuous layer of natural or man-made materials, beneath or on the sides of a surface impoundment, landfill, or landfill cells, that restricts the downward or lateral escape of hazardous waste, hazardous waste constituents, or leachate.

lipid. One of a group of naturally occurring fats or fatlike materials consisting of the higher fatty acids, their naturally occurring compounds, and substances found naturally in chemical association with them. Principle types of lipids include the triglycerides, phospholipids and associated compounds, and the terpenoids.

liquid. A material that has a vertical flow of over 50 mm within a 3-miniute period or a material having 1 gram (1 g) or more liquid separation, when determined in accordance with the procedures with the procedures specified in ASTM D 4359-84, Standard Test Method for Determining whether a material is a liquid or solid.

lithosol. An azonal group of shallow soils lacking well-defined horizons and composed of imperfectly weathered fragments or rock. It usually develops on steep slopes.

lithosphere. The earth's crust enclosing the kernel of the earth of bathysphere. It is commonly considered as extending to a depth of about 80 km from the surface of the earth; however only the outer part of it or biogeosphere is associate with any form of life.

litter. Waste materials thrown randomly over a surface. The term can refer to natural as well as human wastes and to large materials as well as small.

littoral. Pertaining to the benthic environment or depth zone between high water and low water, or to the organisms of that environment.

littoral drift. Sand moved under the effect of longshore current; it carries sand which has been stirred into suspension by the turbulence of the breaking waves. The direction and strength of the waves determine the direction and magnitude of the litho transport as a given time. Determining the direction and average net annual amount of the littoral drift, is important in developing shore protection plans. Onshore and offshore sand movements caused by low swells and steep waves respectively, coupled with littoral drift, help to explain the major shore-line changes on the open coasts of the world.

littoral zone. The shallow, marginal region of a lake, characterized by rooted vegetation; the area where sunlight is able to penetrate to the lake bottom, the zone sustaining a high level of photosynthetic activity. A small shallow pond may consist entirely of littoral zone, while a deep lake with an abruptly sloping basin may posses an extremely restricted littoral zone. Per unit volume of water, the littoral zone yields more biomass than either the limnetic or profoundal zones.

living fossil. Any organism whose closest relatives are extinct and that was once itself thought to be extinct. An example of the living fossil is the coelacanth, a primitive fish that was common in the Devonian era, the first recent living specimen of which was discovered in 1938.

load-on-top system. A code of practice aimed at minimizing pollution from oil-carrying ships; it involves passing the washings from tank cleaning operations and residue from discharge of the original ballast water to an empty cargo tank nominated as the 'slope tank'. Fresh oil cargo is loaded on top of the final residue left after further discharges of water, the resulting mixture being acceptable to refineries despite some additional cost in removing the salt and water. Under the International Convention for the Prevention of Pollution from Ships, 1973; all oil-carrying ships will be required to be capable of operating with this method of retention, or alternatively to discharge to recreation facilities.

loam. A soil containing sand, silt, humus and clay in roughly equal proportions.

location of industry. The factors influencing the location of industry may be defined as:

(a) availability and cost of raw materials of satisfactory quality and security of future supplies;

(b) adequacy of local resources such as water supply and facilities for waste disposal;

(c) availability of labour having regard both to number and degree of competence required;

(d) delivery costs of sending the final product to markets of sufficient size and certainty, and competitiveness of the product in those markets;

(e) transport and communications; 6. load-bearing requirements for site;

(f) availability of local specialized industries and services;

(g) level of local costs generally (rents, rates, wages, etc.);

(h) cost of site development (land cost, levelling, filling, drainage, roads, etc.);

(i) availability, reliability and cost of fuel;

(j) availability of housing, local transportation, schools, religious places such as temples or churches, hospital and recreation facilities;

(k) planning and developing restrictions and inducements; and

(l) the possibility of development of site for additional plant in due course of time.

Clearly the 'weightage' given to each of these items will vary according to the type of business activities involved. The Primary reason for a plant location study by a company is to find a site at which a plant of suitable size can produce the highest return on invested capital; the aim is to establish the optimum location. The problem of location involves highly complex studies concerned not only with present but also future conditions and changing pattens, and often involves difficult decisions.

Planning and industrial development cannot be dissociated from the concept of the socially-responsible utilization (or conservation) of resources, and with larger objectives which may be regarded as desirable by some, such as 'zero population growth' or 'zero industrial growth' and a stable standard of living. These concepts, accepted as social objectives, would restrict industrial development to industrial change in a qualitative sense associate with only small or zero quantitatively expansion. There is certainly an increasing tendency in public policy towards the exclusion of certain industries from certain areas on the simple proposition that the social penalties would outweigh any social gains. The nature of a 'social penalty' and a 'social gain' is bound to shift with any shift in 'social values', but the general thrust today is undoubtedly in the direction of some restraint on the unbridged industrial expansion.

Lodofenphos. A non-systemic contact and stomach insecticide and acaricide, used mainly for control of stored products pests. For crop protection purposes persistence is one to two weeks. If forms colourless crystals, almost insoluble in water, slightly soluble in benzene and acetone. It is stable in neutral media but unstable in strong acids and alkalis. The acute oral LD_{50} for rats is 2100 mg/kg. It has been found to be effective against various pests of stored products and public hygiene, and for crop protection against a wide range of coleopterous, dipterous, and lepidopterous pests.

logistic curve. An S-shaped curve of population growth which is initially show, then steepens, and finally flattens out at an asymptote determined by the carrying capacity of the environment.

London agreetment. The Salient features of London, Agreement (June, 1990) are:

(a) Both CFCs and Halons to be completely phasedout by 2000 A.D.

(b) A 240 million dollar fund to be operated by the World Bank under UNEP (for three years).

(c) Multinational chemical companies to set up joint ventures in developing countries to produce CFC sustitutes.

(d) Urges all the signatories to ensure that best available ozone friendly substutes are transferred to the developing countries.

(e) Developing countries have been allowed a grace period of 10 years (2020 A.D.) to completely phase out CFCs and Halon.

(f) If the developing, countries do not fulfil their obligations, the amendments allow developing countries to withdraw from the Protocol.

(g) Besides CFCs and Halon, the Protocol also cover HCFCSs carbon tetrachloride and methyl chloroform. Montreal Protocol did not envisage any control on them.

London smog. Incidents of acute episodes of pollution associated with natural fog covering London area for four days (5-8 December 1952). An anti-cyclone reached London from the north-west in the early hours of 5th December and then became stationary. On 6th and 7th December, London Airport had a minimum air temperature of about 267 K and the maximum temperature less than 273 K. Soundings showed two inversions one close to the surface and the other caused by descending (anticyclonic) air higher up. By 7th December, the two inversions were very close to each other. The final result was that London was trapped in the pool of cold and stagnant air, with a kind of very effective lid overhead. At that time, the atmosphere contained a large quantity of water in the form of tiny droplets. Nearly 4,000 people died as a result of this atmospheric activity. Subsequent analysis had revealed that between 80 and 90% of the increase in deaths of persons during and immediately after the fog was due to respiratory and cardiovascular diseases, mainly of chronic nature. Over 90% of the increased death were of the people in the age group 45-60, and 70% over the age of 65. At that time, It was concluded that it was impossible to state if, any one pollutant was the major cause of death, but that the irritants mainly responsible were probably derived from the combustion of coal. The maximum recorded concentrations of sulphur dioxide was 1.34 ppm over a 48-hour period. Another acute air pollution incident occurred in London during 5-9 December, 1962. Persistent fog covered the greater part of the country and was particularly dense in the lower Thames valley. In London, concentrations of sulphur dioxide reached an hourly peak of 1.9 ppm, but pollution by smoke was distinctly lower.

The public was alerted by warnings on radio and television and by press announcement; the aged and those suffering from chronic respiratory and cardiac disease were advised to stay indoors. About 700 persons died in the London area due to the effects of the smog, as compared with 4,000 in 1952. The progressive establishment of smoke control areas under the Clean Air Act of 1956 with a consequent reduction of smoke by domestic dewllings, combined with improvements effected by industry, could well have contributed to the lower mortality. There is, however, no really conclusive evidence on this point. Sulphur dioxide levels were certainly no lower than in the 1952 smog. During the period 1952-66, the discharge of sulphur dioxide from chimneys in London increased by about 30%. The interesting point is the concentrations of sulphur dioxide as measured by instruments at breathing level did not increase. As a large part of the increased tonnage discharged to atmosphere can be attributed to the electricity generation from modern power stations, the net result is undoubtedly a tribute to the efficacy of the high chimneys currently employed.

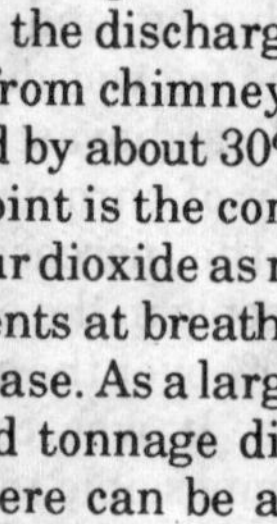

LONG HOPPER CLOSET

long hopper closet. A closet used in early days; it consists of a long inverted stoneware connected to a trap below.

longshore current. An oceanographic term used for the current in a body of water that moves parallel to the shore. These currents result primarily from waves that approach a shore at an angle. Part of the energy of such a wave will be expended on the shoreline, while the rest will be deflected parallel to it. The direction and strength of longshore currents are determined by the angle the wave make with the shore, which in turn depends up on the prevailing wind. Thus longshore currents may reverse from season to season as the prevailing wind changes. These currents are responsible for the transportation of large amounts of sand, silt, and other materials along shorelines, and shape many common shoreline features.

long-term turbidity. A term used in water pollution studies, for the turbidity that does not significantly decrease when a water sample is left undisturbed for a specified period of time, usually seven days. Long-term turbidity is the result of the presence of colloidal clays. It is more important than peak turbidity in determining the water quality and its effect on water-supply systems and aquatic life.

LONGZ model. A standard air-quality model designed to calculate the long-term pollutant concentration produced at a large number of receptors by emissions from multiple stack, building and area sources. It utilizes statistical wind summaries to calculate long-term (seasonal or annual) average concentrations. The model is applicable in areas of both flat and complex terrain, including areas where terrain elevations exceed stack-top elevations. The software requires random-access mass storage capability.

looping. The behaviour of a chimney plume in the presence of superadiabatic temperature lapse rates. Large scale thermal eddies are set up and sporadic puffs of pollutants at high concentration may be brought to the ground at short distances for a few seconds. Looping occurs in the presence of light winds.

Los Angeles smog. Smog of a photochemical nature, largely attributed to the effect of sunlight on motor vehicle exhaust gases. Basic to the Los Angeles control system is a programme of monitoring bcth weather conditions and level of air contamination. The smog problem of Los Angeles persisted after a drastic reduction of major stationary sources of air pollution; which left the motor vehicle as the major probable source. However the cause and effect mechanism, was not at all easy to explain. During smogs considerable increase of ozone and oxidant material occur. The oxidant concentration that can cause eye irritation is regarded as being in the range 0.21 to 0.32 mg/m^3 (0.10 to 0.15 ppm), levels reached very frequently in Los Angeles. The highest value ever recorded in the city was about 1.75 mg/m^3 (0.82 ppm) on 16th December 1966. These were not found in appreciable concentrations at night but only during daylight hours, beginning to form simultaneously throughout the Los Angeles basin in smoggy air, shortly after dawn. These facts suggested a photochemical formation of ozone or oxidants from air impurities by the action of sunlight, sulphur dioxide, nitrogen dioxide and aldehydes absorb ultraviolet radiation in the wave lengths present at ground level and reach in their excited states with molecular oxygen to produce atomic oxygen. Reactions with SO_2 and aldehydes are irreversible, but not so in the case of nitrogen dioxide. In the latter case, the absorption of ultraviolet light leads to the rupture of a bond to form atomic oxygen and nitric oxide. Reaction of the products with molecular oxygen leads to the formation of ozone and the regeneration of nitrogen dioxide. Thus nitrogen dioxide is available for the repetition of the process, unless converted to nitric acid or used up in organic substitution reactions. Hydrocarbons also play an essential part in this reaction, olefins being the most reactive. Ozone formed during the smog accounts for accelerated rubber cracking; while the oxidation of sulphur dioxide to sulphur trioxide with the formation of sulphuric acid aerosol, as well as existing smoke, dusts and fumes, still further reduces visibility. Ozone and peroxy acetyl nitrate (PAN) produce eye irritation, coughing and chest soreness experienced by many Los Angeles residents on smoggy days. It is well established that the automobile was the largest source of air contaminants and leading source of smog-forming hydrocarbons.

loss of head. The loss of head occcurring during the filtration of water as a result of the resistance in the flow of water through the bed. In a pipeflow or channel flow, the loss of head occurs due to the frictional resistance. Thus the pressure head gradually decreases with the length of pipe line of the same diameter

loudness. Annoyance results from both the loudness and the frequency of a noise. Tones which stand out above the background noise, particularly those of high frequency, are usually the most annoying. Loudness depends on the response of the ear to sound and the ear is not equally sensitive at all frequencies.

L_x noise levels. Noise levels in dBA which are exceeded for a specific percentage of the measurement period. For example, L_{10} and L_{90} noise level means that the nose level in dB was exceeded for 10% and 90% of the measurement period, respectively. The advisory council of many advanced countries have recommended the adoption of the L_{10} index for measuring disturbance by traffic noise. It has recommended also that existing residential development should in no circumstances be subjected, as an act of conscious public policy, to more than 70 dB on the L_{10} index unless some form of remedial or compensatory action is taken by the responsibly authority.

lowest achievable emission rate (LAER). In air pollution management, the highest degree of control possible over the emission of pollutants from industrial sources. The LAER for each class of pollutants is defined by the Clean Air Act, to be the most stringent emission standard set for that pollutant by any state implementation plan, or the lowest emission rate for that pollutant achieved in practice anywhere in that country, or whichever is lower. LAER standards may be waived only if the industry can prove that it is impossible to comply with them.

M

macrometeorology. The branch of meteorology which is concerned with the study of large-scale meteorological conditions. The study usually relates to a large geographical region, such as a continent or even the entire globe.

macronutrients. Mineral nutrients utilized by organisms in large quantities, such as carbon, hydrogen, oxygen, nitrogen, phosphorous, sulphur, potassium, and calcium. *See also* micronutrients.

mad hatters disease. A disease suffered by hatters of last century, who became mentally retarded as a result of absorbing mercury used in making felt for hats.

maintenance. The continuation of a species at a particular population density in a given habitat through reproductive behaviour alone.

Malathion. An insecticide derived from diethyl maleate and dimethyldithiophosphoric acid. It is highly toxic by ingestion and inhalation. The action level to malathion is defined as one-half of the recommended time-weighted average (TWA) environmental exposure limit for malathion. Overexposure is defined as either known or suspected exposure that leads to the development of signs and symptoms of absorption of organophosphorus compounds and cholinesterase inhibition. When skin exposure is prevented, exposure to malathion in workplace should be controlled in such a manner so that no employee is exposed to malathion at a TWA concentration greater than 15.0 mg/m^3 of air for up to a 10-hour workshift.

maleic anhydride. A chemical proposed to be assessed as a hazardous air pollutant. Exposure to maleic anhydride in the workplace should be controlled so that no employee is exposed to maleic anhydride at a TWA concentration greater than 1.0 mg/m^3 of air for up to a 10-hour workshift.

malnutrition. A compromised state of human health which results from an inadequate intake of food or an inability to assimilate and metabolize nutrients properly. The most common form of malnutrition is associated with insufficient intake of food or nutrients essential for a balanced development of the body.

management. The systematic control of the collection, source separation, storage, transportation, processing, treatment, recovery, and disposal of hazardous waste. Also termed as hazardous waste management.

manganese. A silver-white metal, member of the transition elements of the *3d* series of the periodic table, falling between chromium and iron. Airborne manganese sources are widespread and its distribution over large distances is favoured by the fact that emitted manganese is predominantly associated with smaller dust particles. When it is present in natural surface-water, manganese occurs in both the dissolved and suspended forms. Anaerobic groundwater often contains elevated levels of dissolved manganese.

Freshwater may contain from one to several thousand micrograms of manganese per litre depending on the location. Higher levels of manganese sometimes found in freely flowing river-water are usually associated with industrial pollution. The reducing conditions that may exist in underground water and in some lakes and reservoirs are conducive to very high levels of manganese.

The metal is derived commercially by electrolysis of manganous sulphate. Its multiple valences make manganese a versatile metal for both analytical and industrial procedures; it can act either as a reducing agent or an oxidizing agent depending on its valence. Its principal uses are in manufacture of manganese salts, as a deoxidizer and purifier in steel manufacture, and as an alloying agent in steel manufacture and in aluminium and magnesium alloys.

Manganese is an essential element in animals and man but only about 3% of ingested manganese is absorbed. It is required as a cofactor in a large number of enzyme systems and plays an important role in the proper functioning of flavoprotenis and in the synthesis of sulphated mucopolysaccharides, cholesterol and haemoglobin, and in many other important metabolic processes. It has recently been suggested that its presence in drinking-water is inversely related to cardiovascular mortality. Absorbed manganese leaves the bloodstream quickly and concentrates in the liver. Manganese concentrated in the liver is conjugated with the bile salts. Manganese has a rather short biological half-life. The storage capacity of the liver for manganese is limited to about 1-1.3 mg/kg (wet weight). In animals, experimentally induced or naturally occurring manganese deficiency has resulted in a variety of symptoms. Although no specific syndrome due to manganese deficiency has been described in man, it has been suggested that there may be an association between manganese deficiency and disorders such as anaemia, bone changes in children and lupus erythematosus.

The main routes of absorption of manganese are the respiratory and gastrointestinal tracts. Owing to the low solubility of manganese in the gastric juice only 3-4% of that orally administered is absorbed by the gastrointestinal tract. Intimately linked with the absorption of manganese is the absorption if iron. Anaemia leads to an increased absorption of manganese is increased more than twofold. Absorption is inversely related to the level of calcium in the diet and directly related to the level of potassium.

Manganese in the body is regulated primarily by excretion rather than by both absorption and excretion. Some of the metal is excreted through the pancreatic secretion and some directly through the wall of the gut. Very little 0.1-2% is eliminated in the urine. Manganeses is regarded as one of the least toxic elements. Chronic ingestion experiments in rabbits, pigs and cattle at 1-2 mg/kg of body weight dose levels have shown no effects other than a change in appetite and reduction in metabolism of iron to from haemoglobin. The acute toxicity due to manganese compounds causes an influenza like illness of metal fume fever in which the patient shivers, and has tightness of the chest for a few hours. The chronic toxicity may affect the nervous system and lungs.

The presence of manganese in drinking-water supplies may be objectionable due to a number of reasons unrelated to health. At concentration levels exceeding 0.15 mg/L, manganese imparts an undesirable taste to beverages and stains plumbing fixtures and laundry. When manganese (II) compounds in solution undergo oxidation, manganese is precipitated resulting in problems of incrustation. Even at concentrations of approximately 0.02 mg/L, manganese will form coatings on piping which may slough off as a black precipitate. The growth of certain nuisance organisms is also supported by manganese; these organisms concentrate managanese and give rise to taste, odour, and turbidity problems in the distributed water.

The guideline value for the drinking-water has been recommended to be 0.1 mg/L based on considerations of the staining properties of manganese. This is a compromise value and obviously, to avoid staining problems concentrations of this metal in solution should be kept as low as possible. The daily atmospheric exposure to manganese of a non-occupationally exposed population living in the non-industrial area has been estimated to be 2-10 μg.

mangroves. Plant communities and trees that inhabit tidal swamps, muddy silt and sand banks at the mouths of rivers and other low-lying areas which are regularly inundated by the sea, but which are protected from strong waves and currents. Mangroves are the only woody species which will grow where the land is periodically flooded with sea water; individual species have adapted themselves to different tidal levels, to various degrees of salinity and to the nature of the mud or soil. Mangroves vary in size from substantial trees up to thirty metres in height down to miniature forms less than waist high. Mangrove swamps and thichets support hundreds of terrestrial, marine and amphibian species. There is reason to believe that many edible marine fish depend on mangrove vegetation, or on the related 'wetlands' between shore and sea, for food and shelter at some stage of their life-cycles. with scattered occurrences elsewhere. Considerable areas of mangroves have been destroyed in recent years, both in many parts of the world, to make way for industrial and housing development, harbors, and aircraft runways.

manhole. A vertical shaft from the surface to the sewer and used for inspection, cleaning, and repair of the system.

marble. Limestone recrystallised by metamorphism to produce a granular mosaic of calcite or dolomite crystals. Colourful streak in marble are due to inclusions of minerals such as mica, pyrite, epidote, quartz, felspar, or iron oxide. Marble is harder than limestone, and often shows no bedding. When bedding exists, it is usually consorted. Pure varieties, without inclusions, are valued by sculptors; veined varieties are used as ornamental stone. This calcic rock is highly vulnerable to damage by acid rain and other forms of air pollution.

marine abrasion. 1. Erosion of a bedrock surface by the to-and-fro movements of an overlying layer of sand under the influence of waves. 2. Erosion of submarine canyons by down slope movement of sediments under the influence of gravity.

marine park. An extension of the terrestrial national park idea to the undersea world; a permanent reservation of part of the sea-bed. Marine parks exist in the United States, Japan, Philippines, Kenya, Israel, and Australia.

marine plain. 1. A coastal plain of marine sediments. 2. A hypothetical wave-cut surface produced during the ultimate stage of marine erosion.

marine pollution. Any noxious and toxic material released intentionally or by accident into seas, oceans and estuaries. Marine pollutions can originate from a number of sources and include sewage and industrial effluent which may be piped directly in to the sea or transported further out at sea by ship and dumped. Domestic and industrial refuse, and until recently nuclear waste, is also dumped at sea by many countries. Oil is another major marine pollutant which may result from tanker collisions, the accidental release of oil from terminals and the illegal cleaning of ships bilges at sea. Between 2 and 5 million tonnes of crude and processed oil are spilled into the seas each year although about two-thirds of the oil of this comes not from ships, but from land-based sources, in particular from the illegal disposal of waste industrial and vehicle oil directly into rivers and drains which ultimately flow into the sea.

marine swamp. An area of low, salty, or blackish water found along the shore and characterized by abundant grasses, trees and similar vegetation. Also known as paralic swamp.

marking. The application of descriptive name, instructions, cautions, weight, or specification marks or combination to be placed upon outside containers of hazardous materials.

marsh. A soft and wet area which suffers from poor drainage and frequent waterlogging. Many marshy areas are completely flooded for part of the year, becoming a little drier periodically. They are generally associated with areas of impermeable rock, and are often flat and low-lying areas of land, where the water-table is near the surface. Some marshy areas are also found in hilly regions where rainfall is very heavy and peat bogs form. They differ from bogs in that circulation is good so that there is a continuous supply of fresh oxygenated water. They are among the most productive of all ecosystems, both in terms of total biomass and in the great variety of organisms that inhibit them. They are also excellent natural water treatment devices, removing virtually all particulates and high proportion of the dissolved solids in the incoming water. It is nearly impossible to drain marshes, by digging deep ditches and lowering the water-table. Environmentalists normally wish to leave marshlands in their present state, whilst farmers often wish to drain them in order to make use of the land.

masking. A decrease of the sensitivity or a change in the quality of the perception of one stimulus by simultaneous action of another. In air pollution context, this term usually applies to odour perception of certain malodorous materials.

mass spectrometry. An analytical technique that is based on the separation, according to their mass/charge quotient, and electrical measurement of ions in an instrument known as a mass spectrometer. Mass spectrometry is an extremely sensitive technique that is applicable to many air pollutants.

mass wastage. The movement of masses of soil or rock under the influence of gravity. Water may be involved as a lubricant, especially in the areas underlain by clay soils, but actually it does not carry the earth material. Slow mass wastage is known as creep, while the more rapid mass wastage is known as landslide. The special types of landslide include the slump, the earthflow and the mudflow. Special types of creep include rock creep, talus creep, and the rock glacier, a slowly moving mass of large and small rocks which acts in most respects like an ice glacier and may in some cases have an ice component.

maximum permissible body burden. The total body content of a radioisotope which, if maintained, will not deliver to permissible.

maximum permissible concentration. The concentration that, if inhaled daily (in the case of workers for 8 hours, and in the general population for 24 hours), dose not, in the present state of knowledge, appear capable of causing appreciable harm, however long delayed, in the target. In setting values for such concentration and in determining the meaning of 'appreciable harm' an authority will have regard, according to the nature of the pollutant, to the need for including a factor of safety, and to the degree of risk that may or may not be acceptable to individuals, population groups (*e.g.*, workpeople), or the general population (proposed definition). *See also* threshold limit value.

maximum permissible dose. The dose of ionizing radiation accumulated in a specified time, of such magnitude that no bodily injury may be expected to result in the lifetime of the person expose and no intolerable burden is likely to accrue to society through genetic damage to his descendants.

maximum permissible level. A term used loosely to refer to the maximum permissible dose-rate of radiation, the maximum permissible concentration of a radioisotope or the maximum permissible degree of contamination of a surface.

mean free path. The average distance that particles of a specified type travel (or types) in a given medium. The mean free path may thus be specified for all interactions (*i.e.*, total mean free path) or for particles types of interactions such as scattering, capture, or ionization. It is an important factor in reactions involving highly reactive chemical species in the atmosphere.

Mecarbam. An insecticide and acaricide with slight systemic properties, used for control of Hemiptera and Diptera. At recommended rates it persists in soil for 4 to 6 weeks. It is a pale brown oil, almost insoluble in water, slightly soluble in aliphatic hydrocarbons, miscible with alcohols, aromatic hydrocarbons, keytones and esters. It is compatible with all but highly alkaline pesticides. The acute oral LD_{50} for rats is 36 mg/kg. It has been found to be effective against scale insects and other Hemiptera, Olive Fly and other fruit flies, leafhoppers and stem flies of rice, and rootfly maggots on vegetables. It is suspected of possessing carcinogenic activity, hence the exposure to workers by all routes should be carefully controlled.

Menazon. A systemic insecticide, used mainly against aphids. It is regarded as non-phytotoxic. It forms colourless insoluble crystals; stable up to 305 K; is weakly basic; and is compatible with all but strongly alkalilne pesticides, but may be decomposed by the reactive surfaces of some inert fillers. The acute oral LD_{50} for female rats 1950 mg/kg. It is most frequently used against aphids, as a seed dressing, as a drench and a root dip, and is also used for woolly aphid on apple.

mercaptan. Any organic compound containing the -SH group. Mercaptans are sulphur analogue of alcohols and phenols. They have objectionable odours and are sometimes added to odourless gases (*e.g.*, natural gas) to give rapid warning of a leak. The unpleasant smell associated with oil refineries is partly due to mercaptans. They are sometime called 'thiols'. Marcaptans may be produced in oil refinery feed preparation units as a result of incipient cracking; the offensive gases are burnt in plant heaters. Mercaptans arising in cracking units are removed by scrubbing with caustic soda, the mercaptans being removed from the spent caustic soda by stream stripping and subsequently burned in a process furnace.

mercury. A heavy liquid metal placed in group IIB of the periodic table. The major source of mercury in the environment is the natural degassing of the earth's crust, quantities ranging between 25,000 and 150,000 tones of mercury per year being released. In addition, many industrial activities not directly related to mercury production or use contribute significant amounts of this element to the environment; these include burning of fossil fuels, smelting of various metals, cement manufacture and waste disposal. In addition, mercury is used in chloralkali plants (producing chlorine and sodium hydroxide), in paints as preservatives or pigments, in electrical switching equipment and batteries, in measuring and control equipment (*e.g.*, thermometers, medical equipment), in dentistry and in agriculture (especially as seed dressings). Mercury can exist in the environment as the metal, as monovalent and divalent salts, and as organomercurials, the most important of which is methyl mercury. Methyl mercury can also be produced from inorganic mercury by the action of micro-organisms. Fish and mammals absorb and retain methyl mercury to a greater extent than inorganic mercury; it is methyl mercury that accumulates along food chains.

An epidemic outbreak of methyl mercury poisoning following ingestion of polluted shellfish and fish has occurred in Japan, associated with some fatal cases and congenital disease. This has been closely linked with heavy industrial pollution in Minamatta Bay. In past, a subsequent reduction in fish consumption had adversely affected Japan's large fishing industry. The presence of unacceptable levels of in flake (school shark) has led to a reduction in the marketing of flake in Victoria. The presence of mercury does not necessarily indicate a condition of pollution; mercury in the ocean, for example, is largely of natural origin. Generally, inorganic salts of mercury (if present in minute quantities) are not a threat to living creatures, and are widely used in agriculture to control disease and pests; in contrast, organic compounds used to control fungal diseases in seeds and growing plants, fruits and vegetables, can be absorbed by humans and are extremely toxic. Alkyl mercury may cause permanent mental retardation.

Mercury serves no beneficial physiological function in man; its physical and chemical states (metal, inorganic compounds, organomercurial compounds) each have intrinsic properties that dictate independent toxicological assessment.

Absorption of inorganic mercury compounds from food is about 7-8% of the ingested dose; in contrast, the gastrointestinal absorption of methyl mercury is practically complete. Absorption of inorganic mercury compounds from water may be 15% or less whereas the methyl mercury is almost completely absorbed. Inorganic mercury compounds are rapidly accumulated in the kidney, the main target organ for these compounds. Absorbed methyl mercury rapidly appears in the blood where, in man, 80-90% is bound to red cells; demethylation of methyl mercury to inorganic mercury occurs at a slow but significant rate. The greater intrinsic toxicity of methyl mercury compared with inorganic mercury is due to its lipid solubility, which permits it to cross biological membranes more easily than inorganic mercury, especially into brain, spinal cord, and peripheral nerves, and across the placenta. Mercury compounds are excreted from the kidney, liver, intestinal mucosa, sweat glands, salivary glands, and through milk; the most important routes are via the urine and faeces.

The major effects of mercury poisoning take the form of neurological and renal disturbances, which are primarily associated with organic and inorganic mercury compounds respectively. In addition to producing general toxic effects, mercury causes gonadotoxic and mutagenic effects and disturbs the cholesterol metabolism. The present studies have revealed that mercury is highly toxic in all forms, both as element and virtually every known compound, whether inhaled, ingested, or absorbed through the skin. Exposure to small amounts of elemental mercury over short periods of time is not normally a problem due to its high chemical immobility. However, the exposure to high amounts or chronic, long-term exposure to small amounts can cause nervousness, irritability, timidness, and tremors. At very high concentration it can cause nerve damage and severe birth defects. For total recoverable mercury, the criterion to protect freshwater aquatic life is 0.00057 μg/L, and concentration should not exceed 0.0017 μg/L at any time; while the criterion to protect saltwater aquatic life is 0.0025 μg/L. For the protection of human health from the toxic effects of mercury ingested through water and contaminated aquatic organisms, the ambient water criterion has been determined to be 144 ng/L; while for the protection of human health from the toxic properties of mercury ingested through contaminated aquatic organisms alone, the ambient water criterion has been determined to be 146 ng/L.

mesoclimate. A local climatic effect due to terrain extending influenced over several km and vertically one or two hundred metres, contrasting with the regional or macroclimate.

mesometeorology. The branch of meteorology which is concerned with the study of medium-scale meteorological conditions. The area covered is typically of the order of a few to some tens of square km

mesopause. The top of the mesosphere at about 80-85 km.

mesophyte. A plant which requires an average amount of moisture; in consequence most trees, shrubs, and herbs, living in climates of moderate rainfall and temperature are mesophytes.

MESOPLUME model. An air-quality model, which is designed to calculate concentrations of sulphur dioxide and sulphate ions over long distances. This model is highly user oriented, and provides a range of flexible options. It has been designed to be driven by user-specified meteorological scenarios, of arbitrary duration, constructed by a suitable meteorological pre-processor, MESOPAC. It outputs spatially-gridded concentration arrays averaged over arbitrary time intervals of one hour or more and is designed to be coupled to a post-processor, MESOFILE, to provide additional graphical and statistical analyses.

MESOPUFF model. A variable trajectory regional-scale Gaussian puff air-quality model, especially designed to simulate the air-quality impacts of multiple point sources at long distances. It is highly user-oriented and provides a range of flexible options. It is designed to be driven by user-specified meteorological scenarios, of arbitrary duation, constructed by a suitable meteorological pre-processor, MESOPAC. It outputs spatially-gridded concentration arrays averaged over arbitrary time intervals of one hour or more and is designed to be coupled to a post-processor, MESOFILE, to provide additional graphical and statistical analyses.

mesosphere. The region of the atmosphere, situated between the stratopause and the mesopause, in which the temperature generally decreases with height.

mesozone. The intermediate depth zone of metamorphism in metamorphic rock, characterized by moderate temperatures 575-775K, hydrostatic pressure, and shearing stress.

metabolism. The sum of the total of the physical and chemical processes by which an organism converts simpler compounds into living, organized substance and then reconverts such material into simpler compounds with release of energy for its use.

metalimnion. The horizontal layer of a thermal stratified lake in which the temperature decreases rapidly with depth. the metalimnion lies between epilimnion and the hypolimnion and includes the thermocline.

metamorphism. Range of processes involving combinations of high temperature, high pressure and chemical action by which rocks in the crust change in nature. Some overlap with diagenesis, but weathering is specifically excluded.

meteoric water. A term used for the water which enters the rocks from the atmosphere, *i.e.,* rain, dew, hail, snow, and also the water of rivers and streams.

meteorological element. An atmospheric variable or phenomenon which characterizes the state of the weather at a specific place at a given time (air temperature, pressure, wind, humidity, thunderstorm, fog, *etc.*).

meteorological influences. The effect of a range of atmospheric characteristics on the dispersal of pollutants, including heat. In respect of air pollution, the concentration of pollutants at or near ground level is a balance between the amount emitted and the degree to which it is diluted and dispersed by the atmosphere, or removed from the atmosphere by gravitation or precipitation. In a modern, industrial society it is only the enormous dilution produced by the atmosphere which renders the situation at all tolerable; without turbulence man could not live in large communities. The most important factor controlling the dispersal of pollution is turbulence. The intensity of turbulence depends on:

(a) wind strength at a standard height;

(b) variation of wind direction with height;

(c) profile of temperature variations with height;

(d) rate at which heat is exchanged between the atmosphere and the ground and outer space

(e) nature of the earth's surface;

(f) profile of wind variation with height; and

(g) cloud formation, rain, etc.

Only in exceptional circumstances will high pollution levels be found when the wind is strong and possessing considerable turbulence. With low wind strengths and reduced turbulence pollution levels frequently increase, the most severe pollution occurs in non-turbulent conditions during an inversion when air temperature, instead of decreasing, increases with height. On the other hand, if the potential temperature gradient is positive, a condition of equilibrium will be reached at which the plume ceases to rise and travels horizontally in an atmosphere of density equal to its own. Vertical movement, whether upwards or downwards, is which it was emitted or at the height to which it succeeded in penetrating. In these conditions an inversion is said to exist. This situation frequently arises on clear calm nights when the ground is cooled by outgoing radiation and the layer immediately above is colder than at higher levels. It also arises when a subsidence inversion occurs at a level well above the ground. In these conditions, plumes tend to follow a meandering path without change in height, a pattern called coning.

meteorological optical range (MOR). The length of part in the atmosphere required to reduce the luminous flux in a collimated beam from an incandescent lamp at a colour temperature of 2700K to 0.05 of its original value, the luminous flux being evaluated by means of the CIE (international commission on illumination) photopic luminosity function. This gives, in effect, an instrumental measure of visibility.

meteorology. The scientific study of the atmosphere; its structure, physical characteristics and phenomena; including the interaction of the atmosphere with the earth's surface and the behaviour of air pollutants after they enter the atmosphere. The atmosphere is regarded as consisting of several more or less concentric layers, the layer adjacent to the earth's surface being the troposphere, followed by the tropopause, stratosphere, mesosphere and ionosphere.

methaemoglobinaemia. The presence of methaemoglobin (a compound of haemoglobin and oxygen, more stable than oxyhaemoglobin) in the blood. It is produced by the action of oxidizing agents on the blood and gives rise in infants to the condition described as 'blue baby'. The most common cause of this disease is the excessive levels of nitrates in water. It is very well established that nitrate can be readily converted in vivo to nitrites as a result of bacterial reduction. In infants, where the stomach acidity is very low, a higher concentration of nitrite is reached, in contrast to the adults in which the conversion from nitrate to ntrite is very less because of the high *p*H of the stomach. The nitrite can oxidise haemoglobin to methaemoglobin, a pigment that is incapable of acting as a carrier of oxygen.

methanol. A colorless liquid, miscible with most of common organic solvents; used as solvent for dyestuffs, oils, gums, resins, waxes, and nitrocellulose. Occupational exposure to methanol should be controlled so that no employee is exposed to methanol at a concentration greater than 262 mg/m^3 of air, determined as a time-weighted average (TWA) concentration limit for up to a 10-hour workshift in a 40-hour workweek, or to more than 1048 mg/m^3 of air as a ceiling concentration for any 15 minute period. The recommended standard is designed to protect the health and provide safety to the workers for up to a 10-hour workshift, 40-hour workweek over a working lifetime. Also known as methyl alcohol; wood spirit; wood alcohol; Colombian spirit.

Methidathion. A non-systemic insecticide, with some acaricidal activity, and capable of foliar penetration. Non-phytotoxic to all plants tested; rapidly metabolized and excreted by plants and animals. It forms colourless crystals, of slight solubility in water, readily soluble in acetone, benzene, and methanol. It is stable in neutral and weakly acid media; but much less stable in alkali. It is compatible with many fungicides and acaricides. Acute oral LD_{50} for rats is 25-48 mg/kg. it has been found to be effective against lepidopterous larvae; foliar penetration enables it to be used against leaf rollers. It is used on a wide variety of crops against leaf-eating and sucking insects and mites, especially against scale insects. Also known as Supracide.

Methomyl. *See* Lannate.

methyl alcohol. *See* methanol.

methyl allyl chloride. This gas has been suggested as a grain fumigant and has been used experimentally in mixtures with other fumigants. In laboratory tests it has ranked above carbon disulphide and ethylene dichloride against eight species of stored product insects. It is nonflammable in concentrations toxic to insects. In field trials in Russia it has shown great promise as a fumigant for cereal grains and pulses and is significantly less expensive to apply than chloropicrin and methyl bromide.

methyl bromide. An organic compound used as solvent and mild fumigent; it is not as toxic to most insect species as are some other commonly used fumigants such as hydrogen cyanide acrylonitrile, and ethylene dibromide. Nevertheless, other properties make methyl bromide an effective and versatile fumigant. The most important of these is its ability to penetrate quickly and deeply into sorptive materials at normal atmospheric pressure. Also, at the end of a treatment, the vapours dissipate rapidly and make possible the safe handling of bulk commodities. Another important property is the fact that many living plants are tolerant to this gas in insecticidal treatments. Methyl bromide is non- flammable and nonexplosive under ordinary circumstances and may be used without special precautions against fire.

Because methyl bromide has a comparatively low boiling point and is not greatly sorbed by many materials, it may be used for low temperature treatments that are not practicable with many other fumigants. Treatments of a wide range of commodities may be conducted at temperatures down to 277 K, or even lower in some instances.

At normal fumigation concentrations, methyl bromide is odourless. This disadvantage is sometimes overcome by mixing it at the time of packaging with a warning gas such as chloropicrin. The chloropicrin usually constitutes 2% of the mixture.

The effect of methyl bromide on man and other mammals appears to vary according to the intensity of exposure. At concentrations not immediately fatal, this chemical produces neurological symptoms. High concentrations may bring about death through pulmonary injury and associated circulatory failure.

methyl chloroform. *See* 1,1,1-trichloroethane.

methylene chloride. A colourless liquid, with ether-like odour; used for decreasing, removing paints, as blowing agent in foams. Occupational exposure to methylene chloride is defined as exposure above one-half the daily time-weighted average (TWA) exposure limit, when there is no exposure to carbon monoxide; because toxicities of carbon monoxide and methylene chloride are additive. When the carbon monoxide levels are more than 9 ppm, occupational exposure to methylene chloride is defined by the equation;

$[C(CO)/L(CO)] + [C(CH_2Cl_2)/L(CH_2Cl_2)] \leq 0.05$; where,

$C(CO)$ = TWA exposure concentration of carbon monoxide; $L(CO)$ = recommended TWA exposure limit of CO = 35 ppm;

$C(CH_2Cl_2)$ = TWA exposure concentration of methylene chloride; and, $L(CH_2Cl_2)$ = recommended TWA exposure limit of methylene chloride = 75 ppm.

In the absence of carbon monoxide, a time-weighte average (TWA) of 9 ppm for up to a 10-hour workday, is applicable, and occupational exposure to methylene chloride should be controlled so that no employee is exposed to methylene chloride at a concentration greater than 261 mg/m^3 of air (75 ppm), determined as a time-weighted average (TWA) concentration limit for up to a 10-hour workshift in a 40-hour workweek.

methyl hydrazine. A colourless, hygroscopic, highly flammable liquid, that is toxic by ingestion and inhalation. It has been found to possess carcinogenic potential in humans. Worker exposure by all routes should be carefully controlled so that so that no employee is exposed to methyl hydrazine at a concentration greater than 0.45 mg/m^3 of air (0.2 ppm), determined as a time-weighted average (TWA) concentration limit.

methyl iodide. A colourless liquid that turns brown on exposure to air and light, and is toxic by ingestion and inhalation. It has been found to possess carcinogenic potential in humans. Worker exposure by all routes should be carefully controlled so that so that no employee is exposed to methyl iodide at a concentration greater than 10.0 mg/m^3 of air (5.0 ppm), determined as a time-weighted average (TWA) concentration limit.

Mesurol. A non-systemic insecticide and acaricide, with a broad spectrum of activity; it is quite persistent and is a powerful molluscicide. It is a white crystalline powder, practically insoluble in water, but soluble in most organic solvents; hydrolysed by alkali. The acute oral LD_{50} for male rats is 100 mg/kg. It is mainly used for control of slugs and snails, can control cutworms and various beetles. Also known as Draza; Methiocarb.

Meuse valley incident. An air pollution incident of the 1930s involving respiratory illness and death. The topography of the Meuse Valley between Huy and Liege, at a distance of about 24 km, is that of a steepsided trench about 1 km wide and 100 m deep. The valley is densely populated and is a centre of heavy industry. From 1-5 December 1930, prolonged stable weather conditions accompanied by the drainage of cold air (katabatic winds) from the uplands into the valley produced a severe inversion with heavy fog. Several hundred people became ill, and many died as a result of respiratory illness. Many cattle had to be slaughtered. An official enquiry begun within twenty-four hours of the end of the fog, put out a report which concluded that the illness and deaths were caused by poisonous waste gas from many factories in the valley in conjunction with unusual climatic conditions. Although it had been impossible to identify any definite compound, sulphur dioxide was thought to be the primary cause. A later investigation revealed that there were 15 factories in the region which could have emitted gaseous fluorine compounds. The conclusion reached was that there was circumstantial evidence that illness was the result of acute fluorine intoxication aggravated by the immense quantities of suspended soot and particles in the atmosphere.

Mevinphos. A contact and systemic insecticide and acaricide of short persistence. Although non-persistent, its high initial kill provides a relatively long period before build-up recurs. It is non-phytotoxic. The technical product is a pale yellow liquid, miscible with water, alcohols, ketones, chlorinated hydrocarbons, aromatic hydrocarbons, but only slightly soluble in alphabetic hydrocarbons. Stable at ordinary temperatures, but hydrolysed in aqueous solution, and rapidly decomposed by alkalis, hence incompatible with alkaline fertilizers and pesticides. It is corrosive to cast iron, mild and some stainless steels, and brass; relatively non-corrosive to copper, nickel and aluminium; non-corrosive to glass, and many plastics, but passes slowly through thin films of polyethylene.

The acute oral LD_{50} for rats is 3.7-12 mg/kg. It is effective against sap-feeding insects (aphids, etc.) at 0.1-0.25 kg/acre, mites and beetles at 0.15-0.2 kg/acre, caterpillars at 0.25-0.50 kg/acre; and some fly larvae; especially useful for giving rapid kill close to harvest. Also known as phosdrin.

mica. Any of a group of monoclinic minerals of the general formula, $(k, Na, Ca)(Mg, Fe, Li, Al)_{2-3}(Al, Si)_4O_{10}(OH, F)_2$. It consists of complex phyllosilicates with perfect basal cleavage, which split into thin elastic laminae and range from colourless to black. An essential feature of mica group is the replacement of one silicon by one aluminium in the silicon-oxygen lattice and a perfect basal cleavage. They lie close to the bottom of the Bowen series, crystallizing out of magma at relatively low temperatures, and are found commonly as tiny flakes scattered through granite and similar igneous rocks. They also form in some metamorphic rocks, notably marble and schists. Crystals of pure mica, known as 'books' due to resemblance of the individual layers to pages, are hexagonal, and may be several metres across.

microclimate. A local climatic effect on a small scale from a metre to a km horizontally effect on a small scale from a height. Vegetation, soil conditions, small-scale topography, structures and industrial activities, may create pronounced microclimatic differences.

micromesh drum filter. Drum type fine screen having non-ferrous wire mesh screen cloth. The drum remaining half-submerged in waste water rotates at a speed of about 4 r.p.m. The screenings when raised above the liquid level are back-flushed into receiving troughs by high pressure jets of water.

micronutrients. Mineral nutrients utilized by organisms only in minute amounts, *e.g.*, iron, boron, copper, manganese, zinc, molybdenum, and chlorine. *See also* macronutrients.

micro-organisms. The microscopic plants (bacteria, fungi and algae) or animals (protozoa, rotifers, crustaceans, and nematodes) found in liquid wastes representing the active agents in biological treatment processes or the participants in the reduction activity.

microphyllous forest. A type of forest found in semi-desert areas, typically in regions with less than 25 cm rainfall per annum. Microphyllous forest occurs extensively in South America, on the Indian sub-continent, and less widely in Africa and Australia. Its appearance is broadly similar in all regions comprising low to medium-sized trees and thorny scrub, all of which show adaptations to survive dry periods. Leaves are small spinney and thickly covered with cuticle to minimize evapotranspiration losses. A thick protective bark is also typical as are deep roots to tap the groundwater supplies. Microphyllous forest can

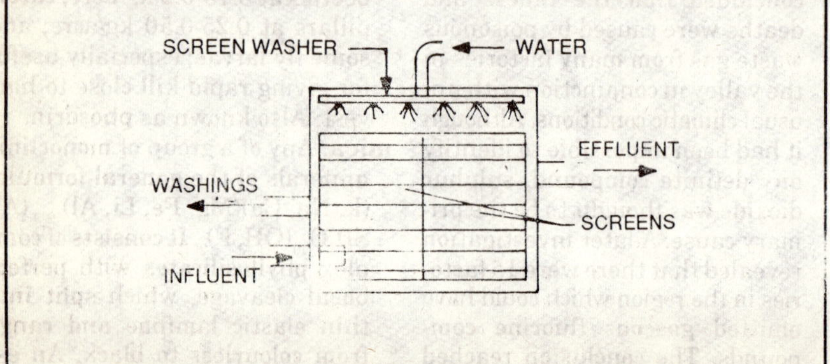

MICROMESH DRUM FILTER

provide some grazing cover in the damper season although if used for agriculture, great care must be taken to prevent overgrazing and consequent soil erosion. This vegetation type has been severely cut over in recent years for firewood supplies, which is partially responsible for the air pollution in the region.

micro-strainer. A rotating drum filter having a fine screen fitted on the periphery of the drum. This is used to remove algae from water prior to its treatment and in polishing activated-sludge effluent. The collected solids are back washed by high pressure jets of water.

midocean ridge. A long submarine mountain chain running through the Atlantic, Indian and south Pacific oceans and associated with divergent plate boundaries. The midocean ridge lies along the active, growing edges of most of the earth's crustal plates. As the plates pull apart, magma wells up from the earth's interior. It is deposited on the edges of the plates as a twin row of basalt peaks that slowly separate as the plates move away from each other. This phenomenon is known as sea floor spreading. As the rock cools and compresses, huge fractures develop in it at right angles to the ridge. It is estimated that entire volume of the oceans passes through the midocean ridge approximately once every 200 million years, and it is now thought that this circulation, rather than the erosion of minerals from the continents by rivers, is primarily responsible for the salty nature of the seawater.

mining overburden returned to the mine site. Any material overlying an economic mineral deposit that is removed to gain access to that deposit and is then used for reclamation of a surface mine.

mining wastes. Unwanted material arising form all classes of mining operations in two principal forms:

(a) rock waste, which may occupy valuable land and disfigure the landscapes; and

(*b*) tailings from mills, which as silt can impede the natural flows of streams.

Tailings may contain chemicals hazardous to vegetation and animal life. Modern mining methods utilize abandoned workings such as shifts, tunnels, and adits to store unwanted waste as backfill, thus conserving space. Great harm to stream life may occur where mill tailings have been piled in proximity to the drainage area of streams, *e.g.*, copper and zinc compounds, lethal to fish, may be carried from the pile to the stream by rainwater. Filtrates may be carried for considerable distances underground to reach wells or other sources of water for livestock and human consumption. Sometimes, old tailing dumps are reworked to recover the metal content. Piles of tailings and other wastes may become mechanically unstable, when saturated with moisture, forming a mid flow that can damage property and life.

mist. A cloud like mass of minute droplets of water suspended in the air near the earth's surface. When air is cooled, it cannot hold as much water vapour. As the water vapour condenses, the drops become visible, forming mist. Mist is like thin fog, with a visibility of at least 1000 m. It is most likely to occur in calm, settled anticyclonic conditions, especially in autumn. It is generally very patchy, occurs most frequently near lakes rivers and coastal areas, where there is more water available and tends to accumulate in hollows. Once a wind starts to blow, turbulence will mix the air, and the mist will clear. In urban areas, where there may be pollution, the mist may become dark and dirty, to form smog. *See also* photochemical smog.

mistral. A cold northerly wind which blows down the Rhone valley. It is caused by cold air from Europe blowing south wards into a low pressure area over the Mediterranean. The depressions occasionally pass along the Mediterranean from the Atlantic, especially during the colder half of the year. When the mistral blows down the Rhone, temperatures fall by several degrees, and the strong winds of up to 60 km/hr make conditions very unpleasant. Most farmhouses have rows of trees on their northern side as protection from the wind, and many fields of fruits and vegetables also shelter behind rows of cypress trees, which always extend from east to west and are very numerous in parts of the Rhone Valley.

mixing layer. The lower part of the atmosphere within which motions are much affected by the vicinity of the surface of the earth and where, as a result, pollutants are dispersed and mixed. For convective conditions, the mixing layer may extend up to several km above the surface but for stable conditions its height may be only some 200 m. In the absence of temperature differences between the air and the surface, mixing is brought about solely by mechanical turbulence and the depth of the mixing layer (the distance between the earth's surface and the upper boundary of the mixing layer) depends on the surface roughness and is proportional to the geostrophic wind speed.

mixing length. The mean length of travel, characteristic of a particular motion, over which an eddy maintains its identity; analogous to the mean free part of a molecule.

mixing ratio. r. For moist air, the ratio of the mass m_w of water vapour to the mass m_a dry air with which the water vapour is associated; *i.e.*, $r = m_w/m_a$.

mobile source. In air pollution control, an automobile, aircraft, or other moving source of air pollution. Mobile sources are point sources in the sense that emissions of each individual source are theoretically controllable, but the fact that there are many of them and that they move around, often makes such control practically impossible. Mobile sources are the single largest contributor to air pollution in most urban areas, and are particularly important as sources of hydrocarbons, nitrogen oxides, and carbon monoxide.

model, mathematical. In air pollution studies, a set of formulas that take into account sources of pollution in a given area, the amounts of pollutants emitted by each, different meteorological conditions and topographical features, and other factors that affect dispersion of pollutants. Such a model can be used for the calculation of pollutant concentrations at any given point in the air.

monitoring. In environmental heath, the repetitive and continued observation, measurement, and evaluation of heath and/or environmental or technical data for defined purposes, according to prearranged schedules in space and time and using comparable method for sensing and data collection (proposed definition).

monitoring programme. The systematic deployment of measuring equipment for the purpose of detecting or measuring quantitatively or qualitatively the presence, effect, or level of any polluting substance. For example, the scientific measurement of pollution has gradually become recognized as an essential pre-requisite to remedial action. The measurement of the general atmospheric pollution to which people are constantly exposed is desirable for the following reasons:

(a) It enables an objective assessment to be made. It is, however, important that measurements should be made in more than one type of district in an area, or a false impression may be obtained as to the amount of pollution to which the inhabitants are exposed.

(b) It enables comparisons to be made with similar areas in other parts of the country.

(c) The information gained assists in making an intelligent decision as to the remedial measures necessary and their order of priority.

(d) It provides a means of judging the success of remedial measures once.

(e) The information is useful to an air pollution control agency considering plans for the industrial, commercial and residential development of an area.

(f) Knowledge of existing background levels of pollution is indispensable to the making of decisions in relation to chimney height proposals.

(g) Facts concerning existing pollution are an essential ingredient in an authority's campaign to convince the public of the need for a remedial programme.

(h) A quantitative picture of the pattern of air pollution throughout the country is a valuable aid to medical investigations into the relationship between air pollution and disease.

(i) It enables increases in air pollution that will result from industrial development in a given area to be predicted.

Monocrotophos. A fast-acting insecticide with systemic, stomach and contact action, used against a wide range of pests on a variety of crops; persistence of 1 to 2 weeks. It has caused phytotoxicity under cool conditions to some apples, cherries, and sorghum varieties and is incompatible with alkaline pesticides. It is a crystalline solid, miscible with water, soluble in acetone, and ethanol, sparingly souble in xylene but almost insoluble in kerosene and diesel oils. It is unstable in low molecular weight alcohols and glycols and is corrosive to iron, steel, and brass, but does not attack glass, aluminium and stainless steel. The acute LD_{50} for rats is 13.23 mg/kg. It is quite effective against a wide range of pests including mites, bugs, leaf-eating beetles, leafminers and caterpillars.

monomictic. 1. Said of a lake with only one yearly overturn. Tropical lakes overturn in the winter and polar lakes in the summer. 2. Said of a clastic sedimentary rock composed of a single mineral species.

monsoons. The seasonal winds known for their effect on the seasons in India and other parts of south-east Asia as well. Monsoons blow from land to sea when high pressure zones develop over the land. Monsoons blow from sea to land when high pressure zones develop over the sea. From June to September the land area of India is warmer than the Indian Ocean, which lies south of the continent. The direct rays of the sun fall on India as the sun moves northward during the summer, and the land heats faster than the water. Then winds blow from the cool Indian Ocean toward the warm land. When the winds reach northern India, they rise to cross the mountains. Air cools as it rises, and its moisture condenses and falls on the lands south of the mountains. During the winter the direct rays of the sun strike the Indian Ocean instead of the continent. The land mass of India becomes colder than the adjacent ocean and winds then blow toward the sea. Winter winds are evaporating because they become warmer as they travel southward, and they are able to hold more moisture. Because of the monsoon winds, India has alternating wet and dry seasons. The rainfall brought by the monsoon conditions in Asia is cyclonic, but there is the addition of orographic (relief) rainfall in the mountains, which for this reason are often much wetter than the lowlands. In addition, the great heat during the day often gives rise to thunderstorms and the convection rainfall occurs. In the smaller continents of South America, Africa, Australia and North America the monsoonal effects are less marked. These smaller continents do not have such wet summers or such dry winters, and are sometimes referred to as eastern marginal rather than true monsoon.

morbidity rate. The incidence of sickness in a population.

Morocide. A non-systemic acaracide (also effective against powdery mildews) and mainly used against red spider mites. Non-phytotoxic to a wide range of apples, pears, cotton, and citrus; some risks of damage to young tomatoes, grapes and roses. It is a white crystalline powder practically insoluble in water but soluble in most of the organic solvents. It is unstable in concentrated acids and dilute alkalis, suffers slight hydrolysis on long contact with water and is slowly decomposed by UV light. It is noncorrosive and compatible with formulations of insecticides and non-alkaline fungicides; with organophosphorous compounds it may be phytotoxic. Acute oral LD_{50} for rats is 120-165 mg/kg. It has been found to be effective especially against red spider mites. Also known as Binapacryl.

mortality rate. The rate of removal of individual from a population by death.

motor vehicle. It includes a vehicle, machine, tractor, trailer, or semitrailer, or any combination thereof, propelled or drawn by mechanical power and used upon the highways in the transportation of passengers or property. It does not include a vehicle, locomotive, or car operated exclusively on a rail or rails, or a trolley bus operated by electric power derived from a fixed overhead wire, furnishing local passenger transportation similar to street-railway service.

motor vehicles act, 1988. This Act has come into force from 1st July 1989. The salient features of the provisions of the Act, besides other things also include the requirements to be observed in matter of vehiclesfitness. Some of the features are as follows:

1. For registration of a new vehicle, the vehicle is to be produced before the registering authority for inspection to satisfy that the vehicle is fit for registration. The certificate of fitness is to be issued for a new vehicle for a period of two years. Thereafter, the renewal shall be for a period of one year till the vehicle attains the age of 10 years.

2. Regarding construction, equipment and maintenacne of the motor vehicles, from October 1, 1989 every motor vehicle shall comply with the following emission standards:

(a) Idling emission limit for four-wheeler petrol driven vehicle shall not exceed 3% of the volume. (b) idling emission limit for two-wheerers and three-wheelers petrol driven vehicles shall not exceed 4.5% by volume.

3. Transportation of goods of dangerous or hazardous nature to human life has been regulated under the Act. The vehicle carrying such goods should have prescribed labels indicating the nature of hazardous goods. The packages should also bear such labels. The driver should know the fundamentals in case of the vehicle is involved in accident. Driver should have minimum Matriculate standard qualification.

4. Every vehicle is required to meet the safety standards of components. Every vehicle manufacture shall have to certify that every part used in the vehicle complies with the standards relatable to such components laid down by Bureau of Indian Standards.

5. A prototype of the vehicle to be manufactured by the manufacturer will have to be tested by VRDE, Ahmadnagar, ARAI, Pune or CMTTI, Bundi or any other agency specified by the Central Government.

6. The horn to be used is to be in accordance with the approved specifications of Bureau of Indian Standards.

7. New items are included for offences and penalties in the Act. Amounts for different types of offences have been specified.

To help the owners of car, scooter maintain the prescribed level of exhaust emissions, the Directorate of Transport in Delhi has established the Pollution Checking Centres at each of its offices in Delhi. Besides this, mobile teams are also covering different parts of the city. Delhi Administration has also been providing free facilities at different Petrol Stations all over the city since November 1987 for checking exhaust carbon monoxide and hydrocarbon levels from cars and scooters.

movement. That hazardous waste transported to a facility in an individual vehicle.

MPTDS model. An air-quality control model which is a modification of MPTER model, and is used to account explicitly for gravitational settling and/or deposition loss of a pollutant. Surface deposition fluxes can be printed under an optional output feature. It is a multipoint source code with an optional terrain adjustment feature. Its execution is limited to a maximum of 250 point sources and 180 receptors.

MPTER model. A multiple point-source Gaussian model with optional terrain adjustments. It estimates concentrations on an hourly basis for relatively inert pollutants; and utilizes Pasquill-Gifford dispersion parameters and Briggs plume-rise methods to calculate the spreading and the rise of plumes. The model is most applicable for source-receptor distances less than 10 km and for locations with level or gently rolling terrain. Terrain adjustments are restricted to receptors whose elevation is not higher than the lowest stack top. In addition to terrain adjustments, options are also available for wind-profile exponents, buoyancy-induced dispersion, gradual plume rise, stack downwash, and plume half-life.

mud valve. A type of valve used for removing sludge or mud along with water from the bottom of a reservoir or basin.

mulch. Any suitable soil-protecting material such as straw, plastics or paper; one of the methods of checking wind erosion is to plant suitable grasses and to enable them to live through the dry season by covering them with mulch.

multiplier effect. The way in which the creation of one or two industries may encourage the setting up of other industries in the same area. For example, a steelworks may provide raw materials for an engineering works, which may provide machines for a textiles factory, and so on. Once started the effect will continue, because there will be a need for transport, schools and hospitals which will provide more jobs and also create a good local market. More people will be encouraged to move in to the area, and possibly additional industries will be attracted. Soon administration will be necessary, providing yet more jobs.

mutagen. Any physical or chemical agent that causes a modification of deoxyribonucleic acid (DNA) in such a way as to affect the hereditary characteristics transmitted by genes or chromosomes. Some of the typical mutagens are *X*-rays, ultra-violet rays, heat, alkylating agents, esterifying agents, nitrous acid, and hydroxylamine. If the mutagen is a chemical, it is capable of passing through the barrier of the cell, and reaching the nucleus, where it reacts chemically with the DNA molecule to alter its structure, replacing apart of it or breaking it into two parts that then recombine in a different pattern. The effects of a mutagen do not show up in the individual who has been exposed, but in that individual's offspring, where they usually take the form of birth defects. Since, cancer is also a form of cellular abnormality, the same agent is both a mutagen and a carcinogen. *See also* alkylating agents, nitrous acid, heat, radiation, and *X*-rays. Environmental Protection Agency has prepared a list of various mutagens along with their threshold values.

mutagenic agent. *See* mutagen.

mutation. A change in the character of a gene that is perpetuated in subsequent divisions of the cell in which it occurs; a change in the sequence of base pairs in the chromosomal DNA molecule. It may be caused by the application of an external stimulus, *e.g.*, irradiation to the germ cells. Natural mutation can also occur spontaneously, and not due to an artificial external stimulus; while somatic mutation occurs in the general body cells (as opposed to germ cells).

mycorrhyza. A fungus living in a symbiotic association with the roots of a vascular plant. Approximately 90% of all known vascular plants form mycorrhyzal relationships, and most plants that form these relationships cannot live in soil that has not been inoculated with spores of one or more of the particular fungi they associate with. Often the relationship is highly specific, with a fine species of fungus never found without its plant associate and vice-versa.

myiasis. Disease of the man and animals due to the infestation by the larvae of Diptera which are not necessarily parasitic. Most cases of human myiasis are accidental infestations of the intestine through swallowing larvae in the food; others are infestations of the wounds and sores.

myxomatosis. A disease of rabbits, caused by a virus and marked by fever, inflammation, and often death.

N

Naled. A non-systemic contact and stomach insecticide and acaricide with some fumigant action; used mainly under glass and in mushroom houses. The technical product is a yellow liquid, insoluble in water, slightly soluble in aliphatic solvents, and readily soluble in aromatic solvents. It is stable under anhydrous conditions but rapidly hydrolysed in water (90-100% in 48 hours at room temperature), and by alkali; stable in glass containers, but in the presence of metals and reducing agents, rapidly loses bromine and reverts to dichlorvos. Acute LD_{50} for rats is 430 mg/kg; it is mainly used against glasshouse and mushroom pests.

naphtha. A term applied to a variety of distillates obtained from either petroleum or coal tar. In petroleum industry, a light distillate having a distillation range similar to gasoline. Heavy naphtha and solvent naphtha, coal tar distillates having distillation ranges of 433-493 K and 433 K, respectively.

naphthalene. A white crystalline solid obtained from coal tar, possesses characteristic aromatic odour. The available data for naphthalene indicate that acute and chronic toxicity to freshwater aquatic life occur at concentrations as low as 2300 and 620 μg/L, respectively; and would occur at even lower concentrations among the species that are more sensitive than those tested.

natality rate. The rate of addition of new individuals to a population by birth.

national estate. Those components of the cultural and natural environment which are of such value to the nation or any part of it, that they should be conserved, managed and presented for the benefit of to he community as a whole. Components possess aesthetic, historical, scientific, social, cultural, ecological or other special values and include parks and reserves, beaches and coastlines, certain forests, rare species, buildings and gardens of special merit, sites of archaeological interest, along with scenic aspects of routes, urban areas of social character, museums, are treasures, areas of major wilderness, potential and rare ecosystems.

Measures to protect the national estate include planning controls and schemes, special funds to finance or subsidize acquisitions and other necessary conservation work, research and investigation into the effects of developments of various kinds, and tax and rating concessions.

national park. A relatively large area of land set aside for its features of predominantly unspoiled natural landscape, flora and fauna, permanently dedicated for public enjoyment, education and inspiration and protected from all interference, other than essential management measures, so that its natural attributes are preserved. The main principle of national park management is preservation to the greatest possible extent of the natural condition of these parks. The various categories for the management of the national parks are:

1. *Primitive areas.* The areas of substantial size with well defined natural boundaries within which development of roads, tracks or structures is not permitted, scientific work is discouraged, and commercial development (such as tourist resorts, beekeeping, grazing and commercial fishing) is completely excluded.

2. *Primitive and recreation areas.* The area that resembles a primitive area, but the major difference being sufficient development of walking tracks, shelter sheds and directional signs to enable public use and enjoyment of the area on foot. Vehicular access is not provided, but scientific work may be permitted.

3. *Recreation areas.* These areas are limited in size, not exceeding 400 acres or half of the park area (whichever is less). Facilities for recreation in a natural setting (*e.g.*, camping, picnicking and boating) and public access are provided. As the demand for this type of recreation is likely to outstrip the capacity of national parks to cater for recreation without detracting from other national park values, the department of forestry and other authorities are providing alternative bushland recreation areas.

4. *Scientific areas.* The areas which are preserved as samples of the natural environment for scientific study (which is allowed under permit). Minimum access and shelter facilities may be provided to this kind of area.

5. *Historic areas.* Measures considered necessary (including pollution control measures) to preserve the historical significance of an historic area are permitted.

national wastelands development board (NWDB). The Board established in 1985 to formulate action plans necessary to arrest land degradation and deforestation. Besides this it also looks for regeneration of degraded forest areas and reclamation of ravines, usar lands, arid tracts, mine spoils etc. In the initial four years the Wastelands Development Programme was mainly focused on tree planting. However after an indepth review in 1989-90 the programme was suitably restructured.

The current mission of the NWDB is to check and degradation, bring wastelands into sustainable use, increase biomass availability and restore ecological balance. During the last seven years the NWDB has initiated and promoted several activities and has demonstrated that it is possible collectively to meet the challenge of regenerating India's wastelands.

natural enemy. A predator, parasite, or pathogen that is indigenous to the same region as another species of living thing, and which will attack the other species under natural conditions. A species and its natural enemies have generally coevolved so that their numbers remain in approximate balance with each other and with the environment, thus, species introduced into regions where their enemies are absent are likely to overbreed, leading to an irruption, or population explosion. Such explosions are best controlled by introducing one or more natural enemies.

natural gas. A combustible gas that occurs in porous rocks and is found with or near accumulations of crude oil. Typical natural gas consists of hydrocarbons having a very low boiling point. Methane makes up approximately 85% of the typical gas. Ethane may be present up to 10%; and propane up to 3%. Butane, pentane, hexane, heptane, and octane may also be present in small amounts. Traces of carbon dioxide, nitrogen, helium, and hydrogen sulphide are also present in the natural gas. It is sootless and essentially odorless, and has twice the calorific value of manufactured gas. It is the most convenient and the most readily controllable of all fuels, and is also the cheapest source of energy for many purposes, since production, transmission and distribution require far fewer man-hours than coal and petroleum, salaries and wages are a relatively small item.

Most gas reserves were discovered during searches for petroleum, and about 35% of all gas is obtained as a sideline to oil production. For many years natural gas was discarded as a nuisance and as a waste by product of petroleum, but it is now regarded as a precious source of energy, and hence is saved and sent to market by pipeline.

Natural gas has two modes of occurrence: it is found by itself in distinct gas reservoirs; and it is found with petroleum. Gas from oil wells, known as wet gas is rich in volatile gasoline. It is run from well to gasoline plant, where the gasoline is extracted. Free gas, often known as dry gas is usually ready to go directly into pipelines.

natural gasoline. A gasoline of low octane number made by extracting and liquefying the C_4 and higher hydrocarbons occurring in natural gas. It is not suitable for automotive use but is blended with petroleum fractions for use as a source of petrochemicals.

natural increase. The rate of population growth, determined by subtracting the mortality rate from the natality rate.

natural pollutants. 1. Substances of natural origin present in the earth's atmosphere which may, when present in excess, be regarded as air pollutants. These include:

(a) ozone formed photochemically and by electrical discharge;

(b) sodium chloride, or sea salt;

(c) nitrogen dioxide, formed by electrical discharge in the atmosphere;

(d) dust and gases of volcanic origin;

(e) soil dust from dust storms;

(f) products of forest fires, and

(g) bacteria, spores and pollens.

2. As in the case of air, excessive contamination of water may arise from natural sources; pollution of this kind is often associated with

adverse weather conditions and is intermittent in character. During a storm, silt, vegetable matter and manure may be washed into a river. The erosion of river banks and valley slopes can lead to significant pollution of this kind. Drainage from peaty areas is liable to contain much vegetable matter and organic matter. An excessive growth of weeds and other vegetable life may take place in a stream or river caused an obstruction of the free flow of water; when such vegetable matter dies it can seriously deplete the amount of dissolved oxygen in the river is due to ground water drainage through pyrites. Many rivers, receive and carry tons of sulphuric acid each year; this acid load from mine drainage travels for several km before it is completely neutralized. *See* air pollution; water pollution.

natural product. As customarily used by chemists, this term refer to organic materials originating in or extracted from plants and animals; it includes such basic industrial materials as petroleum, cotton, wool, rubber, coal, leather, sugar, and wood, as well as fatty acids, hormones, enzymes, alkaloids, vitamins, *etc.*

natural radiation. Ionizing radiation arising from extraterrestrial sources and from naturally occurring radionuclides contained in earth crust, air and living organisms.

natural resource. Any portion of the natural environment such as air, water, soil, forest, wildlife, and minerals.

natural selection. The agent of evolutionary change by which the organisms possessing advantageous adaptations in a given environment produce more offspring than those lacking such adaptations.

nature conservation. The main purpose of this type of conservation is to preserve more or less natural plant communities (and possible modified vegetation as well, in some instances) as representative examples of their kind.

nearshore. A widely used term denoting a zone beginning at the low tide line and continuing offshore for an indefinite but generally short distance. The breaker zone, longshore drift and waves long shore currents are found in the nearshore region.

negative price. A concept used in economic studies; an inputted price for, for example, unwanted waste products. There is a strong underlying similarity between the concepts of negative prices and effluent taxes; the latter are a possible alternative to subsidies and standard setting as a means of controlling air and water pollution.

neighborhood noise. A term used by the Noise Advisory Council of many developed countries, to cover a great variety of sources of noise which may, and frequently do, cause disturbance and annoyance to the general public in their homes and going about their lawful occasions. They include, for example:

(a) factory noise;

(b) noise from demolition, construction and road works;

(c) noise generated from ventilation and air-conditioning plants in buildings of all kinds;

(d) noise generated from activities such as sports, entertainment and advertising; and

(e) human noise arising from lack of consideration for others (such as loudspeakers, noisy parties, slamming of car doors, farewell hooting, and the like). The term does not embrace industrial noise, aircraft noise, and traffic noise.

nematicide. Any chemical used to destroy plant parasitic nematodes.

neritic zone. The relatively warm, nutrient-rich, shallow-water zone overlying the continental shelf; the marine counterpart of the littoral zone of a lake. Terminating at the edge of the continental shelf, sunlight normally penetrates to the ocean bottom, permitting photosynthetic activity and promoting the growth of a vast population of floating and anchored plants. The total amount of biomass supported by the neritic zone is greater per unit volume of water than in any other part of the ocean. *See also* abyssal zone, euphotic zone.

nerve gas. One of a group of exceedingly toxic gaseous compounds. Chemically, nerve gases are esters of phosphoric acid derivatives; they immobilize the nervous system by preventing the enzyme cholinesterase from deactivating the acetylcholine formed by nerve impulses. They are often referred to as cholinesterase inhibitors.

net reproduction rate. The average number of female babies that will be born to a representative newly born female in her lifetime, if existing reproduction and mortality rates continue. If each 1,000 girls born in 1990 ultimately produce 1,500 female babies, the net reproduction rate will be 1.5. A net reproduction rate permanently greater than 1 means ultimate population growth, although this may be ignored if the existing age structure is unfavorable to growth; conversely, a net reproduction rate less than 1 means ultimate population decline.

neuston. The micro-organisms inhabiting the surface film of a body of water. Most neustons are members of the *Protista* kingdom. Hyponeustons are aquatic organisms that live on the underside of the surface film; they generally differ from those inhabiting the rest of the body of water. Epineustons live on the upper surface of the water film. They are generally aerial organisms that have adapted so that they can use the surface film as a substrate, usually by developing a broad foot of the lipid tissue. They are much more specialized than the hyponeuston, and will not be found in other environments.

neutral gradient. *See* lapse rate.

neve'. A term used for a mass of hardened snow at the source or head of glacier; it refers to overall snow cover that exists during the melting period and sometimes from one year to another.

new tank system. A tank system or component that will be used for the storage or treatment of hazardous waste and for which installation commenced after July 14, 1986; except, however, for purpose of Sections 264.193(g)(2) and 265(g)(2), a new tank system is one for which construction commenced after July 14, 1986.

niche. 1. The overall place of an organism in the structure of a community, including both the space its occupies, and the role it plays in maintaining the community's balance. 2. A shallow cave re-entrant produced by weathering and erosion near the base of a rock face or cliff, or beneath a waterfall.

nickel. A silvery-white metal which takes a brilliant polish; placed in group VIII of the periodic table. The chief uses of nickel are as an alloying metal in stainless steel, magnets, and resistance alloys; in cladding and other protective coating; in special types of batteries; and in powder form as a hydrogenation catalyst.

Nickel is present in most foodstuffs, but at levels below (and often well below) 1 mg/kg. Little is known about the chemical form of nickel in food, although it is probably partly complexed with phytic acid. Dietary contributions have been reported ranging from less than 200 to 900μg/day. A typical diet might contribute about 400 μg/day. Nickel concentrations of 100 μg/L and 50μg/L have been reported in wines and beers respectively.

It has been reported that about 10-20% of the nickel content of cigarettes (typically around 3 μg per cigarette) can be inhaled. This appears to be mainly as a volatile nickel compound, nickel carbonyl. A typical weekly intake for someone who smokes 20 cigarettes a day might be 40-80 μg of nickel.

Nickel is almost certainly essential for animal nutrition, and consequentially it is probably essential to man. Absorption of nickel through the gastrointestinal tract seems to be very low, *i.e.,* 1% or even less, although higher absorption values have been reported, *i.e.,* 10%. There is little evidence of accumulation of nickel by various tissues. No significant accumulation of nickel was observed in rats fed nickel in drinking-water at a concentration of 5 mg/L. It is clear that at least in the animal body a mechanism controls excessive intake of nickel. Certain disease states in man do give rise to elevated nickel in tissue; the reasons, however are not understood. Nickel is readily excreted, mainly in the faeces, with smaller quantities in the urine and sweat.

Nickel is a relatively less toxic element. The levels of nickel found in food and water are not considered a serious health hazard however, high doses (1600 mg/kg in the diet) were shown in early animal studies to cause minimal toxic effects. Certain nickel compounds have been shown to be carcinogenic in animal experiments. However, soluble nickel compounds are not currently regarded as either human or animal carcinogens. As in the case of other divalent cations, nickel can react with DNA and at high concentrations can result in DNA damage as shown in vitro mutagenicity tests. Dermatitis is most commonly associated with industrial exposure. However, the same effects have been observed from dermal contact with coinage or jewellery. High-level occupational exposures have been associated with renal problems, and effects such as vertigo and dyspnoea have been observed.

Occupational exposure to nickel should be controlled so that no employee is exposed to nickel at a concentration greater than 15 μg/m^3 of air, determined as a time-weighted average (TWA) concentration limit for up to a 10-hour workshift in a 40-hour workweek, over a working lifetime.

Many compounds of nickel are water-soluble, therefore contamination of water can arise; significant problems are associated with industrial discharge to rivers of effluents containing nickel compounds. Level as high as 1 mg/L have been reported in surface-waters although the levels are generally much lower, *e.g.*, 5-20 μg/L. For the protection of human health from the toxic effects of nickel ingested through water and contaminated aquatic organisms, the ambient water criterion has been set to be 7.1 μg/L; while for the protection of human health from the toxic properties of nickel ingested through the contaminated aquatic organisms alone, ambient water criterion has been determined to be 140 μg/L.

nickel carbonyl. A compound of nickel, which has been classed as potential occupational carcinogen. Occupational exposure to nickel carbonyl should be controlled so that no employee is exposed to nickel carbonyl at a concentration greater than 0.35 mg/m^3 of air (0.05 ppm), determined as a time-weighted average (TWA) concentration limit for up to a 10-hour workshift.

nicotine. A compound formerly used as a glasshouse fumigant. The most convenient method of volatilizing it is by the use of pressure-cans; these are ignited to send off dense clouds of smoke which contain the vapours of nicotine concentrated to send off dense clouds of smoke which contain the vapours of nicotine. It was found that in a glasshouse, the nicotine concentrations fell off rapidly and little or none remained one hour after discharge. When the nicotine was evaporated slowly, concentration was maintained only as long as evaporation continued and the introduction of fumigant was equal to the loss through leakage. Delicate flowers and tender shoots may be injured by nicotine applied in any way.

night-soil. Human excretion of faecal matter and urine. It may be spread on the fallow fields; mixed with earth and used as manure and mulch, or spread on to drying beds called sewer farms.

NIOSH. Abbreviation for the U.S. *N*ational *I*nstitute for *O*ccupational *S*afety and *H*ealth. It evaluates all available research data and criteria and recommends standards for occupational exposure.

nitrate and nitrite. Nitrates are widely present in substantial quantities in soil, in most waters, and in plants, including vegetables. Nitrates are products of oxidation of organic nitrogen by the bacteria present in soils and in water where sufficient oxygen is present. Nitrites are formed by incomplete bacterial oxidation of organic nitrogen. One of the principal uses of nitrate is as a fertilizer; most other nitrogen-containing fertilizers will, however, be converted to nitrate in the soil. Nitrates are also used in explosives, as oxidizing agents in the chemical industry, and as food preservatives. Some nitrates in the environment are produced in the soil by fixation of atmospheric nitrogen (bacterial synthesis). Some nitrates and nitrites are formed when oxides of nitrogen produced by the action of lightning discharge or via man-made sources are washed out by rain. Nitrates and some nitrites are also produced in the soil as a result of bacterial decomposition of organic material, both vegetable and animal. Because nitrates are widespread in the environment, they are found in most foods, in the atmosphere and in many water sources.

Fertilizer use, decayed vegetable and animal matter, domestic effluents, sewage sludge disposal to land, industrial discharges, leachates from refuse dumps, and atmospheric washout all contribute to these ions in water sources. Changes in land use may also give rise to increased nitrate levels. Depending on the situation, these sources can contaminate streams, rivers, lakes, and groundwater, especially wells. Contamination may result from a direct or indirect discharge, or it may arise by percolation over a period of time, sometimes after many years. The levels of nitrates in polluted water are almost invariably very much higher than the levels of nitrites.

Because none of the conventional water treatment and disinfection practices modify the levels of nitrate to any appreciable extent, and since nitrate concentration is not changed markedly in water distribution systems, the levels in tap-water are often very similar to those for source water. For nitrite, the levels in tap-water are likely to be markedly lower than in source waters because of oxidation during water treatment, particularly when water is chlorinated. It is very difficult to define a range and average exposure to nitrate or nitrite in water because the concentrations vary widely depending on the water source.

Considerable quantities of nitrates and lesser amounts of nitrites are present in certain foods and in general the major source of human intake of both nitrates and nitrites is food. in certain crops the nitrate levels may be as high as 100 mg/kg. Certain vegetables, including cabbage, celery, lettuce, potatoes, several root vegetables, and spinach, contain relatively high levels of nitrate.

A further important source of ingested nitrates and nitrites is saliva, human beings secrete about 10 mg of nitrate-N per day, of which about 2 mg/day is reduced to nitrite, the nitrate in the saliva is essentially derived from food sources mainly vegetables.

Apart from natural sources of oxides of nitrogen and nitrates in the air, there are some important man-made sources; in particular the products of combustion of fossil fuels (coal, oil, gas) and from the chemical industry. Inorganic and organic forms of nitrates occur; these and the oxides of nitrogen will be inhaled and some will be absorbed by the respiratory system, producing a mixture of nitrates and nitrites in the body. It has been estimated for areas with elevated levels of nitrogen compounds in the air, that if all these compounds were absorbed by an adult, it would amount to an intake of approximately 0.1 mg of nitrate-N per day.

Oxides of nitrogen and nitrate aerosols are produced in a burning cigarette, but in comparison with food and water, the quantities contributed by smoking tobacco are regarded as relatively small.

The metabolism of ingested nitrate is not fully understood; it seems that absorption takes place in the upper portion of the small intestine and that excretion is primarily if not exclusively, through the kidney. It is well known that nitrate is absorbed in the upper gastrointestinal tract and concentrated ultimately into saliva by the salivary glands. The nitrate metabolism in man has not been studied fully, and the results of animal experiments are not very reliable when extrapolated to man.

A very important consideration is the fact that nitrate can be readily converted in vivo to nitrite as a result of bacterial reduction. Exposure to high levels of nitrate has been shown to give rise to large increases in the concentration of salivary nitrite. Reduction of nitrate to nitrite also occurs elsewhere in the body, including the stomach; little conversion takes place unless the pH is greater than 4.6. In infants, where the stomach acidity is normally very low, about pH 4 or higher a high yield of nitrite is obtained. In contrast, the acidity of an adult stomach is pH 1-5 and less conversion of nitrate occurs.

The formation of nitrite is especially important for two reasons. Firstly, it can oxidize haemoglobin to methaemoglobin, a pigment that is incapable of acting as a carrier of oxygen. Secondly, under certain conditions nitrites may react in the human body with secondary and tertiary amines and amides (commonly derived from food and other sources) to form nitosamines, some of which are considered to be carcinogenic. This process occurs in acidic solution within the pH range 1-5 characteristic of the normal acidity range in a human stomach. The reaction rate is greatest at pH 3.5 or less.

Since ingested nitrates can be readily converted to nitrites, either in the mouth or elsewhere in the body where the acidity is relatively low (high pH), it is possible that nitrosamines some of which may be carcinogenic will be produced. It has been shown that the formation of mutorsamines may be increased in individuals with balder infections and people suffering from achlorohydria (a condition of low stomach acidity). In the case of bladder infections it is probable that the nitosamines produced there would be absorbed into the blood.

nitric acid. A mineral acid used for numerous industrial applications. Occupational exposure to nitric acid is defined as exposure to airborne concentration of nitric acid at or above one-half of the recommended workplace environmental limit. It should be noted that a potential exposure to oxides of nitrogen exists whenever airborne nitric acid is present in the working environment. Occupational exposure to nitric acid should be controlled so that no person is exposed to nitric acid at a concentration greater than 5.0 mg/m^3 of air (2 ppm), determined as a time-weighted average (TWA) concentration limit for up to a 10-hour workshift in a 40-hour workweek, over a working lifetime.

nitrification. The microbial conversion of ammonium and nitrite compounds of nitrates, generally by soil nitrifying bacteria.

nitriles. Organic compounds containing cyano group, C≡N, as the characteristic functional group. They may release cyanide on hydrolysis. Ten nitriles which have been included in the recommended standard include: mononitriles (acetonitrile, propionitrile, *n*-butyronitrile, *iso*-butyronitrile); the cyanohydrins (glycolonitrile and acetone cyanohydrin); and dinitriles (malononitrile, succinonitrile, adiponitrile, and tetramethyl succinonitrile). Whenever there is simultaneous exposure to several nitriles, or other sources of cyanides, the total effect is additive, and the environmental limit is defined by the relation:

$E_m = (C_1/L_1) + ... + (C_n/L_n)$, where,

C_1 = concentration of the main component of the mixture,

C_n = concentration of the other constituents of the mixture, with *n* having values from 2 to *n*.

L_1 = permissible exposure limit for the main component,

L_n = permissible exposure limits for other constituents, with *n* having values from 2 to *n*, and E_m should never exceed 1.

The recommended workplace exposure limits for some nitriles are:

Name	mg/m^3	ppm
Acetonitrile	34	20
Propionitrile	14	6
n-Butyronitrile	22	8
iso-Butyronitril	22	8
Glycolonitrile	5	2
Acetonecyanohydrin	4	1
Malononitrile	8	3
Succinonitrile	20	6
Adiponitrile	18	4
Tetramethyl-succinonitrile	06	1

nitrilotriacetic acid (NTA). A proposed substitute for phosphate as a builder in detergent. However, reservations about potential harm to the environment of this alternative has prevented its adoption.

nitrobenzene. A yellowish liquid, obtained by the nitration of benzene; used in the manufacture of aniline, azobenzene, benzidine, quinoline, and a number of dyestuffs, solvent for cellulose ethers, and ingredient in metal and shoe polishes. It is quite toxic by inhalation, ingestion, and skin absorption. It has been proposed to be assessed as hazardous air pollutant. The available data for nitrobenzene indicate that acute toxicity to freshwater aquatic life occurs at concentrations as low as 27,000 µg/L; and would occur at even lower concentrations among the species that are more sensitive than those tested; while the acute toxicity to saltwater aquatic life occurs at concentrations as low as 6,680 µg/L, respectively; and would occur at even lower concentrations among the species that are more sensitive than those tested. No data are available concerning the chronic toxicity of nitrobenzene to sensitive aquatic life.

nitrogen. A comparatively unreactive element which comprises 78% by volume of air. It is as essential to vital processes as are oxygen or carbon, for it is a constituent of amino acids and proteins, the basis of all animals life. These compounds are synthesized by plants from nitrogen 'fixed' in the soil by certain bacteria. Nitrogen, under standard conditions, is a colourless, odorless, and tasteless gas. The gas is slightly soluble in water (2.35 parts nitrogen in 100 parts water at 273 K), the solubility decreases with increasing temperature (1.55 parts nitrogen in 100 parts water at 293 K). There are two naturally occurring isotopes, ^{14}N and ^{15}N, with ^{14}N by far the most abundant (99.635%). Four radioactive isotopes have been identified, ^{12}N, ^{13}N, ^{16}N, and ^{17}N, all with extremely short half-lives measured in seconds or minutes.

When molecular nitrogen is subjected to the actions of a condensed electrode discharge, or to a high frequency electrodeless discharge, it is partially changed to an activated, unstable condition, from which on standing it returns to its normal state with the emission of a golden-yellow afterglow. In elemental form, nitrogen is used as a protective blanket for highly reactive chemicals, as a blowing agent in formed plastic, as a scavenging and carrier gas, and in special types of refrigeration. Nitrogen forms dinitrogen complexes with a number of metals of VIII group transition metal family. Such complexes occur in low oxidation state of the metals. It has no active toxicity and is noncombustible. It is only hazardous in steel industry in that reducing atmosphere of pure nitrogen, such as may be found in some heat-treatment furnaces. During arc-welding and cutting operations, oxides of nitrogen may be formed, which are hazardous in confined and ill ventilated places. The prolonged low-level exposure to the air containing relatively higher nitrogen content may produce brown staining of the teeth and skin, along with permanent lung damage.

nitrogen compounds in atmosphere. Five principal nitrogenous species exist in the atmosphere; these are: molecular nitrogen (N_2), ammonia (NH_3), nitrous oxide (N_2O), nitric oxide (NO), and nitrogen dioxide (NO_2).

Molecular nitrogen, N_2, is a permanent gas in the atmosphere yet some 100 tones a year are converted to reactive species in lightning strikes. Another apparently small amount of molecular nitrogen is converted to reactive nitrogen by nitrogen-fixing bacteria. N_2O is also relatively less reactive though it is also produced and consumed by soil bacteria. It has a relatively constant concentration of about 0.25 ppm, and its main contribution to pollution is decomposition in stratosphere, producing N_2, O or NO and N. Generally, it may be excluded from the smog producers, but does influence the ozone balance in the upper stratosphere.

Ammonia, NH_3, is a useful though extremely variable nitrogenous compound. Most of its production has been attributed to the ammonia release from animal urine. It is a known product of the deamination of proteins and in the oceans there are bacteria capable of producing ammonia from nitrates. In its way it is the 'de-acid' agent of the atmosphere as it combines in the gaseous phase with sulphuric acid and sulphur dioxide and neutralize their acidity. It also tends to catalyze the oxidation of sulphur dioxide in water droplets. One way or the other it tends to form the ubiquitous ammonium sulphate particles that are major components of almost every aerosol; also it is a good fertilizer. About 0.3% of ammonia is man made, being manufactured by Haber process from nitrogen and hydrogen; it is even injected directly in to the soil as fertilizer. In the atmosphere, ammonia is quickly removed by clouds, rain or acidic gases, and so is highly variable. In the lower levels of the atmosphere it has a residence time of few hours though in a clear, dry environment it may remain for weeks.

The nitrogen containing species nitric oxide (NO) and nitrogen dioxide (NO_2), combined with hydrocarbons, produce ozone and undesirable substances that are eye irritants and pose health problems. Generally NO is formed during high temperature combustion, mainly from motor vehicle exhausts but including stationary combustion. The nitric oxide reacts in the Stewing pot with hydrocarbons and sunlight to produce nitrogen dioxide which in turn reacts with a host of reactive species to produce quite undesirable materials but principally ozone, O_3. The various reactions may be summarized as:

NO_2 + UV light = NO + [O]

$[O] + O_2 + M = O_3 + \cdot M$

$O_3 + NO = NO_2 + O_2$

Nitric oxide is man's greatest single contribution to the pollution but at the same time a series of other reactive species are formed, so that with in a few hours most of the nitric oxide is converted into nitrogen dioxide. It is not clearly understood as to how reaction proceeds, but certainly assorted forms of elemental oxygen and free radicals such as $\cdot HO_2$ and $\cdot OH$ react with hydrocarbons and produce intermediates. It is also possible that sulphur dioxide is also involved in the reactions. Some nitrogen containing organic compounds are also formed, one of them is peroxyacetal nitrate (PAN). The result is that people experience eye irritations that may be so severe that driving is no longer possible. Plants suffer and become burnt, and crop yields are reduced; in particular tomatoes and petunias are affected. *See also* nitrogen oxides.

nitrogen cycle. The general biological series of changes in nature by which the elemental nitrogen of the atmosphere is converted into compounds; used in the nutrition of plants and animals, and ultimately liberated again as free elemental nitrogen. Major events in the natural cycle are the fixation of the atmospheric nitrogen by natural electrical discharges such as lightning, washing of the nitrogen compounds into the soil by rain, then their assimilation for plant use by certain bacteria, followed by their elaboration in the plant into a form available for animal nutrition. The animals produce nitrogenous wastes, and ultimately its body also is decomposed by bacteria; in both cases the nitrogenous end products return to the soil or to the atmosphere to repeat the cycle.

nitrogen fixation. Utilization of

the nitrogen of the air by plants to form critically important compounds; the conversion is performed by certain types of bacteria which live symbiotically on the root hairs of plants, thus enabling them to synthesize nitrogenous compounds (proteins). The term is also applied to various processes for chemically manufacturing ammonia and other nitrogen compounds.

nitrogen oxides. Oxides formed and released in all common types of combustion; they are formed by the oxidation of atmospheric nitrogen at high temperatures and are introduced into the atmosphere from automobile exhausts, furnace stacks, incinerators and other similar sources. The oxides include nitrous oxide, nitric oxide, nitrogen dioxide, nitrogen pentoxide, and nitric acid. Nitrogen dioxide can be injurious to health when inhaled; nitric acid being produced on the lung tissue with the moisture in the lungs. Nitric oxide can combine with the haemoglobin of the blood to form an addition complex. The oxides of nitrogen undergo many reactions in the atmosphere. In the presence of sunlight and hydrocarbons they catalyze the formation of the irritant, ozone. Nitric oxides are released whenever combustion occurs at high temperatures, as in conventional power stations, boiler plants, vehicle and aircraft engines, the chemical industry and to a lesser extent domestic heating systems. Nitric oxides are toxic gases, including in particular nitrogen monoxide (NO) and nitrogen dioxide (NO_2), which attack the mucous membranes of the respiratory organs and encourage catarrhal and other infections. Together with the organic constituents of exhaust fumes, they are prime producers in sunlight of photochemical smog. It has been established that as little as 0.1 ppm of nitrogen dioxide in the air can result, over a period of one to three years, in an increase in the incidence of bronchitis and have an adverse effect on the lung performance of children. For persons already suffering from chronic bronchitis, breathing is made more difficult by a rise in the nitrogen dioxide content of the atmosphere. In tests with animals, 0.25 ppm of nitrogen was found to produce changes in the pulmonary tissues, and 0.5 ppm to cause inflammatory reactions and cell changes. The influence of the nitrogen dioxide concentration on the children's breathing capacity was thus clearly demonstrated. In the case of children and adults alike, the frequency of acute disorders in the respiratory organs was significantly higher in the district with a high nitrogen dioxide content than in the two areas of low pollution. A higher sickness frequency was also regularly recorded when the 24-hour average value of nitrogen dioxide concentration exceeded 0.06 ppm. Measures are being widely introduced to restrict the formation of oxides of nitrogen in motor vehicle exhaust gases and boiler-plants. Occupational exposure to oxides of nitrogen is defined as exposure to oxides of nitrogen at a concentration greater than one-half the recommended environmental limit. Occupational exposure to nitrogen dioxide should be controlled so that no employee is exposed to nitrogen dioxide vapours at a concentration greater than 1.8 mg/m^3 of air (1 ppm), determined as sampling time of 15 minutes. Occupational exposure to nitric oxide should be controlled so that no employee is exposed to nitric oxide at a concentration greater than 30.0 mg/m^3 of air (25 ppm), determined as a time-weighted average (TWA) concentration limit for up to a 10-hour workshift in a 40-hour workweek. *See also* Los Angeles smog; London smog; nitrogen compounds in atmosphere.

nitrophenols. Compounds obtained by the nitration of phenol and its derivatives; frequently used in the manufacture of dyes, insecticides, and organic synthesis. The available data for nitrophenols indicate that the acute toxicity to freshwater aquatic life occurs at concentrations as low as 230 μg/L; and would occur at even lower concentrations among the species that are more sensitive than those tested; while the acute toxicity to saltwater aquatic life occurs at concentrations as low as 4,850 μg/L; and would occur at even lower concentrations among the species that are more sensitive than those tested. No data are available concerning the chronic toxicity of nitrophenols to sensitive aquatic life. For the protection of human health from the toxic effects of 2,4-dinitro-*o*-cresol, ingested through water and contaminated aquatic organisms, the ambient water criterion to be 13.4 μg/L; while for the protection of human health from the toxic properties of 2,4-dinitro-*o*-cresol, ingested through contaminated aquatic organisms alone, the ambient water criterion has been determined to be 765 μg/L. For the protection of human health from the toxic effects of 2,4-dinitrophenol ingested through water and contaminated aquatic organisms, the ambient water criterion to be 70.0 μg/L; while for the protection of human health from the toxic properties of 2,4-dinitrophenol, ingested through contaminated aquatic organisms alone, the ambient water criterion has been determined to be 14.3 μg/L.

nitrosamines. Any of a series of compounds in which NNO is attached to an alkyl or aryl group. Such compounds are formed by the reaction between an amine and nitrogen oxides or nitrites. They mainly occur in many food products, whisky, herbicides, and cosmetics, as well as in industrial environments such as tanneries, rubber factories, and iron foundries. Nitrosamines have been found to be carcinogens, and have been listed as potential occupational pollutants. For the maximum protection of human health from the potential carcinogenic effects due to exposure of *N*-nitrosodimethylamine through ingestion of contaminated aquatic organisms and water, the ambient water concentration should be zero on the nonthreshold assumption for this compound. However, zero level may not be attainable at present time. Therefore, levels that may result in incremental increase of cancer risk over lifetime are estimated at 10^{-5}, 10^{-6}, and 10^{-7}. The corresponding criteria are 14.0 ng/L, 1.4 ng/L, and 0.14 ng/L respectively. If the above estimates are made for the consumption of aquatic organisms only (excluding consumption of water), the levels are redefined as 160,000 ng/L, 16,000 ng/L, and 1,600 ng/L respectively.

For the maximum protection of human health from the potential carcinogenic effects due to exposure of *N*-nitrosodiethylamine through ingestion of contaminated aquatic organisms and water, the ambient water concentration should be zero on the nonthreshold assumption for this compound. However, zero level may not be attainable at present time. Therefore, the levels that may result in incremental increase of cancer risk over lifetime are estimated at 10^{-5}, 10^{-6}, and 10^{-7}. The corresponding criteria have been set to be 8.0 ng/L, 0.8 ng/L, and 0.08 ng/L respectively. If the above estimates are made for the consumption of aquatic organisms only (excluding consumption of water), levels have been redefined as 12,400 ng/L, 1,240 ng/L, and 124 ng/L respectively

For the maximum protection of human health from the potential carcinogenic effects due to exposure of *N*-nitroso-di-*N*-butylamine through ingestion of contaminated aquatic organisms and water, the ambient water concentration should be zero on the nonthreshold assumption for this compound. However, zero level may not be attainable at present time. Therefore, the levels that may result in incremental increase of cancer risk over lifetime are estimated at 10^{-5}, 10^{-6}, and 10^{-7}. The corresponding criteria are 64.0 ng/L, 6.4 ng/L, and 0.64 ng/L respectively. If the above estimates are made for the consumption of aquatic organisms only (excluding consumption of water), the levels are redefined as 5,868 ng/L, 587 ng/L, and 5.87 ng/L respectively.

For the maximum protection of human health from the potential carcinogenic effects due to exposure of *N*-nitrosodiphenylamine through ingestion of contaminated aquatic organisms and water, the ambient water concentration should be zero on the nonthreshold assumption for this compound. However, zero level may not be attainable at present time. Therefore, the levels that may result in incremental increase of cancer risk over lifetime are estimated at 10^{-5}, 10^{-6}, and 10^{-7}. The corresponding criteria are 49,000 ng/L, 4,900 ng/L, and 490 ng/L respectively. If the above estimates are made for the consumption of aquatic organisms only (excluding consumption of water), the levels are redefined as 161,000 ng/L, 16,100 ng/L, and 1,610 ng/L respectively.

For the maximum protection of human health from the potential carcinogenic effects due to exposure of *N*-nitrosopyrrolidine through ingestion of contaminated aquatic organisms and water, the ambient water concentration should be zero on the nonthreshold assumption for this compound. However, zero level may not be attainable at present time. Therefore, the levels that may result in incremental increase of cancer risk over lifetime are estimated at 10^{-5}, 10^{-6}, and 10^{-7}. The corresponding criteria are 160 ng/

L, 16 ng/L, and 1.6 ng/L respectively. If the above estimates are made for the consumption of aquatic organisms only (excluding consumption of water), the levels are redefined as 919.000 ng/L, 91.900 ng/L, and 9,190 ng/L respectively.

nitrous acid. One of the mutagens which is known to deaminate adenine and cytosine slowly. At low *p*H, it is so strong that DNA or a living cell is destroyed. It has been seen that if DNA possessing transforming activity is exposed to mild deamination conditions, a slow inactivation occurs concomitantly with deamination of only one or a few molecules of adenine and guanine. The observation has been utilized for the demonstration that such sublethal deamination of infective RNA of tobacco mosaic virus produces viral mutants in whole cells, whose bacteriophage and other viruses, and in DNA having transforming activity. The production of mutations by treatment of 'naked' RNA and DNA in vitro with nitrous acid, is of particular interest; it clearly indicates that, at least in these cases, no other part of the cell need undergo a primary change in order for the mutational injury to be registered. The replication of nucleic acids is also not necessary for such registration, although it may be necessary for the final step. Moreover, the possibility of subjecting only the nucleic acids and not the whole cell to the mutagen may considerably broaden further experimental possibilities. According to recent reports, the mutagenic action of nitrous acid on DNA in vitro is possible only after the two strands of DNA have been separated. One change in nucleic acids produced by nitrous acid and suspected to be mutagenic involves deamination of adenine to hypoxenthine. Ordinarily, on replication of a DNA strand, adenine chooses thymine as a partner in the opposite strand, that is being synthesized. However, hypoxenthine may be sufficiently different from adenine to introduce an error in base pairing (cytosine instead of thymine) and such an error may be mutation. Another possible change is the deamination of guanine to xanthine; however recent studies indicate that such a change may be lethal rather than mutagenic. The third possible change is deamination of cytosine to uracil, which can also produce errors in base pairing.

noble gases. The gaseous elements helium, neon, argon, krypton, xenon, and radon. They were formerly referred to as the inert gases, but the use of this term is now deprecated. All the noble gases occur in the atmosphere, although (with the exception of argon) only in trace amounts.

noise. 1. Any disagreeable or undesired sound. 2. Sound, generally of a random nature, the spectrum of which does not exhibit clearly defined frequency components. By extension, noise may consist of electrical oscillation for an undesired or random nature, Many authorities now consider noise as defined in (1) to be a pollutant. Noise as defined in (2) is important in instrumental techniques of analysis. The various sources of environmental noise may be classified as: aircraft, road traffic, road repair, and maintenance work; industry and commerce, domestic and residential construction and demolition work; entertainment activities such as musical concerts, advertising and sports activities; and exhaustive industries. The human ear is capable of hearing a very wide scale of loudness of sound from the softest sound- the threshold of hearing- to the intense and distressing roar of jet aircraft which is 10^{13} times as loud. The range is quite unmanageable in arithmetic sense and a logarithmic has to be used, called decibel scale which indicates hoe many times louder a noise is than the basic reference point. The pitch of the sound is governed by the number of waves emitted by the sound source per second. The range of sound detectable by human ear lies between 16 Hz and 16,000 Hz. Excessive noise produces:

(a) noise induced hearing loss which may be temporary or permanent;

(b) psychological effects such as stress, fatigue, loss of efficiency,

(c) interference with communications.

The only deleterious effect which is measurable is hearing loss. The threshold limit value or upper limit for noise for 8-hours per day for a working lifetime has been estimated to be 90 dB. Noise levels below this are unlikely to affect hearing adversely in most people but the higher the noise levels above 90 dB the greater the risk of hearing loss.

noise exposure forecast (NEF). A technique for predicting the subjective effect of aircraft noise on the average person, exposure levels being expressed in NEF units. Factors which are taken into consideration are the frequency of aircraft movements and their distribution by day and night; the magnitude and duration of aircraft noise as determined by type, weight and flight profile; and the distribution of the noise energy over the spectrum of audible frequencies. In applying the NEF technique, a pattern of contour lines is drawn on the map of the area surrounding the airport.

noise induced hearing loss. Hearing loss which workers exposed to steady noise in the course of their occupations develop gradually over a long period. First appears as a loss of auditory sensitivity in the region 4,000 Hz and progressively affects higher and lower tones with increased exposure to noise.

noise level. The ratio of the root-mean-squae value of the amplitude modulated component in the frequency range 50 to 15,000 Hz, to the root-mean-square value of the carrier in the absence value of the carrier in the absence of any applied modulating signal. Usually expressed in decibels.

noise number index (NNI). An index for the measurement of disturbance from aircraft noise. The index takes into account the average peak noise level at the ground due to a passing aircraft and also the number of aircraft which fly past. It is based on the equation;

$$NNI = PNdB + 15 \log N - 80$$

where, *PNdb* = the logarithmic average of aircraft noise in perceived decibels and, *N* = the number of aircraft heard on an average summer day between 800 and 1800. NNI contour values can be plotted around airports, and permitted land use patterns controlled accordingly. Thus, where NNI values exceed 60, land use is confined to warehouses, industry or transport. Between NNI values of 45 and 60, no new residential development is permitted and all; existing houses, schools and hospitals must be fitted with sound insulation of the highest standard. Between NNI 35 and 45, new residential construction is permitted but only if the design includes full sound insulation.

noise pollution level. An index used to measure noise irritability, calculated by empirical formula that takes in to account the greater irritability of impact sound as opposed to steady-state sound.

noise quieting. The reduction of reverberant noise level in a room, usually by applying sound absorbent treatment to the surfaces, so that it is no higher than the direct noise level.

noise rating. A system whereby manufacturers indicate on their products the noise level emitted at a fixed distance from the appliance.

noise susceptibility. Susceptibility to hearing impairment by noise. There is a wide range of noise susceptibility between "tender" and "tough" ears, but there is no sure way of identifying the "tender"ears except by periodic audiometric checks.

noise zoning. The statutory classification of areas according to usage; this method allows higher noise levels in areas where their effect will not be noticed but maintains lower levels in more sensitive areas such as suburban residential sites and rural areas. An inherent problem in zoning lies in the difficulty of accurately defining the zones and of setting the boundaries between adjacent zones. Noise zones are not necessarily compatible with established land-use zones. *See* neighborhood noise.

nonattainment area. In air pollution control, any area of the country that does not meet one or more of the primary ambient quality standards as defined in the Clean Air Act. Permits for new stationary sources of pollutants or for significant modifications of existing ones, may not be issued in nonattainment areas unless:

(a) an implementation plan exists with a timetable for reaching attainment;

(b) the new plant or modification installs pollution-control equipment that meets lowest achievable emission rate standards; and

(c) pollution from existing sources is reduced sufficiently that the overall air quality does not diminish.

nonbulk packaging. A packaging that has (a) an interval volume of 450 litres (118.9 gallons) or less as a receptacle for a liquid; (b) a capacity of 400 kgs (881.8 pounds) or less as a receptacle for a solid; or (c) a water capacity of 1,000 pounds (453.6 kgs) or less as a receptacle for a gas.

noncombustible refuge. Solid wastes that will not burn in a conventional incinerator. Good incineration practice sorts out noncombustibles from combustibles before incineration in order to minimize problems afterwards.

nondegradable pollutant. Any pollutant that is not readily broken down or otherwise chemically altered by exposure to the natural environment. Nondegradable pollutants remain potentially harmful as long as they are present in the natural environments such as air, soil, or water.

non-destructive activation analysis. Activation method of analysis in which selective measurement of activity of element to be determined is carried out by physical methods without chemical separation of irradiated sample.

nondestructive testing. A type of materials testing made on a finished product rather than on a sample, which involves no damage to the product. Examples are radiography, *X*-rays, and infrared radiation. Although there are several methods used for nondestructive testing six are widely applied in industry: visuloptical, liquid-penetrant, magnetic-particle, eddy-current, ultrasonic, and radiographic.

nonflowing artesian well. An artesian well in which the hydrostatic pressure is not great enough to elevate the water above the land surface; the water does however, rise above the local water table.

nonpersistent pesticides. Phosphate-based pesticides currently being used to rapidly replace chlorinated hydrocarbon pesticides. Although nonpersistent pesticides may have a much shorter half-life than the persistent ones, they create temporary hazards to persons applying them on crops, because these pesticides are of the same family as chemicals in nerve gas.

nonpoint pollution. In the pollution of water bodies by diffuse sources such as agricultural or urban runoff or aerial deposition. Conveyances for runoff, such as drainage ditches and storm sewers, are generally called nonpoint sources. Nonpoint pollution is usually the most important overall source of contaminants in the water bodies. It is much more difficult to deal with than is pollution from point sources, because the pollutants come from a large number of small, often unidentifiable sources, making treatment of waste stream impossible.

non-renewable resources. Natural resources which, once consumed, cannot be replaced *e.g.*, a ton of coal once consumed is gone forever in that form. Mineral resources generally are regarded as wasting assets of this kind. However, it is difficult to predict what the consequences of exhausting particular resources would be. For any particular mineral the exhaustion process would be gradual, accompanied, ceteris paribus, by a steady rise in its price. A rising relative price intensifies exploration and ensures treatment of lower grades of ore; recycling and reclamation of scrap and residues are also encouraged. Meanwhile developments in substitute materials and processes and in the pattern of demand could mean that a mineral considered indispensable at one stage could become redundant at another.

non-washer dust separators. The cyclone, in gas cleaning, is a dust separator or droplet separator using essentially the centrifugal force derived from the motion of the gas. A dust separator consisting of several cyclones in parallel is known as multicyclone. In the inertial separator particles are removed by a combination of inertial and centrifugal forces resulting from a sudden change in direction of flow of the gas, together with impaction of the particles on a target. In the electrostatic precipitator the gas is passed between sets of electrodes across which a very high constant potential is maintained. The dust particles become charged and adhere lightly to one set of electrodes; they are removed by sharp tapping, causing them to fall into containers. Although expensive to install, electrostatic precipitators are relatively cheap to operate and are one of the most efficient means of removing fine dust from gases, although strict maintenance is necessary to ensure unimpaired efficiency. They are widely used in power stations burning pulverized fuel, cement works, steel works, etc. *See also* impinger.

normal erosion. Wearing away of topographic features by prevailing agencies in the temperate climate. The term is open to criticism because erosion as found in temperate areas may in fact be abnormal or because one mode of erosion is just as normal as another.

normal pressure. The standard pressure equal to one atmosphere to which measurements of volume, especially of gases, and other experimental work which may vary with pressure changes, are usually referred. It is the pressure of a column of mercury 760 mm high at sea-level at a latitude of 45.

1 atmosphere = 1.01325 10^5 Pa.

normal soil. A soil whose profile is more or less in equlibrium' with the environment, and which shows the effects of the environment on its development from the parent material.

noxious gas. Any gas or vapour having a more or less toxic effect when inhaled. The term is restricted to gases resulting from chemicals or chemical reactions that occur either naturally or as by-products of industrial manufacture or use. It does not include so-called poison gases made specifically for military purposes, nor the asphyxiant gases, which have no positive toxicity.

noxious industry. *See* offensive industry.

nuclear energy. Energy of a higher order of magnitude than that of chemical reactions; the latter is derived from the formation and rupture of bonds (electrons) and amounts to about 5 eV per bond, whereas the former is evolved from the nucleus of the atom, yielding, for fission, about 200 million eV per nucleus. Nuclear energy is released either by splitting (fission) of an unstable, heavy nucleus (uranium-235 or uranium-233 and plutonium-239) or by union (fusion) of the hydrogen isotopes deuterium and tritium to form helium.

nuclear fission The splitting of the nucleus of a heavy atom into two fragments of approximately equal mass, usually by neutron bombardment. *See* nuclear reactor.

nuclear fuel. Material containing fissionable nuclides in chemical form and geometrical shape ready for use in the particular type of nuclear reactor. Principally, the three fissile isotopes uranium-235, uranium-233, and plutonium-239 are used as nuclear fuel.

nuclear fuel cycle. The sequence of processes which nuclear fuel undergoes, from the mine to fuel fabrication plant, nuclear reactor, and finally to reprocessing plant. The cycle also includes the transportation of fuel between each process and the disposal of the radioactive waste produced by each process.

nuclear fusion. A thermonuclear reaction involving the fusion of positively charged hydrogen nuclei (protons) to form helium, with evolution of energy. A temperature of several million degrees is necessary to overcome the repulsion of the positive charges. This process occurs in the sun, where it is catalyzed by carbon. Uncontrolled fusion has been achieved in the hydrogen bomb, the initiating temperature being supplied by a fission reaction. Research is now being devoted to developing a controlled and sustained fusion reaction, using the hydrogen isotopes deuterium and tritium. The most efficient experimental reaction is, for each fusion event. where, *e* represents at least 44 million K. Fusion has two great advantages over fission as an energy source:

(a) it utilizes water and readily available lithium as its raw material instead of scarce and costly uranium; and

(b) it produces no long-lived radioactive fission products, though it does yield high-energy neutrons.

nuclear radiation. A term used to denote α-particles, electrons, neutrons, photons, and other particles which emanate from the atomic nucleus as a result of radioactive decay and nuclear reactions.

nuclear reactor. An assembly in which a fission chain reaction is caused to take place in a controlled manner. The essential components of a reactor are a fissile material for fuel, a moderator, a coolant and a neutron absorbent material to act as a control for the neutron flux in the reactor core. *See* nuclear fission.

nuclear waste. Radioactive waste material s produced as by-products of research and nuclear-power generation. Medical sources are responsible for a small percentage of waste produced, but the greatest amount results from the exhaustion and reprocessing of fissile fuel sources from nuclear reactors, chiefly uranium-238 and plutonium-239. Most nuclear waste is produced by nuclear power stations and after a certain proportion of the fuel rods within the reactor core have been used, they are withdrawn for reprocessing. Typically waste fuel will be stored at the power station in a pressurized buffer storage tube for 28 days following which the fuel rod will be broken down into its component parts in an automated dismantling facility and the irradiated fuel elements stored for 80 days in a water-filled pond to allow for further decay of fission product heating. The spent fuel is then placed in a special steel flask for transfer to a reprocessing plan. At the reprocessing plant up to 97.5% of the uranium and polutonium can be recovered and a small proportion recycled for new fuel. However, for the non-reusable radioactive waste which remains no totally safe method of disposal exists. Nuclear waste is currently stored in slurry or liquid form in surface tanks protected by concrete and lead shields, buried in impermeable strata in deep bore holes as vitrified solids or dumped in steel and concrete containers deep on the ocean bed. nuclear waste is classified into three categories of radioactivity:

(a) high-level waste, with a radioactivity greater than 3.7×10^{10} (Bq)/gallon of slurry;

(b) intermediate waste, with a radioactivity of between 3.7×10^{4} and 3.7×10^{10} Bq/gallon of slurry;

(c) low-level waste, with a radioactivity of less than 3.7×10^{4}Bq/ gallon of slurry.

nuclear winter. A theoretically deduced state which some scientists believe would exist after nuclear war involving major atmospheric nuclear explosions. The devastation caused by the blast combined with the heat generated from the resulting fires, and the death of plants and animals as a result of radioactive fallout would lead to a major increase in the particulate matter in the atmosphere. The lower atmosphere would become so opaque that the transmission of solar energy would be prevented, leading to a substantial lowering of the average air temperature. As the particulate matter will be removed from the atmosphere by gravitational fallout then so the nuclear winter would retreat.

nucleation. The action of special particles, termed 'nuclei', in the passage from the vapour phase of a substance to the liquid or solid phases, or from the liquid to the solid phase.

nucleic acid. An extremely complex compound of high molecular weight which occurs in the nuclei of biological cells; when associated with a protein, the combined molecule is called a nucleotide. They can be partially hydrolyzed to sugar derivatives (ribosides) of purines and pyrimidines (nucleosides), or to nucleotides (phosphate esters of these compounds). The two major types of nucleic acids are ribonucleic acid, which contains ribose, and deoxyribonucleic acid, containing deoxyribose. Both types are of critical importance in cellular biochemistry, as they establish and execute the genetic mechanism of the organism.

nucleotide. A term used for complex molecules which are usually constituents of nucleic acids; they are composed of nitrogen-containing bases (purine or pyrimidine) bonded to either ribose or deoxyribose sugars, phosphoric acid being present to form an ester. The purine constituents are adenine and guanine, and the pyrimidines are uracil and cytosine. A well-known nucleotide is adenosine triphosphate (ATP), which is essential to many biochemical process, including photosynthesis.

nuisance dusts. Excessive concentrations of dusts in the atmosphere or in the workroom air, which may seriously reduce visibility, may cause unpleasant deposits in the eyes, ears, and nasal passages, or cause serious injury to skin or mucus membranes by chemical or mechanical action. A threshold limit of 10 mg/m^3, or 30 mppcf, of total dust 1% quartz, or 5 mg/m^3 respirable dust is recommended for substances in these categories, for which no specific threshold limits have been assigned. This limit, for a normal workday, does not apply to brief exposures at higher concentrations. Neither does it apply to those substances which may cause physiologic impairment at lower concentrations but for which a threshold limit has not yet been adopted.

nuisance organisms. A term frequently used in water pollution; it refers to a morphologically and physiologically diverse group of organisms, which includes planktonic and sessile algae, fungi, crustacea, and protozoa, as well as actinomycetes, and iron and sulphur bacteria. These organisms can cause objectionable tastes, colour, odour, and turbidity and may interfere with treatment processes by blocking strainers and filters. In addition, certain planktonic organisms, although not themselves harmful, may harbour pathogens and protect them against disinfection by chlorine. Most of these nuisance organisms can be controlled relatively easily by the usual water-treatment processes. Furthermore, problems of taste, odour, colour, and turbidity, which may be caused by them, are covered indirectly by the guidelines for the aesthetic characteristics of water. The presence of certain organisms in water may be an indication of corrosion of cast iron or of biodeterioration of construction materials that support the growth of micro-organisms. These include nonmetallic materials, such as plastics, rubbers, jointing compounds, and pipe-lining materials, which provide organic nutrients and thus encourage growth of certain micro-organisms including sometimes coliform organisms and *P. aeruginosa*. Although treatment will normally remove such organisms, they may establish themselves in sediment or slime and on materials within the distribution system, where their presence may support the growth of Asellus and other animal populations. Residual disinfection will help control such infestations, but occasional flushing and physical cleaning of pipe sections with polyurethane foam plugs may be needed. Nuisance organisms may also cause problems with groundwater sources by encrusting well-screens, thus causing loss of yield and impairing the aesthetic quality of the supply. Indeed, their presence may indicate organic pollution of the aquifer. Routine monitoring of such nuisance organisms cannot be recommended because of their diverse nature and unpredictable occurrence. It is not practicable to specify any quantitative limit for nuisance organisms.

nurse log. In forestry, a fallen tree in the process of decaying that has one or more seedlings established on its upper surface. The seedlings utilize the nutrients released by the decay of the dead tree. Nurse logs are very abundant in rain forests, both because the nutrients are scarce in rain-forest soils due to leaching and because the porosity of the decaying wood makes adequate water retention for seedling establishment difficult in dry climates.

nutrient. Any substance that is essential to the life and growth of plants, or animals, or man either as such or as transformed by chemical or enzymatic reactions. Nutrient requirements differ from species to species, however, due to different proportions of vital elements needed by different organisms and the different forms in which assimilation of them in to the body takes place.

nutrient budget. An estimate for a particular living system setting out the amounts of essential mineral nutrients which are taken up or lost.

nutrient cycle. The transfer of nutrients in an ecosystem from one stage to another. For example, leaves fall to the ground to be broken down by the bacteria and provide nutrients to the soil, which then sustain plant growth. The growing plants take energy from the sun, and provide food for the animals which live in the ecosystem.

nutrients. *See* eutrophication.

nutrient stripping. Tertiary treatment of waste waters, either to reduce the rate of eutrophication of receiving waters or to permit the re-use of water for domestic purposes. Constituents of interest are those responsible for stimulating excessive growth of algae namely compounds of phosphorus and nitrogen. Methods range from chemical coagulation to advanced treatment processes presents an additional problem.

Nymphalidae. A family of large and handsome butterflies including the Fritillaries and the Vanessids. They belong to the so called 'four-legged' group, the front legs being greatly reduced and functionless. Most of theses butterflies are brightly coloured. The Fritillaries form a natural group all very similar in the pattern of their wings; the Vanessids, sometimes known as aristocrats are very variable and generally beautifully patterned. Some of the species are very sensitive, and have disappeared as a result of deforestation and pollution.

O

oak ridge formula. An empirical formula used to calculate ground-level concentration of pollutants poured from a chimney opening.

obligative organism. An organism that must live in a certain way. The term usually refers to obligative anaerobe; that is, an organism usually a bacterium, that must live in an oxygen-free environment and is killed by exposure to free oxygen. Such organisms lack the enzyme necessary to convert hydrogen peroxide, a bactericide that is a common product of bacterial respiration in oxygen to water and oxygen. They are poisoned by their own wastes. The category includes various pathogens.

occlusion. 1. The process of progressive decrease of area of the warm sector (*i.e.*, that part of a depression in which the warm air mass is contained between the leading warm front and the following cold front) at the earth's surface, and its ultimate disappearance, by the junction of the cold air masses which initially precede the warm front and follow the cold front. 2. The front between these two cold air masses, after their junction . Also termed as occluded front.

occupational air. Air present inside plants, factories, offices, and heavily crowded places such as railway stations and service establishments. If air becomes heavily polluted, the workers should move to ambient air.

occupational noise. Any noise including vibrations from jackhammers, created inside or outside the industrial establishments, in the course of manufacture. This includes the sound of ball meeting bat, but the crowd's roar is not regarded as occupational noise.

occupational pollution. Pollution encountered by the employees during their working periods; such as dust inhaled by the workers in mining and digging operations.

octane number. A number on a conventional scale expressing the knock resistance of a fuel for spark-ignition engines. It is determined in test engines by comparison with reference fuels. There are several methods of test; consequently the octane number quoted should by accompanied by reference to the method used. The term arose through the use of 2, 2, 4-trimethylpentane (*iso*-octane) as a reference fuel, to which the octane number of 100 was assigned (as opposed to 0 for heptane).

odorant. A material that has a distinctive, sometimes unpleasant, odour and that may be added to odourless materials to give warning of their presence (the term odorizer is also used for the latter application). In most areas, the addition of an odorant to natural gas (to avoid the danger of explosions resulting from undetected leaks) is mandatory.

odour intensity index. In the test method of the American Society for Testing and Materials (ASTM), the number of times that an odorant must be diluted by a factor of 2 in order to reach the threshold concentration.

odour nuisance. Any distinctive, unpleasant odours resulting from manufacturing or natural process. Rendering, smelting, and refining are industries that create odour nuisances as well as air and water pollution. In most of the cases, the odour nuisances are not harmful to human health.

odour threshold. In principal, the lowest concentration of an odorant that can be detected by a human being. In practice, a panel of sniffers is normally used and the threshold taken as the concentration at which 50% of the panel can detect the odorant (although some workers have also used 100% thresholds).

offensive industry. Any business which by reason of the process involved, or the methods of manufacture, or the nature of the raw materials or goods used, produced or stored, is likely, as a result of the inadequacy of the available means of control, to cause effluvia, fumes and odours of a character offensive to persons on adjacent land. Historically, the offensive trades have included those dealing in the by-products *e.g.*, blood, hides and bones, and the process for dealing with condemned meat and fish. Also known as noxious industry.

oil. A nonspecific term applied to several groups of organic mixtures having quite different chemical composition and properties. Oils are liquids at room temperature, becoming increasingly viscous to semisolid at lower temperatures. The most important groups are;

(a) the mineral oil (petroleum, shale oil) which are mixtures of hydrocarbons;

(b) the vegetable oil (cotton-seed, soybean, etc.) which are mixtures of unsaturated fatty acids, many of which are edible;

(c) the animal oil (sperm and fish oils), also containing fatty acids; and

(d) the flower oil (essential oils), in which terpenes predominate (though derived from vegetations, they are classified separately from vegetable oils.

oil equivalent. In principal, the mass of a standard oil that would on combustion produce the same quantity of heat as a given mass of a given oil. In practice certain arbitrary rules are applied in calculating oil equivalents and there differ from one country to another.

oilex system. A method for cleaning oil-water interfaces created by oil spills, using polymers. When the oil comes in contact with the polymers, it sticks to the polymer material and the water runs off.

oil pollution. A pollution problem related mainly to the growth of the tanker trade and particularly with the development of giant tankers; statistics have shown that the incidence of oil spills at sea is increasing.

oil seepage. The slow natural release of oil from rocks in to the marine or terrestrial environment. Estimates of the global input of the oil to the oceans from natural seepage vary widely but may be of the order of $0.2\text{-}6.0 \times 10^6$ tones per year.

oil shale. A kerogen bearing finely laminated brown or black sedimentary rock that will yield liquid or gaseous hydrocarbons on distillation. It does not contain free oil. It appears to form in a special kind of anaerobic environment and is not commonly found in association with coal-bearing strata.

oil slick. A phenomenon caused by the activities of ships in ports and at sea, by small or large effluents from shore installations, and by offshore drilling activities. The slicks are normally small in area and are generally degradable by ocean's natural self-cleansing mechanisms, even though the slicks wrecks havoc with the plankton in their vicinity.

oil spill. The pollution of large water bodies such as sea, occurring when a tanker or other vessel containing petroleum accidently discharges its cargo into the ocean, a bay, estuary or other body of water. The present methods can successfully combat small spills. Major spills destroy marine plants and marine life, blacken coastal beaches and litter the sea with tar balls before the spills disappear.

oil spill absorbents. The materials that can successfully absorb the oil. These are classified as:

(a) lightweight porous inorganics, such as glass wool and vermiculite;

(b) natural organic absorbants, such as sawdust, peat and straw;

(c) inorganic solids, such as silica and talc; and

(d) polymers, such as polyurethane and polyethylene foams.

oil spill combustion. A technique for controlling spills where natural or supplied oxidants, coupled with wicking agents, are added to cause the oil spill to burn.

oil trap. Any barrier to the upward movement of oil or gas, allowing either or both to accumulate. A trap includes a reservoir rock and an impermeable roof rock; the contact between these is concave downward.

oligotrophic. Applied to a body of water containing relatively low amounts of nutrients, and usually with considerable dissolved oxygen in the bottom waters. *See* eutrophication.

old-age. A term applied to the final stage in the cycle of erosion in which the surface has been brought to almost base level. It may also refer to that stage of stream development in which sediment builds up and water flow decreases.

oligotrophic lakes. Lakes which do not produce abundant organisms in relation to their volume and which always posses abundant oxygen in their lower regions are called oligotrophic (little-producing) lakes; they are usually deep lakes. Like other deep lakes, during the summer they often have at the bottom a region of cold water (the hypolimnion) which is of greater volume than that of the upper region of warm water (the epilimnion). The hypolimnion in oligotrophic lakes con tains considerable oxygen at all times. Separating the epilimnion and hypolimnion is the metalimnion, a layer in which the temperature of the water falls very rapidly with increasing depth. Within the metalimnion is a zone of maximum rate of decease in temperature called the thermocline. In this zone the decrease in temperature must be at least 1°C per metre of increase in depth. A relatively shallow (though still deep) lake may be oligotrophic because there are so few organisms produced that little oxygen is expended in their decay on the bottom, while a deeper lake may be more productive of organisms but remain oligotrophic because the hypolimnion is so large that there is ample oxygen to decay the organic matter without undue depletion of the oxygen. There may be other factors involved in creating oligotrophic conditions, such as the shape of the lake basin, direction of the prevailing winds with respect to the orientation of the lake, and amount and nature of chemicals and organic materials washed into the lake. However, the classification is still based on productivity as indicated by the resulting condition, oxygen is never depleted in the hypolimnion.

Omethoate. A systemic insecticide and acaricide with a broad range of action and little phytotoxicity, except to some peach varieties. It is a colourless oily liquid, readily soluble in water, acetone, ethanol and many hydrolysed by alkali. Acute oral LD_{50} for rats is about 50 mg/kg. It has been found to be effective against a wide range of insects particularly caterpillars.

once-through cooling. The standard method for disposing of waste heat from a power plant. Water is drawn from a lake, river, or estuary, passed through the steam condenser where its temperature is raised, and is then returned to the body of water from which it was drawn.

onground tank. A device meeting the definition of tank and that is situated in such a way that the bottom of the tank is on the same level as the adjacent surrounding surface, so that the bottom cannot be visually inspected.

on-site. The same or geographically contiguous property that may be divided by public or private right-of-way, provided the entrance and exit between the properties is at a corossroads intersection, and access is by crossing, as opposed to going along, the right-of-way. Noncontiguous properties owned by the same person, but connected by a right-of-way controlled by that person and to which the public does not have access, is also considered on-site property.

opacity rating. A measure of the opacity of an emission; the degree of obscuration (of the vision of an observer) that is equal to the apparent obscuration produced by smoke of a given Ringelmann number. *See* smoke; chert.

open burning. The combustion of any material without the following characteristics:

(a) control of combustion air to maintain adequate temperature for efficient combustion;

(b) containment of the combustion reaction in an enclosed device to provide sufficient residence time and mixing for complete combustion;

(c) control of emission of the gaseous combustion products.

operator. The person responsible for the overall operation of a facility.

opportunity-cost. The real cost of satisfying a want, expressed in terms of the cost of the sacrifice of alternative activities.

organic. Pertaining or relating to a compound containing carbon as an essential constituent arranged in chains and/or rings; also containing hydrogen with or without oxygen, nitrogen, or other elements.

organoleptic. Relating to an attribute perceptible by the sense organs. In air pollution contexts, the attribute of a product is usually odour.

organophosphorus insecticides. A diverse group of non-persistent synthetic chemical poisons which act chiefly on the nervous system; the group includes fenthion, malathion, and parathion. These compounds have phosphorus chemically bonded to the carbon atoms of organic radicals, and are effective as both contact and systemic insecticides and against insects and mites. Many of these compounds are very toxic to mammals and birds and have to be handled with care. Doses may be accumulative. The systemic compounds are very effective against sap-sucking insects. All the organophosphorus compounds are relatively transient and are soon broken down to become non-toxic. In comparison with the persistent chlorinated hydrocarbons great care in timing and applications is required in the use of these compounds for effective results. The mode of action in both insects and mammals appears to be inhibition of acetyl cholinesterase (or some very similar enzyme).

organotin compounds. A group of compounds having at least one covalent bond between carbon and tin. An action level is defined as half the recommended time-weighted average (TWA) work place concentration limit. The occupational exposure to organotin compounds means any work involving handling, storage, use, or manufacture of organotin compounds at a concentration above the action level, or if the skin or eye contact with organotin occurs. Occupational exposure to organotin compounds should be controlled in such a manner so that no employee is exposed to organotin compounds at a concentration greater than 0.1 mg/m^3 of air, determined as a time-weighted average (TWA) concentration limit for up to a 10-hour workshift in a 40-hour workweek, over a working lifetime. The recommended standard is designed to protect the health and provide safety to the workers for up to a 10-hour workshift, 40-hour workweek over a working lifetime.

orographic cloud. Air which is compelled to rise over a barrier of hills or mountains may be forced aloft until the dew-point level is reached. Condensation will occur, and cloud will form on the hills. The amount of ascent necessary to produce condensation will depend upon the degree of humidity. The degree of stability controls the cloud types. If the air is comparatively stable, then layer cloud with a flat base is formed. Where there is marked instability within the air mass the air may go ascending, and cloud of great vertical thickness may result.

orographic precipitation. A meteorological term for the precipitation caused or intensified by the upthrust effects on the air of highlands. Heaviest orographic rainfall along a mountain front usually is not far above the point where the precipitation begins, although its elevation varies with the season, exposure, and latitude.

osmium tetraoxide. An hazardous compound used as catalyst in organic synthesis; highly toxic by ingestion and inhalation. Occupational exposure to osmium tetraoxide should be controlled in such a manner so that no employee is exposed to this chemical at a concentration greater than 0.002 mg/m^3 of air (0.0006 ppm), determined as a time-weighted average (TWA) concentration limit for up to a 10-hour workshift in a 40-hour workweek, over a working lifetime. The recommended standard is designed to protect the health and provide safety to the workers for up to a 10-hour workshift, 40-hour workweek over a working lifetime.

outer core. the outer or upper zone of the earth's core, extending from a depth of 2900 km to 5100 km and including the transition zone. It is equivalent to the *E* layer and the *F* layer. It is presumed to be liquid because it sharply reduces compressional-wave velocities and does not transmit shear waves.

outfall sewer. A pipe or conduit used to transport either raw sewage, or treated effluent, to a final point of discharge into a body of water.

outwash. Soil material washed down a hill by rainwater and deposited upon gently sloping region.

outwash cone. A cone-shaped deposit consisting chiefly of sand and gravel found at the edge of srinking glaciers and ice sheets.

over burden. Waste overlying the stone in a quarry or open pit mine; worthless surface material covering a body of useful mineral.

overfit stream. A misfit stream that is too large to have eroded the valley in which its flows, or whose flood plain is two small for the size of the stream.

overpack. An enclosure that is used by a single consignor to provide protection or convenience in handling of a package or to consolidate two or more packages. Overpack does not include a freight container.

owner. The person who owns a facility or part of a facility.

oxalic acid. A hazardous compound used in metal equipment and automobile radiator cleaning, leather tanning, stripping reagent for permanent press resins, bleaching of textiles, and in the recovery of rare earth elements. Occupational exposure to oxalic acid should be controlled in such a manner so that no employee is exposed to this chemical at a concentration greater than 1.0 mg/m^3 of air, determined as a time-weighted average (TWA) concentration limit for up to a 10-hour workshift in a 40-hour workweek, over a working lifetime. The recommended standard is designed to protect the health and provide safety to the workers for up to a 10-hour work-shift, 40-hour workweek over a working lifetime.

oxidation. In its original use, oxidation meant simply combination with oxygen. Its use has, however, been considerably widened to cover a great many processes similar to oxidation, such as chlorination, and other processes of combination with strongly non-metallic elements, which add electrons readily. In fact the term oxidation in its broadest sense means simply a chemical reaction whereby electrons are removed from one or more of the atoms of a substance. It is, of course, most frequently accompanied by a simultaneous process, in the same reaction, whereby another substance or substances gain the electrons and thus undergo reduction; therefore, calling the process oxidation, under these circumstances, simply means that it is this part (*i.e.*, loss of electrons) of the particular process that is of greatest interest. Removal of hydrogen atoms (each having one electron) from a hydrogen-containing organic compound (dehydrogenation) is a form of oxidation; it is effected by a catalytic reaction with air or oxygen, as in the oxidation of alcohols to aldehydes. Free radical chains play an important part in the oxidation of such organic compounds as rubber, drying oils.

oxidation ditch. A modified form of activated sludge process. In essence, it is an extended aeration process, capable of taking shock laidings without upset. The ditch is operated as a closed system.

oxidation pond. A shallow lagoon or basin, about 1.5 metres deep, within which waste water is purified, through sedimentation and both aerobic and anaerobic biochemical activity over a period of time; used in favourable climates. (See diagram on the next page.)

oxidative fermentation. Decomposition of hexoses to compounds of simpler structure, occurring under action of bacteria, in which initial degradation of carbohydrate is similar to alcoholic fermentation; final stage leads, however, to products of higher oxidation number.

Oxydemeton-methyl. A systemic and contact insecticide and acaricide, used against sap-sucking in-

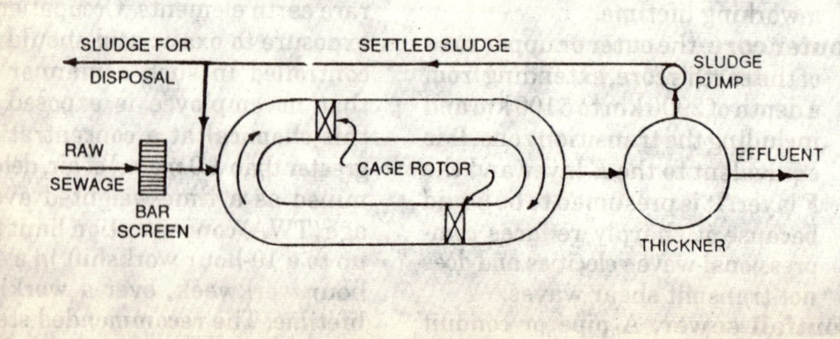

OXIDATION DITCH

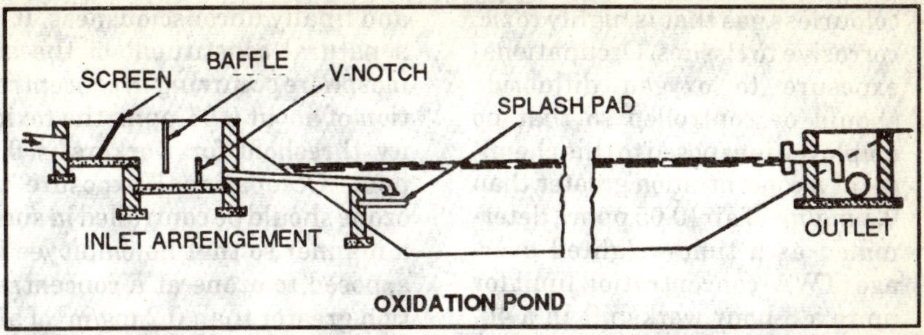

sects and mites, with a fast kill and moderate persistence. It is a clear brown liquid, miscible with water and soluble in most organic solvents except light petroleum. It is hydrolysed by alkali. The acute oral LD_{50} for male rats is 65 mg/kg. Effective against aphids, and red spider mites on most crops, also leafhoppers, whiteflies, psyllids, thrips, some flies, sawflies. Also known as metasystox.

oxides of nitrogen. *See* nitrogen oxides.

Oxydisulphoton. A systemic insecticide and acaricide particularly suitable for seed treatment against virus vectors. It is a pale coloured liquid, slightly soluble in water, readily soluble in most organic solvents. The acute oral LD_{50} for rats is about 3.5 mg/kg; particularly effective against sap-sucking insects and mites. Also known as Disyston.

oxidizing enzyme. An enzyme that catalyzes an organic oxidation, *e.g.*, oxidase, phenolase.

oxygen. A gas comprising about 50% by weight of the earth's crust and oceans and thus is the most abundant terrestrial element. Gaseous oxygen constitutes 21% by volume of the air near the earth's surface, much of which is formed by photosynthesis of plants; water contains 88.8% oxygen by weight. It is vital to all animal and most plants as the supporter of respiration-metabolism processes. The main hazard of oxygen is not poisoning by the excess of the gas but due to lack of it. Enclosed spaces such as vats, tanks, sewers, etc., may have insufficient oxygen present to support life due to replacement by other gases which may or may not be toxic by themselves, *e.g.*, carbon monoxide is toxic and will kill, carbon dioxide is nontoxic but will not support life. If the concentration of oxygen falls below 14% of the atmosphere, humans become irrational, dangerous to themselves and other people, and finally become unconscious and may die from asphyxia. Special hazards are attached to such occupations as diving and tunnelling and call for very special medical facilities. In industry, generally the greatest hazard from the use of oxygen lies in its power to cause spontaneous fire and explosion with other chemicals and materials, and to cause smouldering objects to burst in to flames.

oxygen absorbed. The amount of oxygen in parts per million absorbed by a sample of water from acidic potassium permanganate in 4 hours at 300 K.

oxygen difluoride. An unstable

colourless gas that is highly toxic, corrosive to tissues. Occupational exposure to oxygen difluoride should be controlled so that no employee is exposed to this chemical at a concentration greater than 0.1 mg/m^3 of air (0.05 ppm), determined as a time-weighted average (TWA) concentration limit for up to a 8-hour workshift in a 40-hour workweek. Also known as dissolved oxygen sag.

oxygen sag curves. Graphical curves which relate the dissolved oxygen content of water against time flow, within the context of the process of self-purification, following the discharge of pollut-. ants into a stream. Also known as dissolyed oxygen sag.

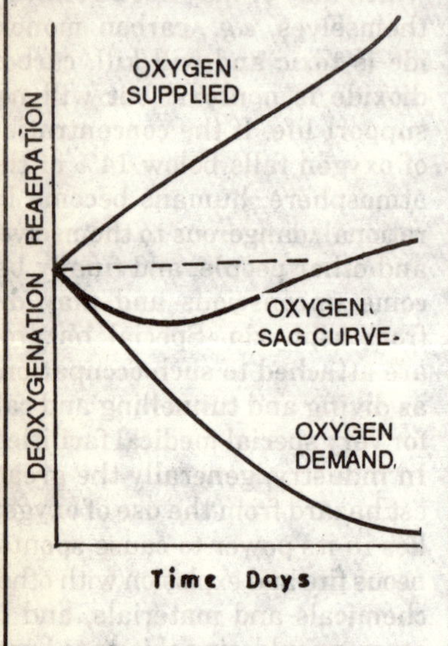

OXYGEN SAG CURVE

ozone. A triatomic molecule of oxygen. Above minimal levels, it is an irritant to human beings and animals. Higher concentrations cause headache, giddiness, pains in chest, difficulty in breathing, and finally unconsciousness. It is a natural constituent of the atmosphere occurring in concentration of about 0.01 ppm; the toxicity threshold for workers is 0.1 ppm. Occupational exposure to ozone should be controlled in such a manner so that no employee is exposed to ozone at a concentration greater than 0.2 mg/m^3 of air (0.1 ppm), determined as a time-weighted average (TWA) concentration limit for up to a 8-hour workshift in a 40-hour workweek, over a working lifetime. *See also* Los Angeles smog.

ozone depletion. The depletion of ozone is a result of three simultaneous phenomenona the very low temperature in the antarctic (200K or lower), the presence of stratospheric clouds at this time, and the existence of a polar vortex which provides a containment wall. The polar stratospheric cloud is itself a results of the low timperatueres; it sponges nitrous oxide from the atmosphere and thus removes from the scene the species that could have tied up carbon monoxide, Also, laboratory meaurements have confirmed that there are heterogenous reactions on the surface of such clouds releasing chlorine in the presence of sunlight to attack ozone. There is no doubt that the hole is the creation of human activity. The free flow of technology to develop ozone-friendly alternative to CFCs. HCFC-22 with an ozone depletion potential of 1.20 of that of CFC-11, has been suggested as an interim substitute. In India, the National Chemical Laboratory at pune and the Indian Institute of Chemical Technology at Hyderabad, have mounted efforts to develop better alternatives. One such product is HFC-134a (a compound without chlorine or bromine) whose ozone depletion potential is virtually zero and is being examined as a replacement for CFC-12. Another is HCFC-123 with an ozone depletion potential of 1/50 of CFC-11. This is a subject for the simulataneous study of lubricating oils and modifications to compressors, heat exchangers, motors, insulations, etc. *See also* ozone layer.

ozone layer. An atmospheric layer lying between about 10 and 50 km (above the surface of the earth), in which the amount of ozone is relatively high. The maximum concentration generally occurs at the height of about 20 or 25 km. The ozone layer is formed by the action of ultraviolet (UV) radiations on atmospheric oxygen, and is thought to act as a shield that removes harmful UV radiations from incoming solar radiations; the strongest evidence to date being an 'ozone hole' that has been found to develop over Antarctica each spring as the so called 'polar stratospheric clouds' (PSCs) disperse. The size of the hole waxes and wanes in near-perfect correspondence with the concentration of CFCs in polar atmosphere. It is thought that these man-made products reach Antarctic through the atmospheric circulation and become trapped on the surfaces of the ice crystals that make up the PSCs, where they apparently undergo reactions with nitrogen oxides trapped on the same crystals to create ozone-destroying chlorine monoxide. These compounds are stable in lower atmosphere but are broken up by the UV radiations when they reach the upper stratosphere; and the active free radicals thus formed react with the ozone and lower its concentration levels. The result is likely to be an increase in UV radiations at the surface of the earth, affecting the environment. It is expected to produce skin cancer, cataracts, and a general lowering of the ability of the immune system to combat disease. Natural ozone itself is not limited to stratosphere. On special meteorological instances, stratospheric air may intrude into the troposphere and bring the ground levels of the ozone to 30 ppm. Also known as ozono-sphere. *See also* ozone depletion.

ozonosphere. *See* ozone layer.

P

package treatment plant. A compact, transportable, factory-made, sewage treatment unit capable of achieving a specific effluent quality; it may be deployed to serve a housing estate for a temporary period prior to the installation of a trunk sewer.

packaging. The assembly of one or more containers and any other components necessary to assure compliance with the minimum packaging requirements of this subchapter and includes containers (other than freight containers or overpacks), portable tanks, cargo tanks, tank cars, and multitank car tanks.

palatable species. A species of plant that is preferred over the other species by browsing or grazing animals, and which can be eaten first if available. Palatability is determined by a complex set of factors, including general chemistry of the plant, the effects of soil chemistry and water supply, the growth form, and the nutritional needs of the grazing or browsing species. In general, it appears to correlate most strongly with succulence, protein content, and percentage of ash. The animal's preferences as determined by heredity, of course, also plays a vital role; for example, forbs are preferred over grasses by sheep, and grasses over forbs by cattle, though these species have similar nutritional needs. Palatable species are always first to disappear from an overgrazed range.

paleoclimatology. The study of climate through geologic time, extending back to the Precambrian. Basic data are derived from the analysis of sedimentary rocks, their contained fossils, and other sedimentary features.

Palmer bowlus flume. A device for measurement of flow in a variety of open cahnnels. The principle is based on venturi flume. Such a flume is sometimes installed in a manhole to measure the flow in a sewer.

pan. 1. A natural shallow depression often occupied by a lake. if the lake waters evaporate in time the depression will be lined with salt crystals and it is called salt pan. 2. The upper portion of the *B*-horizon of soils in temporate climates may be hardened or cemented by precipitation of salts previously leached from *A*-zone. The hardened zone is called pan or hard pan.

pandemic. A term used for conditions that occur over a broad geographic area and affect a major part of the population.

pangaea. A supercontinent that existed about 300 to 200 million years ago during Mesozoic time when all continents were joined. The northern portion, named Laurasia, was sometimes partially and sometimes completely separated from the southern portion, named Gondwanaland, by a large sea called Tethys.

panplain. A type of erosion surface, resulting from lateral plantation by meandering streams (hence the process of panplanation); peneplains are characterized by:

(i) steepsided residual hills,

(ii) the presence of almost perfectly level surfaces rather than the gently undulating landscapes likely to result from mass wasting of interfluves, and

(iii) occurrence in series (that is, one above the other, a logical impossibility if the dominant pores in their formation is down wearing).

These features could arguably be explained if lateral plantation, leading to the back wearing of interfluves, were the most active process in the late stage of the cycle of erosion. However, alternative explanations have since been proposed.

paper and pulp industries waste treatment. The paper and pulp industries wastes also account for water pollution. Cellulose in the form of wood, straw, rag, jute, esparto, hempo is discharged during manufacture of pulp, treatment of pulp and finally manufacture of paper from pulp. The *p*H value of the wastes lies between 7.5 to 9.5 and B.O.D. is 150-1000 ppm. If these wastes are directly discharged into streams, they will impart turbidity, colour and hardness; increase slime, growth. The treatment of paper industries wastes include screening. setting, floatation, filtration, lagooning and aeration followed by coagalution, anaerobic digestion, trickling, filters.

parathion. Generic name for O,O-diethyl-O-*p*-nitrophenylphosphorothioate; mainly used as insecticide and acaricide. It is highly toxic by ingestion, inhalation, and by skin contact, and is effective as a contact and stomach poison against many species Special precautions are necessary to prevent inhalation and skin contamination. Occupational exposure to parathion is defined as any work involving handling, sto-rage, processing, blending, mixing, use, or manufacture of parathion. Occupational exposure to parathion should be controlled in such a manner so that no employee is exposed to parathion at a concentration greater than 0.05 mg/m^3 of air, determined as a time-weighted average (TWA) concentration limit for up to a 10-hour workshift in a 40-hour workweek, over a working lifetime. *See also* organophosphorus insecticides.

parathion-methyl. A non-systemic, contact and stomach insecticide, with some fumigant action, and a range of action similar to that of parathion but of lower mammalian toxicity. It is a non-phyto-toxic chemical. The technical product is a brown liquid of about 80% purity, scarcely soluble in water, slightly; soluble in light petroleum and mineral oils, but soluble in most other organic solvents. It is hydrolysed by alkali at a faster rate than parathion, and readily isomerizes on heating. Compatible with most other pesticides. The acute oral LD_{50} for male rats is 14 mg/kg; for female rats 24 mg/kg. It is hazardous to wild life but is of brief persistence. As for parathion but not effective against Acarina.

partial closure. The closure of a hazardous waste management unit in accordance with the applicable closure requirements of Part 264 or 265 of 40 CFR at a facility that contains other active hazardous waste management units. For example, partial closure may include the clusure of a tank (including its associated piping and underlying containment systems), a landfill cell, surface impoundment, waste pile, or other hazardous waste management unit, while other parts of the same facility continue in operation in the future.

partial life cycle toxicity tests. The toxicological tests involving the each of several groups of individuals of one species that are exposed to different concentrations of a toxicant throughout part of a life cycle which include life stages observed to be especially sensitive to chemical exposure.

particle size analysis. In pollution control, the study of the measurement of the dimensions and the determination of the shape of particles; the whole of the operations by which a particle size distribution can obtained. The presentation is made in the form of a table of numbers, or a graph of the experimental results obtained using a method or an apparatus capable of measuring the equivalent diameter of particles in a sample of capable of giving the proportion of particles for which the equivalent diameter lies between defied limits.

particulate matter, suspended. All solid and liquid particles in the air that are small enough not to settle out on to the earth's surface under the influence of gravity; also defined as the material that can be removed from air by passing it through a suitable filter. *See also* aerosol; dust.

particulate pollution. Pollution caused by the release of particulate material into the atmosphere by man-made processes. Airborne particulates can have a wide range of deleterious effects on human health, plants, materials and the climate. As far as human health is concerned, particulates enter the respiratory tract during inhalation. The size of the particles inhaled determines the extent of penetration into the respiratory system; for example, particles over 5 µm in diameter are stopped by the hairs lining the nasal passages and are deposited mainly in the nose and throat. Particles ranging in size from 0.5-5.00 µm may penetrate as far as the narrowest passages (bronchioles) in the lungs where most are deposited on the walls in mucus, which is in turn removed by tiny hair (cilia) within a few hours. Particles less than 0.5 µm in diameter reach the air sacs deep in the lung tissue and may settle there some being absorbed into the blood. The effect of particulates on human health depends on their air pollutants present. The particles may be intrinsically toxic because of their chemical or physical characteristics, for example asbestos and beryllium, or the particles may carry adsorbed molecules which are irritating or toxic to lung tissue, for example aromatic hydrocarbons such as benzopyrene, or tetraethyl lead from motor vehicle exhaust.

In plants, the deposition of particulates on leaf surfaces interferes with photosynthesis by reducing incident solar radiation, resulting in reduced growth rate. In materials particulates may accelerate corrosion of metals, especially in the presence of sulphur-containing compounds. They may damage buildings, sculpture, and other structures, and react with painted surfaces. The deposition of particulates on textiles requires more frequent cleaning which weakens the fabric materials.

Climate is also affected by particulates in the atmosphere which influence the amount and type of solar radiation reaching the earth's surface as a result of light scattering and absorption by the particulates. Particulate pollution may reduce visibility and decrease the incident slolar radiation, creating a greater need for artificial illumination. The formation of clouds may be influenced by particulates when they act as nuclei upon which water condensation can take place. Patterns of precipitation over cities and adjacent countryside show a correlation with atmospheric particulate levels. Worldwide climatic change may also be related to particulate pollution; the reduction in the solar radiation reaching the earth's surface may be disturbing the heat balance of the atmosphere by causing an atmospheric temperature decrease which may more than compensate for the greenhouse effect of increased atmospheric carbon dioxide levels.

pasteurization. Heat treatment of liquid or semiliquid food products for the purpose of killing or inactivating disease causing bacteria.

pathogenic organism. Etymologically, any disease-producing agent; in common usage the term is restricted to a living organism (usually a microorganism) that causes communicable diseases such as cholera, bacillary dysentery, typhoid fever, typhus fever, bacterial food poisoning, malaria, yellow fever, amoebic dysentery and infective hepatitis. Wide varieties of pathogenic bacteria, viruses and parasites, are responsible for food- and water-borne diseases.

pathological waste. Infectious or potentially infectious waste, the disposal of which could be a public health hazard or nuisance; it includes hospital wastes, some laboratory wastes, municipal waste, and any other material infected with bacteria and viruses.

pathotoxin. A chemical of biological origin, other than an enzyme, that plays an important role in plant disease. Most pathotoxins are produced by plant pathogenic fungi or bacteria but some are produced by higher plants.

Pearth system. A system consisting of recirculating the sludge digester gas with the help of a compressor and releasing it to lower scum level to promote rapid digestion by circulating the actively digesting sludge. Also known as PFT system; named after Pacific Flush Tank Company,

peat formation. Decomposition of

vegetation in stagnant water with small amounts of oxygen, under conditions intermediate between those of putrefaction and those of moldering.

pedosphere. The portion of the biosphere that contains soil. The ground covering the surface of the earth consists of loose and solid stone, rock, and humus. The temperature changes, the freezing and thawing of water in rock fissures, and the dissolution and crystallization of salts reduce the rock to such an extent that loose weathering products are formed. Under the influence of weathering elements such as oxygen, carbon dioxide, water and many minerals on the surface, further reaction products are formed. The layer of weather-worn material so created comes to be occupied by lower and higher order organisms, by whose exudation and intake of mineral nutrients the decomposition is carried further. Excrement, dead plants, and animal remains form the organic substance which is decomposed by microorganisms and other soil-dwellers in to carbon dioxide or transmuted in to humus. The outcropping geological seams are thus reconverted in to the soil by weathering and new clay formation, the decomposition of organic matter and humus formation, and transposition of the soil components. The soil is thus a complicated dynamic system in which physical, chemical, and biological processes are interconnected.

pentaborane. A compound of boron and hydrogen that is highly toxic by ingestion and inhalation. Occupational exposure to pentaborane is defined as any work involving handling, storage, processing, or use of pentaborane. Occupational exposure to pentaborane should be controlled so that no employee is exposed to pentaborane at a concentration greater than 0.01 mg/m^3 of air (0.005 ppm), determined as a time-weighted average (TWA) concentration limit for up to a 10-hour workshift in a 40-hour workweek.

pentachlorophenol. A hazardous chemical discharged from the chemical industry; used as insecticide for termite control; as fungicide for protection of timber from fungal rots and wood-boring insects. It is strongly phytotoxic, and is used as a pre-harvest defoliant and as a general herbicide. It forms colourless crystals; volatile steam; almost insoluble in water; soluble in most organic solvents. It is non-corrosive in the absence of moisture, solutions in oil cause deterioration of natural rubber but synthetic rubbers may be used in equipment and protective clothing. The acute oral LD_{50} for rats is 210 mg/kg; it irritates mucous membranes and causes sneezing, the solid and aqueous solutions stronger than 1% cause skin irritation. Effective against termites and other wood boring insects; use restricted by strong phytotoxicity.

The available data for pentachlorophenol indicate that acute and chronic toxicity to freshwater aquatic life occur at concentrations as low as 55 and 3.2 μg/L, respectively; and would occur at even lower concentrations among the species that are more sensitive than those tested. The corresponding values for saltwater aquatic life are 53 and 34 μg/L, respectively.

perceived noise level. Sound pressure level of a reference sound (consisting of a band of randon noise between one-third of an octave and one octave wide, centred on 1000 Hz) which is subjectively judged to be equally noisy as the sound being measured. The perceived noise level of a broad-band noise having no strong pure-tone components is usually estimated from measured values of band pressure level over the audio range using accepted calculation proceducers.

percentage of hearing loss. According to Fletcher's original point eight rule, the hearing levels at 500, 1,000 and 2,000 Hz were average and multiplied by 0.8 to determine the percentage of the auditory area lost in the speech range. The hearing levels at 500, 1,000, 2,000 and 4,000 Hz for each ear were averaged. The worst car was considered only one seventh as important as the better ear in assessing the binaural loss. The frequencies were weighted so that 500 Hz counted for 15%, 1,000 Hz for 30%, 2,000 Hz for 40% and 4,000 Hz for 15%. Hearing impairment begins at 26 dB hearing level (averaged over 500, 1,000 and 2,000 Hz). For every decibel that the estimated hearing level for speech exceeds 26 dB, 15% is allowed up to the maximum of 100%. This is reached at 93 dB. The wrost ear is considered one fifth as important as the better ear in assessment of the binaural hearing impairment.

percolating filter. In pollution control, a bed of inert material provided with means of distributing sewage over the surface. The surface of the medium becomes covered with a film of micro-organisms which effectively purify the sewage under aerobic conditions. *See also* trickling filter.

percolation. The process by which water passes down through the pores into the soil and through cracks and joints in the rocks. The water moves downward under the influence of gravity. The rate of percolation depends upon the rock type as well as the amount of rainfall. Percolating water can carry dissolved chemicals, and may cause leaching.

perezone. A zone in which sediments accumulate along coastal lowlands; includes lagoons and brackish-water bays.

permeability. The capacity of a porous rock, soil, sediment, or any material, for transmitting a fluids without damage to the structure of the medium. It depends up on the size and number of the connections between the openings in the material rather than on the size and the number of the openings themselves. Permeability may be achieved by rock being either porous or previous. The essential feature of a bed of permeable rock is that the liquid it contains may be extracted by pumping. Permeability in a rock is measured in darcies.

permit. An authorization, license, or equivalent control document issued by EPA or an approved state agency to implement the requirements of this part and parts 271 and 124. Permit includes permit-by-rule (270.60) and emergency permit (270.61). Permit does not include RCRA interim status or any permit that has not yet been the subject of final agency action, such as a draft permit or a proposed permit.

permit-by-rule. A provision of the regulations stating that a facility or activity is deemed to have a RCRA permit if it meets the requirements of the provision.

peroxyacetic acid. A highly reactive, hazardous compound used as an oxidizing agent in organic synthesis; classified as potential occupational carcinogen. It is also formed by the action of UV radiations or ozone on the acetic acid vapours, during the formation of photochemical smog.

peroxyacetyl nitrates (PAN). A component of photochemical smog and the primary plant toxicant of smog-type injury. It has been estimated that the field levels of 0.01 to 0.05 ppm will injure sensitive plants, causes eye irritations and other health effects. *See* Los Angeles smog.

persistence. An important characteristic of a pollutant in an environmental medium (air, water, or soil) or in living tissue; substances that persist (remain active for a long lime) in a toxic form, such as certain heavy-metal metabolites, organo-chlorine compounds, and polychlorinated biphenyls (PCBs) are particularly hazardous.

person. An individual, trust, firm, joint stock company, federal agency, corporation (including a government corporation), partnership, association, state, municipality, commission, political subdivision of a state, or any interstate body.

Personnel or facility personnel. All persons who work at or oversee the operations of a hazardous waste facility, and whose actions or failure to act may result in noncompliance with the requirements of Parts 264 or 265 of 40 CFR.

pesticides. A broad term that includes all chemical agents used to kill animal and vegetable life which interferes with agricultural productivity; thus, insecticides, herbicides, fungicides, and rodenticides are special types of pesticides, regardless of their mode of action. Of these compounds, synthetic organic chemicals are the most important, in terms of growth rate as well as consumption, and potential for contaminating the environment. Synthetic organic pesticides are produced, usually, as concentrated materials which are later 'formulated' before application. The formulation consists of mixing the concentrated material with such diluents as clays, talcs, water, kerosine and other solvents. The purpose of formulation is to assist the even distribution of a small amount of active chemical over a large area at a re-determined rate per unit of area. Pesticides may be detected in water, soil, and food (including milk, meat, fruits, and fish living in polluted waters) particularly in rural the areas where they are widely used for agricultural purposes. Insecticides may be classified as:

(a) chlorintated hydrocarbon (organochlorine) types,

(b) organo-phosphorus types, and

(c) carbamates and others.

It should be emphasized that pesticides are extremely diverse group of substances. There is a potential of wide variety of toxic effects throughout the group. For many pesticides, the possibility of dermal exposure and subsequent absorption presents a greater problem to users as well as workers than does through inhalation. In addition, many establishments by their nature manufacture or formulate a vast number of pesticides with varying toxicities, the possible synergisms of these combinations of substances are unknown. Pesticide residues are absorbed by lichens from the environment and through them reach higher animals and eventually, human beings. Similarly, pesticide residues in water, diatoms and planktons reach higher animals through the consumption of aquatic flora and fauna. Pesticides often translocate from soil and food crops. Humans consuming it have high amount of pesticides accumulated through translocation become victims of toxic effects of pesticides. The sale of pesticides should be strictly regulated under state laws that require products to be registered and all label directions approved. No new pesticide may be registered without positive evidence of its safety to people, crops, domestic animals, wildlife, and the environment generally. *See also* chlorinated hydrocarbons; insecticides; organo-phosphorus insecticides.

Pestox. A systemic insecticide and acaricide with little contact effect; it has been found to be highly effective against sap-feeding insects and mites; non-phytotoxic at insecticidal concentrations. It is a brown viscous liquid, miscible with water and most organic solvents; slightly soluble in petroleum oils, and readily extracted from aqueous solution by chloroform. The acute oral LD_{50} for male rats is 9.1 mg/kg. It is usually employed against aphids and red spider mites on a variety of crops. Also known as Scgradan; System.

petrifaction. A fossilization process whereby inorganic matter dissolved in water replaces the original organic materials converting them to a stony substance.

petrochemical. A chemical intermediate obtained directly from petroleum or natural gas by cracking or pyrolysis, or an end-product derived by subsequent chemical processing. The term is so general that its usefulness has been questioned by some authorities. The primary petrochemicals are methane, ethane, propane, ethylene, acetylene, benzene, hydrogen, *etc.*, from which numerous chemicals are produced by a variety of reactions. Petroleum-derived materials that are used directly as energy sources (gasoline, fuel oil) are not usually considered to be petrochemicals.

petrol. A mixture of paraffins and aromatic hydrocarbons, the exact composition of which vary with the source of origin. In addition, it contains sulphur derivatives. Commercial petrol contains various additives to give better performance, one of the most important being tetraethyllead, for its antiknocking property. Benzol, which is largely benzene, toluene, and xylene is also added to it. Petrol is narcotic and can cause unconsciousness. Inhalation of petrol fumes over a long period can cause blood changes due to benzene; this can also cause bone marrow aplasia and aplastic anaemia. By ingestion, the gastrointestinal system can be upset.

petrolatum. A purified mixture of hydrocarbons consisting of a semi-solid whitish or yellowish mass. Also known as vaseline; petroleum jelly.

petroleum. This term literally means 'rock oil'. Petroleum is thought to have originated from decomposition of animal life which inhabited the ocean floor in early geologic periods. It is a complex mixture of a number of hydrocarbons, mainly paraffins, aromatics and cycloparaffins. The molecules of some of its components contain up to 50 carbon atoms. It is not only the primary source of automotive fuel but of thousands of organic chemicals used in medicines, plastics, dyes, solvents, lubricants, etc. 2. A general term for all naturally occurring hydrocarbons in gaseous, liquid as well as solid state.

petroleum gas. Any of a number of flammable gases obtained by refining of petroleum and used both for organic synthesis and in liquefied form as fuels. Most important are butane, *iso*-butane, and propane; and the unsaturated butylenes and propylene. Methane is obtained not only from petroleum, but also from other sources such as coal and natural gas.

petroleum industry pollution. The petroleum industry is characterized by the regular discharge of hydrocarbons and other organic compounds, sulphur dioxide and fine dust. In the refining process, the crude oil is heated and vaporized and then condensed again at various temperatures. In this way the varying fractions, from highly volatile gasoline to heavy heating off, are separated. In the process, tar-like bitumen is left behind for further processing in its turn. In order to produce the energy needed to vaporize the crude oil, the distillation residues are used in the refineries as the main fuel. These residues contain large quantities of sulphur, which, after combustion, finds its way into the atmosphere in the from of sulphur dioxide. In addition, according to where it comes from, the material consumed can contain larger or smaller quantities of fine dust, which is also given off with the flue gas. The second group of components in air pollution by refineries are organic substances such as hydrocarbons. These are discharged in the main from various sources, at ground level, spread over the entire area of the works, such as storage tanks, flanges, safety valves, vents, seals, settling tanks and torch flares. These organic gases and fumes are in some cases very pungent, and so can cause serious nuisance in the vicinity of the refinery. Between 0.4% and 1% of the crude oil put through a refinery is given off in the from of organic vapours into the environment. Assuming it to have been no more than 0.4%, discharges of organic gases and vapours from leaky pipeline and valves come to about 0.80%, the process gases of the torch to about 0.23%, and the heating gases of the torch flares and the discharges, from the waste water treatment to 0.02% each. On the average the torch has a combustion efficiency rate of no more than 50%-70%. This gives an average discharge rate of organic gases and vapours of 4.3 tons per day per million tons annual average crude oil throughput for the refinery. It has been estimated that, at present that one-third of production losses by the petroleum industry pass into the atmosphere as hydrocarbons.

***p*H.** A scale indicating the acidity or alkalinity of aqueous solutions. *p*H value is designated as a number from 1 to 14, which represents a logarithmic scale indicating the concentration of hydrogen ions. These number are actually exponents expressing the molar concentration; water molecules dissociate into H^+ and OH and recombine at such a rate that there is at any instant a concentration of these ions of 1/10,000,000 mole per litre, *i.e.*, $1/10^7$ or 10^{-7}. This is the neutrality point of pure water (*p*H 7), at which the concentrations of H^+ and OH^- ions are equal. When an acid is added to the water, numbers from 1 to 7 are used to indicate the acidity of the solution, *i.e.*, the predominance of hydrogen ions; if alkalies are added to the water, numbers from 7 to 14 indicate the alkalinity, *i.e.*, the predominance of hydroxyl ions in the solution. A *p*H of 1.0 is represented by 0.1 N hydrochloric acid, and a *p*H of 14 is that of 0.1N sodium hydroxide solution.

Unpolluted rivers generally vary in *p*H value from about 5.0 (acid moorland peaty streams) to about 8.5 (chalk streams). Acid water draining from an abandoned coal mine may have a *p*H value as low as 2.0; this drainage water is actually a sulphuric acid solution. In order that the normal biological and chemical processes which occur in a river or during sewage treatment should not be adversely affected, the river water or sewage should not vary greatly from neutral, *i.e.*, *p*H 7.0. For this reason, river authorities usually set limits between *p*H 6.0 to *p*H 9.0, and sewage authorities between *p*H 5.0 and *p*H 10.0.

The *p*H of the water has a major effect on the type of fish and other aquatic species present. Alkaline sreams are usually found in localities where the rock and soil contain calcium carbonate. Rain, with its normally small amout of carbonic acid (H_2CO_3), dissolves the calcium carbonate present and forms calcium bicarbonate.

phase. A homogeneous part of a system that is divided from another homogeneous part of the system by a boundary. For example, an enclosed mixture of ice, water, and water vapour exists in three phase-a solid phase, a liquid phase, and a gas phase.

Phenisobromolate. A popular contact acaricide with residual activity, applied on many crops. It is a crystalline solid, insoluble in water; but readily soluble in most organic solvents; stable in neutral media. The acute oral LD_{50} for rats is 5000 mg/kg. It is of promise for use against mites on pome and stone fruits, citrus, hops, cotton, beans, cucurbits, tomatoes, and strawberries.

phenol. A colourless, hazardous solid with a characteristic disinfectant properties. It is soluble in water, alcohol, and oil; it is obtained from fractional distillation of coal tar, from benzene, and monochlorobenzene. It exerts a strong corrosive action on body tissues including the skin, gastrointestinal tract and lungs. It is capable of absorption through intact skin. If swallowed, it is a violent poison for which there is no satisfactory antidote. In case of acute poisoning, the mouth, lips, and the skin are stained white and become hard, and the pulse becomes rapid and feeble. Occupational exposure to phenol should be controlled so that no employee is exposed to phenol at a concentration greater than 20.0 mg/m^3 of air, determined as a time-weighted average (TWA) concentration limit for up to a 10-hour workshift in a 40-hour workweek, or to more than 60 mg/m^3 of air as a ceiling concentration for any 15 minute period. The recommended standard is designed to protect the health and provide safety to the workers for up to a 10-hour workshift, 40-hour workweek over a working lifetime. The available data for phenol indicate that acute and chronic toxicity to freshwater aquatic life occur at concentrations as low as 10,200 and 2,560 µg/L, respectively; and would occur at even lower concentrations among the species that are more sensitive than those tested.

The available data for phenol indicate that acute toxicity to saltwater aquatic life occur at concentrations as low as 5,800 µg/L, and would occur at even lower concentrations among the species that are more sensitive than those tested.

Phenthoate. A non-systemic insecticide and acaricide with contact and stomach action. It may be phytotoxic to some peach, fig and grape varieties, and may discolour some red-skinned apple varieties. It is a crystalline solid, almost insoluble in water, but miscible with most organic solvents. The acute oral LD_{50} for rats is 250-300 mg/kg. It is effective against caterpillars, aphids, jassids, mites, and is also used for the protection of stored grain.

phenyl mercaptan. A derivative of phenol in which oxygen has been replaced by sulphur. It is highly toxic by skin contact, inhalation and ingestion. The occupational exposure to phenyl mercaptan should be controlled so that no employee is exposed to phenyl mercaptan at a concentration greater than 2.0 mg/m^3 of air (0.5 ppm), determined as the time-weighted average (TWA) concentration limit for up to a 10-hour workshift in a 40-hour workweek.

phon. A unit of loudness level employed when a plane-progressive 1000 Hz comparison tone, coming from directly in front of an observer who listens binaurally, is employed in the measurement of loudness level.

phonemic regression. Symptom, affecting the aged, of difficulty in comprehending words even when they are heard well.

Phorate. A persistent systemic insecticide used for the protection of seedlings form sap-feeding and soil insects; some fumigant action. In temperate climates effective soil persistence of 15-20 weeks is expected. It is a clear liquid only slightly soluble in water, but miscible with carbon tetrachloride, dioxane, xylene, and vegetable oils.

It is hydrolysed by alkalis and in the presence of moisture. The acute oral LD_{50} for male rats is 3.5 mg/kg; for females 1.6 mg/kg. It is effective against aphids, wireworms, various fly maggots (Frit, Carrot), capsids, leafhoppers, and various weevils.

Phosalone. A non-systemic insecticide and acaricide used on deciduous tree fruits, field and market garden crops, against a wide range of pests. It persists on plants for about 2 weeks before being hydrolysed. It forms colourless crystals; insoluble in water and light petroleum, but soluble in acetone, benzene, chloroform, ethanol, methanol, toluene and xylene. It is stable under normal storage conditions, non-corrosive, and compatible with most other pesticides. The acute oral LD_{50} for male rats is 150 mg/kg. it is effective against a wide spectrum of pests-caterpillars on fruit, cotton bolloworms, fruit fly maggots, aphids, psyllids, jassids, thrips, various weevils and red spider mites. Also known as Zolone.

phosgene. A colourless gas with a pleasant odour in low concentrations, but becomes pungent in high concentrations; used in the synthesis of many organic compounds. It is many times more poisonous than chlorine and causes intense irritation of the respiratory tract. At low concentrations, the gas is not easily detected and the poisonous effect may be delayed for 24 hours. Acute poisoning due to phosgene leads to irritation of nose, throat, and lungs; and the eyes become red and tear-filled. Occupational exposure to phosgene is defined as exposure to airborne concentration of phosgene at or above one-half of the recommended workplace environmental limit. Occupational exposure to phosgene should be controlled so that no employee is exposed to phosgene at a concentration greater than 0.1 ppm, determined as a time-weighted average (TWA) concentration limit for up to a 10-hour workshift in a 40-hour workweek, or to more than 0.2 ppm as a ceiling concentration for any 15 minute period. The recommended standard is designed to protect the health and provide safety to the workers for up to a 10-hour workshift, 40-hour workweek over a working lifetime.

Phosmet. A non-systemic acaricide and inecticide, used at concentrations safe for a variety of predators of mites and thus useful for integrated control programmes. It is a white crystalline soild, with an offensive odour, scarcely soluble in water, but more than 10% soluble in acetone, dichloromethane and xylene. The acute oral LD_{50} for male rats is 230 mg/kg; it is readily degraded both in laboratory animals and in the environment. It is used mainly against phytophagous mites; when used as recommended should not affect mite predators. Also known as Imidan.

Phosphamidon. A systemic insecticide and acaricide, rapidly absorbed by the plant, but only a little contact action. It is non-phytotoxic except to some cherry varieties and sorghum varieties related to Red Swazi. It has no fumigant action. It is a pale yellow oil, miscible with water, and readily soluble in most organic solvents except saturated hydrocarbons. It is stable in neutral and acid media but is hydrolysed by alkali; compatible with all but highly alkaline pesticides. It corrodes iron, tinplate and aluminium, and is packed in polyethylene containers. The acute oral LD_{50} for rats is 28.3 mg/kg. The half-life in plants is about 2 days. It is quite effective against sap-feeding insects and leaf-eating ones; particularly aphids, bugs, many caterpillars (but not Noctuidae), rice stem borers, thrips, Colorado Beetle, and phytophagous mites.

phosphate ethers. The organic derivatives of phosphoric acid, used as fire resistant hydraulic fluids. The accidental ingestion forms the main hazard and has been responsible for several outbreaks of paralysis where it was used as a cooking oil. Occupational exposure to tri-*o*-cresyl phosphate should be controlled so that no employee is exposed to tri-*o*-cresyl phosphate at a concentration greater than 0.1 mg/m^3 of air, determined as a time-weighted average (TWA) concentration limit for up to a 8-hour workshift in a 40-hour workweek, over a working lifetime.

phosphine. A colourless gas with garlic odour, it is extremely toxic in high concentrations. It is dangerous because of fire, explosion and toxic hazard. The occupational exposure to phosphine should be controlled in such a manner so that no employee is exposed to phosphine at a concentration greater than 0.4 mg/m^3 of air (0.3 ppm), determined as a time-weighted average (TWA) concentration limit for up to a 10-hour workshift in a 40-hour workweek.

phosphoric acid. A colourless, odourless, viscous liquid; used in making fertilizers, soaps and detergents, pickling of metals, pharmaceuticals, sugar refining, electroplating, and water treatment. It is toxic by ingestion, inhalation, and irritant to skin and eyes. Occupational exposure to phosphoric acid should be controlled in such a manner so that no employee is exposed to phosphoric acid at a concentration greater than 1.0 mg/m^3 of air, determined as a time-weighted average (TWA) concentration limit for up to a 10-hour workshift in a 40-hour workweek.

phosphorus. A non metallic element having several allotropic forms differing in their crystal structure. The white allotrope is pyrophoric, but the black does not ignite easily. Phosphorus also resembles carbon in its tendency to form covalent bounds, though it does not bond to itself as readily as carbon. Phosphorus is an essential nutrient for plants and animals and has complex metabolic function (as adenosine triphosphate) in addition to its hardening effect on bones and teeth (as hydroxyapatite). Phosphorus is required by every living plant and animal cell. Deficiencies of available phosphorus in soils are a major cause of limited crop production. Phosphorus deficiency is probably is the most critical mineral deficiency in grazing livestock. The biological role of phosphorus include:

(a) the anabolic as well as catabolic reactions as exemplified by its essentiality in high energy bond formation, *e.g.*, ATP (adenosine triphosphate), ADP (adenosine diphosphate), etc., and the formation of phosphorylated intermediates in carbohydrate metabolism;

(b) the formation of other biologically significant compounds, such as phospholipids, important in the synthesis of cell membranes;

(c) the synthesis of genetically significant compounds such as DNA and RNA;

(d) contributing to the buffering capacity of body fluids, cells, and urine; and

(e) the formation of bones and teeth.

The most of the phosphorus in the vertebrate body is contained in the hard tissues. The nutrient requirement for phosphorus depends upon the particular species and the physiological status of the animal. During growth, lactation, gestation, and egg-laying, a higher phosphorus content of the diet is generally required.

In elemental form it is highly toxic, and some of its organic compounds (nerve gases and insecticides of the parathion type) are lethally poisonous. The chief uses of elemental phosphorus are in the manufacture of numerous compounds (phosphoric acid, combinations with halogens, sulphur, *etc.*, and organophosphorus compound) as a semiconductor and catalyst, in pyrotechnic devices, and in deoxidizing metals. Phosphorus-containing fertilizers, such as single superphosphate, wet process ortho-phosphoric acid, triple superphosphate, ammonium phosphate and nitrophosphate do not require elemental phosphorus (or the resulting pure P_4O_{10}) in their preparation, but are manufactured by directly reacting phosphate rock with requisite chemicals, such as H_2SO_4 or HNO_3. Occupational exposure to yellow phosphorus should be controlled so that no employee is exposed to yellow phosphorus at a concentration greater than 0.1 mg/m^3 of air, determined as a time-weighted average (TWA) concentration limit for up to a 10-hour workshift in a 40-hour workweek.

phosphorus cycle. Phosphorus is present in the biosphere almost exclusively in the form of phosphate. Calcium, iron, and aluminium form phosphates that are almost insoluble in water. The bulk of the phosphorus present on the earth is consequently integrated in rocks, soils, and sediments and distributed fairly uniformly over the entire earth. During the course of the evolution of the earth, deposits have formed at various locations, of the phosphorus-rich minerals, which are exploited as natural reserves for the steadily rising phosphorus requirement of the man.

Phosphorus is obtained by the plants mainly as phosphate ion. Owing to the poor solubility of phosphorus compounds in water, only a few phosphate ions are available in the solution in the ground. The availability of phosphorus is highly dependent on the form of phosphorus and *p*H of the soil. When the plants die, the organic matter is returned to the soil and there decomposed by the bacteria and fungi. In this process, part of the phosphorus incorporated in the plants is absorbed by the micro-organisms, and the rest is released, which passes to the ground. Depending upon the soil conditions, this phosphorus is again established in the form of iron, calcium, and aluminium phosphate. If the plants are consumed by the animals, the phosphorus contained in them is ingested by the animal organisms, and ultimately returned to the soil in excrement or with the carcass.

In the atmosphere, phosphorus is largely combined with aerosols. Its displacement in this form is of consequence only in dust and sandstorms, and volcanic eruptions. When the air turbulence subsides, dust particles settle down again. Phosphorus normally enters the stream and river currents only through erosion of soil containing phosphorus compounds. It tends to dissolve in water and is absorbed by the water plants. In natural ecosystems, the subsequent delivery of phosphorus into the biosphere results primarily from weathering of phosphorus bearing rocks. Under certain conditions, in water meadows for example, the supply of phosphorus in sludge may play a vital role in the provision of phosphorus to the vegetation, while removal of phosphorus is significant only in extremely dry regions with little plant growth and a high incidence of wind erosion.

phosphorus oxychloride. A colourless, fuming liquid; used in the manufacture of cyclic and acyclic esters for plasticizers. It reacts violently with water. It is toxic by ingestion, inhalation, and irritant to skin and eyes. Occupational exposure to phosphorus oxychloride should be controlled so that no employee is exposed to phosphorus oxychloride at a concentration greater than 0.6 mg/m^3 of air (0.1 ppm), determined as a time-weighted average (TWA) concentration limit for up to a 10-hour workshift in a 40-hour workweek.

phosphorus pentachloride. A light yellow, fuming solid; used in the manufacture of many compounds including pharmaceuticals. It reacts violently with air and water. It is toxic by ingestion, inhalation, and irritant to skin and eyes. Occupational exposure to phosphorus pentachloride should be controlled in such a manner so that no employee is exposed to phosphorus pentachloride at a concentration greater than 0.1 mg/m^3 of air (0.1 ppm), determined as the time-weighted average (TWA) concentration limit for up to a 10-hour workshift in a 40-hour workweek.

phosphorus pentasulphide. A light yellow, hazardous solid with a pungent smell; used in the manufacture of insecticides and pesticides. It reacts vigorously with air and water. It is toxic by ingestion, inhalation, and irritant to skin and eyes. Occupational exposure to the phosphorus pentasulphide should be controlled in such a manner so that no employee is exposed to phosphorus pentasulphide at a concentration greater than 1.0 mg/m^3 of air, determined as a time-weighted average (TWA) concentration limit for up to a 10-hour workshift in a 40-hour workweek.

phosphorus trichloride. A clear, colourless, fuming liquid with a pungent smell. It reacts vigorously with air and water. It is toxic by ingestion, inhalation, and corrosive to skin and tissues. Occupational exposure to phosphorus trichloride should be controlled so that no employee is exposed to phosphorus trichloride at a concentration greater than 1.5 mg/m^3 of air (0.2 ppm), determined as a time-weighted average (TWA) concentration limit for up to a 10-hour workshift in a 40-hour workweek.

photochemical reaction. A reaction brought about or markedly accelerated by exposure to electromagnetic radiations in the spectrum of visible light, the ultraviolet, and (rarely) the near infrared. This type of reactions are initiated by absorption of photons with appropriate energy by at least one component or reacting system composed of atoms or molecules. Such reactions are responsible for the production of photochemical smog. *See also* photochemical smog.

photochemical smog. Smog is formed from atmospheric pollutants that are generated under the influence of solar radiation while photochemical smog manifests itself in the from of a more or less dense haze, covering the town, which restricts visibility by the blurring if contrasts due to dissipation of light. The dissipation of light is caused by aerosols generated by chemical reactions occasioned by smog. These chemical reactions are highly complicated, and have not been fully analyzed to this day. The initial products include various hydrocarbons, sulphur dioxide and nitrogen oxide. Thus unburned standard gasoline alone contains over 200 different hydrocarbons in the categories of aliphatics, olefins and aromatics. Greater still is the number of hydrocarbons that, because of incomplete combustion, are emitted in exhaust fumes. The first reaction stage is the formation of oxidizing substances under the influence of photodissociation. The most important reaction is probably the formation of ozone. Another important factor is the oxidation of sulphur dioxide to sulphur acid in sunlight. In the process ozone is produced as a by-product. In the second phase of the reaction, the ozone combines as an oxidizing agent with many initial products of atmospheric pollution, whereby new, often highly corrosive pollutants are formed. In the following processes certain important reactions and initial products are represented. By the reaction of excess ozone with nitrogen dioxide, nitric acid is formed under the following formula: The corrosive nitric acid occurs in the same way as sulphuric acid in the form of aerosols. Owing to the effects of ozone and other oxidizing agents on hydrocarbons, chemical radicals are formed. These include alkyl, alcohol,oxide,peroxide, acetyl group, formic and pereoxyacyl radicals. These radicals are chemically beings directly or produce further chemical reactions in conjunction with other substances, as a result of which new noxious substances will be formed. Overall, the number of possible photochemical primary and secondary reactions in the smog has been estimated to be several hundred. *See also* aerosols.

photosensitization. The initiation of a chemical reaction by irradiation of an intermediary substance. The intermediary absorbs the radiation and initiates the process by collisions with the reactants, thereby transferring part or all of its excess energy to the reactants. Such reactions are quite frequent in the atmosphere, and to some extent responsible for the formation of photochemical smog.

photosynthesis. The synthesis of carbohydrates (sugars, starches, and cellulose) performed in the cells of plants, in the presence of sunlight. The plants absorb water through the roots and absorb carbon dioxide through the pores called stomata in leaves. These combine to give carbohydrates and oxygen. Most photosynthesis occurs within the chloroplast of green plant cells and the overall process may be divided in to two sets of reactions, the first requiring light and the second occurring even in absence of light. where, (CH_2O) represents one-sixth of a glucose molecule. The absorption of light radiation that is necessary for photosynthesis is effected by chlorophyll, the green leaf-colouring pigment in the plants, which is stored in the chloroplast contained in the plant cell. This occurs primarily in the plant cells which are directly exposed to the light. The energy absorbed by these pigments is utilized in removing electrons from water molecules and eventually liberating oxygen in the water-splitting reaction. The displaced electrons are conveyed through an elaborate electron transfer system to ultimately reduce pyridine nucleotide chemical compounds to $NADPH_2$ (hydrogenated nicotinamide adenine dinucleotide phosphate). In order from each electron to be displaced from water, two photons of energy is required. The $NADPH_2$ molecule provides the reducing power for the reduction of carbon dioxide to sugar. High-energy adenosine triphosphate molecules are also formed during the transfer of electrons in two photosystems so that stored energy is available for the subsequent dark phase carbon dioxide reduction reactions. Thus two electrons are required to form one molecule of $NADPH_2$ and $1/2O_2$. Therefore four electrons, and hence, two $NADPH_2$ molecules are need to complete the overall reduction of carbon dioxide to (CH_2O) and oxygen. Since the displacement of four electrons from water requires the absorption of eight photons, then at least eight photons of light energy need to be sequestered for the photosynthetic reduction of one carbon dioxide molecule and the liberation one oxygen molecule.

Photosynthesis in green plants depends on certain external factors, such as light, the carbon dioxide content of the air, atmospheric humidity, and temperature. Generally, it can be mentioned that the rate of photosynthesis rises with the increase in the strength of radiation. Above a certain saturation value, however, it will not continue to rise with any further increase in the intensity of the light. The saturation values are different for the different species of plants. They are lower for instance, for the plants that grow in shade, in comparison to the plants that need more sunlight to grow. A limiting factor for the level of photosynthesis rate in the plant's natural location is frequently the carbon dioxide content of the atmosphere, which is generally 0.3%. In greenhouse, the carbon dioxide level of air can be raised, and under favourable radiation conditions, the photosynthesis will thereby be increased. The humidity of the air affects the aperture of the stomates in the leaves and with it the absorption of carbon dioxide. While the photochemical reactions of photosynthesis are considered to be independent of temperature, the dark reactions vary in amount with a temperature increase of 10°C by the factor 2.

The photosynthesis performance of green plants is quite impressive. On an hourly basis, 1 m^2 of leaf surface produces about 1 g of sugar. On the basis of annual assimilation performance of the total vegetation coverage in the world, it amounts to about 100 billion tones of carbon. This is about 100 times the amount of the total coal output of the entire world. The effective rate of energy conversion in photosynthesis works out at about 30%. The highest effective rate is attained in tropical forests, in which the plant growths are disposed in various stages and are thus able to utilize the incident sunlight to the best advantage.

phototropism. The alteration of the growth form of a plant in response to light. Most plants are positively phototropic; that is, they tend to grow toward light, elongating and bending their shoots so that their leaves and flowers get full-light exposure. The phenomenon seems to be controlled by the movement of auxins from light to dark areas of the plant, so that the cells in the dark areas are stimulated to lengthen faster than those in light areas. This differential growth causes a bending of the stem towards the light.

Phoxim. An insecticide of brief persistence and no systemic action, with low mammalian toxicity, effective against a broad range of insects; most useful against soil insects and stored products pests. It is a yellow liquid virtually insoluble in water, slightly soluble in light petroleum, soluble in alcohols, ketones, and aromatic hydrocarbons. Stable to water and acid media, but unstable to alkali; believed to be compatible with most pesticides of a non-alkaline nature. The acute oral LD_{50} for rats is more than 2000 mg/kg. Effective against a broad range of insects, especially stored products pests and insects affecting man. It has also been successfully used against soil pests (dipterous maggots, rootworms and wireworms). It is effective as a contact and stomach poison against many species Special precautions are necessary to prevent inhalation and skin contamination.

phreatic explosion. A volcanic eruption or explosion, of steam, mud, or other material that is not incandescent; it is caused by the heating and consequent expansion of ground water due to an underlying igneous heat source such as lava. Such eruptions are usually not accompanied by the usual products of volcanic eruption.

phreatic water. Originally applied

only to water that occurs in the upper zone of saturation under water-table conditions. but now applied to all water in the zone of saturation. Thus, it is synonymous with groundwater.

phthalate esters. The compounds obtained by the action of phthalic anhydride (or phthalic acid) on certain alcohols and phenols. The available data for phthalate esters indicate that acute and chronic toxicity to freshwater aquatic life occur at concentrations as low as 940 and 3.0 μg/L, respectively; and would occur at even lower concentrations among the species that are more sensitive than those tested. The available data for phthalate esters indicate that acute toxicity to saltwater aquatic life occur at concentrations as low as 2,944 μg/L, and would occur at even lower concentrations among the species that are more sensitive than those tested. For the protection of human health from the toxic effects of dimethyl phthalate ingested through water and contaminated aquatic organisms, the ambient water criterion has been estimated to be 313 mg/L; while for the protection of human health from the toxic properties of dimethyl phthalate ingested through contaminated aquatic organisms alone, the ambient water criterion has been determined to be 2.9 g/L. For the protection of human health from the toxic effects of diethyl phthalate ingested through water and contaminated aquatic organisms, the ambient water criterion has been estimated to be 350 mg/L; while for the protection of human health from the toxic properties of diethyl phthalate ingested through contaminated aquatic organisms alone, the ambient water criterion has been determined to be 1.8 g/L. For the protection of human health from the toxic effects of dibutyl phthalate ingested through water and contaminated aquatic organisms, the ambient water criterion to be 34.0 mg/L; while for the protection of human health from the toxic properties of diethyl phthalate ingested through contaminated aquatic organisms alone, ambient water criterion has been determined to be 154 mg/L. For the protection of human health from the toxic effects of di-2-ethylhexyl phthalate ingested through water and contaminated aquatic organisms, the ambient water criterion to be 15.0 mg/L; while for the protection of human health from the toxic properties of di-2-ethylhexyl phthalate ingested through contaminated aquatic organisms alone, the ambient water criterion has been determined to be 50.0 mg/L.

physical construction. The excavation, movement of earth, erection of forms or structures, or similar activity to prepare an HWM facility to accept hazardous waste.

physical quality of life index (PQLI). An index designed to measure the physical well-being of the population of a nation. It is calculated by the use of three indices, each of which is given equal weight; child mortality, literacy, and life expectancy. Each country is rated on scale of 0-100 for each of the indicators and a man value is then taken to give the PQLI rating of 77 has been set to represent basic human needs although approximately 66% of the world's population presently fall below this figure. The PQLI index provides a more useful indicator to the physical progress than the exclusively economic indicator of the gross national product figure.

physico-chemical treatment. A process of treating waste water (usually industrial effluent) by physical and chemical action. Appropriate chemicals are added to the waste water followed by passing through screen and grit chamber, prior to clarification. The clarified liquid is filtered and then passed through a bed of activated carbon or through a carbon adsorption unit. Finally, it is kept in a holding pond wherefrom the treated effluent goes out.

physiological acoustics. The study of the physiological response to acoustic stimuli.

physiological noise. Noise generated when an earphone is applied to the ear, being caused by pulsation of blood vessels.

phytoplankton. The plant component of plankton, consisting chiefly of microscopic algae, such as diatoms and dinoflagellates. Near the surface of the sea there may be many millions of such plants per cubic metre. Members of the phytoplankton are of great importance as they form the basis of food for all other forms of aquatic life, being the primary producers.

pickling. 1. Descaling and cleaning of metallic surfaces with a strong acid such as sulphuric or

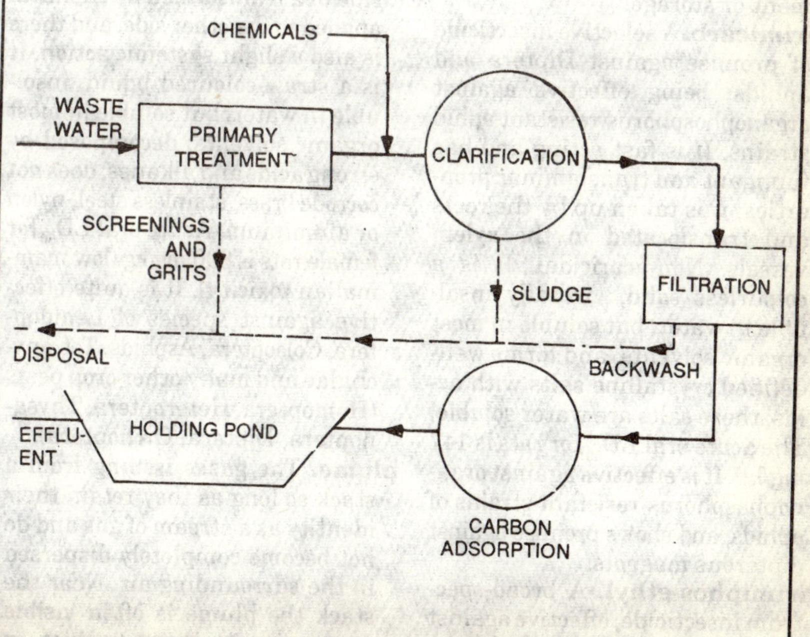

PHSICO-CHEMICAL TREATMENT

hydrochloric acid. 2. Preservation of certain food products by the use of various spices, sodium chloride solution, vinegar (acetic acid), or sodium benzoate in low concentrations. Salt solution is also used in the preliminary treatment of skins for the tanning process in leather technology.

picornavirus. One of a group of small RNA-containing viruses commonly present in the alimentary and respiratory tracts of vertebrates. They cause mild infections of these tracts but the group also includes the polioviruses, which attack the central nervous system causing poliomyelitis; and the causal agent of foot and mouth disease in cattle, sheep, and pigs.

pile. Any noncontainerized accumulation of solid, nonflowing hazardous waste that is used for treatment or storage.

Pirimicarb. A selective insecticide of promise against Diptera and aphids, being effective against organophosphorus-resistant aphid strains. It is fast acting and has fumigant and translaminar properties; it is taken up by the roots and translocated in the xylem vessels. Non-acaricidal. It is a colourless solid, virtually insoluble in water, but soluble in most organic solvents, and forms well-defined crystalline salts with acids; these salts are water soluble. The acute oral LD_{50} for rats is 147 mg/kg. It is effective against organophosphorus-resistant strains of aphids, and shows promise against dipterous maggots.

Pirimiphos-ethyl. A broad-spectrum insecticide, effective against soil-inhabiting Diptera and Coleoptera. No phytotoxicity has been recorded using recommended rates; high rates of seed dressing have resulted in seedling abnormalities though. It is stable for 5 days at 350 K. In the pure state it is a pale straw-coloured liquid; insoluble in water but miscible with most organic solvents; corrosive to iron and unprotected tinplate. Acute oral LD_{50} for rats is 140-200 mg/kg. It is effective particularly against soil-inhabiting Diptera and Coleoptera; effective as foliage spray at conventional rates against species of Lepidoptera, Coleoptera, Homoptera and Tetranychidae. Also known as Primicid.

Pirimiphos-methyl. A fast-acting, broad-spectrum insecticide of limited persistence, with both contact and fumigant action; non-phytotoxic. It penetrates leaf tissue to the extent that an insect on one side of a leaf is killed by chemical applied to the other side, and there is also a slight systemic action. It is a straw-coloured liquid, insoluble in water, but soluble in most organic solvents; decomposed by strong acids and alkalies; does not corrode brass, stainless steel, nylon or aluminium. Acute oral LD_{50} for female rats is 800 mg/kg (low mammalian toxicity). It is quite effective against species of Lepidoptera, Coleoptera, Asphids, Tetranychidae and many other crop pests (Homoptera, Heteroptera, Thysanoptera, Diptera, Orthoptera).

plume. The gases issuing from a stack so long as they retain their identity as a stream of gas and do not become completely dispersed in the surrounding air. Near the stack the plume is often visible owing to water droplets, dust, or smoke that it contains, but it often downwind long after it has become invisible to the eye (it can, however, be detected and followed by suitable instruments). Fanning plume is the plume that fans out horizontally into a thin layer under stable atmospheric conditions that restrict its spread vertically. The effect is enhanced in buoyant plumes that have already spread considerably by turbulence while rising, before levelling out where the atmospheric and plume temperatures are equal. A fanning plume can cause intense pollution if it impinges on a building or hillside. Looping plume is the name given to a plume that appears to be following a sinuous path, usually with irregular undulations. The up and down motion starts as soon as the gas issues from the stack and is caused by atmospheric eddies, often the result of thermal convection. It is an optical illusion that any particular parcel of gas follows a sinuous path as it moves downwind; if it forms the top of a wave near the stack. it remains as the top of a wave as it moves downwind. It is the sinuosities that move with the wind, growing in size as they travel. Looping is seldom observed from a stack taller than 100 m.

plutonium. A radioactive and fissionable element of trans-uranium series. Plutonium-239 emits an α-particle from its nucleus in normal radioactive disintegration, for which it has a half life period of 24,131 years. However, by the action of slow neutrons, the nucleus of the plutonium atom disintegrates in an entirely different way to form a number of products consisting of elements having mass number of the order of one half that of plutonium. This process is accompanied by an over-all loss of mass which appears as energy. It is mainly used in electric power generation reactors. Technically most important of them, Pu-239, has a half-life of 24,400 years. As it is highly fissionable by slow neutrons, Pu-239 is used as nuclear fuel and to make atomic bombs. It is easier to extract than uranium (U-235), and its critical mass amounts to no more than 8-16 kg, compared with a critical mass for uranium of 50 kg. Pu-239 is now obtained in large quantities from nuclear reactors, especially from fast breeder reactors. A fast breeder contains 1 ton of plutonium in its fuel rods. Radiologically, plutonium, which burns in the air to from aerosols capable of penetrating into the lungs, is one of the strongest poisons known. When they get into the human organism, quantities of as little as one ten-millionth part of a gram are sufficient to cause cancer, for plutonium emits α-rays of limited range which are capable of very high radiation doses locally. It has been demonstrated that the margins for plutonium hitherto considered tolerable, and the legal limits prescribed by law for plutonium, are in fact too high by a factor of 300,000. Plutonium is discharged into the environment in limited quantities by reprocessing of nuclear fuels. There is likely to be in the future a substantial increase in the transport of plutonium to reprocessing centers by load and rail, so that the possibility of releases of plutonium by leakage or owing to terrorist activities cannot be ruled out. The dangerous nature of plutonium having in particular for the long life-span of its isotopes, is one of the main arguments against using nuclear fission as a source of energy.

pluvial. 1. Pertaining to rain or, to precipitation. 2. Said of a climate characterized by relatively high precipitation. 3. Said of a geologic process or feature resulting from rain, *e.g.*, pluvial denudation from land sliding and gully erosion.

pneumatic sewage ejector. A device used for lifting a sewage volume from a lower level to a higher level of a sewer line under moderate head. First, the sewage fills a chamber through a non-return valve. At a certain level of sewage in the chamber the float opens the air valve and compressed air is admitted into the chamber which forces the sewage to flow up.

pneumoconiosis. A general term describing occupational diseases of the lungs found in miners and others who work with fine dust materials, or live in such atmosphere. It is characterized by a chronic inflammation of the lungs, which may develop in to tuberculosis, emphysema, or bronchitis.

point source. Any discernible, confined, and discrete conveyance, including, but not limited to any pipe, ditch, channel, tunnel, conduit, well, discrete fissure, container, rolling stock, concentrated animal-feeding operation, or vessel or other floating craft, from which pollutants are or may be discharged. This term does not include return flows from irrigated agriculture.

polishing filter. A filter bed of gravel and sand, through whch effluent from a sewage treatment plant is passed for further clarification removing BOD and suspended solids.

pollen. The fine powdery substance produced by seed plants, each particle containing a male cell for the purpose of fertilization. Many pollens cause hay fever, sometime of a very severe nature, in sensitized persons, for whom pollens constitute the worst of the air pollutants.

pollutant. A contaminant whose presence is damaging to the quality of environment. These are substances that are useful in some context but have escaped from that context into other parts of the environment where they are harmful instead of useful; or they are waste products that have been inadequately disposed of or contained.

polluter pays principle. The idea that the generator of pollution should bear the cost to which it gives rise. The principle would exclude, for example, government grants to polluting firms to pay for the installation of pollution reducing equipment. Since the incidence of taxation is not necessarily the same as the point at which the tax is levied, care needs to be taken in assessing the implication of the principle. If the polluting firm is not a price-taker, it will pass some of its tax on to its customers in the form of a higher price. For example, the imposition of the tax on the emissions in to the atmosphere from heavy vehicle exhausts, would lead to a higher price charged for transportation.

pollution. The introduction of pollutants into a liquid or gaseous medium, the presence of pollutants in a liquid or gaseous medium, or any undesirable modification of the composition of a liquid or gaseous medium. For purposes of air pollution control, an 'undesirable modification' is one that has injurious or deleterious effects. Air pollution is defined as 'the presence in the outdoor atmosphere of one or more contaminants, such as dust, fumes, gas, mist, odour, smoke, or vapour, in quantities, of characteristics, and of duration such as to be injurious to human, plant or animal life or to property, or which unreasonably interferes with the comfortable enjoyment of life and property'. Atmospheric pollution is a major problem faced by all nations of the world. Rapid urban and industrial growth has resulted in vast quantities of potentially harmful waste products being released in to the atmosphere. Societies have been reluctant to accept, or have simply failed to recognize, the limitations of the cleansing properties of the atmosphere. The consequence has been that air pollution has affected the health and well being of the people, has caused widespread damage to vegetation, crops, wildlife, materials, buildings, and climate, and has resulted in depletion of the scarced natural resources needed for long term economic development. The worst pollution has occurred in and around urban industrial areas. The seriousness of pollution for urban communities, as shown by the effects of short-term pollution episodes or accidental release of large quantities of a pollutant, has led to the introduction of national pollution control policies, which have largely been aimed at tackling local pollution problems.

pollution, exotic. Pollution that drifts into a given area from a source outside that area.

pollution from petroleum industry. The petroleum industry is characterized by the regular discharge of hydrocarbons and other organic compounds and of sulphur dioxide and fine dust. Crude oil imported from the oil-producing countries is processed in refineries into various petroleum products, in particular heating oil and gasoline. In the refining process, the crude oil is heated and vapourized and then condensed again at various temperatures. In this way the varying fractions, from highly volatile gasoline to heavy heating off, are separated. In the process, tar-like bitumen is left behind for further processing in its turn. In order to produce the energy needed to vapourize the crude oil, the distillation residues are used in the refineries as the main fuel. These residues contain large quantities of sulphur, which, after combustion, is discharged into the atmosphere in the form of sulphur dioxide. In addition, according to where it comes from, the material consumed can contain larger or smaller quantities of fine dust, which is also given off with the flue gas. The second group of components in air pollution by refineries are organic substances such as hydrocarbons. These are discharged in the atomsphere from various sources, at ground level, spread over the entire area of the works, such as storage tanks, flanges, safety valves, vents, seals, settling tanks and torch flares. Some of these organic gases and fumes are very pungent, and therefore, can cause serious nuisance in the vicinity of the refinery. Between 0.4% and 1% of the crude oil put through a refinery is given off in the from of organic vapours into the environment. Assuming it to have been no more than 0.4%, discharges of organic gases and vapours from leaky pipeline and valves come to about 0.80%, the process gases of the torch to about 0.23%, and the heating gases of the torch flares and the discharges, from the waste water treatment to 0.02% each. On the average the torch has a combustion efficiency rate of no more than 50-70%. This gives an average discharge rate of organic gases and vapours of 4.3 tons per day per million tons annual average crude oil throughput for the refinery. It has been estimated that one-third of production losses by the petroleum industry pass into the atmosphere as hydrocarbons.

In India, the major controversy over the locations of a petrochemical complex at Mathura, endangering Taj Mahal and the bird sanctuary at Bharatpur, is also an indication of public concern about the hazards of air pollution due to the petrochemical industry. The expert committee set up by the government of India and its Italian consultants expressed the view that high air pollution levels at Agra are on account of foundries, railway marhshalling yards for coal locomotives and two thermal power plants. Many experts have expressed their view that Taj Mahal is threated by the Mathura refinery complex.

pollution from spraying. An example of serious irreversible damage to the environment caused by an industrial product which was previously regarded as neutral in its effects is the spray gun, which is in increasing use today for a variety of purposes. As a propellant, the spray gun contains chlorofluorocarbons (CF_2Cl_2 and $CFCl_3$). When the spray gun is used the propellants are released into the atmosphere. Until recently it was believed that the compounds were so stable that they would not be absorbed or reduced by either plants, soil or water. They were consequently regarded as harmless. In 1974, it was discovered that chlorofluorocarbons could cause serious disturbances in the environment. The vapours of these compounds rise into the stratosphere and damage the ozone belt surrounding the earth; the ozone belt intercepts a large part of the ionizing radiation coming in form outside and so reduces damage to the earth by this radiation. The process proceeds as follows: the chlorofluorocarbon molecules are broken down by the strong ultraviolet radiation in the stratosphere. In this way chlorine atoms are released, which break down ozone molecules by a catalytic process. It is assumed that some 10 ozone molecules per second are broken down in this way.

pollution potential. A term sometimes applied to meteorological condition that, given the existence of pollutant emissions, would be conducive to the occurrence of severe air pollution.

pollution rose. A diagram similar to the wind rose in which the length of each radius is proportional to the average degree of pollution when the wind blows from the direction indicated. The average pollution on days of calm is written inside of different widths drawn along the lengths of the radii.

pollution standard index (PSI). In air pollution control, a measurement of the air quality mandated by the amendments to the Clean Air Act, in order to allow standardization of comparisons of pollutant levels from community to community. The PSI is based on five criteria pollutants, which are, sulphur dioxide, nitrogen dioxide, ozone, carbon monoxide, and total suspended particulates. Each of these pollutants is assigned a number from 0 to 100 based on its measured level taken as percentage of the regulatory standard for health effects. For example, if the ambient level of sulphur dioxide is 45% of that judged to be harmful to human health, the sulphur dioxide number would be 45. The five numbers are then added together to obtain PSI. The values below 100 are regarded as healthful, from 100 to 199, unhealthful; from 200 to 299, very unhealthful; and over 300, hazardous.

polychlorinated biphenyls. Polychlorinated biphenyls (PCBs) find numerous applications in electrical industry, especially in the manufacture of transformers and capacitors. When these appliances are short-circuited, considerable amount of PCBs is released in air and soil. These compounds are leached from soil into water and water sheds, and contaminate water resources also. Thus PCBs enter into human body through food, air, and water. One of the potential sources of these compounds in food items is wrapping paper and cartons made from recycled carbonless paper. Fresh water fish, shrimp, and fish eating bowls are also found to accumulate high amounts of PCBs. Dairy products such as butter, cheese, and milk, obtained from cattle feeding on PCBS contaminated fodder and water have been found to contain appreciable amounts of PCBS. It has been found that the common varieties of fish can bioaccumulate more than 100,000 times the level of PCBs, found in surrounding water and forms a potential source of PCBs ingestion by human beings.

polycyclic aromatic hydrocarbons (PAH). A variety of chemical compounds such as benzopyrene, dibenzopyrene, dibenzoacridine, occupational exposure to which can cause cancer in man. The available data for polycyclic aromatic hydrocarbons indicate that acute toxicity to saltwater aquatic life occur at concentrations as low as 300 μg/L, and would occur at even lower concentrations among the species that are more sensitive than those tested. No data are available concerning the chronic toxicity of polycyclic aromatic hydrocarbons to sensitive saltwater aquatic life. For the maximum protection of human health from the potential carcinogenic effects due to exposure of polycyclic aromatic hydrocarbons through ingestion of contaminated aquatic organisms and water, the ambient water concentration should be zero on the nonthreshold assumption for polycyclic aromatic hydrocarbons. However, zero level may not be attainable at present time. Therefore, the levels that may result in incremental increase of cancer risk over lifetime are estimated at 10^{-5}, 10^{-6}, and 10^{-7}. The corresponding criteria are 28.0 ng/L, 2.8 ng/L, and 0.28 ng/L respectively. If the above estimates are made for the consumption of aquatic organisms only (excluding consumption of water), the levels are redefined as 311 ng/L, 31.1 ng/L, and 3.11 ng/L respectively.

polynology. The study of pollens and spores in a historical context through observations on pollen grains and other spores preserved in ancient peat and sedimentary deposits; the findings are widely used to interpret past environmental conditions.

polytetrafluorethylene. A white granular powder which is not affected by any known solvents or chemical reagents with the exception of fused alkali metals. It is extremely resistant to heat and shows no structural change between 200 K and 600 K. Above this temperature it becomes a firm rubbery mass, and if further heated, gives off invisible fumes containing fluorine compounds, which if inhaled, produce an influenza-like attack. No threshold limiting value has been recommended regarding the toxicity, but air concentrations should be minimized.

pop. Light, short, abrupt, explosive sound such as that made by drawing a cork or the bursting of corn when roasting.

pop music. Music, usually vocal, intended to interest the majority of young people. It usually has an immediate but short-lasting appeal. It employs strong rhythms, and the instrumentalists rely heavily on electronic techniques in the production and modification of the sounds recorded which are almost invariably very loud.

population. A number of interacting and interbreeding organisms of the same species forming a group, separated more or less clearly from other groups of the same or other species; a discrete, dynamic unit of a species.

population explosion. A phenomenal increase in the rate of natural growth of the world population. While the time required for population to double was about 1500 years during the period 8000 B.C. to 1650 A.D., it now takes only about 35-37 years. This rapid increase of population is due to a combination of the application of modern drugs and large scale public health measures (control of specific diseases and improved sanitation) which have depressed death-rates and extended the span of human life without any accompanying fall in birth rates.

population genetics. The subject concerned with the transmission of characteristics from one generation to the next at the level of populations rather than of individuals. It has several points of contact with demography. In theory, since detailed demographic statistics are an invaluable aid to population genetics, and since genetic structure is fundamental to any population, the scope for convergence in the two disciplines should be great, but in practice genetics has made only a very limited impact on the mainstream of demographic study.

potassium. A very abundant element, ranking seventh among all the elements in the earth's crust, 2.59% of which is potassium in combined form. In sea water, potassium is present up to 380 ppm. Potassium, is one of the reactive of the alkali-metal group. There are three naturally occurring isotopes, K-39 through K-41, of which K-40 is radioactive ($t_{1/2}$=1.3109 years). In ordinary potassium this isotope represents only 0.0119% of the content. There are four other known isotopes, all radioactive, K-38 and K-42 through K-44, all with relatively short half-lives-measured in minutes and hours. Potassium is a silvery-white metal, can be readily moulded, and cut by a knife, oxidizes instantly on exposure to air, and reacts violently with water, yielding potassium hydroxide and hydrogen gas, which burns spontaneously in air with a violet flame due to volatilized potassium. In these respects, potassium behaves much like sodium. The element is preserved under kerosene

potassium-argon dating. A method of dating geological specimens based on the decay of the radioisotope potassium-40 to argon-40. The half-life of potassium-40 is about 1.3109 years and an estimate of the ratio of the two isotopes in a specimen give an indication of its age.

potential temperature. Gradient of temperature in the lowest layers of the atmosphere, the difference between the adiabatic lapse rate and the actual atmospheric lapse rate. When the gradient of potential temperature is zero, the buoyancy of mass of rising gas is constant and there is no theoretical ceiling. If the gradient is negative, the buoyancy of the gas will increase as it rises, and if it is positive it will decrease and there will be a height at which the buoyancy vanishes.

potentiation. When two chemicals are acting on the same or different organs or systems, one chemical is made more effective in the presence of other chemical. This potential sensitizing effect of chemical agents could become a major problem to toxicologists. One must distinguish between a substance acting as a primary irritant and one acting as a sensitizing agent. The primary irritant elicits its effects immediately on one application. The sensitizing agent may show no primary irritation, but when applied or injected may combine with a protein molecule and acts as an antigenic agent. This, in turn produces antibodies. If the compound is applied again or injected, an antigen-antibody reaction may occur, producing either minor or serious allergic conditions which could lead to death or crippling illness.

Poza Rica incident. An air pollution incident involving respiratory illness and death. At Poza Rica, Mexico, on 24 November 1950, about 22 persons died and 320 were hospitalized as a result of the malfunction of an oil refinery sulphur recovery unit; large quantities of hydrogen sulphide were discharged into the atmosphere. Meteorological data indicated that a pronounced low altitude temperature inversion prevailed at that time. Unlike other acute air pollution incidents, a single source and air pollutant were responsible for the incident.

precipitation. The thickness of the layer of water which accumulates on a horizontal surface, as the result of one or more falls of precipitate, in the absence of infiltration or evaporation, and if any part of the precipitation falling as snow or ice were melted. Practically all the precipitation of the earth is the result of the adiabatic cooling of ascending air masses. The major regions of ascent are:

(a) Zones of converging horizontal air flow (equatorial and cyclonic low-pressure areas giving convectional and frontal rains).

(b) Areas along the windward sides of mountain ranges (orographic rainfall).

The principal factors which influence the distribution of precipitation over the earth can be listed as follows:

(a) The location of the belts of ascending air.

(b) The character of the moisture-bearing winds.

(c) The distance from the ocean-that is, the distance from the main source of water in the atmosphere.

(d) The height of the land over which the moisture-laden winds blow.

(e) The temperature of the air; this governs the moisture content.

The principal rainfall regimes are outlined below:

Continental rainfall. The distance from the oceans is the chief factor governing precipitation. Normally the main rainfall is in summer when the high seasonal temperature results in a maximum absolute humidity, and when there is a flow of air into the continental low-pressure area.

East-coast rainfall. In low latitudes the east-coast belts tend to have a high rainfall. This precipitation results from the on-shore trade winds. In mid-latitudes the precipitation is the result of monsoon wind systems, with the in flowing mass of warm, moist air in summer and cyclonic low-pressure conditions in winter.

Equatorial rainfall. This is characterized by abundant precipitation and the absence of a dry season. The rainfall is convectional, but may be frontal where the convergence of the air masses along the intertropical front occurs.

Mediterranean rainfall. The precipitation is confined mainly to the winter season, when the areas (western sides of land masses 30° to 40° of latitude) come under the influence of the cyclonic low-pressure belts. The dry summers are associated with the subsiding air of the sub-tropical high-pressure belts.

Polar rainfall. Low temperatures and the consequent low absolute humidities give rise to small precipitation amounts. Anticyclonic pressure controls and also militates against the conditions favouring precipitation. The maximum precipitation probably occurs during the season of higher temperatures when there is more moisture in the air and when the cyclonic influence can reach farther poleward.

2. In gas cleaning, an operation in which particles are separated from a gas stream in which they are suspended, by the action of an electrical field or thermal gradient.

3. Precipitation of particulate matter by an electric field between electrodes; the particles become positively charged and migrate to the negative electrodes, where they are collected. *See* dust separator.

precipitation, thermal. A form of precipitation based on the fact that suspended particles subjected to a high thermal gradient migrate from a zone of this temperature to that of low temperature.

precipitation, thermal. A process consisting of the separation of particulate matter from air and other gases under the influence of a sufficiently steep thermal gradient. In the thermal precipitator (a sampling instrument), the air or gas is drawn slowly through a narrow chamber across which extends a heated wire, the particulate matter being deposited union the adjacent collecting surface.

preservative. Any substance that prolongs the useful life of an organic material, usually in low concentrations; though generally applied to food additives such as benzoic acid, acetic acid, and ascorbic acid, which have antimicrobial and antioxidants value, the term applies equally well to antioxidants used in petroleum products, rubber, and similar materials.

pressurized water reactor PWR. A nuclear reactor in which water is the coolant and the moderator, but in which the water maintained at a high pressure in order to prevent it boiling. The pressurized water is passed through a heat exchanger to generate steam for producing electric power in a conventional turbo-generator.

prevailing wind. That wind, indicated by direction, at a certain place or in a certain area, which has a considerably higher frequency than any other. *See also* wind rose.

primary air. Air mixed with a combustion gas as it enters a burner or introduced under the grate when coal is burned as a fixed or fludized bed. This term is also used for the air used to atomize liquid fuels or to inject pulverized fuel.

primary forest. Any original, virgin forest unmodified by deleterious human activity. It is probable that no primary forest now exists as even the most remote areas of forest, such as that in the Amazon basin, have been subjected to airborne pollutants and chemical residues from agricultural regions.

primary pollution. Pollution resulting directly from any substance which has been released into the atmosphere in harmful concentration. The primary pollutant may already be present in the atmosphere, such as carbon dioxide, but only becomes toxic when additions to it causes it to rise above its natural concentration. It may also involve the direct release into the atmosphere of a chemical substance not normally present in the air, for example, hydrogen fluoride released from large coal-fired furnaces.

primary treatment. The first stage

of the process of treating the sewage. As sewage enters a plant for primary treatment, it flows through a screen which removes large floating objects such as rags and sticks that may clog pumps and pipes. The screens vary from coarse to fine-forms those consisting of parallel steel or iron bars with openings of about 1 cm or more to screens with much smaller openings. Screens are generally placed in a chamber or channel in a position inclined with respect to the flow of the sewage to make cleaning easier. The debris caught on the upstream surface of the screen can be raked off manually or mechanically. Some plants use a device known as a comminutor which combines the functions of a screen and a grinder. These devices catch and then cut or shred the heavy solid material. In this method the pulverized material remains in the sewage flow to be removed later in a settling tank.

After the sewage has been screened, it passes through a grit chamber where sand, grit, cinders, and small stones are allowed to settle to the bottom. A grit chamber is especially important for cities with combined sewer systems because it will remove the grit or gravel the washes off streets or land during a storm and ends up at the treatment plants. The unwanted grit or gravel from this process is usually disposed of by filling land near a treatment plant. In some plants, another screen is placed after the grit chamber to remove any further material than might damage equipment or interfere with later processes. With the screening completed and the grit removed, the sewage still contains suspended solids in the form of minute particles of matter that can be removed from the sewage by treatment in a sedimentation tank. When the speed of the flow of sewage through one of these tanks is reduced, the suspended solids will gradually sink to the bottom. This mass of solids is called raw sludge.

Various methods have been devised for removing sludge from the tanks. In older plants it was removed by hand. After a tank had been in service for several days or weeks, the sewage flow was diverted to another tank. The sludge in the bottom of the out-of-service tank was pushed or flushed with water to a nearby pit and then removed for further treatment or disposal. Although 30% of the municipalities in even advanced countries give only primary treatment to their sewage, this process by itself is considered entirely inadequate for most needs. Municipalities and industry, faced with increased amounts of wastes and wastes that are more difficult to remove from water, have turned to secondary and even advanced waste treatment. *See also* secondary treatment; tertiary treatment.

production ecology. A study of the more complex life communities, or biomes considered as trophic association or food cycles; it is concerned essentially with the dynamic structure of the system whereby regulation is effected, rather than with the actual operation of the regulation processes on individuals within populations. The name production ecology results from an increasing preoccupation with the supply, or production, of food and ultimately with the flow, or exploitation, or energy within trophic cycles.

production residues. Wastes arising in production and distribution processes.

product standard. Derived standards or working levels of pollutants applied to products such as food or detergents. The maximum acceptable level or potential pollutants in the specified product is designed to ensure that under specified circumstances primary and secondary ambient quality protection standards are not exceeded.

propellant. 1. A term use in aerosol technology to denote a gas used to drive or push various materials through an orifice in the form of a spray or foam. Propellants of this type are gases such as carbon dioxide, air, nitrous oxide, butane, and propane. 2. In combustion technology, the term refers to rocket fuels of various types, among which are liquid hydrogen peroxide, hydrazine, boron hydride, *etc.*, and solids such as plasticized nitrocellulose and ammonium nitrate.

portable tank. A bulk packaging (except a cylinder having a water capacity of 1,000 pounds or less) designed primarily to be loaded onto or on or temporarily attached to a transport vehicle or ship and equipped with skids, mountings, or accessories to facilitate handling of the tank by mechanical means. It does not include a cargo tank, tank car, multiunit tank car tank, or traile carrying 3AX, 3AAX, or 3T cylinders.

Prothoate. An acaricide and insecticide with systemic action, used mainly against phytophagous mites and some sap-sucking insects. It is a colourless crystalline solid, virtually in soluble in water, but miscible with most organic solvents. It is stable in neutral moderately acid and slightly alkaline media, but is rapidly decomposed in strong alkali. The acute oral LD_{50} for male rats is 8 mg/kg. It is effective for protection of fruit, citrus and vegetable crops from tetranychild and some eriophyid mites, and some insects, notably aphids, Tingidae, Psyllidae, and Thysanoptera.

pseudomonas aeruginosa. An organism often occurring in the faeces of man but in much lower numbers than coliform organisms. It is an opportunist pathogen of the very young and old and those already debilitated by disease, being frequently isolated from persons with urinary tract infections and skin burns. The organism occurs in raw water, usually in the presence of coliform organisms. However, in drinking-water it may occur in the absence of coliform organisms and the ability of some materials used in the construction of distribution and plumbing systems to support the growth of the organisms may account, in part for this. Although the presence of the organism in potable water should not be ignored, it should not be used for the routine examination of water for the presence of faecal pollution. Examination for *P. aeruginosa* may be of value in certain circumstances, as for example, in the reconstitution of rehydration mixtures, baby foods, and pharmaceutical preparations, as well as in the surveillance of hospital water supplies and bottled water.

psychosocial stressors. Stimuli suspected of causing diseases which originate in social relationship or arrangements and affect the organism through the medium of the higher nervous processes.

publicaly owned treatment works. Any device or system used in the treatment (including recycling and reclamation) of municipal sewage or industrial wastes of a liquid nature that is owned by a state or municipality (as defined by Section 502(4) of the Clean Water Act). This definition includes sewers, pipes, or other conveyances only if they convey wastewater to a publicaly owned treatment works providing treatment.

pulverization. In pollution control, an intermediate step only in refuse disposal which consists in reducing refuse to small-size particles; it is particularly valuable in conjunction with transfer stations and land-fill methods, reducing the volume of refuse to be handled. Also known as milling; shredding.

pumping station. In pollution control, an installation comprising a wet-well, pump and pressure pipe, often located underground, operated for the purpose of raising sewage to a higher elevation. A pumping station, located at a low point in a catchment, may be used to despatch sewage to a treatment plant elsewhere. *See* sewage treatment.

putrefaction. Decomposition of organic matter in an anaerobic state releasing foul-smelling gases and incompletely oxidized products. It is important to distinguish between putrefaction and the process of anaerobic digestion; an anaerobic digestion process permanently removes the offensive odour of many organic wastes so that they can be used on agricultural land without causing nuisance.

putrescible wastes. Wastes which consist mainly of plant or animal residues and which undergo degradation by bacteriological action; *e.g.*, animal residues, cannery wastes, fats, fish residues, fruit and vegetable wastes, etc.

pyridine. A slightly yellow or colourless, flammable liquid having nauseating odour; used in the synthesis of vitamins, rubber chemicals, dyes, and fungicides. It is toxic by ingestion and inhalation. Occupational exposure to pyridine should be controlled so that no employee is exposed to pyridine at a concentration greater than 15.0 mg/m^3 of air (5 ppm), determined as a time-weighted average (TWA) concentration limit for up to a 10-hour workshift in a 40-hour workweek, over a working lifetime.

pyroclastic. A geological term designating detrital volcanic materials explosively erupted; formed by fragmentation as a result of volcanic action; ejected, transported aerially and deposited upon land surfaces, or in marine waters. Pyroclastic materials may be classified according to size, origin or petrograhic composition, as described below:

(a) bombs and blocks, the fragments having size between 64 mm and a few metres;

(b) lapilli, the fragments having size between 64 and 2 mm;

(c) volcanic ash, the fragments having particle size between 2 and 0.25 mm;

(d) volcanic dust, the fragments of size less than 0.25 mm;

(e) pumice, a light coloured, highly vesicular glassy material; commonly rhyolitic in composition; and

(f) scoria, a vesicular material, usually heavier, darker, and more crystalline than pumice.

Both pumice and scoria may exist as pyroclastic material or as froth or lava flows. Ashes, pumice scoriae, and bombs are formed from ejected fragments of fluid lava. Other ejecta, including lapilli and blocks, consist of fragments of all sizes thrown out in a completely solid or semisolid state.

pyrocone. A type of small incinerator installed at the base of a solid waste chute in multistoried buildings, hospitals and public buildings.

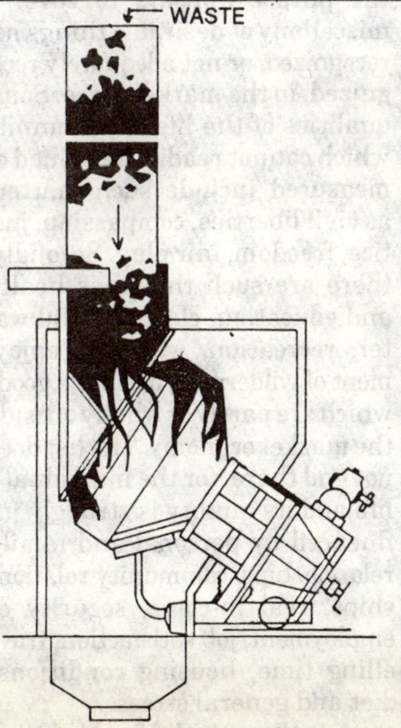

PYROCONE

pyrolysis. A chemical change brought about by heat alone; in the case of inorganic materials (limestone or metal ores) it is synonymous with calcination. It is distinguished from combustion by the fact that oxidation does not occur. It is usually applied to the conversion of organic compounds not only into smaller and simpler compounds but also into substance of lower molecular weight than the original compound. It can be utilized for the reforming of material in an inert atmosphere to produce combustible gases, volatile fluids, bar and charcoal. For the treatment of wastes and refuge, the solid domestic refuse is placed in a retort and heated without additional air to temperatures between 770 K and 1275 K, its weight being reduced by 90%. The solid residue remaining is then disposed of at land-fill sites. Industrial wastes can be reduced by up to 65% in volume. It is a potentially valuable method of obtaining valuable products from refuge. Also known as destructive distillation.

pyrolysis reactor. A fludized-bed reactor in which the heat transfer rate is rapid. It gives low liquid yields and high gas yields from municipal solid wastes. The hot gas can be used to pyrolyse the feed in the bed. The char produced should be removed from the bed so that pyrolysis gas does not react with oxygen.

Q

q. A measure of the ability of a system with periodic behaviour to store energy equal to 2 times the average energy stored in the system divided by the energy dissipated per cycle.

quaking bog. A peat bog floating or growing over water-satatutrated land which shakes or trembles when walked on.

qualitative analysis. An analysis which seeks to determine what components are present in significant amounts in a substance or mixture of substances such as air, water, soil, effluents, etc. Such analysis is designed to indicate the presence or absence or specific chemical species, and not their respective quantities. *See* quantitative analysis.

quality class (QC). A general method of indicating the general growth performance of a strand of trees. The QC value is calculated from the relationship between the average height of 40 trees of the same type and their age. Generally, the faster the rate of growth the higher the quality class. Many QC calculations have been made for specific tree types and average growth rates. In the forestry system such calculations have been made for all the main commercial species and five QC divisions established ranging from QCI (best) to QCV (poorest). QC values are not comparable between different species and are of only limited use as indicators of future timber yield from a forest.

quality of life. A term referring to the living conditions along with other considerations such as the noise and pollution levels, aesthetic environment, the access and easy approach to the countryside, sanctuaries etc. In popular usage, the phrase appears to cover a miscellany of desirable things not recognized, or not adequately recognized, in the market place. Some qualities of the life a community which cannot readily be valued or measured include such matters as civil liberties, compassion, justice, freedom, fair play. Secondly, there are such things as health and education, clean air and water, recreation, wild life, enjoyment of wilderness, desirable goods which are partly or wholly outside the market economy. The list does not end there, for the individual's life and its quality is strongly influenced by personal and family relationships, community relationships, real in-come, security of employment, job satisfaction, travelling time, housing conditions, diet and general stress.

quantitative analysis. In pollution control, the term refers to the analytical methods or procedures which seek to determine the relative amounts of significant compounds present in substance or mixture of substances such as air, water, soil, and effluents discharged from industries, and municipal wastes. The various analytical techniques employed for this purpose are colorimetry, spectrophotometery, gas chromatography, ion chromatography, polarography, spectrofluorimetry, turbidometry, mass spectrometry, etc. *See also* qualitative analysis.

quick water. The part of a stream characterized by strong current.

quinoline. A basic heterocyclic nitrogenous compound occurring in coal tar and obtained from it, but generally prepared synthetically from aniline. It is a strong base and is used as a preservative, in the manufacture of dyes, and to a limited extent as a medicine. It has been classified as potential occupational carcinogen.

Quinomethionate. A selective as well as non-systemic, acaricide; and a fungicide that is specific to powdery mildews. It forms yellow crystals, practically insoluble in water and springly soluble in organic solvents. In chemical properties it is closely related to thioquinox, but is more stable to oxidation. The acute oral LD_{50} for rats is 2500-3000 mg/kg. It controls red spider and other phytophagous mites on a wide range of crops; and powdery mildews. Also known as Morestan.

quinone. A dihydroxy aromatic compound, used in the manufacture of dyes and hydroquinone, as fungicides, in photography, and as an oxidizing agent. It is quite toxic by inhalation, ingestion, and strong irritant to skin and mucous membrane. The occupational exposure to quinone should be controlled in such a manner so that no employee is exposed to quinone at a concentration greater than 0.4 mg/m^3 of air (0.1 ppm), determined as a time-weighted average (TWA) con-centration limit for up to a 10 hour workshift in a 40-hour workweek, over a working lifetime. According to the report of Toxic Subustances Control Act (TSCA) Interagency Testing Committee to the administrator, and Environmental Protection Agency (EPA), it has been found in effluents discharged from industries and included in the category of hazardous waste.

R

race. 1. A group of organisms with similar characteristics but not distinctive enough to be classified as a species or subspecies. 2. A strong current of water flowing through a narrow channel, *e.g.*, a tide race; also the constricted channel in which such a current flows.

Rad. The unit of absorbed radiation dose; a dose which results in the absorption of 100 ergs/g of specified material.

radial drainage pattern. A drainage pattern characterized by radiating streams diverging from a high central area. Also known as centrifugal drainage pattern.

radial flow. Pertaining to spoke-like flow of reservoir fluids radially pointing inward toward a well-bore area.

radiation balance. The energy needed to sustain life on the earth is provided by solar radiation. This consists of electromagnetic radiation of different wavelengths, from shortwave Röentgen rays (*X*-rays), which are absorbed in the upper atmosphere, to longwave radio waves. Before the solar radiation reaches the earth's surface, it is diverted by the air molecules; as a result of it, a part of the incoming solar radiation is reflected back immediately into the outer space. The earth's surface also reflect back part of the radiation. In the cloudy sky, there is additional reflection due to the layer of clouds. As a consequence of all these collectively known as albedo, the earth reflects about 34% of the inflow of the energy. About 20% of the energy produced by the solar radiation is absorbed by the gaseous molecules (such as carbon dioxide, water vapours, oxygen, ozone, methane, etc.) present in the atmosphere, and causes a rise in temperature. Directly or by diffusion in the earth's atmosphere, 46% of the solar radiation arrives at the surface of the earth and is absorbed by it after deduction for the reflection attenuation. The earth would get constantly hotter if an energy flow were not directed from it to the universe, whereby the energy absorbed from the sun is emitted again into the outer space. There is thus an exchange of energy between the universe and the earth, as a result of which the solar inflow and the thermal outflow tend to balance each other.

radiation fog. A common type of land fog produced by radiation cooling of relatively shallow layers of quiet, humid air overlying a chilled land surface. Night-time conditions which favour radiation fogs include a surface inversion of temperature, a cloudless sky, and slight air movement (but not an absolute calm). The inversion is necessary to prevent the fog from rising. Cloudless skies promote fog because a low cloud cover absorbs a large part of the earth's radiation and reradiates it back to the earth's surface, where it is absorbed and consequently acts to reduce the net loss of heat. Slight air movement is a requirement because fogs of the radiation type cannot form when the wind velocity is greater than 10-15 km/h; at higher speeds the turbulence associated with the wind carries heat downward and thus prevents formation of an inversion. Slight turbulence and mixing appear to be necessary however, in order to develop a fog of moderate density.

Radiation fog is build up by gravitation. For this reason they are most prevalent in valleys and depressions where air drainage causes the colder, heavier air to collect. Often the slopes and uplands of a region are clear while the adjacent lowlands are fogged in, so that from an elevation one sees many lakes of fog occupying the surrounding depressions. On a convex land surface air drainage reduces the likelihood of temperature inversion and radiation-fog formation. This type of fog has a distinct diurnal periodicity and is usually short-lived. It grows and deepens from the ground upward as the night progresses only to burn off and disappear as the temperature inversion is dissipated and the fog droplets are evaporated by the warming air during the following morning. Radiation fog is at its worst in the vicinity of large cities, where the air is rich in hygroscopic particles derived from coal and oil smoke and the exhaust fumes from cars. These abundant condensation nuclei result in tiny fog particles, which make for greater density of the fog, or smog.

radiation pollution. The pollution occurring as a result of radiations of any potentially harmful nature. In practice, the harm arises from a combination of intensity, wavelength, and time of exposure. Although the mutagenic effects of radiation have been recognized for a long time, the exact mechanism of their action is not completely known. Various explanations have been offered, mainly on the basis of *in vitro* effects of radiation on DNA. Thus *X*-rays and other ionizing radiations are known to produce in aqueous solutions free radicals such as ·OH, ·HO_2, which are short-lived and reactive; these supposedly could react somehow with DNA, causing mutation and, in stronger doses, death of the cell.

radiation source. A term referring to usually, an artificial sealed source of radioactivity used in teletherapy, radiography, as a power source for space batteries, or various types of industrial operations, According to some authors, accelerators radioisotopic generators, and natural radionuclides may also be considered as radiation sources.

radiation standards. Exposure standards, permissible concentrations, rules for safe handling, regulations for transportation, regulations for industrial control of radiation, and control of radiation exposure by legislative means. These are based on rates of injury under certain known conditions.

For example, the U.S. Council on Radiation Standards has set the standard for 0.5 milliard an hour for a colour television set at 5.0 cm from any accessible location. But even such a conservative figure could cause a number of genetic problems for watching 20 or more hours a week from a distance of 2.5 metres.

radiation units. Units of measurement used to express the activity of a radionuclide and the dose of ionizing radiation. The units curie, roentgen, rad, and rem are not coherent with SI units but their temporary use with SI units has been approved while the derived SI units becquerel, gray, and sievert have become familiar.

The becquerel (Bq), the SI unit of activity, is the activity of a radionuclide decaying at a rate, on average, of one spontaneous nuclear transition per second;

$$1 \text{ Bq} = 1 \text{ s}^{-1}$$

The former unit, the curie [Ci], is equal to 3.7×10^{10} Bq. The gray (Gy), the SI unit of absorbed dose, is the absorbed dose when the energy per unit mass imparted to matter by ionizing radiation is 1 joule per kilogram; 1 rad = 10^{-2} Gy.

radiative capture. A nuclear capture process whose prompt result is the emission of electromagnetic radiation only.

radioactive. Possessing, or pertaining to, radioactivity. Sometimes only the prefix 'radio-' is used to describe radioactive nuclides or the substances containing them, *e.g.*, radiocarbon is an abbreviation for radioactive carbon.

radioactive age The age of a mineral, fossil, or wooden object as estimated from its content of radioisotopes. This method assumes that the content of radioisotopes has remained unchanged except for radioactive decay.

radioactive clock. A radioactive isotope such as potassium-40 which spontaneously decays to a stable end product at a constant rate, allowing absolute geological age to be determined.

radioactive contamination. The radiation released upon the disintegration of radioactive atomic nuclei takes the form of particulate or wave radiation of very high energy. When this radiation impinges on living cells, various interactions can result. The most important of these is the ionization of atoms. If this process of ionization of atoms takes place in living tissue, in certain circumstances a variety of damage may result.

radioactive dating. A technique for measuring the age of an object or sample of material by determining the ratio of the concentration of a radioisotope to that of a stable isotope in it; for example the ratio of carbon-14 to carbon-12 reveals the approximate age of pieces of wood and other archaeological specimens. Most widely used radioactive dating techniques include: carbon-14 dating; lead-lead dating; potassium-argon dating; rubidium-strontium dating; thorium-lead dating; and uranium-lead dating. The absolute age of a sample determined by different techniques show some descrepancies. The radioactive dating techniques are also known as isotopic age determination methods; radiometric dating methods; nuclear age determination; radiogenic dating methods.

radioactive debris. Radioactive material which is carried through the air from site of a nuclear explosion.

radioactive decay. The spontaneous transformation of a nuclide into one or more nuclides, accompanied by either the emission of particles from the nucleus, nuclear capture or ejection, of orbital electrons, or fission. Also known as decay; nuclear spontaneous reaction; radioactive disintegration; radioactive transformation.

radioactive element. An element capable of changing spontaneously into another element by the emission of charged particles from the nuclei of its atoms. In case of some of elements, such as uranium, all known isotopes are radioactive, while for others, *e.g.*, potassium, one of several isotopes is radioactive.

radioactive emanation. A radioactive gas given off by certain radioactive elements; all of these gases are isotopes of the element radon. Also known as emanation.

radioactive equilibrium. A state ultimately reached when a radioactive substance of slow decay yields a radioactive product that may also decay to give a further radioactive substance, and so on. The amount of any of the daughter radioactive products present after the equilibrium has been reached, remains constant and the loss due to decay being counterbalanced by gain.

radioactive mineral. Any mineral species that contains uranium or thorium, as an essential component of the chemical composition; for example, uraninite, pitchblende, carnotite, coffnite, and autunite.

radioactive series. A series of radioactive nuclides in which each member of the series is formed by the decay of the nuclide before it. The series ends with a stable nuclide. Three radioactive series occur naturally, those headed by thorium-232 (thorium series), uranium-235 (actinium series), and uranium-238 (uranium series). All three series end with an isotope of lead. The neptunium series starts with the artificial isotope plutonium-241, which decays to neptunium-237, and ends with thallium-81.

radioactive waste management. Liquid, solid and gaseous radioactive wastes are produced at all stages of the nuclear fuel cycle. Three basic philosophies are applied to the management of these wastes:

(a) Dilute and disperse; some of the low-level liquid and gaseous wastes produced at nuclear facilities are released directly into the environment where they are diluted into bodies of water or air.

(b) Delay and decay; some radioactive wastes containing radionuclides with short half-lives are stored until their radioactivity has decayed to relatively innocuous levels before further treatment or handling; for example, irradiated fuel assemblies are stored under water in cooling ponds at the reactor or reprocessing plant prior to reprocessing.

(c) Concentrate and contain; highly radioactive wastes are treated by various chemical and mechanical means to produce a high-level liquid waste fraction, which then requires special treatment for long-term storage and disposal.

radioactivity. The spontaneous emission of ionizing particles and rays following the disintegration of certain atomic nuclei. Man is continuously exposed to ionizing radiations from natural sources; radioactive substances are widely distributed in rocks, soils, water and air. Sedimentary rocks areas contribute an average dose of about 45 millirems/year. Higher background levels are to be expected in area containing deposits of uranium, thorium and radium, perhaps several times as much. Natural γ-radiation directly from the earth and from buildings represent usually about one-half of the total external radiation to which populations are exposed. All food and drinking water contains minute quantities of radium which are ingested into the system; the variations in content depend upon the radioactivity of the rocks and soils from which they are derived. Radon in the atmosphere and cosmic rays also contribute to the general level of radiation.

The world average dose received from natural and unavoidable background radiation by the individual is estimated to be about 150 millirems/year. This may vary from between 80 to 300 millirems depending upon the composition of the ground, building materials, altitude, foodstuffs, and so on. Sources of additional radiation to which a person may be exposed include the various forms of radiation used in medicine and industry, the radioactive isotopes produced in nuclear reactors, accidents in nuclear reactors, and fall-out resulting from the explosion of nuclear weapons.

radiocarbon dating. A method of estimating the age of carbon containing substances which have formed within the last 70,000 years and which have utilized carbon dioxide from the atmosphere or some other portion of earth's dynamic reservoir, based on the decay of carbon-14. The impact of cosmic rays on the earth's atmosphere causes a very small proportion of nitrogen atoms to transform into carbon-14 atoms. Some of these radioactive carbon atoms find their way, via carbon dioxide and photosynthesis, into living trees.

radiommunoassay. An analytical technique for the sensitive quantitative determination of the trace amounts of hormone (or some other biomolecule) by its capacity to displace the radioactive form of combination with its specific antibody.

radionuclide. A general term for unstable nuclide undergoing spontaneous radioactive transformation with emission of particle or photon.

radio opaque. Not appreciably penetrable by *X*-rays or other forms of radiation.

radiosonde. A small radio transmitter carried by a balloon by means of which observation may be obtained from the atmosphere at various heights. Observations are usually of pressure, temperature and humidity.

radiospectrum. The entire range of frequencies in the radio range to about 300,000 megahertz. Also known as radio-frequency spectrum.

radium. A strongly radioactive element, occurring in extremely small percentages in uranium ores (pitchblende and carnetite). Radium is formed by radioactive transformation of uranium, about 3 million parts of uranium being accompanied in nature by one part radium. The radium isotope of mass number 226 occurs in the uranium ($2n + 2$) alpha-decay series. Its half-life is 1,620 years, and it yields radon-222 by α-disintegration. Other naturally occurring isotopes of radium are Ra-228 in the thorium series, half-life 6.7 years, producing actinium-228 by-decay which yields by-decay thorium-228, which in turn yields 224 Ra half-life 2.64 days, giving radon-220 by-decay.

radium-D. An isotope of lead; atomic number 82, mass number 210.

radium-G. An isotope of lead; atomic number 82, mass number 206. Also known as radium lead.

radon. An element placed in group zero of the periodic table; emitted as a radioactive gas from the soil into the atmosphere. It is also released during the combustion of fossil fuel, and for this reason there is more radon in the air over cities than in country air. Radon is the heaviest of all gases with a density of almost 10 grams per liter (air = 1.3 g/L). The isotope Rn-222 is formed by the α-disintegration of Ra-226. Actinon, its isotope of mass number 229, is produced by alpha disintegration of Ra-223 (AcX) and is a member of the actinium series. Similarly, thoron, its isotope of mass number 220, is a member of the thorium series. Since the name 'radon' may be considered to be specific for the isotope of mass number 222 (from the radium series), the term 'emanation' is sometimes used for element with atomic number 86 in general.

rain. The drops of water falling from the sky. They are formed by the condensation of water vapour in the atmosphere, caused by the cooling of air. Small droplets form clouds, but as the drop grows in size, they become too heavy to float, and so they descend to the ground. There are two different hypotheses regarding the mechanism of rain drop formation. According to the first, all the droplets present in the cloud are not of the same in size. The larger droplets fall faster than the smaller ones, so that a bigger drop will overtake and absorb all smaller ones lying in its downward path, unless an air current forms around the falling drop that causes part of the smaller droplets suspended in air to be bypassed, so that the actual agglomeration is smaller than it might be. Nevertheless, a big cloud whose droplets have a long way to fall and are sufficient in number will still produce raindrops in this manner. In addition, in a rising cloud there will be considerable up currents by which big drops will be held in suspension while smaller ones are caught up and merge with the big ones. If the individual drop becomes too big it will loose its stability and burst, and the fragments will again be caught up and merged until they eventually fall from the cloud in big drops. This kind of raindrop formation is likely to occur in hot and humid atmosphere over the tropic region. The second hypothesis is based on the observation that in temperate zone all the clouds from which rain falls in big drops consists, at the higher levels, of ice crystals. In the temperate zone the ice phase is obviously a precondition for the formation of big raindrops. Just as in the case of condensation, a condensation nucleus (dust particle) is necessary, similarly, for the transition from liquid to the solid state, a freezing nucleus is needed. The temperature at which the transition occurs from the liquid to the solid phase, depends on the size and structure of the molecular lattice of the nucleus. The freezing nuclei effective in the temperate zone generally allow a supercooling of the water droplets to 258 K (-15°C) before the ice formation sets in. Upon formation of the ice crystals they go on growing rapidly and in consequence fall faster and absorb additional supercooled droplets on their way down, which in turn contribute to the growth of the crystals. The more droplets that adhere to it, the faster a crystal falls and the less time remains for the formation of the crystal form, so that out of the original crystal a shapeless, unwieldy lump of ice is formed, which melts at less than the atmospheric limit and becomes a raindrop.

rain crust. A type of snow crust formed by freezing of surface snow that had been melted by liquid precipitation.

raindrop erosion. The displacement of soil particles by the impact of large raindrops, particularly under conditions of bare soil affected by intense conventional rainfall. The raindrops have the effect of detaching individual particles, which are then affected by a preferred movement down slope, and helping to seal the soil surface by forcing the finest particles into the voids, reducing infiltration, and increasing the surface runoff.

raindrop formation. *See* rain.

rain forest. A dense, luxuriant, closed mesomorphic community; a global vegetation type containing many tree species associated with high rainfall and humidity, and a relative absence of frosts. The distribution depends upon altitude, moisture availability, the nature of the soil, the aspect of the slope, the incidence of fire, damage by tropical cyclones and the impact of man. There are many types of rain forest, though it is usual to consider three major divisions; tropical, subtropical and temperate. The preservation of different types of rain forests has become an important environmental issue.

rainout. A process in which particles in the higher troposphere may act as nuclei on which water droplets form, later to fall as rain. *See also* washout.

rain shadow. A dry region on the lee side of a topographical obstacle, generally a mountain range, where rainfall is significantly less than on the windward side.

rainwash. A very thin sheet of water, at least a few mm in depth, running over a slope, and with the capacity to transport fine soil particles. It may be generated as infiltration excess flow or as saturation overland flow.

reaction. 1. Any chemical change, regardless of rate, amount of product formed, or whether it occurs naturally (as in plant and animal metabolism) or is purposely induced in a laboratory or in large-scale production. Chemical reactions involved only the electrons of an atom, and the energy absorbed or emitted is small compared with that of nuclear reactions. 2. Disintegration of the nucleus of an atom either by natural radioactivity or by fission due to bombardment with high-energy particles. A thermonuclear reaction involves the fusion or union of hydrogen nuclei to form helium, with evolution of energy. *See also* chain reaction; fission; fusion.

reactivity. In general, the tendency of a substance to combine spontaneously with the gases present in the atmosphere or with its surroundings, or to undergo a chemical change, under proper conditions of temperature and pressure. The U.S. National Fire Protection Association has classified various materials on the basis of their chemical reactivity from fire-fighting point of view, as follows:

4. Materials that in themselves are readily capable of detonation or of explosive decomposition or explosive reaction at normal temperatures and pressures.; includes materials that are sensitive to mechanical or localized thermal shocks.

3. Materials that in themselves are capable of detonation or of explosive decomposition or of explosive reaction but that require a strong initiating source or that must be heated under confinement before initiation; includes materials that are sensitive to thermal and mechanical shock at elevated temperatures and pressures, or that react explosively with water without requiring heat and confinement.

2. Materials that are normally unstable and readily undergo violent change but do not detonate; includes materials that can undergo chemical change with rapid release of energy at normal temperatures and pressures, or that can undergo violent chemical change at elevated temperatures and pressures; also includes those materials that may react violently with water or that may form potentially explosive mixtures with water.

1. The materials that in themselves are normally stable but that may become unstable at elevated temperatures and pressures, or that may react with water with some release of energy but not violently.

0. Materials that are normally stable even under fire exposure conditions and that do not react with water.

reactor. A device for maintaining a controlled nuclear reaction, chiefly for electric power production, but also for the production of radioisotopes and military equipment. The essential components of a power reactor are:

(a) a fissionable element, or fuel, such as uranium-235 or plutonium;

(b) a neutron source to initiate the reaction;

(c) a moderator to retard fast neutrons for more efficient fission;

(d) a coolant (water or liquid sodium);

(e) control rods made of cadmium, which absorb neutrons and thus maintain any desired level of output.

rebound. The elevation of a part of the surface of the earth during or following the removal of overlying material or the filling of an underground cavity.

receptor. The organism, population, or resource, exposed to specific risks from pollution or other adverse influences. Also known as target.

reclaiming. Any of various processes for recovering the values from scrap or used materials so that they can be incorporated in the manufacture of new products.

recombinant DNA. Genetic materials transferred from the genes of one species to those of another by uniting a portion of the DNA of one organism with extranuclear section of DNA from another organism. The technique has made possible the synthesis not only of certain complex molecules (proteins) but also of entirely new life forms (bacteria).

rectification. 1. The interaction of a partial condensate with the vapour rising through a fractionating column, resulting in further enrichment of the vapour in the low boiling component. 2. The adjustment of alcoholic content, of alcoholic beverages etc., to obtain a product of predetermined strength.

recycling. The return of discarded or waste materials to the production system for utilization in the manufacture of goods, with a view to the conservation as far as practicable of nonrenewable and scare resources. Recycling goes beyond the re-use of a product (such as glass milk bottles) and involves the return of salvaged materials, such as paper or metals or broken glass, to an early stage (pulping or melting stage) or of the manufacturing process. Some recycling has always been profitable to certain industries (*e.g.*, the return of steel scrap to the steel industry); opinion now seems to favour an increased tempo and scale of recycling to conserve resources for the future of mankind beyond what may be profitable in the shorter term. The capacity of an industry to recycle is in many cases limited by technical as well as economic consideration. On the other hand, the glass industry is already recycling considerable quantities of broken and used glass; the aluminium and steel industries find it economically acceptable to encourage the return of aluminium and steel scrap. Plastic and rubber industries are also recycling the used containers and other articles.

red-tide. Descriptive effect of the red-brown colour of dense populations of marine protozoa which can occur under exceptionally favourable conditions of water temperature, salinity, and/or nutrient salts. The accumulation of metabolic wastes in these conditions may cause massive fish mortality.

reducer. In biology, a hetertrophic individual which utilizes the chemical energy of organic matter while breaking it down or reducing it to more simple substance.

reduction. 1. Addition of hydrogen to, or subtraction of oxygen from a substance. Though reduction can be regarded simply as the removal of oxygen, it also has a broader meaning; the acceptance of one or more electrons (or their equivalent) from another substance. Oxygen is not essential to the reaction. Reduction can also be effected by addition of hydrogen to a molecule. 2. Lowering the valence of an element in combination, as reducing ferric chloride to ferrous chloride. 3. Both the preceding processes, and the complete reactions of which they are a part, involve an interchange of electrons between atoms, where upon the atom gaining the electron or electrons is reduced, and the atom losing the electron or electrons is oxidized.

reduzates. Sediments that have accumulated under reducing conditions, and which are therefore typically rich in organic carbon and iron sulphide; black shale and coal are examples.

re-entrainment. The return of particles, subsequent to their deposition on a collecting surface, to an air stream in which they were previously suspended.

refining. 1. In the petroleum industry, this term refers to chemical reactions performed for removal of certain unwanted impurities on the various fractions from petroleum by distillation; these include cracking, reforming, polymerization, dehydrogenation, etc., usually with catalysts, for production of gasoline and other derivatives. 2. In metallurgy, the term also implies the removal of impurities by various separation techniques, important among which are electrolysis used for aluminium, copper, and the precious metals and a specialized operation called zone refining.

refrigerant. In general, any substance used to attain reduced temperatures. In specific sense, a fluid used for heat-transfer purposes in refrigerating equipment. The substances most frequently used for this purpose are fluorinated hydrocarbons, and they are also widely used as propellants in aerosol spray dispenser cans. They should be referred to either by their chemical names or by their international designations, which consist of a number preceded by the letter R (examples: R12 is dichlorodifluoromethane; R22 is chlorodifluoromethane). Fears have been expressed that fluorinated hydrocarbons propellants released from spray cans, drifting upward in the atmosphere, might be instrumental in reducing the amount of ozone in the ozone layer, thus permitting a greater proportion of the solar ultraviolet radiation to reach the earth's surface, with serious consequences for health.

refuse. The complete range of unwanted or undesirable material generated in the course of producing, processing and consuming useful products.

Reinluft process. A process for removing (and recovering) oxides of nitrogen, sulphur, and phosphorus from stack gases. The gases are mixed with oxygen and converted to a higher oxidation state (a catalyst may be used to increase the efficiency of conversion) and passed upward, in counter current fashion, over a down ward-moving bed of a special type of carbon in a multi-chambered adsorber. The oxides are absorbed at different temperatures. Finally they are swept out of the carbon bed at high temperature in a stream of nitrogen or carbon dioxide and reduced. The process may be carried out in the presence of water vapour, in which case the corresponding acids, rather than the gaseous oxides, are recovered.

regeneration. 1. The process of returning a changed material or natural product to its original state or condition after it has been chemically modified for processing purposes. Regeneration should not be confused with reclaiming, which only partially restores the original properties of a material. 2. Renewing or reactivating a catalyst, molecular sieve, or ion-exchange medium (zeolite) by any of several methods. Catalysts fouled with coke or other deposits are regenerated by treatment with hot reactive gases such as oxygen, hydrogen steam, etc.

relative biological effectiveness. The ratio of the dose (in rads) of γ-radiation from cobalt-60 to the dose (in rads) of any type of ionizing radiation which produces the same, specified, biological effect.

relative humidity. The ratio between the actual weight of water vapour in a given volume of air and the amount which would be present if the air was saturated at the same temperature, expressed as a percentage. The total amount of water vapour that a given volume of air contains (expressed in grams per cubic metre) is called the absolute humidity. The humidity measurements are of great significance for several reasons:

(a) the amount of water vapour present in a given volume of air is an indication of the atmosphere's potential capacity for precipitation;

(b) water vapour, in its power to absorb radiation, is a regulator of heat loss from the earth;

(c) the amount of water vapour present in the atmosphere decides the quantity of latent energy stored up in the atmosphere for the growth of storms; and

(d) the amount of water vapour present is an important factor affecting the human body's rate of cooling.

The relative humidity depends depends both upon the absolute humidity and the temperature; if the moisture content remains the same, then the relative humidity will decrease as the temperature rises and will increase as the temperature falls.

rem. Abbreviation for 'Röentgen *e*quivalent *m*an'; a obsolete unit of dose of ionizing radiation; equal to absorbed dose of any ionizing radiation causing the same biological effect as 1 rad of *X*-ray radiation with specific ionization of 100 ions pairs in water layer of 1 nm thickness.

renewable energy. Flows of energy occurring naturally and repeatedly in the environment. The various renewable energy sources include, the sun, geothermal energy from within the earth, tidal range power from the rise and fall of tides resulting from the attractive forces and orbital energy of the moon and the earth acting together and with respect to the sun, and wind energy. These sources and flows are contrasted with non-renewable finite sources, *e.g.*, fossil, nuclear, chemical and other sources whose energy is released by the action of man. Renewable supplies are continuously available and therefore can not be depleted. If averaged over world population, the total renewable energy flows would equal approximately 30 MW per person. This is about 10,000 times more power than the 3 kV required per person for a developed life style. Thus the amount of renewable energy is more than adequate as an energy source, and the technical problem becomes that of making the power compatible with requirements such as heat, transport, and electricity.

Of the various renewable sources, solar flow of energy is dominant and may be divided in to many interrelated subsidiary flows which include;

(i) solar radiation, *i.e.*, visible and near visible wavelengths of the solar spectrum, having thermal and photoactive properties;

(b) thermal flows from the absorption of radiation in the atmosphere and at the earth's surface;

(c) photosynthesis from photoactive properties of radiation, sustaining the growth of plants and subsequent release in the biosphere and biofuel use;

(d) hydropower from the evaporation of water and condensation as rainfall onto elevated ground;

(e) wind power from the thermally induced motion in the atmosphere; and

(f) wave power from the motion of wind over water.

reportable quantity. RQ. The reportable quantity that may be harmful, and discharge of which is a violation of the law and requires notice. Any person incharge of a vessel or an onshore or an offshore facility in quantities equal to or exceeding in any 24-hour period the reportable quantity determined by this part, immediately notify the appropriate Government agency of this discharge.

representative sample. A sample of a universe or whole (*e.g.*, waste pile, lagoon, groundwater) that can be expected to exhibit the average properties of the universe or whole.

reserpine. A water-soluble alkaloid, used as antihypertensive agent and tranquilizer. It has been classified as potential occupational carcinogen.

reservation. The withholding from use and exploitation of areas and resources which it is judged should be held back either against future needs or because they are best kept as they are; areas so treated are called 'reserves', *e.g.*, forest reserves.

residence time. In air pollution studies, the length of time during which a given molecule of an air pollutant remains in the atmosphere (it may, at the end of that time, be replaced by another molecule, so the residence time is not the duration of air pollution). In chemical engineering, the term is applied to the length of time that a given material remains in a vessel through which it is flowing.

residual. In pollution control terminology, a quantity of material or energy which is left over or wasted, when, in the course of human activity, inputs are converted into outputs in production and consumption. The examples of this type are, waste-heat and gaseous pollutants from thermal power plants, slag from metal ore refining. Outputs have prices in normally existing markets; residuals do not. Through a change in economic circumstances or technological advance, a residual may become an output. Scrap metal or glass recovery at a refuse plant converts a waste into an output. *See also* recycling.

residual chlorine. The amount of chlorine remaining in potable or industrial water, after chlorine or sodium hypochlorite has been added to it in a water treatment plant. This may be present in the form of free chlorine residual or combined chlorine residual. This is usually kept at 0.2 to 0.3 mg./L after 30 minutes contact period. The residual chlorine helps to prevent further contamination during its passage from treatment plant to the consumers.

residual use. A use other than a beneficial use in of respect of water, *e.g.*, the disposal of liquid effluents.

residue. The hazardous material remaining in a packaging, including a tank car, after its contents have been unleaded to the maximum extent practicable and before the packaging is either refilled or cleaned of hazardous material and purged to remove any hazardous vapours.

resorcinol. A dihydroxy phenolic compound used in the manufacture of resorcinol-formaldehyde resins, dyes, pharmaceuticals, and adhesives. It is toxic and irritant to eyes and skin. Occupational exposure to resorcinol should be controlled so that no employee is exposed to resorcinol at a concentration greater than 45.0 mg/m^3 of air (10 ppm), determined as a time-weighted average (TWA) concentration limit for up to a 10-hour workshift in a 40-hour workweek, over a working lifetime.

resource management. The introduction and enforcement of restraints, including specified technical practices, to safeguard the future of renewable resources and uphold the principle of sustained yield.

response time. The time which elapses after a sudden change in the quantity being measured up to the point at which the measuring instrument given an indication which does not differ from the correct indication corresponding to the new value of the quantity by an amount greater than a given value.

In order to determine the response time, it is necessary to fix for each category of instrument:

(a) the initial value from which the change in the quantity measured must be made,

(b) the value of this change, and

(c) the difference between the current indication and the indication at the end of the period takes as being the response time.

The response time is therefore the time required for a readout device to reach a specified fraction of its final value in response to a step-function input (*e.g.*, a sudden increase in pollutant concentration) to the detector. If this fraction is specified as 0.63 ($1^{-1/e}$), the response time is equal to the time constant; if, as is often the case, it is specified as 0.98, the response time is approximately equal to four time constants. The response time is of critical importance when components are assembled to form an analytical system, *e.g.*, when a recorder is added to a detector and amplifier. A short response time is important in real-time measurements, particularly those involving hazardous pollutants. (The response time is sometimes, particularly in US, referred to as the fall time when it follows a decrease, and the rise time when it follows an increase, in the quantity being measured.)

retention time. In pollution control terminology, the duration of time necessary for the fermentation of a given quantity of substrate to an end product. In the case of anaerobic digestion to biogas, the total time period for virtually complete digestion may be up to 90 days when operated as a batch fermentation. In continuous or semicontinuous operation, a given amount of input feed is introduced into the vessel during the course of each day and equal amount of digester contents are withdrawn, so that once the fermentation is established, the rate of gas production remain steady. The retention time then equals the capacity of the digester divided by the feed rate (volume/time). The loading rate (concentration) is particularly important since at high loading rates the retention time is reduced. Thermophilic digestion at temperatures around 320 K can reduce the retention time of a mesophilic digestion by 50% or more.

reverse osmosis plant. A system consisting of a semi-permeable cellulose acetate membrane module in a pressure vessel. The driving force to extract dissolved solids from a waste is the reverse osmosis pressure. A schematic arrangement of a reverse osmosis plant is shown in the following illustration:

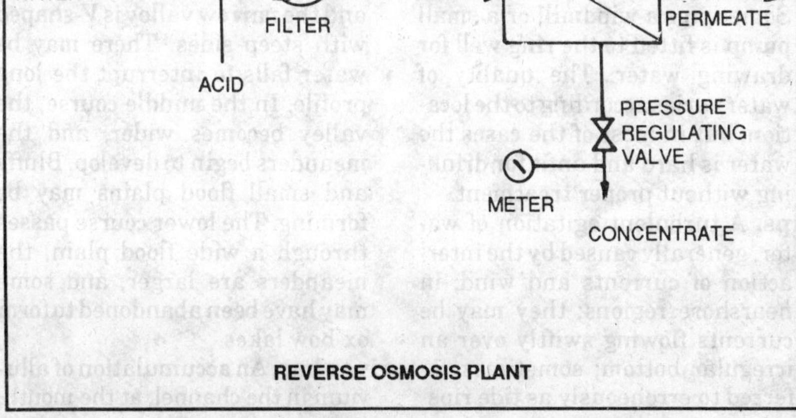

REVERSE OSMOSIS PLANT

Rexco. A proprietary solid smokeless fuel prepared by carbonizing coal in a vertical cylindrical chamber about 7.5 metres high. Carbonization is achieved by burning fuel gas within the top of the chamber and passing the hot products of combustion downwards through the charge of coal.

Rhizobium. A bacterium existing in symbiosis with the leguminous plants such as lucerne and soyabean. It can fix atmospheric nitrogen in the root nodules of the associated plants, the nitrogen compounds formed being utilized by the legume, which in turn supplies energy-rich sugars to the bacteria via photosynthesis. The efficiency of nitrogen fixing can often be improved by the inoculation of more effective strains than those naturally colonizing the plant.

rill erosion. The formation of numerous, closely spaced rills due to uneven removal of surface soil by streamlets running water.

ring well. A type of dug well used in remote and rural areas, for drawing ground water. Its diameter ranges from 1 to 3 metres, and the depth varies from 6 to 14 metres. Sometimes a windmill or a small pump is fitted to the ring well for drawing water. The quality of water varies according to the location, but in most of the cases the water is hard and unfit for drinking without proper treatment.

rips. A turbulent agitation of water, generally caused by the interaction of currents and wind; in nearshore regions; they may be currents flowing swiftly over an irregular bottom; sometimes referred to erroneously as tide rips.

rip-up. A sedimentary structure formed when currents lift plates or discs of finely laminated and partially consolidated sediment and transport them to a new site of deposition. The individual plates or clasts may themselves by referred to as rip-ups.

risk. The expected frequency of undesirable effects arising from a given exposure to a pollutant.

river. A channelled flow of water, which moves downhill because of gravity. Most rivers flow in the sea, although there are some which flow into lakes, and some flow into deserts, where they evaporate to leave salt flats or very saline lakes. Most rivers flow throughout the year, although the amount of water flowing through the river varies depending upon the climatic factors, especially the rainfall, and the season. The source of a river is generally in an area of high ground, it may be a spring, a lake, a marshy patch, or a place where the water table reaches the surface. From its source, it usually flows through the mountains, then through an upland area, and finally onto a lowland. The upper parts of a river are usually rocky and turbulent, and the narrow valley is *V*-shaped with steep sides. There may be water falls to interrupt the long profile. In the middle course, the valley becomes wider, and the meanders begin to develop. Bluffs and small flood plains may be forming. The lower course passes through a wide flood plain; the meanders are larger, and some may have been abandoned to form ox-bow lakes.

river bar. An accumulation of alluvium in the channel, at the mouth, or along the banks of a river or stream. At low water, it is commonly exposed and constitutes a navigational obstruction.

river basin. The area drained by a river and all of its tributaries.

riverbed. The channel which contains, or formerly contained, a river. The suspended insoluble matter present in the effluents discharged into the rivers, settle at the riverbed.

river capture. The capture of a river's water supply by a second river, which works back uphill by headward erosion and intercepts flow. Also known as river piracy.

river terrace. A near-level surface in a river valley, usually covered by a thin layer of gravel or alluvium. At the rear of the terrace there is a steep bluff leading up to higher ground; at the front, there is a steep drop either to the river or the flood plain. Many river terraces result from lateral plantation at a time when the river was graded to the higher base level. Subsequently, the river under went rapid vertical incision, leaving the former valley floor upstanding as the terrace. Sometimes, the river terraces are formed when the phase of the extensive valley-floor aggradation is followed by a phase of degradation.

river tide. A tide occuring in rivers emptying, directly into the sea, showing the characteristic modifications of ocean tides; the speed at which the tide travels upstream depends on the depth of the channel, the further upstream the longer the duration of the falling tide and shorter the duration of the rising tide, and range of the tide decreases with distance upstream.

river valley. An elongated depression in the earth's surface, carved by river or stream erosion in conjunction with mass wasting or collapse of river banks.

ROADCHEM model. An air-quality control model which is a version of ROADWAY model, and incorporates the chemical reactions involving NO, NO_2, and O_3 as well as advection and dispersion of NO, NO_2, CO, and O_3. It utilizes surface-layer similarity theory to produce vertical wind and turbulence profiles. The temperatures at two heights and wind velocity are required inputs for this model. These values are generally obtained from instruments on a tower upwind of the roadway.

ROADWAY model. A finite difference air-quality control model which predict pollutant concentration near a roadway. It utilizes surface layer similarity theory to produce vertical wind and turbulence profiles. The temperatures at two heights and wind velocity are required inputs for this model. These values are generally obtained from instruments on a tower upwind of the roadway.

rod float. A wooden rod designed to float vertically with most of length submerged under water due to the weight attached to its bottom; used to measure the average velocity of flow of a stream throughout the submerged depth.

Röentgen. R. The amount of radiation which on passage through dry air under standard condition, produces an electrostatic unit of ions, of either plus or minus charge, per cubic cm.

In SI system, 1 R = 0.258 mC/kg.

Röentgen ray. The familiar *X*-ray, a type of radiation produced whenever cathode rays impinge on any solid substance such as the walls of a gas-discharge tube or upon abstacles placed within their path.

rotary meter. A current meter used to measure the current in a flowing river or stream.

rotary pump. A pump with gears which delivers large volume of water at a low head.

rough fish. Fish undesirable as food or for other activities such as sports. Most destructive of all rough fish is the carp; it may uproot extensive quantities of vegetation.

Royal Commission Standards. Standards for the quality of sewage works effluents recommended by a Royal Commission on Sewage Disposal which was appointed in Britain in 1898 to report on the methods available for the treatment and disposal of sewage and trade wastes. The Commission recommended standards for sewage effluents discharging to inland streams (other than storm water sewage). The type of treatment envisaged was sedimentation and complete biological treatment, and the standards included, maximum biochemical oxygen demand (BOD) of not more than 20 g/m^3 and a maximum concentration suspended solids of not more than 30 g/m^3, by weight, where the dilution factor was not less than 8:1. The Commission also suggested a limiting concentration of 40 to 60 g/m^3 of suspended solids for trade effluents discharging into the inland streams, the exact value depending on the nature of the effluent. The aim of the standards was to avoid nuisance. These standards are still considered fairly good even today, although an increasing number of situations demand more rigid standards and hence tertiary treatment.

run. 1. The stretch of a waterline or sewer line. 2. The layout of cables or pipelines in a building.

runoff. Any rainwater, leachate, or other liquid that drains over land from any part of a facility. Most of water in the hydrological cycle falls on the land surface as rain, snow, sleet, or hail. Some of this water evaporates into the air. A part of it is consumed by the plants and animals, and some sinks into the ground, where it is held in the openings in the rocks for some time. But almost 40% of the water that falls on the ground, flows back to the sea by way of surface and underground streams. Several factors that affect runoff are: amount and type of rainfall; slope or gradient of the area receiving the rainfall; type of surface and material over which the water flows; and the amount and kind of vegetation in the area.

run-of-wind. A term applied to the distance defined by tv, where t is time in seconds and v is a constant wind velocity in m/s. If the wind velocity is not constant, integration over the time period involved is necessary.

S

sabin. A unit of sound absorption equivalent to absorption through 1 ft^2 of an opening.

saccharin. Generic name for the anhydride of *o*-sulphamidebenzoic acid; mainly used as a non-nutritive sweetener. According to National Academy of Sciences, U.S., saccharin is a weak carcinogen in animals and a potential human carcinogen. Therefore, the products containing saccharin must have a warning label. Its name has also been included in the list of Carcinogen Assessment Group of Environmental Protection Agency.

sacrificial. A term used to denote a type of galvanic corrosion in which a coating, most commonly zinc, is attacked in preference to the underlying metal, that is, the coating is sacrificed, in order to preserve the base metal.

sacrificial anode. The anode used in cathodic protection of pipes and other metallic substances against corrosion.

sacrificial protection. The protection of iron surface by coating with zinc or any other more electropositive metal.

safrole. Trade name for 4-allyl-1,2-methylenedioxybenzene; used in perfumery and soaps, and in the manufacture of heliotropin; it has been found to possess carcinogenic activity in humans.

salinity. The total content of dissolved mineral constituents, of all kinds, in water. Normally the problem of excessive salinity in rivers does not arise. Rain and other forms of precipitation are relatively free of minerals; it is when these waters come into contact with the earth that the process of mineralization begins. The natural sources of salinity include springs passing through rock formations which contain soluble salts. Other sources of salinity include domestic and industrial wastes, oil-well brines, and mine water. The use and re-use of water, particularity where irrigation is carried out, increases the threat of excessive salinity which makes water unsuitable for public supply and for further irrigation. Water containing more than 500 ppm of dissolved solids is not considered desirable for domestic supplies. Water containing more than 2,000 ppm is considered to be unsuitable for irrigation under average conditions, in the long term. High levels of salinity in soil water in many countries, is a major environmental hazard associated with agriculture, and particularly with irrigation. In many areas the ground-water is naturally saline.

Average salinities in most of the

r…ers are generally less than …00 g/m³ of total dissolved solids. Factors contributing to this salinity include flows from tributary catchments, ground water inflow, surface drainage, and sub-surface drain effluents from irrigated areas. The salinity problem of the polluted rivers is particularly important because of the number of agricultural and urban users who are supplied from it.

saltation. Transport of a sediment in which the particles are moved forward in series of short intermittent bounces from a bottom surface. The size of particles can be saltated usually depends upon the velocity of the current and its density, *e.g.*, water will saltate larger particles than air at the same velocity.

salt dome. A circular piercement structure produced by the upward movement of a pipelike plug of salt. They form from the thick layers of rock salt that mark some diverging contiental margins. Subsidence of these continental margins carries the rock salt to great depth and allows it to be covered with a wedge of sedimentary rock perhaps 5-10 km thick. The sedimentary rock on top of the salt layer is denser than the salt, and under the great pressure caused by the weight of the overlying rock, the salt begins to deform plastically and flow upward. Large columns of salt rise from the top of the salt bed and then break off, perhaps assuming a streamlined tear-drop shape one or more km in diameter. As the salt continues to rise, it deforms the surrounding sedimentary rock, forming folds and faults that create oil traps, some of which may be under an overhanging mushroom-shaped top that is characteristic of some salt domes.

When the salt rises into the zone of active ground-water circulation near the surface, it dissolves. Therefore, many salt domes never reach the surface. If the rock salt contains gypsum, it may develop a cap rock on its upper surface as the halite dissolves, but the less soluble gypsum does not. Gypsum, contains sulphur in the form of calcium sulphate, that may form native elemental sulphur when it contacts bacteria and petroleum. Salt dome cap rocks, therefore, often contain thick beds of bright yellow sulphur. Salt domes then supply a variety of valuable resources. Oil and gas are found around and above the domes. The salt itself is mined by drilling into it and dissolving it with hot water. Some salt domes deform the surface. Some of the low, round islands in the costal swamps of Louisiana were pushed up by salt domes. If solution of the salt by ground water is very rapid, the overlying rock may subside, so some salt domes are marked by surface depressions. Most salt domes are found by geophysical surveys, however. The density of rock salt is 2.2 g/cm³, a value that does not change even if the rock salt is compressed. Sedimentary rocks within the Gulf coast belt of domes have densities of 2.0 g/cm³ at the surface increasing to values of 2.5 or greater at depth due to compaction. The salt dome rises because it is out of isostatic equilibrium with the heavier rock around it.

salting out. An operation used chiefly in the soap industry involving the incorporation of common salt in the product at the end of the mixing cycle to cause aggregation of the desired ingredients and thus the separation of these ingredients from unwanted reaction products. This principle can be successfully applied for removing certain pollutants from the industrial effluents.

salt marsh. An area of coastal marsh which is flooded by the sea from time to time. Special salt-resistant plants colonize the areas at; they trap silt and help to build up the land. Many of the coastal marshes can be reclaimed once the land has become well vegetated.

saltwater habitats. An ecological term for the organisms and various forms of life, in saltwater such as seas and oceans, and covers about 70% of the earth's surface, the most extensive of the major habitats. More different phyla of animals live in the sea than on land. Within limited areas, the seas are much richer with life than are equal areas on land. Yet there are fewer species in the seas, marine organisms accounting for only 20% of all species. Because of the generally uniform conditions and the lack of isolation in the continuous water medium, seas do not favour the development of species as much as does land. Only a few kinds of flowering plants live in the sea. Marine plants are mainly algae, and the most numerous of these are macroscopic species that form the vast floating pastures of phytoplankton. These small plants account for most of the photosynthesis in the sea and form the base of the food chain for marine life. Seaweeds that grow in shallow seas are macroscopic types of algae with fleshy bodies. Some of them, the giant kelps, grow to more than 60 metres long. They are anchored to the bottom by rootlike holdfastsa, and their fleshy, leaflike bodies float at the surface by air-filled bladders. Where abundant, these giant seaweeds make forests in the sea.

Despite its immensity, sea is a relatively uniform habitat. Though there are local variations, the salt content is fairly constant, about 3.5%. Tropical seas have an average temperature of about 285 K, while in arctic seas the temperature is always near freezing. But in the same area, the temperature of the water in the sea rarely varies much more than 5 degrees from season to season.

sampling, continuous. In pollution control, sampling without interruptions throughout an operation or for a predetermined time, that is, uninterrupted sampling of air, usually at a fixed rate. Where the sample can be analysed continuously, the stream of gas may be passed through a measuring instrument continuously. Otherwise, the sample is collected in an uninterrupted fashion for a given period and the entire sample is finally analysed to give the mean composition of the air over whole period.

sampling, cumulative. A process or system in which the sample is accumulated either by sampling continuously or for finite periods at regular intervals to give a single sample whose composition is regarded as representative of the whole period of its accumulation.

sampling, in-situ. In pollution control, sampling of a property of a medium (for example atmosphere) by using sensors or detectors at the actual place where sampling is desired.

sampling, instantaneous. In pollution control, obtaining a sample of an atmospheric air in a very short period of time, such that this sampling time is insignificant in comparison with the duration of the operation or the period being studied. It implies sampling at one point in time. Instantaneous sampling is possible with electrical and optical devices.

sampling, intermittent. In pollution control, sampling successively for limited periods of time throughout an operation or for a predetermined period of time. The durations of sampling periods and of the intervals in between are not necessarily regular and are not specified. In contrast to continuous sampling, intermittent sampling means that sampling occurs at intervals for only a fraction of the total time.

sampling, running. In pollution control, withdrawal of a portion of the atmosphere over a period of time with continuous analysis or with separation of the desired material continuously and in a linear form such as withdrawal of the atmosphere accompanied by absorption of a component in a flowing stream of absorbent or by filtration in a moving strip of paper. Such a sample may be obtained with a considerable concentration which occur during the period of sampling.

sand trap. A trap used in a drainage system to arrest sand and grit.

sanitary land-fill. *See* land-fill.

Santa Barbara blow-out. An incident which occurred on 28th January 1969, while the Union Oil Company was drilling its fourth well from an offshore rig located about 13 km from the shore of the Santa Barbara Channel, off the coast of California. Pressure in the hole rose suddenly, blew out all the drilling mud, and crude oil spurted from the ocean floor. The blow-out continued for ten days. The first slick of oil reached about 24 km from the drilling platform, some five days after the blowout; three days later it arrived at Santa Barbara, surging on to the beaches, promenades, and jetties. Seagulls avoided the oil, but many grebes dived into it and died slowly. Santa Barbara was declared as a disaster area. The Union Oil Company spent more than $5 million making good the damage, collecting blackened birds, washing and caring for them. Dispersives were sprayed on the oil. Tons of straw were blasted at high pressure on to water, beaches, rocks and docks, functioning as blotting paper. The straw was later collected and removed. Blackened sand was removed from the beaches. The oil well was sealed with mud and cement, but cracks continued to occur in the ocean floor around the platform causing seepage; special measures were adopted to deal with this seepage. *See also* oil pollution.

saprophyte. A plant which lives on decaying organic matter; most saprophytes are fungi.

saturation index. An index used to indicate the saturation of a sample of water with respect to calcium carbonate;

$I_s = p\mathrm{H}$ of water - pH of water at which it should be in equilibrium with calcium carbonate.

A zero index means the water is in equilibrium with calcium carbonate. A negative index indicate the water to be under-saturated with calcium carbonate and a positive index indicates just the opposite.

scale. 1. A deposited layer or incrustation of calcium carbonate or calcium sulphate (or any other water insoluble substance) on the lining of boilers or in water pipes, resulting from prolonged contact with hard water. 2. A type of paraffin wax which retains several percent of liquid distillate; scale wax has a lower melting point, 325 K, than fully pressed and refined wax and is type commonly used for packaging, candles, etc.

scattering. A process in which a change in direction or energy of an incident particle or incident radiation is caused by a collision with a particle or a system of particles. Mie scattering is the scattering of electromagnetic radi-ation by spherical particles, there being no particular relationship between particle size and the wavelength of the radiation. It is of considerable importance in air pollution studies. Light is effectively scattered by particles about 0.1-1 μm in diameter; the resulting loss of visibility is a function of the particle radius squared. Rayleigh scattering is the scattering by particles whose radius is less than about one-tenth of the wavelength of the radiation (*e.g.*, the scattering of light by oxygen and nitrogen molecules in the air).

scavenger. 1. Any metal or alloy or alloy which has the ability to remove traces of gaseous impurities from molten metals by combination or adsorption 2. In radiochemistry, substance used to remove unwanted radioactive impurities by their co-precipitation or adsorption. The scavenger is usually a precipitate with a well developed surface. 3. A chemical compound reacting at high rate constant with specified free radicals.

scent test. A drain test carried out by pouring a strong scent into a drain and plugged. The next manhole is opened out and investigated whether there is any smell of the scent coming out of the manhole. The test is carried out to ensure the flow of sewage through the drain stretch.

schedule of compliance. A schedule of remedial measures included in a permit, including an enforceable sequence of interim requirements (for example, actions, operations, or milestone events) leading to compliance with the act and regulations.

Schöenherr process. One of the processes used for the production of nitrates directly from the air by the combination of oxygen and nitrogen under the action of an electric arc.

screen analysis. The classification of material by size, accomplished by shaking it on screens of successively smaller sizes, and collecting separately the portions that fail to pass through the various screens.

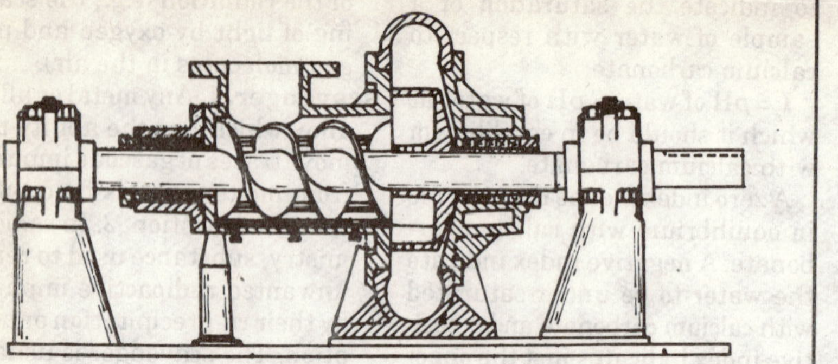

SCREW PUMP

screw pump. A non-clog type sewage pump equipped with screw-feed mechanism, that macerate solids before they enter the pump chamber.

sea-breeze. The movement of air from sea to land. On clear days the land usually heats faster than water. The lowest air layer adjacent to the land warms quickly; this is displaced by inflowing heavier and cooler sea air. *See* land breeze.

sea-water distillation. A purification process involving the evaporation of sea-water and subsequent condensation of the vapour; the undesirable suspended and dissolved solids remain as the residue.

secondary forest. The vegetation type which usually replaces primary forest following its removal. When forest disturbance has been small the secondary forest may bear a strong visual resemblance of the original forest although species diversity, layering, energy flow patterns and faunal diversity will inevitably have been simplified. In other instances when vegetation is allowed to recolonize an area of former agriculture (as in tropical slash-and-burn clearings) the resulting vegetation reveals considerable lack of diversity and far fewer animal species (particularly bird and arboreal species of monkey). At best, those areas of forest now called natural, are merely very old secondary woodlands.

secondary pollution. Atmospheric pollution resulting from the chemical reaction(s) between two or more sources of primary pollution or between primary pollutants and naturally occurring atmospheric elements. The most notorious secondary pollutant is photochemical smog.

secondary treatment. A series of biochemical, chemical and mechanical processes used in sewage treatment which remove, oxidize, or stabilize non-settleable, colloidal, and dissolved organic materials found in sewage, following primary treatment. The two techniques most commonly used are either treatment on trickling filters or the activated sludge process. These carry out in a controlled manner, the biological assimilation and degradation processes that occur in nature. Trickling filters; also known as biological filters, consist of beds of coarse material over which the sewage is sprinkled at a uniform rate,they are generally not less than 2 m deep and circular in plan. The activated sludge process of sewage treatment is in effect an artificially accelerated self-purification process, promoted by oxidation. As in the case of the trickling filter, the impurities in the sewage are oxidized mainly by the action of aerobic bacteria. The most common methods of introducing oxygen into the sewage in the activated sludge process is to blow compressed air through porous plates placed in the bottom of the tanks; under-water paddles assist in the distribution of air and help to keep the sludge in suspension. The sewage, after passing through the activated sludge tanks, is allowed to settle in secondary sedimentation tanks; after a suitable retention time the activated sludge (other than that mixed with fresh sewage) is pumped to sludge digestion chambers.

sediment. 1. Solid material that has settled down from a state of suspension in a liquid. 2. A mass of organic or inorganic solid fragmental material transported and deposited by wind, water, or ice, chemically precipitated from solution, or secreted by organisms, and that forms in layers in loose unconsolidated form, such as mud and sand.

sedimentation. A separation operation in which particles dispersed in a liquid medium are allowed to fall to the bottom of a container, by gravity. It differs from precipitation in respect to the time required; precipitation is quite rapid, whereas sedimentation may take hours or even days if the particles approach colloidal dimensions. In sludge treatment plants it is employed for the removal of settleable solids within primary or secondary treatment plants using settling tanks; the low velocity of the sewage flowing through the system allows particles to gravitate to the bottom, permitting ready removal as sludge.

sedimentation analysis. The mechanical analysis based on difference of rate of sedimentation of particles of investigated substance dispersed in a given medium in order to determine concentration of particles of different size.

sedimentation constant. A quantity obtained in investigating the behaviour of colloidal particles under the action of forces, chiefly centrifugal forces.

seepage pit. A buried perforated tank or gravel-filled cavity allowing effluent, *e.g.*, from a septic tank, to seep into the surrounding soil. Also known as soak pit.

selenium. A semiconducting element, placed in group VIA of the periodic table; classed as a nonmetal. It is mostly recovered as a byproduct of copper ore refining. As a result of geochemical differences, levels of selenium in soil and vegetation vary within broad limits. The chemical form of selenium, and thus its solubility is another decisive factor both as regards its entry into the food chain and its presence in water. Environmental processes can decrease selenium solubility converting soluble selenate compounds or some selenites into compounds of very low solubility such as elemental selenium or selenides (or even selenites of certain metals). Selenium is usually present in water as selenite or selenate, the chemical form being influenced by such factors as *p*H and by the presence of salts of certain metals such as iron.

Its electrical properties make it particularly suitable for use in rectifiers; its electrical conductivity is increased on exposure to light by the effect of photons, which proliferate electrons and energy deficits (holes) within the atoms. Selenium is thus used in photocells, solar batteries, and similar devices. It has specialized applications in rubber vulcanization and as a colorant in glass and ceramic products. In terms of abundance, selenium ranks 34th among the elements occurring in the earth's crust.

Dietary intake of selenium depends on food consumption patterns and selenium levels in foodstuffs, the latter being determined mainly by the character of the foodstuff and by geochemical conditions. Vegetables and fruits generally represent a poor dietary source of selenium levels in contrast to grain, grain products meat (particularly internal organ meat) and seafood, which contain substantial selenium levels, usually well above 0.2 mg/kg on a wet weight basis. The chemical composition of the soil and its selenium content have a marked influence on the selenium content in grain from different countries, ranging from about 0.04 mg/kg to 21 mg/kg. Its compounds are toxic, and may cause severe burns of the skin and eyes and intense pain around finger nails. Sudden inhalation of a large amount of selenium dioxide fume causes severe lung irritation.

Soluble selenium salts, such as sodium selenite, are readily absorbed in the gastrointestinal tract of rats. Absorption exceed 95% whether the diet contained 20μg or 4000 μg of selenium per kg. About 93% of selenium was absorbed by man when milligram doses of sodium selenite were administered in aqueous solutions. Thus humans, like rats exhibit no homeostatic control limiting gastrointestinal absorption of large amounts of selenite.

Absorbed selenium is widely distributed in organs and tissues, with high levels present in the liver and kidneys. Selenium penetrates through the placenta and also into the milk the extent depending on the chemical form. Within the body, two primary metabolic pathways predominate. One is direct incorporation into or binding by proteins. The other, reduction followed by methylation is responsible for the production of dimethylselenide and trimethylselenonium ions. When its rate of formation exceeds the rate of further methylation to a urinary metabolite trimethylselenonium ion, the volatile dimethylselenide is exhaled. Under the conditions of exposure prevailing in the general population urinary selenium excretion predominates.

The rate of selenium elimination depends on the chemical form in which selenium is administered and on the selenium nutritional status. Available human data indicate that selenium administered as selenite is excreted more rapidly from the body than when given in organic form, such as selenomethionine. In rats, the biological half-time of selenium decreased dietary selenium levels.

For total recoverable inorganic selenite the criterion to protect freshwater aquatic life is 35 μg/L as a 24-hour average and the concentration should not exceed 260 μg/L at any time. The available data for inorganic selenite indicate that acute toxicity to freshwater aquatic life occur at concentrations as low as 760 μg/L, and would occur at even lower concentrations among the species that are more sensitive than those tested. No data are available concerning the chronic toxicity of inorganic selenite to sensitive freshwater aquatic life. For total recoverable inorganic selenite the criterion to protect saltwater aquatic life is 54μg/L as a 24-hour average and the concentration should not exceed 410 μg/L at any time. The ambient water quality criterion for selenium is recommended to be identical to the existing drinking water standard which is 10 μg/L.

self-absorption. The reduction in radiant power at the centre of emission lines, resulting, from selective absorption of radiation emitted by the hot central core into the cooler outer vapour of the source envelope.

self-cleansing. The general tendency of a body of air to recover naturally from contamination by waste gases. Pollution in many forms is continually being introduced into the atmosphere. If the atmosphere did not have certain self-cleansing powers its condition would quickly become intolerable. Particles of sufficient size are removed from the atmosphere by gravitation Smaller particles (say 20 μm) may be removed from the atmosphere by impaction on the surface of the earth or vegetation or on buildings. Rainfall also plays a part in collecting and removing particles; gaseous contaminants may be absorbed in rain and fog. The character of pollutants may be modified by photochemical or chemical reactions which may accelerate or retard the effect of pollutants on man, animal or vegetation. The balance is much affected by the meteorological factors and topography of the city or town under consideration. Some localities are normally poorly ventilated with a resultant aggravation of their pollution problems. Others are well ventilated and can dispose of more pollutants by dispersion into the atmosphere for a comparable level of pollution. The frequency, intensity and duration of temperature inversions in the atmosphere (when the temperature of the atmosphere increases instead of falling with height which has the effect of inhibiting the upward diffusion of gases) is a major factor influencing the dispersal of pollutants. The atmosphere is a dynamic system. It steadily absorbs and relinquishes a range of solid, liquid and gaseous pollutants from both natural and man-made sources. While being dispersed through the effects of turbulence, some of these pollutants will react between themselves and with other substances, both chemically and physically, yielding a variety of other compounds. Whether or not in their original form some of these pollutants will eventually reach a sink (such as the ocean) or a receptor (such as man or vegetation). The description self-cleansing appears to have been attached to bodies of air, while the equivalent expression self-purification, has been used for bodies of water. *See also* self-purification.

self-diffusion. Spontaneous displacement of chemical components in their own medium caused by thermal movement of particles, *e.g.*, self-diffusion of lead ions in crystals of a lead salt.

self-purification. The general tendency of a body of water to recover naturally from contamination by organic wastes; thus when a river receives, continuously or intermittently, quantities of organic wastes it will tend to purify itself and recover naturally in the course of time. This process of self-purification depends very largely upon biochemical reaction in which bacteria(and other micro-organisms) in the presence of sufficient dissolved oxygen use the organic matter as food, breaking down complex compounds into simpler and relatively harmless products. Other factors such as dilution, sedimentation and sunlight also play an important part in the self-purification process. However, the dominant requirement is a sufficient quantity of dissolved oxygen. If this is used up, that is the rate of absorption of oxygen exceeds the rate of replenishment, self-purification will cease and a septic condition will prevail. Septic conditions are associated with offensive odours, floating masses of black sludge and the termination of aquatic life. The organisms contributing to the process of self-purification include fungi, algae, bacteria, protozoa, crustaceans, shell-fish, worms, insect larvae, snails, fish, dig predatory animals and waterfowl. The last two are the terminal members of the biological self-purification chain in the water.

In water and sewage, the bacteria, algae and fungi absorb dissolved and dispersed organic and the inorganic constituents. In the metabolism of the organisms, these substances are incorporated into the body matter or ultimately broken down into water and carbon dioxide for the purpose of providing energy. In order to sustain these processes, dissolved oxygen is absorbed from the water. Owing to their autotrophic manner of feeding, the algae containing chlorophyll are in a position by day to return the oxygen so absorbed. If the water is quite rich in nutrients, *i.e.*, overloaded with plant nutrients such as nitrogen or phosphorus, these can well be an explosive proliferation of algae. This will result in a shortage of oxygen as, owing to the limited absorptive capacity of the water, once saturation points is reached the oxygen produced by day will by give off in the form of gas. The absorptive capacity depends largely on the water temperature. At higher temperatures, the saturation point is reached more rapidly. If algae are present in the water in over abundance, the oxygen requirements at night will lead to a severe oxygen deficiency. The protozoa, which absorb bacteria and algae as nutrients, are also able to utilize dissolved organic substances to some extent. Crustaceans, snails and worms feed on undissolved, deposited or suspended matter. They also ingest protozoa. Bigger cursaccans and insect larvae, for their part, feed on small curstaceans, worms and also on protozoa. Fish and waterfowl, which are also liable to fall victims to predatory animals in their turn, often prey on curstaceans and worms. The intensity of self-purification is determined not only by optimum functioning of the living communities but also by the conformation of the river-bed. In naturally formed riverbeds, that is to say, in waters with large surfaces and strong turbulence (irregular strong water currents of high turbulence), the higher input of oxygen makes for more favourable living conditions for the organisms than are found in corrected or dammed river courses. Even minor changes in one or another of the determining biological, chemical or physical factors can completely upset the self-purification capacity of the waters.

The oxidation of organic matter during self-purification is effected in two stages:

(i) Carbonaceous oxidation stage, in which most of the organic carbon is oxidized to carbon dioxide. Water and ammonia are also formed from the hydrogen and nitrogen of organic matter.

(ii) Nitrification stage, in which biochemical oxidation of ammonia to nitrous and ultimately nitric acid occurs, and the residual organic carbon is consumed.

Finally, a dark brown or almost black complex organic material remains, known as humus. Deposited by the river bed, it is very resistant to further decomposition by micro-organisms. Humus contains carbon, hydrogen, oxygen and nitrogen with a C:N ratio of about 10:1. A shallow, fast-flowing watercourse will purify itself in a much shorter period of time than a watercourse which is deep and sluggish, through a higher rate of re-aeration. The speed of chemical or biochemical reactions increases with a rise in temperature; hence the process of self purification will tend to be more rapid in the summer months than in the winter months. The speeding up of the process will increase the amount of dissolved oxygen required in any given length of river or stream. However, since warm water contains much less dissolved oxygen than cold water, a heavy pollution load has a greater likelihood of deoxygenating a river or stream in the summer than in the winter, thereby creating septic conditions. In addition, lower summer rainfalls may result in lower dilution factors. *See also* self-cleansing.

semipermeable membrane. A membrane or septum through which a solvent but not certain dissolved or colloidal substances may pass through; used in osmotic pressure determinations. Many natural membranes are semipermeable. Also known as semipermeable diaphragm.

sensitivity. In sensory analysis, the ability to perceive, identify, and/or differentiate, qualitatively and/or quantitatively, one or more stimuli by means of the sense organs. In analytical chemistry, the sensitivity of a procedure is (for a simple procedure) the slope of the calibration curve, *i.e.*, the differential of the measure with respect to concentration, dx/dc. It is not the smallest amount, or lowest concentration, that the procedure will detect; the correct name for the latter quantity is limit of detection.

sensitization. The process of rendering succeptible to the action of some force or state, as radiant energy, acidity, etc. In colloid chemistry, effect of certain substances added in very small quantities to sol on its sensitivity to action of electrolytes.

separate system. A drainage system in which foul sewage and surface-water are conveyed in separate pipes.

separator. An apparatus for separating any one or more of the following of a from a gaseous medium in which they are suspended or mixed:

(a) solid particles (filter and dust separator),

(b) liquid particles (filter and droplet separator), and

(c) gases (gas purifier).

See also dust separator; efficiency; filter; gas purifier; gas washbottle; washer.

septic. A biochemical condition depending on anaerobic bacterial activity, characterized by putrefaction.

septic sewage. A sewave becomes septic due to formation of carbon dioxide and other compounds which ar inimical to bioligical oxidation, when anaerobic digestion takes place due to stagnation of sewage in a sewer line or in a channel or clarifier with sludge accumulations or due to entry of a large volume of supernatant liquor from sludge digester to primary settling tank.

septic tank. A watertight sedimentation tank for organic wastes in which the sludge settling on the bottom is allowed to digest and liquefy by anaerobic bacterial action. The tank may be emptied at interval by a special vehicle, or the effluent may pass into a seepage tank or system of agricultural pipes for final absorption into suitable ground. If an all-wastes septic tank is combined with a sand filter and a chlorination unit, it resembles a miniature sewage works capable, with good maintenance, of handling the wastes from an individual premise or small group of premises.

sequestering agent. A type of chelating or coordination compound (also called a metalion deactivator) which immobilizes (sequesters) the metal ions by binding them into complexes that are both stable and soluble. As a result, the ions are prevented from acting as oxidation catalysts and from forming insoluble precipitates. Ethylenediamine-tetracetic acid (EDTA) and nitrilotriacetic acid (NTA), are the common examples of this type. Sequestering agents are employed for industrial water softening.

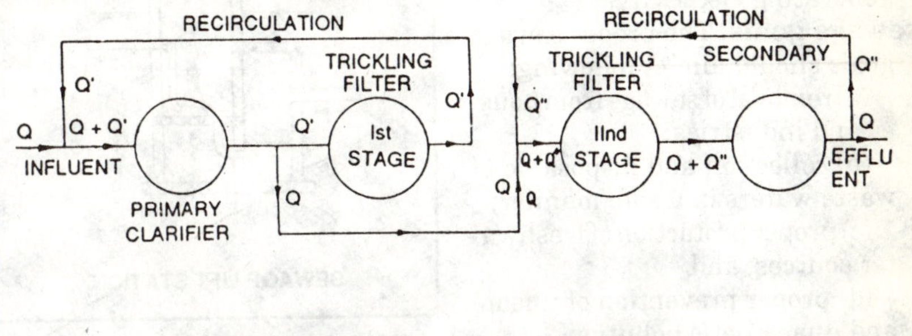

SERIES-PARALLEL TRICKLING FILTER

series-parallel trickling filter. A process of treatment of sewage by two-stage trickling filters with series-parallel arrangement; Its biological oxygen demand removal efficiency is 90 to 95%.

sessile. A term describing permanently attached; stationary; or on a base without a stalk.

settling tank. A tank either rectangular or circular, in which suspended particles settle down and the clarified liquid flows out from top.

sewage. The contents of sewers carrying the waterborne wastes of a community. Sometimes the term foul sewage is used to distinguish between sewage, as defined here, and the contents of sewers carrying surface or storm water only.

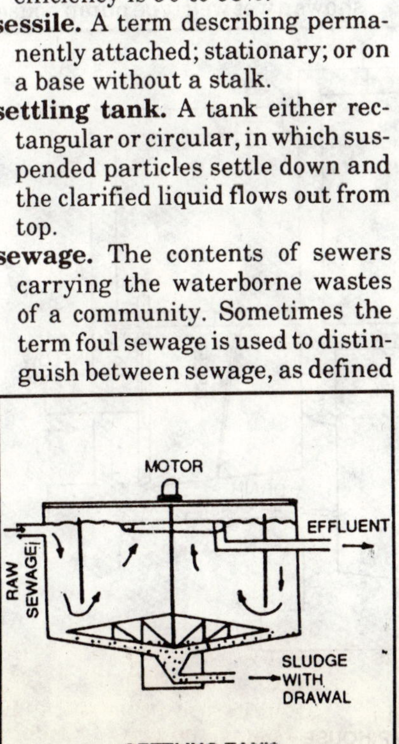

SETTLING TANK

sewage accelerator. A device that combines air diffusion and agitation. The impeller of the accelator is placed close to the bottom of the tank. Air is mixed with the settled sewage entering at the bottom of the tank.

sewage farming. An alternative method of sewage treatment, by land irrigation especially in sandy soil which is capable of taking hydraulic load. the nutrients present in the sewage increase the fertility of the soil. The land should be irrigated with sewage alternately with a proper time gap in between, in order to avoid sewage sickness of the land. This can be successfully employed in areas of low rainfall.

sewage fungus. Unsightly slimes resulting sometimes from the pollution of rivers discharges of organic matter.

sewage gas. The gas generally methane (or mixture of methane (65%), carbon dioxide (32%) and hydrogen sulphide), formed during the bacterial decomposition of sewage and sludge. The gas can be used for cooking, heating, and generating electricity.

sewage goals. The proper sewage goals should aim at following:

(a) removal of sewage from houses and industries;

(b) collection and disposable of waste waters in a safe manner;

(c) proper protection of freshwater sources; and

(d) proper prevention of unsafe and unaesthetic pollution.

sewage lift station. A pumping station installed in sewer network to lift the sewage from a lower level to a higher level, with a view to avoiding too deep excavation for laying sewers. Such a lift station is required to be installed when a sewer invert reaches 6 metres or more below the ground surface.

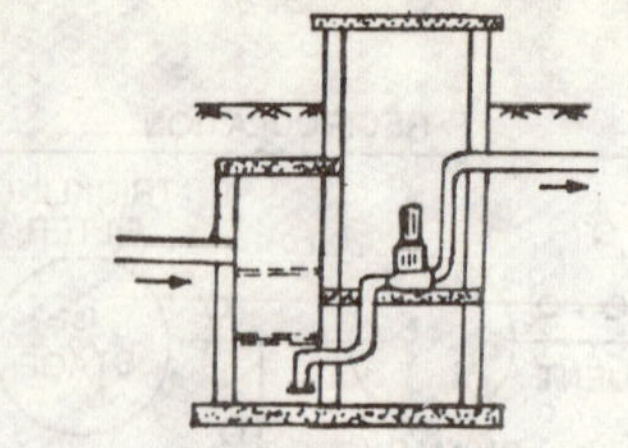

SEWAGE LIFT STATION

sewage pump house. A pump house close to a sewage treatment plant or outfall to pump the sewage from a lower level to a higher level. This may be a dry well type or wet well type. The illustration shows a wet well type pump house.

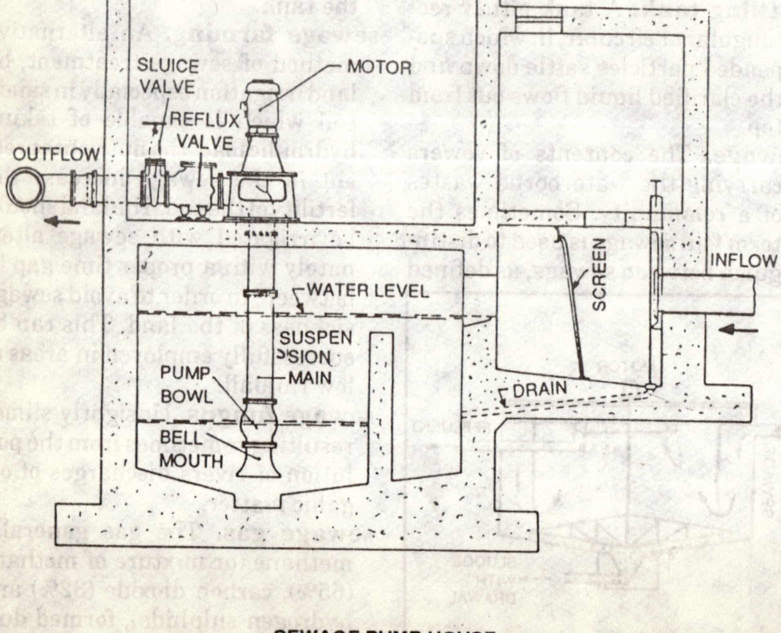

SEWAGE PUMP HOUSE

sewage purification. Until relatively recent times, the self-purification capacity of static running waters was still sufficient to reduce the contaminants contained in them. Loading the waters with sewage from different sources has proliferated, however; and owing to the accretion of these contaminants, the reduction processes in the waterways have either come to a standstill by the extermination of micro-organisms or been intensified by the increase in nutrients. With the multiplication of organisms, more oxygen has been extracted from the waters. The self-purification capacity of the waters has been overloaded, and the regenerative powers of the waters have been disrupted. The immediate consequences of such pollution have been the extermination of fish life, deposition of mud, and putrefaction processes. The most serious loading of the waters stems from domestic and industrial waste disposal. *See* primary treatment; secondary treatment.

The water purified by the primary and secondary treatment, passes finally to the biological stage, which comprises a restoration basin (percolating filter) and a second filter, or final sedimentation tank. In the restoration basin, bacteria and other micro-organisms convert the suspended and dissolved matter into removable sludge by absorbing the particles and dissolved matter as a nutritive substratum and by forming cell lumps as they proliferate, which, owing to their increase in weight, sink to the bottom. The whole process, is facilitated and intensified by artificial induction of air by means of bellows, rotors and cylinder pumps. In order to ensure that the micro-organisms required for decomposition are present in sufficient quantities, parts of the micro-organisms sludge deposited on the floor of the secondary filter tank are returned to the restoration basin. The purified water on the surface of the secondary filter tank is fed in to the receiving stream. The sludge from the primary and secondary settlers is digested in septic towers with the aid of anaerobic bacteria. By this process, methane gas is formed which can be used to provide energy for the plant. Earlier the digested sludge was usually dried out in beds to compact it. In new plants, the preference is for mechanical dehydration plants, such as centrifuges and presses, because of the smaller space they take up. The dehydrated sludge can then be further processed together with household refuse. Under optimum conditions the mechanical-biological sludge drying plant can achieve a purification performance of over 90%. For future purposes, however, this performance level is still too low, so that a further stage, the chemical stage, needs to be added. The chemical precipitation process employed serves to eliminate phosphates and other (especially industrial) pollution. With the aid of microsieves and similar technical appliances, organic resides can be further reduced. In addition, a hygienic improvement in the sewage may be achieved by means of chlorination, radiation, heating or ozonization.

sewage sludge composting. A method of composting undigested sewage sludge without using admixtures. The raw sewage is spread over a drying bed, which is subsequently ploughed, harrowed, and rototilled, and then set up in windrows. Ripe, usable, hygienic compost, with excellent fertilizer values, is produced by this process in about 4-5 months.

sewage treatment. The modification of sewage to make it more acceptable to the environment. Sewage treatment may be divided into four main stages:

1. *Primary treatment.* The removal of suspended matter by physical and mechanical means, *e.g.*, screening, grinding, flocculation or sedimentation.

2. *Secondary treatment.* The removal of finely suspended solids and colloidal matter, and the stabilization and oxidation of these substances and the dissolved organic matter by means of air and the activity of living organisms.

3. *Tertiary treatment.* The attainment of higher effluent standards for many purposes.

4. *Sludge disposal.* The disposal of the suspended matter removed.

A decision as to the stages of treatment to be adopted depends on what is to become of the final effluent. A town situated close to the sea may discharge its sewage without pre-treatment at a suitable distance out to sea; this approach is known as disposal by dilution. Where conditions are not satisfactory for this method of disposal, the final effluent which will be discharged into a watercourse undergoes at least two stages of treatment.

sewer bricks. The special type of bricks having low absorptive power and high resistance to abrasion; employed in the construction of sewer treatment plants.

sewer chimney. When a street sewer is at a great depth, a vertical pipe of smaller diameter with branches encased in concrete, called a chimney is used to facilitate house sewer connection as shown in illustration. The house sewer is connected to the branch at the top of a chimney.

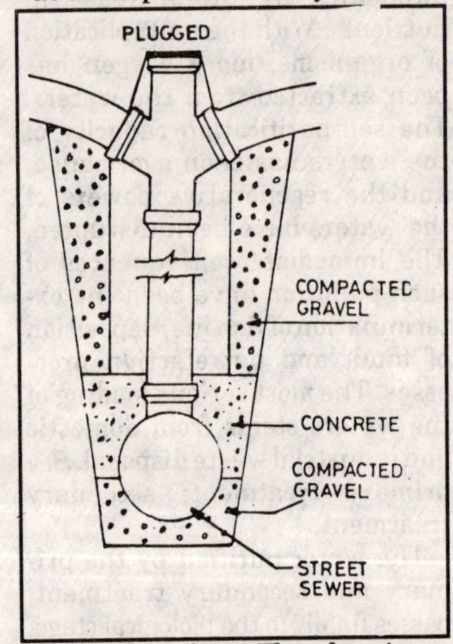

sewer cleaning. The cleaning of small diameter sewers by rodding or by dragging some sewer-cleansing apparatus or device through them. Medium size sewers can be cleaned with the help of movable scrapers. Plows and scrapers ar dragged through sewers to loosen sludge banks within the sewer line. Large diameter sewers can be cleaned manually or mechanically by means of cable and windlass or hydraulic sand ejector or turbine machine.

sewer corrosion. The corrosion of sewers taking place due to the action of hydrogen sulphide gas. The gas evolved gets mixed with methane and carbon dioxide coming out from sludge decomposition, which is corrosive to pipes. Also, hydrogen sulphide can be biologically converted to sulphuric acid, which corrodes sewers.

sewer junction. A typical sewer junction of three sewers meeting at a place. Difficulties arise in providings supports for the partial arches whose supports are cut away in making the junction. It is therefore necessary to build a masonry chamber enclosing the entire junction and with a vault roof spanning all the

sewers. The bottoms of the junction are the mathematical intersections, executed in masonry. Bell mouth arch is used to span the opening.

sewer laying. The laying of a sewer is shown in illustration. On completion of digging preparation of bed roughly by dresing, sight rails or batten boards are placed across the trench at intervals supported on both sides on uprights as shown. Then, the centre line of the sewer is marked on the sight rail by nailing an upright cleat. A cord is stretched between two such cleats. Then, the sewer grade is checked by resting an adjustable bonding rood over the invert of the sewer grade is checked by resting an adjustable bonding rod over the invert of the sewer and keeping it vertical.

sewer nomenclature. The designation of different sewers in a sewer network. The lateral sewers feed a branch sewer and the branch sewers discharge into a trunk sewer. The intercepting sewer receives sewage from turnk sewers and lead to either an arterial sewer or an outfall sewer.

sewer pill. A ball-shaped skeleton frame almost of same diameter of sewer is allowed to pass through the sewer along with the flow of sewage. During its travel it cleans the sewer walls.

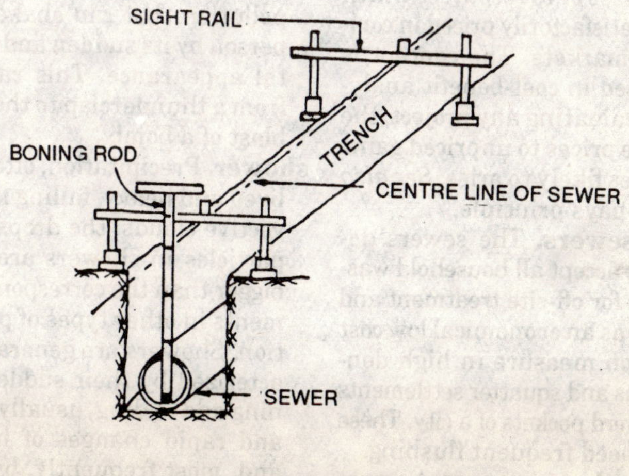

SEWER LAYING

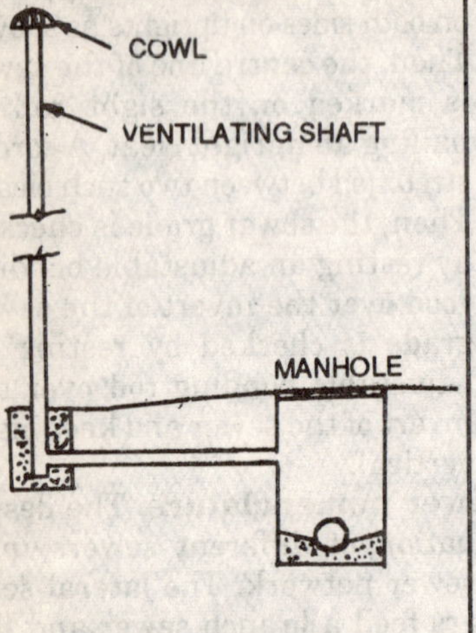

SEWER VENTILATION

sewer ventilation. The ventilation of sewers is sometimes made by providing a ventilating shaft and connecting it to the manhole chamber to drive out the dangerous explosive or corrosive gases. Thus, accumulation of such gases within the sewer line is prevented.

shadow price. A price or value imputed to unpriced social benefits or losses or to resources which are not satisfactorily priced in commercial markets. The concept is much used in cost-benefit analysis. In evaluating any project, the attribute prices to unpriced gains and losses likely to arise. *See also* polluter pays principle.

shallow sewers. The sewers designed to accept all household wastewaters for off-site treatment and disposal as an economical low cost sanitation measure in high density slums and squatter settlements in unsewerd pockets of a city. These sewers need frequent flushing.

shell phosphate process. A scrubbing process for the removal of hydrogen sulphide. In this process, a solution of tripotassium phosphate is employed, which reacts with hydrogen sulphide, producing sulphur, which can be recovered. This helps to reduce the cost of wet scrubbing pollution control operation.

shelter belt. Belts of trees purposely planted to provide protection against prevailing winds; soil erosion is retarded by this technique and crop yields generally improved.

shielding. Protection of the personnel by placing adequate thickness of the appropriate materials around nuclear reactors, and sources of high-energy *X*-rays and radioactive emanations. Lead is most frequently used for *X*-ray protection because of its high density.

shipworms. Troublesome mollusks related to oyster and the clam, that undergo metamorphosis into wormy shapes as they wore into wood.

shock pollution. A form of noise pollution that can shake up any person by its sudden and accidental appearance. This can range from a thunderclap to the sudden blast of a bomb.

shower. Precipitation, often short-lived and heavy, falling from convective clouds; the drops or solid particles in showers are usually bigger than the corresponding elements in other types of precipitation. Showers are generally characterized by their sudden beginning and ending, usually by large and rapid changes of intensity, and, most frequently, by the appearance of the sky; namely, rapid alternations of dark, menacing clouds (cumulonimbus) and of clearances of short duration.

side-entrance manhole. A deep manhole in a trunk sewer having access through the side of the inspection chamber.

sieving. The process of separating a mixture of particles according to their size by one or more sieves. Size analysis by sieving, the division of a sample by sieving into size fractions, and the reporting of results. The International Standard nominal aperture for test sieves are 128 in number, ranging from 22 μm to 12μm.

silica gel. An amorphous form of silicon dioxide that is widely used as a dehydrating agent and as a gas adsorbent in certain methods for the measurement of air pollutant. The term 'silica gel' is a misnomer, since the material is not in fact a gel (although it passes through a gel stage in the course of manufacture).

silver. A white metal, softer than copper and harder than gold. When molten, silver is luminescent and occludes oxygen, but the oxygen is released upon solidification. As a conductor of heat and electricity, silver is superior to all other metals. It has antiseptic properties which are utilized in medicine and dentistry, and it plays an essential part in the formation of photographic images. The other applications are in special batteries, alloys and linings for chemical equipment. Silver forms compounds with the halogen elements, oxygen, and nitrogen. The light-sensitive halides are used in photography; the iodide is effective in atmospheric nucleation for rain-making.

Silver occurs naturally in elemental form and as various ores, such as argentite and horn silver; it is also associated with lead, gold, copper, and zinc ores. Silver is present in the earth's crust at a concentration of about 0.1 mg/kg. It is used as a component of various alloys and solders in photography, electrical equipment, electroplating, for fungicides, silverware, jewellery, coins, and dentalware,. Because of their bacteriostatic properties, silver salts are used for water disinfection and as prophylactic agents.

Levels of silver in natural waters are very low. There is insufficient information to provide precise levels in water, but published data suggest that few water sources contain more than 1 μg/L of silver and levels greater than 10 μg/L are rare.

The conventional water-treatment practices have been shown to be effective in removing silver from water and, consequently, many treated waters contain very low levels of silver. However, because some metals (such as lead and zinc) used in distribution systems may contain traces of silver and also because in some countries silver oxide is used to disinfect water supplies silver levels in tap-water may sometimes be elevated. Levels exceeding 50 μg/L have been recorded on rare occasions, particularly when silver-containing point-of-use water purifiers have been employed to obtain drinking-water. The average levels in tap-water are low and certainly less than 1 μg/L. Assuming a consumption of 2 litres per day the average daily exposure from drinking-water would thus not be likely to exceed 2 μg.

Relatively, little is known about the absorption and metabolism of silver in humans except that individuals absorb the metal selectively. Animals seem to absorb about 10% of any ingested silver. Silver can be detected in various organs; the liver and spleen especially seem to concentrate the metal. In humans, more than 50% of the body burden can be found in the liver 16 days after exposure. Inhaled silver is also absorbed to a slight extent. Silver combines with the sulfhydryl component of some enzyme systems and other biologically important chemical groups, thus influencing the precipitation of proteins and inactivating some enzyme systems. Animal experiments have also shown that silver interacts metabolically with copper and selenium. Most of the absorbed silver is excreted almost exclusively with the faeces, and only small quantities are permanently retained by the tissues the exception being the skin, where larger amounts of silver can accumulate. Silver that is available for excretion has a biological lifetime in the body ranging from a few days to a few weeks.

There is no evidence that silver is essential to the human organism. Cases of fatal poisoning have been recorded but only with extremely high doses. The main effect of silver is discoloration of skin, hair, and fingernails (argyria). This has been detected when silver arsphenamine has been administered as a medication. A single dose of 1 g of silver, injected as silver arsphenamine can produce this effect. The effect has also been observed in workers industrially exposed to silver, the condition is rarely encountered, however. It is possible that argyria may occasionally mask some mild systemic effects. There is no evidence that ingested silver is carcinogenic.

The available data indicate that chronic toxicity to freshwater aquatic life may occur at a concentration as low as 0.12 μg/L. For saltwater aquatic life the concentration of total recoverable silver should not exceed 2.3 μg/L at any time. The ambient water quality criterion for silver has been recommended to be identical to the existing drinking water standard which is 50.0μg/L.

silver thaw. An atmospheric condition when, after a period of cold weather and below-freezing temperature, a mass of warm air passing over the region will cause frost or glaze to form on objectives that are still at a low temperature. A silver thaw usually lasts only a few hours, because the warm air soon warms all exposed objects above 273 K.

silvicide. Nonselective herbicides which kill or defoliate woody plants, bushes and small trees. Ammonium sulphamate has been used effectively for this purpose. Defoliants such as picloram may also be classed as silvicides if the trees die as a result of its application.

sink. 1. In atmospheric chemistry, an area or part of the earth and its atmosphere in which, or a process by which, one or more pollutants is removed from the air. Moist ground, for example, forms an important sink for sulphur dioxide. 2. A swallow-hole or doline. 3. A collapse depression on the flank of a volcano. 4. A depression with no outlet, as where a desert stream comes to an end or disappears by evaporation.

sinking. A technique for controlling oil spills, in which materials are dropped into the oil that will trap the oil molecules, making them heavier than water. The oil along with the sinking agent, is precipitated and settles down under the influence of gravity, and is subsequently biologically degraded by the aquatic life. The use of sinking agents is undesirable because of the possible harm caused by them to the benthos.

sirocco. The hot, dry and sometimes dusty southerly wind blowing from the Sahara; it is experienced in North Africa, Sicily and southern Italy. It is most frequent in spring when the drepession are most active, and the Sahara has already become very hot. The sirocco often has a low relative humidity; it can cause plants to shrivel, and is unpleasant for humans. Sometimes it carries large quantities of dust from Sahara.

site. In the air pollution literature, unless otherwise stated, the location of a measuring instrument.

sky cover. In surface weather observations, a term used to denote one or more of the following:

(a) the amount of sky covered but not necessarily concealed by clouds or by obscuring phenomena, *i.e.*, any atmospheric phenomenon that obscures a portion of the sky from the point of observation;

(b) the amount of sky concealed by obscuring phenomena that reach the ground; or

(c) the amount of sky covered; or concealed by combination of (a) and (b).

Opaque sky cover is the amount of sky cover that completely hides everything above it; transparent sky cover is that portion of sky cover through which higher clouds, blue sky, etc., may be observed; and total sky cover is the two taken together. Sky cover, for any level aloft, is described as thin if the ratio of transparent to total sky cover at and below that level is one-half or more.

Sky cover is reported in tenths, so that 0.0 indicates a clear sky and 1.0 (or10/10) indicates a completely covered sky. According to the summation principle used in U.S. weather observing practice, the sky cover at any level is equal to the summation of the sky cover of the lowest layer plus the additional sky cover provided at all successively higher layers up to and including the layer in question. Thus, no layer can be assigned a sky cover that is less than a lower layer, and no sky cover can be grater than 1.0. If, at any level the ratio of transparent sky cover to total sky cover is one-half or more (excluding transparent portions of surface-based obscuring phenomena), the layer at that level is classified as thin.

slash-and-burn. A method of land clearance in which vegetation is cut, allowed to dry, and then fired prior to cultivation of the soil and the planting of crops. It is common in tropical regions where shifting cultivation and rotational bush fallow are practised.

sleek. The polychromatic film of oil

or grease appearing on the surface of a water body, signalling pollution.

sleet. In meteorology, the term referring to frozen rain. Sleet differs from hail in being simply frozen raindrops, rather than complex concentric structures. It is formed when the falling rain encounters a layer of air next to the ground, in which the temperature is below freezing, and freezes as it falls, reaching the earth as an ice pellet of the same size as the raindrop that began the descent.

slip. The proportion of the grit and dust (or other pollutant) in stack effluents, that is not trapped by dust-collecting or other equipment and that therefore passes out of the stack.

slough. 1. A marshland or tidal waterway which usually connects other tidal areas; often more or less equivalent to a bayou. 2. Rock material that has crumbled from the sides of a borehole; it may obstruct the hole or be washed out in the drilling mud.

slow sand filter. A shallow basin, partly filled with sand and provided with an under-drainage system which is used for the purification of surface-waters intended for domestic water supplies.

sludge. 1. A soft or muddy bottom deposit as on tideland or in a stream bed. It consists of large amounts of organic matter mixed with silt, clay, and sand, and with enough water content to remain in a semisolid state. 2. The solid material removed from the streams of sewage by a sewage treatment plant. It consists primarily of fecal matter, but may also contain food matter from garbage disposals, silt, sand, bits of leaves etc., living micro-organisms, especially algae and bacteria, that have entered the sewage at various points along its path; and chemical precipitates of industrial effluents.

sludge cake. A final biochemical reduction stage in sewage treatment. Raw sludge is a semi-liquid whose solids content varies with the source which may be primary sedimentation, trickling filtered or activated sludge process. The primary purpose of sludge digestion is to change the offensive fresh sludge into an innocuous residue, the organic matter in the fresh sludge being broken down and stabilized by bacteria and other micro-organisms. The digestion of sludge also results in a reduction in volume and improved ability to

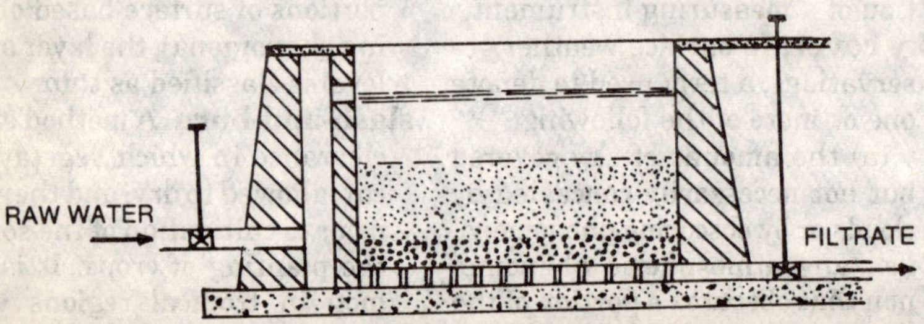

SLOW SAND FILTER

drain and dry. The products of digestion are withdrawn as gas, supernatant liquor and digested sludge. The proceeds from the sale of sludge, if any, help to reduce the overall cost of processing.

The factors having the greatest influence on the rate of digestion are temperature and acidity. To achieve the best results the temperature is maintained at not less than 300 K and the sludge should always be slightly alkaline. In colder climates artificial heating of the sludge is necessary. In the process of sludge digestion the heavier solids separate from the liquid and settle to the bottom whilst floating solids rise to the surface to form scum. The space between the two layers of solids is occupied by a liquid known as supernatant liquor. In most treatment plants the supernatant liquor is drawn off and returned to the primary setting tank. Properly digested sludge is almost black in colour, containing up to 95% water. To remove water, the sludge is spread on drained sand-drying beds. Mechanical methods of dewatering sludges are becoming popular in comparison to drying beds, because they occupy less site space and are independent of weather changes.

Dried Sludge can be used as filling or as a soil builder; it possesses some fertility value. Considerable research is being devoted to work on the treatment and disposal of sludge disposal, as this process frequently involves greater difficulties than any other water treatment operation. Sludge disposal may account for about 25 to 50% of the capital and operating costs of treatment. It is not, however, directly connected with water pollution unless allowed to enter a stream or other body of water. Sometimes the final sewage effluent may be disinfected by chlorination. To ensure an effective destruction of 99.9% of the sewage bacteria, it is necessary to have a chlorine residual of 0.2 to 0.4 parts per million after 20 to 30 minutes of contact.

sludge digestion. Digestion of sludge by anaerobic decomposition which produces sewage gas and reduces the volume of sludge.

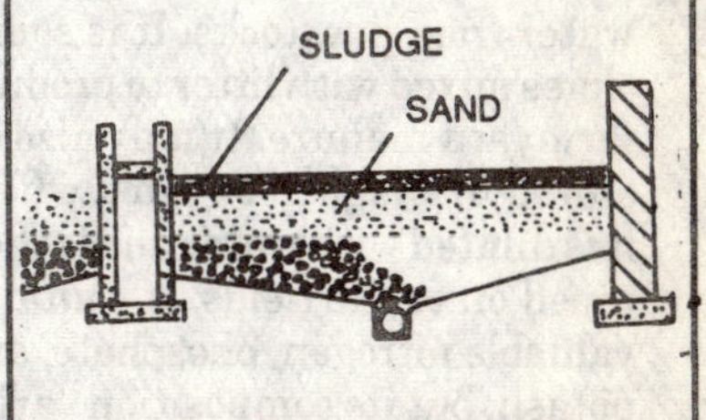

SLUDGE DRYING BED

sludge drying bed. A bed of sand and gravel with under-drainage system, used for drying digested sludge from the digester.

sludge gas. *See* sewage gas.

sludger. 1. A scraping tool used for taking out drilled material from a hole in rock prior to inserting explosive for blasting. 2. A sand pump or a sludge pump.

sludge slurry. A sludge containing a high moisture content as obtained from a clarifier or digester. *See also* slurry.

sludge thickener. A hopper-bottom cylindrical tank in which concentration of primary and secondary sludge takes place with the help of slowly rotating vertical members and squezes with rake blades.

sludge volume index. SVI. The volume in ml. occupied by aerated mixed liquor containing 1 g of dry solids after 30 minutes setting. Also known as Mohlman index. when SVI exceeds 100, setting characteristic is poor and when above 200, bulking of sludge takes place.

slurry. 1. A dilute suspension of particulate solids in water, for example, the aqueous dispersions of clay, fibre particles, or metal powders. 2. A semi-fluid mixture of faeces and urine, often containing rain water and washing down water from livestocks. It is sometimes mixed with litter to produce farmyard manure. It may also be stored in a lagoon or tank, where it is diluted with water and is then piped on to the fields. It contains valuable nitrogen, phosphate, and potash; but its composition varies according to the type of livestock, diet, dilution, etc.

slush. Snow or ice on the ground that has been reduced to a soft, watery mixture by rain, warm temperature, or chemical treatment.

small bore sewers. The sewers used to carry the effluent of septic tank and also the waste water from pour flush toilets in high density slums having no sewerage system. The small bore sewers are connected to the nearest sewerline. This system is marginally cheaper than conventional sewerage system.

smog. A term applied to fog heavily polluted by smoke, particularly under condition of temperature inversion in winter. The term is also applied to the lachrymatory haze produced by photochemical reactions that occur under the influence of strong sunlight in air polluted by automobile exhaust gases under temperature inversion conditions. The latter type of smog is usually referred to as photochemical smog or oxidant smog.

smog index. A mathematical relationship by which the presence or absence of photochemical smog can be determined. Such indices are based on the relationship between smog and the meteorological conditions that are conducive to its formation and take into account factors such as temperature, relative humidity, wind speed, and degree of temperature inversion.

smoke. An aerosol composed of colloidal particles of combustion products dispersed in air combined with the gases resulting from combustion, thermal decomposition, or evaporation. Specialized types of smoke include the fumes from heated metal surfaces and so called military or chemical smoke, which is evolved by reaction of appropriate compounds. The definition of the term in air pollution legislation may vary, but is generally related to emission that can be seen issuing from a stack or chimney. Smoke is undesirable for several reasons:

(a) as visible evidence of incomplete combustion it involves a significant waste of fuel;

(b) in boiler heating surfaces, it reduces the heat transfer rate, increases fuel consumption, and maintenance costs;

(c) being dirty and sometimes greasy, it possesses a high soiling capacity;

(d) it contains substances such as benzopyrine, suspected of possessing carcinogenic activity; and

(e) it obscures sunlight, generates murk and gloom, and increase the intensity and duration of fog.

In addition to carbon, tar and ash, droplets containing dissolved salts and sulphuric acid have been recognized as common constituents of urban air. The vast majority of smoke particles are much less than 1 μm in size and may only be examined in any detail by an electron microscope.

The air pollution control bodies have accepted the view that, with few exceptions, no industrial chimney need normally emit more than a light haze of smoke if the combustion arrangements are adequate and properly operated. The exceptions are:

(i) the emission of dark smoke for occasional short periods when fires are being lighted, or raked, or during soot blowing, or in cases of mechanical breakdown; and

(ii) the emission of dark smoke from industrial processes in which, according to present knowledge, the prevention of dark smoke entails special technical difficulties.

Industrial steam-raising plant does not present special technical difficulties and smoke can be avoided by the employing fuel efficient boilers and latest techniques of efficient combustion. The efficient combustion depends upon:

(a) a sufficient supply of air (oxygen) in relation to the amount of fuel to be burned;

(b) an intimate mixing of fuel and air to ensure that every particle of fuel of molecule of volatile gas receives a sufficient amount of air;

(c) an adequate temperature not only to initiate combustion but to sustain it; and

(d) a sufficient amount of time to allow combustion to be completed before any combustible gases impinge on cool, flame-quenching surfaces.

In practice an excess of air is necessary over the theoretical amount required to achieve intimate mixing. Given sufficient air, efficient combustion then depends on time, temperature and turbulence. See *also* air pollution.

smoke abatement. Legal measures that may by taken (on community, regional, or national level) to control smoke emissions and thus reduce pollution by smoke. In some European countries, the term smoke control is used for such measures.

smoke control zone. Any geographically defined region, usually an urban area, within which it is illegal to produce smoke from chimneys. Many countries have introduced Clean Air Act in order to reduce the quantity of particulate matter in the atmosphere and thus reduce the frequency of smogs which were known to be a major health hazard. The creation of smoke control zones within which smoke control orders apply have done much to improve the atmosphere in urban areas.

smudging. The practice of making smoke to produce an artificial cloud, in an attempt to reduce heat loss from the ground and prevent frost damage to crops.

snout. The downstream end of a glacier. It is an area of melting for most part of the year, and a river is likely to be flowing from underneath the ice, often through a cave. Masses of morainic debris may make the end of the ice look very dirty, and there will be depositional material all around the snout, and also further down the valley, if the glacier is in a period of retreat.

snow. A type of precipitation consisting of water vapour which has frozen into ice crystals. Several ice crystals join together to form a snowflake, which will gradually fall down to earth. Some snowflakes may melt as they fall, especially if the temperature is only just down to freezing point. Under such condition sleet occurs, and for the same reason it is possible for clouds to give snowfall on mountains, while producing rainfall on adjacent lowland areas.

soak pit. *See* seepage pit.

sodium. An element placed in group IA of periodic table. It is present in a number of minerals and seawater. Overall, sodium represents about 26 g/kg of the earth's crust. Sodium and its salts are used for a variety of purposes, including the de-icing of roads, in paper, glass and soap industries, in pharmaceuticals, water treatment, and food industry. It is present in water owing to the high solubility of its salts and abundance of mineral deposits. Seawater contains about 10 g/L of sodium. Coastal areas, windborne sea spray can make important contribution, either by fallout on to land surfaces where it drains to the water source or from washout by rain from the air to surface water sources. Discharge of effluents (domestic as well as industrial) to rivers is another important source of sodium in water.

In most developed countries, the water supplies contain less than 20 mg/L of sodium, but in many countries sodium levels do exceed even 250 mg/L. Apart from saline intrusion and natural contamination, salt used for de-icing roads, water-treatment chemicals such as sodium carbonate, sodium bicarbonate, sodium hydroxide, provide, as individual chemicals, a relatively small contribution, but collectively, the amounts can be significant. Most people are exposed to less than 50 mg of sodium per day by drinking tap-water (based on a consumption of 2 litres per day). Sodium is also naturally present in all foods. The manner in which food is processed, controls the final sodium content of the food. For different individuals, there can be fairly wide range of exposures to sodium. Since sodium is readily absorbed after ingestion, uptake can be considered to be equivalent to the exposure to the element. It is the most abundant cation of plasma and extracellular fluid in man. It is present in bones, in cells, and in most tissues. The level of sodium in extracellular fluid is maintained by the kidney under the influence of endocrine, cardiovascular, and autonomic regulatory mechanisms. In general, sodium compounds are not acutely toxic due to the efficiency with which kidneys excrete sodium. Excessive intake of sodium chloride causes vomiting. Other acute effects include convulsions, muscular twitching and rigidity, cerebral and pulmonary oedema. The effects on infants are different because of the immaturity of infant kidneys. It has been found that severe deterioration of chronic congestive heart failure can result from excessive salt intake, and ill effects due to high levels of sodium in drinking water have been reported. Infants with severe gastrointestinal infections can suffer from fluid loss leading to dehydration and raised sodium levels in plasma; permanent neurological damage is common under such conditions. Although there is no association between hypertension and some diseases, such as coronary heart diseases, genetic differences in susceptibility, possible protective minerals (potassium and calcium), and methodological weakness in experiments make it difficult to quantify a relationship. Sodium levels in drinking-water are generally only a small contributor to dietary sodium.

sodium fluoracetate. A rodenticide marketed under the designation '1080'; it is manufactured from ethyl chloroacetate and potassium fluoride which react to give ethyl fluoracetate; this is then hydrolyzed with sodium hydroxide in methyl alcohol. It is highly toxic and is very stable. Its toxicity for rabbits is very high and indeed is one of the main tools of rabbit control in many countries. It is distributed in chopped carrot. Strict regulations in all the countries should govern its use. The occupational exposure to sodium fluoracetate should be controlled in such a manner so that no employee is exposed to sodium fluoracetate at a concentration greater than 0.05 mg/m^3 of air, determined as a time-weighted average (TWA) concentration limit for up to a 10-hour workshift in a 40-hour workweek, over a working lifetime.

sodium hydroxide. One of the most important commercial compounds of sodium, used in the manufacture of soaps, detergents, rayon, cellophane, and a large number of other compounds. It is corrosive to tissues in the presence of moisture, and is a strong irritant. Occupational exposure to sodium hydroxide is defined as exposure to airborne concentration of sodium hydroxide at or above one-half of the recommended workplace environmental limit. Occupational exposure to sodium hydroxide should be controlled in such a manner so that no employee is exposed to sodium hydroxide at a concentration greater than 2.0 mg/m^3 of air, for any 15-minute period.

softener. This term is widely used in chemical technology in its common meaning to denote a material or agent which is added to a product or process to increase the pliability or plasticity of any substance. A special usage is in the treatment of water in which the term 'water softener' is applied to a substance used to remove undesirable salts.

soft pesticides. Any pesticide that breaks down readily in the environment, yielding harmless decay products.

soil. Product of weathering of the bedrock before removal by erosion. The upper portion of the regolith capable of supporting plant life. It forms the upper layer of the mantle rock of the earth, consisting mainly of very small particle of inorganic mineral matter plus humus; the depth of soil varies up to several metres and is the material from which roots derive both food and moisture. The 'top soil' is the soil that is cultivated; it is more fertile and contains more organic matter than the subsoil which lies beneath it. Soil creep is the almost impermeable but continuous movement of surface soil down slopes, under the influence of thermal and precipitation effects. *See also* pedosphere; soil conservation; soil erosion; soil horizon.

soil and land pollution control. The pollution of the land and soil can be controlled by adopting precautionary measures such as:

(a) use of pneumatic pipes for the economic collection and disposal of wastes;

(b) land filling (biological method of treatment, and incineration are some of the best possible ways of wastes disposal;

(c) pyrolysis (combustion of wastes or anything in the absence of oxygen) for the disposal of wastes;

(d) recycling of the wastes from packaging industries, such as paper, plastics and glass should be done;

(e) the use of night soil *i.e.*, untreated domestic sewage should be minimised; and

(f) biodegradable materials should be developed and used to minimize soil pollution.

soil conservation. The devising and implementing of system of land-use; and management so that there will be no loss stability, productivity, or usefulness of the soil in relation to the selected purpose. Control of soil erosion is state responsibility and all countries have implemented soil conservation programmes aimed at repairing the structural damage which has occurred already and at the development of policies for improved systems of land use to prevent further deterioration. There is, however, as serious continuing problem of loss of productive land due to soil erosion. Conservation tillage practices have been introduced in many parts of the country. The tillage practices involved are mainly stubble mulching and minimum tillage; these represent some of the most important soil conservation measures in the grain-growing areas. The adoption of these practices contributes greatly to the reinstatement of natural hydrologic and hydraulic regimes, and consequently reduces soil erosion rates.

soil erosion. The loss of soil as a result of natural and human activities. The natural erosion is the starting point of pedogenesis (creation of soils) which is indispensable to sustain human life; on the other hand, accelerated erosion due to bad soil management, deforestation, brush and forest fires, overgrazing and poor agricultural practices destroys the soil, with far-reaching consequences. Among the most important measures for combating soil erosion are: re-afforestation, reduction of overgrazing, return of manure to the land, terracing of mountain slopes and contour ploughing.

soil horizon. A layer of soil that is distinguishable from adjacent layers by characteristic physical properties such as colour, texture, or structure, or by chemical composition, including content or organic matter and degree of acidity or basicity.

soil pollution by agricultural practices. Modern agricultural practices are mainly responsible for polluting soil. Insecticides and a host of chemical fertilizers which are used in modern agriculture, are gradully making land infertile by changing the chemistry of soil. The increasing use of artificial fertilizer of global scale to fortify the soil which also pollute the soil to some extent because of presence of some impurities in it. Most of these have been stable chemicals. It is interesting that these stable chemicals remain unchanged without degradation in soil, but the nitrates plays and important role because of there are some possibilities of the nitrate to be washed out into the rivers, lakes etc. and effect their quality. The nitrates activities are mainly due to careless appliances. These as a whole exert cumulative effect. As we know that, purity exceptionally made a place in this so called rapid development stage in every field by man. So, the fertilizers are also got contaminated by other synthetic organic chemical results ultimately in polluting the soil. Among the greater causes of concern in the field of agricultural pollution of soil, the pesticides are of great value in polluting the soil because when they control insect borne diseases and protect the crops, the remanant of these pesticides such as of DDT, BHC, aldrin, dieldrin, endrin etc. may get absorbed into the soil and through which root crops grown in soil may got contaminanted. As we know that pesticides are not only responsible for killing of living organism present on the soil surface. But through tilling and irrigation on the land, they reach even the deep down the earth and destroy, still more living forms. It is not only the limit of pesticides born pollution of soil but some micro-organisms in the soil also loose their capacity of nitrogen fixation. Farmings are not less active in polluting the soil then fertilizers and pesticides. The wastes from cattle sheds and poultries, if not disposed off suitably on to land, it will be the ground for flies, insects etc. which are the carriers of pathogenic organism and ultimately they will to cause serious problem for public health.

soil pollution by domestic wastes. The household activities provide a major amount of solid rubbish (*i.e.*, non-putrescible wastes, which may be combustible or non-combustible. Comustible wastes usually include cloth, paper, wood, leather, garden wastes etc., while non-combustible wastes usually comprise stones, metals, glass, ceramics, dirt, masonary and some chemicals also). But some common domestic wastes which usually play a vital role in polluting the soil are food scarps, vegetable remains, groceries, packing materials, paper, remnants of used coal, ash, wood metals, plastic, glass etc. Most of them are included in the list of non-reusable, and these form the mass of materials of municipal refuse. Those places where these wastes are not properly disposed off, become the homes of rats, flies, bacteria, mosquoitoes etc. and are responsible for causing many human diseases. In dumping domestic wastes areas the large number of rats carry insects and other microorganisms which are mainly responsible for causing human disease viz. plagua. The flies in domestic wastes areas have potential of causing human diseases, they carry pathogenic organism which cause will known diseases like dysentery, diarrohea etc. Thus it is of great concern that, if these domestic wastes are not disposed off properly, this can prove dangerous for our environment and growing population.

soil pollution by industrial wastes. The industries like pulp and paper mills, oil refineries, power and heating plants, chemicals and fertilizer plants, iron and steel plants, plastic and rubber producing complexes etc. are the main sources of land pollution. These industrial wastes contain toxic metals. Solid-waste pollution has been more advanced in the metropolitan cities. It is important to mention here that disposal problems of the industrial wastes become very difficult. It is because of a greater production of waste per unit area, and a decrease proportion of land available for its disposal. Thus, the increased industrail application of air and water pollution controls will also cause an increase in solid wastes which have been destined for land disposal. The industrial wastes containing hazardous chemicals transmitted to man from the soil or crops resulted in causing various diseases.

soil pollution by smelting and mining complexes. Smelting and mining complexes are engaged in soiling the surrounding areas through discharging the heavy metals like cadmium, zinc, lead, copper, arsenic and nickel. It is well known fact, that these heavy metals are very toxic to man, animals and vegetation and act as phytotoxic even in small quantities. These toxic heavy metals enter our body. Some of the organometallic compounds such as methyl mercury and tetraethyl lead are the most toxic compunds known.

soil remnant. An elevated island of soil protected by vegetation that has survived while the unprotected soil around it has been washed away by erosion. Soil remnants are indicative of a badly deteriorating range. This term has also been applied to the pedestals of soil that develop beneath pieces of lag gravel.

soil scarification. Disturbance of the soil or ground surface, especially when the disturbances are not of uniform dimension and spacing. Soil scarification may be accidental, as when felling trees or yarding logs in forestry, or it may be deliberate, as in the practice known as chaining, where a heavy chain dragged between two tractors churns up the soil surface and clears it of bushes and small trees. Light scarification is often good for the soil, loosening and turning it over and helping to prepare it for further planting.

sol. A term used to denote a liquid colloidal dispersion of solid particles, for example, gold, in water the dispersion is stabilized by electric charges, either all negative or all positive, the particles being kept from colloiding or flocculating by mutual electrical repulsion. The 'sol' state is opposed to the 'gel' state, in which the dispersion is a thick, semisolid mass. The word is a shortened form of solution, not of solid.

solar energy. The energy of the sun which reaches and earth in the form of short-wave radiation, visible light and near-ultra-violet light. After penetrating the atmosphere, part of the energy heats the surface of the earth and part of it is re-radiated back in the form of long-wave radiation and absorbed by water vapour and carbon dioxide in the atmosphere. The latter radiates again about half of the captured energy back towards the earth's surface. The warming caused by trapped energy is known as greenhouse effect. The possible utilization of solar energy for the generation of electricity is receiving an increasing amount of attention in India and elsewhere where sunlight is abundant. While sunlight is essential to living things, it is thought to be the most frequent cause of skin cancer.

solar pond. An experimental means of storing solar energy in either fresh or salt water. The 'pond' is a large, suitably lined open container of varying dimensions.

solar still. A device for converting sea water into fresh water by evaporation. The sea water is collected in one or more pools and a transparent cover made of glass or plastic is placed over it. Heat from the sun evaporates the water, leaving behind a residue of salts; the vapours from the evaporated water condenses on the surface of the receiving tank.

solid. A material that has a vertical flow of 2 inches (50 mm) or less within a 3-minute period or a separation of 1 gram (1 g) or less of liquid when determined in accordance with the procedures specified in ASTM D 4359-84 standard test method for determining whether a material is a liquid or soild.

solid waste. A solid waste as defined in Section 261.2 of 40 CFR.

solid waste management. A planned system of effectively controlling the production, storage, collection, transportation, processing and disposal or utilization of solid wastes in a sanitary, aesthetically acceptable, and economical manner. It include all administrative, financial, legal, and planning functions, as well as the physical aspects of solid waste handling.

solid waste management unit. Any discernible waste management unit at a RCRA facility from which hazardous waste or constituents might migrate, irrespective of whether the unit was intended for the management of solid and/or hazardous waste.

The solid waste management unit definition includes:

(a) Containers, tanks, surface impoundments, container storage areas, waste piles, land treatment units, landfills, incinerators, underground injection wells, and other physical, chemical and biological units, including those units defined as regulated units under RCRA.

(b) Recycling units, wastewater treatment units, and other units that EPA has generally exempted from standards applicable to hazardous waste management units; and) areas associated with production processes at facilities that have become contaminated by routine, systemic, and deliberate discharges of waste or constituent.

soild waste pollution. The soild waste includes glass containers as bottles, croleries, plastic containers, polythene and other packing materials that are used and then thrown away as garbage. These pile up at public places and cause obstruction in daily life. Besides these there are also other used things like automobile spares, machines, cycle parts etc. that are thrown as junk. The wastes from building material (during construction and demolition), sludge, dead animal skeletons, heaps of crop residues also contribute to solid waste.

To slove these problems technologies have been developed to recycle most of the solid waste items. Thus paper cans, newspapers and other waste paper may be easily recycled. Metallic components of vehicle spares,may be recycled by cheap methods. However, there is problem of recycle of heavy metals, plastics, nylon, polythene etc. To control solid waste pollution, following methods have been suggested:

(a) recycling,

(b) burning of waste and utilising heat to warm residential units and, generation of electricity,

(c) composting of organic waste for preparation of manure and biogas.

solid wastes. All material of a solid or semi-solid character that are no longer considered of sufficient value to retain.

sonic boom. A phenomenon caused by supersonic aircraft crashing the sound barrier, *i.e.*, flying faster than the velocity of sound (about 1,200 km/h).

sorption. A general term employed for description of ability of taking up given substance (sorptive) from liquid bulk by another condensed phase. This term is also used by chemists in cases when it is not clear whether adsorption or absorption is involved, or when both are occurring simultaneously. It is used to combat water and air pollution.

sound and noise. Sound is the result of any oscillation of air molecules that is perceptible to the organs of hearing. It is measured by reference to the pulsating load pressure generated in the air. To facilitate comparison of readings on a standard basis over the whole field, the sonic pressures are set out in a logarithmic scale. While the sonic pressure that a sound wave exerts on the eardrum can be measured objectively; there is no unit of measurement that can be applied to the physiological effects of sound or noise on the human organism. The unit of measurement used to record the acoustic pressure level is the decibel (dB). High audio frequencies are more clearly perceptible than lower frequencies. To allow for this circumstance in obtaining a sound, evaluation curves have been prepared depending on the audio frequency. In general, the evaluation is made according to a curve bearing the letter *A*, and the result of sound-level measurements are recorded accordingly in terms of dB (*A*). The evaluation curve is so devised that an increase in the sonic pressure level that seems to the individual to amount to a doubling of the sound volume is expressed in the scale as a rise of 10 dB (*A*). Apart from the intensity of sound, its duration is also a factor in determining the noise effect, so it is evacuated according to the duration of the average sound level over a period (average level, equivalent duration sound level). To enable consideration to be given to further factors such as the height and number of peak levels (for assessing sleep disturbance). Their impact whether they are customary in the district, and the nature and commercial background of the noise, an assessment level is established based on the average level. This should provide a measure by which to judge the physiological effect of a noise level. At present several divergent bases are in use for measurement and assessment purposes. The 'phon' unit, which was frequently used previously, corresponds in general terms to the decibel unit in regular use today.

The term noise is difficult to define precisely, as in addition to measurable factors various subjective elements, such as the personal attitude and the general physical and mental makeup of the party concerned, also play a part. A good definition of the term is: 'by noise is understood such sounds as influence the physiological functions of the organism unfavorably, and such as exert a psychic influence on people, and disturb, annoy, anger or frighten them, and damage their hearing'.

spallation. The smashing of atomic nucleus into several fragments by high energy particles. This type of nuclear reaction result from bombardment of atoms with high energy projectiles, such as 200 meV protons and 400 meV alpha particles, whereby nuclei having atomic numbers 10 to 20 lower than the bombarded nucleus are obtained. Spallations differ from nuclear fission process in that the reaction is not self sustaining and that the changes in nuclear mass in spallation are not large as usually encountered in fission.

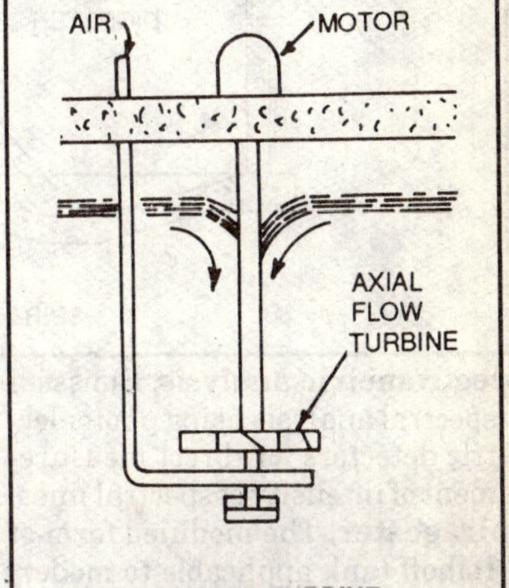

SPARGED TURBINE

sparged turbine. An axial flow turbine used for aeration of sewage.

spectrofluorimetry. Measurement of intensity of split fluorescence spectrum. This term is frequently applied in context of fluorimetric analysis utilizing spectrofluorimeter. Also known as spectrofluorimetry. This technique is employed to determine many pollutants in the industrial effluents.

spectrographic analysis. Spectroanalysis based on measurement of sample emission spectrum record on photographic plate.

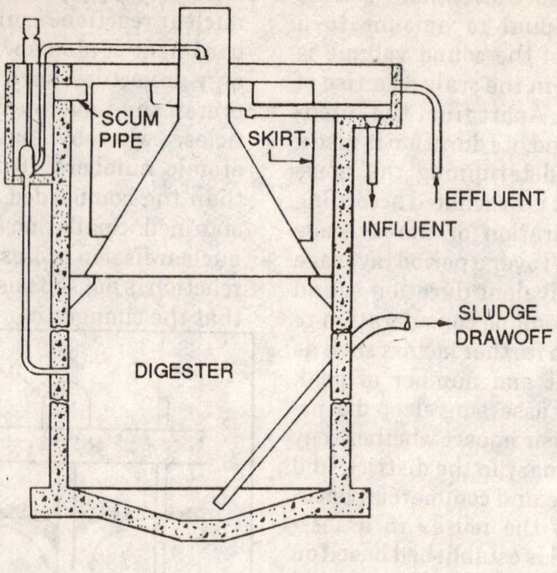

SPIRAGESTER

spectrometric analysis. Emission spectral analysis using photoelectric detectors for direct measurement of intensity of spectral lines.

spiragester. The modified form of Imhoff tank applicable to moderate size installations. It has three compartments viz., flow-through chamber, digestion chamber, and scum chamber. The sedimentation and digestion of sludge takes place in separate compartments of the same tank.

spontaneously combustible material. A solid substance (including sludges and pastes) that may undergo spontaneous heating or self-ignition under conditions normally incident to transportation or may upon contact with the atmosphere undergo an increase in temperature and ignite.

spraying. *See* pollution from spraying.

spur. 1. The group of ionic and free radical products of radiolysis located close to one another in zone of primary ionization of high energy particle or photon. Spur region diffuses with time and eventually becomes indistinguishable with bulk of liquid. 2. An area of high ground which protrudes into an area of lower ground such as a river valley. Spurs alongside valleys are gradually eroded by the river but in the upper and middle courses especially, they often form interlocking spurs. In glacial valley many of the spurs will have been truncated.

sputter. A method of producing systems containing very small particles of metals, as, *e.g.*, metals sols, by passing an electrical arc between two metallic electrodes placed the surface of a liquid or, sometimes, in a gas.

stabilizer. Any substance added to another substance or mixture to prevent or retard a chemical or physicochemical change, at least for a considerable time. As this function can occur in many different ways, the term is a very general one, which includes antioxidants, inhibitors, emulsifiers protective colloids, etc.

standard. Levels of exposure to pollutants which should not be exceeded; standards may be statutory or presumptive. Two levels have been adopted by the U.S. Environmental Protection Agency:

1. primary levels judged necessary to protect health with an adequate margin of safety, and
2. secondary. levels judged necessary to protect public welfare from any known or anticipated adverse effects. These are essentially environmental quality standards. Standards may also prescribe the contents of products, *e.g.*, the amount of phosphates in detergents, or pesticide residues in foodstuffs. They may also take the form of emission standards, *e.g.*, the upper limits of what may be emitted from the exhausts of motor vehicles or from the chimneys of industrial plants. *See* product standard.

standing crop. The biomass or organic matter present on a given area at a given time; it usually varies in quantity with the season.

static stability. A fundamental concept in meteorology; it refers to what happens to a parcel of air after it has been given an initial vertical displacement, either upwards or downwards. If, after an upward displacement, the parcel is found to be warmer (less dense) than its surroundings, its buoyancy will make it move farther from its original position; it will continue to move until its temperature (and density) become equal to that of its surroundings. In this instance in which a parcel moves farther from its original level, the surrounding atmosphere is said to e statically unstable (or just unstable). If after displacement, however, the parcel is found to be colder (more dense) than its surroundings, its buoyancy will tend to return the parcel to its original level; the surrounding atmosphere is then said to be statically stable (or just stable). In the intermediate stage when the vertical motion is neither encouraged nor opposed, the atmosphere is said to be neutrally stable. The concept of static stability is of considerable importance in the study of the dispersal of air pollutants in the atmosphere. See *also* air pollution.

steepness of slope. A characteristic of land expressed in terms of percentages, *e.g.*, a 10% slope is one which drops 10 metres over a horizontal distance of 100 metres. Intensity of water run-off and soil erosion are partially dependent on the relative slope of the terrain.

storm sewer. A sewer designed to handle the runoff that results from precipitation (rain, snow, hail, *etc.*), as opposed to one designed to handle domestic or industrial wastewater. Storm sewers are usually considerably larger than sewers that handle wastes. They are generally built in a network parallel to that of wastewater sewers, but are emptied directly in to the receiving waters instead of going through the sewage treatment plant.

storm surge. A rise above normal water level on the open coast due only on the water surface; includes the rise on level due to atmospheric pressure reduction as well as that due to wind stress. Also known as storm wave; surge.

storm tank. A tank, usually located at a sewage treatment works, provided for storage and partial treatment of excess storm sewage prior to discharge to a watercourse or other body of water.

storm water. Natural water from the surface of the ground, paved areas and roofs.

storm water overflow. An arrangement whereby all excess flow of sewage an surface-water in a combined sewer system is by-passed to watercourse. A common engineering practice has been to provide for the interception and treatment of a sewage and surface-water flow equal to two or three times the average dry-weather flow; all flow in excess of this amount is directed to a water course. Storm water overflows may be provided at several points in a system. Of major concern during periods of overflow or surcharge are the flooding of basements with a mixture of sewage and storm water, and the additional pollution load imposed on water courses. It is not feasible to design systems which will accept the maximum possible flow, due to the large volumes of run-off which occur in very short periods of time. One solution is to completely separate the sewage and surface-water systems, so that no storm water enters the sewage system; another lies in the provision of holdings tanks or ponds to receive excess storm water and release it slowly to treatment plants or watercourses.

STP. Conventional abbreviation for standard temperature and pressure. The standard temperature is 273.16 K and the pressure is 1 atmosphere.

stratocumulus. The cloud type consisting of large, globular masses, soft and grey in appearance. The masses are often arranged in a regular pattern.

stratosphere. The upper layer ot the atmosphere lying above the troposphere (above about 11 km altitude) in which the temperature remains constant with height and no convection occurs. The mean temperature is reached at about 48 km, which marks the stratopause. This rise in temperature is essentially due to the absorption of the UV radiation from the sun by ozone molecules.

stratus. A uniform layer of cloud which resembles fog, but which is above ground level.

stream. A body of running water or any other moving liquid under the influence of gravity to lower levels in a narrow, clearly defined natural channel.

stream capacity. The ability of a stream to carry detritus; expressed as per unit time at a given point.

stream channel. A long, narrow sloping trough-like depression where a natural stream flows or may flow.

stream erosion. The progressive removal of exposed matter from a surface of a stream channel by a stream.

streamflow. A type of channel flow, applied to surface runoff moving in a stream.

streamflow regulation. One of the methods of water quality control in which good quality stored water, is added to a stream at times of deteriorating stream water quality. There are three aspects to an effective streamflow regulation scheme:

(i) the deterioration of downstream water quality must be determinable;

(ii) good quality, impounded water must be available for release and must be released as required; and

(iii) there must be a beneficial effect downstream from the release of impounded water. *See also* beneficial use; water pollution.

stream load. All the material that is transported by a stream. The dissolved load consists of material in ionic solution; the ions are part of the fluid and move with it. They are derived from groundwater that has filtered through weathering soil and rocks. The suspended load is comprised of clay, silt, and sand particles so fine that they remain in suspension almost indefinitely.

street gulley. A receptacle or a chamber with an entry point with grate and an outlet pipe connecting the street sewer. This is constructed at the edge of a road and under the road surface to receive the discharge from gutters and to convey it to the sewer.

stress. The non-specific response of a body or organism to any demand made upon it, primarily preparing the organism for physical activity, *e.g.*, fight or flight. Stress is one of the mechanisms suspected of leading to disease in modern life.

strong outside container. The outermost enclosure that provides protection against the unintentional release of its contents under conditions normally incident to transportation or may upon contact with the atmosphere undergo an increase in temperature and ignite.

strontium. A comparatively soft metal of the alkaline-earth group, placed in group IIA of periodic table; similar in many respects to calcium. In terms of content in sea-water, the element ranks 11th, with an estimated 8208 metric tons in a cubic kilometre of seawater. It is quite reactive and quickly forms an oxide coating when exposed to dry air. It has strong reducing properties, decomposing water to evolve hydrogen; it must be protected from moist air by storage under naphtha. There are four stable isotopes, Sr-84 and Sr-86 through Sr-88, and seven known radioactive isotopes Sr-82, Sr-83, Sr-85, and Sr-89 through Sr-92, all with relatively short half-lives measurable in hours or days, except Sr-90. The latter isotope represents a hazard from nuclear blasting activities because of its long half-life, tendency to contaminate food products, such as milk, and retention in the body.

strontium unit. A measure of the concentration of strontium-90 in an organic medium (*e.g.*, milk, bone, soil, etc.) relative to the concentration of calcium in the same medium.

subacute toxicity tests. The adverse effects tests produced after subacute exposure, eliciting subacute toxicity. Subactue toxicity results from repeated exposures over a period of several days or months. Such studies are carried out at three or more dose levels in two or more species, as in animals, one species is non-ordent. One of the major objectives of subacute toxicity is to establish a dose which could be classified as a no effect dose or that dose which, if exceeded can be considered harmful to man.

sublimation. The direct transition, under suitable conditions between the vapour and the solid state of a substance. At pressures near the triple point the heat of sublimation is approximately equal to the sum of the heats of fusion and vaporization. In physical and chemical literature, it is customary to regard as sublimation only the transition from solid to vapour, not from vapour to solid; but meteorologists do not make this distinction.

subsidence inversion. A temperature inversion formed in the atmosphere usually well above the earth's surface, as a result of the slow descent of air which becomes warmer through adiabatic compression.

subsoil. The layer which is situated below the top soil. It may not contain any organic matter, but is likely to include fragments of rock. It is approximately equivalent to the *C*-horizon.

subsoil water. The geological name given to water occurring naturally in the subsoil.

substitutions effects. The environmental consequences of substituting, for example, one form of control or methods of disposal for another. Scrubbing water gases converts an air pollution problem into a liquid waste problem, while the installation of domestic garbage disposal units converts a solid waste disposal problem into a liquid waste disposal problem.

succession. The replacement of one community or population by another as a result of changes in the environment.

sullage water. Household water, other than sewage; contaminated water from kitchens, bathrooms and laundries. In unsewered areas, sullage water is often discharged directly to creeks. *See also* combined sewer;, septic tank.

sulphate. The anion (SO_4^{2-}) formed from the ionization of sulphuric acid. The sulphates of alkali metals are soluble in water, the sulphates of lead, barium, and strontium are insoluble. Dissolved sulphate is considered to be a permanent solute of water. It may, however, be reduced to sulphide, volatilized to the air as hydrogen sulphide, precipitated as an insoluble salt, or incorporated in living organisms. Sulphates are discharged into the aquatic environment in the wastes from many different industries. Atmospheric sulphur dioxide (SO_2), formed by the combustion of fossil fuels and emitted by the metallurgical roasting processes, may also contribute to the sulphate content of surface water. Sulphur trioxide (SO_3), produced by the photolytic or catalytic oxidation of sulphur dioxide, combines with water vapour to form sulphuric acid, which is precipitated as 'acid rain' or snow.

Data concerning the daily dietary intake of sulphates are scarce. Sulphate compounds used in US as additives in foods are estimated to contribute an average of 453 mg to the daily sulphate intake. Daily intake of sulphate from drinking-water, depends upon the source and quality of water, and is extremely variable. Sulphate is poorly absorbed from the human intestine; it slowly penetrates the cellular membranes of mammals and is rapidly eliminated through the kidneys. The reported minimum lethal dose of magnesium sulphate in most of the mammals is about 200 mg/kg of body weight. Sulphate dose of 1.0-2.0 g have a cathartic effect on humans, resulting in the purgation of the alimentary canal. Infants ingesting sulphate equivalent to 21 mg/kg of body weight per day may also suffer from this effect. Magnesium sulphate at concentrations above 1000 mg/L acts as a purgative in normal humans, but concentrations below this are apparently physiologically harmless. Sensitive people are responsive to magnesium sulphate levels as low as 400 mg/L and new users or those consuming occasionally may be affected by concentrations in excess of 700 mg/L. The human system adapts in the course of time to higher concentrations of sulphate in drinking-water.

Taste threshold concentrations for the most prevalent sulphate salts are: 200-500 mg/L for sodium sulphate; 250-900 mg/L for calcium sulphate; and about 400-600 mg/L for magnesium sulphate. Essentially on the basis of the above values, which are also applied to the cathartic effect of sulphate, the guideline value of 400 mg/L has been proposed.

sulphite-reducing clostridia. The anaerobic spore-forming organisms, of which the most characteristic, *C. perfringens (C. welchii)*, is normally present in faeces though in much smaller numbers than *E. coil*. Clostridial spores can survive in water longer than organisms of the coliform group and they can resist disinfection if the concentration, contact time, or *p*H is unsatisfactory. Their persistence in disinfected waters may thus indicate deficiencies in treatment. However, it would not be desirable to consider these organisms for the routine monitoring of distribution systems since they tend to survive and accumulate; they may thus be detected remote in both time and place from the original source of pollution and consequently give rise to false alarms.

sulphur. A yellow solid element placed in group VIA of the periodic table. Its low melting point permits extraction in liquid form by pumping superheated water into the limestone deposit. Both rhombic and monoclinic forms contain S_8 molecules, when melted, produce the same liquid, which is also composed of S_8 molecules. As the temperature of the liquid is raised, S_8 rings are broken into chain by the thermal collisions. The stable isotopes of sulphur are S-32, S-33, S-34, and S-36. There are three known radioactive isotopes S-31, S-35, and S-37, with S-35 having the longest half-life. It is present in coal and oil, being derived from the substances from which they were formed. The sulphur may be either chemically or physically mixed with the fuel. The sulphur content of coals ranges from 0.3 to 3.5%. Sulphur is present in coal in three forms:

(a) pyrites;

(b) sulphates, present only in very small quantities and rarely exceeding 0.03%; and

(c) organic sulphur compounds, cleaning processes having virtually no effect on this type of sulphur.

The ratio of pyritic to organic sulphur varies considerably. High-rank coals tend to be low in sulphur, medium-rank coals high in sulphur, while low-rank coals appear to be fairly average. During the combustion of coal, most of the sulphur is released to the atmosphere, mainly as sulphur dioxide together with a small amount (1 to 3%) of sulphur trioxide With coal and coke burned in domestic heating appliances, about 20% of the sulphur is retained in the ash or clinker. In industrial boilers and furnaces, only about 10% of the sulphur is retained in the ash. The crude oils of the middle East have an average sulphur content of about 2.5%; most of this sulphur appears in the final products, being less than 1% in diesel and gas oils and up to 4% or more in residual oils. During the combustion of oil virtually the whole of the sulphur is released to atmosphere, mainly in the form of its oxides.

sulphur cycle. The circulation of sulphur atoms brought about mainly by living things. The decomposition of proteins containing sulphur (*e.g.*, egg albumin) under aerobic conditions results in the formation of sulphates which are odourless and relatively harmless. However, when such proteins undergo decomposition by anaerobic bacteria the foul-smelling gas hydrogen sulphide is produced. Other malodorous sulphur compounds may also be produced under certain conditions, *e.g.*, methyl mercaptan (CH_3SH) is produced when a river or other body of water is devoid both of dissolved oxygen and nitrate. Sulphur circulates globally between air, land, and sea. A large part of the sulphur in the global atmosphere (as distinct from the atmosphere of towns) is emitted originally as hydrogen sulphide from natural sources; much of this hydrogen sulphide is converted later to sulphur dioxide. Sulphur, either in the form of sulphur dioxide, sulphur trioxide, hydrogen sulphide, or sulphate salts, is removed from the atmosphere in rain, drizzle and fog, and by gaseous absorption in the oceans. Only about one-third of the discharge to atmosphere is due to combustion processes, the balance being attributable mainly to release from sea-spray and biological decay.

sulphur dioxide. A colourless, pungent gas formed when sulphur burns in air. It is considered to be one of the most important air pollutants; most of the sulphur dioxide in the general atmosphere comes form the combustion of the sulphur present in most fuels. Sulphur dioxide is formed by the combustion of fossil raw materials which, because of their organic origin, contain sulphur, and by various processes in the chemical industry. The dangerous nature of sulphur dioxide in due to the fact that it penetrates the respiratory tract and damages the numerous small delicate cilia of the bronchial mucous membrane, whose task it is to expel dust and aerosol particles. Owing to the effects of sulphur dioxide, inhaled dust and soot particles remain in the lungs and pursue their toxic activities there. Apart from its damaging effects on health, sulphur dioxide also exercises an influence on vegetation. It is highly probable that a synergism with fluorine waste gases plays some part in the damage to plants by sulphur dioxide. The damage manifests itself in discoloration of the tips of the leaves to complete bleaching of the leaves. The patches may be red, brown or yellow. The leaves then dry up, curl and fall off. Coniferous trees are particularly seriously affected, and may die off altogether.

Finally, sulphur dioxide is known to have a destructive effect on other inorganic materials. Many edifices from the Middle ages, which had survived undamaged for centuries, have suddenly begun to disintegrate in recent decades. Sulphur dioxide and waste gases are particularly prone to attack limestone and marble; since sulphur dioxide combines with water to form sulphurous acid, which attacks calcium carbonate (lime, marble). Exposure to sulphur dioxide is defined as exposure to airborne concentration of sulphur dioxide at or above one-half of the recommended workplace environmental limit. Occupational exposure to sulphur dioxide should be controlled in such a manner so that no employee is exposed to sulphur dioxide at a concentration greater than 5.0 mg/m^3 of air (2 ppm), determined as a time-weighted average (TWA) concentration limit for up to a 10-hour workshift in a 40-hour workweek, over a working lifetime.

sulphur tetrafluoride. A highly toxic gas, that is strong irritant to eyes and mucous membranes. It is used as a florinating agent for making water and oil repellents, and lubricity improvers. Occupational exposure to sulphur tetrafluoride should be controlled in such a manner so that no employee is exposed to sulphur tetrafluoride at a concentration greater than 0.4 mg/m^3 of air (0.1 ppm), determined as a time-weighted average (TWA) concentration limit for up to a 10-hour workshift in a 40-hour workweek, over a working lifetime.

sulphur trioxide. A constituent of flue gases from sulphur bearing fuels, frequently to the extent of 3 to 5% of the sulphur dioxide present. Several mechanisms appear to contribute to its formation; in every case a supply of oxygen is necessary. Thus the reduction of excess air tends to inhibit the formation of this corrosion-promoting gas. According to U.S. National Ambient Air Quality Standard (NAAQS), the amount of sulphur oxides in air should not exceed 365 μg/L for any 24-hour period. *See also* aerosols; photochemical smog.

summer feeding. The supplying of water to marshland in the summer, usually by impounding river water to prevent natural drainage and the lowering of the water table.

sump. A pit or underground chamber into which water, hazardous waste, or sewage is collected and then pumped to a higher head for further transporation of water or sewage.

sump pump. A pump provided for emptying a sump.

superadiabatic lapse rate. A lapse rate greater than the dry adiabatic lapse rate, *i.e.*, greater than 10° C per kilometre. The dry adiabatic lapse rate is often exceeded by a factor of several times close to a land surface which is strongly heated by solar radiation. Turbulence in the atmosphere is strong and the dilution of water industrial gases more rapid than in average or neutral conditions.

superboom. The magnified shock wave arising when waves from a number of points along the path of an aeroplane travelling at supersonic speed all meet in phases at one point on the ground.

supernatant liquor. The liquid that leaves a digester by the overflow pipe when fresh sludge is introduced into it. The liquid is normally offensive in odour having suspended solids 0.05 to 0.10% and total solids 0.10 to 1.20%. It is discharged into the influent of primary clarifier. when the liquid contains more than 0.5% of total solids, it may cause floatation of sludge in primary clarifier.

superphosphate. A mixture of compounds obtained as a result of a long established process for the production of chemical fertilizers is the treatment of phosphate rock with concentrated sulphuric acid. The product of this reaction, as practiced in industry is a mixture of calcium sulphates and calcium phosphates containing more or less of the acid salts, which is called superphosphate.

surface-active agent. This term and its condensed synonym surfactant conventionally refer to substances that reduce the interfacial or surface tension of liquids; it could logically be applied to catalysts also, since their action depends directly on surface activity. These compounds are used to combat oil pollution

surface currents. The currents set in motion in the tropics by the powerful trade winds and by differences between the density of tropical waters and polar waters. Cold water is more dense than warm water. Furthermore, sea level is slightly higher in the tropics than in polar latitudes and water tends to flow down this slight decline. Sea level is a few centimetres higher in the tropics because daily rainfall adds water to the surface of the sea faster than the water can spread out horizontally. Also, heat from the sun causes tropical waters to expand and to have a greater volume than polar waters.

Trade winds, the easterlies blow steadily from northeast to southwest in the northern hemisphere. They blow from southeast to northwest in the southern hemisphere. Trade winds drive the ocean waters before them. But rotation of the earth deflects ocean currents even more than it does air currents. Movement at the surface of the sea is almost due west in both hemispheres in the zone of the trade winds. The westward moving currents meet the continents which form barriers. Water is turned toward the north and toward the south. Along the eastern coast of North America the Gulf Stream a warm, swift current carries water northward. The Brazil current moves water southward along the eastern coast of South America. Similar currents in the Pacific Ocean carry water along the eastern coast of Asia.

In both hemispheres, the surface currents move poleward until they reach the zone of the westerly winds. Then the currents are carried eastward in front of the westerlies until they meet another continent. When eastward moving currents come in contact with a continent, some water flows poleward. The rest flows toward the equator. In the zone of the trade winds this water meets and joins the westward flowing currents. Major surface currents follow a circular path around a central, relatively quiet body of water in both the Atlantic and Pacific oceans.

surface impoundment. A facility or part of a facility that is a natural topographic depression, man-made excavation, or diked area formed a natural topographic depression, man-made excavation, or diked area formed primarily of earthen materials (although it may be lined with man-made materials), that is designed to hold an accumulation of liquid wastes or wastes containing free liquids, and that is not an injection well. Examples of surface impoundments are holding, storage, settling, and aeration pits, ponds, and lagoons.

surface water. Water which fails to penetrate into the subsoil and flows along the surface of the ground, eventually entering a lake, river, or creek. It describes water from a perennial flowing stream; water stored behind a rock bar, weir or dam placed across a stream; and water collected from a small drainage area. *See* ground water.

surface wind. A wind blowing near the earth's surface. It is measured in principle at a height of about 10 metres above the ground in an open situation.

suspended solids. Solids in a liquid that can be removed through sedimentation or filtration.

suspension. Disperse system in which particles of solid dispersed phase have dimensions greater than 500 nm.

suspensoid. Historical term denoting an irreversible lyophobic sol. It should not be confused with suspension, that is, mechanical suspension.

sustained yield conservation. That aspect of conservation which seeks wise use and containing productivity of renewable natural resources; originating with forestry, the principle has been extended to other fields.

SVI. sludge volume index, An empirical measurement index defined as the volume in ml. occupied by 1 g of mixed liquor solids (activated sludge) by dry weight after settling in 1000 ml. cylinder for 30 minutes. On this basis, the rate of sludge return and plant operation are controlled. In practice, it is the percentage volume occupied by the sludge in a mixed liquor after 30 minutes settling.

SVR. sludge volume ratio, The volume of sludge blanket maintained at the bottom of a thickener divided by the volume of thickened sludge removed daily. The SVR normally ranges between 0.5

and 2 days. The lower values are required in hot climates.

swill. The name given to waste food from kitchens used for feeding pigs. It should be sterilized before feeding by through boiling, for at least 1 hour, to prevent the transmission of infectious diseases.

swish. Sound, such as the rustling of slik, or the sound made by cutting the air with a lash or by the swift passage of a bird; the gentle agitation of liquids such as the breaking of small waves.

syndrome. A set of concurrent symptoms or signs of a disease.

synecology. The study of relationships between communities and their environments.

syneresis. Separation of water or other suspending liquid from a uniformly dispersed colloidal gel, with resulting contraction of the gel. This action is probably caused by a decrease in the capacity of protein portion of the gel to bind water, induced by change in *p*H, temperature, surface tension, etc.

synergistic effect. The tendency of chemicals and processes to react together to form possibly unforeseen combinations which may have a wholly new or markedly more powerful effect than the substances or processes taken separately. Synergistic effects occur in the formation of photochemical smog. A synergistic effect may link different elements in the total biosphere utilizing, for example, organic substances and the characteristics of light. The formation of highly toxic methyl mercury, through the interaction of organic matter and mercury, is another example of a synergistic effect.

systemic poison. A poison that is spread throughout the body of a living organism. The term is used both for poisons that act systemically (*i.e.*, that affect all parts of an organism) and for compounds that spread systemically without harming an organism but happen to be poisonous to the organism's enemies. Systemic poisons are useful as pesticides for ornamental plants but their use on fodder and food plants is not recommended.

T

2,4,5-T. An abbreviation for 2,4,5-trichlorophenoxyacetic acid, the active ingredient in herbicide products used in forestry and other applications to control woody weeds such as brambles. US Environmental Protection Agency has imposed a ban on the use of this compound on the grounds of a report concluding a correlation between its usage and miscarriage in women.

tailings. The portions of washed ore that are regarded as too poor to be treated further; also called debris.

tank-mixing. A relatively new practice of mixing crop-protection chemicals before spraying on field crops, particularly cereals. The benefits include saving in time, labour, water and fuel, reduced wear and tear of machines, and less crop damage through wheelings.

tank sewer. A civil engineering term for a storage tank for storing sewage, when in an outfall system the high tide rises above the crown of the outfall sewer and it is not possible to discharge the sewage. This is usually built near an outfall.

tank system. A hazardous waste storage or treatment tank and its associated ancillary equipment and containment system.

tannins. A group of naturally occurring organic compounds characterized by amorphous, hygroscopic, usually brown coloured and astringent of precipitate gelatin from solution. Tannins convert hide into leather; precipitate many alkaloids and glycosides from solution, form insoluble compounds with lead and copper; react with ferric salts to produce deep blue or green colours. In alkaline solution they absorb oxygen, and produce a deep red colour with ammonia and aqueous potassium ferricyanide. Tannins are classified as water pollutants as these are frequently encountered in effluents from the industries.

tapered aeration. A modified form of activated sludge process in which compressed air is supplied at a higher rate at the inlet end of the aeration tank and is gradually decreased towards the outlet end of the tank. Thus, the rate of aeration is tapered. The tank is partitioned into three or four compartments.

tape sampler. A device used for the sampling of particulate level of the atmosphere. A known volume of air is passed through a paper tape which is advanced in discrete time intervals from a supply cell to a tape-up cell. The air particulates are collected on the paper tape forming a spot. Spots so obtained are evaluated by analyzing the amount of light that can be transmitted through spot.

tark screen. A very fine screen with mechanical cleaning device. The sewage passes through the performated surface of a drum rotating slowly with its long axis normal to the direction of flow. The sewage which enters into the drum, leaves it through one end and at right angles to its original direction of flow. The screenings collected at the top of the drum are swept by brushes mounted on an endless chain.

tarnish. A grey-to-black film of sulphide formed on surfaces of silver and gold when exposed over a period of time, to polluted atmosphere containing sulphur or its compounds such as hydrogen sulphide and sulphur dioxide. Most tarnishing is due to sulphur dioxide in the air or to sulphur compounds in eggs or other food products in contact with silverware. It does no permanent damage and can be effectively removed with suitable cleaners/removers. A transparent water-insoluble film is sometimes applied to reduce susceptibility to tarnish.

tax incentives for environment protection. Incentives provided by governments through the credits, tax relief, or accelerated depreciation, for the purpose of stimulating investment in pollution control equipment in industrial plants. Several federal government have strongly resisted special concessions to industry for this purpose, adhering to the principle that the polluter should pay. *See* polluter pays principle.

technical name. A recognized chemical name currently used in scientific and technical handbooks, journals, and texts. Generic descriptions authorized for use as technical names are organic phosphate compound, organic phosphorus compound mixture, organic phosphorus compound mixture, methyl parathion, and parathion.

technological effects. The effects which alter the total production possibilities or the total welfare opportunities for consumers in the economy. Classical examples are air and water pollution; the effects are borne by persons and firms other than those who cause the pollution and in consequence production and consumption opportunities elsewhere in the economy are reduced. Also known as real effects.

tectonic lakes. Lakes formed in basins created by movements of the earth's crust. Occasionally, as the earth's crust shifts, a fissure may form or a narrow strip of the land may sink. This process is known as faulting. Such fissures of sinks may fill with water and form lakes known as rift lakes. As one might expect, these lakes are long and narrow. They may also be deep, and the deepest lakes known are of this type.

Tedion. A systemic acaricide toxic to the eggs and all stages of phytophagous mites except adults. At acaricidal concentrations it is nonphytotoxic. It forms colourless crystals, almost insoluble in water, slightly soluble in alcohols and acetone, more soluble in aromatic hydrocarbons and chloroform. It is resistant to hydrolysis by acid or alkali, is compatible with other pesticides, and is non-corrosive. The acute oral LD_{50} for rats is more than 5000 mg/kg. It is effective against eggs, larvae, nymphs of phytophagous mites, but not adults; it has been recommended for application to fruit, citrus, tea, cotton, grapes, vegetables, ornamentals and nursery stock. Also known as Tetradifon.

teleoclimate. The micro-climate at the boundary between living organisms and the environment.

temperature. The property of a body or region of space that determines whether or not there will be a net flow of heat into it or out of it from a neighboring body or region and in which direction (if any) the heat will flow. If there is no heat flow the bodies or regions are said to be in thermodynamic equilibrium and at the same temperature. If there is a flow of heat, the direction of the flow is from the body or region of higher temperature. The temperature of a body is a measure of its 'hotness', which can be defined as a property determining the rate at which heat will be transferred to, or from it. Temperature is thus a measure of the kinetic energy of the molecules, atoms or ions of which matter is composed. The basic physical quantity, thermodynamic temperature, is expressed in Kelvins.

temperature inversion. In the air layer on the earth's surface a temperature gradient is formed in which the temperature falls by day as the height above the earth's surface increases, whereas at night the temperature rises as the altitude increases. This process is known as temperature inversion. If in the course of the following day the ground warms up again, the night's inversion will be cancelled by the supply of energy from the ground to the cold air above it, and the normal temperature gradient will be restored. The form of such inversions depends to a large extent on the structure of the terrain and the climatic conditions and is not for the most part very stable. The situation is different when a layer of cold air flows away over a warm airmass so that an extensive inversion of temperature occurs. Such weather conditions can be very persistent, lasting perhaps days or weeks. The significance of the inversion for the exchange of gas in the air layer near the ground lies in the difference in specific gravity of colder and warmer gases in the same combination. Cold air heated up by the ground rises and cools. If it reaches the layer of warm air, because of its lower specific gravity and further rise of the cold air as it warms up is now checked. Thus, above the boundary layer no exchange of the gas can occur.

terpenes. The class of organic compounds characterized by the presence of the repeating units of isoprene. The name terpene used properly, refers to the hydrocarbons which are exact multiples of the skeletal isoprene unit. However the name terpene, sometimes used loosely include not only hydrocarbons but also other functional types of naturally occurring organic compounds which contain the reoccurring isoprene skeletal. In the strictest sense, the name terpenoid or isoprenoid should be used instead of the more loosely applied usage of terpene. Terpenoids are divided into subclasses as:

(a) Hemiterpenoids,
(b) Monoterpenoids,
(c) Sesquiterpenoids,
(d) Diterpenoids,
(e) Sesterterpenoids,
(f) Triterpenoids,
(g) Tetraterpenoids, and
(h) Polyterpenoids.

The terpenes are also emitted from plants as a part of plant life processes, particularly when they are damaged or defoliated; they include β-pinene, myrecene, and limonene. Since these compounds contain one or more double bonds that are extremely reactive with photochemical species, including ozone. In atmosphere, they are a source of haze in scarcely populated areas or urban areas that are thickly wooded. They may be a major sink for ozone; their reaction rate is such that their concentrations are around 50 $\mu g/m^3$ even though their emission rate is comparable to that of methane.

tertiary treatment. Any sewage purification process which is capable or removing over 98% of the pollutants from sewage, following a secondary treatment plant. During the past few years several methods by which effluents from percolating filters may be improved or 'polished' have been examined. These methods have included the use of microstrainers for the treatment of effluent direct from the filters and the treatment of humus tank effluents by irrigation over land and by passage through slow sand filters, lagoons, or pebble-bed clariers. Polishing is also described as advanced water treatment or tertiary treatment.

Using a polishing process, a effluent may be much improved, both the BOD and the suspended solids beings less than 10 ppm. For example, treatment by addition of ferric alum, followed by filtration and chlorination will yield a clear colourless water free from bacteria contamination suitable for many industrial purposes. Rapid sand filters are also used in tertiary treatment. Most of the straining is effected by the top layers of sand. Rapid filters are easier to clean in comparison to the slow sand filters and the area required is much less. About a 40-70% reduction in BOD and a 70-90% reduction of suspended solids is achieved by this method. A considerable amount of interest has recently been shown in the application of upflow filtration techniques for the tertiary treatment of sewage works effluent.

tetanus. A bacterial disease of livestock and man which enters the body *via* wounds, particularly from the soil. Muscles become stiff, spasms may occur, and the muscles which close the jaws may become continuously contracted. Also known as lockjaw.

tetrachloroethane. A colourless, nonflammable, and corrosive organic solvent; used for cleansing and degreasing metals, paint removers, varnishes, lacquers, extraction of oils and fats, insecticides, weed killer, fumigant, and as an intermediate in the manufacture of a number of organic compounds. It is toxic by ingestion, inhalation, and skin absorption. Occupational exposure to tetrachloroethane, because of systemic effect and dermal irritation produced by the contact of tetrachloroethane with the skin, is defined as work in an area where tetrachloroethane is stored, produced, processed, or otherwise used. When skin exposure is prevented, occupational exposure to this compound should be controlled so that no employee is exposed to tetrachloroethane at a concentration greater than 1.0 ppm (6.87 mg/m^3) determined as a TWA concentration for up to a 10-hour work shift, 40-hour workweek. Also known as 1,1,2,2-tetrachloroethane; acetylene tetrachloride; *sym*-tetrachloroethane.

tetrachloroethylene. A colourless, nonflammable, and hazardous organic liquid with ether-like odour; proposed to be assessed as a hazardous air pollutant. It is used as dry-cleaning solvent, vapour-degreasing solvent, vermifuge, and as heat-transfer medium. It is a moderately toxic substance and is irritant to eyes and skin. Occupational exposure to tetrachloroethylene is defined as exposure at a concentration greater than the action level (TWA) environmental limit. The occupational exposure to this compound should be controlled in such a manner so that no worker is exposed to tetrachloroethylene vapours in excess of 50 ppm (339 mg/m^3) determined as a time-weighted average (TWA) concentration for up to a 10-hour workday, 40-hour workweek, greater than a ceiling concentration of 1000 ppm (678 mg/m^3) determined by 15-minute samples, twice daily.

The available data for tetrachloroethylene indicate that acute and chronic toxicity to freshwater aquatic life occur at concentrations as low as 840 μg/L, and toxicity to saltwater aquatic life occur at concentrations as low as 450 μg/L. For maximum protection of human health from the potential carcinogenic effects due to exposure of tetrachloroethylene through ingestion of contaminated water and contaminated aquatic organisms, the ambient water concentration should be zero based on the nonthreshold assumption for this chemical. However, zero level may not be attainable at the present time. Therefore, the levels that may result in incremental increase in cancer risk over the life time are estimated at 8 μg/L, 0.8 μg/L, and 0.08 μg/L respectively.

Tetrachlorvinophos. *See* Gardona.

Tetradifon. *See* Tedion.

tetraethyl lead. A petroleum additive; used to reduce the tendency to 'knocking' or detonating. Since 1959, another antiknock additive, tetramethyl lead has been added to certain grades of petrol. The amount of additive used has tended to increase The combustion of leaded petrol is the major source of lead in the atmosphere of urban areas. While the question of the likely hazard to health arising from the inhalation of lead compounds by the public at large remains unresolved, unleaded or low-lead gasolines are being introduced in United States and many European countries. This decision was based upon the need to remove lead because it reduces the effectiveness of catalytic devices used on cars to restrict the emission of carbon monoxide and hydrocarbons. The use of unleaded or low-lead petrol is not without some disadvantages; essentially it implies a reduction of compression ratios to cope with lower octane fuel, accompanied by increased petrol consumption. Conversely, to bring an unleaded fuel up to 90 octane rating, (standard petrol has an octane rating of about 90-95) would involve refiners in additional costs which may be recollected from the consumers.

Tetrasul. A non-systemic acaricide, highly toxic to eggs and all stages of phytophagous mites except adults. At the correct dosage it is non-phytotoxic. As it is highly selective it does not pose a hazard to beneficial insects or to wild life. It is a brown crystalline solid, only slightly soluble in water, moderately soluble in acetone and ether, but soluble in benzene and chloroform and stable under normal conditions, but should be protected against prolonged exposure to sunlight; it is oxidized to its sulphone, tetradifon. It is non-corrosive, and compatible with most other pesticides. The acute oral LD_{50} for female rats is 6810 mg/kg. It is effective against eggs, larvae and nymphs of most phytophagous mites, but not adults. It has been recommended for use on fruit and cucurbits at the time when the winter eggs are hatching.

thallium. A metal placed in group IIIA of the periodic table; it has low melting point (576 K), and is used in the metallic form as alloys of bismuth, cadmium and zinc. It is quite poisonous, its compounds have been used as rodenticides and insecticides. The available data for thallium indicate that acute and chronic toxicity to fresh water aquatic life occur at concentrations as low as 1400 and 40 μg/L respectively, and would occur at lower concentrations among the species that are more sensitive than those tested. Toxicity to one species of fish occurs at concentrations as low as 20 μg/L after 2600 hours of exposure. For the protection of human health from the toxic properties of thallium ingested through water and contaminated aquatic organisms, the ambient water criterion is determined to be 13 μg/L. For the protection of human health from the toxic properties of thallium ingested through contaminated aquatic organisms alone, ambient water criterion has been determined to be 48 μg/L.

thalweg. A geological term having several meanings. 1. The line connecting the lowest points along a stream bed or valley; a longitudinal profile. 2. The line of continuous maximum descent from any point on a land surface, *e.g.*, the line crossing all contour lines at right angles. 3. The ground water stream percolating beneath and in the same direction as a surface stream. 4. The deepest or best navigable channel used in defining water boundaries between states.

thaw lake. A shallow, rounded depression containing a circular or semi-circular pond in a lowland periglacial region. Thaw lakes are very common features of thermokarst, and result from the surface thawing of frozen ground (for example, at points where the vegetation cover has been disrupted). This produces localized collapse, and the formation of an irregular depression which becomes occupied by meltwater.

therm. An obsolete unit of heat equivalent to 1,000 large calories used in expressing the calorific value of foods. In SI system, it has been replaced by kilojoules.

thermal erosion. The environmental degradation of the permafrost resulting from human activity. The removal of surface vegetation cover, which has an insulating effect for underlying permafrost, prior to the construction of buildings, roads and bridges as well as the laying of underground services can result in the downward extension of the active layer. During the summer, this disturbance can cause the active layer to become a quagmire with the thawed soil being very susceptible to erosion by meltwater. Thermal erosion can be prevented by constructing roads and railways on insulating gravel beds which protect the underlying permafrost. House and other buildings along with services can be erected on piles which allows the free movement of air beneath them and prevents damage to the permafrost.

thermal inversion. The condition in which warm air in a valley is sandwiched between two layers of cold air and acts like a lid in the valley.

thermal pollution. The transfer of heat from industrial processes of bodies of water or air in such quantities as to be detrimental to the environment. Effluents having a significant effect on the temperature of a river may effect the oxygen content of the water and may create many other adverse conditions. At sufficient high temperatures, fish may die; fish population could be destroyed also by the lethal effects of increased temperature either on another animal on which they feed or on their own spawn. Heat will accelerate the decomposition processes taking place in water; in relation to oxygen-sag curves, the effect will be to lower the curve and also to depress the saturation line. In the presence of sufficient oxygen, it appears that heat alone will shorten the stretch of river affected by the pollution load, accelerating purification. In a river with a light pollution load this would be beneficial; however, in a river with a heavy pollution load the effect is likely to be harmful. The harmful effects may include a reduction of the oxygen concentration in g/m^3 below the level critical to the organisms living in the water. A sufficient loss of oxygen will result in anaerobic conditions. Sewage fungus, found frequently in polluted rivers, grows rapidly in warmed water. Power stations use large quantities of water in condensers for the cooling and condensing of exhaust steam from the turbines. Two general methods are in use:

(a) Direct cooling, in which water is pumped from a river or other source, used once for cooling purposes, and returned at once to the sea, river, estuary or lake. In passing through the condensers, the temperature of the water is usually raised by about 10°C.

(b) Indirect cooling, in which water is pumped from a river or other source, used many times for cooling purposes, and is finally dissipated to the general atmosphere as steam from large open cooling towers. The use of large cooling towers, common in many developed countries, to dissipate the recovered waste heat eliminates the thermal pollution problem. However, make-up water for a cooling tower system is taken from the river or stream, eliminating its subsequent use by those down-river.

thermal power station pollution control (a) The heated effluents can be discharged into the lake, river or any other large waterbody; at one end the water for cooling purposes may be drawn at the other end.

(b) The quantity of impurities discharged into water basin such as in lakes, canals etc. should be diminished by decreasing the discharged of impurities in them and by purifying waste water.

(c) Dry methods of ash storage should be employed in which ash and slag are pelletized and then stored on waste land.

(d) These stored ash should be used as building materials.

(e) The modern state of gas purifying techniques should be applied to reduce appreciably the concentration of impurities in waste gases.

(f) Electrostatic precipitators should be employed to ensure a high degree of gas cleaning.

(g) Thermal power plant complex wastes should be disposed off in the cenented pools.

(h) The stored ash should be used as manures, as it is already in practice in Japan and other developed countries.

thermal precipitation. One of the methods available for collection of particulate pollutants from ambient atmosphere. Thermal precipitates operate on the principle that small particles, under the influence of a string temperature gradient between two surfaces, have a tendency to move towards the lower temperature and get deposited on the colder of there two surfaces. There temperature gradients are normally of the order of 300°C per cm.

thermal treatment. A form of hazardous water destruction involving heating waste. Such incineration can destroy 99% of the organic wastes.

thermocline. 1. A layer in a thermally stratified body of water in which such a gradient occurs. 2. A temperature gradient as in a layer of sea water, in which the temperature decrease with depth is greater than that of the overlying and underlying water. Also known as metalimnion.

thinner. A low-viscosity liquid such as hydrocarbon (naphtha, benzene, etc,) and turpentine, which are added to oil-base paints to adjust their viscosity to a suitable point for application. These substances are generally volatile and some of them are suspected to be carcinogen.

thiol. Any of a class of organic compounds containing -SH group. These compounds have very strong pungent and repulsive smell. They were formerly called mercaptans. Because of the systemic effects, absorption through the skin on contact and possible dermal irritation, occupational exposure to thiols is defined as work in any area where thiols are produced, processed, stored, or otherwise used. The occupational exposure to thiols should be controlled so that no employee is exposed to benzenethiol at concentrations in excess of 0.5 mg/m³ of air, determined as the ceiling concentration for any 15-minute period. The occupational exposure to aliphatic thiols should be controlled in such a manner so that no employee is exposed to thiol at concentrations in excess of 1.0 mg/m³ of air, determined as the ceiling concentration for any 15-minute period. In case of a mixture of air contaminants an employer should compute the equivalent exposure as follows:

$$E_m = [C_1/L_1] + [C_2/L_2] + [C_n/L_n]$$

where, E_m = the equivalent exposure for the mixture,

C = the concentration of a particular contaminant,

L = the exposure limit in parts per million for that contaminant. The recommended exposure limits for some aliphatic thiols are given below:

Thiol Ceiling Concentration Limit

Name	CCL in mg/m³
1-Methanethiol	1.0
1-Ethanethiol	1.3
1-Propanethiol	1.6
1-Butanethiol	1.8
1-Pentanethiol	2.1
1-Hexanethiol	2.4
1-Heptanethiol	2.7
1-Decanethiol	3.6
1-Undecanethiol	3.9
1-Hexadecanethiol	5.3
1-Nonanethiol	3.3
1-Dodecanethiol	4.1
1-Octadecanethiol	5.9
Cyclohexanethiol	2.4

Thiometon. *See* Ekatin.

Thioquinox. A non-systemic acricide effective against eggs; and a fungicide specific against powdery mildews. It is a brown powder, practically insoluble in water and most organic solvents, but is very slightly soluble in ethanol and acetone; it is stable towards temperature and light and resistant to hydrolysis, but susceptible to oxidation without any reduction of biological activity. The acute oral LD_{50} for rats is 3400 mg/kg; some operators. It is specific against eggs of phytophagous mites; and the powdery mildews. Also known as Eradex.

thorium. A relatively heavy, radioactive metal, occurring in monazite sands, and is associated with the rare-earth elements of the lanthanide series. It emits an alpha particle and forms meso-thorium 1 (radium 228), which is also radioactive, having a half-life of 6.7 years, emitting a beta particle. Since Th-232 captures slow neutrons to form by a series of nuclear reactions, thorium can be used as a fuel for nuclear reactors of the breeder type.

threshold limit value. TLV. The quantity referring to the airborne concentrations of substances and represent conditions under which it is believed that nearly all workers may be repeatedly exposed day after day without any adverse effect. Because of wide variation in individual susceptibility, however, a small percentage of workers may experience discomfort from other substances at concentrations at or below the threshold limit; a smaller percentage may be affected more seriously by aggravation of a preexisting condition or by development of an occupational illness. *See also* TLV-STEL.

threshold of discomfort. Minimum effective (root-mean-square value) sound pressure of a specified pure tone which gives a sensation of discomfort in the ear. Averages about 120 decibels sound pressure level at most frequencies for normal subjects.

threshold of feeling. Minimum effective (root-mean-square value) sound pressure of a specified pure tone which gives a sensation of feeling in the ear. Averages about 120 to 130 decibels souond pressure level at most frequencies for normal subjects.

threshold of hearing. The pressure at which a sound source, in the absence of background noise, first becomes audible. In the average young adult with normal hearing, it has been found to be a sound pressure of approximately 0.00002 N/m^2 in the frequency region of greatest sensitivity (around 3,000 Hz). As the sound pressure increases, the sound becomes louder until at a pressure of approximately 20 N/m^2 the sound can be almost felt. This is known as the 'threshold of feeling'. Thus the amplitude of sound pressures in the audible range, from the threshold of hearing to the threshold of feeling, varies enormously. To present this variation in a more convenient scale, a logarithmic, the decibel (dB), which is one-tenth of a bell, came into common use. *See* decibel, sound wave.

throughflow. Sub-surface movement of water in a downslope direction, by contrast with the vertical movement of percolating rainwater towards the water table. Throughflow may be concentrated in the subsoil, especially where it lies above relatively imper-meable bedrock, and may follow natural pipes in the soil (percolines). Throghflow is probably a far more important process than overland flow in the disposal of rainwater in hill-slopes in humid temperate regions.

tilted plate separator. A parallel plate separator used for removal of free oils from refinery effluents. It consists of corrugted plate modules installed at 45° to the horizontal.

TLV. *See* threshold limit value.

TLV-STEL. Abbreviation for *T*hreshold *L*imit *V*alue-*S*hort *T*erm *E*xposure *L*imit. It refers to concentration to which workers can be exposed continuously for a short period of time without suffering from (a) irritation, (b) chronic or irreversible tissue change, or (c) narcosis of sufficient degree to increase the likelihood of accidental injury, impair self-rescue, or materially reduce work efficiency, and provided that the daily TLV-TWA also is not exceeded. It is not a separate independent exposure limit; rather it supplements the time-weighted average (TWA) limit where there are recognized acute effects from a substance whose toxic effects are primarily of a chronic nature. STELs are recommended only where toxic effects are reported from high short-term exposures in either humans or animals. A STEL is defined as a 15-minute time-weighted average exposure that should not be exceeded at any time during a working day even if the 8-hour time-weighted average is within the

TLV. Exposures at the STEL should not be longer than 15 minutes and should not be repeated more than four times per day. There should be at least 60 minutes between successive exposures at STEL. An average period other than 15-minutes may be recommended when this is warranted by observed biological effects.

tinnitus. Sound in the ears or in the head, a common symptom associated with disorders of hearing or balance. Usually originates in the labyrinth, the auditory nerve or the auditory centres of he barin, in which case it is know as subjective tinnitus. Frequent tinnitus is caused by muscular spasms or by circulatory sound sources and can be heard by others. This type is called objective tinnitus.

Tokyo-Yokohama respiratory disease (T-YRD). Originally called Tokyo-Yokohama Asthma, a respiratory complaint associated with the Kanto Plain or Tokyo-Yokohama area. Surrounded by a mountain barrier to the north and west, and the ocean to the east and south, the Kanto Plain suffers a serve air pollution problem; most industry is located near the sea and burns fuel oil and soft coal. The complaint is characterized by severe cough, wheezing, persistent shortness of breath and reduced oxygen uptake. However, most sufferers are cigarette smokers, indicating a combined overburdening of the system. The only satisfactory method of treatment has been the removal of the patient from the area. Such problems are faced in many other large cities having acute air pollution.

***o*-tolidine.** An industrial chemical suspect of carcinogenic potential for humans; the suspect of inducing cancer is based on either

(a) limited epidemiologic evidence, exclusive of clinical reports of single cases, or

(b) demonstration of carcinogenesis in one or more animal species by appropriate methods.

Worker exposure by all routes should be carefully controlled to levels consistent with the animal and human experience data. The occupational exposure to *o*-tolidine should be controlled in such a manner so that employees are not exposed at a concentration greater than 20 μg/m^3 of air, determined as a ceiling concentration in a 1-hour sampling period, and skin contact with *o*-tolidine should be avoided. The recommended standard is designed to protect the health and provide for the safety of employees for up to a 10-hour workshift, 40-hour workweek, over a working lifetime. The synonyms for *o*-tolidine includes 3,3-dimethylbenzidine; 4,4-diamino-3,3-dimethylbiphenyl; diorthotoluidine; azoic diazo reagent; gold diazo reagent; nitro coupling reagent; direct blue 63; fast blue R base; and benzo fast blue R.

toluene. A colourless, flammable, aromatic hydrocarbon; classified as hazardous air pollutant; finds numerous industrial applications. Exposure to toluene means exposures to a concentration of toluene equal to or above one-half the recommended workroom environmental standard. The occupational exposure to toluene should be controlled in such a manner so that employees are not exposed at a concentration greater than 375 mg/m^3 of air, determined as a ceiling concentration in a 1-hour sampling period, and skin contact with toluene should be avoided. The recommended standard is designed to protect the health and provide for the safety of employees for up to a 8-hour workshift, 40-hour workweek, over a working lifetime.

The available data for toluene indicate that the acute toxicity to freshwater aquatic life occurs at concentrations as low as 17,500 µg/L and would occur at even lower concentrations among species that are more sensitive than those tested. The acute and chronic toxicity to saltwater aquatic life occur at concentrations as low as 6300 and 5000 µg/L respectively. For the protection of the human health from the toxic properties of toluene ingested through water and contaminated aquatic organisms, the ambient water criterion is determined to be 14.3 mg/L; while for the protection of human health from the toxic properties of toluene ingested through contaminated aquatic organisms alone, the ambient water criterion has been determined to be 424 mg/L.

***o*-toluidine.** An aromatic compound containing amino group, has been included in the list of potential occupational carcinogens. The suspect of inducing cancer, is based either

(a) limited epidemiologic evidence, exclusive of clinical reports of single cases, or

(b) demonstration of carcinogenesis in one or more animal species by appropriate methods.

The workers exposure by all routes should be carefully controlled to levels consistent with the animal and human experience data.

Torrey canyon disaster. An incident which occurred on 18 March 1967, when the Libean oil tanker Torrey Canyon went aground on the Seven Stones reef, about 24 km northeast of the Sicily, liberating its cargo of Kuwait crude oil. On the afternoon of 24 March, there was a slick of oil about 64 km long off lands end with an average width of perhaps 16 km. Initially, detergent was sprayed on the oil floating on the sea to emulsify and sink it. Subsequently, the ship was bombed, some of the oil being burned, the remainder being swept away by the sea. The burning consumed perhaps one-third of the total cargo. A great deal of the oil finally landed on the Cornish beaches; this too was very largely dealt with by the use of a solvent emulsifier mixture. Some of the oil drifted across the English Channel necessitating prompt action by the French Government to safeguard the beaches and oyster fisheries of Britain. *See also* oil pollution.

total bacteria count method. An important method by which the total number of bacteria is counted which are present in 1 ml of water. In this method, usually 1 ml of diluted water (1 ml of sample water is diluted to 100 ml) is mixed with 10 ml of gelatine and then kept in incubator at 37°C for about 24 hours. The sample is taken out from the incubator and the bacterial colonies are counted; the dilution factor and number of colonies usually give the total number of bacteria present in every mililitre of water sample which is undiluted.

total dissolved solids. TDS. A term frequently used in the studies related to water pollution; it refers to the inorganic salts and small amounts of organic matter present in water. The principal ions contributing to TDS are carbonate, bicarbonate, chloride, sulphate, nitrate, sodium, potassium, calcium, and magnesium. Total dissolved solids influence other qualities of water, such as taste, hardness, corrosion, properties, and tendency to incrustation. Total dissolved solids in water may originate from natural sources, sewage effluent discharges, urban runoff, or industrial waste discharges. Waters in contact with granite, siliceous sand, well-leached soil, or other relatively insoluble material have TDS levels of less than 30 mg/L. Waters in Precambrian shield areas generally have TDS levels less than 65 mg/L. Waters in areas of Paleozoic and Mesozoic sedimentary rock have higher TDS levels, ranging from as little as 195 to 1100 mg/L, carbonates chlorides, calcium, magnesium, and sulphates are the principal ions present. In addition to these natural leaching processes, sewages and industrial wastes may lead to further increases.

Under arid conditions, the TDS of the smaller streams may increase to levels of 15 g/L. Elsewhere, levels in excess of 35 g of TDS per litre have been recorded in brine waters. The use of salt for snow and ice control on roads during winter weather contaminates both surface and groundwater sources, increasing the TDS of waters noticeably in some countries. There is no evidence of deleterious physiological reactions occurring in persons consuming drinking-water supplies that have TDS levels in excess of 1000 mg/L. The results of certain epidemiological studies would appear to suggest that TDS in drinking-water may even have beneficial health effects.

The common dissolved mineral salts are claimed to affect the taste of water. The palatability of drinking-water according to the TDS level has been rated as:

Excellent:
less than 300 mg/L

Good:
between 300 and 600 mg/L

Fair:
between 600 and 900 mg/L

Poor:
between 900 and 1200 mg/L

Unacceptable:
greater than 1200 mg/L.

Water with extremely low TDS levels may also be unacceptable because of its flat, insipid taste. Certain components of TDS, such as chlorides, sulphates magnesium, calcium, and carbonates, affect corrosion or incrustation in water distribution systems. Although no deleterious physiological effect has been recorded with total dissolved solids in water above 1000 mg/L, it was considered that it would, as a rule, be unacceptable to exceed this level, which is recommended as a guideline value.

total pollution loading. A concept which regards the aggregate mass of a specific pollutant, discharged to the environment in a given time period, as more important than the concentration of a pollutant as a basis of environment protection legislation. The total loading on any one segment of the environment becomes the basis of control.

totally enclosed treatment facility. A facility for the treatment of hazarodus waste that is directly connected to an industrial production process and that is constructed and operated in a manner that prevents the release of any hazardous waste or any constituent thereof into the environment during treatment. An example is a pipe in which waste acid is neutralized.

Toxaphene. Generic name for technical chlorinated camphene, contains 67-69% chlorine; mainly used as insecticide. It has been found to be carcinogenic in animals, especially in mice.

For toxaphene the criterion to protect freshwater aquatic life as derived using standard guidelines is 0.013 mg/L as a 24-hour average and the concentration should not exceed 1.6 mg/L at any time. For saltwater aquatic life, the concentration of toxaphene should not exceed 0.070 mg/L. For the maximum protection of human health from the potential carcinogenic effects due to exposure of toxaphene through ingestion of contaminated water and contaminated aquatic organisms, the ambient water concentration should be zero based on the nonthreshold assumption for this chemical. However, zero level may not be attainable at the present time. Therefore, the levels that may result in incremental increase in cancer risk over the life time have been estimated at 10^{-5}, 10^{-6}, and 10^{-7}. The corresponding criteria are about 7.1 ng/L, 0.71 ng/L, and 0.07 ng/L respectively.

toxicant. An agent that can produce an adverse response (effect) in a biological system, seriously damaging its structure or function or producing death. The adverse response may be defined in terms of a measurement that is outside the normal range for healthy organisms. A toxicant or foreign substance may be introduced deliberately or accidently into the ecosystem, impairing the quality of environment and making it unfavourable for organisms.

Toxicants enter ecosystems from (i) nonpoint sources such as agricultural runoff, dredged sediment disposal, and atmospheric fall out, and (ii) point sources such as discharges (effluents) from manufacturing plants, hazardous waste disposal sites, and municipal waste treatment plants.

toxicity tests. The test used to evaluate the concentrations of the chemicals and the duration of exposure required to produce the criterion effect. Toxicity tests are also used to detect and evaluate the potential toxicological effects of chemicals on organisms. Since these effects are not necessarily harmful, a principal function of the tests is to identify chemicals that can have adverse effects on organisms. These tests provide a data base that can be used to assess the risk associated with a situation in which the chemical agent, the organism, and the exposure conditions are defined.

toxicology. The science that deal with the study of the nature, action and relations of poisonous substances and the methods for detecting and treating poisoning. *See also* TSCA.

toxic waste. Any discarded material, commonly from industrial or commercial processes, capable of causing injury or deaths to living organisms. The term is sometimes confused with hazardous wastes which refers to all substances, including toxic wastes that present an immediate or long-term human health risk to the environment.

toxin. 1. In general, any poisonous substance. 2. A plant poison of unknown composition. 3. A poisonous substance produced by microorganisms is called bacterial toxin.

toxophore groups. The portion of a bacterial toxin which has the specific poisonous properties shown by the toxin.

trace elements. The term mainly referring to five elements necessary for plant nutrition which are present in the soil in minute concentrations (less than 1000 parts per million). These are generally considered to be boron, copper, zinc, manganese, and molybdenum, Trace elements should not be confused with tracer elements.

tracer element. A radioactive isotope, either natural or artificial, introduced into a system to determine its behaviour in and reactivity with the other constituents present. This is made possible by the emission of radiation from the tracer which is detected by a sensing device, so that the movement of the isotope can be followed continuously. The terms labelled or tagged are frequently used to designate these elements or the compounds in which they occur.

trade wastes. Wastes of organic as well as inorganic origin discharged by industrial and commercial enterprises. Organic wastes are discharged on a considerable scale by the food industries such as canneries, dairies, breweries, and fishmeat factories. Other contributors include paper-mills, tanneries, petrochemical industries, textile industry, and laundries, Inorganic wastes include acids, alkalies, cyanides, sulphide, sulphates, nitrates, chlorides and the numerous compounds of lead, arsenic, iron, nickel, copper, chromium, and zinc. *See also* water pollution.

trade wind. These belts extend is from the doldrums to about 30° latitude both north and south of the equator. In the northern hemisphere, the trade winds blow from northeast to southwest. In the southern hemisphere, trade winds blow from southeast to northwest. Trade winds also are known as the easterlies. Notice that winds are named for the direction from which they blow. In the zone of the easterlies winds are deflected toward the west. Here the air flows from a zone in which the rotational velocity is less than it is at the equator.

The zone of the westerlies lies between 30° and 60° latitude. Air currents descend to the earth's surface at 30° latitude. Part of the air turns southward as the trade winds; part of the air flows northward as the westerlies. Westerly winds blow from a zone in which the velocity of rotation is greater than the velocity of the zone toward which the air is flowing. Winds are deflected towards the east. In the northern hemisphere, westerly winds blow from southwest to northwest. In the southern hemisphere westerly winds blow from northwest to southeast.

The zone of the westerly winds is noted for its changeable weather. Eddies are revolving masses of air called cyclones (sie klohns) and anticyclones. Cyclones are local areas of low pressure and warm air. Anticyclones are local areas of high pressure and cold air. Cyclones and anticyclones tend to follow one another across the continents from west to east. They travel with the major wind system. Locally winds blow from the high pressure center of an anticyclones toward the low pressure center of a cyclone. Cold and warm air are brought into contact by the winds of the cyclones and anticyclones. Day to day weather changes result from this mingling. The masses of cold air drift into the zone of the westerlies from the polar regions. Masses of warm air reach the westerly zone from the tropics. Storms and turbulence result from the mingling of air masses in the zone of the westerlies.

transfer facility. A facility operated for the purpose of transferring refuse from collection trucks and other vehicles to larger capacity trucks. The larger trucks transport the refuse to a distant disposal site. The purpose of this arrangement is to assist in minimizing overall collection and disposal costs per ton of refuse handled.

transformer hum. Acoustic noise caused by mechanical vibration of transformer laminations under the influence of the alternating magnetic fields passing through them. Electrical noise in the form of oscillating currents electromagnetically induced into parts of an electrical circuit by the leakage of oscillating magnetic fields from a transformer.

transport vehicle. A cargo-carrying vehicle, such as an automobile, van tractor, truck, semitrailer, tank car, or rail car, used for the transportation of cargo by any mode. Each cargo-carrying body (trailer, rail car, etc.) is a separate transport vehicle.

transportation. A phase of sedimentation concerned with movement by natural agents of sediment or any loose or weathered material from one place to another.

treatability study. A study in which a hazardous waste is subjected to a treatment process to determine:

(a) whether the waste is amenable to the treatment process;

(b) what pretreatment (if any) is required;

(c) the optimal process conditions needed to achieve the desired treatment;

(d) the efficiency of a treatment process for a specific waste or wastes; or

(e) the characteristics and volumes of residuals from a particular treatment process; and

(f) exemptions are linear compatibility, corrosion, and other material compatibility studies and toxicological and health effects studies.

A treatability study is not a means to commercially treat or dispose of hazardous waste.

treatment zone. A soil area of the unsaturated zone of a land treatment unit within which hazardous constituents are degraded, transformed, or immobilized

1,1,1-trichloroethane. A toxic and irritant, chlorinated aliphatic hydrocarbon; proposed to be assessed as a hazardous air pollutant; used as solvent for fats, oils, waxes, resins, and other products. The inhaled vapours of this compound rapidly enters the bloodstream and are transported to the tissues. The metabolism takes place in the liver. The immediate effect of 1,1,1-trichloroethane intoxication is the loss of consciousness, followed by coma and death. The mean lethal dose in man has been estimated as 650 mg/kg of the body weight. Occupational exposure to 1,1,1-trichloroethane should always be controlled in such a manner so that no employee is exposed at a concentration greater than 1910 mg/m^3(350 ppm) of this compound in air, determined as a ceiling concentration in a 15-minutes sampling period. The recommended standard is designed to protect the health and provide for the safety of workers for up to a 10-hour workshift, 40-hour workweek, over a working lifetime. Also known as methyl chloroform.

trichloroethylene. A colourless, volatile, nonflammable, photoreactive, chlorinated hydrocarbon; proposed to be assessed as hazardous air pollutant. It finds numerous applications in metal degreasing, solvent extraction of oils, fats, and waxes, cleaning and drying electronic components, adhesives, and in textile processing. Occupational exposure to trichloroethylene is defined as exposure to half of the time-weighted average limit of trichloroethylene in air or greater. Occupational exposure to trichloroethylene should be controlled so that employees are not exposed at a concentration greater than 100 ppm in air, determined as a time-weighted average (TWA). No worker should be exposed to a peak concentration of trichloroethylene of 150 ppm, as measured by a maximum sampling time of 10 minutes. The recommended standard is designed to protect the health and provide for the safety of employees for up to a 8-hour workshift, 40-hour workweek, over a working lifetime.

The available date for trichloroethylene indicate that the acute toxicity to freshwater aquatic life occurs at concentrations as low as 45000 µg/L and would occur at even lower concentrations among species that are more sensitive than those tested. The acute toxicity to saltwater aquatic life occur at concentrations as low as 2000 µg/L. For the protection of human health from the toxic properties of trichloroethylene ingested through water and contaminated aquatic organisms, the ambient water concentration should be zero based on the nonthreshold assumption for this chemical. However, zero level may not be attainable, and therefore, the levels that may result in incremental increase of cancer risk over the life time are estimated at 10^{-5}, 10^{-6}, and 10^{-7}. The corresponding criterion are 27 µg/L, 2.7 µg/L, and 0.27 µg/L respectively.

Trichloronate. A persistent (in soil) non-systemic insecticide recommended for control of root maggots, wireworms, and other soil insects; acts as contact and stomach poison. Recently shown to be effective against Stem Eleworm. The foliar uses of this formulation are under test. Soil applications have given up to five months residual control. It is a brown liquid, practically insoluble in water, but soluble in acetone, ethanol, aromatic solvents, kerosene, and chlorinated hydrocarbons. It is hydrolysed by alkali. The acute oral LD_{50} for rats is 16-37 mg/kg. The acute dermal LD_{50} for rats is 135-340 mg/kg. It is effective against root maggots, wireworms and other soil and grassland insects; also gives control of some nematodes; very persistent in soil; probably effective against cutworms, termites, and Collembola. Also known as Agritox, Agricil, Phytosol.

Trichlorphon. *See* Dipterex.

Tricyclohexyltin hydroxide. An acaricide effective against the motile stages of a wide range of phytophagous mites. No phytotoxicity reported on deciduous fruit or on glasshouse crops, but some spotting on citrus fruit has been observed. It is a white crystalline powder, insoluble in water, poorly soluble in most organic solvents, but 22% w/v soluble in chloroform; stable to ambient temperatures, and in neutral and alkaline media; degraded on exposure to UV light in thin layers. The acute oral LD_{50} for rats is 540 mg/kg. It is effective anainst motile stages of phytophagous mites, but not the eggs. Also known as Plictran.

trickling filter process. An aerobic process used in secondary treatment plants for the processing of sewage. Trickling filters consist of beds of coarse material (generally 50 to 100 mm crushed stone) over which the sewage is sprinkled at a uniform rate; they are generally not less than two metres deep and circular in plan. Settled sewage may be applied to the bed either by mechanical distributors or by fixed nozzles so designed and spaced as to ensure proper distribution of the sewage over the whole area of the bed. The use of plastics (such as polyvinyl chloride) the beds of trickling filters roughly doubles the surface area on which the biological process takes place. The efficiency of standard trickling filters varies from 85 to 95% BOD reduction, 90 to 95% suspended solids removal, and from 80 to 98% bacteria removal. This secondary stage may be followed by tertiary treatment. Also known as biological filter process.

trickling filter sludge. The humus obtained from flim sloughing of a trickling filter. The volatile solids content is 45 to 70%. This sludge is digested with the primary sludge in digestion tanks.

trigger factor. Any environmental factor which has increased or decreased to the point where it precipitates a hitherto latent response or process . The onset of trigger factors may be swift, as when a wind above a critical speed causes vegetation to be blown over. Alternatively, the trigger factor may accumulate slowly in the environment, causing change to occur but which goes unnoticed until a threshold is reached, at which damage symptoms become evident; for example, air pollution levels may gradually increase resulting in internal damage to vegetation until a critical value is passed and symptoms of visible damage are noticed.

tritium. T. A radioactive isotope of hydrogen with a half-life of about 12 years. It arises in nuclear power stations in large quantities. Its distribution in environment is very difficult to check simply because its weak β-rays cannot be measured with normal actinometers. When it is present uncombined as a form of elementary hydrogen, it can penetrate steel, concrete and other protective screens. Present-day nuclear power stations (1000 megawatts) discharge 100-1000 Ci of tritium into the environment in waste water every year. Still larger quantities of tritium are discharged from reprocessing plants. These range from 10,000 to 20,000 Ci for the fuel of a nuclear power station of 1000 magawatts. Tritium produces only a low radiation charge, and until recently it has consequently been regarded as a relatively harmless radioisotope. It is now recognized that tritium can also affect living tissue by processes known as transmutations. In the radioactive decay process, tritium atom emits an electron and is converted into stable helium.

tropopause. The boundary between the troposphere and the stratosphere. It is about 16 km at the equator, and about 6 km at the poles.

troposphere. The portion of the atmosphere next to the earth's surface, in which temperature generally decreases rapidly with altitude, clouds form, and convection is active. In middle latitudes the troposphere includes the first 10-12 km above the earth's surface. Atmospheric turbulence is most noticeable in the troposphere. Air is constantly rising, descending, and moving horizontally.

trunk sewer. A major sewer collection flowing from a large area.

TSCA. Abbreviation for *T*oxic *S*ubstances *C*ontrol *A*ct of United States. It established an Interagency Testing Committee (ITC) to make recommendations to the administrator of EPA of chemical substances to be given priority considerations in proposing test rules. The ITC also may designate chemicals for priority considerations by EPA within 12 months of the date of designation. The total number of designated chemicals on the list may not exceed 50 at any one time. For each designated chemical EPA must, within 12 months, either initiate rule making or publish in the Federal Register its reason for not so doing.

Another section of this act, that is, The Preliminary Assessment Information rule requires chemical manufacturers (including certain producers and importers) to submit information on chemicals. The informations sought from the manufacturers usually include the data on the quantities of the chemical manufactured, the amounts directed to certain classes of uses, and the potential exposures and envi onmental releases associated with the manufacturer's own and his immediate user's processing of chemicals. Another section of this rule requires the submission of unpublished health and safety studies on specifically listed chemicals by chemical manufacturers.

processors, and others in possession of such studies, which is further used to support the investigations of the risks posed by chemicals and, in particular, to support its decisions whether to require industry to test chemicals.

tube settler. A device used for sludge treatment; based on the principle of shallow depth settling of suspended particles in water. In an inclined tube settler, the tubes are inclined at an angle of 45-60° to the horizontal. A flow pattern is established in which the settling solids are trapped in a downward flowing stream of concentrated solids. The capacities of the existing basin can be increased by 50-150% with improved effluent quality by providing striply inclined tubes with the clarifiers or horizontal sedimentation tanks.

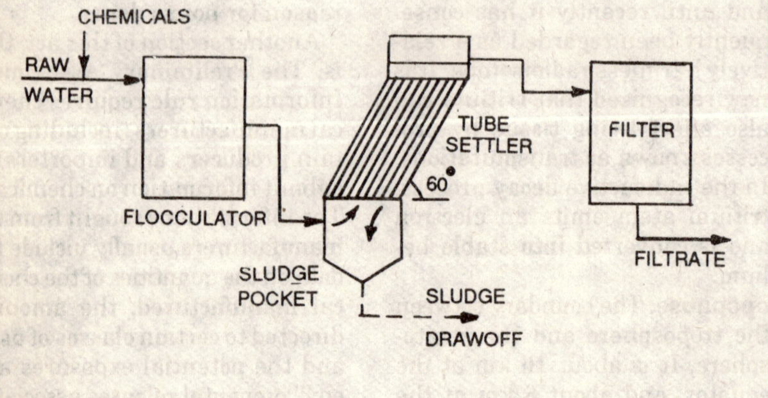

TUBE SETTLER

tungsten carbide. *See* hard metal.

tunnelling. A form of erosion related especially to one kind of soil; the erosion goes on below the surface and may not show until the surface collapsed into the tunnel. The subsurface disperses during wet weather, a mud spring appearing at a point lower down the slope. In this way, a whole hillside may become undermined. An initial counter measure is to keep a cover of vegetation. *See also* soil erosion.

turbidity. In water pollution terminology, the visible pollution due to suspended material in water causing a reduction in the transmission of light. Turbidity in water is caused by the presence of suspended matter, such as clay, silt, colloidal organic particles, plankton, and other microscopic organisms. It is a parameter whose significance is to a large extent dependent on the measurement technique. The total intensity and angular distribution of light scattered from turbid water (or any other liquid) represent the overall effects of intra-particle and inter-particle interactions. The particles that cause turbidity in water range in size from colloidal dimensions to diameters of the order of 0.1 mm. They may be divided into three general classes:

(a) clays;

(b) organic particles resulting from decomposition of plant and animal debris; and

(c) fibrous particles such as asbestos minerals.

Clay particles generally have an upper particle-size limit of about 0.002 mm diameter. Soil particles derived from the land surface by erosion constitute the major part of suspended material in most natural waters. Clays and organic particles are also often found together as a clay-organic complex. Humic substances have a much higher ionic exchange capacity than inorganic clays, and in many instances the effect of humic components predominates. Organic turbidity resulting from the accumulation of higher microorganisms may occur in such large amounts that waters become turbid. Examples of turbidity due to microorganisms are the summer blooms of blue-green algae in surface water, algal debris, and the detritus from iron bacteria in distribution systems(red-water is such a manifestation). Raw-water turbidity can vary from less than 1 NTU to greater than 1000 NTU.

The removal of turbidity may be achieved by simple filtration, or more effectively, by a combination of coagulation, sedimentation, and filtration. Filtration through sand beds or other single medium filters can consistently produce a water with a turbidity of 1 NTU or less. The turbidity of water is related to or affects many other indicators of drinking-water quality. The particulate matter may also be a source of nutrients and protection for micro-organisms. There is evidence that a large part of the colour in water arises from colloidal particles, 50% of such colour being due to a colloidal fraction of humic substances. True colour is, therefore, defined as the colour of water from which the turbidity has been removed. The relationship between high turbidity in both raw and filtered water, and taste and odour has also long been recognized, and suspended particulate matter in a potable water supply renders the water unattractive to the consumer. The presence of turbidity can have a significant effect on the microbiological quality of drinking-water may be complicated by the presence of turbidity. In water, microbial growth is most extensive on the surfaces of particles and inside loose, naturally occurring, floc and floc formed during coagulation treatment. The microbiological growth is facilitated because nutrients are adsorbed on to surfaces and attached bacteria are thus able to grow more efficiently compared with those in free suspension. Similarly it has been demonstrated that river silt readily adsorbs viruses. In the water-treatment process of coagulation, bacteria and viruses become trapped in the floc formed and are removed along with turbidity.

turbidity current. A density current in water or air; specifically a bottom-flowing current laden with suspended sediment, moving swiftly down a subaqueous slope and spreading horizontally on the floor of the body of water, having been set in motion by locally stirred-up sediment that gives the water a density greater than that of the surrounding clear water. Such currents are known to occur in lakes, and are believed to have produced the submarine canyons notching the continental slope. The term is applied to a current due to turbidity, not to one showing that property. Turbidity currents are capable of eroding the floor of the basin or slope and are responsible for transferring large quantities of shallow-water sediment into deeper zones. The recognition of the work of turbidity currents has revolutionized ideas on rates of sedimentation and the depths water in which sediments were deposited.

turbidity rod. The rod lowered into the water and the depth at which the platinum needle ceases to be seen under standard light; indicates the turbidity of water.

turbulence. The random movements of the air which are superimposed upon the mean wind speed. The individual movement is called a turbulent eddy which may have almost any size and may move in any direction at any speed. *See also* meteorological influences.

turbulence clouds. The clouds formed as result of irregular turbulence which is continually being formed in the up-currents and dispersed in the down-currents. The two conditions that enable the turbulence clouds to form are:

(a) the humidity must be high enough for the dew point to be reached near to the surface; and

(b) turbulence must be sufficient for the air to be carried up to the dew-point level.

If the layer immediately above the turbulence level is unstable, the large up-currents would commence and the turbulence cloud would rapidly change from a layer type, so producing large, towering, heap-type clouds. Turbulence cloud, by the very character of its formation, is low cloud and it is usually of the layer type. The base may be between the surface and 600 m; the vertical thickness may vary from a few metres upto 1000 or 1500 m, depending upon the degree of stability of the lower layers. Since the clouds are continually undergoing formation in the ascending currents and dispersal in the down-currents, there is rarely sufficient activity within them to produce precipitation.

TWA. The *T*ime-*W*eighted *A*verage concentration for a normal 8-hour workday and a 40-hour work which nearly all workers may be repeatedly exposed, day after day, without adverse effect.

Tyndall effect. The reflection or scattering of light by colloidal particles suspended in a gas or liquid· the suspension, particles (which are too small to be seen in an optical microscope) indicate their presence by reflecting the light at various angles, depending on their position relative to the incident beam. As a result, a visible path or cone of light appears. A similar effect is observed when an intense and narrow light beam is passed through a dark room.

U

ultimate median tolerance limit. The concentration of a chemical at which acute toxicity ceases. Also known as incipient lethal level; lethal threshold concentration; and symptotic LC_{50}.

ultrasonic cleaning. The removal of surface layers of grease and dirt from materials, particularly metals, by their exposure to intense ultrasonic waves in a cleaning fluid, the probable cleaning mechanisms being acceleration of the fluid particles and cavitation at the metal surface.

ultrasonic coagulation. The formation of clusters of particles from individual solid particles suspended in a liquid or gaseous medium, when the medium is irradiated with intense ultrasound.

ultra sound. Mechanically induced sound pressure waves which are above the upper limits of hearing in humans; while the waves which are below the threshold of hearing are termed as infra sound. Ultra sound is produced either as a continuous or pulsed beam which has a variety of uses in industry such as drilling, welding plastics, mixing liquids, and in detecting cracks in rolled metals. It also has a wide medical use in the treatment of injury, and in the detection of disease. The hazards due to ultra sound include dizziness, somnolence, fatigue, nausea, and noise in the ears of operators exposed to the waves. Where parts of the body are directly exposed to the ultra sound beams, pains may be produced and there may be disruption of the tissues.

ultraviolet radiation. U.V. Electromagnetic radiation in range of wavelength between 100 nm to about 400 nm. Most UV radiation for practical use are produced by various types of mercury-vapour lamps. Ordinary glass absorbs UV radiation and therefore lenses and prisms for use in the UV are made from quartz. Sufficient technology exists to prevent adverse effects on workers, but technology to measure ultraviolet energy for compliance with the recommended standard is not adequate, so work practices are recommended for control of exposure in cases where sufficient measurement or emission data are not available.

For the ultraviolet spectral region of 315 to 400 nm, total irradiance incident on unprotected skin or eyes, based on either measurement data or on output data, should not exceed 1.0 mW/cm^2 for periods greater than 1000 s, and for exposure times of 1000 s or less, the total radiant energy should not exceed 1000 mW.s/cm^2 (1.0 J/cm^2). For the ultraviolet spectral region of 200 to 315 nm, total irradiance incident on unprotected skin or eyes, based on either measurement data or on output data, should not exceed levels described below:

If the ultraviolet energy is from a narrow band or monochromatic source, permissible levels for a daily 8-hour period can be read directly from the following table:

nm	*mJ/cm²*	S_λ
200	100.0	0.03
210	40.0	0.075
220	25.0	0.12
230	16.0	0.19
240	10.0	0.30
250	7.0	0.43
254	6.0	0.50
260	4.6	0.65
270	3.0	1.00
280	3.4	0.88
290	4.7	0.64
300	10.0	0.30
305	50.0	0.06
310	200.0	0.015
315	1000.0	0.003

2. If the ultraviolet energy is from a broad-band source, the effective irradiance (I_{eff}) relative to a 270 nm monochromatic source is calculated from the formula:

$I_{eff} = I_l S_l D_l$

where, I_{eff} = effective irradiance relative to a monochromatic source at 270 nm,

I_l = spectral irradiance,

S_l = relative spectral effectiveness, and

D_l = band width.

If radiation intensity from a point source is known at some distance from the worker, for example, from measurement at another point or from output data at a known distance from the ultraviolet source, attenuation of the from that point to the worker can be calculated from the principle that radiation decreases with the square of the distance.

umbrella separator. In air-lift pumping of water, an umbrella-shaped plate placed at the top of the eductor pipe, against which the rising stream of mixed water and air strikes, and water gets collected in a tank.

underground flow. The direction of flow of ground water can be traced using dyes, salts, or electrolytes. Deep well current meters, salinity apparatus with water samplers are also used for testing inderground flow.

underground injection. The subsurface emplacement of fluids through a bored, drilled, or driven well: or through a dug well, where the depth of the dug well is grater than the largest surface dimension.

underground tank. A device meeting the definition of tank whose entire surface area is totally below the surface of and covered by the ground.

underground water. Water other than surface-water being drawn from relatively shallow wells or boreholes, and from deep artesian bores.

underwater ambient noise. Noise, of any origin, other than that caused by energy scattered from the signal wave. The general background noise when no signals are being transmitted, and enough time has been allowed for all reverberation to die away.

underwater noise. Any underwater acoustic disturbance other than

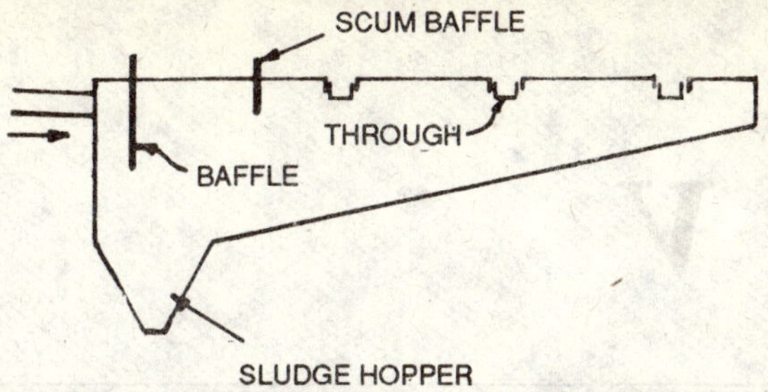

UNIFLOW SETTLING TANK

the wanted signal. It includes thermal noise reverberation, biological noise, etc. Noise which persists in the absence of the signal is called background or ambient noise. Reverberation noise is caused by scattering of some of the energy of the signal itself.

unfit-for-use tank system. A tank system that has been determined through an integrity assessment or other inspection to be no longer capable of storing or treating hazardous waste without posing a threat of release of hazardous waste into the environment.

uniflow setting tank. A specially designied settling tank to reduce the detention period and cost of construction by decreasing the depth gradually towards the effluent end without affecting the uniform velocity the uniform velocity through the tank. This is provided with link-belt sludge removal equipment. This tank can be used for primary as well as secondary sedimentation.

unstable equilibrium. An equilibrium state of a system in which any departure of the system from equilibrium gives rise to forces moving the system further away from the equilibrium. This type of equilibria are frequently encounterd in air pollution management.

uppermost aquifer. The geologic formation nearest the natural ground surface that is an aquifer as well as lower aquifers that are hydraulically interconnected with this aquifer within the facility's property boundary.

uptake. The absorption of a chemical into extracellular fluid for systemic circulation; its further action is governed by metabolic pathways.

urban heat island. A zone of excess warmth within a city over the suburban and rural environs. The warmer air in this region rises upwards and then spreads radially outwards. The colder air from the surrounding countryside at the surface flows inwards towards heat island to replace the rising and outspreading warm air. This occurs when the heat islands are intense. This circulation is known as Urban Heat Island Effect.

urban renewal. The renovation of the decaying central areas of large cities by the demolition or upgrading of existing dwellings, reduction of street congestion, and general improvement in environmental conditions. Urban renewal is one of the major causes of pollution in cities.

V

vacuum filter. A cylindrical drum filter having a filter medium of synthetic fibre-woven cloth of wire-mesh fabric enveloping the drum. The drum is dipped into the vat of sludge, and slowly rotates, a part of the circumference is subjected to an internal vacuum by which the sludge is drawn to the filter medium. This type of pumps are used for dewatering the sludge.

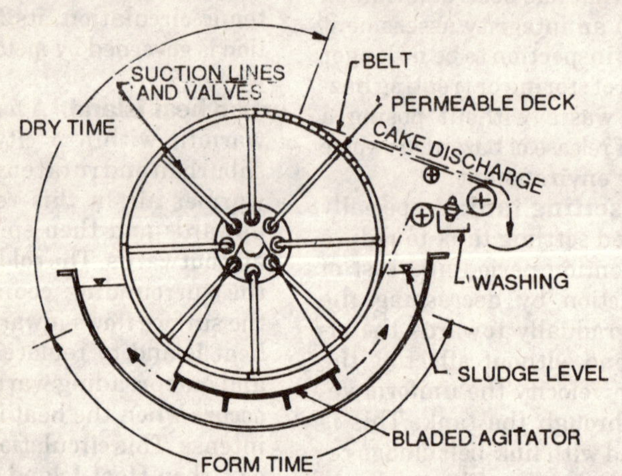

VACUUM FILTER

vadose water. A term for water percolating downwards through the rock to the zone of saturation, that is, water present between the water-table and the surface of the earth. *See also* ground water; surface water.

vanadium. A metallic element placed in group VB of the periodic table. It is used in the manufacture of alloy steels, as catalyst, and as target material for X-rays. The occupational exposure to metallic vanadium and vanadium carbide should be controlled so that the employees are not exposed at a concentration greater than 1.0 mg of vanadium per cubic metre of air measured as a time-weighted average (TWA) concentration for up to a 10-hour workday, 40-hour workweek, over a working lifetime. The occupational exposure to vanadium compounds should be controlled in such a manner so that the employees are not exposed at a concentration greater than 0.05 mg of vanadium per cubic metre of air measured as a ceiling concentration during any 15-minute sampling period. The standard is designed to protect the health and provide for the safety of employees for up to a 10-hour work shift, 40-hours workweek, over a working lifetime.

veering wind. The clockwise change of direction of a wind, *e.g.*, from N through NE; an opposite change of direction to backing. The same definition applies whether in the northern or southern hemisphere.

vinyl acetate. A colourless, highly flammable, hazardous liquid, used in the manufacture of a large number of chemical products, also used in latex paints, paper coating, adhesives, textile finishing, and glass inter layers. The exposure to vinyl acetate in the workplace should be controlled so that no employee is exposed to concentrations greater than 15 mg/m^3 of air, (4 ppm), measured as a ceiling concentration in samples collected during any 15-minute period. The recommended standard is designed for the safety of employees for up to a 10-hour workshift, 40-hour workweek, over a working lifetime.

vinyl chloride. One of the most versatile monomers, used for the manufacture of polyvinyl chloride, and copolymers. No employee may be exposed to vinyl chloride at concentrations greater than 1 ppm averaged over any 8-hour period, and no employee may be exposed to vinyl chloride by direct contact. It is recognized to have cocarcinogenic potential in humans. For maximum protection of human health from the potential carcinogenic effects due to exposure to vinyl chloride through ingestion of contaminated water and contaminated aquatic organisms, the ambient water concentration should be zero based on the nonthreshold assumption for this chemical. However, zero level may not be attainable at the present time. Therefore, the levels that may result in incremental increase of cancer risk over the lifetime are estimated at 10^{-5}, 10^{-6}, and 10^{-7}. The corresponding criteria are 20 mg/L, 2.0 mg/L, and 0.2 mg/L respectively. The risk estimate range is presented for information purposes and does not represent any agency judgement on an acceptable risk level. It may be further mentioned that no information is available about the effect of this compound on salt water organisms and no statement can be made concerning acute or chronic toxicity.

vinyl cyclohexene dioxide. An industrial substance mainly used in the manufacture of a large number of polymers. It is strong irritant to skin and tissues, toxic by ingestion and skin absorption. It has been suggested that no employee may be exposed to vinyl cyclohexene dioxide vapours at the concentrations greater than 60 mg/cm^3 (10 ppm) averaged over any 8-hour period, and no employee may be exposed to vinyl cyclohexene dioxide vapours by direct contact. It is recognized to have cocarcinogenic potential in humans.

virus. A filterable micro-organism, invisible by ordinary microscopy, capable of multiplying locally in the cells; of the body and forming inclusion bodies in the cells; a virus disease is one caused by a virus. There is general agreement that present sewage treatment processes do not entirely remove the virus hazard, although some studies indicate that if chlorination is used efficiently and earlier treatment stages are adequate, the virus hazard is considerably reduced. Most of the human faecal or entering viruses found in sewage are enterovirus members of the picornavirus group (polio, coxsackie and echo viruses); they fall in the size range 23-30 nm.

viscous liquid. A liquid material that has a measured viscosity in excess of 2.500 centistokes at 25 degrees C (77 degrees F) when determined in accordance with the procedures specified in ASTM Method D 445-72 Kinematic Viscosity of Transparent and Opaque Liquids (and the Calculation of Dynamic Viscosity) or ASTM Method D 1200-70 Viscosity of Paints, Varnishes, and Lacquers by Ford Viscosity Corp.

volatile organic compounds. In pollution control, an organic compound that evaporates easily. Technically, such compounds are defined as organic compounds with a vapour pressure of 1,300 pascals (about 1% of atmospheric pressure at sea-level). Compounds that fit this description are often considered in the same category for regulatory purposes due to their similar physical behaviour in the atmosphere.

volcanic lakes. The lakes produced by the volcanic activity. Once a volcano becomes extinct, its hollow interior may fill with water. Frequently these lakes, like rift lakes, may be very deep, although they are circular in outline.

volcanic water. Water within or derived from magma at the earth's surface or at a comparatively shallow depth. Also, juvenile water of volcanic origin.

vortex pump. A sewage pump having nonclogging type recessed impellers mounted outside the flow path of sewage between the pump inlet and discharge. Thus, solids equivalent to the pipe diameter can be passed through it.

W

warble. The singing, whistling, gentle, continuous sound or song with trills, quavers or melodic embellishments; a continuous sound or tone varying regularly in frequency or pitch such as that produced by a wobbulator.

washer. A general term for a dust collector, a droplet separator, or a gas purifier operating with a liquid as the collecting medium.

washout. The process of removal of dust, in particular radioactive dust, from the atmosphere by rain. The term is commonly applied to the removal of all particulate matter from the atmosphere by rain. Many authorities apply the term 'rain out' for the removal of pollutants from clouds (by condensation of water vapour on the particles by their incorporation in raindrops as the latter being formed), and the term 'washout' to the removal of pollutants from the air below the cloud level by the rain as it falls.

waste. Any matter, whether liquid, solid, gaseous, or radioactive, which is discharged, emitted, or deposited in the environment in such volume, constituency or manner as to cause an alteration of the environment. The concept of a waste embraces all unwanted and economically unusable by-products at any given place and time, and any other matter which may be discharged, accidentally or otherwise, to the environment. *See* recycling.

waste anesthetic gases. Gases and vapours that are released into work areas associated with, and adjacent to, the administration of a gas or volatile liquid used for anesthetic purposes. At present, six most commonly used anesthetic agents are: nitrous oxide, halothane, enflurane, methoxyflurane, diethyl ether, and cyclopropane. Occupational exposure to waste anesthetic gases includes exposure to any inhalation anesthetic agents that escape into locations associated with, and adjacent to anesthetic procedures. Such locations should include, but should not be limited to, operating rooms, delivery rooms, labour rooms, recovery rooms, and dental operations. The occupational exposure to halogenated anesthetic agents should be controlled so that no worker is exposed at concentrations greater than 2 ppm of any of the halogenated anesthetic agent, based on the weight of the agent collected from a 45-litre air sample by charcoal absorption over a sampling period not exceeding one hour. Occupational exposure to nitrous oxide should be controlled so that no worker is exposed at

TWA concentrations greater than 25 ppm during anesthetic administration. The standard is designed to protect the health and safety of workers during their working lifetime in locations where anesthetic gases and vapours occur.

waste disposal unit. A unit to dispose off wastes. For easy disposal of rubbish, garbage, etc. except papers, tins and glasses down the drain, a grinder driven elecrically is installed near the kitchen into which all sorts of rubbish, garbage, etc. are ground and drained out through the drain.

waste management. A term describing a comprehensive, integrated, and rational systems approach towards the achievement and maintenance of acceptable environmental quality. It involves the preparation of policies; determination of environmental standards; fixation of emission rates; enforcement of regulations; monitoring air, water, and soil quality, and noise emissions; and offering advice to government, industry, land developers and public.

waste liquid. Polluted water with foul smell, discharged from industries and houses.

waste pipe. A pipe carrying foul water or waste liquids from bath, latrine, kitchen, etc., to the drain. Also known as soil pipe.

waste preventer. A cistern for flushing water from closet. Each time after use, the water closet is flushed with a definite amount of water either by pulling the chain or by lowering the lever attached to the cistern.

waste water. A genereal term for water containing biodegradable or foul matter.

waterborne bacterial pathogens. Faecal pollution of drinking-water may introduce a variety of intestinal pathogens-bacterial viral and parasitic-their presence being related to microbial disease and carries, present at that moment in the community. Intestinal bacterial pathogens are widely distributed throughout the world. Those know to have occurred in contaminated drinking-water include the stains of *Salmonella, Shigella, enterotoxigenic Escherichia coil, Vibrio cholerae, Yersinia enterocolitica and Campylobacter* fetus. These organisms may cause diseases that vary in severity from mild gastroenteritis to severe and sometimes fatal dysentery cholera or typhoid. Other organisms naturally present in the environment and not regarded as pathogens may also cause occasional opportunist disease. Such organisms in drinking-water may cause infection predominantly among people whose local or general natural defence mechanisms are impaired; this is most likely to the case in the very old the very young and patients in hospitals for example with burns or on immunosuppressive therapy. Potable water used by patients for drinking and bathing if it contains excessive numbers of organisms such as pseudomonas, *Flavobacterium, Acinetobacter, Klebsiella,* and *Serratia* may produce a variety of infections involving the skin and mucous membranes of the eye, ear, nose, and throat. The modes of transmission of bacterial pathogens include ingestion of contaminated water and food contact with infected persons or animals and exposure to aerosols. The significance of the water route in the spread of intestinal bacterial infections varies considerably, both with the disease and with local circumstances. Although *Shigella* may be waterborne, but water is not usually the main route for the spread of shigellosis, but rather person-to-person contact in crowded living conditions in contrast cholera is usually waterborne and salmonellosis is food-borne. Among the various waterborne pathogens there exists a wide range of minimum infectious dose levels necessary to cause a human infection. With *Salmonella typhi* ingestion of relatively few organisms can cause disease; with *Shigella flexneri* several hundred cells may be needed whereas many millions of cells of *Salmonella* serotypes are usually required to cause gastroenteritis. Similarly with toxigenic organisms such as enteropathogenic *E. coli* and *V. cholerae* as many as 10^8 organisms may be necessary to cause illness. The size of the infective dose also varies in different persons with age, nutritional status, and general health at the time of exposure. The significance of routes of transmission other than drinking-water should not be underestimated as the provision of a safe potable supply by itself will not necessarily prevent infection without accompanying improvements in sanitation and personal habits.

waterborne diseases. Diseases such as cholera, typhoid fever, dysentery, gastroenteritis, hepatitis and bilharziasis, which are commonly transmitted through contaminated water supplies. While the classical water-borne diseases have been virtually eradicated from many of the developed countries, these diseases are still endemic in other parts of the world. Bilharziasis (caused by schistosomes or blood flukes) is commonly transmitted in tropical countries by bathing in polluted canal water. Urban filariasis (caused by filariae or nematode worms and associated, inter alia, with that breeds in polluted water. Although water transmission is thought to cause only a very small fraction of the disease hepatitis, nevertheless a major epidemic of infectious hepatitis did occur in Delhi, India, in 1955 and 1988, in circumstances suggesting that the treatment of highly polluted water had been successful in controlling bacteria, but not the hepatitus virus. There are Some common water-borne diseases are:

Cholera. This water-borne disease is mainly caused by bacteria. It is often fatal if it is not treated well. There are various symptons, of the this disease the most common symptoms are severe vomiting, diarrhoea, dehydration etc.

Bacterial dysentery. This disease is mainly caused by the several species of becteria. Diarrhoea is the most common symptom of this water borne disease.

Typhoid. It is on of the most common water-borne disease caused by the bacteria.

para typhoid fever. This disease is usually caused by the attack of several species of bacteria. The main symptoms of the is disease are severe vomiting, diarrhoea etc. in man.

Ameobic dysentery. The most

common organisms to cuase Ameobic dysentery are protozoa. The main symptom of this disease is also diarrhoea, but prolonged diarrhoea in man in most possible way of detection of a patient suffering from Ameobic dysentery.

Infectious hepatitis. The organaism involved to cuase this disease is virus. It is the most common in most of this diseae are when man has yellow jaundice skin, enlarged liver, vomitting and often the apdminal pain. More readily identificable group of vacteria, which are generally known by us as cothfrom. Since these micro-organisms are normally present in the intestinal tract of human and animals. The large number of collifoms in water acts as an indicator of contamination of water by untreated sewage. Chlorination of drinking water to protect the humans and animals from the attack of various diseases are usually applied. Recent studies show that though chlorination of drinking water is done to save the population from various disease but chlorination itself usually gave rise to other pollution problems.

water content. The quantity of water present in a system (or substance). It is usually expressed as percent; the weight of water in a wet mass divided by the dry mass and multiplied by 100. Also known as moisture content.

water-cooled grease trap. A trap used for the separation of greqase from sullage water, in which cooling the interceptor aids grease separation.

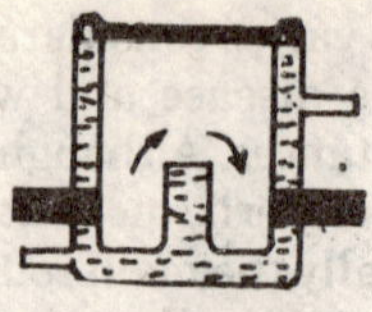

WATER-COOLED GREASE TRAP

water-formed deposits. Any accumulation of insoluble material derived or deposited from water, or formed by the reaction of water with the surfaces with which it comes into contact; deposits may be classified as corrosion products, biological deposits, scale or sludge.

watermass. A body of a water identified by its temperature-salinity curve on chemical composition, and normally consisting of a mixture of two or more water types.

water polluting agents. Bacteria or viruses present in such concentrations or numbers as to impair the quality of the water rendering it less suitable or unsuitable for its intended use and presenting a hazard to man or to his environment. Pollution may be caused by:

(a) Bacteria, viruses and other organisms that can cause disease, *e.g.*, cholera, typhoid fever, and dysentery.

(b) Inorganic salts that cannot be removed by any simple conventional treatment process, making the water less suitable for drinking, for irrigation and for many industries.

(c) Plant nutrients such as potassium, phosphates, and nitrates which, while largely inorganic salt, have the added effect of increasing weed growth, promoting algal blooms and producing, by photo-

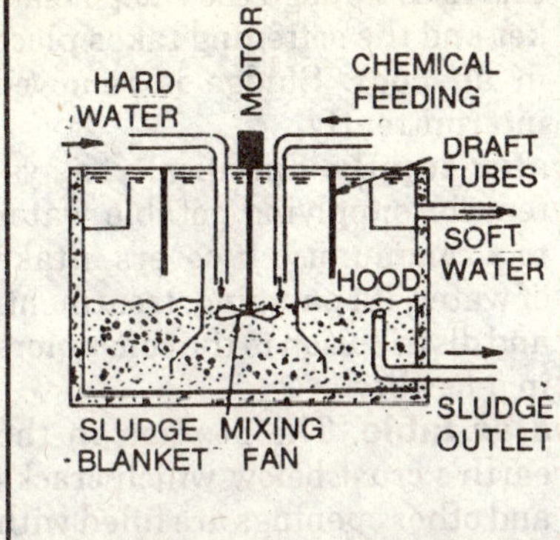

WATER SOFTENING ACCELERATOR

synthesis, organic matter which may settle to the a lake.

(d) Oily materials that may be harmful to fish and other forms of aquatic life, cause unsightliness, screen the river surface from the air thus reducing re-oxygenation, accumulate in troublesome quantities, or have high oxygen demand.

(e) Specific toxic agents, ranging from metal salts to complex synthetic chemicals.

(f) Waste heat that may render the river less suitable for certain purposes.

(g) Silt that may enter a river in large quantities causing changes in the character of the river bed.

water pollution. Most of the major cities of the world are situated on river banks or close to water bodies. Not only the water supply in adequate quantiry, essential for the health and well-being of a community, but a good water front offer facilties of water transport as well as the dirainage varied from the large perspectives of economic development water resources are agents of power generation and contribute directly, to productivity. However, over a period of time with repid urbanization and industrialisation, The intensity of use of river water has often gone far beyound the tolerance limits.

The rapid industrialization has created multifarious problems for

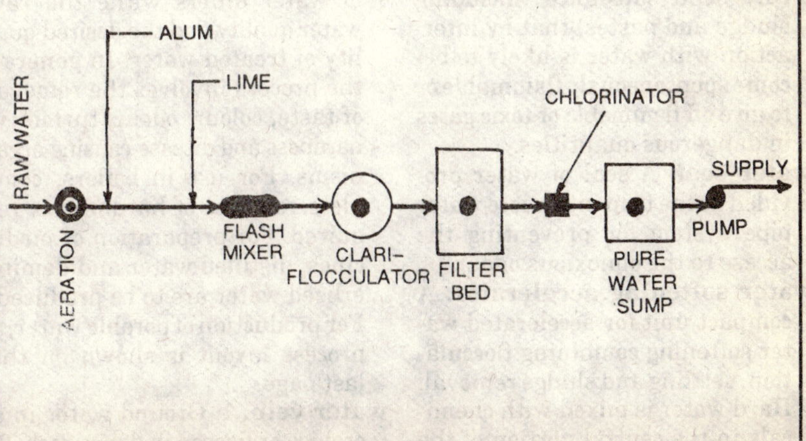

WATER TREATMENT

the disposal of indistrial wastes. Indistrial pollution results to 10 percent to 15 percent of the total river pollution at an average but it is quite deadly due to the highly toxic substances dumped into the rivers resulting in fish mortality, Cattle deaths, spreading of deadly disease like "Minimata" caused due to the mercury poisoning of water, Jaundice, gas problems, skin diseases, and many more similar diseases. So, care is to be taken that the sources of water are not contaminated by the sewage. The organic, inorganic and radioactive substances present in the industrial waste in minute suspended or colloidal form and microorganisms pollute the sources of water, where these are dumped into water bodies. The waste water from various industries in having many of the same problems, plus some additional ones. The type of contaminant is dependent upon the particular industry and the particular process employed.

water reactive material (solid). Any solid substance (including sludge and pastes) that by interaction with water is likely to become spontaneously flammable or to give off flammable or toxic gases in dangerous quantities.

water seal. A seal of water provided at the trap in a waste water pipe system for preventing the access to the obnoxious odour.

water softening accelerator. A compact unit for accelerated water softening combining flocculation, settling and sludge removal. Hard water is mixed with chemicals in the central portion of the tank and the sludge previously formed is churned by a rotating fan. The hard water with chemicals rises through the sludge blanket and the softening takes place in an hour. Sludge is removed intermittently.

water supply. Specifically, a system for supplying potable water to a community. It covers intake of water, its pumping, treatment, and distribution to the consumers in a locality.

water table. The position in the earth's crust below which cracks and other openings are filled with water. Above the water table (zone of aeration), the interstices in earth materials are partly filled with air. In the zone of saturation the interstices are completely filled with water. This zone extends from the water table downward. The position of the water table below the ground surface is a function of the topography of an area and of local climatic conditions. The lowest level to which a water-table falls in any locality is known as the permanent water-table.

water treatment. The treatment of water differs withe the raw water quality and the desired quality of treated water. In general, the process involves the removal of taste, colour, odour, turbidity, hardness and disease-causing organisms. For use in boilers, complete removal of hardness is required. For preparation of medicines, distilled water and demineralized water are to be produced. For production of potable water, a process layout is shown on the last page.

water vein. 1. Ground water in a crevice or fissure in dense rock. 2. A term generally applied to any body of ground water, in part because dowsers commonly describe water occurring in veins. The term is not in common use in hydrology.

wave basin. A basin close to the inner entrance of a harbour in which the waves from the outer absorbed, thus reducing the size of the waves.

weather. The state of the atmosphere at a certain time or over a certain short period as described by various meteorological phenomena such as atmospheric pressure, temperature, humidity, rainfall, cloudiness, and wind speed and direction. Weather has direct effect on personal comfort. *See also* climate.

weathering. The initial stage of denudation, wearing down of rocks on the surface without their being moved by temperature effects, wind, precipitation, living agents, and chemical action. An essential feature of the process is that it affects rocks in situ; and no transportation is involved. This is the factor which distinguishes it clearly from erosion. The main types of weathering are:

(a) *frost weathering,* resulting from the freezing and expanding of water in the joints breaking the rockmass into individual blocks or fragments;

(b) *root wedging,* resulting from the growth of tiny roots which wedge joints apart from the pressure of their expansion; and

(c) *spheroidal weathering*, resulting from the expansion of the rockmass as it chemically weathers. The temperature variations related to forest and brush fires may physically weather rock by thermal expansion and dehydration.

West-Gaeke method. One of the most widely employed methods for the determination of sulphur dioxide in air. The air sample is bubbled through a solution of dipotassium tetrachloromercurate,. The solution is then treated with bleached para-rosaniline and formaldehyde, producing an intense bluish-purple colouration, which is finally determined spectrophotometrically.

wheeler filter bottom. An arrangement in undrainage system of filter beds, comprising conical or pyramidal openings in the concrete bottom with the vertex of the cone or pyramid down. The openings are filled wih heavy balls carefully placed ot achieve the function of a strainer.

whisper. Hushed speech sound produced by using the breath and lips, but with no vibration of the vocal chords.

white noise. Noise whose spectral density is substantially independent of frequency over a specified but broad frequency range.

wind. The movement of air from one place to another. Air moves from higher pressure to lower pressure in an attempt to balance out the pressure differences. As the wind travels it is diverted to its right in the northern hemisphere or to its left in the southern hemisphere. If the isobars are close together, the pressure gradient will be steep, and the wind will be strong. *See also* anabatic wind; geostrophic wind; gradient wind; katabatic wind; prevailing wind; and surface wind.

windbreak. A line of trees planted to provide shelter from strong and persistent winds. Some windbreaks are planted to protect soil and prevent erosion.

wind chill. A measure of the combined cooling effect of low temperature and wind.

wind crust. A type of snow crust, formed by the packing action of wind on previously deposited snow; wind crust may break locally but, unlike wind slab, does not constitute an avalanche hazard.

wind gap. A shallow, relatively high-level notch in the upper part of a mountain ridge usually an abandoned water gap. Most wind gaps are produced by glacial breaching; river capture; climatic changes, accidental diversion.

window. 1. A break caused by erosion of a thrust sheet or a large recumbent anticline that exposes the rocks beneath the thrust sheet. 2. The unfrozen part of a river surrounded by river ice during winter season.

window ice. A thin deposit of ice which forms by the freezing of many tiny drops of water that have condensed on the indoors side of a cold window surface.

wind rose. A diagram indicating the frequency and strengths of winds in a definite locality for a given period of years. It is convention to consider the wind direction as the direction from which the wind blows, *e.g.*, a northeast wind will carry pollutants to the southwest of the source. *See* prevailing wind.

windrow. 1. Any accumulation of material formed by wind or tide action. 2. A long pile or stack with sloping surfaces; used for composting solid wastes.

wind shear. The space variation of the wind vector, or of a component of the wind vector, in a specified direction. The vertical wind shear is the rate of change of wind velocity with vertical distance above the ground.

wind slab. A type of snow crust; a patch of hardpacked snow, which is packed as it is deposited in favoured spots by the wind, in contrast to wind crust.

wind tunnel. A duct through which air can be passed at a steady rate and that is used for the investigation of airflow patterns. If a scale model of, say, a factory (with miniature stacks that emit smoke) is placed in a wind tunnel, the dispersion of the smoke (and the effects of the factors such as stack geometry and efflux velocity) can be investigated.

wind wane. A device used to indicate the direction from which the wind is blowing. It generally consists of a pivoted rod that can rotate freely about a vertical axis, having an airfoil or fin at one end and a pointer at the other. It can also be attached to a recording device.

wood wool slab. A wooden slab prepared from wood shavings compressed together; used as insulating boards, partitions, false ceilings, sound proofing and decorative purposes.

World Environment Day. 5th of June every year, which has been adopted by the U.N. conference on the 'Human Environment', to mark the beginning of the first conference, and as a means of focussing attention on national and world environment problems.

X

Xeret. A suborder of the soil order Vertisol; formed in a Mediterranean climate; wide surface cracks open and close once a year.

xeric. 1. Of or pertaining to a habit having a low or inadequate supply of moisture. 2. Of or pertaining to an organism living in such an environment.

xeric site. A site for growing trees or other vegetation that is dryer than normal, either because not enough rain falls or because the rain that falls, does not remain in the soil.

Xeroll. A suborder of the soil order Mollisol, formed in a xeric moisture regime; may have a calcic, petrocalcic, or gypsic horizon, or duripan.

xeromorphic. A term applied to the plants which appear to have ability to restrict water loss during adverse conditions; a plant displaying this characteristic is described as a xerophyte.

Xerult. A suborder of the soil order Ultisol, formed in a xeric moisture regime; brownish or reddish soil with a low to moderate organic carbon-content.

X-rays. Electromagnetic radiation of shorter wavelength than ultraviolet radiation and longer wavelength than gamma radiation. The range of wavelength is 10^{-11} m to 10^{-9} m. The atoms of all the elements emit characteristic X-ray spectrum when they are bombarded by electrons. These rays can pass through many forms of matter and therefore used medically and industrially to examine internal structures. X-rays are known to produce free radicals which are shot-lived and reactive; these may react with DNA, causing mutations and, in stronger doses, death of the cell.

xylene. An aromatic hydrocarbon obtained from the fractional distillation of petroleum; find numerous applications as aviation gasoline, solvent for alkyd resins, lacquers, and enamels. It is moderately flammable and toxic by ingestion and inhalation. Exposure to xylene is defined as exposure above half the recommended time-weighted average environmental limit. The occupational exposure to xylene should be controlled so that no worker is exposed to xylene at concentration greater than 100 ppm (about 434 mg/m^3) determined as a time-weighted average (TWA) exposure for up to a 10-hour workday, 40-hour workweek, with a ceiling concentration of 200 ppm (about 868 mg/m^3) as determined by a sampling period of 10 minutes. The standard is designed to protect the health and safety of workers over a working lifetime.

Y

Y. A branch pipe leading off a main pipe, usually at 45° to the main line.

yankee gutter. A wooden gutter made by metal sheathing. The metal sheet is held in a position by an upright wooden block at the edge of the pitched roof.

yap. Short sound such as the shrill, fussy barking of a small dog.

yazoo stream. A tributary that flows parallel to the main stream for a considerable distance before joining it at a deferred junction; especially such a stream forced to flow along the base of a natural levee formed by the main stream.

yell. High-pitched, shrill shout or cry, usually of pain, anger or fright.

Yokkaichi asthma. Severe asthma caused by oxides of sulphur in Yokkaichi, site of the largest petrochemical complex in Japan.

Yorkshire fog. A perennial, soft, downy grass (*Holcus lanatus*), common in poor pastures and an indicator of lime deficiency in the soil. Also known as meadow soft grass.

ytterbium. A rare-earth metal, obtained from several ores (monazite, gadolinite). It is subject to attack by acids and is soluble in ammonia. It forms compounds with oxygen, the halogens, and with carbon and other nonmetals. Its most important use is as a doping agent for garnet crystals composed of mixtures of rare earths. It is not toxic and has several radioactive isotopes, one of which is used in radiography of metal parts and in medical diagnostic work.

yttrium. Though it is not one of the rare-earth metals, yttrium, is very similar to them and is always associated with them in such ores as monazite and gadolinite. The major use of the metal is as an additive or alloying ingredient with a number of other metals; additions of small percentages increase resistance to oxidation at high temperatures and have other beneficial effects upon the alloy systems to which it is added. It is a decay product of strontium-90 which has been considered as a radiation pollutant from fallout, and that may cause cancer.

Z

zeolite. A large group of hydrous aluminosilicates of alkali metals (especially sodium, potassium and calcium), characterized by their reversible loss of water of hydration, and by their fusion with a bubbling action when strongly heated. They form a well-defined group of species that are closely related to one another in composition, in conditions of formation, and hence the mode of occurrence. Their general formula is: $A_mB_rO_{2r}$·xH_2O, where, *A* is mainly Na and Ca (K, Ba and Sr to a lesser extent), *B* is Si+Al where, Si:Al is 1:1, and the (Al+Si): 0 ratio is always 1:2. The compositional ranges of individual eolite species, however, are narrow, which is indicative of a narrow range of stability for each of the species and also may serve as an explanation for the existence of a larger number of species within the group. Zeolites may be deposited from the late magmatic solutions, by hydrothermal solutions, or they may be formed during diagenesis. Many are products of alteration of feldspars, feldspathoids, or volcanic glass. They are especially common as amyg-dules, fracture fillings, and fillings in other cavities in many kinds of rocks, especially in bas-alts. They are characteristic of a low-temperature, low-pressure metamorphic facies, known as zeolite facies. They also occur in some metalliferous veins, especially where the gangue is calcite, and in the deposits of hot springs, where they have in some cases been formed within the historic time and are still being formed. The zeolites are commonly associated with calcite, prehnite, pectolite, apophylite, and the datolite. Zeolites find numerous applications as ion-exchangers, as soil conditioners, and as acid-resistant adsorbers in gas drying.

zeolite facies. Metamorphic rocks formed in the transitional period from diagensis to metamorphism, at pressures of 200-3000 bars and temperatures of 475-575 K.

Zerlate. *See* Ziram.

zero curtain. The layer of ground between the active layer and permafrost where the temperature remains nearly constant at about 273 K.

zero discharge. In pollution control terminology, the total/complete elimination of all traces of a particular pollutant from the effluent from a particular source. Zero discharge standards are difficult to implement due to great efforts required to remove each additional increment of a pollutant as its level in the environment approaches zero. At a certain point, the environmental gain achieved by removing more of the substance usually will be offset by the environmental harm caused by generating the proportionately large amounts of energy or producing machinery and chemical substan-ces needed for the removal process. Thus, zero discharge standards are appropriate only for persistent toxic substances, which are harmful even at very low concentration levels.

zig zag filter. An air pollution filter made up of zigzag pieces placed on wires. The flow of polluted gases striking the pieces, and the particulates that are separable impinge on the surface and are dropped down into a collector by gravity.

Zimmerman Process. A sewage treatment process achieving oxidation of organic material in a closed vessel under high pressure and temperature. The process is used on pulp and paper mill wastes, textile wastes, etc.

zinc. An element placed in group IIB of the periodic table. It is an abundant element and constitutes about 0.04 g/kg of the earth's crust. Its presence has been detected in industrial waste water from galvanizing and plating plants, rubber and polymer processing, and rayon manufacture. It is also present in meats, dairy products, cereals and nuts. Food is by far the largest source of zinc for humans. The average daily intake for a normal human has been reported to be about 12 mg. It is an essential element for both animals and man and is necessary for the functioning of various enzyme systems, including alkaline phosphatase, carbonic anhydrase, and alcohol dehydrogenase. In small quantities zinc is considered to be non toxic. The low toxicity of zinc and efficient homoeostatic control mechanisms make chronic zinc toxicity from drinking water and dietary sources an unlikely hazard in man. Symptoms of zinc toxicity in man include vomiting, dehydration, electrolyte imbalance, abdominal pain, dizziness, and lack of muscular coordination. Daily doses of about 150 mg of zinc interfere with copper and iron metabolism because zinc is considered as a metabolic antagonist of both these metals. However, where dietary intake of copper and iron are adequate there is little problem with high zinc doses. Zinc is also a metabolic antagonist of cadmium. According to some researchers, the high zinc intake may be expected to afford atleast some protection against the toxic effects of cadmium exposure from the environment. Zinc imparts undesirable astringent taste to water. The water containing zinc at concentrations in excess of 5 mg/L may appear opalescent and may develop a greasy film on boiling.

zinc dimethyldithiocarbamate. *See* Ziram.

Zinophos. The technical name for a soil insecticide and nematicide, of relatively brief persistence. It is a brown liquid, fairly soluble in water, miscible with most organic solvents; readily hydrolysed by alkali. The acute oral LD_{50} for rats is 12 mg/kg, with the dermal LD_{50} being 11 mg/kg. Soil application is effective against symphylids and cabbage root fly (drench); the granules are recommended for use on cotton, cucurbits, groundnuts, brassicas and tomato. Also known as Nemafos, Thionazin.

Ziram. Technical name for zinc dimethyldithiocarbamate; used as fungicide; stable under normal conditions but is decomposed by acids. It is compatible with most other fungicides except those containing either heavy metals such as copper, iron, mercury, or lime. Some of the common trade names of ziram include Corozate, Cuman, Fuklasin, Hexazir, Karbam, Milbam, Niagara, Vancide, Zerlate, Zirberk, Zitox, etc. It is toxic to mammals, if consumed orally. The acute oral LD_{50} for rats is 1400 mg/kg. Daily ingestion of as much as 1/5 of the LD_{50} dose of ziram produced death within 30 days in some of the test animals.

Ziram is quite stable at room temperature. It is not affected by most of the dilute acids but is decomposed by concentrated acids and caustic alkalies. It is generally employed in the form of wettable powder containing 70-90% of the active gradient. It is slightly toxic to plants, especially to those sensitive to zinc.

Zirberk. *See* Ziram.

zirconium. A metal placed in group IVB of the periodic table. It possesses good mechanical properties. It is found in nature as zircon, zirconium silicate. After separation of the hafnium by solvent extraction of the tetrachlorides of the two elements, it is reduced to metal by magnesium (Kroll process). It has very low neutron absorption capability and thus an important application is in cladding uranium fuel element in nuclear reactors, usually in the form of a series of alloys trademarked. It is also used in the manufacture of corrosion-resistant equipment for the chemical industries. The element is a suspected carcinogen, and its use is not permitted in cosmetics. It is flammable and explosive as dust or powder. The occupational exposure to zirconoum should be controlled in such a manner so that no employee is exposed to zirconium (in any chemical form) at a concentration greater than 5.0 mg/m^3 of air, determined as a time-weighted average (TWA) concentration limit for up to a 10-hour workshift in a 40-hour workweek, over a working lifetime.

Zitox. *See* Ziram.

Z-M system. A novel approach, according to which raw sewage is subjected to all-chemical treatment. In the first stage, the raw sewage is treated with lime and the large organic molecules are broken down. In second stage, the small molecules are absorbed by activated carbon.

Zobar. Technical name for a weed killer; it comprises an aqueous solution of diethylamine salts of polychlorobenzoic acid; toxic by dermal contact and ingestion.

Zolex. Technical name for an aromatic solvent; proposed as an alternate for xylene.

Zolone. *See* Phosalone.

zonal soil. According to early classification systems in United States, a soil order including soils with well-developed characteristics that reflect the influence of agents of soil genesis.

zone. A band, belt, layer, or strip of earth material such as rock or soil. In paleontology, the term zone refers to the division of epochs. Zones are grouped into epochs, epochs are grouped into periods, and periods are grouped into eras.

zone of aeration. A subsurface zone containing water below atmospheric pressure and air or gases at atmospheric pressure.

zone of engineering control. An area under the control of the owner or operator that upon detection of a hazardous waste-release, can be readily cleaned up prior to the release of hazardous waste or hazardous constituents to groundwater or surface water.

zone of leaching. The top layer of the soil, characterized by downward movement of water. Part of the rain falling on the ground percolates downward through the soil, which tends to leach or wash down, some of the soil materials to the lower levels. In a wet and humid climate, clay minerals and iron oxides, and dissolved calcite, are leached downward.

zone of saturation. A subsurface zone in which water fills the interstices and is under pressure greater that atmospheric pressure. If a well were filled in this zone, ground water would fill the lower part of the well. The water level inside the well marks the upper surface of the zone of saturation. Above the zone of saturation, the rock openings are filled partly with water and partly with air.

zone of silence. Lack of sound at a particular place close to a source because of the refraction of the sound waves away from that zone by temperatuer differences in the atmosphere.

zoonoses. A group of infectious diseases transmitted from animals to humans.

zymogenous flora. The name given to the organisms found in the soil following the addition of readily decomposible organic matter such as animal wastes.